INTERNATIONAL HANDBOOK OF READING EDUCATION

INTERNATIONAL
HANDBOOK OF
READING
EDUCATION

Edited by JOHN HLADCZUK
and WILLIAM ELLER

Foreword by JOHN RYAN

Greenwood Press
Westport, Connecticut • London

Library of Congress Cataloging-in-Publication Data

International handbook of reading education / edited by John Hladczuk
  and William Eller ; foreword by John Ryan.
    p.   cm.
  Includes bibliographical references and index.
  ISBN 0–313–26253–5 (alk. paper)
  1. Reading. 2. Literacy—Government policy. 3. Literacy
programs. I. Hladczuk, John. II. Eller, William.
LB1050.2.I58   1992
428.4—dc20   91–10420

British Library Cataloguing in Publication Data is available.

Library of Congress Catalog Card Number: 91–10420
ISBN: 0–313–26253–5

First published in 1992

Greenwood Press, 88 Post Road West, Westport, CT 06881
An imprint of Greenwood Publishing Group, Inc.

Printed in the United States of America

The paper used in this book complies with the
Permanent Paper Standard issued by the National
Information Standards Organization (Z39.48–1984).

10 9 8 7 6 5 4 3 2 1

This book is dedicated
to readers, reading educators,
and literacy workers throughout
the world.

Contents

Foreword

Reading, until quite recently a subject of interest mainly to teachers and specialists, is now a nationwide and, indeed, a worldwide concern. In 1990, proclaimed International Literacy Year (ILY) by the United Nations, special programs and campaigns to promote literacy and education were conducted in more than one hundred countries. International Literacy Year had one simple but vital message: education *matters*. Nothing is more essential to our progress, as individuals and societies, than the development of human competence and potential through education and training. And literacy, the ability to read and write, is the vehicle of education, the means through which ideas, information, knowledge and wisdom are expressed and exchanged. Education is the door to the future and literacy is the key.

The challenge of creating a literate world is enormous. Nearly a billion adults, more than one in four, are illiterate and over 100 million children between the ages of six and eleven years are without schools to attend. Yet, the task is essential. Hopes for a more just, productive and peaceful world depend upon economic, social and cultural transformations that are impossible without widespread education. Education is a part—often a large part—of the solution to nearly all the major problems confronting humanity: peace, population growth, preservation of the environment and all other undertakings that call for collective reflection and action. Thus, the growing interest in education and, more particularly, in the most basic of educational skills, reading, is neither surprising nor misplaced. Reading is our common concern and collective responsibility.

This volume, containing twenty-six case studies on countries in all parts of the world and at all stages of development, makes a rich and timely contribution to the discussion of reading goals, policies, practice, research and results. Inevitably, these studies differ considerably in length, scope and style as well as in the amount and type of information provided. This, in large measure, reflects the vast differences among national educational systems as well as in the information available regarding them. To assemble a case study on the United States one must, for example, sift and select from a plethora of qualitative and quantitative information of many kinds. By contrast, preparing a study on Lesotho calls for the diligent digging out of facts and figures and a skillful stitching together of the various bits and pieces into an informative narrative.

As interest in reading has risen, the controversy surrounding the subject has also grown. Is there a reading problem? If so, what is it and what should be done about it? These are the issues explicitly or implicitly addressed in these case studies. As experts in the reading education programs of their respective countries, the contributors are—at least in certain cases—partisans in a growing international debate on how reading is and should be taught. Their views may—and in some cases certainly will—be contested by other experts. Such debate is a sign of concern and, hence, of health and vigor. Most of the contributors are reporting on countries of which they are citizens. In a few cases, where such is not the case, the reader may wish to speculate on how the view of an "outsider" may differ from that of an "insider."

One of the special merits of this study is that it examines a diverse sample of countries: continental nations and island states, nations with hundreds of millions of citizens and others with hundreds of thousands, countries in which the traditional economy dominates and others which have entered a post-industrial age, countries that proclaim themselves socialist and others that are avowedly capitalist, nations old and new, countries north, south, east and west. How do these nations, that vary so vastly, deal with the common task of teaching their citizens to read? The accounts provided here are informative and often fascinating. The contributors and editors alike are due a vote of thanks for making available, in convenient form, information that previously would have been impossible or nearly impossible to assemble.

To provide a comparative perspective, the editors have invited the contributors to deal with a number of central issues: reading policy, language issues, the instructional process, goals of reading, teacher education, adult literacy, assessment of achievement and reading research. Each contributor, however, examines these issues in his or her own way. This seems a judicious compromise in that it permits the reader to follow common themes throughout the twenty-six studies while at the same time alerting him that there is much that is specific to particular languages, cultures, states of development and perspectives on reading. A strict uniformity of presentation cannot be achieved in a world as diverse as ours.

Language issues, in widely varying forms, are one of the themes mentioned in all studies and emphasized in several. In societies that are monolingual, or think of themselves as such, the issue of language is often lost sight of. Yet, it is central and indispensable. One can teach reading in many ways, but one cannot do so without a medium, a language. In the United States, the dominant language issue has been that of "English as a second language" and is seen as one of the treatments administered in the "melting pot." While this perspective persists, it is increasingly at odds with reality in many parts of the country where bilingualism is being reinforced by both immigration and a growing pride in one's native language. Even in the United Kingdom, the homeland of English, indigenous languages such as Gaelic and Welsh, and languages of immigration, usually of Afro-Caribbean and Indian origins, are of growing significance. Approximately four percent of children in schools in the United Kingdom come from homes where English is not the first language. Yet, compared to Zaire which has an estimated 200 to 400 spoken languages—the number depending on how "language" is defined—the United Kingdom is linguistically homogenous. French, the official language of Zaire—used in government, business and in secondary and higher education—is spoken by only three million persons, approximately ten percent of the population. Swahili, the largest indigenous language, has an estimated eight million speakers. Under these circumstances, it is probable that the mother tongue will not be the language in which literacy will be achieved. It is likely, as well, that the first language of literacy will itself serve mainly as a bridge to literacy in the official language.

In parts of the developing world, as these studies reveal, the progress of literacy depends in good measure upon the formulation of appropriate language policies. The choices confronting policymakers are not easy. Language issues are not only complex, but often, as in the case of India, contentious. Language is part of one's cultural identity, not something external. Thus, while language surveys and analyses of policy options can and do serve useful purposes, they are insufficient by themselves. What matters are not only the objective facts, but also the subjective feelings. Teachers in industrialized countries who must cope with classrooms of children whose native language is not the medium of instruction—an increasingly common phenomenon in inner cities—will discover from these case studies that, in the world as a whole, their situation is not the exception, but the rule. This will not solve their problem, but it may help to put it in perspective.

Readers may find surprising the attention devoted in certain studies to adult literacy, especially in the industrialized countries. The extent of illiteracy in the developing nations is widely recognized and easily explained. In Africa, the large-scale expansion of education dates from the post-colonial period, that is, the 1960s. Up to that time, access to education was reserved to a small minority destined to become the future clerks of a colonial administration. Hence, few had either the opportunity to read and write or, given the paucity of reading materials, the motivation to do so. But how can one explain the phenomenon of illiteracy in industrialized countries—nations in which, with few exceptions, schooling has been both free and compulsory for over a century, nations, one might add, which, until a few years ago, were convinced that illiteracy was a part of their past, not their future? In Germany, for example, the last census of the Imperial era, conducted early in the century, showed literacy to be nearly universal. Now, one hears estimates of millions of illiterates, including native-born Germans as well as immigrants. Is this evidence that the Germans are not reading as well as their forbearers or rather proof that their counting has improved?

Certainly, the present debate turns, in part at least, on the distinction between "literate" and "functionally literate." Unesco defines a literate person as one who "can with understanding both read and write a short simple statement on his everyday life." But to be functionally literate an individual must be able to "engage in all those activities in which literacy is required for effective functioning of his group and community and also for enabling him to continue to use reading, writing and calculation for his own and the community's development." The technological transformation of society has, evidently, created a large and growing gap between the meaning of literacy and functional literacy. It is not the failure of education, but the growing complexity of living and, especially, working environments that is the main cause of the rapid growth in the estimated number of functional illiterates in so-called "advanced" societies.

But is this the whole of the problem? I fear not. Doubtless the problem also has something to do with the fact that most citizens, both in developing and industrialized countries, live not in an "information age," as is ceaselessly asserted, but in a "media age," in which a few selected kernels of information are repeatedly processed until little intellectual nutrition remains and then are carefully packaged and served to the public on television. If fluent and critical reading depends, as much research suggests, upon the information, knowledge and wisdom one brings to the text, then the overindulgence in the "empty calories" served up by the media and the declining consumption of the mind-building proteins that derive from reading are indeed a cause for alarm. The most fundamental educational skill is not reading, but thinking. Reading is important precisely because it provides food for thought in nourishing doses. Our concern with the atrophy of reading skills and habits is prompted and justified by the realization that we are dealing not with a mere technical failing, but with a serious threat to the intellectual underpinnings of democratic society. If we must depend upon the mass media for information and enlightenment, then *1984* is not a past date, but a future menace.

One of the underlying themes explored from many angles in the various national studies is the process through which reading skills are acquired. In its simplest terms, the question is whether reading is taught or learned. Those who emphasize teaching tend to advocate phonics, the formal teaching of grammar and rigorously structured programs. The advocates of "emergent literacy," by contrast, see learning as a natural and spontaneous human vocation, a process of "drawing out" more than "filling up." What they see as of primary importance are supportive learning environments, stimulating interaction and encounters with "real" books, not primers. Ironically, such student-centered curricula tend to place more rather than less demands upon teachers. The teacher's role is transformed from "presenter" to that of guide and facilitator. Hence, rather

than merely following a textbook, he or she must master the subtle art of facil-
itating the learning process and diagnosing its difficulties. Student-centered approaches will generally require smaller classes, a wider range of instructional
materials and better trained teachers. Unfortunately, all of this entails greater
expense and as such is not viable for developing countries where providing every
child with his or her own primer is still a challenge.

Most of the issues raised in these case studies will be familiar to the reading
specialist and reading teacher. What especially will interest such specialists is
the manner in which familiar ideas work, or fail to work, in unfamiliar settings.
The great debate in reading in English-speaking countries, for example, has
evolved around the pros and cons of teaching phonics. This issue, however, has
entirely different implications for the teaching of languages that are strongly
phonetic and syllabic. The Cuba study emphasizes the centrality of a phonetic
approach in the teaching of Spanish. An even stronger case could be made for
certain African languages in which, in theory at least, there is a perfect correspondence between phoneme and grapheme.

In the matter of defining literacy, the general tendency, especially in the
industrialized countries, has been toward more complex and sophisticated definitions. Instead of seeking to draw a dividing line—with those to the north
literate and those to the south illiterate—there is a growing effort to construct
learning profiles indicating what parts of the population can and cannot perform
tasks commonly encountered in everyday life. By contrast, the Chinese definition
of literacy seems simplicity itself. To be literate an urban dweller must be able
to recognize 2,000 ideograms and a rural dweller 1,500. Given that the meaning
is embedded directly in the characters or ideograms, whereas the letters of the
alphabet are merely intermediaries that must be grouped to yield meaning, the
Chinese approach seems logical and justified. The recognition that the knowledge
of more characters is required to operate in complex urban environments than
in simpler rural ones also seems intuitively correct.

Some of the most interesting and insightful differences highlighted in these
case studies pertain not to objective matters of fact, but to subjective interpretation
of findings. The discussion of reading difficulties among Japanese children is a
case in point. We are informed that the Japanese consider reading difficulties a
rarity among their children. Yet, an American scholar, applying more rigorous
testing methods, has found that eight percent of Japanese children are two years
or more behind in reading. What is interesting here is that what the Japanese
view as "normal," an American sees as problematic. To the Japanese, the
children in question are not "problem readers," they are simply marching down
the road to reading at a more leisurely pace. Eventually, it is implied, they will
pick up their tempo and catch up with their confreres. If the Japanese have a
serious literacy problem, we would be quite justified in concluding that their
problem stems, in part at least, from weaknesses in diagnosing reading and
providing remedial treatment. But, in fact, although Japanese children must
master symbol systems (*Kanji, Hiragana* and *Katakana*) to become literate, the

overwhelming majority succeed in doing so by the time they reach adolescence. Hence, the alleged diagnostic weakness is perhaps a major strength, a way of avoiding labeling children as "problems" and setting in train a self-fulfilling prophecy. Any lessons here?

In short, the twenty-six case studies presented here constitute a sort of world-wide odyssey of reading. They provide accounts of how reading is taught in different countries, the objectives of each reading curriculum, which reading problems constitute national concerns, how reading teachers are trained and credentialed, what reading research is underway and many more facts about and insights into the world of reading. These studies constitute a useful complement to on-going research and assessment projects such as the Reading Literacy Project of the International Evaluation of Achievement. They also suggest the extent to which the world of reading is diverse and how even the simplest comparisons between and among countries become complex. What is common to nearly all the studies is the growing recognition of the importance of reading. In the information-based societies of the twenty-first century, for which the school children of today are being prepared, reading will be not only an educational skill, but a life skill, essential for success and, perhaps, even for survival.

NOTE

The opinions expressed above are the responsibility of the author and do not necessarily reflect the views or policy of Unesco.

Preface

This book is an attempt to survey reading education worldwide. In our selection of countries we strove to ensure representativeness across the geographical, economic, and political continuums. In order to achieve that end we initially had to deal with the dilemma of whether to take the easier route of getting Western scholars who were purportedly knowledgeable of the various countries we selected or whether we should try to find scholars indigenous to the countries in question. We opted for the second alternative. Consequently, the chapters in this book are written almost exclusively by scholars in the countries represented. In an effort to standardize the responses across the countries, we submitted to each scholar an outline, a list of topics, and a predecided format.

In many projects such as this—and particularly this one because we are dealing almost exclusively with indigenous scholars—the editors are almost entirely dependent on the contributors to portray the subject in a way that reflects the representativeness of the country in question. Thus, we do understand that there may be disagreements in the areas of interpretation, portrayal, and analysis with respect to a given country. We do believe, however, that the international scholarly community has the sufficient means to air such disputes.

It should also be noted that recent geopolitical changes in several of the countries that are featured in this volume will undoubtedly affect the educational systems of these countries in ways that could not have been foreseen by the contributors.

Acknowledgments

This project has not been an easy one. Yet, we believe that the end result has made it all worthwhile and more. We have perspectives on countries that we may not have had if all the chapters had been written by Western scholars.

To that end we have a lot of people to thank. First and foremost we thank our contributors—all of them. They have performed magnificently. We would also like to thank our translators who have performed above and beyond the call of academic duty. They are Susan Sokolowski for the chapter on Switzerland; John Poritsky for the Soviet Union; Jing Wang for the People's Republic of China; Jeanette Molina for Costa Rica; and Soungalo Ouedraogo for the chapters on France and Portugal.

A great number of other people have contributed to this book. We thank the following people: Dr. John Ryan, Secretariat, International Literacy Year, Unesco, Paris; Dr. Ralph Staiger of Newark, Delaware; Dr. Ho Truc, First Vice-Minister of Education in Hanoi; Carlota Tunnermann of the Nicaraguan Consulate in Washington, D.C.; Fred Morales in San Jose, Costa Rica; Dr. Franciszek Januszkiewicz at the Research Institute for Science Policy and Higher Education in Warsaw; Loomis Mayer, formerly of Greenwood Press; Mildred Vasan also of Greenwood Press; Dr. John Elkins of the University of Queensland in Australia; Dr. Jacques Fijalkow of the University of Toulouse, Toulouse, France; Dr. H.-G. Hofmann, Director of the Institute of the Akademie der Padagogischen Wissenschaften in what was formerly East Berlin; Ramon Sanchez Parodi and Ariel Ricardo, both of the Cuban Interest Section in Washington, D.C.; Professor Saran Gopinathan of the Institute of Education in Singapore; Dr. C. S. Daswani in New Delhi, India; Sean Cao, Mark Chowaniek, Lucy Collins, and Tu Ly of Buffalo, New York; Christina Moreno of Monterrey, Mexico; Dr. Salif Ouedraogo and Dr. Sibry Tapsoba, both of Ouagadougou University in Burkina Faso; Professor Nouchine Ansari of the Children's Book Council of Iran in Tehran; Professor Ada Honegger-Kaufmann in Zurich, Switzerland; Dr. Lettie Tjon A. Toe of the Department of Education in Paramaribo, Suriname; Dr. Frank Greene of McGill University in Montreal, Quebec, Canada; Professor Jaap Tuinman of Simon Fraser University in Burnaby, British Columbia, Canada; Professor Judit Fulop-Kadar of Magyar Pedagogia Tarsasag in Budapest, Hungary; Professor Torleiv Hoien in Bryne, Norway; Dr. Frits Gillebaard of Buffalo, New York; Rosemary Andrews of Lakewood, New York; Dr. Vasily Tsaryov of the USSR Academy of Pedagogical Sciences in Moscow; Ruthie Pizarro at the State University of New York at Buffalo; Wilfried W. Dwarkasing of Miami, Florida; Professor Alvaro Marchesi Ullastres and Professor Abgel Gonzales Rivero, both of the Ministry of Education in Madrid, Spain; Professor Anil K. Sinha, Director of Adult Education in New Delhi, India; Professor Alfred Oftedal Telhaug in Norway; Professor Rachel Cohen in Boulogne, France; Professor An-Magritt Hauge of the Norwegian Institute of Special Education in Hosle, Norway; Professor Ruphang Sodemba of Communication Media Nepal in Kathmandu, Nepal; Professor Ali S. Basalah in Saudi Arabia; Professor Carmen Moreno of Mexico City, Mexico; and Jose M. Ruijter of UNICEF in Harare, Zimbabwe. Finally, we would also like to thank Nancy Meyers at the State University of New York at Buffalo; Amy Epstein of St. Louis, Missouri; Jason Epstein of Knoxville, Tennessee; Sharon Hladczuk of East Amherst, New York; and Alexander Hladczuk also of East Amherst, New York, for their help on this project. We believe that we were able to remember everyone. However, as so often happens in any sort of acknowledgment we may have overlooked some people. We hope they accept our apologies.

Introduction

SETTING THE STAGE

To tell people alive today that they should sit up and pay attention to the overly worn phrase "the world has grown smaller" could border on the abusively reiterative were it not for developments around the world.

The most significant development is the apparent end to the cold war. Yet, the end of the cold war is a result of even greater factors. The advent of *glasnost* and *perestroika* in the Soviet Union, and the democratization efforts in Eastern Europe and the reunification of Germany have given new meaning to the saying "the world has grown smaller."

The world's reduced size has brought with it a greater openness and dialogue on the human condition which, in turn, are resulting in new and increased efforts to better the lot of humanity.

The failure of totalitarian governments has begun to release energies which, if properly directed, can only add to the personal and social development of mankind. One such direction is in the area of literacy—the process of learning to read. With the serious deterioration of communism as an enduring political philosophy and the consequent evolution toward forms of social democracy, the importance of being able to read—or at least of being functionally literate—has taken on a new urgency.

As dictatorships either fall or evolve, the burden of government, commerce, education, and social welfare increasingly becomes the responsibility of the individual citizen. This person will need to be able to weigh choices, to analyze situations critically—in short, people will need to be informed. They will need to be able to read, at first gaining functional literacy but soon thereafter parlaying those basic reading skills into far more sophisticated abilities so as to comprehend the whole world of language in front of them.

We believe that this book is at least an appropriate aid and perhaps even a vehicle to allowing educational planners an opportunity to see how a broad cross-section of the world is handling the process of learning to read. We provide coverage of every continent as well as First, Second, and Third World countries. We have also included a number of interesting contrasts—for example, North Korea and South Korea, Germany and Switzerland, Portugal and Brazil.

Just as the world has grown smaller, so too has the field of education. Through this book we hope to begin to counter the development of centripetal forces in education, a disturbing trend that has recently become visible in at least the United States. Centripetalism occurs when failing schools increasingly revert to simpler materials and less demanding programs. Another characteristic is a shunning of the innovative for the tried (but not necessarily true). Therefore, with this book we hope to shed some light on reading practices around the world, with the hope that they may begin to have even the smallest impact on reading education.

THE TOPIC UNDER STUDY

We are studying the phenomenon known as reading on a worldwide basis and generally by scholars indigenous to the country in question. Specifically, we focus on some of the crucial factors associated with reading as a function of gender and on the educational continuum from emergent literacy and early reading readiness programs to adult education. It follows, then, that the topic and factors under study are also related to the outline of the book. Thus, any meaningful discussion of reading education on a country-by-country basis must first examine not only the languages of the country, but also the nature of reading policy and the goals of reading education. In this way we will be able to translate policy and goals into numbers, materials, programs, and research. In the world of numbers we are interested in the rates of illiteracy, reading disabilities, and the financing of reading education.

In this book we examine materials involved in diagnosing reading disabilities and teaching reading. In the area of programs, our focus is on both reading readiness and teacher education. Finally, we have tried to expose researchers to each other by providing the opportunity to discuss research orientations.

OUTLINE OF THE BOOK

This book examines reading education in twenty-six countries based on a standard format. Of course, not all the contributors were able to follow the outline strictly as it was presented to them. In these cases we have made every attempt to make these chapters conform to the outline. Generally, each chapter contains an introduction followed by sections on ten factors associated with reading: the language(s) of the country in question; reading policy; the goals of reading; illiteracy; questions pertaining to the rate and diagnosis of reading disabilities; reading readiness programs; the teacher qualification procedure; the source and availability of materials in reading; the financing of reading education; and research thrusts in the field of reading. Each chapter ends with a summary and a brief bibliography of important reference sources.

As a result of this logical presentation, several trends have become apparent. Though often interrelated, these trends can generally be discussed across the ten associated factors examined in this book.

TRENDS

A trend is often much like an average; it should not be interpreted in an all or none fashion. Like an average it is a written reflection of the high and low, with the mean point falling somewhere in an area of discernible magnitude. For example, although reading policy is found to be quite centralized throughout the countries studied in this book, in some instances the reading education policy is quite decentralized. This does not, however, keep us from stating that the trend in reading policy is toward centralization.

The first factor, language, becomes an issue in relation to the existence of minority groups in a country or simply the sheer number of languages found there. Japan and Cuba, for instance, have a relatively simple language situation compared to Zaire.

Second, in many countries reading education policy tends to emanate from a relatively centralized system. A prominent exception is the United States which has a decentralized process.

Third, the reading goal of all the countries covered here is the same: to equip students and people generally with the skills that will help them in life. Most differences that may occur are the result of degree and not kind; however, in some cases the goal of reading is quite explicitly a political goal.

The fourth factor is illiteracy. The goal is to decrease illiteracy, but in some countries, because of lack of resources, this goal remains just a wish. Related to illiteracy are trends in the area of adult reading education, namely, under-staffing, underfinancing, insufficient materials, and lack of research.

Worldwide, the greatest concern in the area of education, following illiteracy, is reading disabilities. Much effort and money are being spent in addressing this issue, which represents the fifth factor.

Sixth is the factor of emergent literacy and early reading readiness programs. In many countries, either these programs are nonexistent or they remain just a goal or in a rudimentary state.

The remaining four factors—teacher qualification procedure, materials, the financing of reading education, and research—show the greatest variation. These areas reveal a continuum from wealth to dearth, without emerging trends except in the matter of financing reading education where the clear trend is financially downward. Either the country involved has never financed reading education, or it has been unable to afford it.

In the area of teacher qualification we often found that this factor was closely tied to reading policy and the goals of reading. If, for example, reading was not taught as a separate subject, we found that there were no reading teachers as such.

The financing of reading education followed similar lines. If it was an aspect of the curriculum, it was often funded. More often, however, reading education was generally integrated into the overall curriculum.

Reading research fell into the same sort of pattern: either it was basically being done or it was not.

Over and above the trends affecting the ten factors associated with reading, there was at least one overwhelming trend that all our authors believed was very important: that is, the process and the need to read was crucially important.

This then brings us full circle to the point that there is an inextricable relationship between human beings and the ability to read. The future of humankind is tightly woven with its continuing ability to read; literacy must keep pace with the development and growth of society. It is to this goal that our book is committed.

INTERNATIONAL HANDBOOK OF READING EDUCATION

1

Australia

Paul Kidston and John Elkins

INTRODUCTION

The Australian continent has been occupied by Aborigines for perhaps 40,000 years and by 1988 had known only 200 years of European settlement. Thus literacy was imported along with Western culture, and only recently has distinctively Australian literacy education emerged.

Australians number around 16 million people, with extensive immigration in the post–1945 era, adding a multicultural dimension to earlier dominance by Anglo-Saxon peoples. In 1988 immigration was expected to exceed the natural increase in population, bringing literacy challenges because of the many languages used by ethnic communities. The colonization of Australia led to the formation of independent states which introduced compulsory education in the 1870s. When the Commonwealth was formed in 1901, education was designated as a state rather than a federal responsibility. While this arrangement is somewhat similar to that in the United States, a major difference is that in Australia, the state, rather than the local school district, is the main organizational level for education. Thus, state[1] governments provide free and compulsory public education from six to fourteen years, constituting an expenditure of about thirty percent of their budgets. Across Australia there is also a network of Catholic primary and secondary schools as well as a number of private independent schools. State governments, through their Education Departments, attempt to equalize educational opportunities across urban and rural communities by relatively uniform provision of school facilities and by employing teachers subject to transfer within the state. Furthermore, modern technology is being used to bring education to students living in the most remote or isolated parts of the country. Correspondence tuition is coordinated with radio broadcasting (the

School of the Air), telephone conferencing, use of facsimile machines and satellite video, and audio and data communication to help overcome the tyranny of distance.

Education systems do not differ markedly across states, even though there is some variation in the extent of preschool education, age of school start, the number of years required for primary education, and, in some states, specialized Grade 11/12 schools (matriculation colleges).

Ministers of education from the states and Commonwealth confer each year, and, as a result, even more consistency of curriculum is developing across states. This trend has been promoted by the Commonwealth government's involvement in education funding and policymaking since the early 1970s. One aspect of federal intervention has been the funding of higher education, including the universities and colleges that provide courses of initial teacher education and some of the formal in-service courses. Another important influence has been direct grants, both general purpose and specific, to state, Catholic, and independent schools to promote equity and to move schooling toward national goals.

Through its Schools Commission, the federal government initiated programs to support disadvantaged schools, to increase school retention rates in the post-compulsory school years, to encourage the use of computers in the curriculum, to develop special education, and to promote gender equity. The most recent trend has been to foster high technology through curricular emphasis on science and mathematics and the greater participation of girls in studying these subjects.

In recent years action has been taken to reduce the size of the large state Education Department bureaucracies by regionalizing the public school system and by encouraging the greater participation of parents in their local schools.

Of some importance for literacy education is that, historically, there has been a relatively low reliance on standardized achievement testing. Recently, some moves have been made toward statewide testing in basic skills areas in some states, partly for political reasons and partly to focus teachers' attention on reading and writing as part of the press toward high technology solutions to Australia's economic circumstances. As Boomer (1987) has pointed out, although Australian education systems should be made more accountable, they have also had an opportunity to use more valid approaches than is offered by narrow reliance on standardized testing.

Let's now move to a brief consideration of the history of reading education in Australia.

HISTORY OF READING EDUCATION

Since 1970 when compulsory schooling was introduced in Australia, all states have produced their own sets of class readers predominantly derived from British sources. These include a remarkable mixture of narrative, poetic, and expository texts. Very little of the material was written specifically for children, often a common theme being "God, king and country." From the early years of this century, many states have provided enrichment reading through the issue of periodical "school papers." Between the 1940s and 1960s the early reading diet of Australian children was very similar to that experienced by children elsewhere in the English-speaking world. Through the 1950s approaches to beginning reading instruction emphasized phonics. During the 1960s the emphasis moved to "whole word" approaches. Each Australian state adopted and issued for use in all its schools particular reading schemes, for example, *The Happy Venture Readers* or *Ladybird*. In the 1970s all states started to encourage a variety of materials for use in teaching reading. Consistent with the views at the time, educators experimented with schemes (predominantly from the United States) and Scientific Research Associates' reading laboratories that provided detailed specific teaching on a range of reading comprehension skills. From the mid-1970s there has been a remarkable growth in indigenous publication of reading materials. Today in no state do education authorities specify any particular schemes or materials for the teaching of reading.

Sir Fred Schonell (1900–1969) is the major figure in the history of reading education in Australia, even though he carried out most of his work in the United Kingdom. In 1929 Schonell, a young teacher living in western Australia, won a scholarship for overseas study. He went to the University of London where he completed a Ph.D. in 1932 with a thesis on the diagnosis and remediation of difficulties in spelling ("An Investigation into Disability in Spelling"). During the next thirteen years, Schonell developed diagnostic and attainment tests, developed a reading scheme (*The Happy Venture Readers*, 1939) and wrote two major books, *Backwardness in the Basic Subjects* (1942) and *The Psychology and Teaching of Reading* (1945).

When Schonell returned to Australia in 1950, much of the work he had pioneered in the United Kingdom became better known and widely influential in Australia. With Phyllis Flowerdew, he published another reading series *The Wide Range Readers* (1948). In one of his most important actions, Schonell established a Remedial Centre in the University of Queensland which offered the first training course in remedial teaching in Australia. Schonell also fostered the formation of a Council of the International Reading Association which has prospered and hosted the Twelfth World Congress on Reading in July 1988.

LANGUAGES OF INSTRUCTION

The recent *National Policy on Languages* (Lo Bianco, 1987) points out that, although English is the de facto national language of Australia, its status as such has never been explicitly declared. It is the first and usually the only language of about 83 percent of the population.

Widespread provision is made for NESB (non-English speaking background) children, and to a lesser extent for adults, to receive instruction in English as a second language (ESL). One recent issue of the *Australian Journal of Reading* carries eight articles on ESL, including a review by Campagna (1986) on second language programs in each state and territory. In most schools English is the language of instruction, and children are taught to read and write in English. There are a few significant exceptions.

In major cities, particularly Sydney, Melbourne, Adelaide, and Darwin, where there are concentrations of recently arrived migrants in certain schools, bilingual programs are conducted in which reading and writing in the mother tongue are taught alongside English. Many languages are employed, including Greek, Polish, Spanish, Vietnamese, Italian, Thai, Tagalog, and Hakka. Limited amounts of reading material in those languages are available to support the programs.

In the more remote areas of northern, central, and western Australia, bilingual programs are conducted for Aboriginal and Torres Strait Islander pupils in local Aboriginal languages and dialects. At the time of European settlement some 200 to 250 Aboriginal languages representing 600 dialects were spoken, yet today only some 50 are considered viable (Lo Bianco, 1987). Bilingual programs are most widely employed in the Northern Territory where approximately half of the Aboriginal children are enrolled in schools with bilingual programs. Aboriginal assistant teachers, teacher linguists, and community volunteers are engaged in recording the local language and producing vernacular print materials for use in these reading programs. In the Northern Territory ten Aboriginal languages including Warlpiri, Gumarj, Djambarrpuyngu, and Tiwi are being used. Each is unique to a particular area and is utilized by between 300 and 3,000 speakers. In most of these bilingual programs, literacy in English is delayed until the students develop basic competencies with mother tongue materials.

If not an Aboriginal language, the lingua franca of many Aboriginals, particularly in the more remote parts of Australia, is Aboriginal English (in western Australia and Queensland) or Kriol (in the Northern Territory and South Australia). School literacy programs recognize and support the use of these vernaculars while assisting children to learn to read and write in standard Australian English.

READING POLICY

Home and Preschool

Because schooling in Australia is primarily the responsibility of the state governments, each with its own Education Act, there are marginally different provisions regarding the age of entry to formal schooling. The school year commences at the end of January and runs through to mid-December. In most states compulsory schooling begins at age five. Some states are introducing flexible entry to school. Instead of there being one intake per year in January, children may commence school at other times throughout the year, usually immediately after one of the three midyear vacation periods or immediately following their fifth birthday. The reception classes are called variously kindergarten, reception, preparatory, and Year One or First Grade in different states. Regardless of the particular time in the year when children enroll at school, each

January they move on to the next class. Promotion from grade to grade is now usually automatic, although some classes with composite grade levels do offer flexibility to advance or hold back the placement of children.

In the period prior to entry to the compulsory schooling years, there are various provisions for the education of children. For example, in Tasmania, at four years of age children can enter kindergarten classes and at five years the preparatory class, but all children must be enrolled in school by the age of six. In Queensland the state provides an optional one-year preschool program for children between four and five years of age. Every weekday preschools operate a half-day program for children, in preschool units attached to primary schools. These units are staffed by trained preschool teachers and teacher aides. Correspondence course provisions are made for children in small country towns and for isolated families. They are provided books, play materials, audiotapes and videotapes, and the like, to help the parents of these children organize appropriate learning experiences for their preschool children. Throughout Australia many private kindergartens offer programs for children in their preschool year or even earlier.

The concept of reading readiness underwent significant change in Australia in the 1980s. Previously, when the development of discrete skills was considered to be the basis of reading, reading readiness was defined in terms of preparation for those skills. This resulted in an emphasis on visual and auditory perceptual training and the development of psychomotor areas, with lots of specific exercises and worksheets providing training in these areas. Reading is now viewed as part of the language learning process, and the widely held belief in Australia is that interactional learning principles should be used to assist children to become readers. This has meant a dramatic change in the nature of reading readiness activities. Nowadays much less reliance is placed on perceptual training activities. To foster literacy development in the early years, school programs are now built around the notion of extending informal environmental language learning opportunities for children. These programs involve children in being exposed to, immersed in, and engaged with demonstrations in the use of language for appropriate purposes. Increasingly, children are encouraged to write from an early age and to explore play opportunities that involve reading and writing. One of the most important activities for assisting children to become readers is recognized to be reading stories to children. A great deal of emphasis is placed on this activity in programs in the preschool and early school years.

Australia has an extensive network of public libraries. State libraries have a country extension service to enable families in distant places to borrow books when no library is available locally. Public libraries are well stocked with many picture story books for children and books for older readers.

A number of children's television programs in Australia target the preschool audience. The most popular of these programs is the Australian Broadcasting Commission's "Play School" program which has been running on Australian television for three decades. It incorporates book reading and story telling episodes in every program. These children's television programs also incorporate activities involving recognition of the names of the days of the week and nu-

merals, and like exercises. The "Sesame Street" program from the United States
is also a long-running feature of children's television in Australia. These programs reinforce and expand the opportunities provided through the home whereby
children from an early age are introduced to picture story books and to the
process of reading. Through these experiences children learn that books contain
information, that reading is enjoyable, and that stories are structured in a certain
way. They also learn certain print concepts, such as the idea that it is the print
and not the pictures that conveys the message, that print messages are unchang-
ing, and that in reading print the reader begins at the top left of the page and
proceeds left to right, reading the left page before the right page. Early childhood
programs make extensive use of nursery rhymes, song, and poetry as well as
books with highly predictable text structures. In this way children through "the
favorite book syndrome" are encouraged to become familiar with the act of
reading for themselves. School reading programs extend from and build on this
range of experiences which children have had prior to coming to school.

GOALS OF READING

The Primary Years

Responsibility for reading education in primary schools rests largely with class
teachers. From syllabus and curriculum documents that provide guidelines and
from school policies that provide more detailed guidance, teachers construct
programs for teaching reading and draw on published reading schemes as required
in order to achieve their objectives.

Policy is set by syllabus documents or curriculum guidelines that each state
Department of Education develops separately. These documents establish a learning philosophy and make strong recommendations about expected practices. They
vary in format. They are revised from time to time to take account of changes
in research and practice.

Some of the documents produced in Australia deal solely with the teaching
of reading, for example, *Reading K-12* (NSW Department of Education, 1979).
Most other documents of the 1970s, however, focused on reading as part of the
language arts. The *Language Arts Curriculum Guide for Primary Schools*
(Queensland Department of Education, 1974) provided a separate listing for
reading within the language arts area. It stated, that "reading is above all a
thinking process. Its four recognized elements are word recognition, the mastery
of sight vocabulary and word attack skills, comprehension, reaction and integration." This definition is supported by detailed lists of skills and objectives
to be attained by children in these areas in Grades 1 to 3 and 4 to 7. The 1981
Core Curriculum Document T-10 of the Northern Territory provided a separate
description for reading, but it was expected that teachers would integrate reading
teaching along with that of the other language arts. The documents produced in

the early 1980s such as *Language Arts: Reading* (South Australian Department of Education, 1982) placed strong emphasis on a process approach in accord with the prevailing view from research at that time. Currently, the focus that is being incorporated into the new syllabus of western Australia and the Framework documents of Victoria and Queensland recognizes the social context of language use. Emphasis is placed on reading and other language activities being used purposefully within certain social contexts rather than on reading and other language activities being undertaken in decontextualized circumstances. For example, the *P-10 Language Education Framework* (Queensland Department of Education, 1989) specifies the following holistic goal for language education in English: "The goal is language in use, that is by the time children leave school they should be able to compose and comprehend spoken and written English appropriately and effectively in a wide range of literary and non-literary genres in a wide range of social contexts" (p. 24).

In an effort to promote continuity in the curriculum experienced by children as they progress through school, the staffs of many schools have developed school programs or policies that provide a little more specific guidance on the range of suggested learning experiences, available resources, and relevant assessment and evaluation methods to be employed. The teacher's responsibility is to design programs of work in accord with the directions established in syllabus and curriculum documents and in accord with school policies and programs. Published reading schemes and sets of material are used as required within those programs of work.

Schools are now able to select and purchase reading materials of their choice. In some cases the education authority provides a catalogue of recommended schemes. In most states it is recommended that part of the school grant be spent annually on the purchase of reading materials. Many schools supplement this funding with monies raised by parents and citizens associations. From the mid-1970s to the mid-1980s many of the Australian-produced materials were fully developed schemes or programs of work. Some of these were Australian adaptations of overseas schemes, for example, *Reading 360 Australia* (1976 +); yet some were entirely indigenous, for example, *Reading Rigby* (1976 +), *Young Australia* (1980 +), and the *Mt. Gravatt Language Development Reading Program* (1977 +). In the last-named, the lower levels were based on the language patterns derived from a study of the oral language of hundreds of children, and the upper levels were built around the systematic introduction of various literary and nonliterary written genres. In the last few years the nature of the new schemes has changed again in accord with the latest directions from research and theory. Rather than being comprehensive programs of work, the modern schemes are collections of books on separate topics sometimes thematically arranged, designed so that teachers can make flexible use of the materials. Such schemes are *Story Box* and *Story Chest* (1980 +), *Expressways* (1982 +), *Beginnings* (1985 +), *Bookshelf* (1986 +), *Southern Cross* (1987 +), and *Eureka Treasure Chest* (1987 +).

All Australian primary and secondary schools have identifiable school libraries that are quite well stocked with reference and nonfiction materials, fiction books as well as junior fiction collections. As Robinson (1986) points out, there has been a burgeoning of quality literature written for children by Australian authors in recent years. Many schools have full-time teacher/librarians. Most teachers make use of collections of library books as part of their reading program, and increasingly teachers are teaching reading solely from library books (Hancock and Hill, 1988). With many of the modern schemes, however, there is little to distinguish scheme books from library books. Although most teachers appreciate the fairly extensive teachers' manuals in the schemes, which provide a host of ideas on possible teaching activities across the curriculum to build around particular books, few teachers follow these manuals closely. Most teachers select whatever suggested activities fit in with the class program they have designed. In quite a number of published schemes activity books and copy masters are associated with the basic scheme. Although some teachers make extensive use of such activity books, they are no longer normal practice.

Many teachers, particularly in the early years of school, make heavy use of "big books." These are large-format editions either hand drawn or published, approximately 50 centimeters square, of popular books from the scheme. These big books permit group activities around a particular text. The books are shared, and during reading teachers point out particular features about the text. The corporate experience of reading together is enjoyable and provides support for young readers as they learn to process text. Through reading activities based on shared text, teachers can demonstrate the comprehending processes involved in reading, the text processing strategies involved with and predictions based on meaning and grammar, and confirmations based on letter/sound relationships, as well as pointing out to children text features such as letter shapes, punctuation, and paragraphing.

Most teachers still regard phonics instruction as important in the teaching of reading. Quite a few teachers maintain separate sequenced programs of instruction in phonics and letter recognition that may be only marginally related to the text they are dealing with. Most teachers of early grades, however, do provide specific information about letter/sound relationships as a part of shared-text activities. Most teachers of early grades also make use of language-experience activities. That is, children are given opportunities to dictate texts, quite often those associated with pictures they have drawn, to competent writers such as teachers and teacher aides who write down the child's dictated text. Another common practice is group composition whereby the teacher and the class negotiate and appropriate text together and the teacher constructs the text for children on a large sheet of paper or on the blackboard.

In the last few years, with the widespread adoption of "process writing," children have been encouraged from the earliest grades to engage in their own writing. This is seen not only as a means of assisting with writing development but of providing opportunities for children to explore the writing system and to gain knowledge that will assist with learning to read. In Australian primary schools some sustained reading time is commonly set aside within each school day. This set period of time usually totals 15 minutes, quite often after a break, when all children and the teacher read their own self-selected materials. This activity is given different names in different places—for example, DEAR (Drop Everything and Read), RIBIT (Read in Bed It's Terrific), and USSR (Uninterrupted Silent Sustained Reading). Although the children are seldom required to produce reading logs or reports, they may be encouraged to talk about favorite books they have read during this time and to try and encourage other children to read those books.

During the 1960s and 1970s many schools experimented with ability group streaming across year levels or the whole school, for daily reading instruction periods of half- to one-hour duration. This method did not produce the hoped-for dramatic improvements in performance, and with the trend toward integrating reading instruction across the language arts and even more broadly across the curriculum, cross-class streaming has all but disappeared. It is quite a common practice, however, particularly in the middle and upper primary years, for teachers to organize reading instruction within their classes around a number of ability groups. The most common activities undertaken in these groups are "round robin reading" (children take turns reading aloud a sentence or paragraph), silent reading guided by teacher questioning, and read and discuss or "comprehension activities" (children read a passage and answer a number of questions in writing). Increasingly, more time is spent on corporate activities discussing meaning making in a particular text than on self-directed activities. Standard comprehension questions are being replaced by various meaning-exploring activities such as cloze, semantic webbing, plot profiling, and story maps (see Johnson and Louis, 1985) which involve children in lots of discussion as they learn to comprehend.

Secondary Schools

Reading education in secondary schools did not receive much attention in Australia until the last two decades. For example, in 1968 *The Slow Learning Child* carried five articles from a seminar on Reading Problems in High School at which Mildred Dawson, a past president of IRA, was guest speaker. One of the earliest studies was conducted by Atkinson, Cochrane, and Elkins (1968). They described secondary school students who were having extreme difficulties using reading to learn. The group of thirty-two students were taught individually or in small groups for seven weekly sessions of two hours. Most, but not all, improved, and the authors suggested ways of increasing motivation and critical reading skills among high school students.

Morris (1982) evaluated an early attempt to train resource specialists for secondary schools. Since then interest in secondary school literacy, and not just the area of reading problems has grown substantially. Morris and Stewart–Dore (1984) have synthesized much of the content-area reading literature into a package for secondary teachers in all curriculum areas (ERICA [Effective Reading in Content Areas]). They suggest four stages: (1) preparing, (2) thinking through, (3) extracting and organizing information, and (4) translating (reading to writing). Downing and Morris (1984) evaluated ERICA and considered it to be very useful. The Queensland Education Department has incorporated ERICA into an on-going in-service program called "Learning to Learn Through Reading," while several college-level programs for training secondary school teachers have made good use of ERICA.

Despite these efforts, secondary school reading programs are not widespread. Although assistance in reading may be available via resource teachers or volunteers, it is unusual for reading to be programmed as a subject in the secondary school curriculum. Variability in practices is more characteristic of secondary schools than is true of the primary school, where reading is a clearly recognizable part of the curriculum.

Recently, a number of schools have experimented with approaches such as reciprocal teaching (Palincsar, 1987; Palincsar and Brown, 1986, 1987). The success of such approaches fits in well with the trend toward language across the curriculum which pervades the approach adopted for students from non-English speaking backgrounds.

Reading at the Adult, TAFE, and College Levels

At the postcompulsory schooling stage, several programs are available for improving reading. The Australian Council for Adult Literacy provides advocacy for adults with limited literacy. Programs that may receive some government funding often use volunteer tutors who may be given training by specialists. The system of Technical and Further Education (TAFE) Colleges also provides extensive support for adults to improve their literacy.

Adult literacy programs are well developed in Australia under the initiatives of both the government, through the Technical and Further Education system, and advocacy groups such as State and National Councils for Adult Literacy. Wickert and Zimmerman (in press) review adult literacy in the context of adult basic education. As they note, prior to the early 1970s, little provision was made for adult literacy programs, and in some states widespread funding was not made available until the 1980s. Various official reports on TAFE, learning difficulties, and language policy have all recognized the need to make greater efforts in promoting literacy among adults, particularly among migrants, Aborigines, and prisoners (Colston, 1984; Dymock, 1982; Fesl, 1982; Lo Bianco, 1987; Nelson, 1980, 1981). Much still remains to be done in these three areas. Although the limited data available suggest that functional illiteracy may be around 3 or 4 percent in mainstream society, it may be as high as 50 percent in some disadvantaged groups. The policy statement of the Australian Council for Adult Literacy "affirms that all Australians should have the opportunity to acquire the knowledge and skills necessary to manage their own lives and function as participating members of a democratic society.''

A substantial amount of research has been done on adult literacy in Australia. One of the most important studies was conducted by Grant (1987) who used case study methods to evaluate (1) institutional/professional and (2) voluntary/community-based programs. Among his recommendations are that on-going evaluation of programs be continued and that flexible structures be developed for programs, with devolution of responsibility consistent with improved staff training.

At the tertiary level it is expected that students who qualify for entry into a degree or diploma course will have sufficient reading and writing skills to cope with academic demands. While some support is provided for students with limited knowledge of English, and usually some specific assistance is given with study skills and writing term papers, the availability of more comprehensive literacy instruction is variable and limited.

READING DISABILITIES

Special Needs

Although education for children with disabilities is well advanced in Australia, some aspects of literacy education are of concern. The latest technology is available to support the literacy and study needs of students with visual impairments, yet there has been a tendency to undervalue literacy for students with intellectual disabilities. Indeed, it has been found that one major client group of literacy programs for adults is made up of former special education students.

Children with substantial reading and related difficulties (who might be termed learning disabled in the United States) have received considerable attention over the past twenty years. Beginning with a few pioneers such as Fred Schonell at the University of Queensland and M. D. Neale at the University of Sydney, clinics were established to assist children who were having great difficulty learning to read. By the early 1970s most teacher education colleges had some specialist training programs for remedial and resource teachers, and education departments began to provide support particularly at the primary school level. Elkins (1975, 1983) has documented much of the Australian literature on reading disability. It is perhaps important to note that, following upon an inquiry by a Select Committee of the Australian House of Representatives (Cadman, 1976), Australian practice has favored a noncategorical approach to helping poor readers within the regular school system rather than the U.S. model of defining learning disability and funding support within Special Education as part of PL 94–142. States vary in the extent of specialized support services provided for children who are not making good progress in school. All have psychological services that provide specialized assessments of children in need. In the primary school, remedial/resource teachers provide a range of services from withdrawal classes to assisting the class teacher with appropriate programs. Queensland has the most extensive network of such remedial/resource teachers with one in most of the larger schools. Throughout Australia an increasing number of secondary resource teachers and special support teachers are being trained and involved in supporting children with poor reading skills, but this is by no means universal.

One recent trend in the early education years has been the adoption of Clay's Reading Recovery procedure (Clay, 1985) in Victoria and the Australian Capital Territory. Initial evaluations indicate that Reading Recovery has been successfully adapted to the local education system.

TEACHER QUALIFICATIONS

The first study of teacher preparation in the area of reading in Australia appears to have been carried out as a result of the House of Representatives Select Committee on Specific Learning Difficulties (Cadman, 1976). It noted that many submissions claimed that teachers were often ill prepared to teach reading. The Committee asked one of its consultants (Elkins) to survey institutions involved in teacher preparation regarding optional and compulsory coursework on the teaching of reading and on helping children experiencing learning problems.

A wide range was found in the time spent on the teaching of reading, from as little as two hours and a median of ten to twenty hours. These were very low when compared with the Bullock Report's (United Kingdom) 100 to 150 hours or the IRA's six semester hours (60 to 90 hours). With optional courses, around 20 percent of the student teachers did build up their course content to about 100 hours.

Barely three years after the Australian Reading Association (ARA) was formed, a one-day seminar on Teacher Education in Reading was held in conjunction with the ARA Annual Conference at which Alan Robinson from the United States and Donald Moyle from the United Kingdom provided insights from their nations' experience. Parker (1979) outlined ARA policy on teacher preparation which, among other things, argued for a minimum of three courses in reading education for those intending to become primary school teachers and at least one course for those preparing to teach in secondary schools. However, all participants in the seminar stressed the importance of accountability, but argued for rich, varied, and valid approaches to demonstrating whether teachers were able to teach reading and how their preparation could be improved. Elkins (1979) also noted that the teaching of reading had implications for all curriculum areas.

One major study of the preparation of teachers to teach reading was carried out by the Queensland Board of Teacher Education (1979) "to survey the opinions of beginning teachers, lecturers, and school personnel regarding the adequacy and efficacy of training for the teaching of reading and associated language skills provided in universities and colleges of advanced education" (p. 3). A sample of forty-five faculty in ten institutions with primary (K-8) teacher education programs was interviewed on the following issues: aims and objectives, time devoted to teaching reading/language, content of teaching of reading courses, organization of courses, organization at practice school, and liaison between college and school. Interviews on these topics were also conducted with 205 supervising teachers and 44 school administrators. Several issues relating to teacher education generally emerged. The report noted:

There should be a closer working relationship between schools and teacher training institutions in the preparation of teachers for the teaching of reading. An investigation should be made of the ways in which ''theory'' and ''practice''could be further integrated; and practical programs should be planned, implemented and evaluated jointly by colleges and schools.

Training in the teaching of reading should be regarded as a continuous process through-out a teacher's career. An emphasis should be placed on the development of induction and in-service reading programs; practising school personnel should be carefully selected and receive training in their respective roles; and all schools (both primary and secondary) should formulate their own school reading policy (p. 65).

Specific reading and language-related issues were, of course, considered. For example, the faculty believed that helping children who experienced difficulties in learning to read was not a topic to be included in the three-year teacher preparation program. Supervising teachers, however, tended to help student teachers to recognize and assist children experiencing difficulties. College programs averaged 85 hours, but a very wide range was noted (16 to 176 hours). In some cases, it was found difficult to identify time allocated to the teaching of reading, and we may conjecture that it is even more difficult today given the prominence of whole-language approaches. School experience opportunities for teaching reading decreased as grade level increased, and there was little control over which grades student teachers were assigned.

Until the late 1970s secondary school teachers had not generally been given instruction in the teaching of reading, but in some colleges and universities enthusiasts had succeeded in having an allocation of about 5 percent of the curriculum devoted to language and reading. Of course, those who were planning to teach English would have covered topics dealing with reading and writing, but in Queensland not until 1979 did all training programs include a compulsory literacy and language course for all content areas.

A further component of the Queensland Board of Teacher Education study was based on questionnaires completed by 215 first-year primary teachers. The majority (82.3 percent) felt that too little time had been spent on the content and methodology of primary school subjects such as reading and writing, more than half considered their preparation to teach reading and spelling was poor or very poor, and almost half made the same observation about written expression. It might be hoped that new teachers a decade later would have different opinions, but that research remains to be done.

The highest priority needs expressed by first-year teachers were: (1) how to devise a reading program from available resources, and (2) how to manage simultaneously the reading groups in a class. Interestingly, needs were not identified in areas such as the psychology of the reading process, how to promote interest in reading, or how to select and administer reading tests—all topics that presumably had been appropriately dealt with in preservice courses.

One great concern was that during their practice teaching, only 0.5 percent of student teachers identified reading as the most enjoyable subject to teach, compared to 29.8 percent who named mathematics. Moreover, all language arts together warranted the preference of only 5.1 percent. Similar views were held after some months of teaching, with fewer teachers regarding reading as enjoyable to teach versus mathematics, science, music, social studies, physical education, and art. Only 1.4 percent thought reading was easiest to teach, whereas 27.9 percent (the largest group) thought reading was the hardest subject to teach. These results from the 1979 survey suggest that more effort should be devoted to helping student and new teachers to become confident and competent in teaching reading and the other components of the language arts curriculum.

One problem facing teacher educators was noted in a study by Lennon et al. (1985) who found that experienced teachers, who had had little exposure to contemporary reading theory, differed from teacher education students and beginning teachers with regard to many attitudes and beliefs about reading and how it should be taught. Nevertheless, new teachers seemed able to maintain a stance toward teaching reading that was consistent with the psycholinguistic perspective taught during their teacher preparation program, despite the potentially conflicting socializing influence of experienced teachers. However, one area in which new teachers did change was in adopting systematic phonics instruction. It is unclear whether this change stemmed from the influence of experienced teachers or if it was a response to difficulties experienced in teaching reading from a psycholinguistic perspective.

Morris (1988) has published the most recent study of teacher education in secondary school reading. He obtained data from thirty-three institutions training secondary teachers, which offered a total of forty-one programs: nineteen were one-year postbaccalaureate diplomas, five were three-year undergraduate, and seventeen were four-year undergraduate degrees. Almost half (nineteen) made no compulsory provision for studies of the teaching of reading. Morris noted very little consensus as to what prospective secondary school teachers should know about reading. Topics included content area reading, remediation, language in the classroom, and teaching language arts, but few institutions offered coherent curricula. Although these recent data suggest that more programs preparing secondary teachers are inducing coursework concerned with reading than was true a decade earlier, there is still some distance to go before it can be claimed that secondary teachers are being satisfactorily prepared to help students with reading and writing across the curriculum. Despite the clear limitations in teacher education noted in the research reviewed, substantial progress has been made over the past decades and Australian teachers appear to perform comparably with those in similar societies.

READING MATERIALS

Educational Publishing

Most of the Australian book publishers are divisions of or are closely allied to British and American publishing companies; they were established in order to distribute the parent company's publications more efficiently. In the early 1970s, following on the period of statewide adoption of particular schemes when schools were being given a choice in selecting their reading materials, these publishers vied with each other quite aggressively to market a whole variety of schemes published in the United States and the United Kingdom. Jacaranda Press, an Australian publisher, developed the *Endeavour Reading Programme* (1975 +), and soon it was widely adopted by Australian teachers. This bold publishing move encouraged other companies to consider the possibility of developing Australian-originated materials instead of importing materials from their parent companies. *Endeavour*'s success and the popularity of the New Zealand *Ready to Read* materials confirmed that Australian teachers wanted and needed materials that reflected more localized experience. The first moves in this area for most companies were Australianizations of existing overseas schemes—for example, *Reading 360 Australia* (1976) and *Young Australia Language Development Scheme* (Nelson, 1966 +), which was partly an adaptation of the *Young Canadian Readers*. Since that time quite rapid changes have been made in the approach to teaching reading in Australian schools. The approach has moved from the systematic teaching of skills to a focus on process and most recently to an emphasis on literature and nonliterary forms of text. Reference books such as Burnes and Page (1985), Unsworth (1985), and Murray and Smith (1988) are among those that have been produced to guide teachers in pre- and in-service courses in the study of reading teaching. Publishers have worked closely with researchers and teachers to produce materials that have assisted in the translation into practice of current language learning theory. These materials are proving popular in Australian schools as teachers are seeking locally produced materials, not only because of the cultural relevance of the content but also because they are assured that the underlying framework will most closely match the approach they are adopting. Reading educators across the world have praised these materials, and the publishers are now finding considerable interest from the United States, the United Kingdom, and elsewhere. The rapidity with which publishers have been able to produce suitable new materials in response to developments in theory and research has been a significant factor in spreading new ideas about reading teaching across Australia.

RESEARCH THRUSTS IN READING

Reading research has been significant but limited by funding restrictions common to all areas of education. There is little distinctively Australian about reading research carried out here, and most scholars can be placed in one of the major streams of reading research known internationally.

The psycholinguistic perspective has been influential, particularly through Cambourne (1979, 1983, 1985, 1986, 1987) and Bouffler (1984). In recent years, some polarization of views has been evident as the linguistic theories of Halliday and Hasan (1976, 1985) have been followed in investigations of genre development (Painter & Martin, 1986). Halliday has also influenced studies of cohesion (Anderson, 1987a; Smith, 1985; Smith and Elkins, 1984, 1985), while Brennan and Brennan (1984) have conducted studies of the discourse of children's courts.

Computer-assisted reading has been studied by Anderson (1987b, 1988), Schwartz (1984), and Smith and Gray (1983). Cognitive perspectives on reading research are represented by the work of Freebody and Watson (Cooksey and Freebody, 1987; Freebody and Anderson, 1986; Freebody et al., 1986; Watson, 1983), while Freebody, Baker, and Luke have addressed sociolinguistic issues (Baker & Freebody, 1986; Freebody and Baker, 1985; Luke, 1988). Brennan and Brennan (1984) have studied the literacy needs of prison inmates, an area also commented on by Wickert and Zimmerman (in press).

Reading tests have been produced locally by the Australian Council for Educational Research, which has recently published an innovative comprehension test, TORCH (Mossenson, Hill, and Masters, 1987).

The *Neale Analysis of Reading Ability*, the most widely used individual test of oral reading, has recently been republished in a revised edition (Neale, 1988). An adapted cloze procedure has also been used in the *GAP* (McLeod, 1977), *GAPADOL* (McLeod and Anderson, 1972), and *St. Lucia Reading Comprehension* (Elkins and Andrews, 1974) tests. Kemp (1987) has adapted psycholinguistic principles of assessment developed in the United States by Goodman and Burke (1980) and in New Zealand by Clay (1985) to produce a comprehensive structured observational approach to assessing children with reading difficulties.

In-Service Education

A significant feature of the reading education scene in Australia in recent years has been the development and provision of in-service education. The following examples reveal the variety of ways in which this development has occurred.

Tertiary educators have played a leading role through their research activity, as well as their contribution to conferences and leadership of in-service activities for teachers. Bartlett researched methods for teaching students to utilize explicit text structure knowledge as an aid to more effective reading and writing particularly of expository text. This research followed from the work of Meyer (1975) on expository prose predicate structures. Through in-service sessions conducted by Bartlett and his co-researchers and through publishing an extension of the program into a reference book series for teachers, *Knowing What and Knowing How* (Bartlett, Barton and Turner, 1988), this research has been translated directly into an influence on teaching practice. In a similar way, Morris and Stewart-Dore (1984) developed and promoted the program's Effective Reading In Content Areas (ERICA). In some places, state Departments of Education have employed full-time teacher/consultants to conduct in-service workshops so that teachers can be introduced to ERICA and supported as they apply it in their schools. These examples are typical of the research, development, and diffusion model that occurs internationally whereby researchers in tertiary institutions are able to influence practice.

A significant feature of the Australian education scene, particularly since the mid-1970s, has been the initiative undertaken by employing authorities, school systems, and professional associations in the in-service education area. This is particularly apparent with respect to language and reading.

Although responsibility for providing schools lies with state governments, in 1972 the Australian federal government established a Commonwealth Schools Commission and a Curriculum Development Centre (CDC). The CDC provides national coordination of curriculum initiatives across all subject areas. While most of these efforts have involved the development of sets of curriculum materials or guidelines for teachers, many have placed great emphasis on teacher development through participation in action research projects. One such project was the Language Development Project (LDP). Most Australian states contributed to this project by studying and developing different aspects of language teaching.

In the period 1985–1987 the CDC sponsored a national project in which the Departments of Education, Catholic Education Offices, and Independent School Associations in every state and territory of Australia participated in implementing the Early Literacy In-service Course (ELIC). This professional development program for early childhood teachers is concerned with reading and writing. It is conducted by specially selected teachers who have been carefully trained as tutors. These tutors work with groups of about ten teachers drawn from a number of schools in ten-weekly after-school workshop sessions each of 1.5 to 2 hours duration. Five of these sessions deal with reading development and five with writing. Between sessions, participants undertake reading and practical activities in observing children or applying teaching practices. An important feature of this in-service program has been that, during the period of the course and following it, the tutors work with the participating teachers in their classrooms, discussing, demonstrating, and assisting them to translate the ideas of the course into practice. The South Australian Department of Education developed the ELIC based on New Zealand's successful implementation of a similar program called ERIC—Early Reading In-service Course. Over the 1985–1987 period more than 30,000 teachers and school administrators throughout Australia participated in the ELIC course. The national coordination, promotion, and support by every system and participation by the majority of early childhood teachers across Australia have made this a most significant development and a powerful influence on reading teaching practices in Australian schools.

Following from the success of ELIC, a number of education authorities, some with direct involvement and assistance from tertiary institutions, are developing and implementing in-service programs appropriate to middle and upper primary school years—for example, Further Literary In-service Project (FLIP) in Queensland, Language and Learning in the Middle Years (LLIMY) in South Australia, and Continuing Literacy In-service Course (CLIC) in Victoria. Another interesting recent development has been the Tasmanian *Pathways to Literacy* (1988) project, an in-service program that has developed around assisting teachers track the development of children's progress toward literacy.

A major influence on practice has been that provided through the professional associations. The Australian Reading Association, a national affiliate of the International Reading Association, has been conducting annual national conferences since its formation in 1975. These have provided a forum through which hundreds of teachers and teacher educators have been able to share information about the latest in research and practice. The Association's journal, *The Australian Journal of Reading*, and its other publications along with those of other associations with an interest in the area (members of the Australian Literacy Federation: The Australian Association for the Teaching of English [AATE] and the Primary English Teaching Association [PETA]) have had a very significant impact on language teaching. The most striking example has been the transformation of the teaching of writing in Australian schools. PETA sponsored a visit by Donald Graves to enable Australian teachers to learn of his research. The report of this visit (Walshe, 1981) and the reports of projects that resulted from this visit (Butler and Turbill, 1984; Turbill, 1982) were widely read by teachers throughout Australia and became the inspiration for much experimentation under the banner of "process writing." This practitioner-led change was soon supported by education systems in their policy and syllabus documents, by professional associations through a range of new publications, and by tertiary educators providing additional in-service opportunities and supporting action-research.

THE READING OUTLOOK

Future Issues in Literacy Education

Clearly, a great deal of diversity characterizes Australian literacy education. Although there may be reasonable consensus among those educators who participate in the many opportunities for professional enrichment, teachers are given only limited incentives to spend time and money keeping up to date. Consequently, across the profession as a whole there is a spectrum of practice that is not easily characterized in a simple description. Thus, one important issue for the future concerns how the whole profession can be brought to the forefront of contemporary practice. There are signs of reorganization in universities and colleges which may make them more responsive to the in-service needs of teachers, with less emphasis being given to formal award courses and more to in-service programs contracted to school authority specifications. There are dangers if the tail wags the dog in either direction. Do education authorities know what they need? In addition, the growing strength of professional groups such as the Australian Reading Association may lead to even greater innovation from within the profession. Countering these initiatives may be the reduced public expenditure on education, the introduction of fees or taxes to fund higher education, and the reluctance of teacher unions to support higher standards or salary increments for extra academic credits.

A second issue of growing importance is assessment and accountability. To some extent this is a symptom of changing political climate rather than an enduring national characteristic. Evidence from available achievement test data suggests that there should be no undue concern about average levels of reading performance. At the level of particular children the picture is much less reassuring. Well-known limitations of reading tests mean that we may easily overlook students who need special help at particular times. To the extent that Australian schools still identify and support students who need extra assistance, rather than referring them out to specialists, we might hope for the emergence of more grass-roots approaches such as peer-tutoring and volunteers to engage in paired reading. However, if, as seems likely, states mandate testing programs other than those (like NAEP [National Assessment of Educational Progress]) which use "light sampling," then we may see Australian schools slide back into narrow and constraining classroom practices.

Not being subject to tight bureaucratic control, teacher practices and materials selection are open to influence from a number of directions. It has been suggested that publishers may exert a large and perhaps undue influence on school reading programs. This factor is not thought to be a major one, although publishers are indeed exerting increasing influence. Moreover, there is evidence that teachers and teacher educators are prone to polarize positions. One current conflict situation concerns whole language and genre, although there are signs that dialogue is producing greater mutual understanding (Collerson, 1988).

Cambourne (1987) decries the undoubted tendency of some teachers to be skeptical about each new wave of theoretical advance, and claims that their eclecticism leads to "watered-down" theory underlying their practice. Whether we should regard this matter with the same concern, or instead see it as a healthy "feet on the ground" attitude, few observers of Australian education would deny that Australian teachers are inclined to test theory in the crucible of daily practice and evaluate it in the light of their experience.

We might also comment that literacy education in Australia is limited by the extent of literate behavior within the nation as a whole. While highly literate by international comparisons, it is not difficult to find areas in which literacy is deficient. Although reliable data are limited, national values do not place literacy as high as might be. Consequently, not all children generally receive from home, school, or society the examples of literate activities that provide the ideal matrix for literacy learners to develop. Despite the strength of professional organizations like the Australian Reading Association, PETA, and AATE, parents and employers are not aware of the full range of literate behaviors that a nation needs to exhibit if its young people are to prize the acquisition of literacy.

NOTE

1. Here the term *state* also includes the Northern Territory and the Australian Capital Territory which also run education systems.

READING SCHEMES

Beginnings. 1985 + . North Ryde, NSW: Methuen.
Bookshelf. 1986 + . Sydney: Martin Education/Ashton Scholastic.
Endeavour Reading Programme. 1975 + . Brisbane: Jacaranda.
Eureka Treasure Chest. 1987 + . Melbourne: Longmans Cheshire.
Expressways. 1982 + . Brisbane: Jacaranda.
Mt. Gravatt Language Development Reading Program. 1977 + . Sydney: Addison–Wesley/Longman Cheshire.
Reading 360 Australia. 1976 + . Melbourne: Longman Cheshire.
Reading Rigby. 1976 + . Adelaide: Rigby.
Southern Cross. 1987 + . Melbourne: Macmillan.
Story Box. 1980 + . Adelaide: Rigby.
Story Chest. 1980 + . Adelaide: Rigby.
Young Australia. 1980 + . Melbourne: Nelson.
Young Australia Language Development Scheme. 1966 + . Melbourne: Nelson.

REFERENCES

Anderson, J. 1984. Computing in schools: An Australian perspective. In *Australian Education Review*, No. 21. Hawthorn, Victoria: Australian Council for Educational Research.
Anderson, J. 1987a. *Tie tracer*. Brisbane: Jacaranda Software.
Anderson, J. 1987b. Micro tales or the potential of the micro for learning and teaching. *Reading* 21: 14–15.
Anderson, J. 1988. The printout: Computers and the reading teacher: An Australian perspective. *Reading Teacher* 41: 698–699.
Atkinson, J. K., Cochrane, K. J., and Elkins, J. 1968. Retarded readers at high school start—An investigation in diagnosis and treatment. *Slow Learning Child* 15: 67–83.
Baker, C. D., and Freebody, P. 1986. Representations of questioning and answering in children's first school books. *Language in Society* 15: 451–484.
Baker, C. D., and Freebody, P. 1988. Possible worlds and possible people: Interpretive challenges in beginning school reading books. *Australian Journal of Reading* 11: 95–104.

Bartlett, B., Barton, B., and Turner, A. 1988. *Knowing what and knowing how*. Melbourne: Nelson.

Boomer, G. 1987. Organizing the nation for literacy. In *Proceedings of the 13th Australian Reading Conference, Sydney*.

Bouffler, C. 1984. Predictability: A redefinition of readability. *Australian Journal of Reading* 7: 125–134.

Brennan, M., and Brennan, R. 1984. *Literacy and language: The human factor*. Report to the Criminology Research Council on the literacy needs and abilities of prison inmates. Wagga Wagga, NSW: Riverina Literacy Centre.

Burnes, D., and Page, G. 1985. *Insights and strategies for teaching reading*. Sydney: Harcourt Brace Jovanovich.

Butler, A., and Turbill, J. 1984. *Towards a reading-writing classroom*. Rozelle, NSW: Primary English Teaching Association.

Cadman, A. G. (Chairman). 1976. *Learning difficulties in children and adults. Report of the House of Representatives Select Committee on Specific Learning Difficulties*. Canberra: Australian Government Publishing Service.

Cambourne, B. 1979. How important is theory to the reading teacher? *Australian Journal of Reading* 2: 78–90.

Cambourne, B. 1983. Learning about learning by watching little kids writing. *English in Australia* 66: 10–26.

Cambourne, B. 1985. Change and conflict in literacy education: What it's all about. *Australian Journal of Reading* 8: 77–87.

Cambourne, B. 1986. Process writing and non-English speaking background children. *Australian Journal of Reading* 9: 126–138.

Cambourne, B. 1987. A grounded theory of genre acquisition: Learning to control different textual forms. *Australian Journal of Reading* 10: 261–266.

Campagna, H. 1986. Teaching English as a second language around Australia. *Australian Journal of Reading* 9: 186–191.

Clay, M. M. 1985. *The early detection of reading difficulties* (3rd ed.). Auckland: Heinemann Educational.

Collerson, J. 1988. *Writing for life*. Rozelle, NSW: Primary English Teaching Association.

Colston, M. (Chairman). 1984. *A national language policy*. Report of the Senate Standing Committee on Education and the Arts. Canberra: Australian Government Publishing Service.

Cooksey, R. W., and Freebody, P. 1987. Reliability, validity, and characterization of knowledge. *Reading Psychology* 8: 103–118.

Downing, J., and Morris, B. 1984. An Australian program for improving high school reading in content areas. *Journal of Reading* 28: 237–243.

Dymock, D. 1982. *Adult literacy provision in Australia: Trends and needs*. Armidale, NSW: Australian Council for Adult Literacy.

Elkins, J. 1975. Reading disability research in Australia. *Slow Learning Child* 22: 109–117.

Elkins, J. 1979. Where to from here? *Australian Journal of Reading* 2: 46–48.

Elkins, J. 1983. The concept of learning difficulties: An Australian perspective. In J. D. McKinney and L. Feagans (eds.), *Current topics in learning disabilities* (Vol. 1, 179–203). Norwood, N.J.: Ablex Publishing Corp.

Elkins, J., and Andrews, R. J. 1974. *The St. Lucia Reading Comprehension Test*. Brisbane: Teaching and Testing Resources.

Fesl, E. D. 1982. *Bala Bala: Some literacy and educational perceptions of three Aboriginal communities*. Canberra: Australian Government Publishing Service.

Freebody, P., and Anderson, R. C. 1986. Serial position and rated importance in the recall of text. *Discourse Processes* 9: 31–36.

Freebody, P., and Baker, C. D. 1985. Children's first schoolbooks: Introductions to the culture of literacy. *Harvard Educational Review* 55: 381–398.

Freebody, P., et al. 1986. Strategies for distributing time when studying text: An exploratory cluster-analysis approach. *Discourse Processes* 9: 355–374.

Goodman, Y. M., and Burke, C. 1980. *Reading strategies: Focus on comprehension*. New York: Holt, Rinehart and Winston.

Grant, A. V. 1987. *Opportunity to do brilliantly*. Canberra: Australian Government Publishing Service.

Halliday, M.A.K., and Hasan, R. 1976. *Cohesion in English*. London: Longman.

Halliday, M.A.K., and Hasan, R. 1985. *Language, context and text: Aspects of language in a social-semiotic perspective*. Waurn Ponds, Victoria: Deakin University Press.

Hancock, J., and Hill, S. 1988. *Literature-based reading programmes at work*. Melbourne: Australian Reading Association.

Hasan, R. 1984. Coherence and cohesive harmony. In J. Flood (ed.), *Understanding reading comprehension cognition, language and the structure of prose* (pp. 181–219). Newark, Del.: International Reading Association.

Johnson, T., and Louis, D. 1985. *Literacy through literature*. North Ryde, NSW: Methuen.

Kemp, M. 1987. *Watching children read and write: Observational records for children with special needs*. Melbourne: Nelson.

Lennon, J. W., et al. 1985. *The formation of teachers of reading*. In Board of Teacher Education Research Grants Series No. 1 (pp. 39–47). Brisbane: Board of Teacher Education.

LoBianco, J. 1987. *National policy on languages*. Canberra: Australian Government Publishing Service.

Luke, A. 1988. The non-neutrality of literacy instruction: A critical introduction. *Australian Journal of Reading*, 11: 79–83.

McKeown, G., and Freebody, P. 1988. The language of Aboriginal and non-Aboriginal children and the texts they encounter in schools. *Australian Journal of Reading* 11: 115–126.

McLeod, J. 1977. *GAP Reading Comprehension Test*. Melbourne: Heinemann Educational.

McLeod, J., and Anderson, J. 1972. *GAPADOL Reading Comprehension Test*. Melbourne: Heinemann Educational.

Meyer, B.J.F. 1975. *The organization of prose and its effects on memory*. Amsterdam: North–Holland.

Moore, P. J. 1988. Reciprocal teaching and reading comprehension: A review. *Journal of Research in Reading* 11: 3–14.

Morris, A. 1982. The introduction of resource teachers into Queensland state high schools: A critical review. Unpublished Master's thesis, University of Queensland.

Morris, A., and Stewart-Dore, N. 1984. *Learning to learn from text: Effective reading in the content areas*. North Ryde, NSW: Addison–Wesley.

Morris, B. 1988. Preparation of Australian secondary teachers in the teaching of reading. *Australian Journal of Reading* 11: 54–64.

Morris, B., and Stewart-Dore, N. 1984. Content area reading: Extending an inservice program. *Australian Journal of Reading* 7: 140–146.

Mossenson, L., Hill, P., and Masters, G. 1987. *TORCH–Tests of Reading Comprehension*. Melbourne: Australian Council for Educational Research.

Murray, J., and Smith, F. 1988. *Language arts and the learner*. Sydney: Macmillan.

Neale, M. D. 1988. *Neale Analysis of Reading Ability* (2nd ed.). Hawthorn, Victoria: Australian Council for Educational Research.

Nelson, A.J.A. (ed.). 1980. *Adult literacy: Some Australian papers*. Armidale, NSW: Australian Council for Adult Literacy.

Nelson, A.J.A. (ed.). 1981. *On the importance of being literate*. Armidale, NSW: Australian Council for Adult Literacy.

NSW Department of Education 1979. *Reading K–12*. Sydney: Author.

Painter, C., and Martin, J. R. (eds.). 1986. *Writing to mean*. Occasional Papers No. 9. Applied Linguistics Association of Australia.

Palincsar, A. 1987. Reciprocal teaching: Can student discussion boost comprehension? *Instructor* 96, no. 5: 56–58.

Palincsar, A. S., and Brown, A. L. 1986. Interactive teaching to promote independent learning from text. *Reading Teacher* 39: 111–111.

Palincsar, A. S., and Brown, A. L. 1987. Enhancing instructional time through attention to metacognition. *Journal of Learning Disabilities* 20: 66–75.

Parker, R. 1979. Gazing into a crystal ball: The Australian scene. *Australian Journal of Reading* 2: 22–25.

Pathways to literacy. 1988. Hobart: Tasmanian Department of Education.

Queensland Board of Teacher Education 1979. *The preparation of teachers to teach reading and associated language skills*. Brisbane: Author.

Queensland Department of Education. 1974. *Language Arts Curriculum Guide for Primary Schools*. Brisbane: Author.

Queensland Department of Education. 1989. *P–10 Language Education Framework*. Brisbane: Author.

Robinson, M. 1986. *Jim Trelease, The Read-Aloud Handbook: Australian adaptation*. Ringwood: Penguin Books.

Schonell, F. J. 1942. *Backwardness in the basic subjects*. Edinburgh: Oliver and Boyd.

Schonell, F. J. 1945. *The psychology and teaching of reading*. Edinburgh: Oliver and Boyd.

Schonell, F. J., and Flowerdew, P. 1948–1953. *The Wide Range Readers*. Edinburgh: Oliver and Boyd.

Schonell, F. J., and Sergeant, F. I. 1939. *The Happy Venture Readers*. Edinburgh: Oliver and Boyd.

Schwartz, S. 1984. *Measuring reading competence: A theoretical-prescriptive approach*. New York: Plenum.

Singh, M. 1988. Becoming socially critical: Literacy, knowledge and counter-construction. *Australian Journal of Reading* 11: 155–164.

Smith, J. 1985. Semantic aspects of cohesion in text and their relationship to recall. Unpublished doctoral dissertation, University of Queensland.

Smith, J., and Elkins, J. 1984. Comprehending cohesion. *Reading* 18: 153–159.

Smith, J., and Elkins, J. 1985. The use of cohesion by underachieving readers. *Reading Psychology* 6 no. 1–2: 13–25.

Smith, J. A., and Gray, J. M. 1983. Learning about reading, writing and fish with the help of a word processor. *Australian Journal of Reading* 6: 186–192.

South Australian Department of Education. 1982. *Language arts: Reading.* Adelaide: Author.

Turbill, J. 1982. *No better way to teach writing.* Rozelle, NSW: Primary English Teaching Association.

Unsworth, L. (ed.). 1985. *Reading: An Australian perspective.* Melbourne: Nelson.

Walshe, R. 1981. *Donald Graves in Australia: Children want to write.* Rozelle, NSW: Primary English Teaching Association.

Watson, A. J. 1983. *Reading as a conceptual reasoning task.* Report to the Education Research and Development Committee. Sydney: Sydney College of Advanced Education.

Wickert, R., and Zimmerman, J. 1990. Adult basic education in Australia: Questions of integrity. In M. Tennant (ed.). *Adult and continuing education in Australia: Issues and practices.* London: Routledge.

2

Brazil

Francisco Gomes de Matos

INTRODUCTION

Because of the comprehensiveness and complexity of reading education in Brazil, this chapter selectively focuses on aspects of that domain as related to the teaching and learning of Brazilian Portuguese as a native language. Specific reference is made, however, to developments in reading research in English by Brazilians so as to attest to the varied and broadly based interests of reading educators in Latin America's only Portuguese-speaking country.

The data for this survey have been collected primarily from recent Brazilian literature and additionally from personal communications received from some of the most active professionals in reading and reading education in Brazil, including Ezequiel T. da Silva, Regina Zilberman, Mary Kato, Marilda Cavalcanti, Marisa Lajolo, and Olga Molina. Invaluable sources for those interested in the development of reading education research and applications in Brazil are the publications of the Associação de Leitura do Brasil–ALB (the Brazilian Reading Association) with its central office at Faculdade de Educação, Universidade Estadual de Campinas, 13081 Campinas, São Paulo, Brasil. Thorough familiarity with the work of ALB is required for the researcher to be up to date in the theoretical and applications aspects of reading and the democritization of reading (giving priority to the people's educational and socioeconomic rights, and creating conditions for illiterates, semi-illiterates, or functional illiterates to acquire and use the written language).

THE LANGUAGES OF THE COUNTRY

Brazil is a multilingual nation, but it has only one official, national language: Portuguese. The country's other approximately 170 languages are spoken by relatively small groups of Indians. According to Rodrigues (1986), the two most populous indigenous languages in Brazil are *Kaiwa*, used in Southern Mato Grosso State, and *Tenetehava* (Guajajára and Tembé), spoken in the states of Maranhão and Pará. These two languages are the native medium of communication for 14,000 speakers (7,000 each).

The fact that Brazil is a predominantly Portuguese-speaking country does not mean that the problem of literacy and reading education is centered on a white population only. There is a small but dedicated, highly committed group of linguists, anthropologists, literacy educators, and missionaries very much concerned with helping Brazilian indigenous peoples become literate in their own language(s) and, in addition, depending on local conditions, Brazilian Portuguese. For a perspective on issues in bilingual literacy in the Brazilian context, see Gomes de Matos (1983). Besides indigenous languages, immigrants in Brazil use several different languages: Japanese, German, Italian, Spanish, Arabic, and Hebrew. In the larger cities, especially São Paulo and Rio de Janeiro, cultural centers and/or specialized language schools offer courses in the above-mentioned languages, in addition to French, which, after English, is the second most popular foreign language in Brazil.

READING INSTRUCTION POLICY AND GOALS

Brazil has a required core curriculum for elementary and high school education. It is presently being changed and improved through new legislation on relating to educational guidelines and foundations. The curriculum includes Portuguese (the language and literatures of Brazil, Portugal, and other Portuguese-speaking countries), social studies (geography, history, and political organization of Brazil), physical and biological sciences, mathematics, physical education, civics, health education, and, where appropriate, religion. The teaching of at least one foreign language is recommended beginning in the fifth grade and is required through high school. Although this core curriculum is prescribed by the Ministry of Education through resolutions of its Federal Education Council, every school is free to plan and implement its courses and subject-matter methodology. In short, flexibility and adaptation to local conditions are emphasized, preached, and to some extent practiced at state and city levels.

Further evidence of such decentralization is the existence of state curriculum guides such as Proposta *Curricular Ensine de 1° Grau Communicação e Expressão*, Secretaria de Educação de Pernambuco, 1981 [A guide to the teaching of Portuguese—communication and expression—published by the State Department of Education, Pernambuco]. These guides are aimed at primary school teachers working in public schools.

Guidelines are also prepared by state or municipal Departments of Education, such as the state of São Paulo's *Subsídios para implementação do Guia Curricular de Língua Portuguesa para o 1° Grau*, published in 1979.

The development of guides and other educational documents in Pernambuco

State reveals a slow but increasing autonomy in pedagogical decision making, as this listing illustrates:

Currículo da Escola Primária (Primary school curriculum), 1968

Guia Curricular (Curriculum guide), 1977

Proposta Curricular (Curriculum proposal), 1981

Conteúdos Mínimos para o Ensine de 1° Grau (Minimum required contents for primary school education), 1986

Guia da Professora Rural. Experiência Curricular Participativa (A guide for rural teachers. A shared curriculum experience), 1986

Currículo experimental para a Unidade Integrada de Ensine do Território de Fernando de Noronha, UFPe, Projeto Esmeralda, 1987 (An experimental curriculum for use at the Integrated Teaching Program on Fernando de Noronha Island (part of Pernambuco State), designed by the Emerald Project staff. The word *emerald* as used in the phrase *emerald of the Atlantic* is a nickname for that island.

A large variety of guides, guidelines, experimental, cooperatively designed, and used materials are available for teachers of Portuguese in Brazilian public schools. Reading educators in private schools—which outnumber government-run schools—are exposed to teachers' manuals, which are usually less detailed than is the case in countries with a tradition of almost teacher-proof guides or manuals, such as the United States. Accordingly, the goals for reading instruction vary from very simple and intellectually undemanding to problem-solving comprehending, with a preponderance of the simpler materials at the primary education level. As a new generation of textbook authors and Portuguese language teachers appears on the scene, significant, long-range changes are expected to happen.

Typical goals to be achieved by first grade readers are as follows: (1) reading words containing simple syllabic patterns (vowels, vowel combinations, consonant plus vowel, final syllables with the consonants l, m, n, r, s, z, and consonant clusters with l or r; (2) reading simple sentences (often in unconnected series of sentences); (3) understanding the vocabulary in each lesson; and (4) identifying characters and places in short texts.

Upon completion of the fourth grade, learners are expected to understand longer texts, without grammatical simplification or adaptation; to identify the main idea, and give details; to discover cause–effect relationships; to understand the vocabulary, especially synonyms and antonyms for words; and to identify paragraphs.

The reader's experiences from first to fourth grades (approximate ages: seven to ten) reflect goals based on a predominantly·fragmentary view of reading, as well as a conception of the reader's role as that of information-acquirer rather than that of critical constructor and transformer of human subjectivities as stressed by Freire and Macedo (1987).

Goals for reading at secondary school and university levels have recently been made more challenging under the influence of insights from research in reading instruction, cognitive psychology applied to reading acquisition and development, applied linguistics, library science, psycholinguistics, literature, and pragmatics, among some of the interacting fields engaging the attention of the new wave of interdisciplinarians in Brazilian research centers.

For the past fifteen years, this author has designed and implemented reading and writing development programs for graduate students in human sciences (predominantly from psychology). The goal of these programs is to help young adult readers-writers in an academic setting discover, monitor, improve upon, refine, and control their communicative abilities while reading-writing or vice-versa. Not surprisingly, college students have difficulty processing or producing book reviews and articles systematically and in depth. There is a need for practical guides for readers from both the academic and nonacademic worlds. (On the nonacademic, see Mendonca, 1987, and, more ambitiously, Faulstich, 1988). A more urgent need is for cooperative, carefully planned actions to fill a serious gap in the guidance of reading educators: the preparation of professors of reading teacher educators.

How are the educational system and the community helping the trainers of elementary school teachers of Portuguese to perform their formative tasks effectively? This is a challenge for the next decade or so. The interdisciplinary training and preparation of teachers of native languages (reading and writing being enhanced, because of the greater neglect of written communication and the increasing spread of preferentially spoken modes of linguistic interactions) call for serious national and international action. The reading teacher's right to interdisciplinary training and preparation is a matter not only for discussion but for realistic achievement.

SPECIAL READERS: ARE THEY BEING HELPED?

The Brazilian Dyslexia Association (Associação Brasileira de Dislexis—ABD), based in the city of São Paulo, is a nonprofit organization aimed at guiding parents, teachers, and the community in an understanding of dyslexia and in promoting research on the incidence and forms of dyslexia among Brazilians, especially students. ABD has a specialized library and a file (professionals and clinics), and it organizes and co-sponsors seminars for parents and other interested groups. Among topics of interest to its researchers are school failure and learning disturbances, children's perceptual difficulties, and the diagnostic implications of dyslexia. In short, the study, diagnosis, and treatment of language disorders that affect the ability to read has become a top priority for a small but active group of psychologists, educators, speech pathologists, and linguists under the leadership of Elina M. Rosenberg Colorni, ABD's current president.

TEACHER QUALIFICATIONS

To become a qualified teacher in primary education, a person must have at least a Licenciatura de curta duração (a short-term Licentiate Program), totaling

1,200 hours, whereas for teaching in both primary and secondary schools, a candidate is required to have a Licenciatura plena (a long-term or full Licentiate Program) consisting of a 2,200-hour curriculum. Upon completion of a Bachelor of Letters program, the graduate is permitted to do research but not to teach. If, however, an additional two-semester series of courses is taken in psychoeducational areas, the degree to be received is that of Licentiate in Letters, qualifying its holder to teach in an elementary or a high school. In short, a minimum of four academic years is required for a B.A. or equivalent and similarly four years for a Licentiate. (In Brazil, the school year runs from early or mid-February to June and from August to mid-December; universities usually start in March.) Anyone wishing to teach Portuguese as a native language in Brazil would therefore have to spend thirty-four months or eight semesters in a university or college Department of Letters and, for a specialized educational preparation, in a Department or Center of Education. Our of forty-two subjects required of teachers-to-be, thirty-five have to be taken in the Department of Letters (Languages and Linguistics) and seven in the Education Center.

To become qualified as a university teacher, a candidate is expected to have at least a master's degree and to take a written examination in the field in which he or she would like to teach. That procedure is part of a public competition in which several applicants do their best (in an interview, curriculum vitae evaluation, and in a written test) to succeed in securing a position such as Assistant Professor Level 1, the starting point of a university career in teaching and research in Brazil.

Since adult education is a specialized domain, qualifications for teaching in adult education programs (such as EDUCAR Foundation's courses for those aged fifteen and over) are basically the same as those required of elementary and secondary school teachers, with additional, specialized training either in-service or through distance teaching. A noteworthy example of distance teaching is EDUCAR's correspondence course Educando o educador (Educating Educators), which is specially designed to provide teachers living in nonurban areas with good theoretical and practical background in such areas as literacy, educational policies and planning, adult education pedagogical theories and practices, Brazilian Portuguese (with emphasis on reading, specifically the nature, functions, or uses, and strategies of reading techniques for helping young and older adults to read), and mathematics. Government and private foundations are also using television (both commercial and educational) to help promote more productive training not only of adult education professionals but also of literacy and Portuguese language teachers at preschool, elementary, and secondary school levels.

The use of mass communication media for filling gaps in teacher professional preparation, though relatively new in Brazil, shows promise as more and more educators see such creative efforts as aids. Whether the *telecursos* (telecourses) currently shown will help promote positive attitudes toward reading and disseminate a variety of effective reading strategies remains to be seen. One aspect of such combined use of television-viewing and accompanying booklet (problem-solving activities being increasingly included) is significant: it has engaged more people in reading, though for eventually obtaining a high school certificate.

Who reads what with what purpose in Brazil is an important issue. Given the overwhelming influence of television (especially commercially produced) on the leisure habits of Brazilians, the long-range effects of telecourses and teleclasses on individual and community purposes for reading could well merit serious research by professionals in interdisciplinary domains, besides that of communication sciences. Especially representative of the communication sciences' interest in that issue is the work carried out by researchers linked to INTERCOM, Sociedade Brasileira de Estudos Interdisciplinares da Comunicação (the Brazilian Society for Interdisciplinary Studies of Communication), with headquarters at the University of São Paulo. That organization's journal, *Intercom, Revista Brasileira de Communicação*, is a useful source for those interested in such related issues as the newspaper as a tool for developing a broader repertoire of reading strategies and for the critical reading of sociopolitical ideas affecting the conditions of literacy and reading education in Brazil.

Qualifications for being a reading teacher are the same as those required of a teacher of Brazilian Portuguese as a native language. The idea of setting specific requirements for professionals at different levels of reading education (or, more realistically, language education) is only beginning to arouse interest and to generate discussion. The broader issue of the link between reading and writing, the so-called *lecto-escrita*, seems to be of more immediate concern to Brazilian researchers, educational planners, and policymakers.

Anyone wishing to be a reading teacher at different levels of education in Brazil would, therefore, meet the requirements made of elementary, secondary, and university teachers of Portuguese. Oddly enough, many Brazilian teachers of Portuguese often refer to themselves as *composition* teachers (because of their major commitment to or time invested in teaching written Portuguese) but not as *reading* teachers. This partly reflects the supposedly greater prestige attached to writing, as well as the dominant educational philosophies centered on helping learners overcome or correct their common grammatical and stylistic errors. Thus, the view has arisen that the Portuguese language teacher's primary function is to direct, rather than motivate, learners' actions in communicating through a personally meaningful, culturally significant system. Although such views on reading and writing—perceptions by teachers, learners, and the broader community—are being increasingly documented by researchers (Rocco, 1981), a great deal needs to be done for a clearer, more global picture to emerge.

Finally, there is a much larger proportion of female to male teachers among teachers of Portuguese. (Herein are included preschool, literacy, elementary, secondary, and university education.) It would be no exaggeration to state that teaching language education and development—to the extent that there is actual teaching, since learners' contributions are extremely important to their own linguistic and cognitive growth—is a predominantly female profession, with male teachers being outnumbered at all levels. This may account for the children's universal use of the form of address *tia* (equivalent to *aunt* in English but conveying the sense of "member of the family," a true friend) in reference to their teachers.

PRODUCTION OF READING MATERIALS BY RURAL LEARNERS

The Literacy Project for young people and adults in the sugar-growing, industrial city of Cabo, Pernambuco State, northeastern Brazil, is based on Paulo Freire's Model of Critical-Emancipatory Literacy. That undertaking is sponsored by the state Department of Education, the host city's Education Section, and the Ministry of Education's *EDUCAR* Foundation. In 1987 the students produced their own reader (38 pp.), which makes the cogent point that the act of reading and writing is an act of sharing, of a collective effort by all. The cooperatively created material, entitled *Fazendo e aprendendo* [Doing and learning], is the outcome of integrated contributions from streetcleaners, sugar plantation workers, literacy educators, and representatives of the local community. What is a typical text like in such a learner-generated book? Here is the English translation of one such spontaneously produced message incorporated in the reader:

One day I and a friend of mine were fired and went to town to get our indemnity or compensation. We were given the address of the place to go to, but we could not read, so we asked a policeman on the way. He gave us directions but we were not too sure we had understood him completely, so we showed the piece of paper to another man who finally showed us where the place was. We went into the building, got our compensation and went back home. It was then that I realized how important it is to be able to read and write.

ISSUES AND TRENDS IN READING RESEARCH IN BRAZIL

What are some of the topics of major interest to Brazilian researchers in the area of reading education? A sample of current research, sponsored by various official sources or resulting from meeting master's or Ph.D. requirements, can give us an idea of what has been accomplished as well as what has been left out. The lack of a data bank on research in reading in Brazil makes information gathering a slow, incomplete process. Therefore, this listing should be considered reasonably representative, on the basis of this author's selectivity.

Here are ten examples (with author and institutional affiliations):

Researcher: Lilian Lopes Martin da Silva, State University of
                                    Campinas.
Subject: What books senior high school students read:
                                    when, how, why.

Researcher: João Wanderlei Geraldi, State University of
                                    Campinas.
Subject: Guidelines for helping elementary school students
                                    in public schools read novels and plays.

Researcher: Marilda Cavalcanti, State University of Campinas.
Subject: Reader–text interaction: aspects of pragmatic
                                    interpretation.

Researcher: Sumiko Nishitani Ikeda, Catholic University of São
                                    Paulo.
Subject: Production factors that interfere in the legibility of
                                    a text in Portuguese.

Researcher: Maria Lucia R. de Oliveira, Federal University of
                                    Pernambuco.
Subject: Inferring intentions in author–reader interaction.

Researcher: Marisa Lajolo, State University of Campinas.
Subject: Circulation and consumption of Brazilian books for
                                    children.

Researcher: Olga Molina, State University of São Paulo.
Subject: Readability of elementary and high school
                                    textbooks through the cloze procedure.

Researcher: Lúcia Lins Browne Rego, Federal University of
                                    Pernambuco.
Subject: The use of children's literature as a major tool by
                                    trained teachers in the literacy education of
                                    preschoolers in public schools.

Researcher: Terezinha N. Carraher, Federal University of
                                    Pernambuco.
Subject: Understanding reading failure in Brazil.

Researcher: Angela Kleiman, State University of Campinas.
Subject: Helping improve readers' perception of the
                                    discourse function of lexical items.

Of thirty-eight research projects sponsored by the National Institute for Educational Studies and Research of the Ministry of Education, a Brazilia D.F. organization, fifteen deal with reading and twenty-one focus on literacy. Among the topics investigated and described in reports available from that organization, four illustrate the range of interests:

• A sociological approach to reading habits.
• A guide for teachers to meet the needs of readers in elementary and high school.
• The use of visual and phonological strategies in reading and writing Portuguese.
• The interaction of play, work, and creativity in the reading by poor children.

To see how diversified the goals of a single Brazilian researcher can be, encompassing theory, research, and teaching, here is the translated table of contents of a recent book by Kleiman (1989). A Chilean-born, U.S.-trained (University of Illinois, Urbana), resident in Campinas, São Paulo State, Kleiman is the first chairperson of the Department of Applied Linguistics:

Part I: Theory

　　Describing reading.

　　Theoretical models: fundamentals for probing the interaction of theory and practice in the area of reading.

　　On the reader in interactive reading.

Part II: Research

　　Doing research on reading.

　　Strategies for approaching texts: structure, cohesion, and coherence.

　　Conditioning factors in writing summaries: student's maturity or task constraints?

　　Extracting information from texts—theme and readability.

　　Strategies for lexical inference in second language reading.

　　Perception of the discourse function of vocabulary.

Part III: Teaching

　　Teaching reading.

　　Reading and comprehensibility: insights from a study of children's written texts.

　　Coherence and the comprehensibility of texts in textbooks.

　　The teaching of vocabulary through reading.

Of Kleiman's seventy-one bibliographic references, fifteen are Brazilian publications, two of which are master's theses.

To provide a good sample of the breadth of professional investigations by Brazilian specialists in reading education, linguistics, Portuguese language teaching, communication science, and Brazilian literature, here is the translated table of contents of a recent, interdisciplinary book of readings by Zilberman and Silva (1988):

- Reading: why an interdisciplinary approach? (Zilberman and Silva)
- Social conditions of reading (Magda Soares)
- How children learn to read: a platonic speculative issue (Mary Kato)
- Reading and comprehension of spoken and written texts as individual acts of a social praxis (Luis A. Marcuschi)
- Intelligibility, interpretability, and comprehensibility (Eni Orlandi)
- Functional reading and the dual role of texts in school books
- Reading and literature: far more than a rhyme but less than a solution (Marisa Lajolo)
- Social communication: from reading to critical reading (Jose Marques de Melo)
- Pedagogy of reading: change and history (Silva and Zilberman)

Research by Librarians

The librarian's role in reading education in Brazil should be seen as not only taking care of a library and servicing readers with a variety of resources, but also contributing to democratizing reading. We will therefore cite research by such professionals who share with language teachers a serious concern with helping learners become permanent readers, both within and outside the school context. All the examples are of master's theses in library science, representing several universities:

Researcher:	Jeruza Lyra Lucena, Federal University of Paraíba.
Subject:	The school library as a developmental factor in the acquisition of the reading habit.
Researcher:	P.L.V. Amorim Catholic University of Campinas, São Paulo.
Subject:	Libraries and the interaction between television and reading.
Researcher:	Anaiza Caminha Gaspar, University of Brasília, D.F.
Subject:	A study of reading habits in the Benedito Leite Public Library in the urban community of São Luis, Maranhão State Northeastern Brazil.
Researcher:	Marília M. L. Lopes, Federal University of Paraíba.
Subject:	The reading habit among high school students: users and nonusers of public libraries.
Researcher:	Maria Helena de Andrade Magalhães, Federal University of Minas Gerais.
Subject:	Recreational reading at a public municipal elementary school in Belo Horizonte.

Reading educators, cognitive psychologists, applied linguists, and methodologists have been doing their research independently of one another, but as pleas for interdisciplinary action slowly become a reality, broadly based studies of reading and reading education will enhance the hitherto narrowly conceived and delimited investigations. Specialists in library education have been warning reading educators of the inappropriateness of working in isolation. At the Fifth Brazilian Congress of Reading held in Campinas in 1985, this warning echoed very strongly, and its repercussions are beginning to be felt. All the professionals interested in promoting truly meaningful reading should now join hands and help identify, diagnose, and solve the problems of readers and nonreaders at different levels of the educational system as well as outside it. The right to read, rigorously interpreted as the right to read effectively and ecologically, should become a concrete reality in each educational system in the world.

THE OUTLOOK FOR READING AND
READING EDUCATION

According to the 1980 census, out of Brazil's population of 120 million, only 24.8 million were students aged five and over; that is, a mere one-fourth of Brazilians went to school at different levels. Of this school population, 703,200 were preschoolers, 19.7 million were in elementary school, 3.03 million attended high school, while only 1.3 million were at the country's universities (federal, state, private).

Although illiteracy rates decreased from 38.44 percent in 1970 to 31.6 percent in 1980, the truth of the matter is that reducing or seriously decreasing illiteracy has become a top priority in Brazil's new 1988 constitution. According to government plans, this goal will be reached by around the year 2000. Such overly optimistic planning notwithstanding, the cold fact is that Brazil can hardly be said to be a nation of readers. Neither can it be stated that it is *becoming* a nation of readers. There are multiple factors, including the following.

1. Books and other printed materials (magazines, newspapers) are too expensive for at least two-thirds of the population. Subscribing to wide-circulation magazines (*Veja*, for instance, Brazil's counterpart to *Time* and *Newsweek* sells nearly 810,000 copies) is a luxury that only upper-middle-class families can afford. School textbooks are often prohibitively priced, which has led the government to sponsor a free book distribution program to public schools through the Fundação de Assisténcia ao Estudante (FAE), (Foundation for Educational Aid to Students).

2. Illiteracy rates are still very high, despite noteworthy efforts at the federal, state, and municipal levels and campaigns to attract investments from industry and commerce. (Tax-deductible donations are being made to institutions such as the EDUCAR Foundation, which has replaced its predecessor, MOBRAL, with more realistic and flexible policies for coping with illiteracy among Brazilians aged fifteen and over.)

3. Initiatives aimed at democratizing the printed mass media, especially newspapers, are

still scanty and often short-lived. A recent, successful experience in imparting linguistically adapted information to people who seldom or never read newspapers is the
weekly, mural-like paper *Última Página*, published under the auspices of the Pernambuco State government and circulated in contexts where the reading habit is in
critical need of cultivation. Such a high-legibility and linguistically simple newspaper
also enhances what Brazilian educator Paulo Freire has cogently described as the
critical reading of one's world.

4. The ever-increasing practice of xeroxing textbooks (and even works of fiction), rather
than purchasing them, especially among university students, is detrimental to the
acquisition of the reading habit. (Many learners have fragments photocopied rather
than whole texts.) This practice has added a new word to the Portuguese language in
Brazil—*apostila*—which is roughly equivalent to book in mimeographed or xeroxed
form. As explained in (1) above, economic conditions (skyrocketing inflation now
being slowly curbed by governmental measures) are further aggravating the problem
of who can afford to buy books.

5. Brazil has a relatively small number of bookstores and libraries even in its larger
cities. Recife, with a population of over 1.3 million, for example, has only fourteen
bookstores, ranging from Brazil's largest to very small. The ratio of bookstore to
inhabitant is dramatically low: 1 to 100,000.

   For a city its size, Recife has very few libraries, three of which are main libraries
of the Federal University of Pernambuco, Federal Rural University, the Catholic
University of Pernambuco, and one is the Joaquim Nabuco Foundation Blanche Knopf
Library. Only three public municipal libraries are listed in the 1988–1989 Guide to
Recife, published by the Pernambuco Telephone Company.

6. There is a scarcity of Centers for the Promotion of Reading in schools at all educational
levels or in the community-oriented organizations. One Brazilian state, Rio Grande
do Sul, in southern Brazil has been establishing *Centros de Leitura* in some public
schools, while in other states, *salas de leitura* (reading rooms) are being organized
and open to the public. However, such initiatives often lack the necessary institutional
and, more importantly, financial support for their becoming permanently available to
actual and potential readers.

   The embryo of Centers of Reading is sometimes to be found within a university.
In 1981 the Federal University of Pernambuco launched a Program of Reading and
Linguistic Development (PROLEDE), with the goal of promoting the reading habit
among college students. Portuguese language teachers from that same university are
providing educational assistance to 400 elementary school students living on Fernando
de Noronha Island, one hour's flight from Recife, northeastern Brazil. Thus, the Projeto
Esmeralda (Emerald Project) helps nurture a love of reading and writing to children
away from mainland Brazil.

7. Brazil's reading objectives are also being hampered by the lack of specialized preparation (or even training) of the majority of elementary school teachers of Portuguese
in what reading and reading education are. In addition, they are given little training
in how to make and carry out informed, productive decisions about reading instruction
that takes into account not only learners' abilities, interests, needs, and age but also
their rights and responsibilities. Most teachers tend to follow teachers' guides, which
often do not enhance teachers' roles as facilitators of comprehension. Hence, the

reading experience for the majority of children in elementary school turns out to be self-defeating or unmotivating.

All is not lost, however. There are some signs that positive changes are taking place which will counteract such negative factors as lack of prepared teachers and student lack of interest in reading. Some encouraging evidence is presented in the remainder of this section.

In 1981 the Associação de Leitura do Brasil—ALB (The Brazilian Reading Association) was established in Campinas, São Paulo state, to help democratize and improve reading conditions for the Brazilian people. The ALB gives equal importance to both dyslexic and normal readers and is also seeking to improve the quality of research in reading and writing and to disseminate useful findings to teachers and reading educators. ALB has its own journal, *Leitura: Teoria e Prática* [Reading: Theory and Practice], and it organizes a Brazilian Congress of Reading every year, besides co-sponsoring regional meetings. Since it is impossible for most elementary and high school teachers of Portuguese to subscribe to specialized journals, issues of ALB's journal have tended to reach a university clientele. Efforts at overcoming such restricted circulation are being made, with the cooperation of state and municipal Departments of Education.

One of Brazil's best-known television networks, Rede Globo, has launched Book Donations to Schools, comprising carefully selected titles. Represented is literature for children as well as materials designed to help very young children discover the pleasures and values of reading in a world that is becoming increasingly less accustomed to reading for intellectual and spiritual growth.

Brazilian university graduate programs are giving more attention to specialized seminars and courses in the theoretical and practical aspects of reading. Among such active institutions of higher learning are the State University of Campinas (UNICAMP), which hosts the Brazilian Reading Association, the Catholic Universities of São Paulo and Rio Grande do Sul, the State University of São Paulo, the Federal Universities of Paraná, Santa Catarina, Minas Gerais, Pernambuco, and Rio de Janeiro, and the University of Brasília. The rise of a reader-training consciousness among teacher–trainers is a particularly wholesome sign.

The EDUCAR Foundation (the National Foundation for Youth and Adult Education), in close cooperation with state and municipal Departments of Education, is attempting to establish, promote, and sustain the reading habit among Brazilians aged fifteen and over. The Ministry of Education Foundation also capitalizes on television and distance teaching (correspondence) for the recycling of literacy educators. Much less known than its historical predecessor (the MOBRAL Foundation), the EDUCAR Foundation has formidable challenges to meet. Given the new constitution's emphasis on budgetary prioritizing to literacy programs, however, a great deal is expected to be accomplished, particularly in the mid-1990s.

The Fundação Nacional do Livro Infantil e Juvenil (The National Foundation for Children's and Young People's Books), the Brazilian affiliate of the International Board on Books for Young People, has been sponsoring projects for the establishment of sound, long-lasting reading habits among children and teenagers. It is responsible for a variety of activities, such as seminars, roundtables, book exhibits, and the publication of a newsletter and a magazine for teachers of the Portuguese language and literature for children and adolescents.

Inflation and the generally high price of books have not prevented Brazilian publishers from increasing and diversifying titles especially designed for children. The appearance of a new series of children's books, taking into account age levels and cognitive maturity, demonstrates the keen, serious interest of some far-sighted publishers such as Pioneira and Ática, both from São Paulo. Pioneira's "Série Pinju" and Ática's "Série Pique" are two examples of books in which several important components were carefully integrated: linguistic, pedagogical, psychological, artistic, and even ecological. Books for children sometimes feature suggestions for teachers to help their young readers make the most of their reading experiences by activating their creative talents. One example is the "Coleção Carrossel," a series published by Scipione, São Paulo, which targets preschoolers who are starting to read and are being guided in making the transition from processing stories without written texts to textually organized stories.

The undergraduate and graduate curricula of Brazilian Portuguese language and literature includes courses devoted to Brazilian literature for children and adolescents. This literature is slowly but realistically being recognized as an indispensable step toward redefining, restructuring, and revitalizing conceptions of reading that have hindered rather than enhanced progress in this domain. At the Federal University of Pernambuco's B.A. and Licentiate Program in Portuguese, the course Literatura Brasileira Infantil e Juvenil (Brazilian Literature for Children and Youth) is now required of teachers-to-be.

The constructive criticism made by some reading educators, both through their works and their actions (lectures and seminars in many parts of Brazil), is having an impact on those in charge of educational decision making in public and private school contexts. Two such critical voices are Lilian M. da Silva and Ezequiel T. da Silva, from the State University of Campinas and influential board members of the Brazilian Reading Association. Lilian da Silva's appraisal of the questionable practices imposed on readers by many schools (what has been described as the didactics of the destruction of readers) and Ezequiel da Silva's in-depth, sociohistorical analysis of reading and Brazilian reality have helped place reading education in a new perspective, emphasizing the reader's emancipation and power to shape existing living conditions. For a detailed study of their ideas, see Lopes M. da Silva (1986) and Silva (1985, 1988).

A new generation of Portuguese language series for elementary school students has appeared. This series considers reading and comprehension synonymous, and translates the promotion and assessment of reading comprehension into personally and collectively meaningful activities. Although a typology of cognitively challenging exercises, activities, or tasks for helping build comprehension strategies is still unavailable for immediate classroom application in the

Brazilian context, initial efforts are being made to translate such theory into practice. A good example of how to treat texts with dignity and how to challenge young readers to comprehend effectively is Junquéira (1988). Two other positive features of this series are the choice and use of texts from classic and current Brazilian and international literature and its special attention to children's literature as a source for readings.

Syntheses of eminently practical classroom-tested activities are being disseminated among reading educators, teachers of Portuguese, and textbook authors to promote the reading development of Brazilian learners. In the last chapter in Silva (1988), this far-sighted reading educator presents an overview of procedures for reading enjoyment, reading aloud and silently, selecting and using supplementary reading materials, using motivational "baits" for engaging children in reading acts, independent reading, culturally relevant research projects, or tasks for groups of readers in and out of school, in-class book exchange, games and other playful activities that can enhance reading and helping children organize their own mini-libraries. Interestingly, Silva acknowledges using an International Reading Association publication as one of his sources: Dietrich and Mathews (1968).

Reading English as a Foreign Language: Brazilian Contributions

Reading education in Brazil does not occur exclusively through the medium of Brazilian Portuguese. In addition to problems concerning native indigenous languages (out of 170, only 60 have some reading materials, many of which consist of varying portions of biblical texts translated by the missionary-linguists of the Summer Institute of Linguistics [Grimes, 1984]), Brazilian applied linguists and educators are increasingly working in the thriving area of English for Portuguese-speaking students. This EFL-centered activity has produced sustained interest and increasing productivity in both the theory and practice of the reading development of Brazilian learners of English, particularly young adults in universities and in specialized private language schools found in all large Brazilian cities. (Included herein is the network of binational centers, officially recognized by the United States Information Service as well as the British Council-oriented "Cultura Inglesa" schools or centers.)

The professional preparation of teacher–trainers and teachers in English for Specific or Professional Purposes (ESP) has been enhanced by the establishment of a Clearinghouse with its Center for Research, Resources and Information on Reading (CEPRIL) at PUC-SP, the Catholic University of São Paulo. Given the nationwide influence of such an initiative, it would be no exaggeration to state that, while many Brazilian university teachers of English have been given appropriate training and/or preparation in the pedagogy of reading, a relatively smaller number of their Portuguese language counterparts has benefited from such professional advancement. PUC-SP's achievements include the *ESPecialist*, a journal (with contributions in either English or Portuguese) published three times a year. Its December 1986 issue featured an article on developing flexible competence for approaching a text (Abuendia Padilha Pinto) and another article on English and Brazilian public schools (a case for a receptive reading approach, by David and Tania Shepherd).

Cohen (1987), in his review of research on cognitive processing in reading in Brazil, has found that four contributions by Brazilian researchers were written in English. The studies he reviewed focus on lexical processing, test-taking strategies, syntactic processing and the processing of metaphor, and schemata in reading comprehension. In his conclusion, Cohen, an applied linguist from Israel, clarifies the notion that verbal reporting techniques have clearly experienced an upsurge of popularity among Brazilian researchers devoted to the teaching-learning of English and/or Portuguese.

Brazilian university teachers of English are more familiar with theoretical models and practical applications thereof, and teachers of Portuguese are only minimally familiar with such foundational and applicational knowledge. Hence, Brazilian universities should start or strengthen Programs in Portuguese for Professional Purposes, thus filling a gap in reading education at the tertiary level. Again, the Catholic University of São Paulo has been a pioneer in the area of the specialized preparation of adults in the fluent and proficient reading of scientific, technical texts in Brazilian Portuguese. As well-trained teachers of English and Portuguese and other languages in the Brazilian university curriculum (French, Spanish, German) share their experiences, it is hoped that higher standards of teaching reading will be promoted. Only through such cooperative efforts will progress be possible in learning how to teach effectively and in learning from successful learners in action. Although the idea of helping learners learn is not new, its systematic implementation poses serious challenges to educators hitherto accustomed to teacher-dominated methodological approaches. This area of educational reform is just beginning to attract Brazilian educators and shows promise of rapid expansion and diversification.

What Else Is Being Done under the Brazilian Sun?

A purposeful, in-depth reading of the sources included in the References at the end of this chapter will attest to the great variety of initiatives either suggested or underway concerning reading education in the Brazilian context. Before concluding this chapter, however, two more illustrations will be given of the socioculturally relevant activities being carried out by far-sighted Brazilians: on the one hand, by highly literate scholars and on the other, by newly literate or about to be literate people.

CONCLUSIONS

Reading and reading education are far too complex and multifaceted to be described and assessed with a high degree of scientific accuracy in a single chapter. However, within the limitations imposed by the conditions in which most Brazilian researchers work—the difficulty of accessing nationally and regionally representative data and of objectively interpreting current issues and trends—this overview has attempted to achieve both the editors' and the author's goal of presenting a fairly up-to-date, reasonably well-documented, and revealing picture of a domain that is intimately linked to and influenced by Brazil's realization of its individual and collective potential.

The country's economic, political, and intellectual development has been paralleled by the growth in the citizens' right and responsibility to *read* their country, their local community, their school, their place of work, and their home with critically enlightened, responsible eyes. The objective is to contribute to a holistic, endogenous spirit in the nation, while doing their share to strengthen relations among all nations, in the common pursuit of better ways of living.

Educational analysts unfamiliar with Brazil's solutions to its problems might find it too demanding to foresee advances in a country with a high illiteracy rate, a large population of poorly paid teachers, a rising number of dropouts in elementary school, and a generally low level of reading achievement in high school and college. To those like this author, however, who have been engaged in a permanent struggle to assure learners of their active roles as agents of change and improvement of their own conditions, this ideal goal can be realized. How? By taking on the formidable challenge of transforming the present Brazilian educational and political attitude of fewer illiterates into actions that bring about the preparation of truly confident and competent users of Portuguese, especially as readers. The mission of reading educators in Brazil, then, is to help strengthen a national awareness that the real problem is not simply one of there being *minus nonreaders* but of encouraging, preparing, and valuing *more readers* in all contexts. Making the leap from minus to plus with regard to reading education means a thorough commitment to high-quality teacher and learner preparation. To realize that goal, education must be seen and treated not as a special kind of investment, but as the most powerful way for minds to create intellectually and spiritually meaningful knowledge.

POSTSCRIPT

As serious demands grow in Brazil to prepare reading researchers and trainers of teachers, bigger investments are required. To the detriment of such goals, cuts in government funding, which are symptomatic of the current economic crisis which Brazil is undergoing, have started to affect productivity in this otherwise top-priority domain.

At the Seventh Congress of Reading of the Brazilian Reading Association held in Campinas on September 8–10, 1989, one of the meetings featured a diversified group of promoters of reading: newspaper reporters, publishers, librarians, booksellers, authors, television/movie scriptwriters, language and literature teachers, and researchers. They discussed ways of helping nonreaders or occasional readers to become lifetime readers.

Planning and implementing public policies and programs for enhancing reading among people of all ages presuppose a substantial decrease in the high rate of illiteracy that still characterizes Brazil. This is part of an all-out effort in which everyone who is educationally, linguistically, and culturally committed to spreading the joys of reading should strive to improve the orientation of new readers and readers-to-be, and to maximize the quality of reading methods and materials.

Let's paraphrase Cicero: "A country without fluent readers is a country without a soul." Accordingly, let's exchange our results and experiences and promote reading as a universally unifying power.

REFERENCES

Cohen, Andrew. 1987. Research on cognitive processing in reading in Brazil. *Delta*, Revista de Documentação de Estudos em Linguística Teórica e Aplicada, 3, No. 2, PUC–SP, São Paulo.

Dietrich, Dorothy M., and Virginia H. Mathews (eds.). n.d. *Development of lifetime reading habits*. Newark, Del.: International Reading Association.

Faulstich, Enilde L. de J. 1988. *Como ler, entender e redigir um texto*. Petropolis: Vozes.

Gomes de Matos, F. 1989a. Issues and trends in early literacy development in Brazil. In Elisabetta Zuanelli Sonino (ed.), *Literacy in school and society: Trends and issues*. New York: Plenum Publishing Corp.

Gomes de Matos, F. 1989b. Literacy In Brazil: Eight works from the 80s. *Prospects* 19, 4 615–620.

Grimes, Barbara F. (ed.). 1984. *Ethnologue. Languages of the world*. 10th ed. Dallas, Tex.: Wycliffe Bible Translators.

Junqueira, Sonia. 1988. *Portuguese na Sala de Aula*. Primeiro Frau. São Paulo: Ática.

Kleiman, Angela. 1989. *Leitura: Ensino e Pesquisa*. Campinas: Pontes.

Lopes M. da Silva, Lilian. 1986. *A escolarização do Leitor. A didática da destruição da leitura*. Porto Alegre: Mercado Aberto.

Mendonça, Neide. 1987. *Desburocratização linguística. Como simplificar textos administrativos*. São Paulo: Pioneira.

Rocco, Maria T. F. 1981. *Literatura/ensino: Uma problemática*. São Paulo: Ática.

Rodrigues, A. D. 1986. *Linguas brasileiras. Para o estudo das línguas indígenas*. São Paulo: Loyola.

Silva, Ezequiel T. da. 1985. *Leitura e Realidade Brasileira*. 2nd ed. Porto Alegre: Mercado Aberto.

Silva, Ezequiel T. da. 1988. *Elementos de Pedagogia da Leitura*. São Paulo: Martins Fontes.

Zilberman, Regina, and Ezequiel T. da Silva (eds.). 1988. *Leitura perspectivas interdisciplinares*. São Paulo: Ática.

BIBLIOGRAPHY

Associação de Leitura do Brasil. 1985. *5º Congresso de Leiture do Brasil. Anais. comunicações oficiais*. Campinas: São Paulo.

Associação de Leitura do Brasil. 1987. *Leitura Teoria e Prática*, No. 10 (December).

Associação de Leitura do Brasil. 1988. *Leitura: Teoria e Pratica*, No. 11 (July).

Barbosa, M.L.B., and M. C. Cavalcanti (eds). 1984. *Anais do l Encontro Interdisciplinar de Leitura*. Parana: Universidade Estadual de Londrina.

Carraher, T. N. 1987. Illiteracy in a literate society. Understanding reading failure in Brazil. In Daniel Wagner (ed.), *The future of literacy in a changing world*. Oxford: Pergamon Press.

Cavalcanti, Mirilda do. 1989. *Interacao Leitor-Texto. Aspectos de Interpretação Pragmatica*. Campinas, S.P.: Editora da UNICAMP.

Costa, Miriam S. 1987. A practical approach to course design: English for computer science in Brazil. In Sandra J. Savignon and Margie S. Berns (eds.), *Initiatives in communicative language teaching II. A book of readings*. Reading, Mass., Addison–Wesley, pp. 125–145.

Duarte, Sergio Guerra. 1986. *Dicionário Brasileiro de Educação*. Rio: Antares.

EDUCAR. 1986. *The EDUCAR Foundation: Political and Educational Guidelines*. Ministerio da Educacao, Brasilia, D. F.

Franchi, Eglê. 1988. *Pedagogia da alfabetização. Da oralidade à escrita*. São Paulo: Cortez Editora.

Freire, Paulo, and Donaldo Macedo. 1987. *Literacy: Reading the word and the world*. South Hadley, Mass.: Bergin und Garvey.

Geraldi, J. W. (ed.). 1987. *O texto na sala de aula. Leitura e produção*. Cascavel, Paraná: Assoeste Editora.

Gomes de Matos, F. 1983. A checklist of pluridisciplinary criteria for the evaluation of materials used in the teaching-learning of the mother tongue in primary and secondary schools in Brazil. Paris: UNESCO, Division of Structures, Contents, Methods and Techniques of Education.

Gomes de Matos, F., and Nelly Carvalho. 1984. *Como avaliar um livro didático. Língua portuguesa*. São Paulo: Pioneira.

Kato, Mary. 1985. *O aprendizado da leitura*. São Paulo: Martins Fontes.

Kato, Mary (ed.). 1988. *A concepção da escrita pela crianxa*. Campinas: Pontes.

Kleiman, Angela. 1989. *Leitura: ensino e pesquisa*. Campinas: Pontes.

Kramer, Sonia (ed.). 1986. *Alfabetização: dilemas da prática*. Rio: Dois Pontos Editora.

Mendonça, Neide. 1987. *Desburocratização linguística*. Como simplificar textos administrativos. São Paulo: Pioneira.

Ministerio da Educação. 1986. Diretrizes para o aperfeicoamento do ensino aprendizagem da língua portuguesa. Relatório Conclusivo. Brasília, D. F.

Molina, Olga. 1987. *Quem engana quem? Professor X Livro Didático*. Campinas: Papirus.

PUC–SP, Pontifícia Universidade Católica de São Paulo. 1983. *Linguistica (Leitura)*. *Cadernos PUC*. 16. São Paulo: Educ-Cortez Editora.

PUC–SP. 1986. *The ESPecialist*, No. 15. Centro de Pesquisas, Recursos e Informação em Leitura (CEPRIL). São Paulo.

Rego, L.L.B. 1988. *Literatura infantil: uma nova perspectiva de alfabetização na préescola*. São Paulo: FTD.

Rocco, M.T.F. 1981. *Literatura/Ensino: uma problemática*. São Paulo: Ática.

Scliar-Cabral, Leonor, and Loni Grimm-Cabral. 1987. Research on Narrativity in Literacy Improvement. In Gilles Gagne (ed.), *Selected Papers in Mother Tongue Education*. Etudes in Pedagogie de la Langue Maternelle. Dodrecht-Holland: Foris Publications, pp. 125–134.

Silva, E. T. da. 1986. *Leitura na Escola e na Biblioteca*. Campinas: Papirus.

Silva, E. T. da. 1988. *Elementos de Pedagogia da Leitura*. São Paulo: Martins Fontes.

Tasca, Maria, and J. M. Poersch (eds.). 1986. *Suportes linguísticos para a alfabetização*. Porto Alegre.

UFSC, Universidade Federal de Santa Catarina. 1985. *Ilha do Desterro*, No. 13, *Reading/ Leitura*. Florianópolis.

Zilberman, Regina. 1988. *A Leitura e o Ensino da Literatura*. São Paulo: Editora Contexto.

Zilberman, Regina, and E. T. da Silva (eds.). 1988. *Leitura. Perspectivas interdiscipli- nares*. São Paulo: Ática.

3

Canada

Margaret MacLean, Christine Gordon, Chris Hopper, and Larry Miller

INTRODUCTION

In this chapter, rather than viewing reading education in isolation, we use the term *language arts* to describe the current state of instruction in Canada. As opposed to the restricted notion of reading instruction in isolation, the idea of language arts encompasses reading, writing, speaking, and listening, and in many instances has been expanded to include both content and the arts. The term is not simply a matter of semantics, for it accurately describes the trend in Canadian education.

We gathered information for this chapter in several ways: through examination of provincial curriculum guidelines, resource documents, and the results of language arts assessments, as well as discussions with key informants in ministries of education, faculties of education, and, most importantly, practicing educators. Furthermore, we carried out a literature review with the purpose of examining key published articles and essays concerning important issues in language arts education in Canada.

Because the provinces are responsible for education in Canada, it is impossible to describe language arts curriculum, materials, teaching techniques, and assessment results for the ten provinces and two territories at the primary, secondary, tertiary, and adult levels in a complete manner. Thus, this chapter focuses on the important issues that represent trends across the provinces. We counterbalance this key issue approach with examples of situations unique to Canada.

LANGUAGES, GEOGRAPHY, AND POPULATION

Canada's geography, population, and languages relate directly to its educational system. Although it is the second largest country in the world in size, the population is only 26,489,000, and the majority of people live within a 250 kilometer band close to the Canadian–U.S. border, approximately the 49th parallel. The combination of a large land mass and sparse population creates unique situations that range from the need for local control of education to the necessity of distance education. An example of this second situation is found in the far north region which is inhabited mainly by indigenous Inuit and Indian peoples. Although the culture and educational goals of these people, who often live in isolated areas, are different from those of the dominant majority, language arts curriculum, teaching methods, and materials often are selected or developed by the majority.

In 1986–1987, the latest reported statistics, approximately 4,661,300 pupils were enrolled in public schools, with an additional 228,200 students in private schools (Statistics Canada, 1988). Because education is a provincial rather than a federal responsibility, the number of years spent in school varies, although a typical grade span is 1 to 12. Advanced education, either at the community college or university level, is available to qualified students in every province. Typically, children in Grade 1 are six years old, while those in Grade 12 are seventeen years of age. Many provinces support extensive preschool and kindergarten programs that permit children to begin schooling as early as age four.

Language arts instruction is an integral aspect of education from Grades 1 to 6; from Grade 7 upward, western provinces often use the term *English language arts* while in central and eastern Canada the term *English education* is common. However, some provinces offer specific secondary level courses such as literature and writing. In French-speaking institutions in Quebec, the generic term is *français* for both elementary and secondary levels. Even though the terms change as students progress through the grades, the intent of the curriculum—to develop active listeners, speakers, readers, and writers—demonstrates a remarkable consistency in provincial guidelines.

At the federal level Canada is officially bilingual, and the federal government promotes the use of both English and French in the areas that come under its jurisdiction. Education, however, is under provincial jurisdiction. New Brunswick is the only province that is officially bilingual. Quebec is officially unilingual French but extends special status to English. In reality, all provinces offer some educational services to their French or English minorities, although the scope and nature of such services vary widely from province to province.

According to 1986 census data, 60.5 percent of Canadians spoke English as their mother tongue and 24.3 percent spoke French. Although 6 million Canadians are French-speaking, well over 80 percent of them live in Quebec. Both Ontario and New Brunswick have sizable French-speaking minorities, and in those areas contiguous to Quebec, language maintenance is quite strong. In other parts of Canada, however, such minorities have been largely assimilated. The nostalgia for French remains, but school-age children often feel more at home in English.

Canada's bilingual situation highlights an issue related directly to the teaching of the language arts. Language arts instruction in French does not parallel instruction in English. Thus, it is necessary to examine teaching and learning in both linguistic contexts. Furthermore, many school boards outside of Quebec, as well as English language schools in Quebec, have instituted French immersion programs. Approximately 225,000 children are enrolled in these French immersion programs. As in schools where French is the mother tongue, language arts instruction in immersion schools may differ from that offered in schools where only one official language is used. Whether language arts instruction should differ in these immersion situations is a topic of intense debate.

Canada is multicultural, with nearly 3 million people, or 11.3 percent of all Canadians, speaking a language other than English or French as their mother tongue. Approximately 4 percent of the population speak multiple languages (English and/or French plus at least one other language). The federal government of Canada, as well as most provincial authorities, supports a policy of multiculturalism, and many heritage languages are taught in schools. Mandarin Chinese, Japanese, Ukrainian, Greek, Punjabi, Swahili, and Portuguese, to mention a few, are currently taught as heritage languages. Most of these programs are conducted after school and only if sufficient enrollment exists. Although these classes are typically not part of the regular school day, they are clearly popular, and as many as sixty-one different languages are taught in one province alone. However, as with the differences in language arts instruction in French, English, and French immersion, heritage language programs also vary greatly in terms of supporting theory, materials, and instructional techniques.

In their overview Lessard and Crespo (in press) found that policies and practices in multicultural education vary widely from province to province, largely as a response to the presence and recency of arrival of "other" (i.e., non-French, non-English) ethnic groups. Ontario, Manitoba, and British Columbia have official policies on multicultural education and services with a "cultural/intercultural orientation," which goes beyond the mere provision of services in other languages ("linguistic orientation"). The cultural/intercultural orientation that aims to recognize and welcome, rather than assimilate, other cultures "is the dominant one. It seems a question of time before it generalizes and becomes official policy in all parts of the country" (p. 34). Nonetheless, the burden placed on schools remains somewhat contradictory: "they are expected to respond to cultural diversity and contribute at the same time to the promotion of social cohesion and national integration" (p. 35).

It is impossible to discuss language and education without some mention of how differently Quebec reacts compared to the rest of the country. Recent statistics on ethnic origin, mother tongue, and home language show that French is clearly losing ground across the country. In Quebec itself, French has held its ground quite well, but the English minority has grown substantially, especially through the historic assimilation of immigrants. In addition, for many years Quebec has had the lowest birthrate in Canada. In these circumstances, Quebeckers, whatever their political affiliation, widely accept the notion that the powers and policies of the Quebec government, especially in the realm of education, should rightly serve to defend and further the cause of the French language. French is seen as being under siege, and the school is a crucial battleground.

This context explains why Quebec reacts differently in many areas of education. Although French immersion sweeps schools in English Canada, for example, English immersion simply does not exist in French language schools. Indeed, the Ministry of Education of Quebec officially frowns on it, as it does on "cohabitation," that is, the sharing of the same school buildings by children enrolled in French or English school programs. Instruction in English as a second language is not supposed to begin any earlier than Grade 4. Recent provincial legislation directs children whose first language is neither English nor French toward the French school system, reserving English language schools for English speakers.

The feeling that one must fight to defend a language has repercussions that go far beyond educational policies and regulations. Teachers in Quebec have a more visceral attachment to the language they teach. Helping children and young people learn to read, write, listen, and speak effectively is considered more than applying pedagogical principles based on the primacy of communication. It is also ensuring the survival of a whole society and culture.

READING POLICY

Responsibility for Language Arts Policy

The ten provinces and two territories of Canada are responsible for education in general and for setting language arts policy in particular. One territory, the Yukon, rather than developing independent guidelines, has adopted the provincial language arts curriculum of British Columbia. In many provinces, the Ministry of Education, with the guidance of practicing teachers, consultants, and university professors, sets out general principles and tenets designed to guide instruction. Local school districts then develop relevant curriculum based on these provincial guidelines. The process is decentralized further as teachers are expected to translate local guidelines into action in the classroom.

In addition to setting out the general aims and objectives of language arts instruction, many provinces develop support documents to help local school boards and teachers implement the curriculum guidelines. These support documents include background reading on current theory, sample literature units, teaching techniques considered congruent with the provincial guidelines, approved materials, examples of recordkeeping procedures, and bibliographies. Some provinces also provide assessment and evaluation procedures or tests for teachers. Depending on the province, these procedures and/or tests may be required or optional.

GOALS OF READING AND LANGUAGE ARTS

Curriculum

Before beginning our discussion of provincial curriculum guidelines, it is important to note that Canadian educational policy and guidelines make no distinction between males and females. Nor do they make any differentiation between males and females in terms of the curriculum and instruction available to them. Boys and girls are neither separated for instruction in language arts, nor is any attempt made to provide them with different materials.

As mentioned previously, the language arts curriculum is established at the provincial level. In each province, the Department or Ministry of Education prepares curriculum guidelines for the elementary, junior high, and senior high school levels. For the most part, these guidelines are intended as descriptive rather than prescriptive documents.

Most of these curriculum guidelines or programs of study have been revised in the past few years or are in the process of being revised to reflect new ideas and theories concerning language development, language acquisition, child development, and pedagogy. The guidelines usually include a statement of goals, a listing of general/specific objectives, information about recommended or prescribed materials, suggestions for learning activities, teaching and assessment strategies, and objectives or detailed scope and sequence descriptions for language arts instruction at each grade level. Frequently, sample units and examples of typical activities to achieve the goals or objectives are included.

In most provinces, school boards may develop their own guidelines, policies, procedures, and materials that are congruent with provincial guidelines. By encouraging input at the school board level into curriculum development, ministries of education ensure there is considerable scope for local interpretation of provincial guidelines, thus allowing them to reflect the needs of the community and local teachers as well as current language theory.

Although there are differences in language arts curriculum guidelines across the country, key phrases such as *integration*, *holistic approaches*, *transactional teaching*, *process writing*, *response to literature*, and *developmental processes* occur frequently. In some instances, although these exact phrases may not appear in the provincial guideline, the notions they represent fall within terminology used here. The following sections describe the common themes within each of these characteristics.

Integration

In all provinces, the language arts curriculum considers reading, writing, listening, and speaking within the context of communication. In many provinces, viewing is also included in this integrated communication model; currently, even drama, often considered an art, is incorporated into the language arts framework. In French language institutions in Quebec, such areas are dealt with through separate programs, but specific strategies are suggested for integrating them. Most curriculum guides advise that because language is a social behavior, students need many opportunities for speaking, writing, reading, listening, and viewing for a variety of different purposes, different audiences, and in a wide variety of formats. Teachers are encouraged to include language sources such as the student's own language, literature, nonprinted material, computer resources, oral narratives, and a variety of media resources in their language arts program in order to enhance the development of communication skills.

Provincial curriculum guidelines highlight language development which occurs through active involvement in realistic language situations. Thus, teachers are encouraged to take advantage of natural situations in order to assure meaningful participation in all communication strands. Activities such as group work, response to literature, process writing, improvisation, drama, exploratory talk, peer collaboration, and story telling, all of which encourage students to explore different functions and uses for language, are recommended.

Although provinces may include goals and objectives for the separate language strands, most do not recommend teaching elements such as vocabulary, spelling, or grammar as separate subjects. In a few provinces, the guidelines state that one can still teach specific skills lessons to meet the student's particular needs, but the focus should be on integrated learning activities rather than on separate language lessons. This notion is consonant with current theory in the acquisition of the language arts (Calkins, 1986; Pearson, 1984). Generally, the trend in all provinces is toward teaching the language strands in an integrated manner through a variety of purposeful and meaningful communication activities.

Many provinces highlight the importance of integrating language skills and content areas. For example, the language arts curriculum guideline for the Northwest Territories (1988) states that "the development of language skills should occur not only during a designated Language Arts period during the day, but also in the content areas which offer varied and interesting topics to use as the focus of communication activities" (p. 9). This document suggests that teachers must be committed to helping students acquire and apply the language skills necessary to be successful in their subject area. Other provincial guidelines also stress the importance of incorporating a variety of experiences in the classroom that reflect meaningful uses of language across subject areas. For example, British Columbia, Nova Scotia, and Newfoundland recommend that teachers integrate thinking strategies, which are central to success in all subject areas, in the language arts–English curriculum. Within this perspective, emphasis is placed on providing students with opportunities to develop thinking skills within the context of literature, media, and language itself.

Provincial curriculum guidelines tend to recognize the importance of including a wide variety of texts and language sources in order to satisfy the diverse interests, purposes, audiences, and dialects that may exist in a classroom. The curriculum guide for French as a first language in French language institutions in Quebec suggests considering language in its various guises: expressive, directive, informative, and poetic/imaginative (Government of Quebec, 1979; Valiquette, 1979). Other provinces follow Britton's (1970) categories (expressive, transactional, and poetic) to describe various functions of writing and Rosenblatt's (1978) notions of efferent and aesthetic reading.

These uses of language are not to be seen as so many mutually exclusive categories; when we seek to inform, we may also want to do so in a humorous manner. Or reading an adventure story may cause us to identify with a character who shares and clarifies our way of seeing the world. The value of recognizing the different uses of language in real life is to ensure that students are exposed to a rich variety of language types in school. Students will be proficient in language as a whole when they are able to use it effectively for many different purposes. For this reason, the provincial language arts guidelines recommend that students should be interacting with a wide variety of texts.

Quebec's programs for French language arts resemble those of other provinces. The accent is put on "meaningful language" (*discours signifiant*), used for the same purposes for which it would be used outside school, in a variety of communicative contexts. However, the programs also insist on the importance of "objectivation," that is, reflecting on how language is used, and requests that teachers systematically and regularly help students think about how they use language to communicate before, during, and after the act of communicating. The whole program is structured around the various entry points or questions students might ask about the effectiveness of a given language production in a given context.

Holistic Approaches

The countrywide trend, especially at the elementary and junior high school levels, is toward holistic approaches in language arts. However, only two provinces, Quebec (English language institutions) and Nova Scotia, have officially adopted a whole-language curriculum. Nevertheless, guidelines and teacher practice in all provinces have been influenced by the writings of authors such as Graves (1983), Britton (1970), Moffet (1976), Holdaway (1979), Smith (1978), and Rosenblatt (1978). Proponents of a holistic approach argue that children do not learn language by mastering skills, but rather gain competence by using it in a variety of different communication contexts. For example, the proposed policy guideline for Saskatchewan states that children learn language "in interaction with others, not through isolated skills and textbook exercises" (Gambell and Bartel, 1988, p. 2). Two strategies recommended for Saskatchewan schools to promote the development of oracy and literacy are whole-language and language experience. Basic to these strategies is the view that language in school is an extension of learning outside school; thus, the function of school experiences is to build on and extend the language the child brings to the classroom.

Other provinces, while not explicitly mandating any particular holistic approach, recommend activities that focus on the experiential and creative aspects of language development. That is, they focus on using language rather than learning about it. Guidelines recommend that teachers help students discover what they need to know about language through observation, practice, and experience rather than teaching rules in an explicit manner.

Literature plays a significant role in holistic approaches to language development. For example, the Ontario Ministry of Education (1988) has developed a resource guide called "Growing with Books" which is intended to help teachers explore various strategies for using quality literature in the classroom throughout the elementary grades and beyond. The guide includes recommendations about literature as well as a collection of texts written by teachers, librarians, story tellers, poets, consultants, administrators, and researchers. These texts focus on the importance of literature for developing communication and thinking skills.

Although some provinces still use basal readers, these texts have a stronger children's literature focus than found previously. Many of these basals follow a thematic organization and include excerpts from children's books. Teachers are encouraged to supplement basal programs with activities such as shared reading and writing through "Big Books," student-produced materials learning centers, writing groups, improvisation, and thematic units. In addition, teachers are advised to include supplementary materials such as regional literature and children's literature to complement their language arts programs. Ministries of education frequently prepare lists of supplementary materials that they recommend teachers consult to select additional resources for language arts instruction.

The trend toward holistic approaches to language development has shaped the way Canadians look at many issues. For example, in many provinces, the notion of reading readiness, as seen in terms of a score on a reading readiness or reading correlate test, is being replaced by the notion of emergent literacy. British Columbia's recent *Kindergarten Curriculum Guide and Resource Book* (1988) states, "Emergent reading and writing is based on the child making a number of discoveries about print" (p. 48). Backed by such strong policy statements, teachers are encouraged to help develop emerging literacy skills by providing a rich environment of language activities such as reading aloud to children, building on environmental reading and writing, encouraging improvisation, and incorporating language experience stories that include children's natural talk. The explicit teaching of concepts about print is not recommended at the emergent stage of literacy. Rather, teachers are advised to help students develop an orientation to literacy through a variety of reading and writing activities that encourage meaningful communication.

Transactional Teaching

As more provinces move toward holistic approaches, there has been a refocusing of methodologies to stimulate more dynamic communication environments. There is a trend toward more student-centered, transactional teaching and away from more traditional teacher-centered, transmission models of instruction. As Straw (1988) points out, in the transactional model, the task of the teacher shifts from "information transmitter or skill instructor (as in skill development

programs) to knowledge and process facilitator and rich environment builder''
(p. 68). This shift is reflected in Alberta's *Junior High School Curriculum Guide*:
Language Arts (1987) which states that the teacher's role becomes that of a
facilitator, observer, stimulator, ''providing meaningful, interesting situations
in which language use and development is the natural outcome'' (p. 47).

We should not get the impression that no direct teaching is involved in Canadian language arts programs. Although the trend is away from ''telling''
students about language, such practices as modeling, responding directly to
perceived instructional needs, and involving students in reciprocal teaching/
learning situations are common. Moreover, the use of such practices is valued
because they help students, over time, to learn how to assume responsibility for
their own learning. Support for direct teaching, and its proper perspective, is
offered in the Alberta Junior High School guide (1987) which states,

Sometimes direct instruction is required and where necessary, the teacher's role will shift
to one of telling and instruction. However, this direct instruction should always be within
the broader context of meaningful language use. Direct instruction is not an end in itself.
It will arise out of a meaningful language context, and then the learning will be practised
and applied in a meaningful language context. (p. 47)

Through activities such as small-group discussion, thematic study units, personal response to literature, and collaborative writing activities, the focus in
Canada is shifting toward creating nonthreatening learning environments that
encourage risk-taking and active participation among students. In some classrooms, even the physical environment has been structured to support this type
of participation. Rooms often have self-contained libraries, writing centers, flexible seating arrangements, special lofts or areas for silent reading, and media
centers, all of which are designed to foster language use.

Process Approaches to Writing

Most provinces have incorporated a model of the writing process in their
curriculum guidelines consistent with the writings of Graves (1983), Calkins,
(1986), Atwell (1987), Newkirk (1985), Romano (1987), and Smith (1982), to
mention a few authors who recommend activities that encourage students to
brainstorm, draft, revise, edit, and publish/share their writing with a variety of
audiences. This trend toward a process approach to writing requires a significant
shift from teacher as controller/evaluator to students assuming greater control of
and responsibility for their own literacy development. Peer, individual, and
teacher responses to composing are an important component of a process approach to writing. In many provinces, students are encouraged to keep writing
folders, to develop classroom libraries of texts they have produced, and to publish
class or school newspapers—all of which have been produced following the
drafting, revising, and editing of the collaborative model.

Grammar does not appear to be a formal area of study in most provinces.

Rather, it is taught at the point of need in the writing process—for example, during revising and editing. Provincial curriculum guidelines enjoin teachers to insure that language in school be used for the same meaningful purposes as it is outside school. A consequence of the priority accorded to meaningfulness is reflected in the structure of the various curriculum documents. Such concerns as spelling or phonics, which are not meaningful when taught in isolation, frequently are subsumed under the broader concerns of writing and reading. This integration does not deny their importance, but rather sees them as a means to an end, that of using language effectively in literate societies. Explicit knowledge about language is not included in the curriculum of most provinces unless it can be demonstrated that it serves some purpose in helping students learn to use language effectively. For example, the curriculum guides for language arts at the elementary grades in the Atlantic region, such as that of Prince Edward Island, remind teachers that the goal of the program is language development and enrichment rather than language correction. Grammar is to be integrated with other instructional activities instead of being taught as a separate subject.

Response-Centered Approaches to Literature

At the junior and senior high levels in particular, there is a trend toward developing more complex responses to a range of literature as well as trying to increase an appreciation of a variety of different genres. Curriculum guides recommend including sources of literature such as classics, contemporary literature, cultural and ethnic sources, multicultural, adolescent, and children's literature as well as texts produced by students. Some provinces focus directly on the need to include literature by or about French Canadians, Inuits, Indian and Metis peoples, and other cultural groups that make up Canadian society. At the elementary level, personal response is fostered through music, art, and drama as well as discussions and reports of children's literature.

A response-centered approach to literature does not assume that meaning is something that resides only in text or in the reader. Rather, it views the response process as a transaction between the reader and the text. The proposed policy for Saskatchewan comments that "transactional response makes each reader an equal partner in the response process" (Gambell and Bartel, 1988, p. 14). Students are encouraged to develop their own responses to text rather than accepting predetermined responses from outside sources such as the teachers' manual or the classroom teacher.

Several provincial curriculum documents have pointed out that response is rooted in experience, attitudes, psychological, and emotional development. Thus, in order to facilitate response, a teacher must be aware of the complexity of responses to any text that may occur in any class. The teacher's role is to help students select texts to which they may respond in a personal or critical way. For the most part, personal response is the focus of the elementary and junior high school levels of schooling, whereas developing more critical response is part of the senior high program. However, in the senior high instance, there is a clear trend toward more personal response. For example, many students now engage in response journals that reflect their understanding of and attitude toward literature presented in courses. This trend, though more muted, is also evident in college and university English courses.

Developmental Processes

There is a trend across the provinces toward regarding literacy and oracy as a developmental process, with stated goals of helping students develop and use language and literature for personal growth and development. For example, Saskatchewan has identified four phases of oracy and literacy development: emerging, developing, extending, and specialized. According to the proposed policy summary paper, "this developmental sequence encompasses the concept that children arrive in school with an emergent concept of oracy and literacy, that educational development takes place during the elementary years, and that during the middle years oracy and literacy extend more consciously into the supporting domains" (Gambell and Bartel, 1988, p. 8).

At the junior and high school levels, most curriculum guides recommend an increased focus on the more critical aspects of language. For example, the program guideline for French language institutions in Quebec points out that simply *using* language is not sufficient. For learning to take place, students must also observe or reflect before, during, and/or after they speak, listen, read, and write. Another form of this view comes from the Alberta Junior High guide (1987), which even relates reflection to grammar. The guide states, "We need to write a lot; but we also need to *reflect* on our writing; that is to consider it critically with a view to improving the clarity, force or accuracy of the message. Grammar gives us some tools with which to conduct this critical appraisal" (p. 67).

Although most provinces do not explicitly identify different phases of language development, all recognize that language development is a continuous, life-long process and that part of the task of schooling is to help students develop an understanding of and appreciation for communication activities, especially reading. Interestingly enough, although there is a trend toward holism in Canada, the unbalanced focus on reading seems to reflect Orwell's (1945) maxim concerning equality. As he wrote in *Animal Farm*, "All animals are equal. Only some animals are more equal than others" (p. 114). Each of the curriculum guidelines stresses the importance of including recreational as well as informational reading activities in the curriculum in order to encourage students to become life-long readers. There is rarely any similar injunction regarding the other language strands.

Contradictions

Despite the commonalities across the country in language arts curriculum, a number of contradictions are evident, especially in regard to the concept of whole-language education. For example, in interpreting provincial guidelines, some teachers seem to think that process writing, by itself, constitutes whole language. Thus, in practice, the composing aspect of the language arts may be congruent with provincial and local guidelines. However, in a real sense, instruction may be imbalanced, and some components of language arts instruction may continue to adhere to the perspective of isolated subskills. On the other hand, some administrators and teachers worry that too much time is being spent on writing activities and not enough on developing oracy and reading skills.

Some teachers lack the philosophical orientation as well as the in-service support required to implement a whole-language program. To design and carry out such a program, teachers need to understand the fundamental tenets concerning language teaching and learning. Once this framework is understood, teachers then need specific techniques congruent with the overall philosophy. Because the widespread acceptance of whole-language principles is relatively new, persons who acquired their teacher education earlier may require in-service support. Unfortunately, the scope and nature of this type of human support has been uneven across the country.

Another problem is the lack of appropriate materials. In order to implement a whole-language program, teachers need considerable resources. Such traditional techniques and materials as worksheets, prescribed whole-class direct instruction, and teacher-dominated activities do not fit into a holistic view of pedagogy. However, some teachers are reluctant to give up these familiar activities for others involving more student-centered approaches as they lack appropriate replacement materials—especially large stocks of quality literature for encouraging student participation.

There are also many questions regarding *which* literature should be taught in a response to literature program. The issue of literature selection tends to concern secondary and tertiary level teachers because there is a tradition of prescribed anthologies and books at this level. Some individuals are concerned about the abandonment of the classics in favor of more contemporary and/or student-selected texts. Others are concerned that literature is being regarded as merely an adjunct of language development rather than a separate subject. Proponents of this view argue that literary study should be taught separately from language study.

The whole issue of *who* chooses the literature for students is another area of debate. As Gambel and Bartel (1988) pointed out, "students are given the opportunity to develop their own meaning first in transaction with the literacy work rather than having the supposed meaning imposed by the teacher. The teacher's role is to select, and to help students select, literature which they can engage in meaningful response" (p. 14). Certainly, this notion of a teacher as guide who helps students select literature is different from a more traditional model of a teacher who determines what literature should be taught and what kinds of responses are appropriate.

Other contradictions focus more generally on holistic versus skills approaches.

Some teachers want to maintain a "traditional" skills approach to language arts, whereas others want to embrace the more holistic approaches that are supported by provincial guidelines. Those educators with a skills orientation believe that progress in language development has been achieved at the expense of fundamental literacy, for example, spelling and phonics, as less systematic emphasis is put on the relationships between sounds and words. Another group believes that skills approaches do not differ significantly from holistic notions. This group appeals for a blend of the two theoretical stances at either end of the continuum and argues for eclecticism.

In order to help teachers cope with the new demands in terms of holistic approaches, several provinces have initiated a series of support facilities. In English language institutions in Quebec, for example, a Whole Language Support Group helps those teachers who are interested in exchanging information about whole-language practice. Manitoba has a similar organization called the Child-Centred Experience Based Learning Group that responds to requests for in-service help and produces materials for classroom teachers (e.g., *For the Love of Reading*). There are also five Centres of Excellence in English Language Arts in Canada (three in Alberta and two in Quebec). These centers, which are recognized by the National Council for the Teachers of English, are intended to serve as models of effective language arts practice. Teachers are invited to attend the centers to view exemplary practice and materials. At another level, internationally known speakers as well as local experts are frequently invited to language arts conferences and workshops to help teachers become more familiar with key concepts of the theory and practice of holistic approaches to language arts. Support is also being provided in terms of materials as school boards allocate more funds to libraries (except in Quebec, where school libraries have been especially limited by cuts in educational budgets). By providing additional funding to libraries, the school boards are able to increase the quantity of supplementary materials available to the classroom teacher.

Evaluation in a Whole-Language Context

An overview of the state of current assessment and evaluation procedures in Canada will be presented more fully later in this chapter, but because we are focusing on the development and implementation of holistic principles of language instruction in this section some discussion of the salient issues is required. Holistic language instruction is generally accepted in the provinces, but this shift in pedagogical direction away from subskill approaches offers not only promise, but also problems and paradoxes. Nowhere are the problems and paradoxes more apparent than in the area of assessment and evaluation.

Most guidelines recommend that evaluation should be based on the processes of language use as well as the products and should evaluate students' use of higher intellectual skills. Furthermore, many of these same guidelines imply or state directly that evaluation is a continuous, on-going process and should involve input from students, peers, teachers, and sometimes parents. Techniques such as observation, checklists, anecdotal records, interest inventories, questionnaires, reading and writing folders, reading response journals, interviews, and informal tests are frequently recommended as part of this continuous process (Baskwill and Whitman, 1988).

Recent provincial guidelines usually describe the purpose of evaluation as a means of gathering information to use in planning instructional programs for children rather than a procedure for evaluating school districts, individual schools, or teachers. Even when provincewide evaluation is instituted, attempts have been made to eliminate potential invidious comparison among school districts or schools. For example, Ontario recently began large-scale evaluation of reading and writing skills; however, a Ministry of Education directive clearly stated that comparisons among schools or school boards were inappropriate.

Many provinces are struggling with notions of how to develop evaluation procedures that are congruent with literacy practices in classrooms. Options such as writing folders, anecdotal reporting, checklists, and peer and self-evaluation procedures are being considered. One example of the change in evaluation procedures may be seen in recently developed English exams for students in English language institutions in Quebec. By June 1990 students in English language institutions in Quebec were to be allowed to confer, exchange ideas, and edit each other's work in groups during their English school-leaving exam.

ILLITERACY

Adult Literacy

The lack of a standard definition of the term *illiteracy* makes it difficult to assess precisely the incidence of adult illiteracy in Canada (Fagan, 1988). Audrey Thomas, in a report on adult illiteracy in Canada prepared for the Canadian Commission for Unesco in 1983, proposed that anyone over the age of fifteen who was out of school and who had less than a Grade 9 education could be considered functionally illiterate. Typically, government statistics classify anyone with less than nine years of formal schooling as functionally illiterate and anyone with less than five years of formal schooling as a basic illiterate.

Many people argue that completed years of schooling are not adequate indicators of literacy. They contend that functional literacy tasks that assess how well people can cope with the literacy demands of daily life provide more realistic measures of literacy skills. However, the first national literacy survey (Southam News, 1987) that purported to measure functional literacy has been criticized because the tasks required a variety of skills other than reading and writing— such as numerical calculations, world knowledge, and document use (Fagan, 1988). Another criticism of the survey is that it relied on a jury of "average Canadians" to select items that could be used to measure functional literacy. As Fagan pointed out, the "representative jury" consisted mainly of professionals who decided what all Canadians need to know to be classed as literate. He also contended that, in many cases, the literacy tasks selected did not make "functional" sense. Furthermore, there is no indication that the definition used by the jury was any better or worse than more traditional measures based on completed years of schooling.

Despite the criticisms, the survey has generated considerable media attention. This interest, in turn, has led to increased public lobbying of government agencies and has put considerable pressure on all levels of government to improve resources available for literacy training and services. Funding currently is being made available to try to ensure that efforts to coordinate adult literacy initiatives at the provincial and national levels are successful.

Many players are involved in the area of adult literacy. As described previously, education is the constitutional responsibility of the provinces, and, as such, responsibility for literacy rests with this level of government. All provinces offer adult basic education courses (Grades 1–12) which include literacy training, second language instruction, and/or skills upgrading. While each province has a different arrangement for adult literacy training, most of the provinces have adopted a broad-based approach working with school boards, libraries, community colleges, adult correctional centers, and volunteer organizations to provide a wide range of literacy activities in a variety of formal and informal settings.

Throughout the past two decades, adult literacy work within each province was provided mainly on an ad hoc basis. However, several provinces, such as Alberta, Ontario, and Newfoundland, have initiated public awareness campaigns as well as promoted the development of networks of literacy practitioners to coordinate curriculum guidelines, resources, materials, professional expertise, and funding.

Although constitutionally education is not within its jurisdiction, the federal government has indicated that it is committed to work with agencies in the public and private sector. This commitment appears to have developed because of the growing awareness of the need for literacy skills to ensure economic and social growth. In September 1987 the federal government established the National Literacy Secretariat to develop literacy projects in partnership with all sectors of the Canadian community interested in literacy work—such as provincial governments, voluntary organizations, as well as the business and labor sectors. In addition, the Secretariat's mandate includes advising the federal government on major literacy issues and helping to plan Canada's Action Plan for the International Literacy Year in 1990. The Secretariat has already provided funding to several national literacy volunteer organizations for projects such as a bilingual literacy thesaurus, national and international literacy seminars, professional development training programs for literacy practitioners, and networking/advocacy activities.

The Secretariat has also funded a number of joint initiatives with provincial governments to support community-based literacy efforts focusing on organizational development, public awareness, and coordination. Projects include a literacy learners' conference, media publicity, native adult literacy consultation, provincial networking initiatives, materials development, a literacy hotline, and a think-tank forum. These cost-shared projects are designed to support literacy education rather than provide instruction directly.

The Secretariat has also joined with business/labor sectors to develop demonstration or pilot projects in industrial literacy. Working in conjunction with several national literacy organizations, the Secretariat has funded programs to teach literacy in the workplace. Additional funding has also been allocated to initiate research into the nature and extent of illiteracy in Canada.

Besides the provincial and federal governments, another major player in adult literacy work in Canada is the volunteer organization at the community and national levels. Approximately 1,000 organizations throughout the country are involved in providing literacy training. Although the kinds of activities they provide and the methodologies they use vary considerably by region, the volunteer organizations have managed, despite chronic underfunding, to develop innovative approaches to provide literacy training for learners who are often difficult to reach.

The first national conference for adult literacy workers was held in October 1987. The purpose of the conference was to strengthen the movement for literacy in Canada; to shape recommendations and develop action for the next decade of literacy work; and to serve as a think-tank regarding issues in literacy. This session offered the first opportunity for literacy workers to get together to discuss common concerns regarding resources, programs, and funding in Canada.

Frontier College is one of the oldest volunteer organizations in Canada working in the area of adult literacy. Since 1899 it has been involved in literacy work in mining and logging camps, in isolated rural communities, in prisons, and on the streets. In 1975 it was awarded the Unesco medal for its meritorious work in the field of adult literacy. Among its many innovative activities are literacy in the workplace projects, a peer-tutoring program run by and for street people, prison literacy initiatives including an employment/literacy project run by and for ex-offenders, and a native tutoring center.

Other national organizations such as the World Literacy of Canada, the Movement for Canadian Literacy, Laubach Literacy of Canada, and the Canadian Association for Adult Education are involved in a variety of programs designed to upgrade literacy skills, develop training programs for volunteers, prepare learning materials, coordinate practitioners across the country, and lobby the federal and provincial governments for increased support. These national organizations are complemented by provincial groups such as the Alberta Association for Adult Literacy. The goals of the provincial literacy organizations tend to be similar to those at the national level. However, they often possess unique knowledge about the local needs of the population that may not be available to larger groups.

A recent player in adult literacy work in Canada is the private sector. Within the past few years, business and labor have become more actively involved in adult literacy efforts. For example, the book and periodical industry, in partnership with national literacy groups, has initiated a public awareness and fundraising campaign called the Canadian Give the Gift of Literacy project. The aim of the project is to publicize the extent of adult illiteracy in Canada and to raise money for national and community-based literacy groups through public donation and fund-raising efforts in publishing and other industries. A Business Task Force on Literacy has also been established to alert Canadian business about the social and economic costs of illiteracy to Canadian business and to Canadian society in general, and to offer some suggestions for action. In spite of the well-meaning intent of this organization, the results of its actions remain unclear at this time.

TEACHER QUALIFICATIONS

Teacher Education in the Language Arts

Teacher education is a provincial responsibility that is carried out primarily at three different levels. Degrees, such as the Bachelor of Education (B.Ed.), the Master of Education (M.Ed.), and the Doctor of Philosophy in Education (Ph.D.), are earned at universities where faculties of education are part of the larger academic community. At the B.Ed. level of education, both concurrent and consecutive programs are available. In the former program, students earn both a B.A. degree and a B.Ed. concurrently, a process that normally requires three to five years of study depending on the university. In a consecutive program, students first earn a B.A. degree and then engage in a one- or two-year intensive program of study in education.

The amount of instruction a prospective teacher receives in the theory and practice of the language arts varies greatly, not only from province to province but also from university to university. In some institutions, a primary level teacher may graduate with only one course focused specifically on the language arts. On the other hand, a student may have taken as many as three or four specific curriculum courses in the language arts as well as related subjects such as children's literature, the psychological foundations of reading and writing, linguistics, child development, measurement and evaluation, and technology and the language arts. In all institutions, students engage not only in course work but also in a practicum experience. A current trend in teacher education is to conduct more field-based courses in which professors often accompany students to schools, conducting seminars after the practicum.

Teacher upgrading courses, whose curriculum is set out by ministries of education, are offered by a variety of bodies, including faculties of education and local boards of education. In some provinces, teachers may focus on the language arts as a whole or on selected aspects of the language arts such as reading and writing. Upgrading courses may be extensive, requiring as many as 375 contact hours of instruction in order to earn a specialist certification, and most courses carry both a theoretical and practicum component.

Another form of teacher education is carried out at the school board or individual school level. This type of upgrading often is designed in response to current board or school emphases, and although these courses or workshops do not result in certificates or diplomas, they fill important needs. For example, in recent years many boards have conducted workshops on fostering the writing process. Typically, these sessions begin with a major speaker—sometimes the local language arts consultant—who presents an overview of the current state of theory and practice. In the following weeks, teachers participate in in-depth workshops on specific aspects of the topic under study. Teachers tend to value these types of sessions because they frequently are able to use the acquired knowledge and strategies in their classroom immediately.

Because of the special place of the teaching of French in Quebec society, the PPMF (Programme de perfectionnment des maîtres de français), a part-time, off-campus certificate program for the teaching of French language arts in elementary and secondary schools, was offered by participating universities with special funding from the Ministry of Education in Quebec, starting in 1975. Equivalent to one full year of university study and open only to practicing teachers, the certificate has been taken by thousands of Quebec teachers and has had a profound impact on the teaching of French language arts in the province. It has been instrumental in helping teachers understand and put into practice the basic principles of the new curricula.

READING MATERIALS

In most provinces, print sources tend to be recommended rather than mandatory. Although some provinces, such as Alberta, still have a list of prescribed materials, there is a trend toward recommended resources such as printed material, films, and computer software. Most provinces have developed guidelines that will ensure that materials used in schools reflect Canadian content and, wherever possible, are authored, designed, or produced by Canadians. The material should be about Canada, present a Canadian perspective, or be designed to meet Canadian needs. However, while English Canadians may worry about an influx of American language arts and English materials, this has, of course, never been a concern in Quebec. The notion of "Canadian" content is a non sequitur.

Many provinces are encouraging teachers to incorporate literature and other resources that deal accurately and approximately with Inuit, Metis, and Native Indian culture. In New Brunswick, Newfoundland, Nova Scotia, and Prince Edward Island, regional literature reflecting the diverse ethnic heritages and geographic influences in the area is recommended for study. Besides ensuring that classroom materials reflect the multicultural heritage of the country, provincial curriculum guidelines ensure that textbooks and supplementary materials used in language arts classes avoid gender stereotyping.

Although there is a trend away from prescribed materials, some provinces still require teachers, especially at the elementary grades, to use basal programs as core texts. However, current basals are different from the highly structured, artificial anthologies of previous times. Newer basals may include excerpts from classic children's literature, folk tales, myths, legends, fairy tales, fantasy, poetry, songs, interviews, stories by currently recognized authors, and informational text. Anthologies, with content organized thematically, tend to be popular choices for the junior and senior high levels. These anthologies are usually supplemented by novels, poetry, and drama.

The curriculum actually implemented by teachers in their classrooms is determined to a great extent by the language arts materials they have at their disposal. Thus, in the case of the 1979 French mother tongue program in Quebec, the appearance in 1980 of a series of thirty-six well-illustrated booklets for beginning readers was of strategic importance (Richard, 1980). This package of literature allowed teachers to see how the principles of the curriculum could actually be put into practice. Each booklet contained a single text, which was simple but complete in itself. The booklets contained no exercises where language was presented in isolation, such as phonic or syllable practice.

The introduction of these types of material meant that children were reading whole texts from the onset of instruction and could therefore use a variety of strategies to recover meaning, as readers normally do. These booklets were complemented by other materials that put the accent on verifying comprehension and manipulating the structural aspects of language without losing sight of the broader text of which they were a part. The series was well received, and the enthusiasm of teachers who started using it, even before the guidelines became mandatory, helped create the general feeling that the new holistically oriented guidelines would be beneficial for all.

Progress in beginning reading was also aided by the appearance of a popular television program for preschoolers called "Passe-partout," produced by Radio-Quebec in collaboration with the Ministry of Education. An especially intriguing aspect is the general public's acceptance of related materials even years after the initial appearance. Colorful activity booklets, posters, stickers, and even postcards continue to be a common sight at shopping market checkout counters. The series is still regularly broadcast and continues to attract large audiences.

Native Education

The growing trend across the country is toward native control of native education. In the past, the federal government controlled native schools through the Department of Indian Affairs and Northern Development. Within recent years, however, the movement has been toward local or regional band control of schools. Indian cultural survival schools, which concentrate almost exclusively on Indian content and customs, have been established in several provinces. Textbooks and curriculum materials including audiovisual and print materials that reflect the social, historical, and linguistic heritage of indigenous groups are also starting to appear.

Many of the indigenous languages are now taught in schools, usually as separate subjects. Barman, Hébert, and McCaskill (1987), in their report *Indian Education in Canada: The Challenge*, note that "such study has been directed both at revitalizing the language as part of the cultural tradition and at students acquiring some degree of fluency with natural speech" (p. 12). Stairs (in press) supports and extends this notion by pointing out that the issue goes deeper than simply offering native languages. She writes, "We must attend not just to language but to people whose culture is carried in language" (p. 18).

Issues and Trends in Assessment and Evaluation

Because education is a provincial responsibility, no national statistics are available to indicate current achievements in the language arts in Canada. Froese (1984, 1988), who has studied the issue extensively, reported that provincial assessment is dominated by two major types. First, some provinces, through use of standardized tests such as the Canadian Test of Basic Skills or specially designed provincial examinations, determine the language arts abilities of students at various grade levels. For example, in a given year, Grade 3, 6, 9, and 11 pupils may be tested. Second, departmental examinations, often at the high school level, are devised and administered by local school boards and individual schools. Departmental exams are meant to be congruent with provincial curriculum guidelines.

No national, and few provincial, statistics are available indicating the extent of reading disabilities in Canada. The terms *writing disability* or *speaking disability* are almost nonexistent, perhaps because norm-referenced tests in these areas also are almost nonexistent. Identifying and helping so-called reading disabled students thus fall on local school boards and schools where reading disabled students are helped by specially certified teachers who work in a variety of settings including clinics and resource classrooms and alongside the pupil in regular classrooms. Currently, only a few provincewide attempts to help students in need, such as the Newfoundland Reading Recovery Project, are underway.

The development and implementation of whole-language principles and corresponding pedagogical strategies has created a wide gap between current teaching practices and assessment procedures. Most of the instruments used in assessment, especially existing standardized tests, are based on a subskill model of reading and writing. In the area of writing, only English-speaking institutions in Quebec are currently attempting to examine the process as well as the product, although several provinces are revising their procedures to incorporate this distinction. Moreover, as pointed out by Froese (1988), most provinces ignore the assessment of oracy—listening and speaking. However, the recent resource packages developed in western Canada which attempt to show teachers both how to enhance and evaluate oral communication may indicate a growing awareness that more than reading and writing is involved in literacy.

Although the provinces have only recently begun to devise and adapt assessment procedures reflecting current language arts theory and practice, it is clear that many teachers are making changes individually. Key informants describe an increased use of reading and writing folders, anecdotal reporting, checklists, and audiotaping of children engaged in language arts activities. More emphasis appears to be placed on the developmental nature of emerging literacy rather than on identifying children by grade-equivalent test scores. Teachers are also engaging students more in group, peer, and self-evaluation, a trend especially prevalent in assessing writing. These informal assessment procedures appear to be emerging at all levels of schooling, not simply at the primary level as some educators believe.

As described earlier, the trend toward whole-language teaching and testing strategies is not without its critics. Although in the minority, a vocal group of persons both within and outside education favor a return to standardized tests— in reading and writing. These provincewide tests would be administered at the end of the school year, and students failing to attain a certain level of achievement would not be promoted to a higher grade. The critics, often business leaders and newspaper editors, argue that Canadian standards of literacy are declining and that only standardized tests can restore the educational system to its past high standards. Although they call for testing reading and writing, this group of critics seldom mentions the other two sides of literacy, speaking and listening.

French language institutions in Quebec have made considerable progress in developing summative measures consonant with recent language arts curricula. Germain and Lapointe (1984) have produced one of the first sets of writing evaluation procedures that is both relatively simple to understand and broad enough to cover several grades, in this case, Grades 2 to 6. Evaluation criteria are illustrated as they were applied to samples of real texts written by children. Proposed evaluation procedures are presented within a framework suggesting how evaluation can be linked to planning and organizing classroom learning activities. Such material has contributed greatly to the widespread adoption of "descriptive" report cards, where numbers and percentages are replaced by descriptions of what children can actually do.

RESEARCH THRUSTS

Research in the Language Arts

Research into the language arts may be grouped into three broad categories: university-based research, field-based research, and research based on a uniquely Canadian perspective. The first category refers to researchers—most often based in universities—who conduct investigations into the processes of reading, writing, and speaking, and listening. Because Canada has no federally funded centers that focus on research in the language arts such as the Center for the Study of Reading in the United States, researchers tend to pursue individual interests. On one hand, this lack of focus creates a rich tapestry of types of projects, in terms of both subject matter and methodology. On the other hand, a lack of central focus also translates into diverse funding; thus, potentially useful large-scale or longitudinal research projects are rare in Canada. Another factor contributing to the lack of large-scale studies is the relatively small number of funding agencies in the country.

It is outside the scope of this chapter to list all the investigators and topics currently under study in Canada, but a sample of the types of projects indicating the scope of research is possible. Fundamental research includes (1) language acquisition and emergent literacy, (2) strategies used in processing print, (3) the uses of oral and written language, (4) metacognition, (5) schema theory, and (6) building theories of the speaking, listening, reading, and writing processes. In addition, several researchers are investigating the issue of reading disabilities. Subjects for these types of investigations range from preschool children to adults; methodology extends from naturalistic to experimental paradigms.

Based on an understanding of language processes, other researchers are engaged in application projects. Some of these projects include (1) establishing strategies and techniques for teaching reading and writing processes, (2) applying technology to literacy education, (3) developing assessment instruments and procedures, (4) creating response techniques, (5) examining the social context of education, and (6) fostering literacy in the home.

Finally, numerous researchers in Canada are carrying out studies and developing information sources related to the language arts, but perhaps not directly to the processes. These include (1) comparative reading, (2) linguistics (e.g., analyzing the structure of discourse), (3) children's literature, (4) readability, (5) social patterns in classrooms, (6) teacher thinking and decision making, (7) nonverbal behavior, (8) the interests of adult readers, and (9) the history of language arts instruction in Canada.

Investigators who work in the field, that is, directly with ministries of education, school boards, and individual schools, carry out another form of research. This applied research may take the form of curriculum or material development, which is often field-tested in the real world of schools. Researchers in this category may be employed full time by an agency such as an education ministry or a school board. In other instances, university professors or independent scholars are hired to work on a particular issue, project, or problem. A second aspect of this type of pragmatic research relates to children experiencing difficulty in acquiring literacy. In this instance, boards sometimes devise special programs for such children, and researchers often monitor new programs in order to determine their effectiveness.

Teachers who carry out action research in their own classrooms represent a relatively recent, but encouraging, trend. Some of these investigations began as part of a master's or doctoral program, but as teachers gained skill in methodology, more projects were devised to answer questions unique to a particular situation. Because of the immediate impact of teacher-conducted research, educators have praised this trend. Teachers in Nova Scotia have been particularly active in this area, with many sharing their insights by writing for other teachers. Teachers writing for teachers seems to be a natural outgrowth of the classroom-based teacher research.

Because of the current interest in whole language, much of field-based research focuses on developing guidelines, teaching strategies, materials, and assessment procedures for teachers. Recent projects include attempts to (1) help teachers understand the principles of whole language, (2) create predictable, meaningful print sources, (3) develop strategy lessons that focus on the processes of language rather than the product, and (4) devise assessment procedures that can be used with individual children rather than groups and that focus on language processes as well as product.

Many of the topics described in the previous paragraphs have counterparts in other countries, although the Canadian context adds a unique dimension. However, a third category of research relates directly to situations or issues that seem to be distinctly Canadian. Other countries may have similar situations, but the issues in these instances are clear enough to require a Canadian perspective. Examples are the needs, educational values, and learning styles of native people. Other important issues include the nature of bilingual education and heritage language teaching. In certain areas of Canada, students speak in nonstandard dialects; researchers are determining the effect of these dialects on literacy acquisition. Projects in this spirit include (1) the learning style of native people, (2) the best time to begin immersion education, (3) differences in methods and materials in first and second language education, (4) ways of overcoming distance in educating students, (5) the effects of dialect interference in reading standard English, and (6) the effects of first language knowledge on acquiring a second or third language.

As described previously, Canada has no central, federally funded research centers in the language arts area. However, some provinces have funded educational research facilities where some of the studies focus on various aspect of the language arts. For example, Ontario created the Ontario Institute of Education to carry out studies that would guide the province in creating educational policy. Some of the government-sponsored projects related directly or indirectly to the language arts area. Although no other province has such a specific institute, several have created research centers as part of a faculty of education. Such centers exist in Alberta (Centre for the Study of Gifted Education), British Columbia (Centre for Whole Language), Nova Scotia (Language Centre), and Newfoundland (Institute of Educational Research). Dissemination of language arts research is carried out by national journals such as the *English Quarterly*, *Journal of English Language Arts*, and *Reading-Canada-Lecture*. These journals give priority to reporting Canadian research and thinking in the language arts.

Their counterpart in Quebec is *Québec français*, which is widely read by practicing teachers as well as language arts specialists in school boards, universities, and the Ministry of Education.

THE READING OUTLOOK FOR LANGUAGE ARTS INSTRUCTION IN CANADA

Holistic Teaching of Language

Holistic approaches to language arts instruction, based on current theory, are having a major impact on instruction. How long this trend will influence teaching is problematic as several major issues are emerging. First, teachers' understanding of the tenets underlying holistic notions of teaching and learning vary greatly. In some instances, techniques and materials that are clearly more congruent with subskill orientations to instruction are subsumed under the label "whole language." If the idea of "whole language" is not to be reduced to a cliché, more comprehensive teacher education will have to be implemented.

A second concern, also related to holistic notions of the language arts, is support. In the past few years, ministries of education responded promptly and decisively by creating curriculum guidelines and support materials congruent with holistic principles of language and literacy acquisition; however, the next tier of support is also important. Rich collections of children's literature, new information technology, and other tools of oracy, listening, reading, and writing will be required to implement the holistically based curriculum guides currently used or in development.

The mismatch between holistic principles of language arts instruction and current evaluation techniques is a third important issue. If we accept the contention that evaluation strongly influences curriculum, this matter may turn out to be the keystone. As Valencia and Pearson (1986) have pointed out, current methods of assessment are inconsistent with current knowledge of language processes. If language processes and products continue to be evaluated with techniques more suited to subskill notions of instructions, instruction may move in this direction.

The structure of faculties of education in Canada impede the implementation of holistic approaches to language arts instruction. In some universities, separate reading and language arts departments exist within the same faculty, and courses offered reflect these divisions. Alternatively, reading and language arts courses are staffed by the same department but taught as separate courses. Finally, courses may be taught by faculties of education or other departments within a university such as psychology. Curriculum courses with a specific focus, such as reading or writing, tend to support the idea of fragmenting language instruction. There is nothing inherently wrong with courses having distinct titles, especially when we consider such sacred traditions as academic freedom. However, if professors in faculties of education advocate total communication models of language arts instruction, it may be inconsistent to present such models in narrowly defined courses.

The final question concerning holistic orientations to language instruction relates to the junior and senior high school levels of education. Although "language across the curriculum" is an oft-recited intent for junior high and senior high school, there are many barriers to realization of the goal. The specific demands of courses in history, science, and mathematics make it difficult for content teachers to see how "language across the curriculum" can be achieved. Moreover, because content teachers are often specialists, they may lack the necessary knowledge of current language principles and the means to implement them. Finally, dividing teachers into separate subjects, time slots, and classrooms makes whole-language projects more difficult to implement in high schools than in elementary schools.

Technology

All provinces have attempted to make new technology available to teachers. Some provinces, such as Nova Scotia, have focused on teacher education, while others, such as Ontario, have developed hardware and software especially designed for provincial needs. The decentralized nature of Canadian education has worked against the provinces in creating special software congruent with curriculum guidelines or with Canadian content. Ontario mandates computers with provincial specifications; thus, software developed for these machines typically is not available in other provinces where teachers tend to use commercially available computers.

Although teachers call for creative, open-ended software such as data bases, interactive fiction, and simulations, there still is a tendency across Canada to use drill and practice language programs with a subskill orientation. Because many of the programs resemble basal reader workbooks, one of two situations may develop. First, teachers may tend to move back toward fragmented language programs in general. Second, if teachers see the incongruency between the normal activities of the classroom and the available software, they may abandon technology. In the second instance, the valuable aspects of technology that are congruent with holistic principles would be lost as well.

For the most part, recent graduates from faculties of education have engaged in some course work and hands-on experience in using technology. For teachers already in the field, the situation is more variable. Upgrading courses are available, but teachers are not required to take them. Furthermore, although general courses on using technology are offered, few, if any, focus directly on the use of computers in the language arts. If the true impact of new technology is to match its promise, more concerted efforts in teacher education will be needed. Because many upgrading courses in language education are offered throughout the country, the most productive way to promote wider knowledge in using technology may be to make it an integral aspect of these courses rather than to conduct special computer classes.

In French-speaking institutions in Quebec, word processing is by far the most widely used computer application. This use of technology has fired the imagination of French language arts teachers because word processors make it possible to put revision and process into the heart of their teaching of writing. Teachers are offered support in educational word processing through professional associations, local and regional microcomputing centers, school board consultants, and courses offered for credit by various universities either on-campus, off-campus, or through correspondence.

The biggest hurdles to more widespread use of word processing, at least in French language schools, are the lack of sufficient computers and printers, the problems of organizing classroom time and space, the difficulty of fitting an innovation into established curricula and practices, the absence of teaching materials linking French language arts directly to word processing, students' and teachers' conceptions of writing as linear, and computer phobia. Nevertheless, the spread of word processing through the schools has been greatly assisted by the increasing number of students familiar with word processing at home. Just how far word processing can be implemented in schools and whether its presence is permanent are difficult to ascertain.

Bilingualism

In Canadian schools, bilingualism covers a range of different course offerings, including immersion classes, core French, and mother tongue classes. Although bilingual programs have been in existence for more than twenty years, the issue remains a complex social and political one that warrants more analysis than is possible within the context of this chapter. However, we can make a few brief points regarding this issue.

In English Canada, there is a clear, strong mandate for more French language education in English schools. Evidence of the success of these programs comes from colleges, universities, and the workplace where graduates of the programs are coping successfully in their second language. Further evidence comes from research projects over the past decade which have monitored the linguistic, academic, and social/psychological achievements of students in immersion classes. Results from these studies indicate that immersion students achieve high levels of French proficiency, though not native speaker fluency. Their English language development is neither delayed nor restricted, and their attitudes toward French language and culture tend to be more positive than that of students in unilingual English programs. As Hayden (in press) pointed out in a recent paper, "The general consensus of the literature suggests that as children become bilingual, they produce acceptable levels of educational achievement in both languages. It is not surprising, therefore, that educational fingers point to immersion as the great Canadian success story." Hayden goes on to state that "some questions remain, however, as to the efficacy of immersion as a viable educational experience for all children.'' Certainly, as more children enroll in immersion programs, further research is needed to determine to what extent these programs can be adapted to meet the needs of expanded populations.

Heritage Languages

There has been considerable growth and support for heritage language programs within the past decade. Interest in promoting heritage language instruction comes from recent immigrants and from ethnic groups who perhaps generations after immigrating want to reclaim their culture. Support for expanding these programs also comes from research studies indicating that literacy in one's mother tongue enhances the learning of other languages. A Heritage Language Centre has been established in Ontario, and another one will soon be established in Alberta to initiate research and monitor the development of teaching resources. Despite this support, it is not clear whether heritage language programs will ever become part of the regular school day or to what extent the values and cultures of various minority groups will be integrated across the curriculum and be accepted as an integral part of the Canadian mosaic.

Native Education

One of the challenges facing native education centers on preparing educational planners, policymakers, administrators, teachers, and researchers so that native people can develop their own leadership in education. Approximately seventeen Indian education programs exist in Canada. Barman, Hébert, and McCaskill (1987) note that ''the primary goals of all programmes are to increase the representation of Native people in the teaching profession, to improve the quality of education for native children, and to bridge the gap between the school and the community'' (p. 13).

A second challenge is to revise programs in native schools. Most are heavily influenced by structural linguistics and appear to be teacher-dominated and not student-centered. However, there is a trend toward turning these into more ''holistic language programs'' and to focus on peer interaction, experiential learning, natural language, and other teaching strategies that are more congruent with native cultures.

Adult Education

In the past, adult illiteracy programs in Canada have been organized on an ad hoc basis. However, within the past few years several attempts have been made at the provincial and national levels to try to coordinate the provision of programs and materials for adult literacy. These efforts focus on establishing appropriate structures and delivery systems (that is, training and materials) and increasing public awareness of the problem of illiteracy. With the establishment of the National Literacy Secretariat, there is renewed hope that increased funding will be available for applied and basic research in the area of adult illiteracy.

Canadian Content

Over the past ten years, many provinces have instituted several steps to ascertain Canadian content in curriculum materials. These measures have included grants to authors and publishers, in-house creation of materials, software development support, guidelines for curriculum development, and the creation of panels to screen materials for inclusion on approved lists. There are no signs that any of the provinces plans to retreat from guaranteeing Canadian content. Within the country, efforts have been made recently to create materials for special groups of learners such as native people or special programs such as French immersion. However, Canadian content in these instances remains a priority.

A recent free trade agreement between the United States and Canada has caused concern especially among English Canadian educators for Canadian identity in general and for Canadian content in educational materials in particular. The free trade agreement opens markets in both countries to the other party without tariffs and other barriers. How this agreement will affect social programs, regional development programs, medicare, and education in Canada is a matter of intense debate. Whether or not American publishers will demand that Canadian content requirements be dropped or diluted because of the free trade agreement is problematic.

CONCLUSION

This chapter describes the current state of language arts instruction in Canada. There is a clear trend among the provinces to encourage, and in a few cases, to mandate holistic approaches to teaching as opposed to the more traditional skills-oriented approaches. Although this trend appears to extend across grade levels, it is more pronounced in elementary schools. In spite of a general acceptance of holistic practices, some problems have developed in implementation—including a lack of materials such as quality children's literature, teachers' expertise with whole-language approaches, disparate interpretation of holistic principles of language arts instruction, and a lack of congruency between curriculum practice and evaluation procedures. Despite current tendencies, a vocal minority of parents, administrators, and businesspeople are calling for a return to subskill-oriented methods and techniques, including large-scale standardized testing. However, this minority is being challenged by teachers and parents who, for the most part, have welcomed and supported holistic approaches. Some observers would contend that the so-called whole-language movement had its origins among practitioners rather than administrators and curriculum developers.

REFERENCES

Alberta Ministry of Education, Curriculum Branch. 1987. *Junior high school curriculum guide: Language arts*. Edmonton, Alberta: Ministry of Education.

Atwell, N. 1987. *In the Middle*. Montclair, N.J.: Boyton/Cook.

Aulls, M. 1982. *Developing readers in today's elementary schools*. Boston: Allyn and Bacon.

Barman, J., Hébert, Y., and McCaskill, D. 1987. *Indian education in Canada*. Vol. 2: *The Challenge*. Nakoda Institute Occasional Paper No. 3. Vancouver: University of British Columbia Press.

Baskwill, J., and Whitman, P. 1988. *Evaluation: Whole language, whole child*. Richmond Hill, Ontario: Scholastic.

Braun, C., and Neilsen, A. 1980. *First steps to reading: A guide to prereading and beginning reading activities*. Calgary, Alberta: Braun and Braun.

British Columbia Ministry of Education. 1988. *Kindergarten curriculum guide and resource book*. Victoria, B.C.: School Department, Curriculum Branch.

Britton, J. 1970. *Language and learning*. Baltimore: Penguin

Calkins, L. 1986. *The art of teaching writing*. Portsmouth, N. H.: Heinemann.

Cochrane, O., Cochrane, D., Scalena, S., and Buchanan, E. 1984. *Reading, writing, and caring*. Winnipeg. Whole Language Consultants.

Doake, D. 1985. Reading-like behaviour: Its role in learning to read. In A. Jagger and M. Smith-Burke (eds.), *Observing the language learner*. Newark, Del.: International Reading Association.

Fagan, W. T. 1985. Basal reader/language arts materials: A professional responsibility. *Reading-Canada-Lecture* 3, no.1: 29–35.

Fagan, W. T. 1988. Literacy in Canada: A critique of the Southam Report. *The Alberta Journal of Educational Research* 34: 224–231.

Fairbairn, J. 1987. Illiteracy in Canada. *Debates of the Senate* 131, no. 30: 597–600.

Froese, V. 1984. Trends in Canadian provincial reading assessments. *English Quarterly* 16: 4–8.

Froese, V. 1988. Provincial reading/language arts assessment and evaluation. *Reading-Canada-Lecture* 6 no.3: 167–175.

Gambell, T. J., and Bartel, C. 1988. *Policy for English language arts K-12 for Saskatchewan schools summary paper*. May.

Germain, C., and Lapointe, R. E. 1984. L'evaluation de la communication écrite au primaire (2e a 6e année): Grille et guide d'utilisation. Montreal: PPMF, University of Montreal.

Gordon, C. J. 1989. Teaching narrative text structure: A process approach to reading and writing. In K.D. Muth (ed.), *Children's comprehension of narrative and expository text: Research into practice*. Newark, Del.: International Reading Association.

Government of Quebec. 1979. *Programme d'étude Primaire Français*. Quebec: Ministry of Education.

Graves, D. 1983. *Writing: Teachers and children at work*. Portsmouth, N.H.: Heinemann.

Gunderson, L., and Shapiro, J. 1987. Some findings on whole language instruction. *Reading-Canada-Lecture* 5 no.1: 22–26.

Hayden, H. 1985. Reading in French immersion: A pot-pourri of concerns. *Reading-Canada-Lecture* 3, no.1: 49–55.

Hayden, H. In press. French immersion drop-outs: Perspectives on parents, students and teachers. *Reading-Canada-Lecture* 6, no. 4.

Holdaway, D. 1979. *Independence in reading*. Sydney, Australia: Ashton Scholastic.

Hopper, C. 1986. *Le Scripteur*. Laval, Quebec: Editions FM.

Lessard, C., and Crespo, M. In press. The education of recent immigrants/Multicultural education in Canada: Policies and practices. In D. Ray and D. Poonwassie (eds.), *Tomorrow can be better*. Toronto: McClelland.

MacLean, M. 1986. Second language reading research: Pathways through the labyrinth. *Reading-Canada-Lecture* 4, no.1: 32–37.

Mickelson, N. 1987. *Whole language implementation strategies*. Victoria, British Columbia: University of Victoria Centre for Whole Language.

Miller, L., and Burnett, J. D. 1987. Using computers as an integral aspect of elementary language arts instruction: Paradoxes, problems, and promise. In D. Reinking (ed.), *Reading and computers: Issues for theory and practice*. New York: Teachers College Press.

Moffett, J. 1976. *Student-centered language arts and reading, K–13* (2nd ed.). Boston: Houghton Mifflin.

Newkirk, T. 1985. *To compose: Teaching writing in the high school*. Portsmouth, N.H.: Heinemann.

Newman, J. (ed.). 1983. Whole language: Translating theory into practice. Monographs on Learning and Teaching No. 2. Halifax, N.S.: Department of Education, Dalhousie University.

Norman, C., and Malicky, G. 1986. Literacy as a social phenomenon: Implications for instruction. *Lifelong Learning* 9: 12–15.

Northwest Territories School Program Division. 1988. *Junior high English Language Arts curriculum and program guide*. Yellowknife, NWT: Department of Education.

O'Brien, M. 1985. The methodology of adult literacy in Canada: Some concerns. *Reading-Canada-Lecture* 3, no. 1: 21–28.

Ontario Ministry of Education. 1988. *Growing with books*. Toronto: Queen's Printer for Ontario.

Orwell, G. 1945. *Animal Farm*. Harmondsworth, England: Penguin.

Pearson, P. D. 1984. *Handbook of reading research*. New York: Longman.

Richard, L. 1980. *A mot découverts*. Laval, Quebec: Mondia, Editeurs.

Romano, T. 1987. *Clearing the way: Working with teenage writers*. Portsmouth, N.H.: Heinemann.

Rosenblatt, L. M. 1978. *The reader, the text, and the poem*. Carbondale, Ill.: Southern Illinois University Press.

Smith, F. 1978. *Reading without nonsense*. New York: Teachers College Press.

Smith, F. 1982. *Writing and the writer*. New York: Holt, Rinehart, and Winston.

Southam News. 1987. *Literacy in Canada: A research report*. Toronto: Creative Research Group.

Stairs, A. In press. The question of vernacular education. *English Quarterly*.

Statistics Canada. 1988. *Education in Canada: A statistical review for 1986–87*. Ottawa, Ontario: Minister of Supply and Services Canada.

Straw, S. 1988. Our underlying assumption. *English Quarterly* 21, no. 2: 67–69.

Thomas, A. M. 1983. *Adult literacy in Canada: A challenge*. Ottawa: Canadian Commission for Unesco.

Valencia, S., and Pearson, P.D. 1986. New models for reading assessment. Reading Education Report No. 71, Champaign, Ill.: Center for the Study of Reading.

Valiquette, J. 1979. Les fonctions de la communication, au coeur d'une didactique renouvelée de la langue maternelle. Quebec: Direction générale du développment pédogogique, Coll. SREP, No. 16–0125.

Wagner, S. 1985. Illiteracy and adult literacy teaching in Canada. *Prospects* 15, no. 3: 407–417.

4

China

Miao Xiaochun
Translated by Jing Wang

THE LANGUAGES OF CHINA

Chinese is the official language of China and is used by the majority of the population. China is a multiethnic country, however. In addition to the ethnic Chinese (called the Han nationality), there exist fifty-five ethnic minorities (called nationalities) whose population represents only 6.7 percent of China's total population, yet whose residence is dispersed across the entire territory. Today some of these minorities, such as the Hui and Man nationalities, use the Chinese language; the majority of them, however, have their own languages. In autonomous regions (equivalent to provinces) and states (equivalent to districts within a province) with a relative concentration of ethnic minorities, ethnic languages are widely used or have even become the major language in use in some instances. Tibetan in the Tibet autonomous region, Uighur in the Xinjiang Uighur autonomous region, and Mongolian in the Inner Mongolia autonomous region are only three such examples.

Some small ethnic minorities have their own oral language but no written systems. These groups usually converse in their own vernacular, but their children must learn Chinese and use Chinese-medium textbooks after enrolling in elementary schools. For those minorities that have both an oral language and a writing system, the children learn some Chinese in addition to learning the vernacular and receiving education in the vernacular.

The learning and use of ethnic languages in schools varies widely. Some special schools and classes that admit only students from ethnic minorities carry out all their teaching activities in the ethnic language—for example, the Tibetan elementary schools in Tibet, the Uighur elementary and high schools in Xinjiang, and the Mongolian schools and classes in pastoral Mongolia. Starting from

Grades 3 and 4, however, students in these special schools and classes also learn Chinese. Some ethnic schools and classes use ethnic languages to teach ethnic languages, but use Chinese when teaching such subjects as math, physics, and chemistry. The Tibetan high schools, the Tibetan classes in regular high schools, and the Mongolian classes in urban Mongolia are all such examples. The situation varies from place to place at the university level. At Tibet University, the medium of instruction is Chinese except for two areas, Tibetan language and Tibetan medicine. At Xinjiang University, however, Uighur is used in all but two specialties, medicine and engineering.

In short, ethnic languages are widely used in areas where minorities concentrate. Practices show that the lower the grades, the more subjects that are taught in the vernacular. As children progress in grades, they receive more and more education in Chinese.

CENTRALIZATION VERSUS DISPERSION IN THE READING POLICY

Currently, the Chinese policy toward reading education is a combination of centralization and dispersion. For example, with regard to primary and secondary schools, China has always had a unified curriculum for all subjects taught at these levels. This curriculum was developed by the experts and teachers selected by the State Education Commission (SEdC). Within the SEdC, there is a textbook reviewing committee for primary and secondary education, which has a special subcommittee for reviewing language teaching–related textbooks. Once the curriculum for language teaching is designed, it is reviewed first by the special language teaching subcommittee, and then by the textbook reviewing committee for primary and secondary education, after which it is finally approved by the authorities at the SEdC.

The curriculum for language teaching specifies basic objectives and requirements for reading education. It is the basis for teaching, testing, and evaluating teaching quality and textbook writing. Except in ethnic minority schools, all primary and secondary schools in China should follow this curriculum and achieve the objectives outlined in the curriculum.

The curriculum permits the use of different-styled textbooks, the so-called multitextbooks under one curriculum. The curriculum does not mention the specific ways of compiling textbooks. In fact, it encourages all localities, institutions of higher education, research institutes, specialists, and scholars, as well as teachers and private individuals, to write textbooks. It also encourages variations in textbook content and style according to regional and local characteristics. Local schools are urged to choose, write, and adapt as supplementary textbooks those that suit local needs. However, all textbooks, reference materials, and audiovisual materials are subject to approval by the SEdC Textbook Reviewing Committee for Primary and Secondary Schools before they can be publicly distributed.

Shanghai has published a series of guidance books for language teaching, providing detailed explanations of the curriculum for language teaching, in the primary and secondary schools. It is also in the process of compiling language textbooks for schools in the more developed coastal regions. Beijing is preparing a similar series of language textbooks for schools in general situations, and Sichuan Province is writing one for the remote and mountainous regions. All these textbooks include the teaching of reading and composition.

The textbooks currently in use are in a similar situation. In use are a series of unified textbooks compiled by the SEdC, as well as many experimental textbooks written by various localities, institutions, and teachers. Dozens of them have been officially published. Most of these textbooks have combined reading, writing, and basic language training, with emphasis on reading. Some textbooks for secondary schools separate reading and writing, treating them as two separate subjects. A few such textbooks are centered around basic language training (such as word formation and sentence structure).

The autonomous regional governments of the ethnic minority schools set the teaching objectives and requirements for ethnic languages. For instance, Tibet's regional government has established its own curriculum for teaching Tibetan at its primary and secondary schools. Autonomous regions also compile their own textbooks, either on their own or in cooperation with other autonomous regions. As to the teaching of the Chinese language in these ethnic minority schools, the central government has established a unified curriculum, outlining objectives and requirements. Local schools, however, are allowed to make appropriate modifications according to their specific needs and local characteristics. In general minority schools have more flexibility for reading education than Han nationality schools.

OBJECTIVES OF READING EDUCATION

As outlined in the language teaching curriculum approved by the SEdC of the People's Republic of China in December 1986, the objectives of reading education for primary schools are

1. To master the Chinese pinyin system (the Romanized spelling system of the Chinese language), pronouncing syllables accurately and proficiently. Pinyin is to be taught in Grades 1 and 2, and should be reviewed and retained in subsequent grades so as to help pupils learn the Chinese characters, reading skills, and the common dialect (Mandarin).
2. To learn to recognize 3,000 Chinese characters. About 2,400 characters should be learned in the first three grades. However, the curriculum does not specify which 3,000 characters are to be learned. It is required that pupils correctly pronounce syllables, recognize characters, understand word meanings, and master the basic strokes, rules for stroke sequence, radicals, and the overall structures of the characters.
3. To master common vocabulary. Students are to be able to correctly read, write, and understand the vocabulary already learned.

4. To understand the meaning of sentences in text. Specifically, students are to learn to read text aloud both correctly and fluently and with feeling and also read silently, recite, and retell texts. Other skills to be learned are paragraphing the text, summarizing the paragraphs and the main ideas of the text; developing basic analytical and summarizing abilities; reading children's books and magazines, correctly understanding the central ideas; and developing independent reading skills and good reading habits.

The objectives of reading education for secondary schools include the following. Upon graduation from junior high school, students should be able (1) to read ordinary political, technical, literary, and recreational materials; (2) to understand the meaning of words and sentences, and follow the main ideas, structure, development, and writing style of reading materials; and (3) to analyze and critique the content and style of the reading, recite some contemporary and classic (in classic Chinese) works and excerpts, and translate reading excerpts written in classic Chinese into contemporary Chinese. Senior high school graduates should be able to read ordinary political, technical, literary, and recreational materials with relative ease. They should also have the ability to question, analyze and critique, appreciate literary works, and read in simple classic Chinese with the help of reference books.

Additional objectives of reading education at both primary and secondary school levels are to lay down the foundation for writing; to acquire knowledge about society, nature, and humanity through reading; to develop intelligence, especially thinking abilities, through language training and knowledge acquisition; to carry out moral education so that students can gradually learn to love their country and people, work and the sciences, their language and writing system, and socialism; and to develop good characteristics, lofty ideals, morals, and aesthetics.

No uniform requirements for reading education have been set down for higher education. Each institution of higher learning can set its own requirements. The main objectives of college language courses are to raise the students' general academic level, develop their ability to appreciate literary works, improve their writing skills, and carry out moral education. In the minority regions where minority graduates achieve relatively low proficiency in Chinese, colleges offer Chinese language courses. Some even offer one-year preparatory programs for intensive Chinese training. The main objective of such programs is to improve the minority students' reading and writing abilities so that they can use the Chinese medium to complete their college studies.

For adult education, reading objectives are similar to those for comparable levels of reading programs. For example, adult education at the junior high level has similar reading objectives as those for general junior high schools. There is no gender-based discrimination in terms of reading objectives.

ILLITERACY

China defines illiterates and semi-illiterates as those who are twelve years of age or older and do not know characters, or know fewer than 1,500 characters, cannot read popular books and magazines, and cannot write simple messages.

According to the third national census conducted in 1982, the total number

Table 4.1
Percentage of Illiterates and Semi-Illiterates in the Population at Age 12 or Older

AGE	TOTAL	MALE	FEMALE
12	9.58	5.28	14.12
13	9.83	5.26	14.68
14	9.95	5.28	14.92
15-19	9.39	4.24	14.73
20-24	14.32	5.71	23.76
25-29	22.41	9.55	36.10
30-34	26.21	13.19	40.31
35-39	28.00	14.18	43.40
40-44	38.72	22.36	57.41
45-49	52.12	32.23	74.45
50-54	61.67	40.60	85.18
55-59	67.92	47.16	89.74
>= 60	79.39	60.88	95.74

of illiterates and semi-illiterates in China stood at 237,720,787 as of midnight, July 1, 1982, accounting for 23.67 percent of the total population and 31.87 percent of the population twelve years of age or older. Among the illiterate and semi-illiterate population over twelve, males accounted for 19.15 percent and females 45.23 percent. Table 4.1 lists the percentages of illiteracy for various age groups.

Since no new census data have been collected since 1982, we do not have up-to-date statistics on illiteracy and semi-illiteracy. However, it is estimated that the current percentage of illiteracy is a bit lower than that in 1982. For instance, the percentage of illiteracy in Shanghai in 1982 was 16.7 percent, but a sample survey in 1987 showed that this percentage had fallen to 12.42 percent. Currently, it is estimated that China has about 220 million illiterates (including semi-illiterates). Of this number 140 million, or 64 percent, of them are female.

On February 5, 1988, the State Council issued a regulation to eliminate illiteracy. It states that all citizens, regardless of sex and nationality, between the ages of fifteen and forty (except those who are physically unable to receive literacy education) have the right and obligation to receive literacy education. At the same time, it encourages those above the age of forty to participate in the literacy studies. The criteria for becoming a literate are the recognition of 1,500 characters for rural peasants and 2,000 characters for urban residents and enterprise workers, the ability to read simple newspapers and articles, and the ability to do simple bookkeeping and write simple notes and letters.

READING HANDICAPS AND THEIR DIAGNOSIS

Reading handicaps in China are not serious enough to attract the attention of teachers and researchers. Therefore, we do not know their rate of occurrence, nor do we have any tools or methods to diagnose reading handicapped students.

PRESCHOOL READING PREPARATION

China has no direct programs to prepare preschoolers for reading. However, the curriculum for kindergarten formulated by the Ministry of Education (now the State Education Commission) outlines the requirements for children's language abilities, which are mostly aural and oral skills development. The curriculum requires that at the end of kindergarten (six to seven years of age), children should be able to (1) speak Mandarin in daily communication with correct pronunciation and intonation; (2) use certain nouns, verbs, adjectives and adverbs (of different degrees), prepositions, conjunctions, and some synonyms; (3) clearly answer questions and express their own thoughts and demands; (4) somewhat completely and coherently explain the content of pictures, and be able to use newly learned words in the explanation; (5) understand the content of stories, poems, and songs, remember the main plot of stories, and be able to recite twenty-four to thirty poems or songs. In addition, efforts are made to bring up the children in such a way that they like to read picture books and tell stories, and to listen to children's broadcasts and retell what they have heard. This training in oral and language abilities lays a foundation for future reading in primary education.

In major cities, a few kindergartens with superior faculty teach the five to six year olds to read Chinese pinyin, which is an aid in learning Chinese characters. It consists of twenty-six letters and can indicate the pronunciation of every Chinese character. Normally, these twenty-six letters and the rules of pinyin are taught at primary schools, but a few kindergartens have tried to teach their children so as to give the children a head start for future reading courses. There are no unified requirements and criteria in this respect.

In the countryside and remote areas, the requirement for kindergarten education should be the same. However, because teacher quality and physical conditions in these areas are generally substandard, some children cannot fulfill the requirements specified by the curriculum. In addition, most of the children do not attend kindergarten and hence have not received oral training. Therefore, their oral and aural abilities are poorer than those of children in urban areas. In other words, they are not as well prepared for reading.

Preschool reading requirements do not discriminate on the basis of sex.

TEACHER QUALIFICATIONS

On May 27, 1985, the Central Committee of the Communist party of China issued a document relating to educational reform. That document states that China "should try to enable, in five years or even longer period of time, most teachers to be qualified to teach. After that, only those with qualified training or certificate will be permitted to be teachers." In the future, it is specified, primary school teachers should have middle-level normal school training or should graduate from senior high school; junior high school teachers should have training from a teachers' college or graduate from a three-year college program; and senior high school teachers should have normal university training or a bachelor's degree from other universities. For those who do not have the required qualification, the State Education Commission has set up two certificate examinations with teaching material/method and the subject of teaching, respectively, as the main content of the exams. Passing the exams and obtaining the certificate would indicate a basic understanding of the teaching material and method used in the specified subject matter. Those who have one year of teaching experience but do not have the required qualification can apply for this teaching material/method examination. Those who have two years of teaching experience and have passed the teaching material/method examination can apply for the knowledge exam. Obtaining this certificate indicates that the teacher is qualified to teach in the specified subject. Passing this second exam requires a systematic understanding of the knowledge closely related to teaching.

Primary school reading teachers, for example, are examined on basic concepts of psychology and education; the Chinese language; and a choice from geography, politics, history, music, art, or physical education. For junior high school reading teachers, the exam includes basic concepts of psychology and education; modern Chinese; writing; selected works from classic Chinese literature; and selected works from contemporary Chinese literature. Senior high school teachers are examined on basic concepts of psychology and education; classic Chinese; classic Chinese literature; foreign literature; contemporary Chinese literature; and literary theory. All this knowledge is contained in a unified curriculum with reading materials on which the exams are based. The exams for primary school teachers are set up by provincial and municipal education authorities, and those for high school teachers by the State Education Commission. In addition to exhibiting academic knowledge, before obtaining the certificate teachers are also expected to rate high in the area of ideology, morality, and teaching ability; they are examined in these areas by the local school district. After a teacher passes all these exams, he or she can apply for the certificate to the particular school or school district. The application is considered by a special review board before it is reported to superior education authorities for final approval.

With regard to the faculty at higher education institutions, there is no clear educational requirement as yet. Traditionally, outstanding undergraduates could be retained to be assistant teachers. Today some better known universities are requiring the master's degree as a basic qualification for the position. Undergraduates with the bachelor's degree are no longer employed as assistant teachers in these schools. Those junior teachers without master's degree are encouraged to complete, on a part-time basis, all the required courses for their higher degree and to write a thesis. When the thesis is successfully defended, the master's can be awarded. This kind of requirement and practice is gaining popularity.

Teachers engaged in adult education are not subject to any clear qualification requirements. It is understood, however, that these requirements are similar to those for teachers at similar educational levels. For instance, requirements for adult senior high school teachers should be similar to those for regular senior high teachers. The requirements are the same for male and female teachers; there is no discrimination.

With regard to the ratio between male and female teachers, in 1986 female teachers accounted for 40.4 percent of all primary teachers and 28.3 percent of all high school teachers. There is no statistic on the ratio for reading teachers but it is probably similar to the above ratio. The proportion of female teachers may be slightly higher. The ratio of male to female teachers varies a great deal geographically. In major cities such as Shanghai, nearly all the reading teachers in primary schools, especially at the junior level, are female. In contrast, in the countryside and other remote areas, there are more male teachers than the national average.

TEACHING MATERIAL FOR READING

In China, teaching materials for reading in the primary and secondary schools are compiled by experts and teachers according to a national curriculum. Either the State Education Commission or the local education authorities organizes this compilation. At the moment, most of the schools use standard teaching materials; in addition many other experimental teaching materials are compiled locally. For instance, Shanghai, Beijing, Tianjin and Zhejiang Province have jointly compiled a set of teaching materials (including reading and writing) for use in primary schools, and Beijing Central Research Institute for Educational Science has compiled teaching materials for reading to be used at high schools. Other materials are compiled by individual teachers themselves. In addition, there are reference materials for teachers. The National People's Education Publishing House or local education publishing houses publish all these resources.

The situation in universities is a little different. The State Education Commission does not require universities to offer reading courses. Therefore, there is no nationally organized effort to compile reading textbooks. All the reading resources used at universities are compiled by individual universities or faculty members themselves. A few popular ones have been published.

For middle-level adult education, the situation is similar to that of regular middle schools, whereas for college-level adult education the situation is basically similar to that of regular universities.

Teaching materials are ordered by schools according to enrollment and are distributed to students at the beginning of each semester. Most of these materials are in Han Chinese, but in regions where minority nationalities concentrate, some of the textbooks are in the minority languages.

At present, reading materials for students are in nondisposable form only, such as textbooks. There are no disposable books such as workbooks. However, all textbooks have exercises and discussion questions attached to each lesson. Textbooks for primary and secondary schools have comprehensive exercises after every three to five lessons. Some of the exercises are done orally in class, and others are done in written form both in and after class. Because of a recent upsurge of emphasis on knowledge and self-learning, these exercises have attracted greater attention.

FINANCING READING EDUCATION

There is no specified budget or budget item for reading education; rather, it is part of the total school budget. Primary and secondary schools are divided into two categories: public schools and people-run schools. Public schools are sponsored by the government, and people-run schools are run and sponsored by individual enterprises, or communes and production brigades in the case of rural areas. The government sometimes provides subsidies to the people-run schools. China has now instituted a nine-year compulsory education program, with six years in primary and three years in secondary schools. Students do not pay tuition in those nine years regardless of which school they attend. Senior high school students, however, are charged a minimal tuition.

Because higher education is run by the government, the majority of students do not pay tuition. This situation could change in the near future, with all students required to pay for part of their education.

Adult schools, like primary and secondary schools, consist of public and people-run schools. However, students are required to pay a minimal tuition. Regardless of the types of schools, students are responsible for their own books and stationery.

RESEARCH THRUSTS IN READING EDUCATION

Research on reading education at the primary level focuses on the recognition of characters. The Chinese language has a unique writing system. The characters are not spelled with twenty-some letters but have to be learned and remembered one by one. Although all pupils are required to learn pinyin before they learn the characters, pinyin serves as only a tool in assisting the learning of characters, not as a form of written language. Therefore, learning the characters is a very difficult and time-consuming task, especially for pupils in the earlier grades. A popular research topic is to find out how many characters a primary pupil should learn. There are about 120,000 characters in Chinese, but most of them are rarely used. According to the government's official report to the United Nations, the commonly used Chinese characters total about 3,755. Mastering these characters will enable people to read and comprehend 99 percent or more of contemporary publications. Obviously, it is neither necessary nor possible for a primary pupil to know so many characters. It has been proposed that the emphasis of the first two years of primary education be on learning characters and that the pupils be required to know about 3,100 to 3,567 characters. This requirement has put a lot of pressure on the pupils. As a result, the current curriculum has extended the two-year period to three years and only requires primary pupils to know about 3,000 of the most commonly used characters and to be able to use 2,500 of them. Despite this attempt to reduce the burden on the pupils, the question still remains as to how much needs to be taught and how much a primary pupil can accept.

Another problem is teaching method, or the efficiency of teaching Chinese characters. This issue is related to the first in that with the adoption of an appropriate method and improvement in efficiency, it will be possible to teach more characters. For quite a long time, a debate has been on-going between concentrated teaching and dispersed teaching. *Concentrated teaching* emphasizes the rules of character formation and groups together those characters that are similar in structure or pronunciation, or both, so as to teach a large number of characters in a relatively short period of time. During this time, students do not read texts. *Dispersed teaching* emphasizes the meaning of each character in the context. Each of these two methods has its respective advantages. Most teachers and textbooks now combine both methods in teaching, but the basic principle of teaching meaning in context has won increasing recognition.

A popular method used in China today, the stepwise method, directs students to study pinyin first and then to concentrate on learning a group of characters, with each character placed in a phrase to help explain the meaning. Next, students read some texts to consolidate the characters they have learned. Finally, students concentrate on learning another group of characters and another group of texts, and within two years should be able to learn about 2,500 characters and 6,000 phrases. In Grades 3 and 4, students will do extensive reading, including intensive, extensive, and home reading. Since students have already built a large vocabulary, reading at this stage poses little difficulty. By Grades 5 and 6, the teaching emphasis shifts to writing. Most students can achieve good grades with this method.

Yet another method is being investigated. Through this method students are taught pinyin first and are given texts to read in the early grades. Wherever a new word appears, pinyin is used to help students to read, and they will learn the character later. In this way, the teacher can combine vocabulary, reading, writing, listening comprehension, and oral skill training in one lesson. After two years, students can know 2,300 characters, and their reading speed and comprehension are equivalent to, or even better than, those of typical fourth-year students. At the end of the third grade, students can read 127 syllables per minute. However, some people are suspicious of or actually oppose this experiment. They hold that these results have not been reproduced or confirmed and that the results may be due not to the teaching method but to other factors such as increasing student work load, better faculty, or better preclass preparation.

Research on reading education in the middle school focuses on the following issues: the nature and responsibility of reading education; the content and textbooks of reading education; the method and structure of classroom teaching; and measurements of reading proficiency. All but the first issue are also major research concerns for primary education.

THE NATURE OF READING EDUCATION

The debate concerning reading education centers on the question, is reading a course on language or on literature? Presently, most scholars and teachers think that middle school reading education should focus mainly on language rather than on literature. They state that some literary works are acceptable in the textbook so that students can be exposed and trained to understand and appreciate literature. But these works should not be the main focus of the reading course. Some people have proposed that a separate course be offered on literature as an elective.

Furthermore, there is a question of balancing reading and writing. Even though reading and writing are taught in one course with one textbook, it is popularly believed that the two have not been well integrated. Reading should be the foundation of writing. Students should learn writing through reading. For instance, when the reading material is mainly narrative, students should learn the basics of narrative writing and their writing assignments should also be mainly narrative. On the other hand, some people believe that the schools should offer separate reading and writing courses so that neither will be overlooked. Some of the experimental textbooks are compiled based on this belief.

THE CONTENT AND TEXTBOOKS OF READING EDUCATION

How can reading materials be updated so as to reflect the changes in science and technology and in society? Some believe that reading materials should be updated to reflect new ideas, new achievements in science and technology, and new phenomena in contemporary society. They contend that the classic writings, which make up a large percentage of reading materials, are too remote from contemporary life. Students find them difficult to understand and not very useful. Classic Chinese is no longer a communication tool. Hence, its percentage in reading materials should be lowered. In the current curriculum, junior high schools are supposed to teach 110 reading texts, with 22 (20 percent) written in classic Chinese, while the senior high should teach 80 reading texts, with 19 (23.75 percent) in classic Chinese. The percentages have been lowered from 24.4 percent and 36.7 percent, respectively. However, classic Chinese is a valuable heritage of the Chinese culture. It has many advantages in expressing ideas over the contemporary Chinese. Therefore, a Chinese student should have a certain amount of training in classic Chinese. Furthermore, classic writings by well-known writers are usually literary masterpieces. Students can learn from them what they cannot learn from other writings. Therefore, it is also important that a certain amount of classic writings be included in reading texts. The problem of balancing the two still remains to be tackled.

Method and Structure of Classroom Teaching

The Chinese classroom has long been teacher-centered with the gaining of book knowledge as the ultimate goal. This tradition has become a fundamental weakness, since it fails to recognize student initiatives. The emphasis on teachers' preaching rather than on students' reading and learning does not help build up the students' capabilities. Many researchers and teachers now realize that this type of teaching must be changed and that a new structure of classroom teaching must be established with students at the center. Therefore, the questions that researchers are focusing on are how to establish an appropriate relationship between the teacher, students and textbooks, and how to build up self-study. Some researchers hold that the teacher should indirectly guide students in their study instead of asking them to directly follow the teacher. Others think that the teacher should talk less in the classroom and let students spend more time on their own so as to build up their self-study capability. Still others believe that communication between the teacher and students as well as among students themselves should be improved. Many researchers are approaching the issue from theoretical perspectives, and many teachers are conducting various experiments.

Measurements of Reading Proficiency

Even though students are frequently tested and examined, there are no national criteria. The importance of unified scientific criteria in measuring students' reading proficiency is increasingly being recognized, and some researchers are studying this issue now.

At the university level, the debate focuses on whether the goal of reading education is to improve student ability to appreciate literary works or to sharpen writing skills. If the goal is the first, then reading education should be continued. If it is the second, then reading education can be eliminated, especially when high school graduates can achieve relatively good writing skills with improved primary and secondary reading education.

As for adult education, the curriculum and textbooks are basically similar to those of the middle school. The research focus is on how to develop teaching materials and methods that will suit the adult students who usually have richer practical experience and stronger comprehension ability, and who have to study in their spare time.

On the whole, research on reading education at the university and adult education levels attracts less attention than that for primary and secondary levels.

PROSPECTS OF READING EDUCATION

The goal, content, and method of reading education in China are based on the needs of the modernization program.

The goal of reading education is to nurture students' spirit in pursuing new knowledge, independent thinking, and creativity; to develop students' intelligence, memory, imagination, ways of thinking, as well as the ability to discover and solve problems; and to further integrate language training and thought training.

The content of reading education is closely related to current social life and social mentality. However, because China is such a large country, different regions vary greatly in economic development, cultural background, educational foundation, and teacher quality. At the same time, China is a country with many minority nationalities. Therefore, it is not feasible to set nationally unified comprehensive requirements for reading. In the future, a unified curriculum will only set basic requirements and principles for reading education that are achievable for all regions. Future teaching materials will also vary according to local characteristics. This will help improve student initiative in studying and integrating classroom knowledge with their local reality. There will also be many experimental textbooks exploring the best possible way to improve reading education. The future teaching method will try to accommodate variations in student abilities.

In order to reduce the excessive burden on students, it is expected that the basic requirements for primary and secondary education will be lowered somewhat. The learning of classic Chinese will be reduced. Some subjects, such as logic, will no longer be a basic requirement at high schools, but an elective. At the same time, higher education institutions will continue to offer reading education in order to further improve the reading proficiency of college students, especially in classic Chinese and classic literature.

The emphasis in reading education will be placed on building various reading skills. At present, little attention is being given to student ability in scanning and reading speed. This situation will change in the future. Attention will also be given to out-of-class reading. Research on reading education will be further strengthened. Previous research was mainly on teaching, and research on reading materials and methods was not based on knowledge of how students read. This problem is increasingly being recognized. Future research will place more emphasis on the reading process and reading comprehension. Finally, reading tests will be made more scientific, accurate, and reasonable.

BRIEF SUMMARY

Reading education in China is conducted mainly at the primary and secondary levels. Reading, together with writing and language, constitutes a major course: Chinese. They are contained in one textbook.

China is a multinationality country. Many of the minority nationalities have their own oral and/or written languages. Therefore, in regions where minority nationalities concentrate, reading education is conducted in local languages. Students also study Han Chinese and receive reading education in Han Chinese.

China's policy on reading education is a combination of centralization and dispersion. The State Education Commission issues basic requirements and principles as well as textbooks for reading education. It also encourages local schools and districts to compile their own textbooks. This dispersion may further develop in the future.

Specific educational requirements have been set for teachers at primary and secondary schools. Those who do not have the required education must take certain exams to obtain necessary certifications.

The illiteracy rate in China is about 23 percent. Since girls have a lower school attendance rate and tend to stay in school for a shorter period of time, the female illiteracy rate is higher than that of the male.

With most reading education being conducted in the primary and secondary schools, research efforts also focus on these levels. Currently, much research is being done on teaching and little on learning. This situation could be expected to change.

REFERENCES

Chinese Department, Wuhan Teachers College. 1980. *Language Teaching Methods for High Schools*. People's Education Press.

Editorial Board of Research in Education. 1987. *A Collection of Reports on Educational Reforms and Experiments at Primary and Secondary Schools*. Tianjin Education Press.

Education Commission, People's Republic of China. 1986. *Chinese Language Curriculum for Full-Day Elementary Schools*. People's Education Press.

Education Commission, People's Republic of China. 1986. *Chinese Language Curriculum for Full-Day High Schools*. People's Education Press.

An Essay Collection on Language Teaching by Ye Sheng-tao. 1980. People's Education Press.

Guidance for Language Teaching at Elementary Schools (Lower Grades). 1988. Shanghai Education Press.

Guidance for Language Teaching at Elementary Schools (Middle Grades). 1988. Shanghai Education Press.

Guidance For Language Teaching at Elementary Schools (Upper Grades). 1988. Shanghai Education Press.

Guidance for Language Teaching at High Schools (Junior High). Shanghai Education Press, forthcoming.

Guidance for Language Teaching at High Schools (Senior High). Shanghai Education Press, forthcoming.

Journal of Language Learning. 1985–1988. Shanghai Education Press.

Ju Baokui et al. (eds.). 1980. *Observations of Classes Conducted by Outstanding Language Teachers*. People's Education Press.

Li Baochu. 1985. *An Introduction to Reading Education*. Hebei People's Publishing House.

Liu Guozheng, and Chen Zezhang (eds.). 1985. *Progress and Prospects of Language Teaching*. People's Education Press.

Ministry of Education, People's Republic of China. 1982. *Curriculum for Kindergarten Education (Draft)*. People's Education Press.

Mo Lei. 1987. *Measurement of Reading Proficiency, I, II, III*. Zhongshan University Press.

People's Education Press. 1981. *Chinese Teaching and Teaching Materials for High Schools*.

People's Education Press. 1986. *Chinese Teaching and Teaching Materials for Elementary Schools*.

Zhang Dingyuan (ed.). 1983. *An Essay Collection on Reading Education*. Xinglei Publishing House.

Zhang Hongling, et al. (eds.). 1982. *Language Teaching Methodology*. Beijing Normal University Press.

Zhang Zhigong. 1981. *An Essay Collection on Language Teaching*. Fujian Education Press.

Zhong Weiyong. 1983. *Psychology in Language Teaching*. Zhejiang People's Publishing House, 1983.

Zhu Zuoren. 1984. *Psychology in Language Teaching*. Heilongjiang People's Publishing House.

5

Costa Rica

Maria del Carmen Ugalde
Translated by Jeanette Molina

INTRODUCTION

Inability to read in our times is the equivalent of social handicap and, hence, means the illiterate are deprived of many opportunities. Yet, reading involves a series of problems that are not always easy to resolve. In the first place, written and oral discourses are structured very differently. So here we encounter the first problem in reading: obtaining an adequate or good handling and control of the standardized form of the official language used to write, in addition to other linguistic abilities and skills proper to reading.

Understanding a text fully is not easy. Since a great part of the information is not explicitly provided, the reader must constantly infer in order to grasp the whole meaning of the text and, more so, to discover the hidden messages within. This implies that reading requires a series of mental processes in order to learn the message. Therefore, it is not a simple process for either the learner or the teacher.

All these difficulties, and many others, have led to changes in methods and textbooks. When we review the history of reading, we see that we have moved from synthetic to analytical methods. From readers of syllabic games and conjugation of senseless graphemes, we have gone into the use of words familiar to the child. Yet we are still in search of the resources or means that can help us achieve better and more satisfactory results. Since we are constantly remolding the environment, and as society progresses, capable readers are needed to be in tune to these never-ending changes.

Costa Rica has been no exception, having experienced all these changes. Here, too, we have made great efforts in the field of reading. The institutions responsible for the educational system (the corresponding ministry, universities, and con-

sultation or advisory organs) have promoted research, investigations, and evaluations that have led to changes in the methodology and the corresponding books
used in our search for more positive results.

THE LANGUAGE OF THE COUNTRY

The teaching of reading, and all the materials used for this purpose, are in
the official language, Spanish. Nonetheless, there are other existent languages:
Bribri, which is used by a native community of the same name; Cabecar, the
language spoken by the Cabecar Indians; Maleku, the tongue of the Guatuso
natives; Terraba, the language spoken by the Terraba Indians; the Brunka tongue,
spoken by the Brunka Indians; and the Mekateliu spoken by the 100,000 people
of the black community who live in the province of Limon (one of Costa Rica's
seven provinces). The Indian tribes have small populations, and inhabit the
mountains and the Meridional plains.

All of these languages are still at an oral stage and have not been taken into
account in the educational process, except for an experiment being conducted
by the universities within the Bribri community, in which reading and writing
are being taught in Bribri (the Indian language that has been researched and
studied the most). The University of Costa Rica edits a newspaper in the Bribri
language in an effort to rescue the language from possible extinction and to
promote reading in the tribe. The purpose of this experimental project was not
only to observe the results with regard to reading, but also to help maintain the
language and cultural values of these groups. Within the rest of the country,
only Spanish is used to teach reading and writing (literacy).

READING POLICY

The Teaching of Reading

Reading and writing are taught more or less in the same manner throughout
the country. No experimental projects exist in which other methodologies have
been used. Nevertheless, in general, an eclectic method is used. (Details are
provided later in this chapter.)

The Public Education Ministry is responsible for Costa Rica's educational
policies, recruiting all public school personnel (excluding private schools) as
well as directing educational expenses. The Ministry also prepares the study
programs (curriculum) for each elementary and secondary grade. Although the
universities are autonomous, they, too, receive governmental financing. The
Ministry also provides the necessary consultantship (in-service training) in the
different areas to the personnel in service.

Within the area of reading, the Education Ministry recommends and provides
the texts used during the six years of primary education. The Ministry also
produces and furnishes the corresponding didactical guides for the teachers.

Currently, a series published in 1984, entitled "Hacia la luz" is being used to teach reading. This series consists of books for each area and grade. They were made outside the framework of the global method and with the intention of supporting the prevailing eclectic method in reading.

THE GOALS OF READING AND METHODS

The Eclectic Method

Although the eclectic method has been used in Costa Rica since approximately 1970, its use was not uniform for many years. Teachers who had learned to teach reading with other methods continued doing so for quite a while. Nonetheless, today the eclectic method is used in the great majority of the schools in the country. Universities, within their education course offerings to the new teachers, as well as the in-service training and consultantship services provided by the Education Ministry, have helped standardize and generalize the use of this method.

The eclectic method has two basic objectives: to achieve reading comprehension and to prepare the student to discover new words. The method conveys the appropriate resources to succeed in both reading comprehension and the independent discovery of new vocabulary.

Resources That Contribute to Reading Comprehension

The eclectic method, a derivative of the global method, frequently uses short texts that are created and wherein previously elaborated texts are presented. The reading process begins with the teacher reading sentences to students, using vocabulary familiar to them. Only reading materials that present no difficulty in comprehension are presented to the children. Texts known as reading charts constitute the base material (or framework) for most of the reading. They may either be taken from the text used or can be invented by the children themselves, with the teacher's help and guidance. It is of utmost importance that each chart have a specific word, preferably a noun, that will be repeated in each sentence (in accordance with the chart). The same word should be used later on for syllabic study and to generate new words. The word that has to be repeated is known as the common element. There are various types of charts: experience, conversation, sign, concept, picture and word, and preparatory.

The Experience Chart. The experience chart is a small text made up of three or four sentences, written with the participation of all the children in a spontaneous and natural way. It can be a product of the children's experience or the result of a conversation with the teacher. The teacher writes on a chart three or four of the sentences expressed by the children; then the children read the sentences. These charts are used before formally introducing them to reading.

Their main purpose is to expose the child to the text, helping the child to discover that all that is said can be written.

Charts of Conversation. These charts are also used prior to the initial formal reading. The main objective is to stimulate oral expression. Through the use of pictures or sequence drawings, the children are led to describe or invent a story. The story is not written; the teacher asks only that the children express themselves using complete statements, in order to have them come closer to the norms of written discourse.

Sign Charts. These charts are made up of single words. They are not used for reading, but rather to provide orientation for the child. Nevertheless, through association, the children end up reading and recognizing the words. Among the words found in this kind of chart are door, desk, and window.

Concept Charts. These charts are prepared by the teacher in order to clarify vocabulary that is unknown or of difficult comprehension. They are used once the process of initial reading has formally been started and each time a text with new vocabulary is introduced. These charts normally have one word and the corresponding picture or drawing.

Picture and Word Charts. Picture and word charts are similar to the concept charts in the sense that they are used for introducing new vocabulary. The process is as follows: the cards have a word on one side and the corresponding picture on the other side. These charts are useful for students who have difficulty remembering vocabulary.

Preparatory Charts. These charts are used when formally starting reading. If they are taken from the children's textbook, it is helpful to start familiarizing them with the book. If no book is to be used, these charts can come to form a book created by the children themselves, with the guidance of the teacher (who plans the activities). These charts are short texts comprising three to four sentences. They should have a common element, and it is recommended that they have a picture, or drawing, related to the sentences.

<table>
<tr><td>*Rita lleva la bola.*</td><td rowspan="3"></td><td>Rita has the ball.</td></tr>
<tr><td>*La bola es roja.*</td><td>The ball is red.</td></tr>
<tr><td>*Oba, oba es la bola.*</td><td>Look at the ball.</td></tr>
</table>

The amount of vocabulary used, as well as the level of difficulty of the structure, should be controlled. If the preparatory charts have been taken from the text, the students should not receive the book until they have studied the first charts.

Facilitating the Discovery of New Words

Children, or new readers, capable of discovering and decodifying new vocabulary will be able to advance on their own in reading. But first they must know that the text is formed by sentences, that sentences are made up of smaller units called syllables, and that syllables are formed by graphemes. The student must also know that from one word another can be derived and that two words put together can form another. In order to explain those details in Spanish, several resources can be used including phonetic analysis, structural analysis, and configuration key.

Phonetic Analysis.   This resource enables the child to establish a correspondence between the phoneme and the grapheme. It favors decodification, the mechanical aspect of reading. Phonetic analysis begins with syllabic division, taking care of the hierarchy of difficulties, and with the study of vowels. Rarely does it get to pure graphemic analysis; rather, it looks into a syllable taken from a word.

Structural Analysis.   This resource provides for the study of the morphemes that form words. It begins with the study of the most familiar morphemes: plurals, gender, diminutives, and so on. This analysis starts toward the end of the first grade when derived words are introduced, such as *cartero* (mailman) derived from the noun *carta*, which means letter, and the suffix *ero*, which means occupation or trade. It is expected that, following this model, the students will be able to generate similar words.

With time, more in-depth analysis is made. Hence, upon reaching high school years, the students come to know the three procedures in the formation of new words:

Through derivation (root + affix)

Prefix + root	*des + hacer = deshacer*
Root + suffix	*grand + ote = grandote*

Through composition

Word + word	*para + aquas = paraquas*

Through parasynthesis

Word + word + suffix	*por + Dios + ero = pordiosero*

Configuration Key.   The child begins to recognize words and even sentences either by their global form or by association of their forms to some object. Publicists for the configuration key used this resource earlier and more effectively than educators in their interest in getting children to recognize the products they sell. The configuration key gets heavy use at the initial stage of reading. It consists mainly of delimiting (marking) the shape of the word or sentence in order to help the child remember and recognize it by its shape.

Example

bola	ball
La bola es roja.	The ball is red.

General Steps of the Method

1. If the process of reading/writing has already been formally started, the preparatory chart is presented to the child. On the first day the sentences are read, and recognition exercises are provided.

2. The child receives a copy of the text on the second day, proceeding to divide the text into sentences. The children work on exercises of sentence recognition, and on the composition and rearrangement of sentences.

3. Subsequent days are devoted to copying each sentence, one per day.

4. The next step involves the recognition and drawing out of the common element. The children receive dictations.

5. Following the four previous steps, two more charts are presented. Again, there is dictation of the common element.

6. Once the third chart has been worked with, the first chart (which has already been divided into sentences) is brought out again and now divided into words. Then the children work on exercises where they practice making new sentences by recombining the words.

7. The same procedure is followed on subsequent days. The other two charts are divided into words, and new sentences are made by using the vocabulary of all three charts.

8. The fourth chart (made up of four sentences) is presented. The children will read it, divide it into words, work on the recognition of the common element, copy the text, and receive a dictation of the complete text. The teacher spends the necessary amount of time for all these activities. The same procedure is followed for the fifth and sixth chart.

9. Once the first six charts have been studied, phonetic analysis begins. The common elements for all six charts are taken out and divided into syllables. A particular syllable within each word is emphasized. This particular syllable is divided into consonant + vowel. The vowel is pointed out and emphasized. All of the following six syllables have the vowel *a*.

Example

bola	*la*	*l*	*a*
carro	*ca*	*c*	*a*
mano	*ma*	*m*	*a*
casa	*sa*	*s*	*a*

10. The syllables pointed out are then used to form and discover new words.

11. Through the subsequent charts (at this point, if a book is being used, it can be given to the student) the remaining vowels are introduced, (*e, o, i, u*). The procedure followed here will be the same, bringing the students to substitute the vowels within the familiar syllables and producing and discovering new words.

12. As the children progress, more complicated words are introduced such as trisyllabics, mixed syllabics ($C + V + C$), inversed syllabics ($V + C$), and compound syllabics

$(C + C + V)$. New words are discovered and generated by using and combining these syllables.

13. At this point, the preparatory charts are left, and bigger books are introduced. Certain words are selected according to what is going to be studied, and from them particular syllables are taken. These words are called generators, precisely because they serve to generate other words and are used for learning new graphemes that the students have not studied. For example, from the word *zapato* (shoe) the syllable *za* is taken out and studied in order for the pupils to get to know the *z*.

14. Finally, the structural analysis of words begins. Derived and compound words are presented, so as to succeed in getting the students to discover others following the same procedure. For example, *zapato* (shoe) and *zapatero* (shoemaker); *carta* (letter/ mail) and *cartero* (mailman).

15. At this point it is convenient to mention some of the evaluation or assessment procedures used in this initial stage. The context key is used constantly; it consists of presenting a series of familiar but incomplete statements to the student. The child proceeds to choose the correct answer from those given alternatives and writes it in the corresponding blanks.

Example

El carro es de _____.
mano Beto bola

The car belongs to _____.
hand Bert ball

Matching exercises are also used; here the student will associate statements from a column with the corresponding picture or drawing in another column.

Example

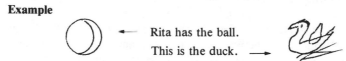

Rita has the ball.
This is the duck.

The steps mentioned correspond to first grade reading. With this method, it is expected that by the end of the school year the child will have learned to read and write. Generally, it is achieved.

Costa Rica does not have the resources to teach those students with difficulties or handicaps as needed. However, some schools have what we call *aula diferenciada* (differentiated classrooms), which are taught by special education teachers.

Reading is just one of the teacher's many areas of responsibility within the subject called Spanish. (The areas are literature, oral expression, listening, writing, orthography, grammar, and reading.) Possibly because of this multiple area coverage within the subject, reading is given emphasis and major concern only within the first two years of school. Throughout the subsequent years of school, reading is cultivated, but neither to the extent nor with the same concern as in the first two primary years.

TEACHER QUALIFICATIONS

The existent study programs used for preparing elementary and secondary level teachers do not provide for a reading specialization. Hence, Costa Rica lacks specialized professionals within the area of reading.

With regard to training elementary school teachers, all three state universities provide for general formation, since these teachers teach within the different subject areas: Spanish, science, math, social studies, and so on.

Within elementary education a teacher can obtain a degree known as the Licenciatura. The program consists of two years to obtain an elementary school teacher's diploma, two more years to obtain the bachelor's degree, and, finally, two more years to reach the degree of Licenciatura, which consists of a specialization within one of the areas or subjects taught in school. In order to receive the Licenciatura degree, the student must present a thesis or graduation project.

The Faculty of Education and Schools of Education are exclusively in charge of the bachelor's degree formation. The student within the Licenciatura program can select some of the courses pertinent to the specialization area he or she chose, besides courses in pedagogy.

Although the number of male teachers has increased in rural areas where the universities have opened schools, the number of females studying education still exceeds that of males by far. Very few men pursue studies or work in education.

Throughout their academic years, students of education take courses that will enable them to teach the different language areas.

Language Arts I. This introductory course briefly covers every one of the areas in language, thereby parting from the idea that it is a means of communication. In this course students learn the general procedure for teaching the four language arts: listening, speaking, reading, and writing.

Didactics of Reading-Writing. This course is offered in the second year of studies. Its principal objective is to get the students to learn the existent reading method (eclectic method). The course also provides general guidelines as to how to work with reading comprehension.

Language Arts II. Offered at the bachelor's level, this course covers in-depth the areas of theory and practice within the areas of language. Students learn to recognize and apply techniques for the development of reading, writing, and oral expression.

Besides these courses, all students must take two "corrective courses" that will help them improve their usage and knowledge of the Spanish language. Another required course is Children's Literature, which is geared toward teaching literature in the elementary school. All these courses correspond to the area of Spanish and give the teacher (or prospective teacher) some necessary training in the field.

Secondary Level Teacher Preparation

Teacher training for the secondary level differs from that of the elementary. Here, the teacher must specialize in one of the subjects. This preparation will be guided by the Faculty of Education or its equivalent and by the faculty in which he or she is specializing. For instance, if a student wants to specialize in Spanish to become a Spanish teacher, he or she must take courses in both: the Faculty of Arts (or its equivalent) and the Faculty of Education. Within the Faculty of Arts the student must take courses in grammar, literature, and linguistics. In the Education Faculty the student needs to take courses in didactics and other topics related to education.

Whatever the specialization, the secondary level teacher preparation takes four years in order for the student to obtain a bachelor's degree in a particular subject. Nevertheless, the universities do not offer a specialization in reading. The development of the skills within this area correspond to the Spanish professor, who deals with reading among all the other areas for which he or she is responsible.

READING MATERIALS

A variety of textbooks are used for both elementary and secondary education in the country. Some are for initial reading/writing and therefore are made up of short simple texts, written by an adult to focus on some aspect of language. Others are texts of literature or informative anthologies, which include questions after each reading (used by the teacher for classwork). There are also reading series, with a variety of exercises that can be used for independent work. Except for the series called "Hacia la luz" (Toward the light), all these texts are published by private corporations. Nonetheless, they have been approved and recommended by the Superior Council of Education (which is composed of a representative of each educational entity of the country).

Books from the series "Hacia la luz" are loaned to the students and are considered school property. The series includes a book for each subject area of each grade. Thus, each area has six books, one for each school year. As the student moves from grade to grade, the text becomes more in-depth within the corresponding subject area. These books also respond to the present programs of study.

Although the Ministry of Education provides and recommends these books, other books may be used. The teacher in initial reading, for instance, can gradually together with his or her students develop a textbook. Although the Ministry of Education wants to standardize the educational process within the country, the teacher can still create and/or adapt within his or her classroom according to need (especially if it's a rural school).

At the secondary level, the reading program is closely related to the study of literary works that are required. In this area, the teacher takes advantage of the literary study to practice and develop skills such as interpretation, text discussion, topic recognition, and grasping of implicit information.

Nevertheless, within the last two years diagnostic assessment has evidenced flaws and weaknesses in various areas. Reading is one of these areas. Presently, reading comprehension is the main concern of those interested in the field. Studies in search of the reasons and possible solutions have already been developed. The different universities of the country, the Public Education Ministry, and the Institute of Research for Education Improvement in Costa Rica (IIMEC) have all joined forces in this task.

CONCLUSIONS

Learning to read, and reading effectively, is of utmost importance in modern living. It is a process of constant improvement, since we can never say that we have learned everything we need to be a good reader. The fact is that reading depends on human production; accordingly, it is subject to changes in human production. For this reason, it is important to frequently revise the teaching process, so as to avoid not fulfilling the requirements of the moment (the now, and today) by updating it.

Costa Rica, as possibly other countries, is making great efforts not only in trying to achieve higher levels of literacy, but also in providing its people with a better education. Having declared education free, compulsory, and paid by the state was a great achievement. Of course, the state cannot provide everything. Nothing can be achieved without the cooperation of the people. Studies are very costly, and so expenses must be shared. The state provides the infrastructure, salaries for personnel, and some materials.

Within the area of reading, the Ministry of Education (as head of the entire educational process) has developed diagnostic tests in an effort to promote and improve reading. These tests are administered countrywide in order to assess the level of development for the skills and strategies needed within reading. (Other areas have also been examined.) The tests have been administered during the past two years, but results have not been as satisfactory as expected. Consequently, in the search for the cause of the problem, many revisions, including those of the methodology, curriculum, and materials, are being implemented. It could be said that Costa Rica is at a stage in which it must stop in order to review what has been done, without losing perspective on what has to be done; and to be able to make future projections. The efforts already completed should not be in vain. An active, agile reader in tune with the moment is needed, but the task of choosing the best way to succeed in this goal is not always easy, inasmuch as when we think we have solved grave difficulties, others often seem to appear.

REFERENCES

Brenes, Porfirio. 1978. *Silabario Castellano*. Editorial Universal.
Chacón, Nora. *Un criterio ecléctico en la enseñanza de la lecto-escritura*. Materal poligrafiado (25 pp.).
Chacón, Nora. 1985. *Lecturas para tarabajo independiente*. Editorial Costa Rica. (Libros; 1–6).

Ministerio de Educación Pública. 1977. *Programas de Español*. Editorial MEP.

Ministerio de Educación Pública. 1984. Departamento de Libros de Texto. *Hacia la Luz*. (1st ed.). San José: Ministerio de Educación Pública. (Libros; 1–6).

Ministerio de Educación Pública. 1985. Departamento de Libros de Texto. *Guía didáctica para el docente* (1st ed.). San José: Ministry of Public Education. (Libros; 1–6).

Rodríguez, Aracelli, and Cabezas, Gamaliel. *Conociendo sílabas*. Editorial Universal (sin fecha de publicación).

Ugalde, M. del Carmen. *Didáctica de la Lecto-escritura. Etapa de iniciación*. Material poligrafiado. (43 pp.).

Ugalde, M. del Carmen. *El lenguaje, caracterización de sus dos formas fundamentales: El código oral y el código escrito*. Material poligrafiado. (22 pp.).

Ugalde, M. del Carmen. *El manejo del texto y su relación con la comprensión lectora*. Material poligrafiado. (25 pp.).

Unesco. 1988. Seminario: "La lecto-escritura como factor de exito o fracaso escolar." (Informe final.) San José, Costa Rica.

Zamora, Relando. 1985. *Como enseñar castellano en I y II ciclos*. 1a. reimp. de la 1a. ed. San Jose, Costa Rica: EUNED.

6

Cuba

Victor R. Martuza

INTRODUCTION

Cuba, a tropical island approximately 46,000 square miles in size, is located in the Caribbean Sea roughly 90 miles south of the United States. The island was a colony of Spain until 1898 when it won its independence and fell under the political and economic influence of the United States, where it remained until 1959 when the Batista dictatorship was replaced by the present political regime of Fidel Castro. Since then, Cuba's closest allies have been the USSR and the socialist countries of Eastern Europe. Because of its colonization by Spain and its pivotal role in African slave trading, the present population of about 10 million is composed mostly of people of Spanish and African descent. The official language of the country is Spanish.

Throughout its history, Cuba's economic fortunes and the material conditions of most of its population have depended heavily on sugar and the vagaries of the world market. In a monocultural economy heavily dependent on manual labor, literacy and education for the masses historically did not have a high government priority. According to the 1899 census, the illiteracy rate for the country at that time was approximately 57 percent. Although this figure declined to nearly 24 percent in 1953 (the last census taken before Castro's revolution), the urban and rural figures were about 11 percent and 42 percent, respectively (Lorenzetto and Neys, 1965), and among the population ten years of age or older, 25 percent had never enrolled in school, 50 percent had dropped out of school before completing their primary education, and only about 20 percent had gone on to further schooling (Jolly, 1964, pp. 164–169). In addition to the near nonexistence of schools in the countryside where the illiteracy rate was greatest, the public school system suffered from administrative waste, corruption, inefficiency, poor teacher quality, counterproductive hiring and tenure arrangements, and a curriculum more suited to the production of the traditional Spanish *pensador* (thinker) than the needs of Cuban society at that time (see, for example, International Bank for Reconstruction and Development, 1951; Paulston, 1971).

Since the triumph of Castro's revolution in 1959, education has consistently been one of the highest priority items on the national agenda.[1] Undoubtedly the most significant single event marking this dramatic change in emphasis was the announcement of a National Literacy Campaign by Fidel Castro before the General Assembly of the United Nations in September 1960. Regarded by many as the first successful national literacy campaign in the history of humankind, this event not only served important political and social ends, but also marked the beginning of the development of a national, unified, free system of education accessible to all citizens, thus, guaranteeing the elimination of illiteracy as a social phenomenon. The importance of this historical event to the Cuban people was recognized concretely and memorialized in the founding of the National Literacy Museum in Havana where the important documents and artifacts of the campaign are housed. The campaign's importance to and influence on the national literacy efforts of other developing countries can be seen in the methods, materials, and organizational strategies they used (e.g., Nicaragua).[2]

The following sections briefly describe the Cuban National Literacy Campaign and the present structure of schooling in Cuba. The remainder of the chapter is devoted to reading education as it currently exists in the various educational subsystems.

THE LITERACY CAMPAIGN

The National Literacy Campaign, which officially commenced on January 1, 1961, marked the beginning of the Cuban "Year of Education." Details of the organization and logistics of this massive effort may be found elsewhere (e.g., Kozol, 1978; Lorenzetto and Neys, 1965; Prieto, 1981a, b) and will not be described here. Instead, attention is focused on the elements that not only made the campaign's success possible, but also had a significant impact on the subsequent development of schooling in Cuba.

After considering a variety of literacy primers available as campaign planning got underway, the technical department of the National Literacy Commission undertook the development of its own primer *Venceremos* ("We Shall Conquer") which consisted of fifteen lessons, each centering on a theme thought to be inherently motivational to the population of Cuban illiterates at the time. The first theme chosen was the Organization of American States, (abbreviated OEA in Spanish) since this organization was known to a large majority of the Cuban population and facilitated the introduction of the open vowels *o/e/a*. The second theme, National Institute of Agrarian Reform (abbreviated INRA in Spanish), was important because of its role in land redistribution prior to and during the campaign. The other themes, as well as a sample lesson, are shown in Figure 6.1.

Cuban educators attribute the success of their teaching method to the use of highly motivational topics; the analytic/synthetic approach to teaching the target letters and the ways of combining them to form new words; the fairly rapid reinforcement received by the learners when they quickly find themselves able to form real words without help; and the correlated teacher's manual *Alfabeticemos* (''Let's Teach How to Read and Write'') which provides literacy teachers with clear and simple guidance in the use of methodology. An inspection of both student and teacher manuals indicates that a great deal of effort went into making them simple enough to be used by literacy workers with minimal training.

The goal of the campaign itself was only to raise the reading and writing abilities of the general population to the first grade level. This goal was largely accomplished through the efforts of a literacy corps consisting of the nation's teachers, students, and other interested adults. When the campaign concluded in December 1961, the number of illiterates had been reduced from approximately 980,000 to 272,000, the latter figure constituting approximately 4 percent of the total population of Cuba at that time (Prieto, 1981a, b).[3]

Attention then turned to *el seguimiento* (the followup), which marked the beginning of the present adult education subsystem, as well as to the schooling needs of Cuba's youth. In the next section, we give a brief introduction to the structure of the Cuban educational system.

THE EDUCATIONAL SYSTEM

The Cuban national educational system is completely centralized. Although there are municipal and provincial education offices, all decisions regarding policy, curriculum, pedagogical techniques, program revisions, and related matters are the responsibility of the national Ministry of Education (MINED) for the preschool through high school levels and of the Ministry of Higher Education (MES) for the postsecondary levels.

Male and female students have the same academic goals at all levels of the system owing to the egalitarian philosophy espoused by the government. Perhaps the best examples of this philosophy are the *schools-in-the-countryside* which accommodate equal numbers of male and female students (see Leiner, 1981, p. 209).

Figure 6.2 shows a diagram of Cuba's national system of public education. At the top of the diagram is the regular education sequence which consists of the day care subsystem, the preschool program, the primary level (Grades 1–6), the intermediate level (Grades 7–12), and the higher education level. The primary level is divided into two cycles consisting of Grades 1–4 (Cycle 1) and Grades 5–6 (Cycle 2). The intermediate level is also divided into two parts: Grades 7–9 (Basic Secondary) and Grades 10–12 (High School).[4]

The day care subsystem currently has 927 centers accommodating approxi-

Figure 6.1
The Primer (*Venceremos*)

     The primer used in the National Literacy Campaign contained 15 instructional units, each dealing with a different topic of importance at that time: "OEA (Organization of American States)," "INRA (National Institute of Agrarian Reform)," "The Cooperative Store," "Every Cuban, A Home Owner," "A Healthy People in a free Cuba," "INIT (National Institute of Tourism)," "The Militia," "The Year of Education," and "Poetry and the Alphabet."

     Each unit begins with a motivational photograph which the literacy worker used to stimulate conversation, to assess the student's level of knowledge about the topic, and to clarify basic ideas. Except for the introductory lesson, the second page (opposite the photograph) contained several simple sentences related to the topic. Finally, there were two or three sets of exercises following a common format, each of which concentrated on one syllable contained in a key concept in the unit. An example of a lesson is presented below. Through the 15 units, difficulty level increased systematically, but a great deal of repetition of previous material was included for practice.

An illustration of the material in the Venceremos primer

A. *The photograph*
    A plowed field with a farmer seated on a tractor and another man standing nearby waving to each other.

B. *The introductory text*
            INRA
    La Reforma Agraria nació en in la sierra.   [The Agrarian Reform was born in the Mountain.]
    La Reforma Agraria da tierra a los   [The Agrarian Reform gives land to the peasants.]
      campesinos.
    La Reforma Agraria avanza.   [The Agrarian Reform advances.]

C. *Exercise Set A*
   1. Vamos a leer [Let's Read.]   La Reforma Agraria
                                     La Re - for - ma
                                     la le li lo lu

   2. Vamos a leer primero, y a leer y escribir despues. [Let's read first, and read and write later.]

Lala	ala	leo
Lola	ele	lea
Lula	ola	lei
Lila	Ela	lio

   3. Vamos a leer primero, y a leer y escribir despues.   El ala   [The wing]
                                                La ola [The wave]
                                                El lee   [He reads]

   4. Ponga la palabra que falta. [Supply the missing word.]
      El _____
      _____ola.
      El_____

   5. Se dictará lo anterior. [The preceding will be dictated.]

   6. Copie con su mejor letra. [Copy with your best handwriting.]

Source: Adapted from INRA (the National Institute of Agrarian Reform), Unit 2 in the *Venceremos* primer (Ministry of Education, 1961b).

Figure 6.2
Structure of the Cuban National System of Education

I. Regular Education

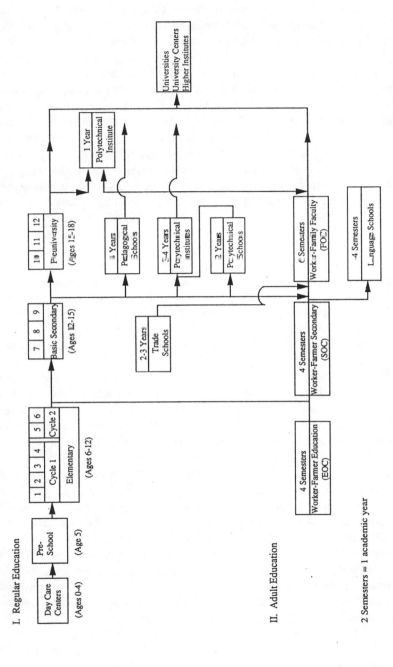

II. Adult Education

2 Semesters = 1 academic year

Source: Organization of Education, 1985–1987: Report of the Republic of Cuba to the 41st International Conference in Public Education.

mately 121,000 students, forty-five days to four years of age, and is staffed by about 21,000 teachers and assistants (MINED, 1988). Since reading education is not part of the day care program, we will not discuss this subsystem further. We will now examine selected elements shown in Figure 6.2 and then provide a brief description of the special education subsystem.

Although a small percentage of children benefit from the day care and preschool programs, the typical Cuban child enters Grade 1 at six years of age and proceeds through the first cycle with the same teacher, being promoted automatically from grade to grade.[5] At this level, emphasis is on the acquisition of basic mathematics and language skills. In Cycle 2, where a richer mixture of subjects is introduced, the main goal is to provide a smooth transition to the more academically rigorous curriculum of Grades 6–9. Following the completion of Grade 9, students may choose a preuniversity school (to prepare for university entrance), a pedagogical school (to become an elementary school teacher), a polytechnic school (to become a skilled worker), or a polytechnic institute (to become a midlevel technician).

The bottom of Figure 6.2 shows the parallel *adult education subsystem* which, at each level, has essentially the same goals as the regular education track. The main differences between the adult education and regular subsystems are the amount of time spent at each level as well as the types of materials and the teaching methodologies used. Notice that all the higher education options available to students graduating from the regular education subsystem are also available to those graduating from the adult education subsystem. The lone exception in the latter case is for those adults who choose the four-semester "foreign language high school" option, which is viewed as a terminal schooling experience.

Within this scheme reading education is regarded as one component of the broader Spanish language and literature curriculum which currently occupies about 22.5 percent of the total class time distributed across grades (Table 6.1). Reading instruction per se occurs only in Cycle 1 of elementary school and its parallel component in the adult education subsystem, that is, Worker–Farmer Education (or Educación Obrero y Campesino–EOC).

The *special education subsystem* consists of 450 special schools that accommodate the following classes of handicap: acoustic, visual, and speech impairment; mental retardation; and chronic behavioral problems. The efficient and rapid development of this subsystem during the current decade has been facilitated by the establishment of diagnostic and orientation centers whose main task is to identify, place and guide students in need of special help. At present, students with these handicaps are not mainstreamed into regular classrooms, but they do have contact with nonhandicapped students through extracurricular activities such as knowledge contests and cultural activities. Although mainstreaming has not been ruled out as a future possibility, the current view is that students in need of special help are best served by programs that target their special needs(Arias, 1989). The structure of this subsystem parallels that of the regular track as shown in Figure 6.2, and the goals at each level are identical.

Table 6.1

Language–Literature Curriculum in Cuban Schools: Number of Hours per Week

Primary Grade	Number of Hours	Secondary Grade	Number of Hours
1	12	7	4
2	12	8	4
3	12	9	4
4	12	10	3
5	6	11	3
6	6	12	2/4*

*There are two hours per week in the first semester and four per week in the second.
Source: Written communication from the Ministry of Education received during Spring 1989.

Following more than a decade of trial-and-error experimentation, Cuban educators began planning a massive national school improvement program called El Perfectionamiento in the early 1970s. This undertaking, implemented during 1976–1981, not only involved restructuring the entire national education system, but also entailed a massive effort in revising all curricula, instructional materials, and teacher preparation programs. During 1981–1986, an evaluation of those efforts was undertaken, and the results are currently being used to further improve all aspects of the educational enterprise. One example, as will be discussed later, is the replacement of all textbooks starting with those at the Grade 1 level during the 1988–1989 academic year.

Beginning with the next section, we turn our attention to the reading readiness and reading pedagogical methods employed at the preschool and elementary school levels, respectively.

THE PHONIC/ANALYTIC/SYNTHETIC METHOD

As part of El Perfectionamiento, Cuban reading experts chose to cast their lot with the phonic/analytic/synthetic method of teaching reading rooted in the work previously done in the Soviet Union by Vygotsky, Luria, and Elkonin. Based explicitly on the psycholinguistic theory of Elkonin, this method assumes that both oral and written language are linked primarily to the sound structure of the word. That is, the fundamental link is not between the printed symbol and meaning, but between sound and meaning.

In general, the method involves the analysis (segmentation) of sentences into words, words into syllables, syllables into phonemes, and the reverse process (synthesis). Because language acquisition is assumed to be primarily oral, the emphasis in both teaching and assessment is on oral activities. Just how this is translated into practice is the subject of the next several sections. For a quick overview of this method, see Pollack and Martuza (1981) and for more in-depth treatments, see either Garcia Pers (1976) or Gonzáles Núñez (1980).

PRESCHOOL

At this level, the students work with the sounds of monosyllabic words, for example, *sol* (sun) and *mar* (sea). As a group, the students pronounce the entire word, stressing the initial phoneme by exaggerating (elongating) its sound (i.e., *ssss*ol). The entire word is then enunciated again with the stress on the second phoneme (i.e., *soooo*l), and so on. There are as many repetitions of the word as there are phonemes, and each phoneme is pronounced as part of the whole word, never in isolation. Visual models consisting of blank cards (one card per phoneme) are used to provide concrete representations of the words. At this level, neither printed letters nor words are used in the instructional process. According to López (1981, p. 238), a child is considered to have mastered the skill of phonemic analysis when he or she "is capable of determining the sound sequence in a word, distinguishing among the sounds, reporting the number of sounds and indicating the position of each in the word."

In order to teach sound/meaning relationships, exercises are used in which one word is transformed into another by the substitution of a particular phoneme. For example, the substitution of the letter *i* for *o* in the word *ajo* (garlic) results in the word *aji* (pepper). Another variant of this method starts with an actual object (e.g., a book), having the children name it, do the type of phonemic analysis described earlier, do a phoneme substitution, and see how the change in sound of the word signals a change in its meaning. The Ministry of Education film *Sonidos y Palabras* provides an excellent introduction to the methodology.

Currently, López and her collaborators (López, 1989) are experimenting with the introduction of a restricted set of printed letters (*m, s, l,* and the vowels) at this level so that the students can get a head start on synthesizing written syllables and words. In addition, they have developed an experimental writing readiness program that is aimed at preparing the students for cursive writing, which is normally taught simultaneously with reading beginning in the first grade. This method involves the use of a pegboard that measures approximately 3 inches by 9 inches. By placing pegs appropriately in predrilled holes on the board, students are able to create wire models of selected cursive writing patterns. The subsequent tracing and copying of these patterns on paper is presumed to provide practice in the eye–hand coordination needed to properly write cursively and also to help students develop concrete mental models that can be employed subsequently as they write.

Since preschool education is only available to approximately 10 percent of the age-eligible students[6] (mostly in urban areas), a new program has been developed in which rural teachers work with groups of local parents, teaching them how to help their children develop these skills. Although the methodologists responsible for developing this program appear to be satisfied with the results obtained so far, solid experimental data that support their optimism are not yet available.

ELEMENTARY SCHOOL

Beginning with the 1988–1989 school year, a greater emphasis has been placed on basic mathematics skills and written/oral expression in Cycle 1. Previous attempts to begin elementary literary analysis at this level are now regarded as unrealistic.

Based on the evaluation that took place from 1981 to 1986, it was concluded that greater emphasis on mastering the mechanics of reading was necessary in Cycle 1 and that the development of an appreciation of literature seemed to be a more sensible priority for Cycle 2. In addition, the special type A and B classrooms (as described by Martuza, 1986), which had existed in the elementary schools to accommodate children having learning difficulties during Cycle 1, have been phased out now that the capacity to diagnose learning difficulties has been improved and the special education subsystem has been expanded (MINED, 1988).

The phonic/analytic/synthetic method, which provides the basis for the pre-school reading readiness program, is carried forward into the work of elementary school. During the first several weeks of Grade 1, which serves as a transition period for students who attended preschool and as a catch-up period for students who did not, phonemic analysis exercises without printed letters are the focus. Following this introductory period, students are introduced to the printed vowels *a, e, i, o*, and *u* followed directly by the consonant *m*. This enables them to begin synthesizing syllables (e.g., *ma*), words (e.g., *mamá*) and finally sentences (e.g., *Amo a mamá*—"I love mama"). During the remainder of the initial twenty-week period of the first grade,[7] additional vowels and consonants are introduced in a logical order, with special attention to difficulties caused by letters like *h* (which is silent) as well as letter sets like *b, v*, and *i, y* which have the same sound. Each student has a letter kit that can be used as an aid in analyzing/synthesizing syllables, words, and sentences. Since cursive writing and reading are taught simultaneously, students also get practice in writing the words they have synthesized using their letter kits. Additional information concerning this approach can be found in the Ministry of Education teacher training film *Adquisición de la Lectura* and the Garcia Pers book (1976) as well as Pollack and Martuza (1981). The similarities between this approach and that employed in the National Literacy Campaign are evident in the analytic/synthetic character of the methodologies, the teaching of reading and writing simultaneously, and the general structure of the lessons.

In the second half of Grade 1, the focus shifts to strengthening previously acquired skills, developing rudimentary comprehension, and exposing students to various literary genres.

One of the best references on teaching and assessment of reading is the book *Didáctica del Idioma Español* by Delfina García Pers (1976), which covers both the theoretical and practical aspects of language, reading, and writing instruction in the Cuban schools, along with lesson plan models for the teacher. According to García Pers (Book 1, p. 112), reading at the first grade level is fundamentally oral and very expressive. By the end of the first grade, the student is expected to pronounce words clearly; use the proper intonation when reading simple declarative, interrogative, or exclamatory statements; and observe pauses where appropriate. In the second grade, a great deal of attention is devoted to pronunciation and articulation, clarification of the uses of frequently confused letters (e.g., *b* and *d, p* and *g, u* and *v*), correction of errors related to the inappropriate addition or omission of letters, and the like. In addition, students are introduced to a variety of literary forms such as prose, narrative, dialogue, and description as well as diverse literary genres such as plays, fables, poems, and science fiction. Extraclass reading activities are initiated in order to promote independent reading.[8]

Beginning in the second and continuing into the third grade, considerable use is made of pronunciation games, rhymes, tongue twisters, team competitions (emulations), and other activities that provide motivational exercises for the individual student as well as the collective.

At the fourth grade level, the text stories become noticeably longer and more complicated. The emphasis at this level is on developing the capacity to do an elementary analysis of literary works, for example, making simple comparisons of one or two characteristics of characters in the same or different stories, and differentiating among works representing different genres.

In the second cycle (Grades 5 and 6), greater attention is paid to silent reading because of its importance as an instrument of self-study, students are introduced to literature appropriate for this transitional stage, and extraclass reading is continued.

García Pers has a great deal to say about oral and silent reading, intonation, and reading for comprehension. In addition, she provides guidance for planning a typical class, including initial preparation, initial reading, analysis and synthesis of the text materials, and followup activities. Other sections of her book deal with topics such as the psychological and social aspects of language, and the physiological bases of language learning as well as the teaching of grammar, orthography, and writing.[9]

INTERMEDIATE LEVEL (BASIC SECONDARY AND HIGH SCHOOL)

At the intermediate level, reading occurs primarily within the context of the literature sequence that spans Grades 7–12. In the previous plan (pre-1988–1989), the seventh grade was devoted to Spanish literature; the eighth, to Latin

American and Caribbean literature; and the ninth, to Cuban literature with an emphasis on literary theory. One unanticipated consequence of this approach was a noticeable decline in the students' reading skills. Under the new plan, the Grade 7–9 courses are called Spanish Literature. The emphasis is on literature appreciation and oral/written expression, with special attention paid to problems related to grammar, spelling, and vocabulary. The strict chronological arrangement of works used previously has been abandoned, thereby allowing greater flexibility in the selection and placement of literary pieces.

The preuniversity program consists of three courses dealing with universal literature as was the case under the previous plan. The selections contained in the text materials are arranged in chronological order, the intention being to help the students realize how literature reflects the major developments in the history of humankind. In order to increase student motivation, particularly when dealing with literary pieces in which students typically display little interest, teachers use out-of-class readings that are more contemporary, including detective stories and works that focus on social issues, in conjunction with visits to museums and other facilities linked to the work being studied. In addition, the textbooks are currently being improved to better accommodate the needs of both student and teacher, as are the correlated guides supplied to the instructors.

SPECIAL EDUCATION

The special education subsystem consists of approximately 450 centers accommodating 47,500 students with a teaching staff of 13,500. Special education schools spanning Grades 1–9 have been set up for mentally retarded, deaf, hard of hearing, blind, weak-sighted, speech impaired, and behaviorally maladjusted students. Special day care centers are also being established. According to Arias (1989), the prevailing view is that the special needs of these students can best be served by providing programs that most directly respond to their difficulties. Since the ultimate objective is to integrate each person into society as an active and contributing participant, the goals for special education students are essentially the same as those for students in the regular track. The teaching of reading in these schools employs the phonic/analytic/synthetic method with adaptations in materials, schedule, and teaching methodology to suit the needs of the particular handicapping condition. For example, while students who are visually or acoustically handicapped follow essentially the same program as those in the general track, the utilization of braille, "talking books," and voice amplifiers is considered to be important in the instructional process. In the case of mentally retarded students, on the other hand, the normal twenty-week acquisition phase at the beginning of Grade 1 is expanded to fifty-six weeks, and the materials used are deemed more suitable to teaching reading to this population, for example, greater use of illustrations and special written materials.

According to Arias and his colleagues, a concerted effort is now being made to develop a screening process that will effectively identify special education students at the first grade level. As economic conditions permit, the intention is to produce large-print books for visually handicapped students and, perhaps at some time in the not too distant future, to experiment with the use of micro-computers for instructional purposes.

Although students who fit the handicapping conditions cited earlier attend special schools, they wear the same school uniforms as their normal counterparts and participate in a variety of joint activities with students from the regular education track, for example, knowledge contests and cultural activities.

ADULT EDUCATION

As seen in Figure 6.2, the three levels of adult education correspond to the elementary, basic secondary, and preuniversity levels of the regular system. According to Rivero (1989) and Gayoso (1989), the reading, language, and literature sequence is very similar to the regular education program. Except at the very beginning of the sequence where different materials and slightly different methods are used to teach reading, the books in the adult education program are based on those used in the regular track. By design, the goals at each level of the adult program correspond to those of the comparable level in the regular program so that regular track dropouts can later resume their studies in the adult track. Therefore, reading instruction as such occurs in the four semesters that constitute the worker–farmer education (EOC) level.

Each reading lesson focuses on a very practical theme like simple machines, inertia, popular Cuban music, and the smoking habit. The structure of lessons during the initial acquisition phase is similar to that employed in the literacy campaign as shown in Figure 6.1. Beyond the initial phase, all lessons share a common structure that consists of oral expression, written expression, grammar, complementary reading, and orthography components. The theoretical aspects of language are subordinated to the practical needs of the workers, and there is a great deal of emphasis on developing speaking and writing skills.

The transition to literature at the upper levels parallels that in the regular subsystem with a selection of literary works that takes into account the interests of the adult population.

The adult education subsystem now has 10,500 teachers at 624 centers ser-vicing 165,000 students (MINED, 1988). The location of many of these centers at work sites enhances the accessibility of education to all workers. Canfux (1981) provides information about the evolution of this subsystem, its programs and instructional arrangements, text materials, and related matters.

TEACHER EDUCATION

Following completion of the ninth grade, the student who wishes to become an elementary school teacher enters one of nineteen pedagogical schools scattered throughout the island. The program in these schools, which has just been expanded from four to five years, consists of a mixture of coursework and graded clinical experiences culminating in practice teaching during the final year. The language and literature component of the program, which contains reading education as an integral element, consists of five courses in Spanish (semesters 1–5), two courses in universal literature (semesters 6–7), one course in children's literature (semester 8), and four courses in methods of teaching the Spanish language (semesters 6–9). In the Spanish language sequence explicit attention is paid to methods of teaching reading. By way of contrast, the Spanish language and literature curriculum for individuals preparing to be intermediate-level teachers consists of courses in literary analysis (semester 1), universal literature (semesters 1–3), Spanish literature (semesters 4–5), Latin American and Caribbean literature (semesters 6–7), Cuban literature (semesters 8–9), elective courses and seminars (semesters 8–9), and methodology for teaching literature (semesters 8–9). This literature cycle is rounded out by coursework dealing with the history of universal art as well as Cuban and Latin American art (Mañalich, 1989). The courses in art are important because of the way art is linked to literature in the textbooks.

As part of an overall attempt to increase the quality of teaching in Cuba, approximately 1,000 graduates of the twelfth grade were admitted into the pedagogical schools for the first time at the beginning of the 1988–1989 academic year. The plan is to increase the number of high school graduates entering the elementary teacher preparation program each year until 1993 when it is intended that all students entering these schools will be twelfth grade graduates, effectively converting them into higher pedagogical institutes. García Pers (1976) has described the reading methods curriculum.

In order to become a teacher at the intermediate level (basic secondary or high school), a student must first graduate from a preuniversity school and then enter one of twelve higher pedagogical institutes in order to specialize in the appropriate subject matter field. Upon graduation, the student is awarded a licentiate degree and is qualified for Grades 7–12. Among the specialties leading to the licentiate degree are Spanish literature, history, mathematics, physics, chemistry, geography, English, labor education, and biology. For the first time in 1990, a licentiate degree in elementary education also became possible, and there are currently about 1,000 students in this program. The curriculum of this degree program is similar to that offered by the pedagogical schools described above and is the first licentiate degree program in Cuba to have a clinical component.

For graduates of pedagogical schools who are practicing elementary school teachers, a six-year licentiate degree program exists. The first four years consist of supervised independent studies and regularly scheduled student–faculty meetings. During the last two years, program participants are given a two-year paid sabbatical from their teaching positions in order to take the intensive coursework required for program completion at a higher pedagogical institute. According to the Ministry of Education, approximately 75 percent of the current elementary school teachers either have a licentiate degree or are enrolled in a licentiate degree program, while 55 percent of the 80,000 intermediate-level teachers have their licentiate degree and the majority of those remaining are enrolled in licentiate programs.

The book *Práctica del Idioma Español* by Migdalia Porro Rodríguez and Mireya Báez García (1988) is included in the study plans for all specialties in the licentiate in education program offered by the higher institutes of education. The course based on this book emphasizes practical uses of oral and written language and aesthetic-literary development. Topics include oral and silent reading, choral and dramatic reading, spontaneous forms of oral expression, public speaking, and oratory. There is nothing analogous to the "reading in the content areas" courses currently popular in the United States. Clearly, the emphasis on the use of oral language permeates the entire curriculum, and reading appears to be regarded primarily as a means of acquiring the information needed for oral discourse. Nevertheless, the emphasis on oral activities such as debate, panel discussions, and the roundtable may provide a vehicle for stimulating interest in reading as well as for developing and refining reading skills for particular purposes.

With respect to preparing teachers for the adult education system, Canfux (1981, p. 231) has indicated that the training of workers who have the ability and interest tends to produce the best results. As Canfux observes,

The screening of new teaching recruits and their initial preparation are carried out in the Initial Preparation Seminars (*Seminarios de Preparación Inicial*). Together with the more advanced preparation seminars (*Seminarios de Preparación Methodológica*) which are conducted by experienced, professional teachers in each municipality, these have constituted a school for training and upgrading the pedagogical skills of thousands of "amateur teachers." The fact that the majority of educational personnel consists of workers and other "amateurs" has required a great deal of flexibility in organizing and scheduling these seminars.

TEXTBOOKS

As part of El Perfectionamiento, an entire new set of textbooks was introduced into the Cuban educational system during the 1976–1981 period. These books, along with teachers' guides and other related materials, were used and evaluated during the subsequent five-year period. According to Rivero (1989), the evaluation had four components: (1) test and questionnaire information from students and teachers throughout the country, (2) controlled experiments, (3) theoretical analysis of the text materials by linguists, psychologists, and pedagogical specialists, and (4) research on specific aspects of the reading process by the higher pedagogical institutes. The purpose of this extensive evaluation was to determine how the materials could be improved. In the case of the reading and literature textbooks, many problems were identified having to do with vocabulary, grammar, story length, sequencing of materials according to difficulty level, and student level of interest in the content of the literary pieces. As a result of this exhaustive effort, textbook revisions are currently at different stages of preparation. In the 1988–1989 academic year, the new first grade reader ¡A Leer! was introduced. New books were expected to be ready for Grades 2, 5, 7, and 10 the following year. Teams of authors are currently working on books for Grades 3, 6, 8, and 11, and the remaining grades will follow shortly. Once the new books are in place, another five-year evaluation cycle will follow, and the entire process will repeat itself.

In most cases, textbooks for the Cuban educational system are produced by writing teams consisting of subject matter specialists. In the case of the language–literature sequence, these teams usually involve notable contemporary Cuban authors (e.g., see Wald and Bacon, 1981). Although contemporary Cuban authors are very cooperative and want to produce quality literary pieces for use in the schools' text materials, they find the writing of stories at a given level of difficulty without sacrificing artistic merit to be a real challenge. In order to deal with this problem, the writers often visit the schools in order to discuss their works with the children. This has the added benefit of developing future readers of their works.

Once the draft of a new text or revision is completed, one or more subcommissions (committees) must review it before it can go on to publication. In the case of the first grade book, the draft was reviewed by a primary cycle subcommission that examines all the books used in Grades 1 through 4. This subcommission, made up of psychologists, pedagogical experts, methodologists, and others, is concerned with questions of horizontal and vertical articulation. After they approved the book, it was then reviewed by the subcommission on Spanish language and literature which functions under the auspices of the Ministry of Education's Central Institute of Pedagogical Sciences (abbreviated ICCP in Spanish). This subcommission analyzes all the materials dealing with Spanish language and literature for Grades 1 through 12 and must put its stamp of approval on the book before it can be published.

Next, the approved materials are turned over to Editorial Pueblo y Educación, the largest publishing house in Cuba. This enterprise, which publishes all the materials for the Cuban educational system, has 452 employees including highly skilled technicians, illustrators, designers, and editorial experts. According to its director Catalina Lagud Herrera (1989), they publish about 1,300 titles annually with about 200 to 300 of them being new. Each year, the total output is approximately 20 million copies, although about 70 percent of these are reprints of existing editions. (A partial listing of materials produced for the Ministry of Education is given in the Appendix.) As indicated earlier, a complete set of replacement texts is being produced during the next several years up to and including the university level where extensive program changes are being made in all disciplines.

RESEARCH

The Ministry of Education's Central Institute of Pedagogical Sciences (ICCP) has primary responsibility for research and evaluation activities in the pedagogical sciences. According to Cuba's Report to the Forty-first International Conference on Public Education (MINED, 1988), the institute works in close partnership with counterpart groups in other socialist bloc countries as well as related national institutions such as the Ministry of Higher Education, the Higher Pedagogical Institutes, and the Ministry of Culture. The research work itself falls within a preestablished framework that is part of the current five-year plan. One of the current research themes is "Improvement of the Efficiency of the National System of Education," and a specific research project is "Study of Ways to Diagnose and Care for Preschool and School-Age Children with Sensory or Mental Handicaps or Psychic Retardation." In addition, as suggested earlier, a great deal of national effort is being invested in the continuous formative evaluation of programs, textbooks, and teaching methodologies. Specific examples include the textbook revision process and the preschool writing readiness program described earlier, as well as the development of a special education screening mechanism for use at the first grade level. Of particular interest at this time is the methodological preparation of teachers. In addition, faculty carries out research at the higher pedagogical institutes, which may or may not be related to projects undertaken by the Ministry of Education.

Finally, the Ministry of Education publishes five periodicals to support and encourage the advancement of education: *Educación* (3 issues/year; 70,000 copies/issue); *Simientes* (3 issues/year; 10,000 copies/issue); *Ciencias Pedagógicas* (2 issues/year; 3,500 copies/issue); *Referitiva de Educación* (4 issues/year; 2,300 copies/issue); and *Pedagógica Cubana* (3 issues/year; 10,000 copies/issue). The last-named periodical was scheduled to begin circulation in June 1989.

SUMMARY

Since the Castro government took power in Cuba in 1959, the eradication of illiteracy and the continuing elevation of the educational level of the general population have been high national priorities. Following a trial-and-error approach to dealing with educational problems during the 1960s, a national school improvement plan (El Perfectionamiento) was initiated in the mid-1970s, marking a shift in emphasis from quantity (i.e., making education accessible to everyone) to quality (i.e., systematically evaluating and revising curricula and pedagogical techniques). The growth of special education along with current attempts to develop a first grade screening procedure, the revision of all text materials and school programs, the development of home-based preschool experiences for children in the countryside, the initiation of a licentiate degree for teachers, and the development of a professional literature to disseminate research and evaluation results as well as to raise the level of discourse in the teaching profession are some of the more obvious signs of the continuing effort to improve the Cuban educational system. In the area of reading specifically, the phonic/analytic/synthetic method continues to enjoy preference, with improvement efforts firmly rooted in programmatic, formative, and summative evaluation activities. Revision of the reading textbooks, modification of courses and course sequences based on evaluative data and theoretical analysis, and recent changes in the teacher preparation courses and programs are just some of the results.

Since the advent of the 1961 literacy campaign, a concerted effort has been underway to make Cuba a nation of readers, and there seems to be steady progress toward this end. Those interested in further study of reading in Cuba should consult the Supplementary Bibliography at the end of this chapter.

NOTES

Cuban educational experts who provided information for this chapter include Mirta Contreras, Noemi Gayoso, Georgina Arias, Rosario Mañalich, Magaly Porto, Delia Rivero, Bertha Rudnikas, Ana María Rojas, Vivian Vázquez, Eva Ramírez, Juan Viscaya, Manuel Ormas, Josefina López, Ana Maria Siverio, Magaly Egurrola, and Guillermo Arias. I am especially grateful to Mirta Contreras and Hermis Campos for their invaluable assistance during my recent visit to Havana, as well as to the University of Delaware Office of International Programs and the Cuban Ministry of Education for the necessary financial and logistical support.

1. For a good retrospective overview of changes occurring in the 1961–1981 period, see Leiner (1981).

2. A useful reference in this regard is the Nicaraguan Ministry of Education (MED) publication entitled *Nicaragua Triunfa en la Alfabetización: Documentos & Testimonios de la Cruzada Nacional de Alfabetización* (San José, Costa Rica: DEI, 1981).

3. *Illiteracy* is still defined in Cuba as the inability to read and write at the first grade level. According to Ministry of Education experts, the most recent census (1981) showed that slightly more than 1 percent of the age ten to forty-nine population were illiterate according to this standard.

4. The preschool, primary, and intermediate levels collectively constitute the General Polytechnical and Labor Education Subsystem.

5. Beginning with the 1988–1989 academic year, some students may be assigned to different teachers at the end of Grade 2.

6. Based on the figures reported in the Ministry of Education publication *Anuario Estadístico*, 1988, p. 34.

7. This period can be extended up to thirty weeks depending on student progress.

8. For information about the nature and purposes of these activities, see Rivero (1979).

9. Until recently, selected characteristics of oral reading performance like intonation, pronunciation, fluency, and reading speed (words per minute) were officially regarded as important indicators of reading achievement. With respect to reading speed, García Pers cites the following quantitative goals for Grades 1–6, respectively: 25–30, 50–60, 70–80, 100–110, 110–120, and 120–130 words per minute. Because of the unanticipated negative effects of these goals on comprehension, they have been dropped and do not appear in the current study plans. It is not clear, however, whether actual classroom practice reflects this shift in policy.

REFERENCES

Arias, Guillermo. 1989. Interviewed by Victor Martuza.
Canfux, Jaime. 1981. "A Brief Description of the 'Battle for the Sixth Grade.' " *Journal of Reading* 25 (December): 202–214.
García Pers, Delfina. 1976. *Didáctica del Idioma Español.* Havana, Cuba: Editorial Pueblo y Educación.
Gayoso, Noemí. 1989. Interviewed by Victor Martuza.
Gonzáles Núñez, Raquel. 1976. "De la frase al sonido, del sonido a la frase." *Revista Educación*, No. 20 (January-March).
Gonzáles Núñez, Raquel. 1980. "El lenguaje: Idea y sonido." *Revista Educación*, No. 37 (April-June).
International Bank for Reconstruction and Development. 1951. *Report on Cuba.* Baltimore: Johns Hopkins University Press.
Jolly, Richard. 1964. "Part II: Education." In *Cuba: The Economic and Social Revolution,* edited by Dudley Seers. Westport, Conn.: Greenwood Press.
Kozol, Jonathan. *Children of the Revolution.* 1978. New York: Delacorte.
Leiner, Marvin. 1981. "Two Decades of Educational Change in Cuba." *Journal of Reading* 25 (December): 202–214.
López, Josefina. 1981. "The Preschool Reading Readiness Program." *Journal of Reading* 25 (December): 234–240.
López, Josefina. 1989. Interviewed by Victor Martuza.
Lorenzetto, Anna, and Karel Neys. 1965. *Methods and Means Utilized in Cuba to Eliminate Illiteracy.* Unesco Report. Havana, Cuba: Ministry of Education.
Mañalich, Rosario. 1989. Interviewed by Victor Martuza.
Martuza, Victor. 1986. "Evaluation of Reading Achievement in Cuban Schools." *The Reading Teacher* 40 (December): 306–313.
MINED. 1988. *Organization of Education 1985–1987; Report of the Republic of Cuba to the 41st. International Conference on Public Education.* Havana, Cuba: Ministry of Education.
Paulston, Roland G. 1971. "Education." In *Revolutionary Changes in Cuba,* edited by Carmelo Mesa-Lago. Pittsburgh, Pa: University of Pittsburgh Press.
Pollack, Cecelia, and Victor Martuza. 1981. "Teaching Reading in the Cuban Primary Schools." *Journal of Reading* 25 (December): 241–250.
Porro Rodríguez, Migdalia, and Mireya Báez García. 1988. *Práctica del Idioma Español.* Havana, Cuba: Editorial Pueblo y Educación.
Prieto, M. Abel. 1981a. "The Literacy Campaign in Cuba." *Harvard Educational Review* 51 (February): 31–39.
Prieto M. Abel. 1981b. "Cuba's National Literacy Campaign." *Journal of Reading* 25 (December): 215–221.
Rivero, Delia E. 1979. "La Lectura Extraclase." *Revista Educación*, No. 34 (June-September).
Rivero, Delia E. 1989. Interviewed by Victor Martuza.
Rodriguez, Elenia. 1989. Interviewed by Victor Martuza.
Wald, Karen, and Betty Bacon. 1981. "New Literacy for New People: Children and Books in Cuba." *Journal of Reading* 25 (December): 251–260.

SUPPLEMENTARY BIBLIOGRAPHY

Abascal Ruíz, Alicia, et al. 1987. *Literatura Infantil*. Havana, Cuba: Editorial Pueblo y Educación.

Almendros, Herminio. 1972. *A Propósito de la Edad de Oro*. Havana, Cuba: Editorial Gente Nueva.

Alpízar, Castillo. 1975. *Para Expresarnos Mejor*. Havana, Cuba: Editorial Científico-técnica.

Cabrera, Orestes. 1982. *Tema de Redacción y Lenguaje*. Havana, Cuba: Editorial Científico-técnica.

García Alzola, Ernesto. 1975. *Lengua y Literatura*. Havana, Cuba: Editorial Pueblo y Educación.

García Alzola, et al. 1979. *Metodología de la Enseñaza de la Lengua*. Havana, Cuba: Editorial Libros para la educación.

García Pers, Delfina. 1976. *Didáctica del Idioma Español*. Havana, Cuba: Editorial Pueblo y Educación.

García Pers, Delfina, et al. n.d. *Orientaciones Metodológicas de Lectura y Literatura Infantil*. Havana, Cuba: Editorial Pueblo y Educación.

García Pers, Delfina. 1980. *Acerca de la Literatura Infantil*. Havana, Cuba: Editorial Libros para la Educación.

González, Raquel, and Ester Ma. Fors. 1982. *Metodólogía de la Enseñanza del Español (1ra parte)*. Havana, Cuba: Editorial Pueblo y Educación.

González Núñez, Raquel. 1980. "El lenguaje: Idea y sonido." *Revista Educación*, No. 37 (April-June).

Grass Gallo, Elida. 1987. *Técnicas Básicas de Lectura*. Havana, Cuba: Editorial Pueblo y Educación.

Guevara, Frank. 1984. *La Locución: Técnica y Práctica*. Havana, Cuba: Instituto del Libro.

Hernríquez Ureña, Camila. 1987. *Invitación a la Lectura*. Havana, Cuba: Editorial Pueblo y Educación.

Maggi, Beatríz. 1988. *El Pequeño Drama de la Lectura*. Havana, Cuba: Editorial Letras Cubanas.

Mañalich, Rosario, et al. 1979. *Metodolgía de la Ensenanza de la Literatura*. Havana, Cuba: Editorial Pueblo y Educación.

Martí, José. 1964. *Obras Completas*. Havana, Cuba: Editorial Nacional de Cuba.

MINED. 1964. *Las Técnicas de Orientación de Grupos*. Havana, Cuba: Editorial del Ministerio de Educación.

Porro, Migdalia, and Mireya Báez. 1984. *Práctica del Idioma Español. (1ra parte)*. Havana, Cuba: Editorial Pueblo y Educación.

Quintero, Aramís. 1977. *Elementos Formales de Apreciación Literaria (1ra y 2da partes)*. Havana, Cuba: Editorial Pueblo y Educación.

Repilado, Ricardo. 1975. *Dos Temas de Redacción*. Havana, Cuba: Editorial Pueblo y Educación.

Romeu, Angelina, et al. 1986. *Metodología de la Enseñanza del Español I y II*. Havana, Cuba: Editorial Pueblo y Educación.

Ruiz, Vitelio, and Eloína Miyares. n.d. *Ortografía Teóricopráctica*. Havana, Cuba: Editorial Pueblo y educación.

Tallet, José Z. 1985. *Evitemos Gazapos y Gazapitos*. Havana, Cuba: Editorial Letras
    Cubanas.
Varios. 1974. *Composición I–II*. Havana, Cuba: Editorial Pueblo y Educación.
Varios. 1979. *Lectura Artística y Narración*. Havana, Cuba: Editorial Pueblo y Educación.
Varios. 1975. *Selección de Lecturas para Radacción*. Havana, Cuba: Editorial Pueblo y
    Educación.

APPENDIX: PARTIAL LISTING OF BOOKS PUBLISHED FOR USE IN CUBAN SCHOOLS

PRIMARY (GRADES 1–6)

Title	Quantity
¡A leer!	280,000
Lectura 1	173,000
Lectura 2	212,070
Lectura 3	254,000
Lectura 4	621,772
Lectura 5	202,070
Lectura Literaria 6	160,700
Blanca Nieves	76,000
Boticas de Hielo	77,000
Para que Ellos Canten	57,280
El Primero de Mayo	88,000
La Caperucita Roja	61,090
El Cochero Azul	89,000
Cuentos de Animales	82,000
Los Cuentos de Compay Grillo	80,000
Cuentos de Guane	80,000
La Gallinita Dorada	61,090
El Gallito Cresta de Oro	79,000
El Gatico	87,000
Fábulas (selección)	80,000
El Guante del Abuelo	111,000
Mashenka y el Oso	82,000
Mi Cocodrilo Verde	89,000
El Nabo	57,675
Nueve Cisnes Blancos	82,000
Rikki-Tikki-Tavi	39,648

El Sol es Tuyo	79,000
El Sombrero Vivo	80,000
Tesoro	111,000
La Tortuga Gigante	8,500
Los Tres Cochinitos	111,000
El Valle de la Pájara Pinta	56,475
Van Hoa Transformó el Odio en Fuego	62,550
Las Aventuras de Tom Sawyer	68,000
La Edad de Oro	114,672
Juegos y Otros Poemas	46,075

INTERMEDIATE LEVEL (GRADES 7–12)

Title	*Quantity*
Español y Literatura	253,145
Literatura Latinoamericana y del Caribe.	173,000
Literatura Cubana	118,597
Español y Literatura	165,245
Literatura Universal 2	64,500
Literatura Universal 3	57,900
El Llamado de la Selva	99,600
Juan Quinquín en Pueblo Mocho	99,600
El Lazarillo de Tormes	72,000
Lázaro, Rinconete y Cortadillo	59,770
Papá Goriot	19,515
Poema del Mío Cid	82,000
La Casa de Bernarda Alba	22,415
Cecilia Valdés (Tomo I)	49,945
Cecilia Valdés (Tomo 2)	50,450
La Celestina	19,960
La Poesía Militante	7,136
El Destino de un Hombre	20,600
El Diario de Ana Frank	99,600
Cervantes Diccionario I	31,000
Cervantes Diccionario II	30,000
Aristos 5 y 6	32,991
El 2 de Mayo	69,000
Fuenteovejuna	35,360

Fausto	19,000
Gobernadores del Rocío y Santa Juana de América	74,000
La Guerra y la Paz (Tomo 1)	15,000
La Guerra y la Paz (Tomo 2)	15,000
La Hija del Capitán	15,000
La Iliada	15,104
El Infierno	15,643
El Ingenioso Hidalgo Don Quijote de la Mancha (Tomo 1)	24,500
El Ingenioso Hidalgo Don Quijote de la Mancha (Tomo 2)	24,500
La Madre	19,500
Martín Fierro	74,000
Otelo	29,290
El Reino de este Mundo	19,080
Reportaje al Pie de la Horca	20,540
El Rojo y el Negro (Tomo 1)	15,000
El Rojo y el Negro (Tomo 2)	15,000
Teatro Bertold Brecht	18,835
Teatro Clásico Francés	28,000
Teatro Escandinavo	19,540
Tragedia Griega	22,690
Un Capitán de Quince Años	99,600
El Viejo y el Mar	18,405
Bertillón 164	52,760
Al Autor y su Obra ANTONIO MACHADO	65,000
El Autor y su Obra BALZAC	15,000
El Autor y su Obra BECQUER	65,000
El Autor y su Obra LA CANCIÓN DE ROLANDO	17,000
El Autor y su Obra CHEJOV	15,000
El Autor y su Obra DANTE	17,000
El Autor y su Obra EURÍPIDES	17,000
El Autor y su Obra FELIX PITA RODRIGUEZ	50,000
El Autor y su Obra GARCÍA LORCA	69,000
El Autor y su Obra GARCÍA LORCA	72,000
El Autor y su Obra HOMERO	17,000
El Autor y su Obra IBSEN	15,000
Literatura Cubana (9no grado)	52,863

ADULTS

Title	Quantity
Lectura para Obreros y Campesinos	10,021
Libro de EOC No. 1	3,614
Libro de EOC No. 2	6,100
Libro de EOC No. 3	7,600
Libro de EOC No. 4	8,300
Ya Sé Leer	15,000
O.M. de Ya Sé Leer	3,000
Español 1 (SOC)	70,900
Español e Historia 1 (SOC)	72,000
Lectura para Obreros y Campesinos	30,000
OM Español y Literatura (Soc 1, 2, 3 y 4)	3,000
Literatura y Español (SOC 3)	18,020
Literatura	58,000
Español y Literatura (FOC 1)	41,540
Español y Literatura Universal (FOC 2)	32,505
Literatura Universal (FOC 3)	22,455
Literatura Universal (FOC 4)	3,000
Literatura 4 (FOC)	27,290
Ortografía (FOC)	37,000

EOC - Educación Obrera y Campesina (Worker–Farmer Education)
SOC - Secondaria Obrera y Campesina (Worker–Farmer Secondary)
FOC - Facultad Obrera y Campesina (Worker–Farmer Faculty)

7

France

Eliane Fijalkow
Translated by Soungalo Ouedraogo

THE LANGUAGE OF THE COUNTRY

The official and institutional language used in France is French, although there are some national minorities in the nation. The language of three of these minorities—the Bretons, Basques, and Occitans is used less and less, but some intellectuals are attempting to revitalize them. These efforts have led to the creation of kindergartens using these languages, as well as to the recent creation of university degrees in these languages (Diplome d'Etude Universitaires Generales de langue basque). Besides these national minorities there are other minorities from recently immigrated populations from such areas as Algeria, Morocco, Tunisia, Spain, Portugal, Italy, Yugoslavia, Turkey, and Southeast Asia.

These minorities are well represented in the schools. In fact, the statistics from the Ministry of Education (for 1986 to 1987, p. 112) show that the enrollment of students of foreign nationalities represents 10.4 percent of the total school population in preschool, elementary, and secondary education. In this melting pot, Algerians are the most numerous (27 percent) and the Southeast Asians are the least numerous (3.3 percent).

These immigrants communicate with each other and with their children in their own language. At home, the mother tongue is more practical because not all members of the family have mastered French. The mother tongue is sometimes taught at school as a subject matter, and in addition, it is used by embassy personnel and by various associations. School programs do not take into consideration the mother tongues of these children who must learn French: "The school provides a means for integration into the French community as well as a culture open to diversity" (Chevenement, 1985, p. 21).

READING EDUCATION POLICY

Reading education policy is very centralized in France, being formulated at the national level. Official instructions are issued in that manner and are mandatory for every teacher in every school of the country.

The curriculum allows the teachers a great deal of freedom because it is very ambiguous. It requires attention to practice of both the oral and written language, study of the language, and practical usage of the language (Chevenement, 1985, pp. 22–27). Methods for reading education are not imposed on the teachers. However, the system does permit a diversity of thought on reading education. That is why a certain evolution can be noticed in the official instruction over time.

One of the first reading methods is the synthetic method. It refers to a combination of the type B + A = BA. It is a simple decoding method in which the child distinguishes the letters without knowing the meaning of what he or she is reading. A second method is called the global method. Decoding is excluded in this method. To learn to read is to grasp meanings. Another method, which is in its infancy, emphasizes the interaction between the following two methods of learning systems: the acquisition of information from the code and the acquisition of information from the meaning. This proposal is discussed in the report for the renovation of national education.

THE GOAL OF READING EDUCATION

If we refer to Chevenement's proposal as it appears in the curricula and in instruction, the objective of education is: "To give the country a strong and active school open to the future." The mission of the school is to prepare children for their role in society. Therefore, it has an unquestionable social mission that can be accomplished through an ability to read and write. Chevenement's policy consists in enabling all children—without exception—to acquire the written language. This mission develops in the early primary grades.

Primary Education

In France primary education consists of five grades. The first two grades are called Cours Preparatoire and Cours Elementaire, respectively, and mark the beginning of reading education. It is imperative that all students be able to read by the completion of these grades. Thus, the official instruction affords two years in order to read and write. However, only at the end of primary education (i.e., the completion of five years of education) does the child have mastery of the written language.

Secondary Education

Junior High School

Following elementary school, the student goes to junior high school which requires four years for completion. Compulsory school attendance ends after the student's sixteenth year.

Reading education is not taught as such in the junior high school, but it remains important. In fact, students who acquire the written language simply to survive scholastically are not able to succeed in their junior high school education. For this reason some junior high school teachers say that many students do not know how to read. The truth is that these students have acquired only the bare minimum; they know how to read but not sufficiently to perform well in their junior high school education.

Moreover, because the number of certain specialized sections has been reduced to these students now attend programs that were not intended for them. Only a small minority of students are affected by this problem, however; there is no reason why these students cannot read. There is no evidence to support the contention that they cannot.

Actually, data run contrary to the teachers' concern on this matter. A study conducted by the Ministry of National Education (MEN, 1988, pp. 126–127) concludes that an improvement in student performance is occurring at this level. Promotion from grade to grade has been improving over time, as seen in the following list.

1973–1974	6°-5°	95.9%
1986–1987	6°-5°	96.0%
1973–1974	5°-4°	72.9%
1986–1987	5°-4°	80.2%
1973–1974	4°-3°	88.0%
1986–1987	4°-3°	96.7%

These data are encouraging and support Baudelot and Establet's (1988) assumptions in their book, *Le niveau monte*.

The High School

The high school system accepts only children who are able to carry out an extended course of study. Students spend three years at this level, which results in their obtaining the BAC degree which gives them access to college. Reading is not a major concern for teachers in the high schools; everyone considers it a "solved problem" by this time.

Education for Boys and Girls

The primary and secondary levels of education are undifferentiated by gender, which means that both boys and girls receive the same education with no restrictions in the subject matter taught except sports activities.

ILLITERACY: HOW IS IT DETECTED?

In France, two populations are distinguished: the illiterate and the functionally illiterate. These terms apply only to the adult population.

Every person who does not know how to read and write is considered illiterate. The functional illiterate is one whose ability is limited to the simple ability to read the written material useful and/or necessary for everyday life. Functionally illiterate persons are those whose level of mastery of written language does not enable them to face the new requirements in reading and writing imposed on them by economic and social change.

The difference between the two populations is as follows. Illiterates are not self-reliant vis-à-vis written materials. They need a "public writer" to fill out forms and to write personal letters. They have developed a "survival competence," however, and can be considered "functionally literate." They can read the simple material they encounter in everyday life.

Detection of Illiteracy

The army is the main source of information on illiteracy among males. The illiterate population is detected during the test for the induction of recruits, organized by the army's psychology services.

Based on army data, sociologists (Baudelot and Establet, 1988; Dumazedier and Gisors, 1984) have found that the illiteracy rate has been stable for many years. It represents less than 1 percent of an age group. Since 1880 the number of illiterates has been declining regularly: less than 2 percent up to 1963 and less than 1 percent thereafter.

With regard to illiteracy among women, there is no source of information available; it is suspected that this rate is lower than the rate in the male population, just as it is in every developed country.

Following a report given to the prime minister (Esperandieu, Lion, and Benichou, 1984), the notion of functional illiteracy became current in France and has now gained significant acceptance among educators, journalists, and politicians. When we hear comments such as: "there are more and more functional illiterates in France," are they true? It appears that no objective research has yet been conducted which would allow us the basis for such an assumption.

The only available information allows us to take the level of instruction into consideration. If we examine the level of instruction over twenty years, (Baudelot and Establet, 1988; Dumazedier and De Gisors, 1984) and the statistics of the Ministry of Education (1988), we realize that this level increases. Therefore, we can conclude that functional illiteracy is decreasing and can be estimated to be about 10 percent. This 10 figure derives from the army (Baudelot and Establet, 1988) and from data concerning out-of-school youngsters who have neither a certificate nor vocational training (MEN, 1988).

For primary education children, we will not use the terms *illiteracy* and *functional illiteracy*; rather, we will speak of the degree of mastery of the written language, which is an issue of great concern in France. It doesn't seem to be an aggravating issue, but there is sufficient concern over the current situation.

Some years ago the repetition rate in schools provided a general idea of the situation regarding the mastery of the written language. The academic authorities no longer allow repetition, and so the observer cannot evaluate mastery of the written language. However, evaluations conducted on grammar and orthography in 1981, 1983, and 1987 on a sample of students finishing primary education (Ministere de l'Education, 1988, p. 120) offered the basis for a comparison over time and revealed a stable trend or an increase between 1981–1983 and 1987.

Other results confirm that trend or tendency. A national evaluation conducted by the Direction de l'Evaluation et de la Prospective in 1987, in order to make an assessment of student acquisition in mathematics and reading at the end of primary education, revealed that in the area of computation there is a good mastery of the four basic mathematical operations: addition, 95 percent; subtraction, 93 percent; multiplication, 88 percent; and division, 75 percent.

In reading, there is a variation related to the difficulty of the text (lexicon and syntax). The results also vary according to type of questions. The achievement rates are higher than 70 percent for questions related to global comprehension and detection of information, but they are lower than 50 percent for those who require in-depth reading and interpretative ability.

Based on this evaluation, we can conclude that, even if a situation is not serious enough, it constitutes a major concern when we look at the achievement rate of in-depth reading.

Secondary Education

No objective evaluation can give us data on the situation of secondary education in France. One evaluation by the Direction de l'Evaluation et de la Prospective of the second year of secondary education was done in 1987–1988 to analyze the written language (lexicon, syntax, orthography); these data are currently being analyzed. A second evaluation, concerning all secondary school students, was scheduled to be conducted during the 1989–1990 school year.

READING DIFFICULTIES AND THEIR DIAGNOSIS

As mentioned above, a child is expected to have learned to read and write during the first two years of primary school education. Therefore, his or her future learning achievement depends on these first two years.

Official research (MEN, 1988, pp. 110–111) was conducted with a sample of 20,000 children selected from the national French population. The figures showed that two years later 20.5 percent of the children were no longer being educated with their age group. These figures are much higher in areas where the majority of the population consists of immigrants. The failure rate is more pressing among this group.

This failure is attributable to numerous variables including psychological, linguistic, social, and educational variables that depend on both the child and the school process. One of the first difficulties that children face is their integration into a culturally different group in which the language and the environment make them suspicious. In other words, their identity is at stake. Would they adapt to the social community offered by the school system or would they remain in their own community?

Knowledge of that population of which the majority are immigrants involves cognitive as well as sociocultural and affective aspects. This leads to new variables that are at least as important as those involved in the child's cognitive environment. It is therefore necessary to have cultural homogeneity before success can take place. The child who finds himself in a culture in which the language and values are identical to those he knows can readily identify with school and be interested in learning to read and write. This homogeneity is, of course, lacking for students from the immigrant population. That is why the failure rate is a little lower among national students at the beginning of their schooling process (Preteur and Fijalkow, 1987).

Students of immigrant families represented only 7.1 percent of the total secondary school population in 1986–1987. This figure demonstrates the difficulty these students have had in staying in school.

Reading Difficulties According to Gender

According to research conducted in France, it appears that girls have a better achievement rate in reading education than boys. Kindergarten and first elementary school year girls display more participatory and cooperative behaviors than do boys. As a consequence, they are more attentive in class than boys. When we take all backgrounds into consideration, we find that 32 percent of the boys are unstable compared to 6 percent of the girls; 19 percent of the boys actively participate in class compared with 39 percent of the girls; and 39 percent of the boys are passive participants as compared with 57 percent of the girls. These facts are related to achievement in reading education.

In the mandatory first school year a correlation has been found between school behavior and achievement in reading education. This correlation is reflected in the official statistics of the Ministry of Education (MEN, 1988, p. 130).

The superiority of girls over boys is also shown at the junior high school level. When we examine the data on promotion, we see that a greater percentage of girls is promoted in both the public and private sector.

	Public Sector		Private Sector	
Level	Boys	Girls	Boys	Girls
6	49.4%	56.4%	54.2%	62.8%
5	42.2%	48.3%	47.1%	55.7%
4	51.9%	54.5%	49.2%	56.6%
3	45.5%	48.1%	43.2%	49.4%

Instruments and Methods Used in Diagnosing Reading Difficulties

Until recently repetition of grade was the most conventional means of diagnosing reading difficulties. The normal course of study, with neither grade repetition nor special courses of study (classes for children having difficulty), involved only 63 percent of the first grade students in 1978–1979 (MEN, 1988, p. 110).

The grade most repeated is the first grade. The student who repeats the first grade has only 4 chances in 10 of reaching the seventh grade. If a student repeats yet another grade after the first grade, the chances of a lengthy process of education is significantly reduced.

This manner of taking repetition into consideration as a means of diagnosis is no longer relevant, for educators are encouraged to promote students automatically, and thus repetition is now considered an exception.

With regard to instruments used in diagnosing reading difficulties, the best known and most popular evaluative tools or instruments for reading education in France are those of Inizan (1963) and of Lefavrais (1967).

DESCRIPTION OF THE TESTS

Inizan's Test

Inizan's test (1963, pp. 65–66) consists of two parts. The first, the Predictive Battery, applies to kindergarten students and puts the child in front of a new task that will lead him to be creative. The second, the reading part called the Reading Battery, concerns the same students one year later in the first grade. It is based on the child's educational knowledge. This second part is used as a validation process or instrument.

CONTENT OF THE PREDICTIVE AND READING BATTERY

Predictive Battery
  Organization in space
    Geometrical Figures

Ability to recognize and distinguish perceptive differences and symmetrical figures

Construction of geometric figures using Koh's cubes

Language

Brief and immediate recall of a short history

Immediate recall of a well-known object

Articulation

Time Organization

Repetition of a rhythm using a percussion instrument

Copy of a rhythmic pattern presented in sequence

Reading Battery

Reading of familiar words

Dictation of familiar words

Reading of unfamiliar words

Silent reading comprehension

The Predictive Battery requires general aspects (space, time) that underlie perceptive aspects (geometric figures, discrimination of symmetric figures, repetition of a rhythm). This test also calls for language ability which is measured through immediate memory (a memory of orthography). The Reading Battery requires more specific knowledge of the written language (to read, to write, to understand).

If the Predictive Battery allows us to evaluate the child's first acquisition of language, the different tasks involved show that Inizan has a visual approach to reading. In fact, he seems to consider reading and writing a purely mnemo-perceptive activity. The concepts are apparent, but these are not what he measures through the different activities presented to the children. The phonetic aspect of the language and every oral activity are not taken into consideration, whereas orality is essential, just as vision is in dealing with the written language. If we examine the children who have difficulties, we realize that these difficulties are related to orality. In reading situations they behave like deaf children, even though no hearing handicap is indicated. Research conducted over the last few years highlights the importance of orality in acquiring reading and writing ability (Fijalkow and Liva, 1988, p. 101).

This first test is, therefore, subject to criticism because it deprives the child of one important component.

The second test, the Reading Battery, is also subject to criticism. In this test the child is put in a situation that is not "natural." She is confronted with words that are deprived of context. If we think that to read and to write is to communicate, the situation in which the child finds herself seems to be meaningless. The communication occurs with sentences but not with words that are isolated one from another. An evaluation in reading and writing cannot depend on the simple knowledge of words whether they are read or written, however, it can depend on comprehension.

Lefavrais's Test

Lefavrais's test (1967) analyzes reading and dyslexia. To determine the reading level of his subjects, the author takes into consideration the optimal speed that a subject can read without making more mistakes than readers of the same mental age. Lefavrais discusses rapid and slow decoding, slow decoding being an indication of possible dyslexia. In his test, a maximum of three minutes is allocated to reading. The number of words to be read in those three minutes is set up, and the number of mistakes during that reading is recorded. This test has been criticized because it implies that the objective of being a good reader is to read fast, whereas many feel that to be a good reader means to be able to understand.

These reading tests are standard in France, but one can only conjecture whether they improve the evaluation of reading knowledge.

Other Informal Materials Used

Beyond repetition and the standardized evaluation instruments, evaluations have been conducted by GAPP (Groupes d'Aide Psych-Pedagogique), a group established in 1970 to help students with reading difficulties. Its prime objective is to improve the student's acquisition of reading and orthography (MEN, 1988, p. 116).

Each GAPP consists of one educational psychologist, one psycho-pedagogical educator, and one psychometrician, and its role is both prevention and adaptation/ remediation. The number of these groups increased from 1,302 in 1978 to 2,066 in 1983 and to 2,800 in 1986–1987. The number varies a great deal from region to region. They tend to be more numerous in areas where difficulties are greater. On the average, a GAPP covers four schools, or 780 students. The average age of the students involved is 6.2 years, which is an optimally early age of intervention.

Another informal evaluation is that of the teacher. He or she decides on the level of the student and identifies the student to GAPP or to the remedial education teachers who teach in the evening classes. Although this approach is not very reliable, it is more easily adapted to the reading difficulties than are the reading tests previously discussed.

What Are the Achievements for Such Efforts?

The role of GAPP is very important. It is through this group that reading difficulties are first identified; they are then remediated outside the classroom. If the situation is serious, medical specialists are called in, and such procedures take place outside the school in the CMPP (Centre Medico-Psycho-Pedagogique).

Today illiteracy is nearly nonexistent in France; nearly everybody learns to read sooner or later. Of course, some people achieve a higher mastery of reading than others, but everyone can handle everyday written material. Functional illiteracy remains, however.

READING PROGRAMS AND PREPARATION FOR PRESCHOOL CHILDREN

The kindergarten system in France takes almost every child ages two to five. The enrollment has increased over time, the percentage being 83 in 1986. The proportions of children attending kindergarten in that year were as follows:

33 percent of children two years old

95.4 percent of children three years old

100 percent of children four years old

100 percent of children five years old

A longitudinal study conducted in the first grade in 1979 and in the fifth grade in 1983 and 1987 examined the length and effect of kindergarten attendance (MEN, 1988, p. 102). It appears that children who had only one or two years of preschool education had lower achievement in French and mathematics, whereas the children with three or four years of preschool education achieved higher than the average. Therefore, preschool education plays a considerable role in educational achievement or failure. It fosters the student's facility in writing. At this level, there is no difference between boys and girls.

In the countryside the kindergartens are only early childhood annexes, but the curriculum is exactly the same as that in the cities.

TEACHER QUALIFICATIONS

The Ministry of Education regulates teacher training for the primary school level. It recruits people who hold the DEUG (Diplome d'Etudes Universitaires Generales) degree—that is, the diploma showing the completion of two years of higher education. Everyone who has this diploma can take the entry test for the teachers' college. The universities offer preparation for this test. Upon the successful completion of this very selective test, theoretical training is given at the teacher training college over a two-year course of study.

This system is in the process of being restructured; by the 1989–1990 school year, the university was expected to replace the teacher training colleges.

With regard to junior high school and high school teachers, no specific pedagogical training exists. Anyone with a university certificate in a given subject matter after three years of study (*licence*) or four years of study (*maitrise*) can teach in a junior high school or high school. However, the candidate must pass one of two recruiting tests which are very selective (CAPES, Aggregation) in order to get a permanent teaching position.

In the future, the teacher in a junior high school and high school will be trained in the universities just as the elementary school teachers are.

Like the secondary school teachers, university teachers do not undergo any specific pedagogical training. However, some reforms are under preparation. Anyone who holds a doctorate can teach at the university level.

The Proportion of Male and Female Teachers

In France no teachers specialize in reading education. Teachers are generalists and must be able to teach reading as well as mathematics, physical education, or music. Official statistics show that 74 percent of primary school teachers are women, but the figures drop off sharply on the high school and university level: 55 and 29 percent, respectively (MEN; 1988, p. 68).

The entry requirements for males and females are the same for all levels of education.

PEDAGOGICAL MATERIALS

The private sector offers teachers educational materials through advertisements and marketing. Every school year the teacher gets materials through the budget. Teachers in primary schools make their own materials. All that is required of them is that they make the materials relevant to the program involved.

Whatever the education level, many products are found in the marketplace, but it is always problematical whether this material is suitable to the students in question. The materials are usually designed for students without major learning difficulties; there is no appropriate material for high-risk students. At all educational levels the available pedagogical materials are only in French. They do not last many years if the quality is poor. The frequent changes of programs and commercial interests are no doubt responsible for this situation.

FINANCING READING EDUCATION

In public primary schools, education is free. The government finances personnel costs whereas the municipalities finance the physical plant. The parents are expected to pay only for some mandatory school materials. Their participation is more and more important, however, as the student progresses in the schooling process.

In private primary schools under contract with the government, the schools receive a subsidy from the Ministry of Education. In addition, the parents pay part of their children's school fees. These schools provide the same programs as the Ministry of Education and submit to control just as the public schools do.

In private schools that are not under contract with the government, the parents pay all their children's school fees; the amount of these fees varies from school to school.

At the junior high school and high school level, teachers' salaries are also paid by the government, but the school buildings are the responsibility of the local communities.

The great majority of France's universities are under state control; therefore, they receive government subsidies. Education is free, but each student does pay an enrollment fee, which is relatively low.

The few religious universities that exist in France are supported by student fees.

THE FOCUS OF RESEARCH IN READING EDUCATION

Research on reading education essentially rests on the following issues: school failure; the teaching and learning process in reading and writing; the opposition between code and meaning; the role of orality and phonological coding; the study of recitation; reading and the deaf student; learning difficulties; the role of the family; motion of the head and eyes; and official evaluation of the results.

OVERVIEW OF READING EDUCATION IN FRANCE

The French education system is largely traditional, but the debate over reading education in the last ten years has led to unquestionable modifications in teaching methods.

CONCLUSIONS

In France, reading education is not considered a specific area, but it is taken into account in the overall educational process. The problem of reading education in France is not serious. Illiteracy has almost disappeared; only functional illiteracy is a big concern.

The research on kindergarten shows that children have greater success in primary school education when they complete the kindergarten activities. This has a positive effect for French students because the great majority of children in France go to school at an early age.

Primary and secondary education is satisfactory for all groups except the slow learners who all the same are able to learn the minimum necessary for everyday life.

Going to junior high school and high school improves the educational level with respect to what was the case a few years ago. According to Baudelot and Establet (1988), the educational level is increasing in France.

REFERENCES

Aubret, J. 1983. Differences individuelles et compréhension du language, *L'Orientation Scolaire et Professionnelle*12 (no.4):283–304.

Baudelot C., and Establet, R. 1988. *Le niveau intellectuel des conscrits ne cesse de s'élever*. Education et Formation.

Chartier, R. (ed.). 1985. *Practiques de la lecture*. Paris: Rivages.

Chauveau, G., and Rogovas-Chauveau, E. 1984. Lire en famille des familles immigrées et l'apprentissage de la lecture. In CRESAS, *Ouvertures: L'école, la crèche, la famille*. Paris: L'Harmattan–INRP, p. 3.

Chevenement, J. P. 1985. *Ecole Elémentaire. Programmes et Intructions*. Ministère de l'Education nationale, CNDP.

Downing, J., and Fijalkow, J. 1984. *Lire et raisonner*. Toulouse: Privat.

Dumazedier, J., and De Gisors, H. 1984. Français analphabètes ou illettrés? *Revue Française de Pèdagogie*:69.

Esperandieu, V., Lion, A., and Benichou, J. P. 1984. *Des illettrés en France*. Paris: Documentation Française.

Fijalkow, J. 1986. *Mauvais lecteurs, porquoi?* Paris: PUF.

Fijalkow, J. 1987. Le rôle des interactions sociales dans apprentissage de la lecture. *Cahiers Pédagogiques* (May-June): 254–255.

Fijalkow, J. 1989a. Dé-lire pour apprendre à lire. *Pour* 120:89–98.

Fijalkow, E. 1989b. Difficultés et stratégies pour entrer dans l'écrit. *Pour* 120: 99–104.

Fijalkow, E., and Liva, A. 1988. Auto-langage et apprentissage de la langue écrite chez les enfants sourds et entendants. *Bulletin d'Audiophonologie* 4–5:434–442.

Furet, F., and Ouzouf, Y. 1977. *Lire et Ecrire*. Paris: Ed. de Minuit, 2 vols.

Herber-Suffrin, C. and M. 1981. *L'école éclatée*. Paris: Stock.

Inizan, A. 1963. *Le temps d'apprendre à lire*. Armand Colin.

Jolibert, J. 1984. *Former des enfants lecteurs*. Paris: Hachette.

Lefavrais, P. 1967. *Test de l'Alouette*. Ed. Centre de Psychologie Appliquée.

Ministère de l'Education nationale. 1988. *Repères et Références Statistiques, sur les enseignements et la formation*. Direction de l'évaluation et prospective.

Poulain, M. 1988. *Pour une sociologie de la lecture*. Paris: Cercle de la librairie.

Preteur, Y., and Fijalkow, J. 1987. Etude différentielle de la lecture et de mathématiques au Cours Préparatoire. *Revue Française de Pédagogie* 79:35–49.

Pynte, J. 1983. *Lire . . . identifier, comprendre*. Lille Presses Universitaires de Lille.

Rossi, J. P. 1985. *Les mécanismes de la lecture*. Paris: Publications de la Sorbonne.

Sprenger-Charolles, L. 1989. L'apprentissage de la lecture et ses difficultés: approaches psycho-linguistiques. *Revue Française de Pédagogie* 87 (April-May-June): 77–106.

Zazzo, R. 1954. Contribution à la psychologie différentielle des sexes au niveau préscolaire. *Enfance* 1 (repris in R. Zazzo, *Conduites et Conscience*, T. I., Paris Delachaux et Niestlé, 1962, 207–221).

8

Iran

Nouchine Ansari and Touran Mirhady

INTRODUCTION

Iran is located in southwest Asia. Its neighbors are the Soviet Union to the north; Afghanistan and Pakistan to the east; beyond the Persian Gulf, Aman, the United Arab Emirates, Saudi Arabia, and Kuwait to the south; and Iraq and Turkey to the west.

The area of Iran is 1,640,000 square kilometers, one-third of which is desert. Most of the population lives on the plains, in rural areas, on the border of the Caspian Sea, and in the industrial centers. Iran has large oil and gas resources. It also has important copper, iron ore, and gold mines.

The majority of the population works in agriculture. Industry, however, also began to develop at the beginning of this century. The population is more than 50 million, about 50 percent of whom are under eighteen years of age. Although the majority of the population are Muslims and Shi'a, there are also Sunnis, particularly in the west of the country. The country also has Zoroastrian, Christian, and Jewish minorities. In 1979 Iran became an Islamic Republic. The constitution and other legislation are based on Islamic precepts. The country is led by the Vali-Fagih, who is selected by a group of religious leaders. The president of the country and members of the Parliament are elected every four years.

LANGUAGE

Iran has a long history and culture, which can be traced back 7,000 years. Written evidence in this area goes back 3,000 years. Ancient Iranians wrote in cuneiform, Avestan, and Aramaic scripts. In ancient times, only religious leaders, scribes, princes, and nobles learned to read and write. A considerable body of literature was produced, the most important of which are the teachings of Zoroaster.

After the coming of Islam more of the common population began to read and write. During the seventh and eighth centuries, the Arabic language and writing was introduced in the country, and as it was the language of the Holy Quran and the lingua franca of the Islamic world many scholars wrote their works in Arabic. With the rise of local governments, the Dari language, which was used mainly in eastern Iran, became the spoken and literary language of the country. It became known as Farsi (Persian). It should be noted that the same language is also used in Tajikistan and Afghanistan. An outstanding body of literature including prose and poetry has been produced in the Persian language. To this day, Iranians can read and enjoy works written more than 1,000 years ago. Finally, despite the fact that many Arabic words have entered the Persian language, they have adapted to Persian grammar and syntax.

Persian is the official and common language of the country and is spoken by the majority of the people. Education from the preschool to the university level is conducted in Persian. Textbooks, almost all radio and television broadcasting, newspapers, magazines—except for a very few—and the bulk of the literary, scientific, and artistic publications of the country are in Persian.

Besides Persian, Azari Turkish, Kurdish, and Baloochi are spoken in various areas of the country. Although there are areas of special concentration, language moves with the population, and thus they have spread and are spoken all over the country. There is, however, no formal education, and these languages are learned orally as mother tongues. Authors in these languages publish their works using the Persian script.

The Assyrians, Armenians, and Jews who live in Iran use their own language and writing. They have special schools, where, in addition to Persian, they teach their own languages.

READING INSTRUCTION POLICY

Iran has a centralized educational system. The Ministry of Education is responsible for the comprehensive organization and administration of the system, overseeing goal setting, curriculum development, textbooks, supplementary reading publications, teacher employment and education, and school administration at all levels. This ministry is the largest in the country. The supervision of the literacy movement, minority schools, private technical schools, and kindergartens which are sponsored privately is also among one of the ministry's responsibilities.

Education is free in Iran according to Article 31 of the constitution. The parent-teacher organizations of the schools are permitted to seek financial and professional help from the parents. These funds may be used for new buildings, restoration, new equipment, laboratories, libraries, and so forth. These contributions were a great help during Iran's war with Iraq (1981–1988).

Recently, legislation for the establishment of nonprofit private schools has been ratified. The parents will provide the budget of these schools.

The educational system is divided into two parts: general and secondary. The general part is subdivided into two sections: primary (five years) and guidance (three years). Since 1963, the addition of a preschool year has been proposed, but has not found wide implementation. Only about 5 percent of the children attend preschool classes. The secondary part is divided into the theoretical, and the service and technical branches, each of which lasts four years.

Under the Islamic Republic, a new educational system was proposed in 1988. This system includes the general part (nine years) divided into three levels: (1) "Base" (*Asas*) for ages six to seven; (2) "Foundation" (*Arkan*) for ages eight to eleven; and (3) "Guidance" (*Irshad*) for ages twelve to fourteen. There is also the theoretical or practical level for ages fifteen to seventeen. At present, preparations for executing the new system are underway. As a whole, the new system is greatly influenced by the educational tenets of Islam and the place of man in Islamic thinking; priority is given to religious and moral education.

THE GOALS OF READING INSTRUCTION

The goals of teaching reading are stressed in a general way in two sections of the proposed system [*Educational System of Iran* (ESI) General Goals, pp. 46–47], namely, in Section C, the educational and scientific goals, and in Section D, on cultural and artistic goals.

Section C: Educational and Scientific Goals

Part 4: The provision of education for every citizen and the eradication of illiteracy.

Part 5: Teaching of the Persian language and writing as the official and common spoken and written language of the people of Iran. Also the teaching of the Arabic language in order to read the Holy *Quran*, [and] other Islamic works and to facilitate the relationship with other Islamic countries.

Section D: Cultural and Artistic Goals

Part 4: Knowledge and transmission of Persian literature as a source of artistic creation and national and social unity of the country.

Part 6: Knowledge of the history, culture and civilization of Islam, Iran and other countries.

These general goals are turned into working objectives at the different levels of education as follows:

Base (ages 6–7)

Part 10:   Stimulating interest for the acquisition of
                                      knowledge.

Part 11:   Stimulating interest in learning the habit of using
                                   books.

Part 13:   Recognizing the difficulties of the child due to
                                   different mother tongues, dialects and its basic
                                   vocabulary, the correct teaching of the Persian
                                   language so as to facilitate communication, and the
                                   acquisition of needed information.

Part 14:   Teaching of phonetics, the alphabet and the signs
                                   of the Persian language and their use in writing and
                                   reading.

Part 18:   Stressing the basic skills for reading, writing,
                                   talking, and listening in order to develop thinking
                                   and social understanding. (ESI, General Education,
                                   pp. 87–88)

Foundation (ages 8–11)

Part 6:   Development of literacy for independent use of
                                   commonly used written sources.

Part 7:   Development of the Persian language and the
                                   advancement of the ability to read and write, so as
                                   to be able to express daily needs in simple style,
                                   correct writing, using readable and beautiful
                                   handwriting. (ESI, General Education, p. 90)

Guidance (ages 12–14)

Part 8:   Strengthening Persian literature, teaching correct
                                   reading methods and the further development of the
                                   previous parts. The teaching of the Arabic
                                   language with special attention to the better
                                   understanding of the Holy *Quran* and *Hadith*
                                   [sayings and deeds of the Holy Prophet
                                   Muhammad and his family] starts at this time. Also
                                   the teaching of foreign languages is to start at this
                                   stage. (ESI, General Education, p. 93)

Theoretical and Practical Level
(ages 15–17)

Part 8:   Developing Persian language and literature and the
                                   Arabic language. Introductory knowledge of a
                                   foreign language in order to be able to read and
                                   understand common, simple texts, basic knowledge
                                   of the grammatical rules in order to facilitate the
                                   use of foreign language texts in advanced studies.
                                   (ESI, Secondary level, p. 113)

These goals, especially with regard to reading, are the same for boys and
girls. A closer look at the ESI, however, reveals that special attention is paid

to education for girls and women. Items 18, 35, 38, 52, 53, and 54 of the ESI refer, respectively, to the Islamic identity of women, educational guidance for girls, strengthening political and social knowledge and self-reliance among girls, paying attention to the differences between girls and boys, solving educational barriers, and providing means especially for the education of girls and of married women.

Only 20 percent of students in the last year of high school are girls, and at present in many professions, especially in the medical field and in education, there is a great need for women. The reason for this attention therefore becomes clear.

Detailed planning for each course at each level is now underway. The contents of school texts have been gradually changed toward the new system during recent years. Hence, it is possible to consider the following aims for reading education at the primary, guidance, and secondary levels.

Primary Level

The aims of primary education are to achieve an ability for reading and understanding newspapers, magazines, and books appropriate to students' knowledge; to develop the ability to read materials and to find out new meanings; to promote the ability to read silently and aloud, cutting and joining words, to read well and without fear among others; to achieve the skill of reading to gain information; to enjoy reading and to get used to reading as a leisure-time activity; to read with purpose and aim; to recognize and appreciate writers and their contribution to learning; and to develop thought, imagination, argumentation, and judgment.

Guidance Level

The objectives of the guidance level are to achieve the skill of reading and understanding simple texts independently; to promote the ability to use newspapers, magazines, letters, circulars, advertisements, simple books, and works pertaining to their employment; and to become acquainted with selected literary classics and contemporary works in both prose and poetry, so as to develop taste and feeling and to create cultural unity with the rich and brilliant Persian literary heritage.

Secondary Level

Students at the secondary school level are encouraged to learn the Persian language in order to express desires, thoughts, and sentiments in a logical, ordered, eloquent way; to achieve skills in reading, writing and note making, summarizing, reporting, speech making and letter writing, and so on; to develop argumentation skills and judgments as to what is true and what is false; to read selected works by classical and contemporary Iranian authors, and become acquainted with famous authors and poets from other countries through the translations of their works, not only to learn literary techniques, but also to relate to the literary heritage of humankind; to develop literary and artistic talents; and to prepare for further studies at the university and continued reading for research in various fields.

In order to achieve these goals, special attention is paid to cultural and spiritual values, civilization and culture throughout the world, international understanding, respect for the law, desire for social life, and mutual cooperation.

The aims of adult reading and adult education are the same as those listed above for the primary level.

ILLITERACY

Literacy, meaning the skill to read, write, make use of written materials, and communicate through writing, was not available to the majority of the people of Iran during many centuries of despotic rule. At the beginning of the twentieth century, the majority of the country was illiterate, with no means for education. Concerted efforts during the past decades have produced considerable changes. According to 1986 statistics (see Table 8.1), 61.9 percent of the population above the age of six are now literate. Literacy among women is 51.9 percent and among men 71.4 percent. These data (see Table 8.2) derive from the Statistical Center of Iran, the Ministry of Planning and Budgeting, and the Adult Literacy Organization.

General education takes eight years to complete in Iran, but the majority of Iranian children remain at school for only the first five years, that is, at the primary level.

Tables 8.3 and 8.4 present data on many of the problems that existed at the various educational levels during the past fifteen years. One reason why the illiteracy rate is so high in the country is the fact that not all school-age children (who by law have to attend school) are able to do so (see Tables 8.5 and 8.6). Since the population of Iran is growing at the rate of 3.72 percent annually, the problem needs to be considered in two respects: (1) Providing the means so that all school-aged children can attend school; and (2) making the duration of school education as long as possible for each child.

Before considering the reading problem in Iran, it is necessary to describe the construction of the Persian alphabet and the various methods of teaching reading. The Arabic script is used for reading and writing the Persian language. However, over the centuries the form of the Arabic letters has changed. At the present two main scripts, namely, Naskh (print) and Nastaliq (manuscript), and a special form called Shekastah (broken) are used in writing Persian. Loan words from Arabic have created a situation in which two different letters are used for very similar sounds. It should also be mentioned that Persian is written from right to left.

Table 8.1

Literate Population Over the Age of 6, According to Sex and Age (1976 & 1986)

SEX AND AGE	1976 Census			1986 Census		
	POPULATION	LITERATE	% OF LITERATE POPULATION	POPULATION	LITERATE	% OF LITERATE POPULATION
Male & Female	27112844	12877075	47.5	38872394	24054306	61.9
6-9	4110345	2942993	71.6	5846420	4846719	82.9
10-14	4303118	3184389	74.0	5965334	5086773	85.3
15-19	2600265	2195979	61.0	5226917	4111254	78.7
20-24	2792215	1392727	49.9	4214309	3007990	71.4
25-29	2111885	880752	41.7	3658969	2229555	60.9
30-34	1706997	597601	35.0	2919415	1565168	53.6
35-39	1626619	459256	28.2	2120487	965549	45.5
40-44	1668685	370807	22.2	1667006	642045	38.5
45-49	1389465	284198	20.5	1593364	476411	29.9
50-54	1329049	344215	18.4	1596700	378455	23.7
55-59	703887	128975	18.3	1353379	291796	21.6
60-64	584144	75214	12.9	1185640	225184	19.0
65 & more	1186470	119969	10.1	1493536	216649	14.5
unknown	0	0	0	30918	10758	24.8
male	13925591	81979987	58.9	19916241	14213684	71.4
6-9	2129177	1727023	81.1	3000436	2648081	88.3
10-14	2258635	1937445	85.8	3086352	2821180	91.4
15-19	1818539	1347985	74.1	2693040	2336182	86.7
20-24	1340858	880277	65.7	2135647	1760798	82.4
25-29	1010195	581441	57.6	1836308	1356995	73.9
30-34	842453	415912	49.4	1466893	998292	68.1
35-39	825340	338307	41.0	1052256	646548	61.4
40-44	895201	287529	32.1	840201	442606	52.7
45-49	751026	218747	29.1	828350	348986	42.1
50-54	731673	196198	26.8	856698	286633	3.5
55-59	396705	105133	26.5	700981	217320	31.0
60-64	301402	61563	20.4	648777	175997	17.1
65 & more	624387	100427	16.1	751866	167190	22.2
unknown	0	0	0	18438	6876	37.3
female	13187253	4679088	35.5	18956153	9840622	51.9
6-9	1981163	1215970	61.4	2845984	2198638	77.3
10-14	2044483	1246944	61.0	2878982	2265593	78.7
15-19	1781726	847994	47.6	2533877	1775072	70.1
20-24	1451357	512450	35.3	2078662	1247192	60.0
25-29	1101390	299311	27.2	1822661	872560	47.9
30-34	864544	181689	21.0	1452522	566876	29.0
35-39	801279	120949	15.1	1068231	319001	29.9
40-44	773484	83278	10.8	826805	199439	24.1
45-49	638439	65451	10.3	7650140	127425	16.7
50-54	597376	48017	8.0	740002	91822	12.4
55-59	307182	23842	7.8	652398	74476	11.4
60-64	282742	13651	4.8	536863	49187	9.2
65 & more	562083	19542	3.5	741672	49459	6.7
unknown	0	0	0	12480	3882	21.1

Source: Statistical Yearbook 1986:98.

Table 8.2
Literate Population Over the Age of 6, According to Sex and Area (per 1,000)

Area	1976 Census			1986 Census		
	Population Above 6	Literate	% of Literate Population	Population Above 6	Literate	% of Literate Population
TOTAL OF THE COUNTRY						
Men & Women	27113	12877	47.5	38872	24054	61.9
Men	13926	8198	58.9	19916	14214	71.4
Women	12187	4679	35.5	18956	9841	51.9
URBAN AREAS						
Men & Women	13183	8628	65.4	21327	15593	73.1
Men	6919	5145	74.4	10989	8852	80.6
Women	6263	3483	55.6	10338	6741	65.2
RURAL AREAS						
Men & Women	13930	4249	30.5	17545	8462	48.2
Men	7006	3053	43.6	8927	5362	60.1
Women	6924	1196	17.3	8618	3100	36.0

Source: Statistical Yearbook 1986:97.

The differences in pronunciation which exist in the Arabic letters have been lost in the Persian pronunciation. In the Persian alphabet three vowels are written and three vowels are not written. At the early stage of teaching, the vowels that are not written are placed as signs above or below the words. Toward the end of the first year of primary school when the child has more or less learned the form of the words, these vowel signs are omitted.

In the Persian alphabet, there are no capital and small letters. The form of some of the letters differs when placed at the beginning, the middle, or at the end of a word. As a result, *mixed* methods are used to teach reading. One is based on sounds or the phonetic method, and the other is based on form or word reading, which is more or less the global method. That is, the reader must

Table 8.3
School Dropouts, Iran, 1966–1984

School Year	Per 1000	Students at 1st Grade			Students at the 1st Year of Guidance School			Students at the 1st Year of Secondary School			Students at the Fourth (Last) Year of Secondary School		
		Total	Boys	Girls	Total	Boys	Girls	Total	Boys	Girls	Total	Boys	Girls
1983–84		1651118	903295	747823	871188	537474	233714	298219	170130	128089	187019	103111	83908
1982–83		1607671	892617	715054	769935	481039	288896	279577	155764	123813	194499	107318	87181
1981–82		1522953	868823	654130	744565	466248	278317	246182	133927	112255	194598	110076	84522
1980–81		1383770	804181	579589	682597	423430	259167	239892	137298	102594	204640	121042	83598
1979–80		1260457	835246	525211	616585	383609	232976	303845	185347	118498	192799	114627	78172
1978–79		1333225	794552	538673	708422	449359	259063	312147	185407	126740	144251	109206	75045
1977–78		1238002	733550	504452	622864	399829	223035	262909	154596	108313	147022	87110	59912
1976–77		1292451	755526	536925	579539	370200	209239	255698	147516	108182	69050	34419	28631
1975–76		1245995	727111	518884	541015	347435	193580	253040	149343	103697			
1974–75		1205540	700599	504941	501538	322852	178686	251767	152206	99561			
1973–74		1176895	704769	472126	474792	306244	168548	149331	85824	63507			
1972–		971250	618130	353120	411123	268542	142581						
1971–72	1136	891561	562848	328713	371699	240793	130906						
1970–71	1231	821985	525454	296531	259218	161751	97467						
1969–70	1189	795384	510622	284762									
1968–69	1091												
1967–68	1037												
1966–67													

Source: ESI, p. 23.

Table 8.4
Birth Rate in Iran, by Sex, 1968–1972 (per 1,000)

Year	Total	Men	Women
1968	1037	529	508
1969	1091	550	541
1970	1189	610	579
1971	1231	636	595
1972	1139	584	552

Source: ESI, p. 23.

Table 8.5
"Real" School Coverage in the 1986 School Year (per 1,000)

AGE GROUP	POPULATION IN NEED OF EDUCATION			POPULATION AT SCHOOL			% OF POPULATION AT SCHOOL		
	town	village	total	town	village	total	town	village	total
Primary	3563	3603	7166	2974	2588	5562	84.4	72.2	78.2
Guidance	1753	1805	3558	484	564	1048	27.6	31.3	29.4
Total	5316	5408	10724	3458	3152	6610	65.1	58.3	61.6

Source: ESI, p. 104.

Table 8.6
"Seeming" School Coverage in the 1986 School Year (per 1,000)

AGE GROUP	POPULATION IN NEED OF SCHOOLING			POPULATION AT SCHOOL			% OF EXTENDED COVERAGE		
	town	village	total	town	village	total	town	village	total
Primary	3564	3603	7166	3601	3632	7233	101.1	100.1	100.9
Guidance	1753	1805	3558	1584	715	2299	90.4	39.6	64.6
Total	5317	5408	10724	5185	4347	9532	97.5	80.4	88.9

Source: ESI, p. 104.

perceive the image or word in the mind in order that the word can be correctly pronounced without the use of the vowel signs.

Over the years, four methods of reading and writing have been used in Iran:

1. The traditional or the analytic method. In this method the complete alphabet with their three forms (beginning, middle, and end) are taught first. Then attention is paid to composition and word teaching. This method was used for centuries.
2. The syllabic method. In this method each letter is combined with six sounds. Word teaching is based on the combination of the syllables.
3. The global method. This method was used for a short period during 1957–1960. At first, the child learned about twenty-five words in their complete form. Then these words were analyzed into syllables and sounds, and in this way the child became familiar with the letters. This method was not used properly; it encouraged memory reading among the first grade children, causing difficulties for some of them for many years.
4. The mixed synthetic-analytic method. In this method the student is first exposed to the complete form of the word, and at the same time the word is analyzed into syllables and sounds. The letters of each syllable are taught, and the student is encouraged to construct new words with these letters.

Constant practice in analysis and synthesis which is practiced in the "mixed" method enables the first graders to achieve a relatively high skill in reading within the first six months, so that they read simple books independently. The difficulty begins when they are confronted with very similar looking letters, various letters for the same sound, and different forms of a letter. Problems are also encountered when the vowel signs are no longer used.

The mixed method, which was first developed by the late J. Baghcheban some sixty years ago, is used in the first grade and in the adult education textbooks throughout the country. In order to facilitate the process, Professor Houshiyar of the University of Tehran established a baseline which helps the child to decide about joining the letters.

The analytical and syllabic methods are still used to teach reading in the villages and at some institutions.

READING DISABILITIES

Reading disability differs at various educational levels. At the primary school level it appears mostly as the inability to distinguish letters and sounds; this memory reading results in the failure to read new words. At the guidance stage students have difficulty reading words in sentences correctly, as well as in reading interrogatory, exclamatory, and imperative sentences. Classical texts, either prose or poetry, are read with difficulty. Furthermore, substantives, adjectives, and genitive cases are not clearly distinguished. Difficulties are also perceived in understanding what is read.

The weaknesses at the secondary level are mainly in the pronunciation of literary words, reading techniques for different subjects, reading composite sentences, and understanding metaphors and other literary techniques. There are several reasons for these weaknesses, the most important of which are as follows:

1. As mentioned before, the construction of the Persian alphabet, the resemblance of several letters to each other, the use of several letters for a similar sound, and the resemblance of some words to each other causes difficulties in reading, especially at the primary school level. The difference between the spoken and the written language used in school texts slows down the reading process to a certain extent. In the spoken language, words are pronounced in a different way (*Shekastah*) and their pronunciation differs in the various parts of the country.

2. The same books and educational materials are used all over the country; this uniformity results in too little stimulation. During the past ten years the language of the school texts has become more difficult, and not enough attention has been given to the needs of the users as regards both content and language. Abstract concepts and difficult literary words diminish the reader's interest.

3. Teachers at all educational levels lack the necessary skills. With tremendously rapid growth of general education in the country, the Ministry of Education has had to hire many untrained teachers. These people, all of whom hold the high school diploma, are thought to be able to read and write Persian and to teach it. This is not the case, however, and has a negative effect on the teaching of reading skills.

4. Special characteristics of the children, including fear, shyness, stress, speech disorders, and a resistance to learning, also retard the reading process. Diagnostic methods are available only for exceptional children such as the blind, the partially sighted, the deaf, the mentally retarded, and the very brilliant. Such cases are discovered through class evaluations, trimestrial examinations, and student homework. The main methods used to help the students are as follows: practice in order to increase concentration and attention while reading; teaching sounds and words in different ways using a variety of equipment and various practical works; independent work with different words; independent and solo reading; use of simple texts for silent reading; practice of word comprehension in the sentence and then in the paragraph; encouragement of free reading; provision of "new word" lists, simple books, and various magazines available for these age groups, for example, the magazine *Rushd* which appears for the primary, guidance, and secondary levels; assignments on writers and poets; the use of plays and creative drama for strengthening oral speech based on reading; and so on.

Many teachers and specialists have recommended that the Institute for Research and Educational Planning use new criteria in text selection, so that textbooks may relate more meaningfully to the interest and ability of children and young adults.

READING READINESS

According to 1988 statistics, the number of preschool children (under six years of age) totals more than 11 million. Nurseries, kindergartens, and preschool classes (for five and six year olds) are available for this age group. Some nurseries and kindergartens are private, and others are government run. They are located mainly in residential areas, in government institutions, and in industrial sectors. They are supervised by the three Ministries of Welfare, Labor, and Education. The majority of the preschool classes are supervised by the Ministry of Education. Less than 5 percent of the children attend such institutions, and of this number only 0.5 percent are from rural areas. The preschool training of the majority of children is still limited to the family and the media such as radio and television.

Preparing the children for reading and writing takes place in the preschool classes and during the first months of the first grade. During this period attempts are made to create a conducive environment, so that the children feel secure and peaceful, join their peers in playing at various activities, and use their mental and bodily strength in many different ways. Here the children become accustomed to correct sitting and rising, order, proper speaking time, finishing sentences, listening with attention, and recognizing and respecting the rights of others. The children also come into contact with both their natural and social environment and are thus able to experiment and discover. Their vocabulary increases, they listen to stories, they do picture reading, and they learn to speak correctly. Their hands become strong enough to hold a pencil and to do simple practices. At this stage children become acquainted with the various sounds at the beginning and end of words. They do so by using picture plates and illustrations, educational, and other picture books.

The preschool class provides teachers the opportunity to discover sight, hearing, and mental weaknesses in the children and to discuss such problems with the parents in order to provide the necessary care or to guide them to special institutions for exceptional children. For blind children attempts are made to strengthen their sense of touch since they will use books in Braille at school. It should be noted that all textbooks are available in Braille.

For the deaf, the preschool year provides the occasion to get acquainted with lip-reading. The deaf are also taught to speak. All the exercises are done through lip-reading; sign language is not used.

For the mentally retarded, instead of the twelve plates used for the ordinary first grade, fifty plates are used, which prepare these children step by step and provide many exercises for reading and writing. Plates begin with physical exercises, and then through stories and strengthening observation, they gradually get to sounds and letters. Each plate is accompanied by an exercise plate.

In this area there is no difference in the programs for boys and girls, or between urban and rural areas. It should be mentioned, however, that preschool education is possible for very few rural children.

The children's programs on radio and television are broadcast nationally and are of relatively high quality, varied, and related to the needs and abilities of the different age groups. These programs are effective for all ages, but especially at the preschool level. Through other media programs as well as by publishing books and articles, attempts are made to reach parents and to guide them as to how they can help their children read. In some cases families have been able to achieve reading and writing skills at the age of four.

TEACHER QUALIFICATIONS

Teacher training in Iran is carried out in the following forms: (1) Child care courses as a four-year high school program, a program that stresses hygiene and child care for children under five with another four-year program underway to train preschool teachers; (2) teacher training centers, which have two-year programs for the primary and guidance levels; (3) rural teacher training institutes; (4) a teacher training university, which prepares high school teachers; and (5) faculties of education that offer programs in preschool education, guidance, and counseling, exceptional children, and other programs at various levels.

All these programs focus on the teaching of reading and writing, and teachers are more or less prepared in this respect. As an example, the education for reading at the teacher training centers is planned with the following objectives:

1. To make available as much information as possible so that student-teachers may become more widely read and self-reliant in reading.

2. To acquaint student-teachers with classical texts, so as to stimulate their interest and raise their reading level.

3. To teach writing style and punctuation.

4. To help the student-teachers increase their reading rate and understand what they read.

5. To encourage the use of speech and writing to the same degree.

6. To help student-teachers become skillful in oral communication.

7. To enable student-teachers to absorb information pertaining to their special area of studies, in order to be able to relate this information in a correct and simple form.

8. To teach student-teachers different ways to transfer knowledge.

All the students at these centers take a course on the "psychology of teaching to read." This course seeks to promote knowledge of teaching reading and writing; to develop different skills in reading Persian; and to solve problems connected with reading. This course contains the following topics: different methods of teaching reading and writing in the world and in Iran, with special reference to three methods, namely, the global, analytic, and mixed; the development of each of these methods; their relation to script and language; the theoretical and practical aspects of their use in Iran; pioneers in their use; practicing the mixed method (which is now used at the primary school); introduction to the other methods using the first grade textbook, other reading materials including the adult education textbooks, basic vocabularies, and so on; language teaching at the primary school level, including such topics as methods of developing speaking, listening and reading skills, vocabulary growth, remedial

Table 8.7
Total Number of Teachers, by Sex, 1989

Sex	Number
Men	302829
Women	261220
TOTAL	564049

Source: Ministry of Planning & Budget.

teaching, stuttering, dyslexia, slow reading, mental disorders, other reading disabilities; and a critical evaluation of the material presented in the course.

Besides this course, the teacher training centers have a special program for the training of Persian literature teachers. At the primary level all courses are taught by one teacher, but at the guidance level teachers teach their own special areas. At the secondary school level, the literature teachers hold a B.A. degree in Persian literature, and there is no difference between men and women. The total number of teachers at the different educational levels is shown in Table 8.7. The much greater number of male teachers is explained when we consider that the ratio of girls to boys fluctuates between one-third and one-half. This fact has also been taken into consideration in planning the ESI.

MATERIALS FOR READING EDUCATION

Textbooks are the main source for reading education at all levels. All the textbooks are prepared centrally by the Office of Research and Educational Planning at the Ministry of Education. The primary school textbook is printed through the Ministry of Education. The schools distribute these books throughout the country. Textbooks for the guidance and secondary school are printed by the Iran Printing and Publishing Company, which is a semigovernmental organization. Reading education is achieved not merely through Persian readers, but also all the texts in use such as those in Islamic cultural and religious studies, science, social science, and mathematics. These works enrich the students' reading skills and contribute to their interests, stimulation, and vocabulary growth. All classes, without exception, have a Persian language text that contains selected passages, words, and grammar. In the second year of the "culture and literature" program at the secondary school there are three books, in the third year five, and in the fourth year six, including a reading anthology, a literature of the Islamic Revolution of Iran, a history of Persian literature, a Persian grammar, Persian literary texts, and literary techniques.

All anthologies contain both classic and modern texts. In the selection of these texts, theosophy, religious aspects, and moral values are stressed. After each lesson new words, questions, exercises, and grammar are given. Whenever needed, information on the life of the author is added.

All the textbooks except those prepared for the teaching of foreign languages, such as English, French, and German, which are used from the second year of the guidance level, are in Persian. Textbooks for the teaching of Azari Turkish and Kurdish are also available. These are published by private publishers and are not used in the official educational system.

Different textbooks are used to teach reading in the adult education programs. Of the two textbooks used for this group, one teaches and the other develops reading and writing. After these books are completed, it is hoped that the young new literate can attend the fourth grade of the elementary school and that the adult new literate can pass the fifth year examination.

For the partially sighted, textbooks are printed in large letters. As mentioned before, all the school texts are also available in Braille as well as on tape.

Deaf children use the same general texts, but each class for the deaf has only eight students. In their education, special stress is put on lip-reading and talking.

For the mentally retarded children, the same textbooks are used as for the general population, but the teaching speed is greatly reduced and exercises are much increased.

Additional reading material is no doubt necessary to sustain and develop reading skills. Magazines play an important role in this respect. The Organization of Research and Educational Planning of the Ministry of Education (OREP) should be given great credit in these areas. OREP publishes the magazine *Rushd* (Growth) at four levels, giving courage from the first grade to the secondary school level. These attractive, well-designed magazines have an average circulation of 700,000. It is the best distributed reading material in Iran. The issues are sold at the minimal price of 15 Rials.

For the new adult literates a magazine called *Now Savad* (The New Literate) is published by the Astan-i Quds in Mashhad. Unfortunately, this magazine is poorly distributed.

Recently, the daily newspaper *Etelaat*, which is one of the highest circulation journals in the country, has begun to devote half a page every week to new literates.

Since the Islamic Revolution, many more books have been published for children. A considerable number of these books relate closely to the vocabulary used in the school textbooks. The Institute for the Intellectual Development of Children and Young Adults (established in 1966) has played a major role in publishing high-quality works at very low prices. The average circulation per title is 50,000. The Institute's series of prereading materials merits special attention.

Some private publishers produce alphabet learners and puzzles that facilitate reading. Alphabet musical tapes are also available.

Much remains to be done in the area of introducing and distributing reading material. Recently, the OREP established a three-level bookshop, called *Rushd*, in order to ensure better distribution of quality works for parents, teachers, and school libraries in Tehran, as well as the rest of the country. Bookshops for children were established in the 1960s.

The Children's Book Council of Iran (CBCI), founded in 1962, has been active in evaluating children's literature. The CBCI's book lists, evaluation criteria, seminars, and workshops have helped improve both the quality of publications and reading. The Association for Research in Education began its activities in 1977, and reading has been a main focal point of its seminars and exhibitions. A recent roundtable focused on "Reading Beyond School Texts: Ways and Methods of Habit Creating."

FINANCING READING EDUCATION

The budget for education is part of Iran's general budget based on taxes and government earnings. At present about 20 percent of the total budget is spent on education, but this is not enough to cover the Education Ministry's constantly growing needs. Separating the budget allocated to reading from the total budget of the Ministry of Education is very difficult. It can only be said that about 45 percent of the budget goes to primary education covering 9 million students, 30 percent is allocated to the guidance and secondary school programs, and 25 percent is used for other ministry expenditures. The Persian language courses, including reading, writing, and grammar, take up about one-fifth of the teaching hours at the primary level, one-sixth at the guidance level, and, with the exception of the culture and literature program, one-seventh of the teaching hours of the secondary level. Since the teaching of reading cannot be separated from other courses, it is not possible to calculate a separate budget for this activity.

READING RESEARCH

Iran has no large body of recent research on reading. What is available can be divided into the following categories: (1) Reading difficulties for those children whose mother tongue is not Persian. Among these the following can be noted: M. Muhiuddin, *The Effect of Turkish Speaking Parents on the Learning of Reading and Writing Among Their Children* (1973–1974); and M. Arefi, *A Comparative Study of Persian Comprehension Among the Bilingual Children in Urumia, Whose Mother Tongue is Turkish and Armenian* (1977). (2) Special issues in literacy and reading such as P. Sandi, *The Evaluation of the Ministry of Labor Literacy Programs* (1970); G. Shahab (Tabari), *Evaluation of the Teaching of Reading Among a Sample of 5th Grade Students in Tehran* (1976); and M. H. Dayani, *Three Formulas for Testing Texts for New Literates* (1988–). (3) Studies on reading interests. The following are master's dissertations submitted to the Department of Library and Information Science, University of Tehran: S. Katebi, *An Evaluation of Students' Reading Interest* (1972); F. Rezwani, *Reading Patterns and Interests Among Users of Public Libraries in Tehran* (1972); P. Bolourchi,

Reading Interest Among the Students of 10 Schools in Tehran (1973); and A. Ja-
farnejad, *Children and Young Adults' Views on the Criteria of a Good Book*
(1976).

THE FUTURE OUTLOOK

In spite of the considerable efforts being made to facilitate the teaching of
reading in Iran, much remains to be done in both quality and quantity. Finding
an effective method that relates well to the language and writing, and generalizing
it throughout the country, has been a very important achievement. Now it is
important to think seriously about the learning problems of those groups whose
mother tongue is not Persian. The Literary Movement Organization's attempt to
compile a textbook designed for use in Azarbaijan where Azari-Turkish is the
mother tongue not only merits attention, but can also be used more widely.

The teaching of literacy methods to all literates may be an effective means of
decreasing illiteracy. This approach is particularly important for those rural areas
that still lack schools and teachers.

Serious attention must be paid to the issue of reading at teacher training centers.
These student-teachers should be better equipped to develop reading skills and
to use various teaching methods. Other programs to be considered are the improvement of textbooks, the development of school libraries, and the production
and distribution of learning equipment and appropriate reading material. Radio
and television have prepared a variety of programs addressed mainly to urban
areas; it is important that special programs now be designed for rural areas as
well.

The various experiments carried out in Iran should be more widely used. For
example, the availability of one hour for free reading in the school program can
raise student interest in the development of reading.

Currently, about fifteen magazine titles are published for children and young
adults. Constant evaluation of these magazines and their wider distribution can
be important in the development of reading. It is also important to think about
the production of reading materials for new literates and all sorts of educational
materials for special groups.

Encouragement and funding for research on the teaching of reading in both
the universities and other research organizations will no doubt shed more light
on many of the present problems and will help the government make better plans
to develop reading skills at all levels.

REFERENCES

Anushihpur, A. 1986. *Guide for teaching Persian at the primary level.* Tehran.
Arbabi, Gh. 1982. *New method for teaching reading and writing.* Tehran.
Ardalan, F. 1963. *Reading in Iran.* Tehran.
Baghchiban, J. 1935. *Guide for teaching the alphabet.* N.P.

Baghchiban, J. 1948. *The alphabet*. Tehran.

Baghchiban, S., and L. Iman. 1962. *Guide for teaching the first grade text book*. Tehran.

Bihruz, Z. 1943. *Learning to read and to write in two weeks*. Tehran.

Burzui, F. 1967. *Guide for the Persian text book of the first grade*. Tehran.

Dayani, M. H. 1988–. *Three formulas for testing text readability for new literates*. Ahwaz.

Iman, L. 1961. *Guide for the teaching of the second grade text book*. Tehran.

Khaliqi, F. 1976. "Z. Bihruz's theories on learning and the natural alphabet." Master's dissertation.

Khanlari, P. 1964. *Linguistics and the Persian language*. Tehran.

Muhhiudin, M. 1973. "The effect of Turkish speaking parents on the learning of reading and writing among their children." Master's dissertation.

Nadiri, I. 1987. *Learning disabilities*. Tehran.

Nihzat Savad Amuzi. 1984. "Guide book for the adult education text book." Tehran.

Nizam, R. 1978. "Shemiran College test for identifying letters and numbers and reading readiness." Master's dissertation.

Omrani, N. 1989. *A bibliography on leisure*. Tehran.

Razmju, H. 1964. *Principles for teaching language and literature at the primary schools*. Mashhad.

Shahab, G. (Tabari). 1976. "Evaluation of reading in a sample of fifth grade students in Tehran." Master's dissertation.

Shakur, S. 1976. "The early stage in reading education." Master's dissertation.

9

Israel

Dina Feitelson

LANGUAGES OF INSTRUCTION

The land that is today Israel was for hundreds of years part of the Ottoman Empire and then, following World War I, for thirty years under British rule. Upon independence in 1948, Hebrew and Arabic became the two official languages of Israel. Both languages are used in everyday life, in street signs and in sessions of Parliament.

One of the first acts of the Parliament of the newly created state was to make nine years of schooling, including a year of kindergarten, in either Hebrew or Arabic, free and compulsory for all. An understanding of the way Hebrew-medium and Arabic-medium education developed is essential for an understanding of today's reading scene. Therefore, we will take a step back in time and review these developments before describing the situation today.

The Teachers Did It: The Revival of Hebrew

According to Fellman (1979), "the successful revival of the Hebrew language is a unique event in sociolinguistic history," for it is the only attested case wherein a language that had ceased to be spoken for nearly 2,000 years was brought back into everyday spoken usage. Hebrew was the language of the Jews in their homeland from about 1200 B.C.E. until the final conquest by the Romans in 70 A.D. After the conquest, the habit of speaking Hebrew in daily life rapidly died out and by about 200 A.D. had ceased altogether (Fellman, 1979). After that date Hebrew became a so-called dead language, although it continued to be used for prayer, correspondence, and the perusal of holy texts.

Hebrew was revived, not as a consequence of a concerted effort by a sovereign state, but rather as the result of the singlemindedness and dedication of a consumptive student and the small band of his followers. Like many before him, Eliezer Ben Jehuda believed that the survival of the Jewish people depended on their rejoining those of their brethren who had remained in their homeland despite foreign conquest. This he argued would not come about unless all Jewish inhabitants of the Holy Land would also adopt a common language, namely, Hebrew. Putting theory into practice, Ben Jehuda married and moved with his young bride, who did not speak any Hebrew, to Jerusalem, first informing her of his vow to speak only Hebrew from the moment of stepping ashore. It was a decision he duly carried out. The inception of Hebrew education is reckoned from the day in 1882 when, a few months after his arrival in Jerusalem, Ben Jehuda was invited to teach Hebrew in a local school. At that time the few existing secular schools belonged to various overseas philanthropic organizations. In each the language of instruction was that of the seat of the sponsors, in most cases French, German, or English. Hebrew was taught as a dead language in the general language of instruction, just as Greek or Latin in European schools of the day. Ben Jehuda introduced the teaching of ''Hebrew in Hebrew,'' thus pioneering the use of Hebrew in the classroom as a living language. Because of his illness, however, Ben Jehuda had to relinquish his position a few months after the seed had been sown. His replacement and teachers of Hebrew in other schools followed in his footsteps. Soon instruction in Hebrew was extended to other subjects as well, with Ben Jehuda once again paving the way by producing a Hebrew textbook of geography.

Further groups of university students, who had been inspired by Ben Jehuda's articles, rallied to his cause. Leaving their homes in Russia, they literally landed at his doorstep. From there they moved to newly established villages to set up schools in which Hebrew became the single medium of instruction. The personal journals which these pioneers left behind give a vivid picture of the nearly insurmountable difficulties they had to overcome. Lacking textbooks and suitable terminology, ''we were half-mute, stuttering, we spoke with our hands and eyes'' (Fellman, 1979, p. 51). Nonetheless, their students started to converse with each other in Hebrew and also introduced the use of Hebrew in their homes.

In 1913, barely thirty years after the young Ben Jehuda had first entered a classroom, the largest of the philanthropic organizations was about to open the first higher institute of technical learning in the country. Since German was the language of the exact sciences in those days, the sponsors decided that German would be the language of instruction in the new institute. In response, teachers, students, and parents throughout the country staged protest meetings, strikes, and walkouts. Moreover, the teachers and entire student body of the only existing teachers' college (which happened to belong to the same organization) abandoned the premises and set up a Hebrew institution in a private home across the street with no funds or backing (Fellman, 1979). Teachers in additional schools, run by overseas organizations, followed suit and started to use Hebrew for all subjects. Not only had Hebrew become the dominant language of instruction, but in the process the poor settlers in a new land had also assumed full financial and ideological responsibility for the education of their children.

Consequently, the British Mandatory Administration that was set up in the wake of World War I found a fully fledged independent Hebrew educational system extending from kindergarten to institutes of higher learning. However, many difficulties had yet to be overcome. For example, vocabulary suitable for modern needs had constantly to be created, and for lack of Hebrew textbooks teachers spent large portions of lessons dictating the contents of what had been learned to their students. Nevertheless, the dominance of Hebrew was never again in doubt.

Education in the British Period

During the thirty years of British rule two parallel school systems arose, each entirely independent of the other. One was the Hebrew school system which continued to expand rapidly. Financed by tuition and self-taxation, it provided nearly universal education. An especially noteworthy feature of this system was the great popularity of kindergartens, most of them private, that children usually attended from age three until they entered school at six. By enabling women to hold jobs, the kindergartens fulfilled an important social function. Yet their educational role was even more important. Operating within the context of an immigrant society with a great diversity of languages and lifestyles, they laid the foundations of a common culture and a shared language. Not only did they prepare their young students for school, but through them kindergartens also became instrumental in establishing Hebrew and local customs in children's homes and the wider community.

In comparison, the second system, the Arab school system, was far less developed. Under Turkish rule, only 8 percent of the Arab school-aged population had attended schools, most of which catered to the elementary level only. The schools that had existed were for the most part run by foreigners, and Arabic was not the main language of instruction. Because of the high tuition fees in most of the schools, the majority of students were male, as education for females was not considered important enough to warrant the expense.

The British administration tried to improve matters. Arguing that the Hebrew school system was self-sufficient, the Mandatory Education Department used its entire budget to set up a network of government Arab schools. Since they were starting from scratch, achievements were rather limited. Education was not compulsory, and in 360 out of a total of 1,000 existing villages there were no schools whatsoever. Furthermore, village schools were mostly nongraded, with only one to two classes, and did not go beyond fourth grade. Complete elementary schools existed only in towns and large villages. Secondary schools were located only in the main cities. Kindergartens, special schools, and any kind of auxiliary services did not exist at all. Schools of a somewhat better quality and most secondary schools belonged to overseas missionary orders, and at least part of the instruction was in a foreign language. Lacking adequately trained Arab educators, the Mandatory Education Department officials were mainly British. This situation created tensions and a general feeling that the educational system was not indigenous but imposed. Despite the forward strides made during the period of British Mandatory administration, education remained the privilege of the few. Toward the end of the Mandatory era, only 30 percent of the Arab school-age population attended schools.

The Situation since 1948

Statehood brought with it free schooling for everyone in either Hebrew or Arabic. Yet once again the accompanying problems were nearly insurmountable.

A network of Arab-medium schools had to be erected nearly from scratch. Not only was there a lack of adequate buildings, but worse still the country had to contend with a dearth of trained teachers and administrators. In the first year of statehood, 90 percent of all Arab teachers were unqualified. In-service training and the opening of an Arab teachers' training college slowly changed the situation. For many years Arab-medium schools were administered by a special department in the Ministry of Education. By now this department has been discontinued and both Arab- and Hebrew-medium schools are now administered jointly by local regional offices. A varying proportion of Arab children, mainly at the secondary level, attend Hebrew-medium or mixed schools. In a few larger cities schools belonging to overseas missionary orders, in which a European language predominates, continue to attract pupils.

Even though all Arab first graders have attended at least one year of kindergarten, they face a grave language problem upon starting to learn to read. In everyday life Arab children speak a local dialect of Arabic that has no written form. However, reading instruction is in classical Arabic that in vocabulary and in many other ways is entirely different. In practical terms this means that children learn to read a language they do not know and do not hear used except during certain lessons in school or, for those among them who are Muslim, in religious observance. In regular conversation both teachers and students use colloquial Arabic. Thus, throughout their entire school careers, comprehension of the texts they read serves as a major stumbling block for many students.

In addition, Arabic script is especially hard to learn. In Arabic most letters are combined even in print. In terms of European languages, this means that from the very beginning children read and write a cursive script. In addition, most Arab letters have four forms that are used according to the position of the letter in the word. The same letter will look different according to whether it is in the initial, middle, or final position in the word. A further difficulty is, that as a consequence of hundreds of years of cursive writing, by today differences among some of the consonant symbols have disappeared. For instance, the five consonants that approximate *b*, *j*, *n*, *t*, and *th* in the Latin alphabet all share the same letter symbol and are told apart only by so-called diacritical markings, in this case different numbers of dots above or below the letter symbol (,,,,). In addition, the three short vowels in Arabic are represented by marks above or below strings of connected consonants. These marks are omitted in everyday writing so that children do not see them in printed matter in their surroundings like newspapers, magazines, or books. When we take all this into account, we find it quite understandable that beginning reading is considered extremely difficult in Arab-medium schools.

Contrary to conditions in the Arab sector, at statehood Israel had a fully-developed, coordinated Hebrew educational system comprising two universities, several teacher training colleges, various kinds of secondary schools, elementary schools, special schools and institutions for the disabled, and an administrative body, that became the nucleus of the Ministry of Education. Kindergartens and preschools were privately owned or run by women's organizations. School attendance was nearly universal. However, the challenges (in themselves rather formidable, though considered feasible in the very first year of statehood) taken on by making nine years of education free and compulsory for all were soon to pale in comparison to what was to come.

Shortly after its inception, the new state was swamped by refugees. During the first three years of Israel's existence, the population doubled, and it doubled once again within the next fifteen years. Moreover, the problems created by the tremendous growth in population were compounded beyond imagination by the demographic characteristics of the majority of new immigrants. The refugees arrived mainly from Arab countries. As a result, a predominantly European-American, technologically highly developed society, changed in less than twenty years to a society in which the families of more than 65 percent of each year's first grade entrants originated from Near Eastern or North African countries. In addition to not knowing Hebrew, in most cases the mothers and most certainly the grandmothers of these first graders were illiterate in any language, while fathers had at best a few years of religious schooling. To try to understand the magnitude of the problems that the society as a whole, and the educational system in particular, faced, we would have to imagine that within three years the population of the United States would increase to 440 million, and within the next fifteen years to 880 million. Imagine further that the majority of new-comers would not only be not English speaking, but also very poorly educated or entirely illiterate in their various native tongues.

A lack of buildings that for years necessitated two-shift teaching; a shortage of teachers that made entire schools depend on newly called-up female soldiers who themselves had finished high school only a few weeks before; and lack of equipment so severe that as a young first grade teacher I had to punish children who used more than a single page for one day's drawing and writing by not allowing them to write the next day—these were thus only part of the picture. More alarming, and less amenable to solutions, were reports of widespread school failure, especially in reading, in a school system with especially high academic expectations, and where reading disabilities had been practically unknown before.

In a society with immigrants from 103 countries, speaking eighty-seven different languages, the fact that once again the number of non-Hebrew speakers actually exceeded that of Hebrew speakers did not threaten the predominance of Hebrew as the common unifying language. Nor did schools feel a need to provide special language tutoring for the new arrivals. As before, children picked up Hebrew in schools, kindergartens, and preschools by immersion and mainly through them the language also filtered to their elders. However, the mere fact of becoming conversant in Hebrew did not in itself catapult students to the level of school performance that had been the norm before mass immigration. To this day the so-called closing of the gap between school achievements of children of highly educated parents originating from developed countries and children from families with scant education originating from developing countries has remained a major challenge for the school system.

Second and Third Languages

During the British period, English was learned as a second language from the fifth grade onward in both Hebrew- and Arabic-medium schools. In addition, in several schools English was the main medium of instruction. English was used extensively in everyday life, and many high school pupils sat for the British matriculation examination in addition to, or instead of, the local high school final examination. This gave them access to universities throughout the British Commonwealth as well as to certain types of professional training and to government jobs. English was studied very intensively, especially at the secondary level, and was a mandatory subject in the local high school final examination. Expected achievements in English were rather high. In fact, the English high school finals included one Shakespearean drama and an extensive list of other literary pieces. During World War II a relatively large proportion of young people joined the British fighting forces, and this, along with the impact of the extensive army installations in the country, further extended the number of those who were very fluent in English, and the motivation of students to become likewise.

In Hebrew-medium schools students started a second foreign language in the ninth grade. According to personal choice, this was either French or classical Arabic. In the French, achievements were quite respectable, with students being able to converse and to peruse literary texts. In classical Arabic, on the other hand, results tended to be disappointing, as outside of class the students had no place to use their newly acquired knowledge.

With the end of British rule, the motivation to learn English and opportunities for its use initially diminished. The great number of students who had, first of all, to acquire Hebrew, and the acute shortage of teachers of English (who after all could not be replaced by untrained female soldiers) were all factors in the decision to reduce the number of years and hours per week of English study. Nowadays, when these difficulties have been largely overcome, the teaching of

English is back to its former status, at least quantity wise. However, the curriculum is somewhat less ambitious than it was in the past and focuses more on student needs and modern literature. Many of the English as second language teachers are native speakers of English, and professional standards are high. Teachers of English maintain organizations according to the level at which they teach, elementary, secondary, or university, publish an English language professional journal, and are internationally active. They have large annual conventions, and there are many in-service training opportunities.

Arabic is started much earlier than before and is compulsory for at least four years. In the sixth grade, children begin colloquial Arabic, and a year later they transfer to modern literary Arabic. Modern literary Arabic is the medium used in newspapers and in the media, and is somewhat different from classical Arabic. Some secondary schools have a strand where students in the tenth, eleventh, and twelfth grade can choose to specialize in Arabic and to take it in their finals.

Starting English in the fifth grade and literary Arabic two years later means that in each case students have to acquire a script that is entirely different from Hebrew. In addition, in other ways, and even in the direction of writing, English differs greatly from semitic languages. Learning English as a second language is thus much more difficult for an Israeli student than is the studying of French or Spanish for an English-speaking student.

In the Arab-medium schools English is the second foreign language. As a minority, children have a greater need for the majority language. Consequently, they start Hebrew in third grade. Depending on how much Hebrew they hear in daily life, many minority children in fact have a working knowledge of Hebrew long before they formally start Hebrew in school.

Arab-medium schools are part of the official educational system. Attendance in different language-medium schools in Israel is not strictly according to ethnic origin. In the past, when secondary Arab education was in its early stages, families tended to send their children to Hebrew-medium schools. With recent great strides in the development of Arab-medium education, this practice has become less common. On the other hand, in some localities there is a trend toward mixed education, and at the tertiary level Christian and Muslim Arabs as well as Druze and other minority groups both teach and study at the seven Hebrew-medium universities. Altogether minorities make up only about 16 percent of the population. In the following sections we drop distinctions between different language groups and discuss the educational scene in general.

READING POLICY AND INSTRUCTION

From its inception and during the first twenty years of statehood, Israel's educational system, including its reading instruction policies, was rather centralized. In the early 1970s the Ministry of Education reversed its policies regarding the respective roles of the main office located in Jerusalem in relation to the six regional ones. Since then the system has become increasingly decentralized, so that today it is almost totally decentralized. Both trends have directly affected reading instruction policies and processes.

The Early Years

In Israel all children attend at least one year of kindergarten, and most are in preschools from age three. Formal reading instruction does not begin until first grade, however.

The young pioneers who laid the foundations of the school system at the turn of the century had left their homes in Eastern Europe in order to set up a new way of life in a new country. Among the traditions they wanted to discard were the long hours of meaningless drill by which they themselves had been made to learn to decipher a dead language. Instead, they were attracted by the new educational theories, namely, the progressive movement as exemplified by the teachings of John Dewey. From this point on children and their own interests would become the focal point of instruction rather than the innate structure of subject matter. Consequently, the educators of the day turned to the incidental activity-experience approach already advocated by Edmund Burke Huey (1908– 1968) and used widely on the American educational scene. Like their American counterparts, they relied on reading matter developed cooperatively by teachers and their pupils on the blackboard or on charts. The preferred units of instruction were short sentences or phrases because they convey more meaning than single words. The teaching of phonics was approached in a somewhat different way than that used by American progressive educators at that time. A couple of days after phrases or short sentences were introduced, single words were extracted from them. From now on these words were used in new combinations. By the time fifty to about one hundred words had been learned in this fashion, teachers started to point out recurring syllables and letters in known words. By about the sixth or seventh month of instruction, children were able to decode texts, including words they had not seen before and words whose meaning they did not know. At this point the children would receive their first classroom reader at a special ceremony attended by their proud parents. In the book-centered culture of the times, this ceremony was in fact somewhat of a rite of passage—henceforth the child was considered a reader. Until then children did not use any commercial reading matter in class. In fact, none existed.

Until the 1950s this way of teaching beginning reading was practically the only one used. Considered highly successful, it was the single one taught in teachers' colleges, and it was required in all first grade readers submitted to the ministry for approval. Although teachers were free to choose the reader they wanted to use, and sometimes first grade teachers in the same school chose different ones, practically all first grade readers on the market closely resembled each other. In the months preceding the introduction of a reader, most teachers introduced the same topics in the same sequence, so that children all over the country sang the same songs and altogether had similar experiences concerning their initiation to school in general and to reading in particular.

An Unexpected Setback

With the advent of mass immigration from Arab countries, the reading situation experienced a completely unexpected setback. Initially, the refugees lived in extremely crowded conditions in huge tents or corrugated-iron-hut camps. Slowly they were resettled in permanent housing. But the reports of a failure rate of about 50 percent in first grade reading, which at first had been attributed to the deprived conditions and trauma suffered by the children, continued. Starting in the second grade, the Old Testament is a core subject; therefore, nonreaders could not be advanced to the second grade. In a school system suffering from a lack of buildings, equipment, and teachers, children could not be held back in first grade, which had formerly been a remedy for the small number of children who had not learned to read satisfactorily in their first year of school.

Within a very few years the problem of nonreaders in the school system became so widespread that the Ministry of Education took the unprecedented step of setting up independent teams of experienced first grade teachers and charged them with developing alternative approaches to first grade instruction. This decision was largely influenced by the results of a study that had investigated the factors that caused school failure.

Ten first grade classes, nine of them from schools in which failure was rampant, were studied intensively throughout the academic year. Children were tested at the beginning, during the course, and at the end of the year. Teachers and children were observed in classrooms, and all children's homes were visited. Teachers were interviewed repeatedly and at great length, and material covered in each class throughout the year was recorded (Feitelson, 1953).

The study resulted in a large number of findings and recommendations, but only those concerned with reading are discussed here. Contrary to expectations, failure and success were not evenly dispersed among the nine matched classes. Instead, the pattern was one of *whole classes* doing well or poorly. Thus, teachers' instructional practices rather than home variables or personal endowment emerged as the dominant factor in children's success or failure. It became apparent that the incidental look and say type of instruction was unsuitable for the idiosyncrasies of Hebrew orthography in which letter symbols resemble each other closely, vowels are mainly combinations of dots placed below consonants, verbs and nouns are conjugated, and a single dot can assume eight different vocal meanings. Teachers who had developed strategies focusing on these difficulties had been the successful ones. At this point the question became not so much what had caused failure in the wake of mass immigration from so-called developing countries, but rather how could a method imported from abroad, that disregarded the idiosyncrasies of the language in which reading was taught, have been successful for such a long period? Further investigation showed that highly motivated and knowledgeable parents had been able to augment school instruction by providing great amounts of additional home teaching that enabled children to overcome the disadvantages of an unsuitable teaching approach. Once the majority of students came from homes in which such help was unavailable, failure in beginning reading became a widespread phenomenon.

The independent teams that had been set up by the Ministry of Education and granted access to several schools each eventually produced four sets of structured instructional materials that closely resembled each other (Bloom, 1966). All of them considerably alleviated the burden on individual teachers by providing guidance and materials from the first day of school onward. The new materials spread very rapidly, so much so that within only four years of their introduction one or the other of the four programs was already in use in about one-half of all first grade classrooms throughout the country. Other educators and publishers followed suit. Today teachers can choose from among more than thirty-five different beginning reading programs, most of which resemble the four initial new programs in at least some aspects.

A survey conducted by the Ministry of Education in 1966 documented the great improvements that had occurred in the wake of the modified teaching approaches. According to the survey, "failure in technical reading, as described by researchers in the fifties, had been overcome" (Adiel, 1968). Once again all children were able to decode by the end of first grade. They progressed to an intensive study of the Old Testament, either in the original or in slightly modified versions, by their second year in school.

The Contemporary Scene

Immigration to Israel continues even if at a slower pace. As was the case before, a large percentage of immigrants come from geographical areas where educational standards are extremely low, for example, the famine-ridden regions of Ethiopia that may be familiar to present readers from the extensive television coverage in recent years. Absorbing children who do not know the language of instruction and whose parents cannot be of help to them thus remains a continuing task of the Israeli school system.

In the wake of developing effective beginners' programs, Israeli educators discovered that learning to decode does not in itself ensure success in coping with reading tasks at later stages of children's school careers. As in many other countries, and among them even countries like Finland where reading instruction is not considered a serious problem, children from nonschool-oriented families tend to fall behind in reading, and thereby in other school subjects as well from the third or fourth grade onward. In Israel children from these kinds of homes make up more than 65 percent of each year's entering first grade cohort.

On the whole, the Israeli school system has been astoundingly successful in coping with the problems inherent in absorbing extremely large numbers of newcomers lacking minimal prerequisites for success in a school system geared to a high level of expectations. Year by year 2 percent more of children whose parents originated from developing countries succeed in their final secondary school exams and make it to university. These children have made steady progress, and many of these former immigrants now hold high office, are members of Parliament and cabinet ministers, or even serve as chief of staff or deputy prime minister. Nonetheless, their numbers among university students is still not commensurate with their percentage in the population. Given the egalitarian outlook of Israeli society, educators, opinion leaders, and the general public consider the glass half empty rather than half full.

For the past decade the efforts of the reading establishment as well as the Ministry of Education were aimed at developing ways and means to increase children's reading comprehension at all grade levels. It is in this area that the great benefits of decentralization have been somewhat diluted by decentralization's accompanying problems. As we saw in relation to decoding, in a centralized school system geared to a population of only 4.5 million, successful practices can spread very rapidly without causing smothering uniformity. By the time fostering students' reading comprehension became a major priority, the school system had become decentralized, with maximal autonomy granted to each individual school. Consequently, principals soon found themselves bombarded by a multitude of different offerings, each promising to be the cure-all. Furthermore, the rate of adoption of these sometimes very expensive programs often depends on their public relations setups rather than on proven benefits.

The present scene is thus one of considerable confusion. On the one hand, school staffs are recurrently pressured by the demands of in-service training and special effort required in the early stages of setting up ever changing new programs. On the other, promising innovations and local initiatives have little chance to spread, so that, despite hectic activity by all concerned, general progress has been rather sporadic and slow.

THE GOALS OF READING EDUCATION

Already in the Quran the Israelites were called the People of the Book. Knowledge of the Old Testament by all was the expected norm even before the spread of literacy to the common people. To this end in ancient times the Holy Script was read aloud to the assembled crowds on the twice weekly market days. A very high level of erudition not only in the Old Testament but also in the commentaries that in time developed in connection with it, the Mishna and the Talmud, continued to be the coveted goal in European Jewish communities throughout centuries of dispersion and in the core of Jewish communities that remained in the Holy Land. With the advent of modern secular education, the basic assumptions of a uniformly high level of education for all were retained as a matter of course. Thus, the first two Hebrew language secondary schools, founded, respectively, in Jerusalem and Tel Aviv forty years before the state of

Israel came into being, were coeducational and had as their declared goal the preparation of their graduates for tertiary education.

Except in the frameworks of second language and adult education, the question of differentiated goals for reading education never really came up for discussion. The perhaps not quite realistic expectation throughout remained that every non-impaired student would reach the highest possible level of reading and after leaving school would engage in reading for pleasure and information.

The one further exception to this general rule are the numerically small, religiously ultra-orthodox Muslim and Jewish educational frameworks, in which boys usually receive a much more thorough grounding in religion than girls, and therefore achieve a higher level of fluency and understanding in dealing with difficult ancient texts. These institutions are not part of the public educational system, nor are they coeducational.

The goals of reading in second language education were never differentiated in terms of the sexes. Nor were they strictly in *second* language education; rather, they were more generally related to the specific role of English as the preferred foreign language during different periods in the development of the school system.

During the British Mandate period, a developing educational system, in the throes of language revival, saw in English a bridge to cosmopolitan culture. Thus, a Shakespearean tragedy, essays by Addison and Burke, as well as poems by Milton, Wordsworth, Shelley, and Tennyson were all part of the curriculum and final examinations of students with a myriad of mother tongues, being educated in Hebrew and living in the Near East. With independence and the great upheavals in educational priorities, more utilitarian goals took precedence. Now fluency in spoken English and modern English usages were deemed more important. Recently, the needs of university students who have to be able to read scientific texts in English have become an additional consideration in defining the goals of English instruction.

The goals of reading education for adults are discussed in the next section within the context of illiteracy.

ILLITERACY

Illiteracy in Israel, as far as it exists, is mainly an outcome of historic factors. When in the first year of statehood Parliament made education up to age fourteen free and compulsory, legislators took cognizance of the fate of youngsters who had not completed school before the new act. Therefore, the act included a provision extending free compulsory education up to age seventeen to anyone who had not successfully completed at least eight grades.

Today, total illiteracy, namely, the inability to identify letters and words, practically does not exist among young people who went to school and are not learning disabled. Functional illiteracy, namely, a reading level below eighth grade among young people, is usually an outcome of very disadvantageous home conditions or of recent immigration. In both cases difficulties are due to language factors rather than to problems in decoding strategies.

As we have seen, age, and more specifically age at time of immigration, is one main determinant of illiteracy in Israel. The second is gender. Traditionally in Middle Eastern societies, education as far as it went, was a prerogative of males. Women were most often totally illiterate. Consequently, total illiteracy among adults in Israel is confined mainly to women, both Arab and Jewish, with the total number decreasing year by year, as the percentage of women who attend school increases.

In 1961, 16.1 percent of the total Jewish population above the age of fourteen had not attended school at all, as against 6.5 percent by 1986. By that time the larger percentages of those who had not attended school were exclusively in the forty-five years old and above cohorts. In the sixty-five years and older age group 20.2 percent of women had not attended school versus 9.4 percent of men. Comparable numbers among combined minority groups are: 49.5 percent in 1961 to 15.8 percent in 1986 who had not attended; larger percentages from thirty-five years of age and upward; and 25.9 percent among the fifty-five to sixty-four year olds, and 52.6 percent among sixty-five years and older males who had not attended school versus 31.6 percent among thirty-five to forty-four, 56.0 percent among forty-five to fifty-four, 70.5 percent among fifty-five to sixty-four, and 83.8 percent among sixty-five years and older females (Central Bureau of Statistics, 1987).

Because of the age groups involved, illiteracy is within the provisions of adult education. Over time two entirely different strands developed as regards educational goals. On the one hand there arose the need to provide knowledge of Hebrew to new immigrants, who were well educated in their native language, especially those in the free professions. Ultimately, a variety of frameworks for imparting Hebrew quickly came into being. These will not concern us here. In the early years of statehood, the other strand dealt mainly with mass campaigns to alleviate total illiteracy among adults who had no formal education, especially women.

It quickly became apparent that uneducated women, burdened with small children, from countries where women traditionally are confined to the household, did not adapt to attending formal lessons at fixed times. This factor, together with the very limited resources available, led to a huge voluntary effort, initiated by private persons and later partly subsidized by the authorities. Volunteers, from retirees to girl soldiers and high school kids, went out regularly to immigrant camps and settlements and taught the rudiments of reading and writing to small groups of women in their own homes.

Since 1977 these efforts have been superseded by formal frameworks set up by the Department of Adult Education in the Ministry of Education. Their goal is to supplement the education of women who have not completed their elementary or secondary education. In this context the transition from illiteracy to literacy is conceived as a continuous path, and the aim is to advance the learner at least beyond "the point of no-return to illiteracy," namely, into someone "for whom reading has become second nature" (Grabelsky, 1983). With the expansion of these new frameworks, growing numbers of women are studying toward completion of an eighth grade curriculum or are going beyond to a high school program.

READING DISABILITIES

Israel has extensive preventive health care. Neighborhood, family-oriented, well baby clinics monitor children's development closely from the early stages of pregnancy throughout their early years. The same health teams continue to see children regularly when they advance to kindergarten and later school. Thus, severe disabilities are detected and attended to well before children enter school. In extreme cases children attend special schools, though in general the tendency is to keep even severely hearing-, sight-, or otherwise impaired students in regular schools, with the aid of personally assigned tutors.

As all five year olds attend at least one year of kindergarten, the schools have a further opportunity to screen children and provide special services to those who strike kindergarten personnel as too immature or in other ways unsuited to progress straight on to the first grade.

Once children enter school, further cases of reading disability can be discovered in one of two ways. First, classroom teachers who feel that a particular child is having extreme difficulties may refer that child to the school reading coordinator, psychologist, or counselor. Any one of these personnel will institute extensive diagnostic testing, so that eventually a suitable remedial program will be set in motion. Second, regional supervisors administer reading tests from time to time to all children in a certain grade in order to assess the general level of reading attainment in their area. Since regional offices as well as individual principals are autonomous, procedures within schools and specific tests used vary.

In general, reading disabilities connected with problems in the area of decoding strategies occur in regular schools only in the first grades. In the later grades problems are exclusively in the area of reading comprehension. There is a growing tendency to introduce programs that foster comprehension skills to all students rather than only to those diagnosed as reading disabled. A variety of specialized programs exist for the latter, and intensive remediation is usually effective.

READING READINESS PROGRAMS

Except for religious ultra-orthodox frameworks for boys, which are not part of the official school system, no instruction is given in reading before the first grade. This is the case even though about 90 percent of three year olds and a higher percentage of four year olds attend preschool, all five year olds attend kindergarten, and a growing number of schools have infant units that combine kindergarten and first grade. Preschools and kindergartens are usually in session about five hours a day, six days a week.

Prevalent reading readiness activities are in some respects rather different from those familiar to educators in other countries. For instance, children do not learn the alphabet. Still, numerous kindergarten teachers do introduce worksheets that contain exercises in directionality, visual discrimination, and the like, and they also use part of their time for face-to-face interaction to train phonic segmentation and other subskills.

There are several reasons why pretraining in decoding skills per se is not introduced before the first grade. Past experience has shown that, although children usually acquire technical reading in Hebrew during their first year in school, without undue difficulty, experimental projects that endeavor to teach decoding in kindergarten are not successful. Furthermore, early childhood educators in Israel tend to feel that decoding is after all only a technical skill and that in view of the needs of children from nonschool-oriented homes the preschoolers' time can be used more profitably by advancing them in other areas.

Studies conducted in the 1950s and 1960s had shown that, unlike children whose parents had immigrated from European countries, children whose parents originated from Near Eastern countries did not tend to engage in make-believe play. As developmental psychologists assume that representational play has important adaptive and developmental functions, the nonemergence of this type of play raises the possibility that the inherent capabilities of children are not fully exploited. Fostering children's imaginative play is therefore an important priority of early childhood education. Another priority is the development of both passive and active language skills. A variety of approaches and materials geared to this end are widely used. An approach that experimental studies have shown to be especially beneficial is daily reading to children from action stories in whole class settings. Contrary to the use of big books which has recently gained favor on the American scene, in the Israeli version teachers do not direct children's attention to the printed symbols in the book they read to them. Instead, they focus on introducing children to literary language and enlarging their knowledge base.

TEACHER QUALIFICATIONS

In Israel early childhood educators and primary teachers are trained in three-year teacher training colleges. Graduates of these colleges receive a teaching diploma that enables them to teach anywhere in the country. Trainees can specialize in a variety of ways. In general colleges students specialize in either the early grades including kindergarten, or in Grades 3 to 6. Then there are specializations in music, arts, crafts, and physical education in either specialized colleges or special departments in the general colleges. Students who take a four-year course qualify as "senior teachers" and draw a higher salary, in addition to having better chances at advancement. In recent years a slow process for accrediting colleges and enabling them to award B.Ed.s has been set in motion. A B.Ed. degree requires four years of study.

All secondary school teachers have to have a university degree. In theory a bachelor's degree suffices only for intermediate schools (seventh, eighth, and ninth grades), and a master's is required for senior high school. In practice, and especially in outlying areas, this structure does not hold, and teachers with only a bachelor's also teach in the final grades. In addition to a university degree, secondary teachers need a teaching diploma. This diploma is acquired by a year and a half course in the Education Department of one of the universities. In certain cases, holders of a teaching diploma in elementary education can transfer to intermediate teaching by taking a special one-year course in one of the accredited teachers' colleges. Conversely, university graduates, especially with higher degrees, who have work experience and wish to change careers, can transfer to teaching by taking specialized training.

Until a few years ago an M.A., M.Sc., Engineering, or otherwise suitable degree sufficed for teaching in most postsecondary institutions. The trend toward academization of many of these frameworks has resulted in the requirement of a doctorate.

Specialization in reading is acquired through in-service training, according to programs developed by the Department for Basic Skills in the Ministry of Education. These in-service courses are rather extended: two years in order to become a primary school reading coordinator, and three years for primary school principals who wish to become leading figures in the field of reading.

As in other industrialized nations, primary teaching, and with it reading instruction, have become largely the province of women, except in religiously ultra-orthodox frameworks for boys where all teaching, even at preschool age, is by males. In Hebrew-medium primary education, out of a total of 32,128 teachers in 1985–1986, 88.7 percent were female. The corresponding figures in Arab-medium education were 42.7 percent out of a total of 6,331. The percentages of female teachers in intermediate and senior secondary grades were, respectively, 69.1 percent and 59.5 percent in Hebrew-medium schools and 22.8 percent and 19.5 percent in Arab-medium schools (Central Bureau of Statistics, 1987). All reading specialists were female.

READING EDUCATION MATERIALS

Except for adult education most textbooks, workbooks, and other materials used in Israeli schools in all subjects and at all levels are published commercially.

In primary education, basal series are very popular. In addition, children might use a grammar and/or spelling book already in the early grades, as well as booklets on topical themes. The variety is great, and schools are bombarded by tempting offers. These often include in-service training, evaluation materials, and the like.

In intermediary and senior secondary education, the emphasis is on literature per se, both originally Hebrew and world literature in translation, as well as more formal texts in grammar, and writing.

In tertiary education texts are used in content areas, including literature.

In adult education, the Ministry of Education develops and publishes part of the available instructional materials, especially in the area of the early stages of reading. A weekly newspaper in easy Hebrew, printed in large letters and partly with vowels, is widely used in both fundamental education and language instruction for immigrants. Teachers in the intermediate grades in some schools also make regular use of this paper.

In general, all reading materials are in the language of instruction—Hebrew or Arabic. In second- and third-language learning, readers and language texts are in the language that is being learned. Thus, students may read a play or poem in translation in the intermediate grades and a further work by the same author in the original a few years later. One publisher specializes in publishing newspapers, in varying levels of difficulty, in English and Arabic for foreign language learning.

Commercial workbooks and handouts prepared and duplicated by teachers are used mainly in primary and adult education and to a lesser extent in the intermediate grades. They are popular with teachers, but because of the high cost involved they are used much less extensively than in the United States.

FINANCING READING EDUCATION

In the early years education was free only up to the eighth grade, or to age seventeen for students who had not completed primary schooling. Later, free education was extended to the tenth grade; today it extends from kindergarten through the twelfth grade—thirteen years. Thus, the Ministry of Education finances practically all education, as well as those frameworks of adult education that include reading instruction.

READING RESEARCH

Research on reading in Israel is characterized not by level of education but by two main directions.

First, many Israeli reading researchers have studied for their doctorate in the United States or have spent sabbaticals at American universities. They follow publications and publish in American professional journals, participate in scholarly meetings, and cooperate with reading researchers in other countries. In general, their studies, both in choice of topic as well as in methodology, follow the lines currently pursued by the international reading research community. Thus, reading is usually treated within the wider contexts of language and literacy development; text processing is studied in relation to factors that might affect it, such as characteristics of written versus oral language, or previous knowledge of different reader populations. One topic that is receiving considerable attention and has not been studied to the same degree in other countries is the influence of language and orthographic idiosyncrasies on perceptual and reading processes.

The second direction of research is evaluation studies of the ever growing number of approaches and programs in the area of reading instruction. Evaluation is sometimes an ongoing component of the development process. In other instances, evaluation follows only after a program has already been in use for some time. In addition, some widely used approaches were never evaluated.

CONCLUSION

Written language has been part of the heritage of the people of Israel for more than 3,000 years. Moreover, contrary to other literate cultures of antiquity, literacy was not a secret art, restricted to a small elite group. Rather, from early on it was seen as the key to the holy scriptures, to be shared as widely as possible. It was this tradition, of passing on the ability to read Hebrew from generation to generation, that made the revival of Hebrew possible after the habit of using Hebrew in daily conversation had died out in about 200 A.D.

The tradition of commitment to learning, and the central role of the Bible in the curriculum from second grade onward, resulted in an educational system with very high standards. In regard to reading, the expectation was that all children would be able to read well before the end of first grade and that reading would remain a favored pastime after the students had left school.

The mass immigration of refugees from Near Eastern and African countries after the establishment of the state of Israel led to unexpected problems in reading acquisition. A radical change in approaches to beginning reading instruction rectified the situation in regard to decoding strategies. However, despite remarkable progress, and a steady increase in the number of students who successfully complete secondary education and enter universities, children from homes where parents cannot help them in their studies still tend to experience difficulties in reading comprehension.

Despite the handicaps of a large segment of the population whose mother tongue is not Hebrew, and a numerical majority of the population who originate from countries where educational standards were not high, interest in books is tremendous. For years Israel has held the record in the Western world in number of books per capita published and sold. Currently, 69 percent of the books published annually in Israel were originally written in Hebrew (Central Bureau of Statistics, 1987).

REFERENCES

Adiel, S. 1968. Reading ability of culturally deprived first graders. *Megamot* (Behavioral Sciences Quarterly) 15: 345–356 (in Hebrew).

Bloom, S. 1966. Israeli reading methods for their culturally disadvantaged. *Elementary School Journal* 66: 304–310.

Central Bureau of Statistics, 1987. *Statistical Abstract of Israel* 38. Jerusalem.

Feitelson, D. 1953–1964. *Causes of school failure among first graders.* Jerusalem: Szold Foundation/Kiryat Sefer (in Hebrew).

Fellman, J. 1979. The teachers did it: A case history in the revival of a national language. In D. Feitelson (ed.), *Mother tongue or second language? On the teaching of reading in multi-lingual societies.* Newark, Del.: International Reading Association.

Grebelsky, O. 1983. A second chance—a new beginning. In O. Grebelsky and R. Tokatli (eds.), *Literacy in Israel: Widening horizons.* Jerusalem: Ministry of Education, Department of Adult Education.

Huey, E. B. 1908–1968. *The psychology and pedagogy of reading.* New York: Macmillan/Cambridge, Mass.: MIT Press.

BIBLIOGRAPHY

Bentwich, J. S. 1965. *Education in Israel.* London: Routledge.

Elboim-Dror, R. 1986–1989. *Hebrew education in Eretz Israel* (3 vols.). Jerusalem: Ben Zvi Institute (in Hebrew).

Encyclopaedia Judaica, 1971. Israel, State of: Education, Vol. 9 928–982. Jerusalem: Keter.

Feitelson, D. 1973. Israel. In J. Downing (ed.) *Comparative reading.* New York: Macmillan.

Feitelson, D. 1980. Relating instructional strategies to language idiosyncrasies in Hebrew. In J. F. Kavanagh and R. L. Venezky (eds.), *Orthography, reading and dyslexia.* Baltimore: University Park Press.

Feitelson, D. 1988. *Facts and fads in beginning reading: A cross-language perspective.* Norwood, N.J.: Ablex.

Kleinberger, A. F. 1969. *Society, schools and progress in Israel.* Oxford: Pergamon.

10

Japan

Takahiko Sakamoto

THE LANGUAGE OF THE COUNTRY

The official language of Japan is Japanese, and there is no other widely used language. Reading education is, therefore, done in Japanese only. Although English is taught from junior high school up, the level is very low and virtually no one is able to use English when they finish compulsory education at junior high school.

Japanese schools do not have a specific subject called "reading." Reading is taught as part of the subject "Kokugo" (Japanese national language), which includes reading, writing, speaking, and listening. There are Kokugo teachers but no reading teachers.

The compulsory education period is nine years starting at six years of age. The first six years are spent in the elementary school system followed by three years in junior high school (middle school). Enrollment in elementary and junior high schools is 100 percent for both boys and girls. After junior high school, youngsters go on to senior high school for three years. The enrollment in senior high is 94 percent. About 31 percent of Japanese youth attend colleges or universities after senior high school.

READING POLICY

It is not easy to determine if Japanese Kokugo instruction (including reading instruction) is centralized or decentralized. It had long been centralized until 1947 (Sakamoto and Makita, 1973). All elementary school textbooks, including Kokugo, were edited and published by the Ministry of Education, and all schools throughout Japan used the same textbooks. After the 1947 education reform inspired by the Allied Occupation, the Ministry of Education stopped editing and publishing textbooks and allowed private companies to publish them. Whether Kokugo instruction can now be described as truly decentralized, however, is problematic because privately compiled textbooks are still subject to Ministry of Education approval. In the early stage of the 1947 education reform, the Ministry of Education published a model for textbooks as well as two official pamphlets, "The Course of Study" and "Textbook Standard." Publishing companies were permitted to compile textbooks following these guidelines. In order to obtain approval from the Ministry of Education, private companies had to follow the guidelines in the two pamphlets strictly; the outcome was a virtual copy of the government's model.

At present the situation is somewhat better, and several series of Kokugo textbooks are published. Individual teachers, however, are not allowed to select their own textbooks. Local committees of education select the texts to be used in their locality. As a result, the same textbook is used by all children in the same grade at all schools in a school district.

THE GOALS OF READING EDUCATION

The goals of reading education are not different for males and females but they may differ somewhat from those in Western countries. Sakamoto (1985) has described this difference. The Oriental way of thinking about reading, he observes, has been passed down from previous generations as part of tradition. When asked why children are taught to read, many Western teachers answer, first of all, that reading is a very important *skill* necessary in pursuing one's studies, job, pleasure, higher level of knowledge, and so on. But Japanese teachers would answer that reading is akin to nutrition and thus is essential for developing a stable, well-rounded personality. If reading is considered merely a skill, the goal of literacy is to educate people simply to utilize their skills when necessary. But if reading is considered an aspect of "nutrition," a merely technically literate person is not sufficient as a goal; instead, the person must be encouraged to obtain reading nutrition as an on-going process.

LITERACY AND READING DISABILITIES

In UNESCO's published results (1964) of comparative research on adult literacy around the world, the Ministry of Education of Japan reported that the problem of illiteracy had been completely solved. This finding was based on two nationwide literacy research studies in Japan.

The first study was conducted in 1948, three years after the end of World War II. This research was based on the 1946 recommendations of the United States Education Mission to Japan, in which "a drastic reform of the Japanese written language" was recommended. In this research "literacy" was defined as "the minimum ability to handle the customary language used in basic mass communication media, specified as (1) newspapers; (2) documents directly relating to citizenry and government; (3) documents basic to economic activities; and (4) private correspondence." Carefully selected samples aged fifteen to sixty-four were tested, and those who scored zero, that is, those who were determined to be unable to read or write Kanji, Hiragana, and Katakana at all accounted for only 1.7 percent of the total sample (male 0.7 percent, female 2.8 percent). If the definition of illiteracy is broadened to add those who can read or write any Hiragana or any Katakana but who are completely unable to read or write Kanji, the illiteracy rate goes up from 1.7 to 2.1 percent.

In 1961 the Ministry of Education of Japan published a report of a literacy study conducted between 1954 and 1956. In this research 1,000 samples in the Kanto area and 1,000 samples in the Tohoku area between fifteen and twenty-four years of age were administered Kanji tests. When "illiterate" was defined as scoring zero points (out of 50 full points), the illiteracy rate was 0.1 percent in Kanto (male 0.2 percent, female 0 percent) and 0.8 percent in the Tohoku area (male 1.2 percent, female 0.5 percent).

Sakamoto and Makita (1973) attribute this high literacy rate to the following causes: (1) The initial use of phonetic symbols, Kana, which are easy to learn; (2) the compulsory education program from the first through the ninth grade constituting a strictly organized system; (3) the great respect of Japanese parents for education and their eagerness for their children to learn (making sacrifices for a child's education being a common part of Japanese parenthood); (4) the availability of many good reading materials at low prices; and (5) the successful movements to stimulate reading, for example, National Reading Week, the reading movement for mothers, the mother-child twenty-minute reading program, reading groups, and book report contest.

Japanese researchers usually feel uneasy when they participate in a comparative reading study with Western, especially American, researchers. The problem from the Japanese viewpoint is that Western researchers sometimes want to make international comparisons of children whose reading ability is low but whose other academic skills are normal. In Japan such children are almost never encountered. When the reading ability of Japanese children is low, their other abilities are almost always low as well. From this perspective, the Japanese generally state that they have no problems of reading disabilities.

Makita (1968) conducted a survey in 1966 to discover the incidence of poor readers among school-age children. He sent questionnaires to a random sampling of school teachers, asking them to report all cases of children without intellectual retardation or visual impairment but to whom teaching reading was difficult. The result, obtained from 247 school teachers covering 9,195 pupils, indicated the incidence of such poor readers was a mere 0.98 percent of the surveyed children. Makita suggested that the nature of the Japanese language itself and its orthography explained this rarity of reading disability. Since this was the first report written in English to describe the rarity of Japanese reading disabilities, it stimulated discussions among Western researchers, many of whom supported the Japanese contention.

Stevenson et al. (1982), however, challenged Makita and his adherents by conducting research in which they compared the reading disabilities of fifth graders in Taiwan, Japan, and the United States. They concluded that "there were children in all three countries who were reading at least two grade levels below their own grade—a common criterion for reading disability," and they reported that the incidence of such readers in Japan was 8 percent, eight times higher than Makita's figure, that the stated rarity of occurrence was not true, and that orthography is not related to reading disabilities. Yamada (1984) introduced the Stevenson report to Japan and warned Japanese school teachers to be sure to identify children with reading disabilities. But both teachers and other Japanese researchers disregarded his warning, perhaps because the 8 percent rate cited by Stevenson et al. was derived not from the results of standardized reading tests but from the scores of an ad hoc researcher-designed reading test.

In addition to this possible lack of objectivity of the tests used, a more important reason for the gap between Makita's 0.98 percent and the 8 percent figure cited by Stevenson seems to be the difference in the definition of reading disability. In *A Dictionary of Reading and Related Terms* (1981) reading disability is defined as (1) an inability to read, often severe, in spite of intensive reading instruction; (2) reading performance below expectancy; (3) reading performance one or more years below one's mental ability; (4) any reading difficulty. These definitions are followed by a note saying, "There is no clear present consensus about the precise nature of reading disability."

It would not be valid to discuss a comparison of reading disability rates without using the same definition in the samples being compared. Makita's definitions seem to approach the first definition mentioned above. Stevenson and others constructed their own reading tests and arbitrarily determined that those children who scored 75 percent or more on their fifth grade-level test were to be considered to be reading at fifth grade level. Thus, their definition is closer to the second dictionary definition given above. If the definition, "two years below the grade level," for example, is employed it could then be stated that reading disabilities have existed in Japan since long ago. Although there are no statistical data on the incidence of such poorly performing children, based on data from standardized reading tests, we can estimate that there were a few such children many decades ago.

What is rare in Japan is the child disabled by disease. Such children, seen in the United States quite frequently, need the special attention of a remedial teacher or need to be treated at a reading clinic by a neuropsychiatrist. Japan has neither remedial reading teachers nor reading clinics because they would not get enough clients to make them feasible.

In Japan parents spend a lot of money for their children's education; as a result, the so-called education business has become prominent in its scope and profitability. Reading ability is, of course, essential for entering a highly regarded senior high school and the better universities as well as for getting a good job. If parents felt their children were even somewhat low in terms of reading ability, Japan would have many reading clinics, reading schools, and the like. As far as can be determined, such institutions do not exist in Japan. The only known reading schools are some recently opened, highly commercial rapid reading schools for businessmen.

READING READINESS PROGRAMS

Japan has no reading readiness programs, for there is no felt need for them. Japanese children begin to read Hiragana, a relatively easy-to-read set of phonetic symbols (Sakamoto, 1980), at age four without any formal reading education (Sakamoto, 1975). Since all books for young children are printed entirely in Hiragana, children can even read a story book before school age.

TEACHER QUALIFICATIONS

Elementary school teachers teach not only Kokugo, but also all the other subjects in the elementary curriculum; hence, there is no special qualification for becoming a Kokugo teacher. In order to become an elementary school teacher, an aspirant must have a teacher's license. According to the Teacher's License Law, the license is given to a person who has studied at a college or university for at least two years, has studied the required subjects for becoming a teacher, and has performed an internship. It is difficult for a two-year college graduate to get an elementary school teacher's license without making a very special effort to take extra credit and courses that are not usually available in the junior college curriculum. Thus, virtually all teachers who have recently obtained their licenses are graduates from the Department of Education of a four-year university. More than 99 percent of Japanese elementary school teachers teach at a public school that is directly administered by the local government. In order to get a teaching job at a public school, a license holder must pass a teacher's employment examination administered annually by a prefectural education board. Those who pass the test are listed for one year as qualified for employment, and a school principal can select new teachers as needed from this list.

In junior and senior high schools, a teacher teaches only one subject, so there is a specific teacher's license of Kokugo. The procedure for becoming a qualified teacher in both junior and senior high schools is similar to that of elementary school. Both sexes have equal opportunity in obtaining teacher's credentials and teaching positions.

READING MATERIALS

The Kokugo textbooks represent the major materials used in reading education at school. They are what could be called "consumable materials" and are given free of charge to each child in all grades of elementary and junior high schools. Parents must pay for senior high Kokugo textbooks, but they are rather inexpensive and affordable in terms of Japanese average income. There is never a problem of their supply or availability.

Workbooks are another popular material in reading education used at home. Since studying at home after school is a very important part of Japanese education, many parents buy these workbooks and encourage their children to use them. They are published by private publishing companies and do not require the approval of the Ministry of Education. Until recently, they have also been used in classes, but teachers are now being encouraged to create similar materials themselves.

FINANCING READING EDUCATION

There is no particular problem in financing basic reading education. Tuition and textbooks are free in the nine years of compulsory education, and although they are not free in senior high schools, the average Japanese family can well afford them.

CONCLUSIONS

Reading education has been successful in Japan in terms of decreasing the number of illiterates, but we still encounter a great problem in this field, namely, an increase in the number of reluctant readers among Japanese children. Sakamoto (1985) has described this phenomenon as follows: "One of the main problems that may still be encountered after the goal of "nation-wide literacy" is attained is that not all people intend to read, even though they have the ability. . . . Thus, what we are facing in Japan is not a literacy problem *per se*, but a problem of reading promotion." The current focal points of reading research in Japan reflect the present status of reading education mentioned above. No study on literacy rate has been reported recently; instead, readership surveys are frequently conducted and reported in order to gauge the level of the Japanese people's fondness for reading. In addition to research on the methods of teaching reading skills, studies on ways to stimulate children to become book lovers are published quite often.

Japanese reading education is now at the stage where reluctant readers are being encouraged to become enthusiastic readers.

REFERENCES

Harris, T. L., and Hodges, R. E. (eds.). 1981. *A Dictionary of Reading and Related Terms.* Newark, Del.: International Reading Association.
Makita, K. 1968. The Rarity of Reading Disability in Japanese Children. *American Journal of Orthopsychiatry* 38: 599–614.

Sakamoto, T. 1975. Preschool Reading in Japan. *Reading Teacher* 29 (3): 240–244.

Sakamoto, T. 1980. Reading of Hiragana. In James F. Kavanagh and Richard Venezky (eds.), *Orthography, Reading, and Dyslexia*. Austin, Tex.: Pro-Ed, pp. 15–24.

Sakamoto, T. 1985. Reading Promotion in the Post-Literacy Age: The Case of Japan. In E. Malmquist (ed.), *The Right to Read: Literacy Around the World*. Evanston, Ill.: Rotary International, pp. 129–140.

Sakamoto, T., and Makita, K. 1973. Japan. In J. Downing (ed.), *Comparative Reading*. New York: Macmillan, pp. 440–465.

Stevenson, H. W.; Stigler, J. W.; Lucker, G. W.; Lee, S.; Hsu, C.; and Kimura, S. 1982. Reading Disabilities: The Case of Chinese, Japanese, and English. *Child Development* 53: 1164–1181.

UNESCO. 1964. *Literacy and Education for Adults*. Bangkok.

Yamada, J. 1984. No, Taro can't read either. *The Science of Reading* 28: 87–92 (in Japanese).

11

Kuwait

Ramadan A. Ahmed

INTRODUCTION

Kuwait (Arabic: Dawlat Al-Kuwait = State of Kuwait) lies in the northwestern corner of the Arabian Gulf, to the north of Al-Hasa Province and the south of Iraq, between latitude 28 and 30 degrees North and 46 and 48 degrees longitude East. It has an area of 17,818 square kilometers. Kuwait covers a strip of flat sand plains, flanked by low hilly ridges. Fertile lands in Kuwait can be found at Jahra Oasis and at some tracts lying in the southeastern coastal part of the country. The country has a curved coastline.

THE POPULATION

The original inhabitants of Kuwait emigrated from the heart of the Arabian peninsula in search of trading opportunities, including Al-Sabah, the rulers of Kuwait who were among the early settlers. Other early settlers came from other areas in the Arabian Gulf. After the development of the oil and other industries, many foreigners came to Kuwait to work in different sectors.

The non-Kuwaiti segment of the present population consists mainly of Arabs from other Arab states and non-Arabs.

According to the preliminary figures of the 1985 census, the population of the country totals 1,695,128 inhabitants. Of this total, only 679,601 (or 40.1 percent of the total population) were listed as Kuwaitis, and the remainder, 1,015,527 (or 59.9 percent of the total population) were foreigners—63.2 percent Arabs, especially Palestinians, Jordanians, Iraqis, and Egyptians, and 35 percent Asian, especially Persians (Iranians), Pakistanis, Filipinos, Sri Lankans, and Indians.

Whereas the annual growth rate for the Kuwaitis reached 4.2 percent in 1985, the annual growth rate for the non-Kuwaitis was only 2.28 percent.

Kuwait is a rapidly changing country especially in the last three decades. The country has great financial resources based on its oil and natural gas industries, and a very high per capita income (which in 1984 was estimated as KD 4,642 or about $17,000). Kuwait has a comprehensive welfare system and free compulsory education for all boys and girls between the age of six and fourteen. Islam is the religion for all Kuwaitis and the majority of the other resident Arabs, as well as a great segment of the non-Arabs living in Kuwait.

STATUS OF EDUCATION IN KUWAIT

The Kuwait government considers education a potent force to support political independence, rebuild human resources, reconstruct society, and establish a national identity. On these bases, the government yearly devotes a great amount of its gross national product to education. For example, education expenditure in Kuwait has ranged from 12.72 (in 1985) to 16.20 percent (1988–1989) of total governmental expenditures (Central Department of Statistics, 1985 census; 1988–1989).

THE KUWAITI EDUCATIONAL SYSTEM

The Kuwaiti educational system resembles that of most Arab countries and consists of the pre-primary, primary, intermediate, secondary, and university level.

The pre-primary level consists of nurseries and kindergartens, mostly privately owned, located in the neighborhoods of the city of Kuwait itself. Children are taken in from as early an age as three and a half and are looked after until they reach the age of admission to primary school. The primary school system, established in 1912 and compulsory since 1966–1967, admits children at the age of six. Its four-year cycle culminates with the Intermediate School Entrance Examination and the Primary School Certificate. The intermediate level encompasses the intermediate school to which admission is based on the Primary School Certificate. This consists of a four-year period of studies at the end of which students, upon passing the Intermediate School Examination, obtain the Secondary School Entrance Certificate.

The secondary level, which students reach through the Intermediate School Certificate, comprises two different systems: (1) The regular academic secondary school system, which has a four-year program leading to the Kuwait School Certificate Examination, the basic requirement for admission to the University of Kuwait, and other nonuniversity institutions of higher learning; this system consists of two branches of study—arts and science. (2) The credit system high school, under which a student must take courses from among those recognized for graduation according to the major chosen. This system also allows students to enroll in other courses that are of interest to them.

Tertiary education is given at the university and an institution of higher learning. Admission is through the high school certificate and varies not only from faculty to faculty but also according to the personnel status of the student. Non-Kuwaitis are held to a higher standard than Kuwaitis according to a scheme that again varies from faculty to faculty.

The University of Kuwait, established in 1966, is made up of seven constituted colleges: Arts, Sciences, Law, Medicine, Commerce and Economics, Engineering, Allied Health and Islamic Studies. Parallel to it is the College of Technology, a two-year institution, which admits students on the same basis but prepares them for careers in technical fields.

Technical education in Kuwait seeks to give the students who failed to continue their intermediate school studies (course) or failed to pass it the opportunity to get technical training for certain professions needed by the society. The schools for technical education are under the supervision of the General Authority for Applied Education and Training. The students qualify to attend these schools if they are Kuwaitis or naturalized Kuwaitis; are at least fourteen years old; have completed not less than the first year of intermediate school; and are mentally and physically able to follow the courses offered.

Kuwait's educational system focuses primarily on theoretical knowledge or general academic studies rather than on empirical and vocational or professional knowledge; the latter fields of knowledge receive less attention owing to many social and economic factors. Recently, some efforts have been made to shift attitudes from general academic studies to vocational and professional studies.

As presently constituted, Kuwait's educational system gives little opportunity to classify students according to their abilities or academic subjects. All students must study all subjects in the same way until the end of the secondary school level. Teachers also deal with students on the basis that they form one unified class, although differences do exist in ability and interests.

Kuwait's educational system is a selective one because many students start in the primary school level, but not all of them pass successfully to the secondary school level. There is also a high dropout rate (wastage) in the primary, intermediate, and secondary school levels. Al-Ahmed and Abou-Allam (al-Ahmed and Abou-Allam, 1987) studied the dropout rate in Kuwait from 1976–1977 to 1985–1986 and found out that the highest dropout rate was found in the secondary school level (2 to 9/10 percent), then in the intermediate school level (1 to 4/5 percent), and finally, in the primary school level (2 to 3 percent). No significant differences were found between males and females concerning the dropout. Al-Ahmed and Abou-Allam also observed that the high dropout rate among students in Kuwait was due to educational factors related to curricula, methods of teaching, ways and systems of evaluation, as well as some psychological and social factors such as the lack of interest and a low perception of the importance of education among parents, especially in the bedouin areas.

There are no approaches other than the two academic approaches (channels) in the secondary school level (i.e., literature and scientific approaches). Although Kuwait is using modern methods, curricula and equipment, they have apparently been added to the educational system without comprehensive study.

Contradictions between daily life and educational requirements still remain. Moreover, there is still a contrast between the official and nonofficial, and governmental and Arabic and non-Arabic education systems and the failure of all to cater to technical and women's education. The attitude toward women's education and vocational and professional education is still negative owing to the dominant values and the old, still powerful Arabian and bedouin traditions.

It seems that the evaluation and testing systems are still in need of improvements and reforms in order, on the one hand, to reach the modern trends in continuing evaluation, and, on the other hand, to decrease the high rate of failure and dropout which leads to disappointment among children. (See Abd el-Motty and Taha, 1980; Abdulghafoor, 1978; Ahmed, 1984; al-Ebraheem,1989; al-Khalaf, 1989; el-Koussy, 1973; al-Sabah, 1989; Siadway et al., 1978.)

LANGUAGES OF THE COUNTRY

As in other Arab countries, Arabic is the official language of Kuwait, with English widely used in the government public sector (government and university) and the public sector (commerce and business) and as a medium of instruction for Arabic speakers. Other languages such as French, Farsi, and Urdu are used according to the nature of the school and ethnic backgrounds.

Reading Policy

The process of reading instruction policy in Kuwait is centralized. All centers or institutions for reading education, as well as libraries and publications that publish according to this policy, are controlled and supervised by either the Ministry of Information or the Ministry of Education.

THE GOALS OF READING EDUCATION

The reading education process policy in Kuwait generally aims at providing learners with the necessary skills and enough information to enable them to deal efficiently with daily life events and to improve their knowledge. Specifically, the goals are to give the students opportunities to achieve high levels of accuracy, intuition, and comprehension in reading; to treat with reading, miscues of Arabic speaking in state primary, intermediate, and secondary schools; and to treat with reading, miscues of Arabic and English speaking in non-Arabic private, intermediate, and secondary schools. It seems that there are no existing differences concerning the goals of the reading education process between males and females in the area of primary education. The purpose of reading education here is to provide children of both sexes with the basic skills of reading. In the area of secondary school education, and partly in the area of the intermediate school education, besides the normal activities of reading education, which are given to the male students, the reading education process tends to focus on female students, on women's roles in the society, past, present, and the future, household affairs, children rearing, and education. In tertiary education, the main goal of reading education is to provide students of both sexes with new sources of academic knowledge and to develop their interest in reading. (See Abdalla, 1985; Allington et al., 1985; Banks et al., 1984; El-Korashy, 1985; Mohammad and Jaber, 1980–1981; Shmas el-Din et al., 1980–1981).

ILLITERACY

Illiterate persons in Kuwait are those people between fourteen and forty years of age who did not receive any education beyond the fourth primary grade level concerning the principles of reading, writing, and arithmetic, and who are not enrolled in any primary school (al-Khalaf, 1989; Ministry of Education, 1984). The rate of illiteracy for both males and females (for those ten years of age and up) decreased from 89 percent in 1961 to 44.6 percent in 1975 and to 26.4 percent in 1985 (1985 census). The rate of illiteracy was higher for females than for males. While the rate of illiteracy in females in 1985 was 47 percent of all female citizens, it was only 32 percent for males.

The 1985 census also showed that the illiteracy rate in the age group sixty years and up was very high. It was 96 percent for females and 72 percent for males (al-Ebraheem, 1989; al-Khalaf, 1989; al-Sabah, 1989).

The campaign against illiteracy in Kuwait began in 1958 when the authorities established two centers for educating illiterate persons. A few years later, night intermediate schools were opened to offer these people a chance to continue their education. In 1962–1963 night secondary schools functioned for males for the first time; six years later, secondary schools were established for females in order to give those who wished to complete their education the opportunity to do so. Intermediate and secondary schools for adults, for both sexes, do not differ much from the ordinary daily intermediate and secondary school. Currently, the number of illiteracy eradication centers is 105; of these, 50 are devoted to females. On the other hand, in 1981 the eradication of illiteracy became compulsory by law (al-Khalaf, 1989; Ministry of Education, 1983 and 1984 and also Ministry of Education, 1970, 1971, 1974, 1975, 1979, 1980, 1981, 1983a, 1984a, 1985, 1986, and 1987; al-Sabah, 1989).

Today, girls attend both state and private Arabic and non-Arabic schools; they also have access to some formal religious training. There is a growing trend to make religious education available to all women regardless of their age and background. In this context, some centers for adult education have been established to provide both girls and women of different ages with sufficient religious education.

The Kuwaiti authorities are attempting to eradicate illiteracy among adults and old people who do not have any chance to obtain education. In this context, the authorities follow the illiterate cases in different institutions and places, such as army and police forces personnel, prisoners, and governmental sectors. The authorities also offer them the appropriate programs. Rewards await those who complete their study successfully. Those who complete their primary education have the opportunity to continue their intermediate, and even secondary, education.

The authorities are also attempting to overcome the sources of illiteracy such as with dropouts, especially among the primary school students (al-Khalaf, 1989). The authorities hope to conquer the problem of illiteracy in Kuwait completely by the year 2000.

Aims of the Anti-Illiteracy Campaign

The government campaign against illiteracy seeks to provide people with the necessary skills of reading, writing, and arithmetic; offer illiterate people the opportunity to gain new skills so that they can improve their lives, to learn how to work efficiently, and to acquire household experiences and healthy habits; help people gain the required skills in spending their leisure time usefully; and help people who wish to continue their education through attending the night intermediate and secondary schools. Currently, there is a growing trend toward using the mass media, especially television programs, to overcome illiteracy in Kuwait, as well as to play a brainstorming role. Moreover, the aims of these television programs are also to conduct a study to determine the obstacles that face people and prevent them from achieving progress—both in Kuwait and the other Gulf states as well. The television program "Open Sesam" is devoted especially to preschool and primary school children; its aim is to develop and encourage children to have access to the reading and writing processes.

A number of problems confront adult education (illiteracy eradication, and night intermediate and secondary schools). These are as follows. The time period for the illiteracy eradication stage is two years, which is too short a period. It has been recommended that this period be expanded to four years. In addition, there is an increasing need to prepare new materials to cope with student needs, interests, and age, and to provide the centers of the illiteracy eradication with modern technical equipment required in the educational process. There is also a shortage of competent educational systems, methods, curricula, and equipment, and of competent teachers, for various reasons. The illiteracy eradication campaign must have qualified teachers, especially in adult education.

Language and reading education should be so structured as to enable students to acquire oral and (nonoral) written reading skills, to express themselves correctly, and to develop their reading interests. Poor attendance, lack of punctuality, and a high dropout rate among students continues, especially among girls (Ministry of Education, 1986). Negative attitudes toward girls' education, stemming from dominant tribal values and old traditions, are still operative. Finally, insufficient reading materials are published in Kuwait to encourage the reading abilities and interests of the young. (Children below fifteen years of age represent about 42 percent of the total population in Kuwait, or 48.6 percent of the Kuwaiti inhabitants and 29 percent of the non-Kuwaitis.) (See al-Khalaf, 1989; Hamada, 1979; Ministry of Education).

READING DISABILITIES AND THEIR DIAGNOSIS

Personnel in some state and private Arabic and non-Arabic schools were interviewed to assess the incidence of reading disabilities in primary, secondary, tertiary, and adult education. With regard to primary education, the main disabilities center on the inability of children to learn how to speak, read and write; the lack of reading interest among the parents and its reflection on the reading education of their children; and reading miscues of Arabic and English speaking in the primary school students.

Among secondary and tertiary school students, the prevalent disability involves a lack of reading interest and motivation. A study carried out in 1985 in Kuwait showed that only 6 percent of the Kuwaiti youth and 2 percent of the non-Kuwaiti youth could be identified as regular readers of newspapers and magazines. The percentage for Kuwaiti and non-Kuwaiti youth males was 4 percent, while the percentage for Kuwaiti and non-Kuwaiti youth females was 5 (in al-Rumaihi, 1985). The country is also plagued by a shortage of competent teachers for various reasons, especially in the field of reading education, and a lack of modern educational systems, methods, curricula, and equipment concerning reading education.

In adult education, the reading disabilities are poor attendance and punctuality; lack of a modern and proper educational system, methods, curricula and equipment; lack of interest and motivation; and failure to devote enough time for reading education owing to family affairs and business.

Some differences exist in the nature and rate of disabilities in reading between males and females in the five areas of reading education. Apparently, reading disabilities occurred more frequently in females than in males in all five areas. These differences tended to be more visible in the state schools than in the private schools, and in the Arabic private schools than in the non-Arabic private schools (Abdalla, 1985; Ahmed, 1986).

The instruments and methods used to determine and diagnose reading disabilities in primary school students are the informal reading inventory; the informal graded word-recognition test; the informal arithmetic test; and calculation of the reading expectancy grade (REG).

Occasionally, remedial teaching programs are used to overcome reading disabilities among students, especially kindergarten and primary school children.

The Center for Child Evaluation and Teaching was established in Kuwait some years ago (Center for Child Evaluation and Teaching, 1988). It was designed to diagnose learning disabilities. The two major components of the center are the Diagnostic Assessment and Evaluation Department and the Educational Testing and Tutorial Department. The center has an English-speaking, Arabic-speaking, and bilingual Arab/English staff. They are trained in the area of diagnostic assessment and the teaching of children with learning disabilities.

El-Korashy (1985) studied reading interests in 585 of the first, second, third, and fourth intermediate grade Kuwaiti female students. The study sought to investigate the relationships between the students' intellectual level and the encouragements given by school teachers and the family, and their reading interests. The results indicated that reading interests in the four samples are influenced first by family, then by teacher's encouragement, and then by the student's own intellectual level in that order. The results also pointed out that the highest correlations were found between the encouragement given by the family and reading interest (where r's were 0.39, 0.40, 0.55 and 0.64 significant at the 0.01 level); then, the correlations between the encouragement given by the school teachers and reading interest (where r's were 0.19, 0.32, 0.44, and 0.51 significant at the 0.05 and 0.01 levels, respectively); and finally, the correlations between the students' intellectual level and reading interest (where r's were 0.16, 0.18, 0.27, and 0.35 significant at the 0.05 and 0.01 levels, respectively).

A study conducted by el-Faky (1977) showed that reading disabilities and education retardation among primary school children in Kuwait are due primarily to family social factors, such as lack of reading interest among parents, different languages and dialects used at home, negative attitudes toward education in general; then to the socialization types used by families in raising their children; followed by family's low socioeconomic status; and, lastly, the psychological factors in the children themselves. A Jordanian study (Freahat and Auda, 1988) supported the above-mentioned study. In this context, el-Faky and Saleh (1978) found positive correlations between preschool experiences and language and intellectual development in kindergarten-level children.

A study conducted in 1985 (Habib, 1985) to assess the intellectual levels in monolingual and bilingual children among Kuwaiti primary school children showed that both males and females who learned the English language as a second language tended to have higher scores on intelligence tests than those who did not learn the English language. The differences between the two groups of children were statistically significant at the 0.01 level.

Ahmed (1989) administered a questionnaire on motives for reading the newspaper to a random sample of 500 Saudi university male students. The students were divided into two groups, according to whether their field of study was related to theoretical or empirical sciences, and multivariate analysis was used to show correlations between the data. It was found that about 82 percent of students read newspapers, of whom 64 percent were regular readers. Those who studied empirical sciences were less likely to read a newspaper on a regular basis and more likely not to read one at all.

READING READINESS PROGRAMS FOR
PRESCHOOL STUDENTS

In Kuwait, as in the other Arab countries, not all preschool children are enrolled in kindergartens or nurseries. The 1975 census in Kuwait showed that only 20 percent of the Kuwaiti and non-Kuwaiti preschool-aged children were enrolled. The percentage for Kuwaiti preschool children in 1985 was 33 (Abdulghafoor, 1978; al-Ebraheem, 1989; el-Faky, 1986). So, the remaining 80 percent do not receive any reading readiness programs.

The reading readiness programs for the kindergartens and nurseries aim at developing and increasing the children's vocabulary, comprehension, and communication skills; developing the children's interest in reading; developing curiosity and knowledge in children; and preparing children for the next levels of education (el-Faky and Saleh, 1978).

The books and materials given in these programs, especially in the non-Arabic private schools, are first books; participation books; ABC books; counting books; and picture books. The children also participate in many social activities.

No differences exist between males and females concerning the reading readiness programs, while slight differences exist in the nature and extent of these programs regardless of the schooling milieu and location in either urban or rural bedouin areas.

TEACHER QUALIFICATIONS

The procedure for becoming a qualified teacher differs from one area of education to another and from state, to Arabic and non-Arabic private schools. In the area of primary education, non-Arabic private schools require that all teachers have a B.Ed. or B.A. degree as well as a special training program certificate. These conditions and terms are not followed strictly in both state and Arabic private primary education. However, el-Faky's study (1986) showed that 52 percent of the teachers at the kindergarten level had a B.A. in psychology or education. Recently, the authorities have tended to raise the levels of qualifications for becoming teachers at the primary education level. Those teachers are expected to have at least the secondary school certificate, and a two-year diploma in teaching, or a five-year diploma in teaching after the intermediate level. Abdulghafoor (1978) pointed out that 60 percent of primary school teachers were Kuwaitis and most of them had the above-mentioned diploma in teaching.

In intermediate and secondary education, teachers should have either a B.Ed., B.Sc., or B.A. degree. Teachers with a B.Sc. or a B.A. degree need to attend a special training program in the teaching process, or they are asked to have a special diploma in teaching which is offered at the College of Education, Kuwait University, in order to acquire the necessary skills for teaching.

As for tertiary education, the required qualifications for teachers are at least an M.A. (for appointment as assistant lecturer) and a Ph.D. for the staff members at the university.

For adult education, teachers should have at least a diploma in teaching along with special training and proper experience in the field of adult education (al-Khalaf, 1989).

Separate qualifications are required for becoming a reading teacher in the five areas of reading education. For example, in primary education, reading education teachers are selected from all the graduates of the Teaching Institute according to their scores in the Arabic and English languages. In intermediate and secondary education, the reading education teachers are required to have a B.A. degree from the Department of Arabic Language (in the case of Arabic reading teachers) and from the Department of English (in the case of English reading teachers). These same qualifications apply for both male and female reading education teachers.

Generally, female teachers outnumber male teachers at the preschool level (nurseries and kindergartens) and in primary education. The ratio is about ten to one. The statistics also show that 67 percent of all female teachers who are working at the preschool education level are Kuwaitis. Male teachers outnumber female teachers in the areas of intermediate and secondary education, with a ratio of about three to one. In the area of adult education, female teachers represent 39 percent of the total number of teachers in this area, and in tertiary education, male teachers outnumber female teachers with a ratio of three or four to one.

In 1986 Kuwaiti female teachers accounted for 48 percent of all female teachers working in preschool and primary education (see al-Ebraheem, 1989; el-Faky, 1986). The number of female teachers increased from 1,180 in 1961–1962 (or 46.3 percent of the total number of teachers in all levels of state education to 14,522 (or 56.6 percent) in 1984–1985. The number of Kuwaiti female teachers increased in all levels of state education from only 55 (or 4.7 percent of the total number of Kuwaiti teachers) in 1961–1962 to 6,363 (or 77 percent) in 1984–1985 (al-Sabah, 1989). There are no available statistics on reading education teachers.

These statistics reflect the rapid increase of female participation in teaching. A recent study (Ahmed, 1989) was carried out in Kuwait on women's work and its relation to motivation, job satisfaction, professional commitment, and problems encountered by women in fulfilling job responsibilities. The results indicated that approximately two-thirds of the subjects preferred to work as teachers. Women generally opt for those jobs that reinforce their dominant role as mothers; other jobs that attract women include research, secretarial work, banking, and nursing.

In the last ten years, a trend toward early retirement has become evident in Kuwait, especially among Kuwaiti teachers. Statistics show that from 1978 to 1988 about 1,500 teachers (or 0.5 percent of the total number of teachers in all levels of education) retired before the normal age of retirement (e.g., after no more than fifteen years of service in teaching). Recently, in one academic year alone (1987–1988), 500 teachers retired (al-Ebraheem, 1989) and about two-thirds of the retired teachers were females. Early retirement among teachers is a negative influence on the education process in Kuwait.

The personal factors leading to early retirement include health conditions; excessive commuting distance; teacher's desire to complete education; lack of interest in teaching as a career; and family disapproval of teaching as a profession for their children.

The social and economic factors include the low perceived image of teachers in the society; failure of the profession to provide self-satisfaction, self-esteem, and self-actualization; low and insufficient salaries; and social denigration of the teacher's job.

The recent policy of the Ministry of Education is to develop self-sufficiency in its qualified Kuwaiti teaching staff mainly in the primary and intermediate school levels and, to a great extent, at the secondary school level. In accordance with this policy and in order to raise teachers' standards in the primary, inter-mediate, and secondary schools, special education institutes, and literacy and adult education centers, the Ministry of Education has decided to hold short training courses. The government of Kuwait has also established a Supreme Council to supervise and organize the process of teacher preparation in Kuwait.

MATERIALS USED IN READING EDUCATION

In both the state and Arabic private schools, as well as in the literacy and adult education centers, the materials used in reading education are provided by the Ministry of Education in Kuwait. Most authors of these materials are Egyp-tians, Jordanians, and other Arabs. In contrast, the materials used in reading education in non-Arabic private schools are imported from either the United Kingdom or the United States except for materials used in Arabic reading as a subject. In tertiary education, the Arab materials for reading education are pub-lished either in Kuwait or in other Arab countries. The English materials are imported from Europe and the United States.

Most of the materials used in reading education in the state, Arabic private schools, and literacy and adult education centers are in Arabic, whereas most of the materials used in the non-Arabic private schools are in the English lan-guage.

Consumable materials (workbooks, handouts, and the like) play a role in reading education in the state, Arabic private schools and literacy and adult education centers. The percentage of consumable versus nonconsumable mate-rials (hardcovers, textbooks, and the like) is about 30 percent, whereas 50 percent of materials used in reading education in the non-Arabic private schools are consumable.

FINANCING READING EDUCATION

At the state primary, intermediate, and secondary school levels, as well as in the literacy and adult education centers, reading education is financed by the Ministry of Education. In both Arabic and non-Arabic private schools, reading education is financed partly by the Ministry of Education and partly by the students' parents themselves. In the tertiary education area, the students themselves completely finance reading education.

THE PRESENT FOCUS OF EDUCATION

Kuwait's primary educational goals are teaching children to read, write, and pronounce correctly, and to understand what they have read; teaching children to avoid miscues in the reading process; increasing and developing reading interests among students at all educational levels; devising tools for diagnosing reading disabilities in students, especially among primary school children; and creating proper methods and ways to treat reading disabilities in children.

NOTE

The author acknowledges the help of the staff members of the Education Research Center, Ministry of Education, Kuwait. The author is also very grateful for the help of many staff members in some schools in Kuwait, especially the valuable help given by Mrs. B. Swanick, head of the English Department, and Mrs. Hala M. Baidas, head of the Arabic Department (The Modern School/Kuwait).

REFERENCES

Abdalla, M. H. 1985. Reading: Its nature and meaning. *The Journal of Education* (Ministry of Education, Kuwait), No. 36 (January): 65–70 (in Arabic).

Abd el-Motty, Yusuf, and Taha, H. J. 1980. Intermediate school level: An evaluative study. Unpublished paper presented at the 10th Week of Education, March (in Arabic).

Abdulghafoor, Fauzia Y. 1978. The development of education in Kuwait 1912–1972. Kuwait: Al-Falah Library (in Arabic).

Ahmed, Ahmed A. 1986. Reading disabilities: Causes and treatment. *The Library Magazine* (Kuwait) 6, No. 11 and 12 (June): 7–9 (in Arabic).

Al-Ahmed, Abdel Rahman A., and Abou-Allam, Ragaa M. 1987. Drop out (wastage) in educational stages in Kuwait from 1976/77 to 1985/86. *The Educational Journal* (Kuwait) 4, No. 14 (Autumn): 13–36 (in Arabic).

Ahmed, M. Abdel Hamed. 1989. The motives of reading newspapers among university students. *Journal of the Social Sciences* (Kuwait) 17, no. 2 (Summer): 225–247 (in Arabic).

Ahmed, R. A. 1984. The place of school psychology in the Sudan at the turn of the century. *School Psychology International* 5, No. 1: 43–46.

Allington, Richard L., et al. 1985. Up and over: Reading for success: Focus. Glenview, Ill.: Scott, Foresman and Co.

Banks, Caroline, et al. 1984. English for changing world. Part I, New edition. Glenview, Ill.: Scott, Foresman and Co.

Center for Child Evaluation and Teaching. 1988. Parents' guide in the field of learning disabilities. Kuwait: Press of the Kuwaiti Scientific Club (in Arabic).

Central Department of Statistics, Ministry for Planning, State of Kuwait. 1985 Census.

Central Department of Statistics, Ministry for Planning, State of Kuwait 1988/89 Statistics.

al-Ebraheem, H. A. 1989. Kuwait and the future: Development and education face to face. Kuwait: That Es-Salasil Press (in Arabic).

el-Faky, H. A. 1977. Problems among primary school children. *Faculty of Arts and Education Bulletin* (Kuwait), No. 12 (December): 33–45 (in Arabic).

el-Faky, H. A. 1986. The status of the Kuwaiti pre-school child. Kuwait: Kuwait Association for the Advancement of Arab Childhood, No. 2 (in Arabic).

el-Faky, H. A., and Saleh, A. A. 1978. Language development in the kindergarten level children in Kuwait. *Faculty of Arts and Education Bulletin* (Kuwait), No. 13 (June): 41–54 (in Arabic).

Freahat, M. H., and Auda, A. S. 1988. The influence of the family factors on the readability in the pre-school children: A field study. *The Educational Journal* (Kuwait) 5, No. 18: 63–88 (in Arabic).

Habib, L. 1985. Intellectual levels in monolingual and bilingual Kuwaiti primary school children. *The Educational Journal* (Kuwait) 2, No. 4 (March): 58–75 (in Arabic).

Hamada, A. A. 1979. Education and training of adults in Kuwait. Kuwait: Mogahwi Press (in Arabic).

al-Khalaf, A.M.A.A. 1989. Educational ideas in the field of illiteracy eradication. Kuwait: That Es-Salasil Press (in Arabic).

el-Korashy, I. Abdel Fattah. 1985. Interest in reading among female intermediate school students in relation to certain variables. *The Educational Journal* (Kuwait) 2, No. 7 (December): 89–106 (in Arabic).

el-Koussy, A. H. 1973. For a self-criticism of education in the Arab Countries. *Prospects* 3, No. 1: 57–66.

Kuwait University. 1989. *The Researcher* 2, No. 1 (March). Issued by Kuwait University, Kuwait.

Ministry of Education, State of Kuwait. 1970. The 5th International Day for eradication of illiteracy (September 8, 1970). Kuwait: Press of the Ministry of Education (in Arabic).

Ministry of Education, State of Kuwait. 1971. The 6th International Day for eradication of illiteracy (September 8, 1971). Kuwait: Press of the Ministry of Education (in Arabic).

Ministry of Education, State of Kuwait. 1974. The 9th International Day for eradication of illiteracy (September 8, 1974). Kuwait: Press of the Ministry of Education (in Arabic).

Ministry of Education, State of Kuwait. 1975. The 10th International Day for eradication of illiteracy (September 8, 1975). Kuwait: Press of the Ministry of Education (in Arabic).

Ministry of Education, State of Kuwait. 1979. The 14th International Day for eradication of illiteracy (September 8, 1979). Kuwait: Press of the Ministry of Education (in Arabic).

Ministry of Education, State of Kuwait. 1980. The 15th International Day for eradication of illiteracy (September 8, 1980). Kuwait: Press of the Ministry of Education (in Arabic).

Ministry of Education, State of Kuwait. 1981. The 16th International Day for eradication of illiteracy (September 8, 1981). Kuwait: Press of the Ministry of Education (in Arabic).

Ministry of Education, State of Kuwait. 1983a. The efforts of the State of Kuwait in the fields of illiteracy eradication and adult education. Kuwait: Press of the Ministry of Education (in Arabic).

Ministry of Education, State of Kuwait. 1983b. The 18th International Day for eradication of illiteracy (September 8, 1983). Kuwait: Press of the Ministry of Education (in Arabic).

Ministry of Education, State of Kuwait. 1984a. Lights on the law of eradication of illiteracy in Kuwait. Kuwait: Press of the Ministry of Education (in Arabic).

Ministry of Education, State of Kuwait. 1984b. The 19th International Day for eradication of illiteracy (September 8, 1984). Kuwait: Press of the Ministry of Education (in Arabic).

Ministry of Education, State of Kuwait. 1985. The 20th International Day for eradication of illiteracy (September 8, 1985). Kuwait: Press of the Ministry of Education (in Arabic).

Ministry of Education, State of Kuwait. 1986. The 21st International Day for eradication of illiteracy (September 8, 1986). Kuwait: Press of the Ministry of Education (in Arabic).

Ministry of Education, State of Kuwait. 1987. The 22nd International Day for eradication of illiteracy (September 8, 1987). Kuwait: Press of the Ministry of Education (in Arabic).

Mohammed, A. T., and Jaber, A. M. 1980–1981. Teacher's guide in reading education for the 4th primary grade. Kuwait: Press of the Ministry of Education (in Arabic).

al-Rumaihi, M. G. 1985. New phenomena in Kuwaiti society and their influences on youth. (Lecture given at the co-symposium of the Departments of Social Work and Psychological Service (Ministry of Education, Kuwait), *Proceedings of Lectures*, September. Kuwait: Press of the Ministry of Education, pp. 363–374 (in Arabic).

Al-Sabah, A.J.A. 1989. Education of Kuwaiti women and its part in the development process: An analytical study 1957–1985. Kuwait: Kuwait Foundation for the Advancement of Sciences (in Arabic).

Shmas el-Din, M., et al. 1980–1981. Teacher's guide in reading education for the 3rd primary grade. Kuwait: Press of the Ministry of Education (in Arabic).

Siadway, A., et al. 1978. Education development. Beirut: Press of the Arab Institute for Development (in Arabic).

BIBLIOGRAPHY

Abd el-Daim, Abd-alla. 1974. Illiteracy in the world and in the Arab countries. *Al-Arabi Magazine* (Kuwait), No. 186 (May): 56–61 (in Arabic).

Abd el-Raheem, Abdullah A. 1981. The oral reading miscues of preparatory and secondary EFL Jordanian students. Unpublished M.A. Thesis, Yarmouk University, Irbied, Jordan.

al-Arnoat, A. 1984. Why do we read? *The Journal of Education* (Ministry of Education, Kuwait), No. 35 (December): 88–95 (in Arabic).

Bistan, A. A. 1984. Educational opinions and attitudes in the field of illiteracy eradication in the State of Kuwait. *Journal of the Social Sciences* (Kuwait), 12, No. 3: 65–106 (in Arabic).

el-Faky, H. A., et al. 1979. A real evaluation for the status of pre-school children in Kuwait. *Journal of the Social Sciences* (Kuwait), 6, No. 4 (January): 45–67 (in Arabic).

al-Fautori, A. 1986. Techniques de motivation a la lecture (TML). *The Library Magazine* (Kuwait), 6, Nos. 11 and 12 (June): 10–21 (translated into Arabic by A. M. Essawai).

Gebrin, Omar. 1976. Dyslexia. *Journal of Education* (Qatar), No. 15 (May): 28–31 (in Arabic).

Hatamleh, I. 1978. A project in developing TEFL reading-readiness material for Jordanian youngsters. Unpublished Ph.D. Dissertation, University of Illinois, 1978.

Hatamleh, I., Gradat, D., and Al-Amiri, Kh. 1986. An analysis of reading miscues in primary school students in Jordan. *The Educational Journal* (Kuwait) 3, No. 10 (September): 77–101 (in Arabic).

Ibrahim, M. A. 1975. Measuring the readability in Jordanian children: An experimental study. Unpublished M.A. Thesis. Jordanian University. Amman, Jordan (in Arabic).

Kaid, Y. M., et al. 1986–1987. Reading disabilities. *Educational Studies* (U.A.E.) 9, No. 2 (1986–1987): 113–121 (in Arabic).

Kashta, A. M. 1982. The evaluation of reading. *Teacher Journal* (Egypt), 13, No. 581 (September): 26–27 (in Arabic).

Khamis, Abdalla. 1982. Learning correct education. *The Journal of Education* (Ministry of Education, Kuwait), No. 22 (July): 44–48 (in Arabic).

Kharma, N. 1981. An attempt to individualize reading skill at Kuwait University. *ELT* 35, No. 4: 398–404.

Khatar, M. R. 1960. Illiteracy eradication in some Arab countries. Cairo, Egypt: International Institute for Functional Adult Education (in Arabic).

al-Khoby, M. A. 1982. Reading problems. *Journal of Education* (Qatar), No. 55 (October): 50–51 (in Arabic).

Klare, George R. 1969. The measurement of readability. (3rd printing.) Ames: Iowa State University Press. Translated into Arabic by I. M. al-Shafai 1988. Rayaddah: King Saud University Press.

League for Arab States. 1976. The strategy of illiteracy eradication. Cairo, Egypt: Dar el-Taaelif (in Arabic).

Magawar, M. S. 1983. Teaching of the Arabic language in primary education: The basics and applications. Kuwait: Dar al-Qalam (in Arabic).

Mahafouz, S. A. 1982. Children's literature and pre-reading stage. *Library Magazine* (Kuwait) 3, No. 4 (May): 14–16 (in Arabic).

Marawan, Nigm el-Din Ali. 1984. Reading and writing in kindergarten level. *Journal of Education* (Ministry of Education, Kuwait), No. 34 (November): 18–24 (in Arabic).

Mukalalu, S. 1980. The oral reading miscues of Jordanian eighth graders in Zerka District. Unpublished M.A. Thesis, Yarmouk University, Irbied, Jordan, 1980.

al-Qabisi, K. 1982. The use of vocabulary in the evolution of reading books in first grade pupils. *The Arab Journal for Educational Research* (Qatar), 2, No. 2 (July): 185–187 (in Arabic).

Radwan, M. M. N.D. Reading education for beginners. Cairo, Egypt: Dar Misr for Publishing (in Arabic).

Radwan, M. M. N.D. Child starts to read. (3rd ed.) Cairo, Egypt: Dar al-Maaref (in Arabic).

el-Rousan, Faarouq F. 1987. Learning difficulties in elementary students from the viewpoint of special education. *Journal of the Social Sciences* (Kuwait), 15, No. 1 (Spring): 145–262 (in Arabic).

al-Samadi, A. M., and al-Rabdi, S. 1988. Reading miscues of Arabic speaking elementary, intermediate and secondary school students in Jordan. *The Educational Journal* (Kuwait), 5, No. 17 (Summer): 99–117 (in Arabic).

al-Sheikh, Abd el-Raheem. 1983. The influence of kindergarten experience on readability in children. Unpublished M.A. Thesis, Jordanian University, Amman, Jordan (in Arabic).

Tea'ama, R. A. 1982. At home the child starts reading. *Al-Arabi Magazine* (Kuwait), No. 278 (January): 120–160 (in Arabic).

el-Topegy, H. H. 1983. Mass media and technology in education in Kuwait. Kuwait: Dar el-Qalam (in Arabic).

12

Lesotho

Roshan S. Fitter

INTRODUCTION

Lesotho Kingdom, a mountainous country, is landlocked and surrounded by the Republic of South Africa. The former British colony known as Basutoland gained its independence in 1966. It covers over 30,300 square kilometers, of which 85 percent constitutes highlands and 15 percent lowlands. The population is 1.6 million (1983 estimate), with an annual growth of approximately 2.32. The capital city, Maseru, has a population of approximately 75,000 people. The majority of the male Basotho work as migrant laborers in the mines, farms, and industries in the Republic of South Africa. For the remaining Basotho, agriculture is the main activity, and, on average, each household owns about 5 acres of land. Unfortunately, only one-third of the land is arable, and the remainder is used as grazing pastures in the highlands. In the countryside, barefooted herd boys tend their herds; women walk long distances to fetch water and firewood, and for most children, primary education ends after their seventh year at school.

TRADITIONAL EDUCATION IN OLD LESOTHO

In the past, learning took place in two stages. Girls received the first stage of primary learning mainly from the mother, while the father taught the boy. The kitchen (the *mokhorong*) was an important place for the girl's primary learning. The boy's learning, which was very rough and hard, took place outside the house. The second stage of learning consisted of initiation (called *lebollo*) in preparation for full manhood or womanhood. For boys, this was done far away from home at *Mphatong*, and for girls, the initiation school was in a special house near the village.

Table 12.1
Statistical Analysis of Student and Staff Enrollment in Lesotho, March 1986

Type of Institution	Number of Institutions	No. of Students		No. of Staff
		Male	Female	
Primary*	1156	142018	177110	5772
Secondary	156	14954	22389	1772
Vocational/ Technical	9	668	767	132
National Teacher Training College (primary level)	1	312	797	93
University	1	571	548	141
Institute of Extra Mural Studies (NUL)	1	817	1359	71

*From the projected population of 273,847 children aged six to twelve years, only 75.8 percent were enrolled in primary schools.

Children between eleven and fifteen years of age went to schools where they were prepared for full adult responsibilities. They also learned basic principles such as secrecy and patriotism, defense and war rites, customs, traditions, and cooperative spirit. Literacy, numeracy, and moral education were usually learned from grandparents.

MODERN EDUCATION

Formal education was introduced by the Christian missionaries who emphasized reading and writing. The first schools were founded by Eugene Casalis and other Protestant missionaries in 1833, and later, Roman Catholic missionaries established their own schools, too. By 1986 Lesotho had more than 1,156 vernacular-medium primary schools, 156 secondary schools, 9 schools offering formal technical and vocational education, including agricultural education, the National Teachers' Training College, and one university, the National University of Lesotho (Table 12.1).

Although children attending mission or government primary schools do not pay tuition fees, their parents are required to pay for school books and uniforms. The Ministry of Education assists schools by paying teachers' salaries and by developing syllabuses and providing instructional materials. Seventeen percent of total government expenditure is for education in Lesotho at primary, secondary, and tertiary levels.

THE EDUCATIONAL SYSTEM: AN OVERVIEW

Schools within the education system in Lesotho, as portrayed in Figure 12.1, have been classified by type and level of education, in accordance with the International Standard Classification of Education (ISCED) recommended for member states by UNESCO.

First Level

Education at the primary level is provided for children from about five to twenty years and above, although the required school-age population is six to twelve years. It covers seven years of basic education in literacy in both English and Sesotho, numeracy, elementary understanding of social studies, sciences, manipulative skills including gross motor, and fine motor skills, and religious instruction. Children who pass the National Primal School Leaving Examination (PSLE) with good grades proceed to secondary or high schools.

Second Level

The second level is divided into three types of education: general secondary; teacher training; and technical and vocational.

General secondary education is subdivided into lower and upper stages. The lower stage is of three years' duration (age thirteen to fifteen years) after primary education and is called the Junior Certificate (JC). The upper stage is of two years' duration (sixteen to seventeen years) after the JC and is called the Cambridge Overseas Senior Certificate (COSC).

Teacher training for primary or secondary school teaching may be taken on completion of the JC or COSC. The duration of the training period is three years. Vocational, technical, or technician training and motor mechanics training may be pursued after PSLE or COSC.

Technical and vocational training is provided in two stages: (1) In the lower stage (entry qualification PSLE or Grade 7), girls study home economics and agriculture and boys leather work and agriculture. (2) In the upper stage (entry qualification JC), the curriculum consists of basic electronics, carpentry and joinery, electrical installation, fitting and turning, plumbing and building. The training period is two to three years. The training period for technician training,

Figure 12.1
Lesotho Education System

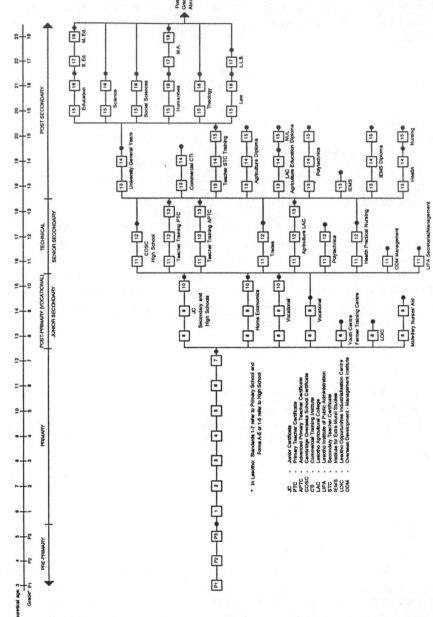

Source: Excerpt from Education Statistics 1986 by Education Statistics Unit, Ministry of Education, Lesotho.

motor mechanics, agriculture business, and the health ministry diploma (entry qualification COSC) is three years.

Third Level

The entry qualification for the third level is COSC, first or second division. The National University of Lesotho caters for higher education needs in the humanities, pure science, education, law, and economic and social sciences. The program is of four years' duration.

LANGUAGE AND EDUCATION

Sesotho and English are the official languages of Lesotho. French is taught as a foreign language in some international schools. Most primary schools are Sesotho-medium from Standard One to Four, with a systematic change to English from Standard Five to Seven. English is also used as a medium of instruction in high schools.

At the end of the seven-year primary school program, pupils must pass the National Standard Seven Examination with very good grades to obtain a place in a high school. Only 40 percent complete Standard Seven, and only 10 percent complete the high school education. The main reason for the high dropout rate is poverty. Secondary education is a five-year course, at the end of which children sit for the National Examination which usually has only a 20 percent pass rate. Of this, only 1.5 percent get into university, and the rest go to other institutes, or centers, or seek employment.

Primary education is universal, but it is not surprising to see herdboys not attending school regularly. The herdboys may be called on to attend to herding by their parents in the event grownups are not available to do such jobs. Young girls may also be called on by their mothers to help with household chores and to take care of smaller children in the family.

Although teachers are required to use English as a medium of instruction in upper primary classes and in secondary schools, it is quite common to see them using Sesotho to a greater degree. Unfortunately, as a result the children fail to acquire fluency and proficiency in English, and therefore children's performances at the National School Leaving Examination which is conducted in English is adversely affected. Consequently, many secondary school pupils without credit in English may be denied admission to university education.

READING INSTRUCTION POLICY

The policy for reading instruction is not clearly defined at all levels of learning. The process is centralized by the Ministry of Education at the primary and secondary school level. Mastery of literacy skills is given top priority in primary school education in Lesotho in order to enable learners to profit from further opportunities for education in or out of school.

Reading instruction at the postsecondary level is processed by the institutions of further studies, whereby reading prescribed textbooks is one of the basic requirements.

THE GOALS OF READING EDUCATION

At each level of education, the goals for reading education are the same for both males and females. At the primary level, reading instruction policy is clearly defined by offering suggestions to teachers for providing learning opportunities to children to acquire fluency and proficiency in reading. One of the objectives for teaching English, as defined in the English Syllabus for Primary Schools (1981), is to develop children's reading skills and to enable them to read and understand information, and to read widely for pleasure.

The goal for reading education in Sesotho is to enable children to read their class readers intelligently so that they can retell stories using figurative language accurately and easily.They should also be able to fill in application forms, to read newspapers and other relevant literature, and to obtain information about current affairs and topics of interest.

Unfortunately, the prescribed books for Sesotho do not have as attractive a format as those for English. Children's books have either black and white pictures, or only two colors. Financial constraints affect the aesthetic quality of books. However, some research is necessary to evaluate the readability and usage of these books by primary school children.

At the secondary level, reading is not considered a separate discipline; rather, it is treated as one of the basic components of English and Sesotho language teaching.

The prescribed books for English and Sesotho literature are studied critically. Very few schools have libraries where children can borrow books to read for pleasure. Some children are members of the Lesotho National Library in Maseru. Obviously, children living outside Maseru do not have access to libraries. There seems to be a strong case for mobile interloan school libraries that can be controlled either by the Lesotho Library Association or by the Ministry of Education. This is very necessary, as children do not have access to books to read for pleasure. Again, it is necessary to investigate the type of books Basotho children like to read, and whether book choices differ between girls and boys.

The postsecondary education for teacher trainees does not explicitly spell out reading instruction policy. Although "Reading Instruction" is one component of the curriculum for language arts, it is lacking in depth, scope, and content. Considering the fact that children are unable to read the prescribed textbooks, it is imperative that "Reading Instruction" be treated as a separate discipline. This would enable trainees to explore different ways of making reading enjoyable through "rotational group activities" that are necessary in overcrowded classes with limited learning resources. Teacher trainees should also have access to books dealing with reading.

The postsecondary agricultural education offered by institutes prepares students for agriculture and mechanization, forestry and rural domestic economy. Technical education prepares students to be skilled craftsmen and technicians. Obviously, more emphasis is laid on practical aspects than on theoretical aspects.

Students in all disciplines are given assignments and reading from the prescribed coursebooks. They have access to over 150,000 books and 1,000 periodical titles covering a wide range of academic subjects. At the Institute of Extra Mural Studies (IEMS), which is widely known for its involvement in a wide variety of educational and cultural projects within Lesotho, more adult females than adult males undertake long or short courses to improve their educational qualifications and professional experience. The numerous projects include Community Development, Adult Education, Credit Union Movement, Society, Development and Peace, Thaba-Khupa Ecumenical Institute, Lesotho Credit Union Scheme for Agriculture, Rural Development, Training of Businessmen, Training of Workers, Labor Studies, Community Needs Assessment, and special projects for the development of villages, including adult literacy classes. IEMS, which is recognized and supported by a number of international development agencies, strives to transfer knowledge of the Basotho, as it believes in the philosophy that development means a better way of life for all (Setsabi). The Institute is also currently involved with the Basic and Non-Formal Education Systems Project (BANFES) program of the Ministry of Education. Practicing primary school teachers have been sponsored for the weekend college courses leading to a Certificate in Educational Leadership.

Another project undertaken by BANFES is the Development of the Primary In-Service Education Program. The purpose of this project is to promote improved instructional opportunities in the basic academic subjects for primary school pupils, facilitate more practical and relevant instruction, and improve managerial efficiency and productivity throughout the education sector. The program is also trying to strengthen the consultancy role of the Education Inspectorate by providing an in-class, in-school program to improve the classroom management and instructional skills of approximately 1,200 lower primary school teachers. Forty to forty-five District Resource Teachers (DRTs), selected from Lesotho's ten districts, participated in a two-part, eighteen-month program. Each DRT was responsible for twenty-five to thirty lower primary teachers.

Yet another program conducted by BANFES is the Non-Formal Education Subproject, which is a joint effort of the Lesotho Ministry of Education and the United States Agency for International Development. The program provides out-of-school education services to adult Basotho who lack adequate education for meaningful employment and personal growth.

The Lesotho Distance Teaching Centre (LDTC), as a nonformal education organization mandated by the Ministry of Education, promotes development in rural Lesotho through four major areas of activity, such as providing literacy

Table 12.2
Pass Percentage Rates at Primary, Secondary, and Tertiary Levels for the National Examinations

Institution	Pass Percentage Rate
Primary	88%

Secondary:
    JC
    COSC
	
	68%
	20%

Teacher Training	81%
Technical/ Vocational	96%

skills, teaching practical skills, offering correspondence courses, and acting as a service agency.

The Learning Post Program, begun in 1981, is conducted by the LDTC, whereby a collection of illiterate learners and their helpers in one or more villages are aided by an administrator from a local school or community and an LDTC field monitor. The focus is on a one-to-one, learner-to-helper teaching method. Currently, there are forty-six Learning Posts in four of the ten districts in Lesotho.

ILLITERACY

To date, no specific studies have been carried out to determine the rate of illiteracy for both males and females at different levels of learning. Standardized tests or instruments in Sesotho and English to measure literacy at different levels of learning are nonexistent. The Education Statistics, 1986 Handbook, has published information about the dropout rate and pass percentage of academic success at primary, secondary, and tertiary levels for the National Examinations (see Table 12.2). The only current source of information about Lesotho's rate of literacy is the 1976 Population Census Analytical Report (Vol. IV, Section 1.8), which states that 36 percent of males and 60 percent of females met a Unesco definition of literacy, based on completion of four years of school. Unless such figures are linked to performance standards, they only reflect assumptions about the literacy skills of Standard Four leavers rather than their actual abilities. In its 1983 publication, *Statistics of Educational Attainment and Illiteracy: 1970–1980*, Unesco defined literacy in two ways: (1) persons are *literate* who can, with understanding, both read and write a short simple statement on everyday life; and (2) persons are *functionally literate* who engage in all those activities in which literacy is required for effective functioning of their group and community, and also for enabling them to continue to use reading, writing, and calculation for their own and the community's development.

The results of the survey of adult literacy carried out by LDTC in 1984 show that, contrary to common belief, Lesotho has a low literacy rate; the rate for simple literacy (reading and writing in Sesotho) was found to be 62 percent, whereas functional literacy (reading, writing, and arithmetic in Sesotho and ability to apply those skills in daily life) was rated at 46 percent. The researchers implied that half the population of Lesotho could be considered literate and that certain subpopulations in the country were in greater need of literacy training, such as men, people in the Sengu River Valley, foothills, and mountains, adults over forty, and herders, farmers, food-for-work participants, and miners. It also recommended that analysis of Lesotho's 1986 population census data raise the cutoff level for literacy to Standard Five.

In the second LDTC report, results of the adult literacy survey were compared with those from the children's literacy survey. The aim was to determine whether adults perform better than children at certain levels of schooling and on what items performance differs. The adults' better performance was not related to schooling, since the difference in performance between two groups of people at the same educational level was so wide. It was reasoned that many literacy skills were acquired informally through shopping, church, clinics, and work in the mines, or perhaps just by coming into contact with print over a certain number of years respondents learned to read simple words.

The literacy assessment instrument used for the study comprised three parts: reading, writing, and numeracy. The reading items had five categories: reading simple words; reading and understanding signs; reading sentences; reading a popular health poster, and reading a letter with comprehension. The writing items included copying words from a card; writing down words dictated by the interviewer; filling out a form, and writing a letter. Arithmetic test items included counting; mental arithmetic; reading numbers; prices and symbols; writing numbers and prices; and written arithmetical problems.

Several other literacy and numeracy studies have identified additional target groups that have had less than adequate educational opportunities and have the greater need for literacy and numeracy training. They are prisoners, women tending rural farms and small businesses, and young women who have dropped out of school for various reasons, including pregnancy. BANFES NFE coordinator has commented on Lesotho's need for nonformal education programs:

We have many adults in Lesotho who are not able to participate fully in Lesotho's society because they cannot read and write and cannot count. For example, if a farmer cannot read and count, how can he calculate the amount of seed and fertilizer plus costs that he will need for a year's supply of crops grown on his land? If he cannot read agricultural newsletters and farm information passed on by the Ministry of Agriculture, farmers associations and cooperatives, then his income capability is affected. Furthermore, his family life is affected and their growth and opportunities are affected. We have many people in Lesotho who lack primary level education, yet they cannot return to school.

READING DISABILITIES

Unfortunately, reading disabilities have not been given due consideration in Lesotho as they have in international schools elsewhere. Teachers in Lesotho fail to realize that learning disability is a processing deficit and that it may result in children experiencing considerable difficulties in reading, spelling, writing, and mathematics.

Learners with reading disabilities at different levels of education usually plough through their courses without any special remedial assistance. Diagnosis becomes more difficult as teachers lack knowledge and skills to help learners to overcome or combat reading disability. Furthermore, at the primary level classrooms are overcrowded and the pupil-teacher ratio is 55:1. This means that the class teacher is unable to offer special assistance to such children. Group teaching techniques are nonexistent as the teachers lack the experience and training for them, owing to the scarcity of support materials or apparatus. However, a couple of schools have involved parents and others. Under the supervision of class teachers, these volunteers provide extra tutoring or hear children read aloud daily.

At secondary and tertiary levels, reading disability would be a serious handicap to learners. Those so affected are usually left on their own to cope with schoolwork. At this level, most students with reading disabilities are those who have not acquired an adequate expressive vocabulary, as some secondary school teachers have stated.

Pertinent information on the incidence of reading disabilities at different levels of learning and between males and females is not available, for reading disability is a relatively new area for most teachers.

The official syllabus for secondary schools expects teachers to devise appropriate remedial strategies for dealing with students' most common errors in speech, reading, and writing. Teachers are encouraged to improve students' proficiency in the language by maintaining a broad level of exposure to the language, particularly emphasizing the personal reading program.

Standardized reading tests are also nonexistent. Teachers tend to rush through the syllabus in order to prepare children for the school examination and national examination. Most of the schools lack reading facilities, such as textbooks, and a variety of reading resources, including the class or school library.

READING READINESS PROGRAMS

Reading readiness programs in pre-primary schools vary from school to school. However, most schools emphasize listening skills as the requisite to language acquisition and skill. The daily routine is heavily loaded with a variety such as stories, poems, traditional songs, and obeying simple instructions and playing language games. Verbal communication is also acquired through drama, news, show and tell, conversations and dialogue, miming, puppetry, and poetry. The majority of the preschools use this approach to develop the spoken language. Reading skill is not emphasized, although some teachers expose children to books and introduce prereading activities to develop auditory and visual perceptual skills. It is common to find children naming and matching colors, discriminating different sounds, matching shapes, ordering sizes, and matching pictures or common words.

The kind and number of such programs vary between urban and rural areas. In urban areas, the preschools have better learning resources, including audiovisual equipment, whereas the scarcity of materials in rural areas forces the teachers to emphasize counting, reading, and writing in the form of repetitive and monotonous drills. Urban teachers tend to use concrete materials, whereas rural teachers stress rote learning such as counting and saying the letters of the alphabet. The same prereading program is offered to boys and girls.

TEACHER QUALIFICATIONS

The National Teachers' Training College (NTTC) provides teacher training for primary school teaching to those who satisfactorily complete the JC or COSC. Those with the JC are trained for a period of three years and are awarded the Primary Teachers Certificate (PTC), which enables them to teach all grades in a primary school. There is also a program for training primary school headteachers, who are awarded the Advanced Primary Teachers Certificate (APTC).

At present, there is no special program or provision for reading education for a candidate to qualify as a reading teacher or reading specialist. Reading teachers or reading specialists are nonexistent. Reading is inadequately covered under the broad heading of language skills. However, the Ministry of Education is attempting to expose teachers to recent innovations in the field of reading and literacy.

The proportion of male to female primary school teachers is 1:4—that is, 23 percent are male and 77 percent female. Female teachers, both trained and untrained, dominate teaching in primary schools. The overall pupil–teacher ratio has remained 55:1, which is very unsatisfactory. Reduction of this ratio is a priority in the fourth Five-Year Development Plan period, and it is intended that it will be reduced to one teacher for every forty pupils.

On the secondary education level, the NTTC trains those with the COSC for a period of three years and awards them the Secondary Teacher Certificate (STC), which enables them to teach the lower secondary classes up to the JC level.

Teacher training for the upper secondary school teachers is conducted at the National University of Lesotho (NUL) for the Diploma in Education (Secondary) and Diploma in Education (Science). Other teaching degrees offered by the university are the B.Ed., B.S.Ed., B.Sc.Ed., PGCE, and M.Ed.

Secondary teachers, like primary school teachers, do not receive any formal training for reading education. No information is available about the ratio of male and female teachers in secondary schools. All that is known is that the proportion of unqualified teachers presently stands at almost 20 percent. The pupil–teacher ratio was found to be 21:1. A shortage of mathematics and science teachers in secondary schools remains.

In the area of tertiary and adult education, in line with the policy of diversification and training in self-reliance, NTTC has designed a program that leads to the Secondary Technical Teachers Certificate (STTC). This program trains teachers in technical subjects at the third grade level. Basic crafts, agriculture, home economics, and commercial studies are included. Boys exceed girls by a large margin on such courses; they make up the total enrollment in bricklaying, fitting and turning, masonry, panel beating, upholstery, architecture, and mechanical engineering. Girls dominate in commercial training—for example, in tailoring, home economics, and dressmaking. This reflects the pattern found in employment. Home economics, bricklaying, commercial studies, motor mechanics, and electrical installation appear to be popular courses.

The Institute of Extra Mural Studies and the National University of Lesotho organize courses for adults at the diploma and degree level. They also conduct in-service workshops, seminars, and meetings for professionals. The National Curriculum Development Centre organizes meetings for curriculum update. The Lesotho Distance Teaching Centre plays a significant role in organizing literacy and numeracy classes. The programs specifically provide basic practical skills to the rural people of Lesotho; offer opportunities for out-of-school youth and adults to develop their literacy and numeracy skills; and provide correspondence courses for private candidates for the Junior Certificate and the Cambridge Overseas School Certificate.

Statistical information about the ratio of male and female teacher participation is not available. No provision is made for teachers to qualify as reading education specialists.

RESOURCE MATERIALS FOR READING EDUCATION AND FINANCE

The National Curriculum Development Centre controls and distributes the source of materials used in reading education.

In primary schools, the Book Supply Unit (BSU) supplies three textbooks (English, Sesotho, and mathematics) to each student. Supplying textbooks to all primary schools is a challenge, and BSU hopes to carry it out successfully. However, parents are required to pay for school books. There is a scarcity of reading materials, and libraries are nonexistent. The class primer is the only book available for reading with understanding and pleasure. Some teachers make a special effort to produce a variety of reading activities. Lower primary classroom walls are plastered with pictures that are labeled. Labeling and general display are of unsatisfactory standards. Handouts are very scarce, the only form available being those that accompany radio broadcast lessons for primary English. Considering the unavailability of commercially made reading materials, there is a need for a special workshop for making reading materials.

Secondary schools are not free, and few parents can afford to pay tuition fees or to buy books for their children. This problem is being partly overcome through the book cooperative organized by each school. Even sanitation facilities are inadequate. In March 1986 only 34 percent of schools had flush toilet facilities, whereas 54 percent had pit-latrine facilities. Only 46 percent had school libraries.

The official syllabus for secondary schools stipulates that students must be trained in the use of effective reading strategies and that they must be encouraged to read extensively outside the classroom, as well as in addition to intensive reading of at least fourteen suitable texts on set drama, set novel, and set poetry.

The reading program covers areas such as consolidation of reading skills, which includes reading quickly and with understanding and critical discussion; intensive reading, which includes in-depth study of reading texts and passages, comprehensive language work, and vocabulary work; class reading, which includes two suitable readers for class reading programs, twelve suitable readers for group and individual reading programs, and ten simple, enjoyable poems; multilevel reading for pleasure and information, which includes group reading and individual silent reading (small sets of books to match the reading level of each group); books and magazines for individualized silent reading; use of encyclopedias, dictionaries, and reference books, incorporating a variety of progressive activities in the use of a dictionary; and listening to stories, including reading appealing books regularly, presenting poetry and excerpts of various kinds of prose, and individuals acting character parts.

Information is not available as to whether students have access to books or whether the activities are being carried out by the teachers.

At the postsecondary level, every institution provides a list of prescribed books to be read by course participants. However, students have easy access to books that can be borrowed from various national, public, and institutional libraries. The Lesotho Teaching Centre has, to its credit, numerous publications—pamphlets, newsletters, reports, manuals, handbooks, posters, brochures, booklets, books, student support materials for JC and COSC students, and radio notes. It has also produced rural education booklets in Sesotho, which cover topics such as Red Cross first aid, crochet, vegetable growing, baby and child care, cookery and cattle diseases. The literacy and numeracy books in Sesotho include literacy and numeracy workbooks, bimonthly newspaper supplement (Moithuti), and leaflets. Of the eighty research reports, at least fifteen are on adult literacy, cover reading habits, understanding print, and learning to read, write, and do arithmetic in village groups.

The National Curriculum Development Centre (NCDC) and the Instructional

Materials Resource Centre (IMRC) develop relevant curricula for schools; design and produce instructional materials; distribute materials to schools; and disseminate curriculum innovations nationwide.

The Book Supply Unit (BSU) handles the materials distribution functions. It ascertains book needs, and stores and supplies books for schools. It also manages the revolving fund, which accumulates as book fees are collected.

The Mathematics and Science Centre develops and disseminates mathematics and science constructional materials made out of simple, homemade equipment.

The Instructional Materials Resource Centre (IMRC) develops and improves educational programs for primary and secondary schools by providing instructional and curricular materials that are relevant to the social and economic needs of Lesotho. The materials produced are printed materials as well as audiovisual materials, such as booklets, handbooks, teachers' guides and charts, and instructional television productions.

The National Library operates branch libraries and also conducts refresher courses for teacher librarians and headmasters. The Library Service for the Prisons is also available to prisoners in Maseru. In addition, efforts are being made to supply reading materials to the handicapped and other patients in the Maseru Health Centres.

READING RESEARCH

There are no records on research in reading education in Lesotho because this is a relatively new field.

In 1976 an exploratory study was conducted on the ability of rural Basotho to understand text and illustrations. The resulting report, "Understanding Print," showed that 55 percent of people over ten years of age could read a passage aloud in Sesotho, but only 27 percent could interpret the meaning of the passage read with a reasonable degree of accuracy.

Another three-stage research project (1976–1978) was launched to discover how the basic literacy skills possessed by Basotho were actually used. The first stage catalogued the uses of literacy and numeracy by Basotho. The second stage investigated the potential of games as aids to literacy teaching. The third looked into how useful literacy and numeracy were to Basotho, whether an extra educational provision was necessary to pick up where schools had missed out, and whether a distance teaching approach would be acceptable to people.

In 1985 an attempt was made to compare the results of an adult literacy survey with a child literacy survey.

The LDTC is at present analyzing the data of another adult literacy survey. Two research studies have been conducted on reading education at the primary school level. One study pertains to Word Recognition Skills of Children in Grade One, and the other is on Reading Skills of Second Language Learners in Grades 1 and 2 in a Multicultural Primary School.

Many studies are required to survey the reading habits of children and adults;

the readability of prescribed textbooks by second-language learners (at the primary, secondary, and tertiary levels); readability and usage of teachers' handbooks by teachers (at all three levels); reading disability and school performance; formal and informal approaches to teaching reading; comparison of reading ability and writing ability; reading ability in English and Sesotho; analysis of reading miscues in English and Sesotho; parental involvement in reading; child-to-child or paired reading or Reading Pal Program; use of supplementary readers or prescribed readers; and effect of peer tutoring on children and adults.

SIGNIFICANCE FOR READING EDUCATION

Until recently, reading, unlike other disciplines, was given very little prominence in Lesotho. More studies have been carried out to survey language development with specific reference to spoken language.

First, when we look at reading education in both primary and secondary classrooms, we can easily see that the reading content of the prescribed pupils' books and teachers' handbooks is often far above the average reading level of children and teachers respectively. The teachers' handbooks are quite lengthy and written in a language which the average teacher may have difficulty comprehending. Research on the readability of teachers' guides is urgently needed.

Second, unrealistic demands are made on teachers, for the syllabuses and books contain more materials than any human being could teach. Furthermore, the syllabus presupposes background knowledge that teachers do not possess. The syllabuses frequently demand approaches and attitudes that are totally different from those held by an average teacher. In schools with limited resources, demands made on teachers, both in preparation time and materials to be collected, may also be unrealistic.

Learning aids or teaching aids are not readily available or may be too expensive to afford. The overenthusiastic curriculum panels drawing on experience from materially rich urban contexts place far too much reliance on the collection and use of "junk" materials. Teachers are often required to make large amounts of apparatus. Where and how teachers can make "reading games" in materially deprived rural environments is rarely specified. With no supply of stationery such as wax crayons, cards, pencils, and paper, the teacher is magically supposed to be innovative, resourceful, and imaginative.

Reading education in Lesotho needs a revolutionary approach. Although some effort has been made to improve the quality of reading education in English, very little has been done to improve reading methodology in Sesotho. Reading education research in both English and Sesotho at all levels of learning will provide information for decision making with regard to the quality and quantity of instructional materials. Examination of current teaching techniques should pave the way to desirable changes.

During the workshop entitled Educational Research Needs and Priorities in Lesotho, held at the Lerotholi Polytechnic in Maseru, Lesotho, on July 9, 1982, one of the first priority areas for research listed was language teaching and learning. There seemed to be a strong desire to study the teaching and learning of both Sesotho and English in schools, with the emphasis on Sesotho as a language for transmission of culture and English as a second language. Among the second priority areas listed was literacy.

BIBLIOGRAPHY

Ambrose, D. P. 1983. *The Guide to Botswana, Lesotho and Swaziland*. Johannesburg, South Africa: Winchester Press.
BANFES (Basic and Non-Formal Education System). *The Non-Formal Education Sub-project*. Maseru.
Educational Research Needs and Priorities in Lesotho. 1982. Proceedings of the Educational Research Workshop held at the Lerotholi Polytechnic, Maseru, July 9, 1982.
Government of Lesotho. 1971. *First Five-Year Development Plan 1970/71–1974/75*. Roma: Government Printer.
Government of Lesotho. 1975. *Second Five-Year Development Plan 1975/76–1979/80*. Maseru.
Government of Lesotho. *Third Five-Year Development Plan 1980/81–1984/85*. Maseru: Government Printer.
Hawes, H.W.P. 1976. *An African Primary Curriculum Survey: Country Profile, Lesotho*. Research report, University of London, Institute of Education (Department of Education in Developing Countries).
Hawes, H.W.P. 1977. *Primary School Curriculum Change in Lesotho: UNICEF's Commitment in context*. London: Institute of Education, Consultant's Report.
Hawes, H. 1979. *Curriculum and Reality in African Primary Schools*. Longman Group Ltd.
Lenaneo: Thuto La Sesotho. 1981. Setsi Sa Sechaba Sa Ntsetso-Pele Ea Mananea Thuto: Muso oa Motlothehi Lesotho.
Lesotho Distance Teaching Centre. 1976a. *A Brief Survey of the Uses of Literacy and Numeracy in Lesotho*. Maseru. 66 p. (mimeo).
Lesotho Distance Teaching Centre. 1976b. *Understanding Print: A Survey in Rural Lesotho of People's Ability to Understand Text and Illustration*. Maseru: Lesotho Distance Teaching Centre.
Lesotho Distance Teaching Centre. 1980. *Bi-Annual Report: Lesotho Distance Teaching Centre*. February 1980–July 1980. Maseru.
Lesotho Distance Teaching Centre. 1985. *Adult Literacy in Lesotho* Part I: *Results of an Assessment of Reading, Writing and Arithmetic Skills*. Part II: *A Comparison of the Results of an Adult Literacy Survey with Child Literacy*.
Lesotho Distance Teaching Centre. 1986. *Bi-Annual Report: Lesotho Distance Teaching Centre*. July 1986–December 1986. Maseru.
Lesotho Distance Teaching Centre. 1988. *Bi-Annual Report: Lesotho Distance Teaching Centre*. August 1988. Maseru.
Lesotho Distance Teaching Centre. *First Evaluation Report: The Learning Post Programme*.

Matsela, Z. A. 1989. *Determination of Sesotho Vocabulary Levels of Standards One and Two Pupils in Lesotho*. Roma: National University of Lesotho.

Ministry of Education, Lesotho. 1987. *Education Statistics 1986*. Education Statistics Unit, Bureau of Statistics.

National Curriculum Development Centre, Ministry of Education. 1981. *Syllabus for English: Primary Schools*.

Sebatane, E. M. 1989. *Teaching/Learning Strategies in Lesotho Primary School Classrooms*. Roma: Institute of Education, National University of Lesotho.

Setsabi, A. M. 1988. In a Wider World IEMS Plays Its Part. In *Light in the Night*. Roma: Institute of Extra-Mural Studies, National University of Lesotho.

Strother, F. S. 1926. *A Night School for Herdboys*. Mission Field (UK), pp. 184–185.

University of London. 1977. *Teaching Mother-Tongue Reading in Multi-Lingual Environments*. University of London, Institute of Education (Department of Education in Developing Countries). Report of a Workshop, March 28–April 1, 1977.

13

New Zealand

Warwick B. Elley

The distinctive features of reading instruction in New Zealand, as in most countries, have arisen largely out of the distinctive features of the cultural and linguistic environment. These features have been modified by prevailing government policies and administrative practices; by the work of prominent teachers and writers; and by input from local research and professional conferences. The shape of the tradition that evolves in the classroom, however, depends considerably on the beliefs and practices of the teachers. This chapter attempts to spell out the distinctive features of reading instruction in New Zealand and to outline some of the forces that have influenced these policies and practices.

THE LANGUAGE BACKGROUND

New Zealand has a population of 3.3 million, approximately 10 percent of whom are Maori and 3 percent Pacific Islanders. The remainder are mostly of British cultural background (referred to locally as *pakehas*) whose ancestors arrived from Britain in large numbers during the middle to late nineteenth century. The country was populated first by the Maoris, a brown-skinned Polynesian race that ventured south from the island groups west of Tahiti in their ocean-going canoes. According to local belief, they settled in New Zealand in about the middle of the fourteenth century. Their language and culture have much in common with other Polynesian groups that have arrived in large numbers over the past twenty years from Western Samoa, Cook Islands, Tonga, Niue, and the Tokelaus. Most of these Polynesian groups have settled in the North Island, making Auckland the largest Polynesian city in the world. English became the official language of New Zealand in 1840 when it became a British colony, but the rapid growth of the Maori and Polynesian populations in the recent past, and the concern of Maori leaders that their language not die out, has produced an activist movement to elevate Maori language to official status and to bring a new emphasis to Maori culture in education and social policy. Similar, but less conspicuous, movements are growing among the migrant Polynesian groups.

In 1987 the Maori Language Act made Maori a second official language for possible use in the law courts of the land. During the 1980s, the emergence of a Maori preschool movement, Te Kohanga Reo (the Language Nest), led to the establishment of dozens of small centers where some 8,000 three to four year olds are socialized into the Maori language and culture through an indigenous immersion program, organized and taught by local Maori mothers, on a largely voluntary basis. These institutions have, in turn, generated a need for bilingual primary (elementary) schools to receive these native Maori-speaking children when they turn five years of age. Indeed, by 1989 there were eleven new bilingual elementary schools scattered throughout the North Island, and large numbers of bilingual classrooms were attached to regular schools. In addition, a small private university has been set up near Wellington to offer courses in Maori in a few selected subjects.

Despite these movements English remains the mainstream language, and the number of fluent Maori language speakers is estimated to be less than 15 percent of the Maori population, according to a sociolinguistic survey conducted in the 1970s by the New Zealand Council of Educational Research. Instructional resources and trained teachers in Maori and other Polynesian languages are still scarce, although recent private initiatives and government policies are alleviating this situation somewhat. However, the English language policies of educators, and sometimes of the Maori leaders themselves, have contributed to a tradition of English instruction in the vast majority of classrooms for over a century. English is still the medium of instruction in over 99 percent of classrooms, and all students are expected to develop fluency in English and confidence in its use.

READING INSTRUCTION POLICY

Because New Zealand has a relatively small population, education policy and funding have traditionally been centralized. Reading provides no exception. The central administrative body, the Department of Education, has always administered the schools, produced curricula and teachers' handbooks, trained teachers, and ensured that standards were maintained in the schools under its care (which cater for some 97 percent of the New Zealand enrollments). In the case of reading, the Education Department's influence has been considerable, as it has not only set out the objectives and trained the teachers, but has also produced the bulk of the reading materials through its central School Publications Branch. Certainly, numerous commercial publishers supplement the reading resources of the schools, but they have minimal influence on the policy or practice, and teachers are free to choose from a wide range of offerings.

Although this situation may sound authoritarian, it should be noted that each school is expected to develop its own local scheme of work, and teachers are encouraged to use their own initiative and to exercise autonomy in developing their own methods and resources to adapt their instruction to pupils' needs. Indeed, the underlying philosophy of reading instruction in New Zealand is that it should be child-centered, with the individual pupil's interests at the heart of the process. It is accepted that not all children learn by the same methods, and although the department promotes some concepts and materials through its inspectors and reading advisers, nevertheless a certain tolerant eclecticism exists, particularly in the case of children with special needs. Moreover, individual teachers have played a major role in preparing materials and formulating policies, as the Department involves them heavily in the development process.

While the tradition of centralization has been preeminent in education, distinct signs of a dramatic shift toward a greater decentralization are evident. A government-appointed commission chaired by Brian Picot produced a report in 1988 (commonly known as the Picot Report), calling for the abolition of the Department of Education, and the decentralization of responsibility and funding for individual schools. The government has accepted the need for such a change and in 1989 was planning its implementation.

The long-term effects of such a change on reading instruction are difficult to predict, but the distinctive beliefs of how children learn language and reading are so widely accepted by New Zealand teachers that it is unlikely to lead to major shifts in philosophy in the near future.

THE GOALS OF READING INSTRUCTION

Although the basic principles underlying reading instruction have been spelled out in many departmental publications and teachers' handbooks, there are few statements of aims as such. Nevertheless, at a recent Unesco international conference, a New Zealand presentation by the Department of Education listed the following aims as "likely to find general acceptance among teachers in New Zealand," and the present writer agrees with this statement. These aims (slightly modified) are:

1. To make reading an enjoyable and purposeful task.
2. To develop a permanent interest in reading.
3. To develop an attitude of demanding meaning—that which is read must make sense.
4. To develop independence in reading—that is, to help the child become self-sufficient in monitoring his or her own reading, and overcoming difficulties met in extracting a message from the written text.
5. To enable the child to select reading materials appropriate to his or her interests and experience.
6. To help the child become a critical reader.
7. To develop flexibility in adapting the rate of reading to the purpose.

8. To bring each child into contact with a variety of books that will enrich or extend his or her experience.

9. To increase the child's resourcefulness in using reading to meet everyday needs.

10. To develop the skill of reading aloud effectively.

The order of these aims is significant. A recent survey of a cross-section of seventy-five primary school teachers (Elley, 1985) showed that teachers of both eight to ten year olds and eleven to twelve year olds gave major weighting to "developing a lasting interest in reading," and only minor interest in "developing the skill of reading aloud." The learning of phonics, or decoding skills, is rarely mentioned as a goal, because teachers normally see this aim as one of a set of word attack skills, to be developed incidentally, if needed. Decoding skills are regarded as a means rather than an end, at all levels. Many would describe the New Zealand orientation as one of "whole-language instruction."

For instance, most teachers of beginning readers would use the language experience approach, in which children participate in a vivid experience which then becomes the focus of oral, written, and reading activity. The Shared Reading Method, developed by Don Holdaway (1979), is often seen as a variant of this approach. Teachers share interesting stories with children over several days and use the language of the book as the basis for natural reading growth, supplemented by discussion, art work, drama, and writing activities.

The goals and methods of reading instruction are identical for both sexes and are similar for all levels of the school. The emphasis shifts from "learning to read" to "reading to learn" in the secondary school. Study skills, or library and research skills, are given considerable weight from about twelve years onwards, and the emphasis shifts gradually from fictional reading to nonfiction, but the central focus on individual need and reading for meaning is retained at all levels, albeit within a wider range of contexts.

Few special reading programs have been set up at the tertiary level, although fewer academic students who enter technical institutes are sometimes given private assistance in reading their course materials.

In 1978 a voluntary adult reading scheme was established following widespread publicity of the plight of adult illiterates. Many such ventures have now been set up, primarily to teach illiterate adults "survival literacy skills" and to improve their English, as for many of them English is their second language.

LITERACY AND ILLITERACY

Although literacy has been highly regarded in New Zealand (see Guthrie, 1981; Purves, 1979), there has been little study of the levels of illiteracy in the adult population. Using attendance in the compulsory school years as a rough criterion, the Department of Education normally reports literacy levels to international bodies as approximately 99 percent. Indeed, virtually all pupils do receive full-time education from five to fifteen years of age, and over 85 percent stay on for their School Certificate Examination, taken in their eleventh year of schooling. On the assumption that one must be literate to attend and profit from a typical secondary education, the 99 percent literacy rate is not an unjustifiable estimate. Nevertheless, it is recognized that a few pupils do emerge from their primary school years with serious reading difficulties. Estimates based on standardized tests show that 4 percent of the children emerging from Form 2 cannot read above level 3 on a criterion-referenced scale of a nationally standardized test. This point suggests an inability to read independently.

The need for a clearer definition of specified levels of literacy and the percentage of people performing at those levels is widely acknowledged. New Zealand is participating in the IEA (International Association for the Evaluation of Educational Achievement) survey of literacy with a view to improving this state of affairs.

Most adult illiterates are believed to come from non-English-speaking backgrounds. Although there may be a disproportionate number of females in this group, the literacy figures for mainstream New Zealanders show that females read more, and with slightly greater success, than males (Elley and Reid, 1969).

There would be virtually no illiterates at New Zealand universities or teachers' colleges, of course, and the figures for technical institutes would be low but not known.

READING DISABILITIES

There is no agreed-on concept of reading disabilities in New Zealand. Although authorities accept the notion that children have varying degrees of success in reading, there has never been an official "magic cutoff point" that separates the failing reader from the remainder. Indeed, the whole notion of remedial reading is regarded with suspicion, and strenuous attempts are being made to avoid classifying children, and labeling them with any pejorative term that might become a stable part of their self-concepts. Thus, official figures on failing children are hard to discover. Nevertheless, the outstanding success of the Reading Recovery Program, pioneered in the late 1970s by Dame Professor Marie Clay of the University of Auckland, has led to government support for a nationwide scheme aimed at reducing reading failure. The recent figures produced as a result of its implementation can be revealing. By December 1987, when the Reading Recovery Program had been operating for four years, a Department of Education report showed that 9,240 six year olds from a population of 49,789 had been identified as "at risk of failure in reading"—after twelve months at school. As the program was accessible to only 71.5 percent of the cohort, the department estimated that 15.7 percent of the six year olds were in need of individual help by age six. As these judgments were made at such an early age, it is probable that many of these children would have "caught up" to their peers without extra help. However, the risk entailed in waiting was felt to be sufficiently great to allow them the individual teacher tuition provided by the Reading Recovery Program.

The figures also show that 64 percent of the children given thirteen weeks tuition (on average) had caught up; another 27 percent were responding well but needed more time; 6 percent had changed schools before completion, and 3.4 percent (of those identified) were in need of specialist help. This represents less than 1 percent of the cohort who were still failing at reading after the age of six and a half years. Followup studies after two years show that most of these gains were maintained (Clay, 1988). Thus, at the time of writing, the Department of Education estimates that less than 2 percent of children need specialist help in the upper primary school. When Reading Recovery coverage is complete, the figure should drop to 1 percent or less. Indeed, a report by Beardsley (1988) on the incidence of failure in the Canterbury (South Island) area found only 2 percent of children reading two years below their chronological age, a large drop from previous years. The percentages for secondary students are probably much higher, but no accurate figures are available. There is no official program for reading-disabled students at tertiary level.

All reading surveys show that larger numbers of boys "fail" in reading. In Beardsley's surveys, nearly 70 percent of the at risk group were boys; in Reading Recovery surveys the percentage is often as high as 80 percent. These figures are typical, regardless of the types of measures used.

To identify pupils for admission to the Reading Recovery Program, Professor Clay's diagnostic survey tests are used. These consist of knowledge of the alphabet, word recognition, concepts of print, writing vocabulary, and running records (or miscue analysis). These tests (or their parallel forms) are normally administered after the Reading Recovery "treatment," to help determine whether pupils are ready to discontinue the program.

Other standardized tests commonly used at higher levels are the Burt Word Recognition Test and the Progressive Achievement Tests of Reading, Vocabulary, and Listening. All these tests have New Zealand norms. Several informal reading inventories are in common use to supplement these measures, and most primary school teachers are now able to administer miscue analyses for diagnosing their own pupils' problems. Several standardized sets of reading passages are available to assist teachers in these analyses.

As noted above, the Reading Recovery Program has been shown to be very successful in helping all but a small percentage of six year olds to become independent readers. Indeed, the program is being "exported" to several other countries.

Those pupils who were not picked up by the "Six Year Net" are often given assistance by departmental reading resource teachers in the upper primary school, or by specialist psychologists if the cases are serious. At the secondary school level, most schools have at least one reading specialist, who gives help to failing readers. Although there are many individual cases of success, the general picture is not nearly as optimistic at these higher age levels.

PRESCHOOL READING

There are no formal reading readiness programs in New Zealand. Nevertheless, most parents read stories to their children regularly and provide them with valuable book concepts and positive attitudes toward books.

Official statistics for 1988 show that 91.4 percent of four year olds were attending some form of preschool institution—kindergarten, play centers, day care centers, or Te Kohanga Reo (the Maori Language Nest) for several half-days a week. While reading is not formally taught in these centers, most children would again be exposed to story reading and much oral language experience derived from it and from other interest themes. No reading readiness tests are used in New Zealand. All children enter school on their fifth birthday. This policy, which is possibly unique, does permit a greater degree of individualization in the early stages of learning to read, and is a cherished tradition in New Zealand schools.

TEACHER QUALIFICATIONS

At the preschool level, candidates for teaching positions in kindergartens are required to complete a two-year period of full-time education in one of New Zealand's six accredited teachers' colleges. Play centers are organized and run by groups of parents who have their own short-term training schemes, whereas Maori parents who are fluent in Maori are given short-term private training schemes to teach in the Te Kohanga Reo.

Primary school teachers are required to complete a three-year training period in a teachers' college, followed by a two-year period of full-time teaching in a state primary school. Alternatively, the college program may be reduced to two years if students enter college with a degree or are judged to be "mature trainees" with relevant work experience. Many primary teachers now take a four-year B.Ed. degree earned jointly at a teachers' college and university.

Polytechnic lecturers typically have relevant professional or trade training and successful experience, as well as a short training course at a national or local tutor training unit. Adult education lecturers normally have a university degree or appropriate professional teaching qualification, whereas adult reading tutors are typically volunteers with relevant experience who are given eighteen to twenty hours of training by the Workers Educational Association (WEA) scheme.

At the primary level, all reading teachers are responsible for reading instruction. The Reading Recovery Program requires that its tutors have a year of full-time training at Auckland after successful teaching experience. Tutors then return to their home base to train local Reading Recovery Teachers, who work with individual children. Reading Resource teachers, of whom there are currently sixty-seven, are successful teachers who have a short in-service course. Secondary reading teachers are typically trained as primary teachers. After a period of in-service specialist training, they transfer to secondary schools to conduct developmental and remedial-type programs. All these qualifications are the same for males and females.

With regard to sex ratios, over 99 percent of primary school reading specialists and nearly 80 percent of secondary reading teachers are female. The ratios for teachers in general are approximately 2:1 in favor of females at the primary level, and 1:1 at the secondary level.

READING MATERIALS

The standard reading materials for instructional purposes at the primary level are the "Ready to Read" booklets for the first two to three years and the "School Journals" for eight to eleven year olds. These materials are produced by the School Publications Branch of the Government Department of Education. They are generally popular with pupils and teachers, as they are attractively illustrated and present themes that are inherently interesting for children. They have also been successfully promoted in Australia, the United States, and several Pacific Islands. A range of commercial publishers, such as Price Milburn-Hygate, Short-lands, Longman-Paul, Wendy-Pye, Ashtons, and McDonalds, provide supplementary reading materials. Teachers are free to select their favorites, and many add more resources from the School Library Service and the "Blown-Up Books" which they often prepare themselves for Shared Reading sessions.

At the secondary level, schools frequently purchase class sets of fictional materials or English textbooks from a variety of commercial publishers, while at the tertiary level and beyond, the students normally purchase their own.

A small number of resources have recently been published in the Maori language at the primary level, and teachers at the few bilingual schools have been very resourceful in preparing their own. However, the vast majority of publications in New Zealand are printed in English only. As a rule, consumable workbooks are not used in New Zealand schools, for the prevailing philosophy of reading encourages the principle that children learn to read by extensive meaningful reading of authentic texts and oral discussion, rather than by artificial written exercises and repetitive phonic drills.

FINANCING READING EDUCATION

Most reading instruction is a charge on the government, through vote education. All teachers, primary and secondary, in public and private schools, are paid from the public purse, and the bulk of standard reading materials and library books are provided by, or purchased with, government grants. Additional materials for class and school libraries are purchased through funds generated by parents through local fund-raising activities.

At the tertiary level, students purchase their own textbooks, but again the government provides standard bursaries to subsidize students' expenses. The costs of tuition are light in comparison with those of other industrialized countries.

Adult literacy programs receive small grants from the government. The bulk of this work is undertaken by volunteer tutors. Each Polytechnic also runs a government-financed ESL program for adult immigrants who need assistance with all aspects of English.

READING RESEARCH

Research in reading in New Zealand in recent years has been linked closely with the efforts of Dame Professor Marie Clay of the University of Auckland. She has thoroughly documented the reading and language progress of children in the first years of school, constructed several diagnostic tests and monitoring devices, and developed the highly successful Reading Recovery Program for failing six year olds. Public concern about weaker readers has encouraged this work, and the Department of Education has promoted the Reading Recovery Program with the resources to expand it to a national network and to various overseas locations. Evaluation of Reading Recovery tuition is a continuing focus of research, as children who have been through the program are followed up and are compared with others who have not.

Another focal point has been the evaluation of the government's in service multimedia packages—ERIC and LARIC—and the whole-language philosophy that underlies them. The pioneering work of reading specialists such as Myrtle Simpson, Ruth Trevor, and Don Holdaway has given rise to a distinctive view of the reading process, outlined earlier. Evaluations of shared reading and other aspects of this approach have been conducted by several researchers, and a series of recent studies on the benefits of teachers' story reading to children, carried out by groups of teachers working with Warwick Elley, of Canterbury University, has supplemented these efforts.

Other research emphases include a series of studies by Tom Nicholson of Waikato University, questioning the Goodman principle that good readers guess from context; by Bill Tunmer of Massey University on the wisdom of teaching children prediction skills; by Stuart McNaughton on the mental processes involved when children make miscues in their reading; and by a variety of researchers on the extent of sex stereotyping in children's reading materials.

The New Zealand Council of Educational Research has initiated several studies on reading standards over time, on readability of children's materials, on children's reading interests, and on the validity of cloze materials. Most of these issues provide the basis for continuing research and help inform the efforts of teachers at primary and secondary levels. Little research is conducted on adult literacy, and some minor efforts have been made on the reading problems of apprentices at polytechnics (Marriott and Elley, 1984).

THE OUTLOOK FOR READING EDUCATION

Reading is one aspect of the school curriculum in New Zealand that has had a positive image for some years. Despite criticism of standards by a vociferous minority, New Zealand children read well, according to international comparisons, and the volume of reading done by adults—as indicated by figures on book sales and library borrowings—is high (see Guthrie, 1981). Children's attitudes toward reading have been generally positive, although recent surveys show they are slipping, especially among boys, as other extracurricular attractions such as television, video, and computer games become more popular (see Elley, 1985).

At the primary level, the spread of Reading Recovery, the presence of rich resources in schools, and teachers' emphasis on promoting a love of reading are all very positive signs for the future role of reading in the later school years and in the community. Although most teachers support a whole-language approach, and teach it competently, there is a growing body of evidence challenging some of its principles. Some features of the Reading Recovery Program itself seem to suggest that many would benefit from a greater emphasis on deliberate instruction on word recognition skills, for instance.

Whether the positive attitudes and skills of primary children can be maintained in secondary schools is hard to predict. Studies of reading standards suggest that they are steady or rising at the primary level, but are slipping slightly at higher levels. In the face of modern technological changes, a divergence may well be developing between the highly literate and those who find they can survive and have satisfying lives with only a modicum of reading ability. Perhaps the current IEA survey of reading literacy will provide more revealing indicators of current and future trends in reading in New Zealand.

SUMMARY

Reading instruction in New Zealand possesses many of the hallmarks of a whole-language, child-centered approach. Prominent catchwords of the official philosophy are interest, meaning, independence, language experience, shared reading, and process writing. At the primary level the priority aims are to entice young children into a lifelong love of reading for enjoyment. These aims are generally accepted by teachers and parents, although periodic calls for a "return to basics" and "higher literacy standards" are highlighted in the media, as they are in many Western countries. Nevertheless, international surveys and overseas observers indicate that New Zealand children do read well, and the volume of reading done in the community is relatively high.

Some children do emerge from the school system with limited skill, but the success of the research-based Reading Recovery Program augurs well for a decrease in reading failure in the future.

The education system is highly centralized, though changing; teachers are well educated and trained in official methodology; and schools are well stocked with high-interest reading materials, although there is a significant lack of Maori language books. In short, New Zealand reading programs have developed out of local needs and traditions rather than from the findings of scholars. As researchers discover more about the nature of the reading process, it will be interesting to observe how well New Zealand policies continue to earn support.

REFERENCES

Books

Beardsley, Nada. 1988. *Report of a Standard 2 Reading Survey in the Canterbury Region*. Christchurch: Department of Education.

Clay, Marie M. 1972, 1979. *Reading: The Patterning of Complex Behaviour*. Auckland: Heinemann Educational Books.

Clay, Marie M. 1976. Early Childhood and Cultural Diversity in New Zealand. *The Reading Teacher* (January): 333–342.

Clay, Marie M. 1979, 1988. *The Early Detection of Reading Difficulties*. Auckland: Heinemann Educational Books.

Clay, Marie M. 1982. *Observing Young Readers, Selected Papers*. Auckland: Heinemann Educational Books.

Department of Education. 1985a. *On the Way to Reading*. Wellington: Government Printer.

Department of Education. 1985b. *Reading in Junior Classes*. Wellington: Government Printer.

Doake, David B., and O'Rourke, Brian T. (eds.). 1976. *New Directions for Reading Teaching*. Wellington: New Zealand Educational Institute, G. Deslandes Ltd.

Elley, Warwick B. 1985. *Lessons Learned about Laric*. Christchurch: University of Canterbury.

Elley, W. B., and Reid, N. A. 1969. *Progressive Achievement Tests of Reading*. Teachers' Manual. Wellington: New Zealand Council for Educational Research.

Elley, W. B., and Tolley, C. W. 1972. *Children's Reading Interests*. Wellington: New Zealand Council for Educational Research and the Wellington Council of the International Reading Association.

Guthrie, John G. 1981. "Reading in New Zealand: Achievement and Volume." *Reading Research Quarterly* 17 (1): 6–27.

Harper, Clive, and Hamilton, Ian (eds.). 1977. *Reading for Secondary Schools*. Wellington: Price Milburn and Company Limited for New Zealand University Press.

Holdaway, Don. 1979. *The Foundations of Literacy*. Auckland: Ashton Scholastic.

Marriott, R., and Elley, W. B. 1984. Teaching from a Learning Point of View. *Tutor* 29 (November): 2–8.

Nicholson, Tom. 1984. *The Process of Reading*. Auckland: Martin Educational.

Nicholson, Tom. 1987. "Good Readers Don't Guess." *Reading Forum N.Z.* 2 (3): 24–27. Also in *Set*, No. 2, 1987.

Purves, Alan C. 1979. *Reading and Literary Achievement in New Zealand*. Wellington: New Zealand Council for Educational Research.

Tunmer, W. E. 1988. "Teaching Prediction Skills: Is it a Good Idea?" Paper Presented at a Conference of the New Zealand Association for Research in Education, Massey University, Palmerston North.

Unesco. 1984. *Textbooks and Reading Materials*. Vols. I–III, Department of Education, Wellington.

Journals and Periodicals

New Zealand Journal of Educational Studies. New Zealand Council for Educational Research, Box 3237, Wellington.

Reading Forum N.Z. New Zealand Reading Association, P.O. Box 19, Matangi, Hamilton.

Set: Research Information for Teachers. New Zealand Council for Educational Research, Box 3237, Wellington.

14

Nigeria

INTRODUCTION

Nigeria, located in West Africa, has an estimated population of 112 million, of which about 50 percent is under fifteen years of age. It consists of twenty-one states and one federal capital territory. Like most African countries, it is multilingual. Estimates of the number of languages range from the very conservative 150 to the more realistic figure of 394 given in Hansford's well-documented compilation of Nigerian languages (Hansford et al., 1976). However, it has been suggested that the use of other criteria like intelligibility and other indices for delimiting language boundaries might yield an even higher figure than Hansford's (Elugbe, 1985, p. 167). Some of these languages are spoken by only a few hundred speakers, while some, such as Hausa, are spoken by as many as 12 million people in Nigeria and in the West African countries adjoining Nigeria.

Based on number of speakers, stage of development, and roles, we can posit three tiers or levels among these languages.

LANGUAGES OF THE COUNTRY

Major Languages

Until 1967, when Nigeria's three regions (North, East, West) were broken up into nineteen states, the country's regional languages were used semiofficially in the then three administrative centers of the regions. These are Hausa, Igbo, and Yoruba. The 1979 constitution declared that the business of the National Assembly would be conducted in those three languages as well as in English, the official language. Each of these languages is spoken by about 10 million people, although they are written by fewer than 10 percent of the speakers (Unoh, 1987).

State Languages

The state languages are used in the twenty-one state Houses of Assembly in addition to English, for example, Kanuri in Borno State, Edo in Bendel, Efik in Cross River, and Ibibio in Akwa Ibom. The languages are also used in state news broadcasts and on the national radio network, the Federal Radio Corporation of Nigeria.

Other Languages

Other languages are spoken in smaller communities with fewer than 100,000 speakers. They may be used, for example, in local courts, village councils, adult literacy classes, and as media of initial instruction in primary schools. Some are neither written nor read. For example, in the Rivers State in the Southern part of Nigeria, these other languages would be those that Kay Williamson (1976) said are spoken by a small group such as the Ibani in Bonny Division and the Ogbogolo in Abua/Odua Division.

Official Language

The official language of Nigeria is English. Nigeria was a British colony until 1960 when it obtained its independence. During the colonial period, the British administration decided that there was a need ''to train a core of clerks, accounting assistants, copyists, messengers, interpreters and telegraph probationers to assist the colonial administration'' (Omolewa, 1975, 104). Since then English has served as the language of commerce, administration, the mass media, and instruction at secondary and higher levels of education. It facilitates communication across ethnic boundaries and makes international communication possible. It has been said to serve the broad functions of accommodation, that is, allowing people speaking different languages to communicate; participation, that is, enabling people to take part in the administration and obtain education in the country; and social mobility, that is, the ability of the speaker to participate fully in the social and political life of the country (James, 1979).

In spite of its multifaceted use, the reality of the situation is that English is still basically the language of the educated elites. Bamgbose has speculated that ''as many as 90 percent of our people in both urban and rural areas are untouched by its alleged communicative role'' (1985, p. 97). This is because use of English has failed to facilitate communication between the educated elites and the vast majority of the people. Its success in enabling communication among various cultural and ethnic groups is therefore limited. In addition, its continued use as the official language is often resented on nationalistic grounds and because of the need for cultural preservation. Consequently, very vocal, though intermittent, calls have been issued for its abrogation and the selection of an indigenous language as the official language. At various times, Nigerian Pidgin, Swahili, and artificial languages like Wazobia and Guosa have been suggested.

Semiofficial Languages

The major Nigerian languages—Hausa, Igbo, and Yoruba—have semiofficial status but are by and large restricted in scope to their regions of origin. Hausa and Yoruba cut across regional boundaries, being spoken in many West African communities for trade and commerce.

Nigerian Pidgin is widely used as an unofficial language of communication across ethnic boundaries, especially in the coastal areas of Nigeria and in the *sabongari*—the stranger settlements of large cities in the north and among the police and armed forces (Bamgbose, 1985). In Bendel State, which is linguistically diverse, Pidgin has attained the status of a mother tongue for some speakers (Shnukal and Marchere, 1983). Nigerian Pidgin is a contact language whose vocabulary comes from English and its syntax from southern Nigerian languages. In spite of its widespread use, it is not accepted as a medium of instruction because its orthography is not yet standardized; it is not used much in writing and, in general, it has a low acceptability. By acceptability we mean that a language has certain features that are considered worthy of emulation by the majority of people in a given speech community. Pidgin is not used officially as a medium of instruction in Nigerian schools, although teachers in areas where Pidgin is predominant may lapse into it when English fails to bring about desired understanding in pupils.

Arabic is also considered important in national and international affairs in Nigeria since a large percentage of Nigerians, especially in the northern and southwestern parts, are Muslims. Consequently, Arabic is taught in Koranic schools, especially reading and writing. A Nigerian ethnic group—the Shuwa Arabs who live in the northeastern part of Borno State—speak Arabic.

Within the formal western school system, Arabic is learned as an optional subject in junior and senior secondary schools. At the end of secondary school education, Arabic can be taken at the West African School Certificate Level and also as a matriculation subject in the Nigerian Joint Admissions and Matriculations Board examinations as a qualifying subject for university education. However, Arabic is not included in the adult literacy programs, and the admission quota for students of Arabic in universities and colleges of education is low, just as it is for Nigerian languages.

The National Policy on Education (1977, revised 1981) states that the medium of instruction in the primary school should initially be the mother tongue or the language of the immediate community. In effect, the introduction to reading and writing is supposed to be in the first language. The national syllabus for primary schools states that the teacher of the mother tongue is expected to put the child through all the prereading and prewriting activities. When the child is introduced to English as a subject in these initial years, the English as a Second Language (ESL) teacher is expected to reinforce the prereading and prewriting skills. Thus, the mother tongue and ESL teachers' efforts complement one another in their general goal of enabling the child to achieve communicative competence.

From the fourth year of the primary school, the medium of instruction becomes English. At secondary and tertiary levels, English is the language of instruction.

In spite of this clear statement by the government on the use of the mother tongue as the initial medium of instruction, the acceptance and practice of mother tongue education is lukewarm. For example, even in the Rivers State where there was significant support for mother tongue education, as illustrated by the state government's sponsorship of the Rivers Readers projects, Williamson discovered that teachers concentrated much more on the teaching of English. Teacher trainees received instruction on the teaching of English but not of the mother tongue and the teachers themselves may not have had much practice in writing their own language (Williamson, 1976). Afolayan discovered that the same situation existed in the case of Yoruba, which is even more widely spoken than the Rivers languages that Williamson worked on (Afolayan, 1976:132).

Consequently, there is a low literacy level in Nigerian languages arising from the stages of development of many of the languages (some have no orthographies) and also from inadequate and ineffective teaching. It is instructive that while the National Policy on Education (NPE) prescribes initial mother tongue education, the primary school leaving certificate examinations and the national common entrance examinations to secondary schools are supposed to be written in English. Parents and even some educators are therefore suspicious of any attempt to introduce the mother tongue as the sole medium of instruction in schools, and their realization that English is a sine qua non for social mobility makes them even less receptive.

A significant problem arising from this multilingual policy on the language of instruction in schools is the sheer number of languages that have to be used. This creates management problems since even speakers of the smallest languages can, by right, insist on the use of their language as a medium of instruction in order to retain their ethnic distinctiveness. As an example, Williamson found that in Rivers State, it was more expedient to adopt a multilingual approach in the Rivers Readers project, that is, to publish as many readers in the languages as necessary and as communities demanded them.

In spite of these misgivings about the quality of mother tongue education and the controversy as to whether or not it confers permanent literacy, the three major Nigerian languages, Hausa, Igbo, and Yoruba, are used as the media of instruction in schools, as are the state languages.

Another interesting dimension to the question of Nigeria's language policy is the stipulation in the National Policy on Education that each child should be encouraged to learn one of the three major Nigerian languages in addition to his or her own mother tongue. Clearly, the government is encouraging planned bilingualism in order to ensure that at some point in the future, one of these major languages will emerge as the natural choice for the official language. The execution of this policy, like the policy on mother tongue education, is beset by numerous problems already highlighted in respect of mother tongue education. Therefore, planners have to be more committed to its effective execution, especially through the mass training of more language teachers. Although Yoruba and Igbo have been used as a medium of instruction in schools since colonial times, many of the other indigenous languages have not.

THE PROCESS OF READING INSTRUCTION POLICY

Okedara's observation that, between 1944 and 1970, "Nigeria's educational plans were intensively guided and largely dependent upon the work of ad-hoc commissions whose recommendations were endorsed in varying degrees for purposes of educational planning" (1986, p. 8) holds true for reading instruction policy. Before 1984, when the Federal Ministry of Education devised a comprehensive national syllabus for primary and secondary schools, reading instruction was decentralized.

Primary education has largely been the responsibility of the state and local governments. Hence, some states designed and produced instructional materials for their own schools. These efforts differed from state to state in terms of scope, depth, and target performance. For example, Williamson noted that, before the Rivers Readers Project was started in 1970, the Nembe, Okrika, and Kolokuma primers which were used in schools in the Ijo-speaking areas were based on "a very old fashioned approach to reading; first the alphabet was taught, then words of two letters were practised, then words of three letters and so on to short folktales and moral or religious texts" (1976, p. 138). There was no textbook, and so the pupils memorized the words and sentences written on the blackboard. As a result, most people became more literate in English (which had the requisite teaching aids) than in the local language. Abiri also noted in 1983 that "the methods employed in the teaching of reading in English and the indigenous languages in Nigeria depend partly on the predilections of each teacher and partly on the course book adopted" (1983, p. 54). The teachers' inadequate training and experience make it difficult for them to cope in a multilingual situation.

The 1984 National Primary School Syllabus on English (SPSSE) centralized the policy on reading instruction for that level of education. Designed to "achieve some measure of harmonisation and uniformity of policies and practices among states of the Federation" (1984, p. 1), it specified goals for reading instruction for each class of the six-year primary education, while, however, providing room for adapting topics, themes, principles, ideas, or concepts to suit peculiar local conditions.

In spite of this attempt to centralize reading instruction, individual teachers still stick closely to the methods prescribed in the English textbooks adopted for use by each state Ministry of Education. In the absence of the English textbooks and teaching aids that should have been produced by the Nigeria Educational Research Council, teachers have resorted to the textbooks they have always used.

At the secondary school level, the national syllabus (1985) again provides an indication of the policy of centralization. The National Curriculum for Senior Secondary Schools in English (NCSSE) adopts an integrated approach to English studies, emphasizing the four language skills and ensuring that the learning of one aspect reinforces the other skills. The section entitled "Comprehension—Listening and Reading" states that the aim is to provide a high level of proficiency in the English language, so as to facilitate communication and personal development. The terminal objectives for each unit of work are specified in terms of communicative tasks, such as recognizing "the main or central points in a given passage" (p. 28).

At the tertiary level, no attention is paid to reading instruction per se except in "Use of English Courses" which are compulsory in all Nigerian universities as part of the general studies program, which is an enrichment program.

THE GOALS OF READING EDUCATION

The National Policy on Education (1977) stipulates a new system of education that is being followed in the country, that is, the 6–3–3–4: six years to be spent in the primary school, three in junior secondary school, three in senior secondary school, and four in the university. As Obanya (1984) has pointed out, the more important feature is not its structure but its emphasis on the diversification of the curriculum, especially the attention given to vocational subjects. According to this policy, the main purpose of primary education, the foundation of the entire educational structure, is to "enable the child to acquire among other things, permanent and functional literacy and numeracy, with emphasis on effective communication, in addition to making him useful to himself and to the society in which he lives (National Syllabus for Primary School English [NSPSE], 1984, p. ii). Reading is seen as an integral part of those skills needed for effective communication. Thus, for the primary school the child is expected to be "able to read correctly and fluently and be able to react sensibly and sensitively to what he has read" (NSPSE, 1984, p. 12).

At the primary school level, therefore, the pupil has to move beyond merely decoding letters to higher order skills of fluent and critical reading. The child is also expected to acquire the language needed to understand content area subjects in primary, postprimary, and tertiary levels of education. At all levels, no distinction is made in the goals for males and females.

Adenuga's study (1986) of reading in Nigeria showed that the teachers in primary school perceived the priority of their own goals of reading instruction as being different from that of the government. They, for example, saw preparation of pupils for examinations as the highest priority, followed by leisure reading, development of reading interest, and functional skills. Intelligent citizenship which was the highest for government was considered to be less important than the other goals (Adenuga, 1986, p. 63).

The National Curriculum for Senior Secondary Schools in English provides for an integrated English studies syllabus that includes, among other skills, comprehension, that is, listening and reading. Its stated aim is to provide a high level of proficiency in the English language so as to facilitate communication and personal development. It therefore builds on the skills already attained at the primary and junior secondary schools. Among its terminal objectives is the stimulation of a love of reading as a pleasurable activity (NCSSE, Vol. 2, 1985, p. vi). The reading comprehension subskills listed are "reading to grasp word meanings in various contexts, to summarize main points, for critical evaluation, for implied meaning, suggestions and writer's purpose" (p. vii).

At the tertiary level, no attention is paid to reading instruction per se. Rather, it is treated as a component of the Use of English courses in the universities, which form part of the General Education Studies program. This covers the broad areas of culture and civilization, government, society and economy, science, land use, and agriculture. The Use of English course, which is compulsory for all students, prepares the candidates to pursue their courses of study in the university through the medium of English. The reading component is designed to enable students to read and comprehend materials in various registers and styles and to deduce meanings at the literal, critical, and creative levels.

Adult Education

Reading education at this level is designed to be used as a tool for the development of individual, societal, and governmental welfare. The adult learners are supposed to be able to read in order to survive in their own environment and to attain permanent literacy. In this way, it is hoped, an enlightened and informed citizenry will be produced. Reading education for this level of learners is designed for professional advancement, recreation, and, above all, social mobilization, in order to make the people more responsive to government efforts in the areas of health, government, agriculture, and commerce.

A recent government-sponsored literacy campaign called Nomadic Education has been directed at a special group, mainly the Cattle Fulani. These are nomadic herdsmen in the northern part of Nigeria who move around with their cattle according to the season. For these people, literacy is designed to be functional, specifically, to make them better and more informed cattle rearers. Since these groups never settle for long in one place, the government has built mobile schools for them and the learning resources are brought to them in their camping sites. The education scheme is designed for the old and young.

For nonformal education such as basic and post-literacy courses, extramural studies, vocational/technical, correspondence studies and external degrees, the goals for reading education are the same as those for the corresponding level in formal education. For example, the extramural studies reading program for students who want to attempt the General Certificate of Education, Ordinary Level, is the same as that for those pupils in secondary schools within the formal education system.

HOW IS ILLITERACY DETERMINED IN NIGERIA?

The definition of illiteracy in Nigeria derives from that of UNESCO in which illiteracy is said to be a state of being in which one is cut off from the written word: that is, is unable to read and write. This rudimentary ability of reading and writing is used as the baseline for defining illiteracy in Nigeria.

Because of the country's multilingual nature, this definition has been further modified as in Laubauch's and Mujahid's definition: "Literacy may be defined in general terms as the ability to read and write a simple message in *any* language [emphasis added]" (1971, p. 536). In effect, literacy can be expressed in any language. It is therefore possible for one to be literate in the mother tongue, and not just in English, the official language.

The level of literacy goes beyond being barely able to write one's name or write a single number, to the less limited ability to read with understanding and write simple statements. New literates in Nigeria are expected to be in a position to further their education through continuous reading and writing.

The permanent literacy stage is measured by the first school-leaving certificate examination, which corresponds to six years of formal schooling (Okedara, 1981b, p. 21). The current practice in the Department of Adult Education, University of Ibadan, Nigeria, is to classify literacy attainment into three levels: beginners, intermediate, and advanced. The first level corresponds to the level of attainment in the first two years of primary schooling in the formal education system; intermediate corresponds to primary 3 and 4 work; and advanced, primary 5 and 6 work. Permanent literacy is reached at the advanced stage and is measured by the first school-leaving certificate examination (Okedara, 1981b, p. 21).

Illiteracy is expressed in terms of inability to communicate through reading and writing in order to gain insights into local, national, and international affairs. Government policy is to eliminate mass illiteracy within the shortest possible time. In 1982 a mass literacy campaign to eliminate illiteracy within ten years was launched.

Apart from basic literacy, the government also places great emphasis on functional literacy, for example, the one designed for soldiers in the Nigerian Army, for tobacco farmers in Oyo North, and for nomadic herdsmen. For these groups, the general practice has been to define and practice literacy education within the utilitarian concept, such as ability to measure accurately, keep records, and read relevant information—in other words, the ability to decode and comprehend materials needed to perform everyday vocational tasks.

Those who acquire basic literacy skills in the mother tongue always express anxiety to become literate in English so that they can attain the major tool for social mobility and greater participation in their profession, government, commerce, and so on (Tomori and Okedara, 1975).

Rate of Illiteracy

There are no figures on illiteracy among specific groups, but Okedara (1986, p. 18) claims that Nigeria's literacy rate is currently estimated at 30.0 percent. According to UNESCO, the number of illiterates aged fifteen and above in Nigeria was 23.1 million in 1970, 27.6 million in 1980, and the projected figure is 29.9 million for 1990. Aware of these statistics, the government included a ten-year mass literacy campaign in the new national policy on education whose aim was to eradicate mass illiteracy. The success of this objective is doubtful, however. Okedara, using the enrollment figures for the first year of the campaign and the poor return rate of the new literates to postliteracy classes (30 percent), concluded that (1) the objective of wiping out illiteracy cannot be accomplished within the target of ten years and (2) the national mass literacy campaign can be said to be inefficiently prosecuted, since a good percentage of new literates relapsed back into illiteracy before they could reach a permanent literacy level (1986, p. 18).

No figures are available, but we have sufficient indications that the rate of illiteracy may be very low at certain levels of education. For example, as cited earlier, Afolayan (1976) and Williamson (1976) pointed out the low literacy levels in both the mother tongue and even in English in primary school. In a presentation at the first Nigerian national seminar on reading in 1982, Omujuwa played a cassette recording of the rendering by final year students of Grade II Teachers' Colleges of graded reading passages in both English and certain Nigerian languages. As was made clear, it was "possible for a professionally trained teacher to be himself completely illiterate in both English and Nigerian languages" (Unoh, Omojuwa, and Crow, 1983, Foreword). Omojuwa attributed the reading problem to the mismatch between educational policy formulation and its implementation. The major problems that scholars have identified are the languages to be used for introduction to literacy, especially in multilingual states; the ownership and curriculum of pre-primary schools where preparation for reading is supposed to start; the availability of materials; the order of introduction of languages with different orthographies and orientations such as English, Nigerian, and Arabic; the minimum standard of literacy in Nigerian languages; and the number of mandatory literacy languages throughout the school system. As Omojuwa concluded:

It seems, on the whole, that literacy, post-literacy and effective reading receive adequate government attention at least in theory, judging by the various provisions made for them in NPE.

Yet, the rate of illiteracy and ineffective reading increases among pupils, their parents, their teachers, students pursuing higher education as well as "educated" adults. Our system of literacy education is without doubt faulty somewhere. (1983, p. 44)

Du-Bey, writing about the situation in Sokoto, stated that "there was an ever increasing number of students entering secondary schooling who were unable to read" (1983, p. 243).

In the absence of statistics, these illustrations may appear exaggerated. What is quite clear, however, is that the level of literacy in the country is of sufficient worry to these educators and planners as to warrant attention. Although we cannot speak of illiteracy at the tertiary levels, we can say that in terms of the development of reading readiness, reading interests, abilities, skills, and habits *at appropriate stages of intellectual development* within a given society, even tertiary students are inadequately prepared. It was this consideration that led Unoh to identify the prevalence of "the reluctant reading and learning syndrome" in Nigeria's educational institutions in his 1980 inaugural lecture. He defined it as "a tendency to limit one's reading and learning to what is specifically required for the achievement of one's limited objectives (e.g. success in specific examinations and/or the procurement of jobs" (Unoh, 1983, 20).

The worsening situation of reading within and outside schools has created great concern in Nigeria. It has given the saying "The Nigerian public is a nonreading public" the status of a canonical statement (Emenyonu, 1983, p. 444) and has led to greater awareness of the importance of studying, teaching, and improving reading at all educational levels as well as in nonformal situations.

READING DISABILITIES AND THEIR DIAGNOSIS

Only a limited number of investigations have been carried out into the diagnosis of reading disabilities in Nigeria. Nearly all those reports are based on isolated studies carried out by staff and students of the University of Ibadan and Ahmadu Bello University. Since these reports cover only a small sample of the country's population, there are no national figures for the rate of incidence of these disabilities. In spite of the limitations of the scope and depth of these undergraduate essays, they still shed some light on the topic as can be seen below.

Primary School

Nkama (1980), in a study of selected primary school children, reported that silent reading errors were more frequent than oral reading errors, whereas Ojelade (1985), in an oral reading test administered to twenty pupils, found that disregard of punctuation was the most consistent error, especially among the boys, accounting for 48 percent of their errors. The girls, who on the whole made more errors than the boys, committed more errors of repetition and addition (52 percent). In the silent reading test, pointing with fingers and head movement were the more prevalent errors. However, the small sample size and the non-standardization of the tests make the study of rather limited application.

Epidi's study (1985) of the link between developmental speech defects and the reading ability of a selected group of primary school pupils showed that speech defects hindered their reading performance. Those with articulatory disorders had problems with oral reading tests such as substituting words, having abnormal repetition, speech blocks, hesitations, and cluttering. Nigeria has few reading or speech clinics that could help such children.

Related research on reading behavior or leisure reading repeatedly highlights the importance of the establishment of remedial centers in Nigeria in view of the complexity of the sources of the reading disabilities of Nigerian children. For example, Akinmola (1980) revealed that language interference, lack of exposure to libraries, and the socioeconomic status of parents affect the reading habits of Nigerian primary school children. She emphasized the need for making diagnostic and remedial services available in institutes dealing with language skills development.

Another problem with diagnostic services is the lack of standardized instruments. Du-Bey (1983) reported that, even though the West African Examinations Council had developed a standardized reading test in 1962, it was unavailable to the classroom teacher, who was invariably incapable of using it anyway. In Du-Bey's experiment at Ahmadu Bello University (ABU) the Informal Reading Inventory was used to determine the level at which the children could read, as well as their level of comprehension. The ABU center had also devised an informal diagnostic test, which includes graded sight vocabulary, oral reading and reading comprehension passages, context clues, and so on. The advantage of this test is that it was prepared specifically for users of English in a second language and thereby avoids the problems of those tests standardized with first language speakers.

Reading difficulties in Nigerian secondary schools have also been investigated, though not on an extensive scale. Tests designed by individual researchers have been used for comprehension (Abioye, 1986), while some tests such as the Gates-McKillop Reading Diagnostic Tests and Baldridge Reading and Study Skills Questionnaire have also been used (Ojo, 1983). Ojo also used a readability test based on the cloze technique devised by the Department of Language Arts in the University of Ibadan. His own study focused on three repeaters of secondary class 2 in an Ibadan school. Although their disabilities were diagnosed, they could not be remediated because of logistic reasons such as transfer of parents and change in school calendar. It would appear that diagnosis is easier than remediation in Nigeria. Studies like Asebiomo's (1981) show that the reading problems of a group of students repeating secondary class 3 were attributable to home background, physical deformity, brain damage, lack of motivation, and immaturity.

Tertiary Level

The reading difficulties prevalent at this level have been studied extensively by Unoh (1972), Chapman-Taylor (1965), McKillop and Yoloye (1962), and various other researchers. Unoh's study is the most significant in this area. He devised his own tests for reading speed and comprehension and for measuring reading difficulties (using Fry's Readability Formula and the Fogg Index). He also adapted and constructed suitable inventories and questionnaires for assessing reading difficulties, reading habits, and leisure inventory. He concluded:

The high incidence of reading difficulties among these students is hardly surprising. . . . What appears remarkable is the emergence of reading difficulties as a continuum in which inability to skim, a slow reading rate, difficulty in understanding and interpretation, and in comprehending main ideas rank very high, while difficulties in comprehension of details, word power or vocabulary and retention or short term memory rank relatively low in that order. (1972, p. 26)

The patterns of reading difficulties and the inefficient reading habits revealed in these studies have been confirmed by later research as will be seen later in the chapter. However, there are no studies of reading disabilities, that is, difficulties serious enough to make the pupils fall below the officially recognized academic cutoff point.

Adult Education

Nigeria has no studies of reading disability in this area of education.

READING READINESS PROGRAMS FOR PRE-PRIMARY SCHOOL STUDENTS

According to the NPE, introduction to literacy begins at the pre-primary level. One of its aims is "teaching the rudiments of numbers, letters, colours, shapes" (p. 10). The stipulated medium of instruction at this level is "principally the mother tongue or the language of the immediate community," that is, one of the indigenous Nigerian languages. To expedite literacy, the NPE states that the government will develop the orthography for many more Nigerian languages and produce textbooks in them.

Until recently (1987) when the government published the first pre-primary syllabus, the government left the ownership and curriculum of pre-primary schools completely to private agencies. Such schools exist mainly in urban areas where the working mothers have to find suitable outlets for young children who are not yet of school age. The majority of Nigerian children (90 percent) in this age group do not benefit from pre-primary education as it is largely an "exclusive elite establishment" (Omojuwa, 1983, p. 38). As a corollary, the preferred medium among its clientele is English, since one of their reasons for patronizing these schools is to give their children a head start in formal education.

The Pre-Primary Curriculum (1987) for Language and Communication skills lists the following reading readiness skills: recognition and tracing of the alphabet, picture and word association, identification of one's own name, word building, play with picture word games, jigsaw puzzles, picture, shape matching and alphabet, and learning of left to right and top to bottom orientation. The teacher is expected to put the child through all the prereading skills in the mother tongue. The NSPSE lists the grounds to be covered in greater detail than the pre-primary one: training in eye movement, visual perception, discrimination of objects, visual memory, sorting out of objects, recognition of shapes and figures, matching of shape and figure, training in auditory perception and discrimination, and so on.

When, in the primary school, the medium of instruction changes to English, the teacher is expected to put the children through all the prereading skills again for reinforcement. In this way, the mother tongue and the English teachers' efforts complement one another.

The programs are the same for males and females for the sexes are not segregated in the schools. As stated earlier, the pre-primary school is an urban, educated, middle-class phenomenon. As a consequence, the typical rural child and the children of the urban poor do not get any training in reading readiness. The children who have been to these pre-primary schools move on to the fee-paying, privately run, English-medium primary schools rather than the public nonfee paying schools, where the standard of reading is predictably poor.

Reading Readiness Programs

Nigeria still has a long way to go in preparing children formally for reading in schools. The factors that are usually considered in reading readiness such as physical, emotional, social, and school readiness, are promoted incidentally, and not as part of a proper, systematic program for preschool children. Thus, for example, while story telling sessions at home may stimulate the preschool child, more likely than not the child may not be exposed to printed books until formal schooling begins (Awoniyi, 1983). The situation is not helped by the confusion over the language medium in nursery schools. Ala's study (1981) confirms the confusion over the language of instruction in nursery schools in the Oyo State of Nigeria.

TEACHER QUALIFICATIONS

Teachers can obtain their credentials in teacher training colleges, advanced teacher training colleges, colleges of education, polytechnic schools (technical education), and university departments of education.

Most of the teachers in primary school obtain the Grade II Teachers' Certificate through a five-year postprimary or one-year postsecondary school program. The second program, a crash course for producing primary school teachers when universal primary education was introduced in 1976, has been phased out. In these colleges the student teachers acquire academic training in the basic subjects as well as professional training. In the southern states, most of the students in these Grade Two Teacher Training Colleges will have gone through secondary school, although they will not have attained high enough grades to enable them to enter higher institutions of learning. The qualifying examinations are set by a federal institution such as the National Teachers' Institute. Unfortunately, primary school teaching is left largely in the hands of teachers with relatively low academic qualifications. The Associateship Certificate in Education is obtained by Grade II Teachers with considerable teaching experience. They undergo two-year sandwich courses such as the one run by the Institute of Education of the University of Ibadan.

National Certificate of Education

Students obtain the National Certificate after a three-year postsecondary course in a college of education or an advanced teachers' college. These institutions are run by state or federal governments, but all the trainees take the same qualifying examinations nationwide.

Recently, the polytechnics started to train teachers of technical subjects at this level in order to provide teachers for the newly introductory technology subjects in secondary schools. They are certified by the National Board on Technical Education. Graduates of these colleges of education and polytechnics teach in secondary schools.

University Faculties of Education

Faculties of education in Nigerian universities produce the majority of teachers in secondary schools. They admit students who have passed a qualifying matriculation examination set by a national body, the Joint Admissions and Matriculation Board, to a four-year degree program, the Bachelor of Education (B.Ed.). In the alternative, the students may be teachers who already possess the National Certificate in Education. The students take a prescribed number of courses in various fields of education such as philosophy of education, sociology of education, methodology, teaching practice, principles of curriculum and instruction, and in addition, prescribed courses in their areas of specialization. In general, they have to take the core courses in the academic disciplines in which they wish to specialize. Their specialty is reflected in their degree, for example B. Ed. (History).

Another way of obtaining qualification for this level is by means of a one year postgraduate diploma in education (PGDE) in a faculty of education. This course is designed for those who have obtained a purely academic degree such as a B.A. in English and have chosen teaching as a career. While they are allowed to teach without this professional qualification, they are encouraged to obtain it in order to advance in their professions.

A few teachers who have obtained the Master's in Education (M.Ed.) also teach in secondary schools, teacher training colleges, and colleges of education.

Tertiary Education

A master's or doctorate in one's discipline is the only qualification required to teach in the university. In other words, no teacher qualification is imposed for university teachers. Only faculties of education indicate a preference for trained and certified teachers. As recently as January 1989, the African Universities Association saw the need to mount a special workshop for the training of university teachers.

Adult Education

The teachers employed in the basic literacy programs are trained after either their Grade II teacher training or their secondary school education in a two-year diploma in adult education, such as the one run in the Department of Adult Education, University of Ibadan.

Continuing Education Programs

Trained teachers working in formal education usually work part-time in continuing education programs.

Qualifications for Becoming a Reading Teacher

Nigeria has no specialist teachers of reading at the primary, secondary, and tertiary levels. At the primary level, all classroom teachers are supposed to be generalists, capable of teaching all subjects in the primary school curriculum. Reading is taught as a skill in the mother tongue or English language class. Abiri has lamented the "unleashing of half-baked and semi-illiterate teachers on school pupils" as a result of the rush to produce enough teachers for the free primary scheme. He continues:

Many of these teachers who can hardly read themselves are naturally incapable of making a success of teaching their pupils to read. . . . It should be remembered that even the few teachers who are good readers and could otherwise be regarded as trained for teaching have usually had no formal instruction in the teaching of reading. (1983, p. 53)

Secondary school teachers are not prepared for reading mainly because it is assumed that the primary school has already provided such a program and the pupils are well equipped to undertake, the varied and complex reading tasks required for general and content area reading. Until 1965 when the Rockefeller Foundation funded the establishment of a Reading Centre in the Faculty of Arts of the University of Ibadan, no attention was paid to the teaching of reading as a special subject. The center was designed:

1. To advise first-year students on methods of study, to improve their speed of English and reading comprehension, and to continue assistance for students in other years who feel the need for special help in this field.

2. To carry out research into ways of improving the teaching of special reading to Nigerian students.

3. To train Nigerian personnel as reading specialists.

4. To act as a resource and guidance center for institutions concerned with improving the teaching of English reading in schools (Department of Communication and Language Arts Handbook.)

Later, the Reading Centre became a full-fledged department, the Department of Language Arts and in 1988, the Department of Communication and Language Arts. Even though the products of this department are equipped to undertake the teaching of reading in secondary schools, most of them function as teachers of English, not reading specialists. Others who can teach reading are the products of the B.Ed. programs in language arts. As Abe noted, "As far as the secondary school is concerned anyone who works in this area (i.e. developmental reading) can be regarded as a pioneer" (1983, p. 201). The qualifications for teachers are the same for males and females.

Proportion of Male to Female Teachers

An impressionistic assessment will reveal that in most of the southern states of Nigeria primary school teaching has become predominantly a female affair. The same holds true for secondary schools, though to a lesser degree. The males are more predominant in tertiary education, especially in the sciences. In the northern states, the Islamic way of life has kept women in the background, leading to a preponderance of males at all educational levels.

As stated earlier, the number of reading teachers is too insignificant to make a comparison of male and female useful.

MATERIALS USED IN READING EDUCATION

Reading materials in Nigeria are produced commercially by various publishers. These materials consist of pupils' books, teachers' books, wall charts, pictures, posters, alphabet friezes, workbooks, worksheets, and supplementary readers.

Major multinational publishers like Macmillan, Heinemann, Evans, Oxford University Press (University Press Limited), and Longmans produce most of these materials, while indigenous publishers like Onibonoje, Fagbamigbe, and Fourth Dimension do not feature in the textbook market. This is understandable because indigenous publishing is a relatively recent phenomenon in Nigeria and the multinational publishers had already captured the highly competitive textbook market before they appeared on the scene.

A 1986 study by Adenuga on the availability and use of books for the teaching of reading skills in primary schools showed that few books were available and that reading in the primary school curriculum was taught mostly in English lessons, and rarely as part of the Yoruba lessons. The books available for teaching reading skills therefore tend to be the regular English coursebooks such as *New Oxford English Course* which was used by 93 percent of the teachers Adenuga sampled. A significant finding was the fact that only 15 percent of the teachers used more than one book apart from the textbook and that these other books were used mainly as a diagnostic tool to detect areas of reading difficulties of their pupils.

Other titles used in schools are *Nation-wide English* by Evans Publishers, *Macmillan Primary English Course* by Macmillan Publishers, and *Lively English* by Oxford University Press. These publishers revise the textbooks as the national syllabus changes, so that they can retain their share of the textbook market. For example, the 1984 National Primary English Syllabus, which adopted an integrated language skills approach, led to such reviews by the publishers. The Nigeria Education Research and Development Council has plans to produce textbooks and materials based on the English language syllabus it produced.

Other sources of reading materials at the primary school level are imported books aimed at teaching specific comprehension skills, such as critical/inferential reading. These are used chiefly in the private primary schools.

The books and materials for teaching reading in the indigenous languages are also published locally. However, there are fewer supplementary readers than there are for English (Unoh, 1983, p. 16).

At the secondary school stage, reading instruction has no definite place on the curriculum. The emphasis in the language textbooks is on aspects of reading comprehension, such as literal recognition, word meaning, and syntax, and rarely on inference, evaluation, and appreciation. Some English language textbooks used in secondary schools, such as *Effective English* published by Evans, teach some of these skills. Materials for diagnosing and measuring activities in the classroom are lacking. Imported kits like the SRA kits are almost unheard of in Nigeria's schools.

There is now available a growing body of leisure reading materials that promote growth in independent reading. These works are commercially produced by publishers and are directed at young adolescents. Examples are the Pacesetters series by Macmillan and Drumbeats by Longman's which are written in English and have attempted to replace the imported popular reading materials such as James Hadley Chase and Denis Robins books with indigenous materials. The provision of general books in Nigerian languages is very low. The publishers themselves are reluctant to produce them because of the limited size of readership and the complex orthographies of the Nigerian languages.

Except in departments specializing in language arts like the one in the University of Ibadan, reading is not taught formally in tertiary education in Nigeria. It may be part of a Use of English course; the materials on reading will therefore be the textbook. However, as a result of the pioneering effort of the University of Ibadan in this department, texts such as *Reading to Remember* and *Faster Reading Through Practice* by Solomon Unoh are now being used in tertiary institutions. These works are in English. A variety of reading skills improvement equipment such as AVR, Eye Span trainers, Reading Accelerators, and Controlled Readers with appropriate Film strips are also available.

Adult Education

Primers are written and published by specialized agencies involved with reading education for adults. For example, international agencies like the UNDP/ World Bank World Health Organization Special Program for Research and Training in Tropical Diseases helped to fund the local production of literacy and numeracy primers on health promotion and control of tropical diseases in primary health care. These works were written by J. T. and C. A. Okedara and Adeniyi (n.d.). Since primers for initial literacy are in the local languages and the literacy projects are government sponsored, the production of the primers and workbooks is funded by state governments or institutes. For example, the Institute of Adult Education, University of Ibadan, produced primers for teaching literacy skills to Oyo North District tobacco farmers in 1970 (Tomori and Okedara, 1975). Publishers are not involved in this arm of reading education.

The Role of Consumable Materials

All the language textbooks series at the primary and secondary levels have accompanying workbooks for pupil use. Adult education primers also provide accompanying workbooks for student practice. Handouts may also be used at the tertiary and continuing education levels. Pictures, charts, graphs, and maps are used to reinforce or develop skills in eliciting information from nonverbal materials. Teachers normally recommend newspapers, magazines, and the like as part of a reading skills improvement program.

FINANCING READING EDUCATION

Reading education is not financed per se in Nigeria but rather as a component of the total educational process. It has not received financial backing primarily because government agencies and administrators are skeptical about the importance of reading as a discipline. Even though educational administrators and even language teachers acknowledge its importance at the primary level, they do not realize that it needs to be taught beyond this level. To promote reading instruction, the financing will have to cover the provision of trained personnel, material resources, and continuing education for teachers, especially content area teachers. Government agencies that should be involved with reading education, such as the Nigeria Educational Research and Development Council (incorporating the Book Development Council), the National Library of Nigeria, and the National Language Centre, will need to be convinced of their role in promoting reading education in the country and therefore of the need to make adequate provisions for its funding. The National Library of Nigeria, for example, has been involved in promoting readership nationwide through its National Readership Campaign and also by funding the first national seminar on reading held in Ahmadu Bello University in Zaria in August 1982.

Direct government involvement is evident in the example of the Rivers State where the state government funded the production of the Rivers Readers after initial support from Unesco and the Ford Foundation (Williamson, 1976, p. 153). Churches have also been involved in funding literacy education and, indirectly, reading education. For example, the Nigerian Baptist Convention has been instrumental in starting literacy classes in various zones in the country.

THE CURRENT FOCUS OF READING RESEARCH

Reading research in Nigeria is still in its infancy. It is limited to those few universities like Ibadan, Ahmadu Bello University, Zaria, and colleges of education that train teachers for secondary schools. The Reading Association of Nigeria, established in 1982, seeks to encourage research in reading as part of its goals. The first national seminar on reading held in Zaria in 1982 featured papers on various aspects of the reading problem as perceived by teachers at the primary, postprimary, and postsecondary level, nonformal education extension workers, authors, and publishers. Before 1982, various studies were done on the identification and correction of reading deficiencies, the development of reading skills, attitudes, habits, and behavior, problems of bilingualism, multilingualism, and methodology in the teaching of reading, and provision of adequate personnel and administrative support for reading.

The earliest works in this area are probably those of Brimer (1959) and McKillop and Yoloye (1962) who conducted a preliminary study on the reading of University of Ibadan students. The establishment of the Reading Centre in the University of Ibadan in 1965 funded by the Rockefeller Foundation led to more research in the area. The main objective of this center was the teaching of reading and study skills in order to aid freshmen in their courses.

Research in Reading at the Primary Education Level

Research on the problems and methods of teaching initial reading in English and Nigerian languages indicates that these problems arise from the multilingual and multiethnic backgrounds of the pupils in states with a heterogeneous population, the confusion over language of instruction, large classes with children of varying abilities, differences between urban and rural areas, quality of teacher training, lack of formal instruction in the teaching of reading, lack of materials, lack of reading proficiency and attainment tests, confusion arising from the child's having to learn more than one orthography and scripts, and even orientation in reading as in the case of English and Arabic. Underlying all these problems are the inadequate or confusing guidelines from educational planners.

These same problems are highlighted in many research studies into reading at the primary level as in Omojuwa's study (1983) of a literacy policy for the Nigerian educational system, Ubahakwe's study (1983) of reading in Igbo, and Abiri's analysis (1983) of the reading methods employed for the teaching of major Nigerian languages. These studies are based mainly on observations of current trends in Nigerian language classrooms, analyses of the linguistic scene in Nigeria, and the components of the language training programs in the teacher training colleges. More recent research into the preparation of pre-primary school children for reading reinforces the findings with respect to the primary school situation (Ala, 1981; Awoniyi, 1983; Egede, 1979; Macaulay, 1983).

Du-Bey's study on diagnosis and remediation in the primary school in the North focuses on the experience of one B.Ed. program aimed at sensitizing students to the problems of reading disabilities among primary school children and giving them some tools and skills for correcting them. It also provides information on undergraduate projects on reading diagnosis and remediation in primary schools in the northern part of Nigeria.

Ikegulu's study (1987) of teachers' perceptions and performance of reading tasks in public primary schools in Lagos showed a discrepancy between what teachers profess and what they actually practice in the reading class. Their age, academic qualifications, and teaching experience were found to have an insignificant effect on their perception and performance of reading tasks. Rather, the decrepit classrooms and lack of adequate funds were found to affect the attitude of staff and students to the learning process.

Other relevant studies dealing with this level of education are those on reading interests (Odejide and James, 1981); readability of textbooks and supplementary readers (Akinpelu, 1983; Kalinda, 1979); children's literature and content area reading (Odejide, 1984); and availability of children's books in English and Nigerian languages (James and Odejide, 1981). In their 1981 study, Odejide and James examined the reading preferences of children in three Media Resource Centres in Ibadan, Oyo State, and Kano based on the students' borrowings and found that there was a clear preference for realistic stories dealing with familiar backgrounds. Although these reflected the range of books available in the centers, Odejide and James found the nonavailability of fictional works in the indigenous languages a worrisome trend since it could lead to the relegation of these languages to the language of texts rather than of creative materials.

The dearth of empirical research into reading problems and remediation indicates the relative novelty of the discipline and the preliminary nature of the research being conducted in the area. What abounds is a superfluity of suggestions on methodology and policies. It is hoped that when reading obtains more recognition as a separate discipline in Nigeria, these gaps in research work will be rectified.

Secondary Education

A considerable amount of materials is available on reading at the secondary school level. The focus of reading research at this level is on the problems of reading in a second language situation. The aspects covered are pupils' reading rate, attitudes, comprehension level, literal, critical, and creative reading abilities, reading interests, vocabulary level, curriculum planning, methodology, and teacher preparation.

The earliest recorded survey of the reading and study skills of Nigerian secondary school pupils (1960) was probably conducted by Prince, a psychiatrist. In his study of the brain-fag syndrome among Nigerian students, he found that as many as 90 percent of the pupils lacked study reading skills. Similarly, Unoh's (1980) study of 450 Nigerian Form 5 pupils showed that their average reading rate of an easy reading passage was eighty words per minute and that their average comprehension was 60 percent. Even though he used an informal reading test that had the advantage of being culturally less alien than imported standardized tests, Unoh still found that the pupils performed poorly. This finding was especially significant in view of the fact that the medium of instruction in secondary schools is English.

Unoh (1980) and Obah (1987) identified the secondary school pupils' typical reading problems as slow, inflexible reading rate, poor comprehension rate, poor recall, uncritical reading behavior, difficulty with creative reading and study type reading, inadequate vocabulary, and inadequate reading interests. Unoh's study was based on the trends in secondary schools in five states in the southern part of Nigeria which has a larger school population than the North and more trained teachers. The results can therefore be extrapolated to apply to the rest of Nigerian secondary schools. Other researchers from relevant disciplines such as educational psychology have identified similar problems (Bakare, 1985).

The inadequacies identified in the reading abilities of these pupils have led researchers to turn to teacher preparation, curriculum design, and methodology. For example, Lawal (1985) provides a sample plan for integrating the literature program into the language program in line with the Junior Secondary School Curriculum prepared by the Continuing Education Studies and the Adaptation Centre of the University of Lagos. This kind of study is typical of many of the works designed for secondary school teachers, for example, "Motivation in Comprehension Lesson" (1975) and Abiodun's "Conduct of Comprehension Lesson in Our Secondary School" (1975). What is lacking are studies into the information processing ability of pupils at this level, or reading problems of the handicapped like Atinmo's study (1987) of the reading ability of the hearing impaired.

A considerable amount of information exists on the environmental factors that impede the development of reading ability (Obah, 1987); the attitudes of secondary students to reading (Abe, 1983); and theoretical issues in reading (Unoh, 1968, 1969). Obianika's 1981 study of the relative effectiveness of the individualized and the conventional approaches to teaching reading in secondary schools is significant in its comparison of methods at this level. It showed that the individualized approach was superior in terms of capacity for developing reading skills and improving reading achievement.

For some time to come, there will likely be continued emphasis on the study of reading problems in Nigerian secondary schools and methods for improving its teaching. This projection is based on the very poor performance of pupils in the West African School Certificate Examinations in English Language.

Tertiary Education

The fact that reading as a discipline in Nigeria was first examined critically with respect to undergraduates is largely responsible for the abundance of materials at this level. The studies cover three broad areas: (1) assessment of student's ability in a variety of reading skills such as comprehension, reading speed, and vocabulary knowledge (Brimer, 1959; Chapman-Taylor, 1962; McKillop and Yoloye, 1962; Obah, 1981; Unoh, 1969, 1972, 1975; (2) the relationship between their language experiences and reading ability (Obah, 1981; Unoh, 1972, 1975, 1977b); and (3) problems and methods of teaching reading skills in the Use of English programs in universities (Arua, 1987; Obah, 1987).

Assessment of Students' Ability in Reading Skills. These studies show the students' rather low level of performance in silent reading, reading speed, vocabulary knowledge, reading rate, summarizing, and interpreting visual information—all vital factors in success in academic programs. These findings from the very early researches continue to be corroborated by later studies such as Nzinga's (1983). This is a worrisome trend, in view of the conscious attempt to teach reading skills improvement in various universities.

Relationship Between Language Experience and Reading Ability. These studies, such as the one conducted by Unoh in 1972, revealed that students' self-reports of their language development and competence in English and their mother tongue were significantly related to their reading abilities as revealed by their performance on reading tests. In spite of the subjectivity of self-reports, they still cannot be ignored, for they may reflect or affect levels of performance or competence in actual language tasks. Obah, in a more recent study (1981), observed that students' perception of their reading task as determined by the linguistic, cultural, and conceptual features of the texts determined their reading performance.

Problems and Methods of Teaching Reading Skills in Use of English Programs in Universities. These studies in general highlight problems of students' low motivation, lack of teaching materials, and instructors' lack of reading skills expertise in Use of English courses. They recommend improvement in teaching methods, provision of reading laboratories, and use of reading machines and better organization of the Use of English courses in the universities.

Teaching of Reading in Language Arts Programs in Colleges of Education

The focus of research into the training of reading teachers is in colleges of education where there is a great awareness that, ultimately, reading improvement in Nigeria's schools will be determined by the quality of training available to teacher trainees. Abe's study (1985) is typical in its analysis of the condition under which Nigerian children learn to read, the problems of training teachers, and the proposal of an instructional methodology program for use in the colleges. Aboderin's earlier work (1983) on the role of the reading teacher in secondary schools provides similar guidelines. This body of research has continued to grow in teacher education departments of universities like Ibadan and Ahmadu Bello University and in curriculum studies departments in other universities.

Adult Education

Reading education research in adult education is limited because of the low level of funding of this area of education and the greater involvement of adult education specialists in the wider issues of financing literacy programs and assessing the quality and quantity and its cost effectiveness in comparison with formal education.

Recreational Reading

Studies in recreational reading highlight the reading habits of adult Nigerians (Ado, 1985; Solaru, 1985); their reading problems (Okedara, 1983); strategies to improve their reading of literature (Emenyonu, 1983); and the provision of general reading materials for the Nigerian public (Areo, 1983). There are as yet no national studies in these areas, and there is a lack of collaboration among scholars working in this area.

Ado's 1985 study of recreational reading among engineering students in the Polytechnic Ibadan showed that, contrary to popular belief, these students do engage in recreational reading for entertainment and for information. Previous exposure to extensive reading before Polytechnic education is an important factor in the amount of recreational reading they do. Marginal research is on-going in the area of reading in foreign languages such as Russian. One such study on the reading behavior, habits, and difficulties among students of the Russian language in the University of Ibadan was conducted by Oni in 1985. He found that the problems the students faced were interference from the mother tongue, lack of people to speak Russian with, lack of motivation on the part of students, and absence of language learning facilities. Students were found to read word by word, to vocalize, and to struggle with the unfamiliar orthography.

THE OUTLOOK FOR READING EDUCATION

The outlook for reading education in Nigeria is quite bright even though two decades of formal instruction in reading as a distinct discipline should have made a far greater impact than it has. Many language teachers and most content area teachers and school administrators still lack knowledge of reading as a special discipline, which needs to be developed at all levels of education. Consequently, there is a lack of administrative support for reading which is reflected in the inadequate budget, material resources, training of personnel, and so on. In addition, reading consultancy services and reading clinics are still lacking. Graduates of language arts who specialize in reading are still employed as language or literature teachers and not as reading specialists. The washback effect that should therefore have been noticeable in the reading ability of pupils in the primary, secondary, and tertiary levels of education is still not visible. The common complaint among the general public remains that the Nigerian public is not a reading public. Major changes in the methods of teaching reading at primary and secondary levels are yet to be made, and there are outcries from the older generation of literate Nigerians about the worsening situation of reading within and outside schools.

Yet, there are signs of hope. Today Nigeria has more specialists in various aspects of language arts than it had a decade ago. These are the graduates of the few universities that have language arts departments. The English studies curricula and curriculum studies programs of some universities include language arts, and the Use of English course, which includes a reading component, is now mandatory in all Nigerian universities.

The greatest hope for the growth of reading as an educational discipline lies in the change in the National English syllabus of primary and secondary schools from the traditional English syllabus to an integrated language arts program. This will require retraining old teachers and preparing new teachers to enable them to cope with the new methods. Colleges of education and teacher education departments have continued their crusade for the improvement of reading skills at all levels. As Unoh (1985) notes, there is a need to move away from the outdated and old-fashioned curricula of colleges of education in Britain to newer programs that will ensure that a teacher training education will be incomplete without training in language arts.

In summary, good quality teacher training, adequate funding of education, and retraining of teachers would brighten the outlook for reading education in Nigeria.

SUMMARY

There are serious inadequacies in the teaching of reading at all levels of education in Nigeria. These inadequacies can be traced to the absence of a coherent language education policy and to the lack of developmental and remedial reading programs, trained personnel, and facilities for extracurricular reading. Much more importantly, there is a lack of awareness of the status of reading as a separate discipline.

Since the 1970s, however, attempts have been made to centralize and improve reading instruction policy and practices especially at primary and secondary schools. These changes should lead to improvements in the discipline. The primary goal of reading education for the young and adults is to achieve better quality citizenship. There is, however, a need for greater cooperation between specialists in reading education and adult literacy in order to enrich the literacy programs. Nigeria has limited facilities for diagnosing and remediating problems and inadequate books and libraries.

It would appear that for a long time to come only those few universities that offer courses in language skills development will continue to provide leadership in teaching and research in reading in Nigeria.

REFERENCES

Abe, E. A. 1983. The Need for and the Problems of Providing a Developmental Reading Programme at the Junior Post-Primary Level. In S. O. Unoh, Ralph Omojuwa, and Susannah Crow (eds.), *Literacy and Reading in Nigeria*, Vol. 1. Zaria: Ahmadu Bello University Press.

Abe, E. A. 1985. Developing a Reading Methodology Programme for Use in the Teacher Training Colleges. *Journal of English Studies* 2 (November): 15–24.

Abiodun, E. A. 1975. The Conduct of Comprehension Lessons in Our Secondary Schools. *Journal of the English Studies Association* 7, Nos. 1 & 2 (December): 81–85.

Abioye, Adisa A. 1986. Reading and Comprehension: Psycholinguistic Competence of Secondary School Students. B.A. Long Essay, Department of Language Arts, University of Ibadan.

Abiri, J. O. 1974. Reading Ability as a Predictor of Performance in University Degree Examinations. *African Journal of Educational Research* 1, No. 2: 197–204.

Abiri, J. O. 1983. Problems and Methods of Teaching Initial Reading In English. In Unoh et al. (eds.), *Literacy and Reading in Nigeria*.

Aboderin, A. O. 1983. The Role of the Reading Teacher in Secondary Schools. In Unoh et al. (eds.), *Literacy and Reading in Nigeria*.

Adenuga, Adeola. 1986. Reading in Nigerian Primary Schools. An Exploratory Study of the Availability of and Use of Books. M.A. dissertation, Department of Language Arts, University of Ibadan.

Ado, Josephine O. 1985. Recreational Reading Among Engineering Students: A Case Study of Ibadan Polytechnic. B.A. Long Essay, Department of Language Arts, University of Ibadan.

Afolayan, Adebisi. 1976. The Six-Year Primary Project in Nigeria. In Ayo Bamgbose (ed.), *Mother Tongue Education: The West African Experience*. London: Hodder and Stoughton.

Agwu, Ada K. 1975. Motivation in Comprehension Lesson. *Journal of the Nigeria English Studies Association* 7, Nos. 1 & 2 (December): 86–88.

Akinmola, O. O. 1980. A Case Study of Reading Behaviour Among a Selected Group of Primary School Children. B.A. Long Essay, Department of Language Arts, University of Ibadan.

Akinpelu, E. O. 1983. Reading English in Post Primary Institutions: An Evaluative Study of Textbooks Available in the Lower Forms. M.A. Dissertation, Department of Language Arts, University of Ibadan.

Ala, F.B.O. 1981. Some Factors Related to Yoruba Language Learning and Usage in the Nursery Schools of Oyo State. M.Ed. dissertation, University of Ibadan.

Areo, A. The Provision of General Reading: Fiction and Non-Fiction. In Unoh et al., *Literacy and Reading in Nigeria*.

Arua, E. Arua. 1987. Teaching Reading Efficiency Skills in Nigerian Universities: The Example of the Obafemi Awolowo University. *Journal of English Studies* 4 (September): 99–110.

Asebiomo, Titi. 1981. A Study of Problems and Treatment Procedures of Selected Secondary School Children. B.A. Long Essay, Department of Language Arts, University of Ibadan.

Asein, Samuel O. (ed.) 1985. *Language and Polity*. Special number of *Review of English and Literary Studies* 2, No. 2 (December).

Atinmo, Morayo. 1987. Reading Ability and Preferences of Hearing-Impaired and Normal Hearing Secondary School Pupils in Relation to Book Selection Criteria. Ph.D. Thesis, University of Ibadan.

Awoniyi, Adedeji. 1983. Pre-reading Activities, Including Readiness Programmes. In Unoh et al. (eds.), *Literacy and Reading in Nigeria*.

Awoniyi, Timothy A. 1976. Mother Tongue Education in West Africa: A Historical Background. In Bamgbose, *Mother Tongue Education*.

Bakare, C. N. 1985. Coping with Reading Problems at the Secondary School Level. Paper presented at a Pre-Conference Workshop for Teachers, 2nd Biennial Conference of the Reading Association of Nigeria, Ibadan.

Bamgbose, Ayo (ed.). 1976. *Mother Tongue Education: The West African Experience*. London: Hodder and Stoughton.

Bamgbose, Ayo. 1985. Language and Nation Building. In Samuel O. Asein (ed.), *Language and Polity*. Special Number of *Review of English and Literary Studies* 2, No. 2 (December).

Brimer, M. A. 1959. Reading Difficulties of Nigerian Students. *Ibadan Journal* (June): 24–26.

Chapman-Taylor, Y. 1965. The Reading Difficulties of University Students and Their Significance for Teaching Reading. Unpublished Manuscript, Ibadan University Reading Centre.

Du-Bey, Olive. 1983. Diagnosis and Remediation in the Primary School: A Case Study of Programme Development in ABU. In Unoh et al. (eds.), *Literacy and Reading in Nigeria*.

Egede, Ejembi. 1979. Teaching Reading to Beginners—A Survey of Methods and Instructional Materials Adopted in Two Nigerian Schools. B.A. Long Essay, Department of Language Arts, University of Ibadan, Ibadan.

Elugbe, Ben O. 1985. National Language and Language Development. In Asein (ed.), *Language and Polity*.

Emenyonu, Patricia. 1983. Promoting the Reading Habit in Nigeria. In Unoh et al. (eds.), *Literacy and Reading in Nigeria*.

Epidi, Gideon T. 1985. The Effects of Developmental Speech Dysfluencies on the Reading Ability of Selected Primary School Pupils in Ibadan. B.A. Long Essay, Department of Language Arts, University of Ibadan.

Federal Ministry of Education Science and Technology. 1984. *National Syllabus for Primary School English*.

Federal Ministry of Education. 1985. *National Curriculum for Senior Secondary Schools*. Vol. 2, *Modern Languages*.

Federal Ministry of Information. 1977. *Federal Republic of Nigeria National Policy on Education, Lagos*.

Hansford et al. 1976. *An Index of Nigerian Languages*. In the Series *Studies in Nigerian Languages* 5:1–204.

Ikegulu, Bene O. 1987. Teachers' Perception and Performance of Reading Tasks in Some Public Primary Schools in Lagos. *Journal of English Studies* 4 (September): 111–126.

James, Sybil. 1979. Three Basic Functions of English Language in Nigeria. In Ebo Ubahakwe (ed.) *Varieties and Functions of English in Nigeria*. Ibadan: African Universities Press and Nigeria English Studies Association.

James Sybil. 1985. Cognitive Demands of Question Papers in JAMB: Implication for Teaching and Learning English in Nigeria. *Journal of English Studies* 2 (September): 25–36.

James, Sybil, and Odejide, Abiola. 1981. A Critical Survey of Nigerian Children's Literature in English and Indigenous Language. *The Reading Teacher* 34, No. 7: 809–814.

Kalinda, C. S. 1979. The Readability of the English Supplementary Readers Used in Selected Primary Schools in and Around Ibadan. M.Ed. dissertation, Department of Teacher Education, University of Ibadan.

Laubauch, R. S. and S. A. Mujahid. 1971. Illiteracy. *Encyclopedia of Education*, Vol. IV.

Lawal, O. O. 1985. Planning a Reading Curriculum for the Junior Secondary School in Nigeria: An Approach Through Literary Texts. *Journal of English Studies* 2 (September): 1–14.

Macaulay, Juliet. 1983. Reading Readiness Programmes and Activities in a Bilingual Environment. In Unoh et al. (eds.), *Literacy and Reading in Nigeria*.

McKillop, Anne, and Yoloye, E. A. 1962. The Reading of University Students. *Reading Education* 3.

Nkama, M. O. 1980. Reading Errors of Selected Primary School Children: Observations on Reading in Second Language Situations. B.A. Long Essay, Department of Language Arts, University of Ibadan.

Nzinga, D. D. 1983. Aspects of Reading Problems and Their Implications for Academic Achievement Among New Entrants at Ilorin University. In Unoh et al. (eds.). *Literacy and Reading in Nigeria*.

Obah, Thelma. 1981. Some Psycholinguistic Factors Affecting Reading Performance— A Study of Nigerian University Students. *Journal of Language Arts and Communication* 2, Nos. 3 & 4: 169–186.

Obah, Thelma. 1987. Improving Reading Ability at the Secondary Level in Nigeria. *Journal of English Studies* 4 (September): 87–98.

Obanya, Pai. 1984. Reflections on the 1982–83 Educational Year. *Nigerian Journal of Curriculum Studies* 2, No. 1 (January): 1–8.

Obemeata, Joseph O. 1981. The Relationship Between Reading Ability and the Intelligence Test Performance of Nigerian Children. *Journal of Language Arts and Communication* 2, Nos. 3 & 4: 187–198.

Obianika, U. B. 1981. The Relative Effectiveness of Two Methods of Inculcating Reading Skills. Unpublished Ph.D. Thesis, University of Ibadan.

Odejide, Abiola. 1984. Nigerian Children's Books and Social Studies in Junior Secondary Schools. *Nigeria Educational Forum* 7, No. 2 (December): 167–172.

Odejide, Abiola. 1986. The Readability Levels of Selected Newspaper Editorials. In S. O. Unoh (ed.), *Use of English in Communication.* Ibadan: Spectrum Books.

Odejide, Abiola, and James, Sybil. 1981. Observations of Reading Patterns and Readership Behaviour in Three Resource Centres in Nigeria. In S. O. Unoh (ed.), *Junior Literature in English.* Ibadan: African Universities Press and Nigeria English Studies Association.

Ojelade, Adebanke K. 1985. Difficulties and Errors in Reading Among Selected Primary School Children. B.A. Long Essay, Department of Language Arts, University of Ibadan.

Ojo, Julius O. 1983. Problems of a Selected Group of Secondary School Students with Reading Disabilities. B.A. Long Essay, Department of Language Arts, University of Ibadan.

Okedara, C. A. 1983. Problems That Adults Face in Learning How to Read. In Unoh et al. (eds.), *Literacy and Reading in Nigeria,* pp. 429–440.

Okedara, J. T. 1981a. *The Impact of Literacy Education in Ibadan Nigeria.* Ibadan: Ibadan University Press.

Okedara, J. T. 1981b. *Concepts and Measurements of Literacy, Semi-Literacy and Illiteracy.* Ibadan: Ibadan University Press.

Okedara, J. T. 1986. *Efficiency in Educational Practice: The Nigerian Experience.* An Inaugural Lecture. Ibadan: Ibadan University Press.

Okedara, J. T., Okedara, C. A. and Adeniyi, J. D. (n.d. *Iwe Kika Fun Awon Agba: Ilera l'ogun Oro Apa Kinni.* Ibadan: Akinola Printing Works.

Olawo, Olafunmike, S. A Case for Reading Consultancy Services: A Critical Evaluation of Problems Encountered in Nigerian Schools. B.A. Long Essay, Department of Language Arts, University of Ibadan.

Omojuwa, Ralph. 1983. A Literacy Policy for the Nigerian Educational System. In Unoh et al. (eds.), *Literacy and Reading in Nigeria.*

Omolewa, Michael A. The English Language in Colonial Nigeria 1862–1960: A Study of the Major Factors Which Promoted the Language. *Journal of the Nigeria English Studies Association* 7, Nos. 1 & 2 (December): 103–117.

Oni, Phillips A. 1985. Reading Behaviours and Difficulties Among Students of a Foreign Language: A Case Study of University of Ibadan Students of Russian Language. B.A. Long Essay, Department of Language Arts, University of Ibadan.

Prince. R. 1960. The Brain Fag Syndrome in Nigerian Students. *Journal of Mental Science* 106: 559.

Shnukal, A., and Marchere, L. 1983. Creolization of Nigerian Pidgin. *English World Wide* 4, No. 1: 17–26.

Solaru, A. T. 1985. Reading in the Nigerian Society: A Survey of the Recreational Reading Habits of Young Professional Adults in Ibadan. Master of Communication Arts Dissertation, University of Ibadan.

Tomori, S.H.O., and Okedara, J. T. 1975. A Comparative Study of the Learning of English as a Second Language by Literate and Illiterate Tobacco Farmers of Oyo North District, Western State. *Journal of Nigeria English Studies Association* 7, Nos. 1 & 2 (December): 89–101.

Ubahakwe, Ebo. (ed.) 1979. *Varieties and Functions of English in Nigeria*. Ibadan: African Universities Press and Nigeria English Studies Association.

Ubahakwe, Ebo (ed.) 1983. Methods and Problems in Teaching and Reading in Igbo. In Unoh et al. (eds.), *Literacy and Reading in Nigeria*.

Unoh, S. O. 1968. A Psycholinguistic Approach to the Study of Reading. *West African Journal of Education* (June): 74–79.

Unoh. S. 1969. *Reading to Remember*. Ibadan: Universities Press Ltd.

Unoh, S. O. 1972. The Reading Difficulties of Students in a Nigerian University: Their Environmental Correlates and Psycholinguistic Implications. Unpublished Ph.D. Thesis, University of Ibadan, 1972.

Unoh, S. O. 1975. Incidence and Patterns of Reading Difficulties Among Students in a Nigerian University. *African Journal of Education Research* 2.

Unoh, S. O. 1977a. On Teaching Reading and Writing for Functional Literacy. *Reading Horizons* (Winter).

Unoh, S. O. 1977b. Relationship Between Reading Ability and Self Reports of Language Development and Competence. *The West African Journal of Educational and Vocational Measurement* 4, No. 1 (August): 30–39.

Unoh, S. O. 1980. Reading Problems in Secondary Schools—Some Observations and Research Findings. *Journal of Language Arts and Communication* 1, No. 1.

Unoh, S. O. 1982. *The Role of Language Arts in Intellectual Development: An Inaugural Lecture*. Ibadan: Ibadan University Press, 1982.

Unoh, S. O. 1985. On Language Arts in Nigerian Colleges of Education. *Journal of English Studies* 2 (November): 37–48.

Unoh, S. O. 1987. Information Dissemination: How Effective Through Local (Nigerian) Languages? In S. O. Unoh (ed.), *Topical Issues in Communication Arts*. Vol. 1. Uyo: Modern Business Press Ltd.

Unoh, S. O., Omojuwa, Ralph, and Crow, Susannah (eds.) 1983. *Literacy and Reading in Nigeria*. Vol. 1. Zaria: Ahmadu Bello University Press.

Unoh, S. O., Omojuwa, Ralph, and Ikonta, N. R. (eds.) 1985. *Literacy and Reading in Nigeria*. Vol. 2. Zaria: Ahmadu Bello University Press.

Williamson, Kay. 1976. The Rivers Readers Project in Nigeria. In Bamgbose (ed.), *Mother Tongue Education*.

BIBLIOGRAPHY

Abiri, J.O.O. 1969. Word Initial Teaching Alphabet Versus Traditional Orthography: The Contractive Behavioural Products of Two Coding Systems in English for Nigerian Pupils. Unpublished Ph.D. thesis, University of Ibadan.

Arua, E. Erua. 1987. Teaching Reading Efficiency Skills in Nigerian Universities: The Example of the Obafemi Awolowo University. *Journal of English Studies* 4 (September): 99–110.

Asein, Samuel O. (ed.). 1985. *Language and Polity*. Special Number of *Review of English and Literary Studies* 2, No. 2 (December).

Awoniyi, T. A. 1982. *The Teaching of African Languages*. London: Hodder and Stoughton Educational Books.

Balogun, I.O.B. 1972. The Intellectual and Residential Correlates of Reading Achievement in Nigeria Schools. Unpublished Ph.D. thesis, University of Ibadan, 1972.

Bamgbose, Ayo (ed.). 1976. *Mother Tongue Education: The West African Experience*. London: Hodder and Stoughton.

Freeman, R., and Jibril, M. (eds.). 1984. *English Language Studies in Nigerian Higher Education*. Proceedings of the British Council NESA Conference Held in Kano, September.

Ikegulu, Bene O. 1987. Teachers' Perception and Performance of Reading Tasks in Some Public Schools in Lagos. *Journal of English Studies* 4 (December): 111–126.

James, Sybil. 1985. Cognitive Demands of Question Paper in JAMB: Implications for Teaching and Learning English in Nigeria. *Journal of English Studies* 2 (November): 25–36.

James, Sybil, and Odejide, Abiola. (1981). A Critical Survey of Nigerian Children's Literature in English and Indigenous Languages. *The Reading Teacher* 34, no. 7:809–814.

Lawal, O. O. 1985. Planning a Reading Curriculum for the Junior Secondary School in Nigeria: An Approach Through Literary Texts. *Journal of English Studies* 2 (December): 1–13.

Obah, Thelma Y. 1981. Some Psycholinguistic Factors Affecting Reading Performance: A Study of Nigerian University Students. *Journal of Language Arts and Communication* 2, Nos. 3 & 4 (April/October): 169–186.

Obemeata, Joseph. 1981. The Relationship Between Reading Ability and the Intelligence Test Performance of Nigerian Children. *Journal of Language Arts and Communication* 2, Nos. 3 & 4 (April/October): 187–199.

Odejide, Abiola. 1984. Nigerian Children's Books and Social Studies in Junior Secondary Schools. *Nigeria Educational Forum* 7, No. 2 (December): 167–172.

Odejide, Abiola. 1986. The Readability Levels of Selected Nigerian Newspaper Editorials. In S. O. Unoh (ed)., *Use of English in Communication*. Ibadan: Spectrum Books, pp. 186–194.

Odejide, Abiola, and James, Sybil. 1981. Observations of Reading Patterns and Readership Behaviour in Three Resource Centres in Nigeria. In S. O. Unoh (ed.), *Junior Literature in English*. Ibadan: African Universities Press, pp. 114–125.

Okedara, J. T. 1986. *Efficiency in Educational Practice: The Nigerian Experience*. An Inaugural Lecture. Ibadan: Ibadan University Press.

Onochie, E. O. 1987. Readability Measures in a Second Language: A Comparative Study of the Fry Formula and the Cloze Procedure. Unpublished Ph.D. Thesis, University of Ibadan.

Tomori, S.H.O., and Okedara, J. T. 1975. A Comparative Study of the Learning of English as Second Language by Literate and Illiterate Tobacco Farmers of Oyo North District, Western State Nigeria. *Journal of Nigeria English Studies Association* 7, Nos. 1 & 2 (December): 89–101.

Ubahakwe, Ebo. (ed.). 1979. *Varieties and Functions of English in Nigeria*. Ibadan: African Universities Press.

Unoh, S. O. 1972a. The Problem of Methodology in Teaching University Students to Read Faster. *West African Journal of Education* 16, No. 3 (October): 309–316.

Unoh, S. O. 1972b. The Reading Difficulties of Students in a Nigerian University: Their Environmental Correlates and Psycholinguistic Implications. Unpublished Ph.D. Thesis, University of Ibadan.

Unoh, S. O. 1977. On Teaching Reading and Writing for Functional Literacy. *Reading Horizons* (Winter).

Unoh, S. O. Reading Problems in Secondary Schools: Some Observations and Research Findings. *Journal of Language Arts and Communication* 1, No. 1 (March): 30–41.

Unoh, S. O. 1982. *The Role of Language Arts in Intellectual Development*. Inaugural Lecture. Ibadan: Ibadan University Press, 1982.

Unoh, S. O. 1985. On Language Arts in Nigerian Colleges of Education. *Journal of English Studies* 2 (December): 37–48.

Unoh, S. O., Omojuwa, Ralph A., and Crow, Susannah, K. M. (eds.). 1983. *Literacy and Reading in Nigeria*. Vol. 1. Proceedings of the First National Seminar on Reading, August 9–13, 1982. Zaria: Ahmadu Bello University Press.

Unoh, S. O., Omojuwa, R. A., and Ikonta, N. R. (eds.). 1985. *Literacy and Reading in Nigeria*. Vol. II. Zaria: Reading Association of Nigeria and Ahamdu Bello University Press.

15

North Korea

Youngsoon Park

THE LANGUAGE OF THE COUNTRY

The national official language of North Korea, like that of South Korea, is Korean. No other languages are spoken in the country; it is a completely monolingual society. The written version of Korean is called *Hangul*, a system invented by King Sejong in 1443. Before Hangul was introduced, the Korean people borrowed Chinese characters for writing, so that until 1443 all documents were written in Chinese. However, Chinese letters proved too difficult to learn, and even worse, the difference between the spoken and the written language made communication very uncomfortable for the people. As a result, only a small percentage of the higher classes could use written language; the rest of the people never learned it.

For this reason, King Sejong, the most admired king in Korean history, was determined to invent a written Korean. The writing system he devised, Hangul, is a phonetic system consisting of twenty-four alphabets that are very scientific and easy to learn and can represent every spoken utterance of Korean. The Korean language is generally known as a branch of the Altaic language family, but Korean linguistic circles have not yet confirmed it.

The Educational System

The North Korean educational system is highly pragmatic. The focus is on technical skills and correct political ideology rather than on academic proficiency. All levels of education are completely politicized and exist to buttress the socialist system. In "Theses on Social Education" published in 1977, President Il-Sung Kim stated that political and ideological education is the most important part of socialist education. Only through proper political and ideological education, he said, was it possible to rear students as revolutionaries, equipped with a revolutionary world outlook and the ideological and moral qualities of communists. Only on the basis of sound political and ideological education would the people's scientific and technological education and physical culture be successful.

In order to fulfill this ideological education, the philosophy of *Juche* or "self-determination" serves as the dominant principle for the North Korean people to follow. According to Kim, the individual is a creative and independent social being; therefore, every individual must have his or her own will and self-determination, Juche. To establish Juche in education, the main emphasis in instruction should be placed on the culture of one's own country, and people should be taught to know their own culture well. In scientific and technical education, for instance, people shouldn't become entranced with abstract theories imported from economically advanced countries or depend excessively on the small elites of theoretically trained experts. Rather, they should be educated so as to be aware of the problems of socialist construction and economic development within Korea, and master the theoretical knowledge themselves in order to overcome these problems.

Closely associated with the central theme of Juche in education is the method of heuristic teaching, which is seen as a means of developing the students' independence and creativity and is a reaction against the traditional Confucian emphasis on memorization of prescribed texts. Heuristic teaching gives students an understanding of what they are taught through their own positive thinking and so greatly helps to develop independence and creativeness. Coercion and cramming should be avoided in favor of persuasion and explanation, particularly in ideological education, and role models such as the anti-Japanese guerrilla fighters should be used as positive examples for students to emulate.

Unfortunately, North Korean educational theory and practice seem to contain two contradictory themes. Social education has emphasized a totally controlled social and cultural environment in which the children have little or no opportunity or time for spontaneous, undirected activity. Heuristic teaching has been based on the idea of Juche, and developing the student's intellectual and critical faculties through discussion and demonstration. Juche in education, however, cannot be equated with freedom, and the "independence of social beings" leaves little room for spontaneity.

The present education system in North Korea has evolved through a number of reforms since 1945. The present system was put into effect in 1972. North Korea's educational structure can be discussed in terms of four major divisions: formal, higher, adult, and social.

Formal Education. For formal education, universal, free eleven-year compulsory education consisting of a one-year kindergarten, a four-year people's school (primary), and a six-year secondary school was established in 1972 (see Figure 15.1).

Figure 15.1
The Education System

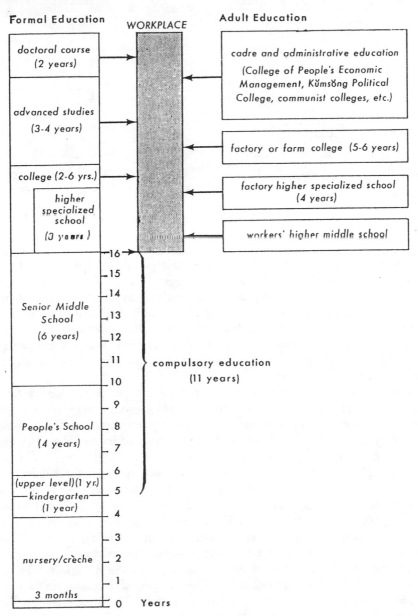

Source: Adapted from Kŭktong Munje Yŏn'guso, *Pukhan Chŏnsŏ: 1945–1980* (Seoul, 1980), p. 595.

Table 15.1
Curriculum of the Four-Year People's School (primary school), 1984–

Subjects	Rate (%)
Korean	32
Math	23
Physical Education	8.4
Music	8.4
Drawing	8.4
Science	6.4
Great Kim Il-Sung	4.2
Special lecture	4.2
Communist Morality	4.2
Health/Hygiene	1.0
10 subjects	100%

The curricula of primary and middle school (secondary) are shown in Tables 15.1 and 15.2, respectively.

After graduating from People's School, students can continue with a regular secondary school education or they can enter a "special" secondary school that concentrates on music, arts, or foreign languages.

Higher Education. According to Il-Sung Kim's report to the Sixth Party Congress presented on October 10, 1980, the number of higher learning institutions increased from 129 in 1970 to 170 in 1980. In addition, 480 new higher specialized schools were established. The number and size of colleges and universities can be expected to expand greatly as the country moves toward the intellectualization of the whole country.

Tertiary institutions include teacher's training colleges, which have a four-year course and produce primary, secondary, and kindergarten instructors; colleges of advanced technology with two- or three-year courses; medical schools with six-year courses; special colleges for the teaching of art, music, and foreign languages; and military colleges and academies.

Il-Sung Kim University, founded in October 1946, is the only true university in North Korea. It is an elite institution whose 15,000 students (12,000 day students and 3,000 night and correspondence students) occupy, according to one observer, the pinnacle of the North Korean educational and social system. Evidence of their privileged status is their exemption from "Friday labor," a duty that even cabinet members and high party functionaries must perform.

The foreign languages offered on the college level include English, Russian, Chinese, French, Arabic, Japanese, and Spanish. English is considered the most important language because of its international status. The Pyongyang Foreign Language Institute and the Foreign Language Teacher's College are four-year institutions. Few students are sent abroad; the largest number in foreign institutions, about 250, are studying scientific subjects in the Soviet Union. The

Table 15.2
Curriculum of the Six-Year Secondary School, 1984–

Subjects	Rate (%)
Math	18.4
Korean language & Literature	11.6
Physics	8.3
Foreign Language	7.5
Chemistry	5.8
Biology	5.6
Geography	5.1
Physical Education	4.5
History	4.2
Chinese letters	3.7
Great Kim Il-Sung	3.0
Special lecture	2.9
Field work	2.8
Technical skill	2.7
Music	2.1
Communist Party Policy	1.5
Communist Morality	1.3
Science	1.0
Art	1.0
Drawing	0.8
Electronics & Agriculture	0.8
21 subjects	100%

second largest group (the number is unspecified) is believed to be in China. In early 1979 about 100 students were studying English in Guyana, the only English-speaking country with which North Korea has close relations. An undetermined number of students from Third World countries study in North Korea.

Adult Education. Because of the emphasis on continuing education among all members of society, adult or work-study education is of great importance. Everyone in the country participates in some educational activity, usually in the form of small study groups. In late 1980 rural people were organized into five-family teams that were the responsibility of a schoolteacher or intellectual. Each teacher was in charge of several such teams, although the five-family teams had a potential surveillance and control function.

The most important adult education institutions in Korea are the factory colleges. In 1960 Kim established twenty of these colleges, and since that date they have trained 22,000 technicians. By 1981 eighty-five such institutions were located in major industrial centers. Their major advantage is that they enable students to learn new skills, techniques, and basic theory without having to quit their jobs.

Social Education. Outside the formal schools is an educational division that is considered extremely important: so-called social education. It encompasses not only extracurricular activities, but also family life and the broadest range of human relationships within Korean society. Educators in Korea have exhibited great sensitivity to the influence of the social environment on the growing child and its role in the development of character.

A special segment of the curriculum for social education is designed to instill communist morality in children. These courses emphasize three sets of values: patriotism, society, and family. Socialist patriotism is explicitly differentiated from traditional nationalism, which is seen as tainted with subservience to foreign powers and cultures. The new patriotism, on the other hand, encourages national pride and identity and self-reliance and holds up Kim as the father of the nation. Social values emphasize the role of the individual in the "Red" society, a love of labor, comradeship among workers, honesty, modesty, and self-sacrifice for the good of the Korean Worker's party. Conversely, Confucian values are denigrated as counterrevolutionary and feudalistic. Family values are taught in the context of nuclear rather than extended families, and the ideals of mutual assistance and respect for elders are promoted.

READING INSTRUCTION POLICY

The process of reading instruction is centralized because North Korea is a communist country. Among communist countries, North Korea is the strictest and most closed society, so much so that the government controls even the people's daily lives.

The government unifies and controls all aspects of existence. People are forced to give loyalty to Il-Sung Kim and the Communist party and to be anti-American, -Japanese and -South Korean. Therefore, the reading material in North Korea is full of praise for the greatness of Il-Sung Kim and Marxism, and paints bad images of America, Japan, and South Korea. Reading instruction is included in language education in North Korea, and language education is part of ideological education. Language is considered to be only a tool to teach the people the ideology of communism and to idolize Kim. During the 1960s, 47 percent of the entire curriculum was devoted to Korean language education for elementary school children since the contents of ideology education are being included in the Korean language course.

In the 1970s, Kim began to be strongly idolized, an adulation that has increased since 1980. As a result, the role of the Korean language course has been reduced, and instead some ideology courses are offered to implement the purpose of ideology education. That is, independent new courses such as History of Great General Kim's Revolution, Great General Kim's Leading Revolutionary Activities, Great General Kim's Childhood, Communist Party's Policies, and Communist Morality have been introduced on both the primary and secondary levels. All these newly developed courses serve as main sources of reading instruction. As such, the process of reading instruction in North Korea is entirely centralized.

GOALS FOR READING EDUCATION

North Korea's goals for reading education are very peculiar but clear: that is, to learn and understand the great idea of revolution as proposed by Il-Sung Kim who has ruled North Korea since 1945 and to strengthen the power of dictatorship and communism in order to let the people know what Kim has said and done. In 1975 a law was passed requiring college students to read 10,000 pages of the many books that extol the greatness of Kim.

North Korea makes no distinction between males and females either in work or education. Of course, North Korea publishes literary works including novels and poems, but even these, in one way or another, are about Kim, the government, or communism.

LITERACY

The rate of illiteracy in Korea is almost 0 percent. In 1947 the North Korean government eliminated illiteracy by law. In order to accomplish this goal, it established 8,000 adult schools throughout the country to teach the Korean language. Later, in 1975, Korea also passed the eleven-year compulsory education law in accordance with Kim's speech in which he proclaimed that "the people must know their language in order to be autonomous and creative."

As a result, there are no illiterate people in North Korea. Today, the North Koreans get at least a secondary education, so that they can read general written materials such as newspapers, magazines, novels, and essays. Furthermore, Kim has emphasized that all writings should be written in easy and general terms using exclusively the Korean language. Therefore, both the South and the North Korean people can read any material written in their language.

PRESCHOOL CHILDREN AND READING PROBLEMS

All North Korean children aged five to six receive compulsory kindergarten education. The curriculum of the kindergarten is shown in Table 15.3. No distinction is made between male and female, or between rural and urban areas, in reading education.

Preschool education in North Korea is also implemented for ideological education, for the political leaders believe that the education of school children is very important in inculcating communist ideology and in the idolization of Kim. Kim says that in order to complete the great revolution of Juche from generation to generation, "We must raise our young children as communistic revolutionary talent."

TEACHER QUALIFICATIONS

Graduates of teacher's colleges (two-year schools) are qualified to teach in primary schools. Since North Korea is a communist country, the government

Table 15.3
The Kindergarten Curriculum, 1984–

COURSE	CONTENTS
Marshall Kim's Childhood	Loyalty Toward Kim
Communist Morality	Loyalty To The Party
Korean	Vocabulary Gaining 2000–3000
Counting	Counting Basic Numbers
Music	Singing Songs
Art	Drawing

Total 1360 hours

nominates a primary school teacher. For secondary schools, a teacher should graduate from a college of education (four-year school) with a special major or from a department of liberal arts and sciences. Because there is no department of reading in North Korea, no special qualifications are required for teaching reading other than being a Korean language teacher.

For teaching on the tertiary level, professors and instructors should hold a master's or higher degree. Probably for adult education anyone who has a college or higher degree is qualified. In Korea, however, both South and North, there is no reading department, nor is there any independent reading instruction program in the universities and colleges; therefore, no systematic reading education is available in Korea. Reading education is included as part of language education.

CHARACTERISTICS OF NATIONAL LANGUAGE EDUCATION IN NORTH KOREA

The characteristics of national language (Korean) education at all levels of schools in North Korea can be summarized as follows:

1. The subject of language education is considered a vehicle for ideological education.
2. The lower level of schooling is emphasized more because government leaders believe that ideological education is more effective and successful for younger children.
3. Reading education is included in Korean language education, and there is no independent curriculum or institution for reading instruction in North Korea.

4. Materials for reading instruction relate mostly to the idolization of Kim and his family, the ideology of communism, anti-Americanism, and an aggressive atmosphere toward South Korea. The materials are devoid of classical literature.

5. All the writings included in the textbooks are written by an unknown group and not by an individual. Therefore, the author's name never appears in a textbook at any level.

6. Writing education is emphasized more than any other aspect of Korean language education.

7. Therefore, reading instruction in a Western sense can be said to be greatly neglected and behind in North Korea.

MATERIALS USED IN READING EDUCATION

Reading materials in Korea are not as diverse as those in Western countries. All the materials are similar and common in the sense that no matter what their formal shape, the theme of the materials must be related to Kim, the importance of solidarity in accordance with communism and the Communist party, and anti-Americanism. The North Korean government publishes many materials designed to propagate Kim's words. These materials are major sources for reading instruction in North Korean schools. In addition, the people must be provided with reading materials on new ideas and tasks in order to promote the society both economically and ideologically, to strengthen the solidarity of the people on the basis of collectivism and the reunification with South Korea by conquest. The reading materials are written mostly in Korean, but some basic reading materials are also available in languages like English, Russian, Japanese, Chinese, and Arabic.

Since the government controls and provides everything, even food, we can conclude that there are no privately published consumable reading materials in North Korea. Even worse, the contents of all materials are very limited in scope and depth because most literary works are written by a group, not by an individual, for individualism is prohibited.

THE CURRENT FOCUS OF RESEARCH IN READING EDUCATION

To date, there has been almost no serious academic research or professional reading education in North Korea. Recently, however, the Communist party and the government have passed a law requiring that college students read 10,000 pages of Il-Sung Kim's works which exclusively contain pages of the ideology of *Juche* which, as described earlier, is anti-American and anti-Japanese, and calls for the respect that is due Kim. Since the North Korean government has increasingly idolized Kim since 1980, most of the contents of all the textbooks at all levels of education (primary, secondary, tertiary, adult, etc.) are still about the greatness of the thought and action of Kim.

Table 15.4 shows the theme of the writings contained in the current North Korean language textbooks (called *Kuko*, meaning national language) for the fourth grade of primary school, which is equivalent to the sixth grade in the United States.

ENGLISH EDUCATION

From 1945 to 1964 Russian was the only foreign language taught in secondary schools in Korea. In 1966 the language education policy was changed so as to teach both Russian and English. Since 1967, the government has allowed students to choose one language among German, French, Japanese, and Chinese as a second foreign language.

In 1978 the North Korean government began to teach English through cable television. In 1979 the Koreans published various English textbooks and reference books and made tape recordings and distributed them on a massive basis. The class hours of English courses have now increased from two to three hours to three to four hours a week, and in college to five hours. In 1980 some special events such as vocabulary contests and the Foreign Language Contest were held in secondary and tertiary schools.

Interestingly enough, however, the reason and purpose of such a strengthening of English is as follows: Kim says "We must determine to fight against the Imperial America and Imperial Japan and in order to do so youth must be able to speak at least a few army words such as 'Your hands up!', 'We will not shoot you if you drop arms and surrender' both in English and Japanese."

With this background the North Korean government offers practice in English education not only to soldiers but also to civilians. In order to train professional foreign language translators, the government sent hundreds of students abroad. For English training, about 200 students have been sent to Iraq, Yugoslavia, and Guyana but not to America, Great Britain, Canada, and other Western nations. The contents of English textbooks also focus on praise of Kim (20 to 35 percent), anti-Americanism (10 to 15 percent), admiration of North Korea, self-confidence of the nation (15 percent), the fight for communism (10 percent), and the fight against Japan (7 percent).

CONCLUSION

As we have seen, reading instruction in North Korea is not only premature but also very peculiar. The content and method of reading education is tragic in every sense except for the lack of illiteracy. There is no known study of reading instruction, in a technical sense, no department of reading, and no academic society of reading instruction.

It is hoped that the current trends in reading instruction in North Korea will gradually change to an extent that will enable the North Korean people to read books outside of their closed society.

Table 15.4
Titles and Themes of Korean Language Textbooks for the Fourth Grade of Primary School, 1984–

Ch.	Title	Theme or Topic
1	We pray for "our master,"	Idolization of Kim
2	The effectiveness of pause	Effective speaking
3	Jung-Il Kim (Son of Il-Sung Kim) sees the pictures.	Praise of Jung-Il Kim
4	To our Mother	Praise of father and son Kim
5	Lining up sentences	Good handwriting
6	Our classroom	Idolization of Kim
7	Diary	[Stressing the spirit of respect for the aged and praise of Jung-Il Kim]
8	The purpose of writing must appear clearly	Effective composition
9	Why didn't Challuki know?	The spirit of cooperation
10	The medicine of love	Praise of Hyung-Jik Kim, father of Il-Sung Kim
11	The speed of reading	Effective reading
12	Guard the headquarter.	The spirit of independence from resisting Japan
13	Familiar sounds "tok," "tok"	Idolization of Kim
14	Seeking writing material	Writing procedure
15	The beautiful road	Idolization of Kim
16	Completely worn-out small Japs	Idolization of Kim
17	Following Mrs. Kim	Praise Mrs. Kim
18	Organizing a writing	Composition drill
19	Visiting Chongbongsukyoung	Idolization of Kim
20	The flower blossomed from our mind	Idolization of Kim

Table 15.4 (continued)

Ch.	Title	Theme or Topic
21	Synonyms and antonyms	Meaning of words
22	The telescope of Marshall	Idolization of Kim
23	Black dog's drawing	Completion of responsibility
24	Characteristics of spoken language	Speaking drill
25	I will raise more rabbit	Completion of responsibility
26	In the learning field	Idolization of Kim
27	How can we write appreciation.	Composition drill
28	Thinking of Soonhi	Hatred of a landlord
29	The flower road	Idolization of Kim
30	The expression of our language	Rhetoric
31	Our father	Idolization of Kim
32	The capital of revolution, Pyongyang	Protection of the national system
33	Three loaves of bread and five apples	Anti-Americanism
34	Simple sentence and complex sentence	Grammar
35	The rainy night	Praise of Jung-Il Kim
36	The gold medalist	Praise of Su-Bok Lee (2)
37	Love of our father	Idolization of Kim
38	Speaking orderly	Speaking drill
39	A tiger caught in trap	Repayment of kindness
40	Sister's picture	Insulting South Korea

REFERENCES

Bunge, Frederica M. (ed.) 1981. *North Korea. A Country Study*. U.S. Government.

Chun, S. T., and D. U. Kim. 1989. *The Current Situation of Language in North Korea*. Seoul: Baikui Publishing Co.

Essac, Alma, and Karim. 1983. *Juche Korean*. Vol. 2. Tanzania: Thakers Limited Printers.

Foreign Language Publishing House. 1982. *Korean Review*. Pyongyang, North Korea.

Kim Hyung-Chan. 1981. For the Heirs of Revolution: Current Educational Practices in North Korea. *Social Education* 45, No. 7.

Kim Il-Sung. 1968. On the Right Way of Maintaining the National Characteristics of the Korean Language. *Munhwahaksup* 3. Pyongyang, North Korea.

———. 1984. *The Works of Il-Sung Kim*. Pyongyang, North Korea: Foreign Material Publishing Co.

Kim Min-su. 1985. *North Korea's National Language Study*. Seoul: Tower Press Co.

Kukdong Munje Yonguso. 1980. *Pukhan chonso, 1945–1980*. Seoul, Korea.

Kurian, George T., ed. 1988. *World Educational Encyclopedia*. Vol. III. Facts on File Publications.

Park Jae-won. 1965. A Content Problem of National Language Education. *Chosuno Haksup*, No. 4. Pyongyang, North Korea.

———. 1968. National Language Education and Cultural Education. *Munhwao Haksup*, No. 3. Pyongyang, North Korea.

Park Sang-hoo, K. Y. Lee, and S. S. Kho. 1986. *Our Nation's Vocabulary Consolidation*. Pyongyang, North Korea: Social Science Publishing Co.

Park Soo-young. 1984. Our Party Which Has Been Practicing the *Juche*. *Munhwao Haksup*, No. 1. Pyongyang, North Korea.

Park Youngsoon. 1989. *A Comparative Study on Language Policies of South and North Korea*. Hyundai Shihak. Seoul, Korea.

Social Science Publishing Co. 1970. *Kim Il-Sung's Ideology on Language and Its Brilliant Performance*. Pyongyang, North Korea.

Research Institute of N. Korea. 1971. *The Great Comrade Kim Il-Sung's Autonomous Ideology*. Pyongyang, North Korea.

———. 1974. *On the Kim's Words "Education and Culture and Art Must Contribute to Man's International Revolutionary View Point of the World."* Pyongyang, North Korea.

———. 1975a. *The Linguistic Theory on the Basis of Juche Ideology*. Pyongyang, North Korea.

———. 1975b. *Reaction Toward Imperial America's Korean Language Erasure Policy*. Pyongyang, North Korea.

———. 1976. *Our Party's Language Policy*. Pyongyang, North Korea.

———. 1977. *A Study of North Korea's Education*. Seoul, Korea.

Study Group of North Korean Language. 1989. *Pukhanui Ohakhyungmyung*. Seoul: Paikui Press Co.

Yoon Young-Kil. 1985. A Study on the Ideology Education Through Language Policy in North Korea. *Kyoyuk Nonchung*, No. 1. Seoul, Korea: Dankook University Press.

16

Portugal

Margarida Alves Martins
Translated by Soungalo Ouedraogo

INTRODUCTION

The Portuguese educational system was reorganized in 1987 as follows: preschool education; basic education, divided into two cycles—elementary education and preparatory; secondary education, also divided into two cycles—general secondary and complementary secondary education; and higher education, comprising university and polytechnical education. Portugal also has a nonformal education system that encompasses many training systems, namely, the apprenticeship system, vocational training, adult education, and youth nonformal education.

In Portugal, mandatory schooling begins at age six, with entry into elementary school, and ends at age fourteen, when the student comes to the end of the first cycle of secondary education (the ninth school year).

Formal Education

Preschool education takes place in kindergarten, which is the responsibility not only of the Ministry of Education but also of other structures such as the municipalities. There are also a great number of private kindergartens. These kindergartens also depend on the Ministry of Education and take children from ages three to six.

In 1986–1987 the enrollment rate (i.e., the ratio between the total number of registered children and the total population of three to five year-old children) was 29 percent. The variations between the different districts of Portugal were very great—from 13 to 60 percent. A study conducted in 1987–1988 demonstrated that the percentage of children who actually went to Ministry of Education kindergartens was 86.2 percent of the total number of kindergarten-aged children. Thus, a high percentage of children do not have their first contact with the education system until age six when they enter primary school.

Elementary education, which is mandatory for all six-year-old children, is organized into two cycles (school phases) of two years each (the first, second, third, and fourth years of school). It takes place in public and private schools which take children from ages six to nine.

Education is compulsory in Portugal until age fourteen; no student can be dismissed before this age. In 1986–1987 of all the school-age students, the percentage of ten- and eleven-year-old children at school was 37.2 percent, and the percentage of twelve- to fourteen-year-old children at school was 9.5 percent. The enrollment rate at the elementary school level was 104.6 percent in 1984–1985 for continental Portugal. (The enrollment rate is greater than 100 percent when estimates of the resident population are used.)

Preparatory education is also compulsory. It lasts two years (the fifth and sixth school years), and it takes place either in preparatory schools (85.4 percent) or through television education programming (14.5 percent). The children who go to preparatory schools are usually ten to eleven year olds.

After their fourteenth year, children can still go to "special" schools until they reach eighteen (0.6 percent in 1986–1987). The enrollment rate in preparatory education was 56.9 percent for 1984–1985 for continental Portugal.

Secondary education begins after these two cycles, which are called basic education. It is divided into two cycles. The first is called *general secondary education* and was made compulsory in 1987. It takes place in secondary school and lasts three years (the seventh, eighth, and ninth school years). These schools take twelve- to fourteen-year-old children. The repetition rates (repetition rate $= Tj = Rj + 1$; $Rj + 1 =$ those who repeat in the year $j + 1$; $Ej =$ the number of registered students in the year j) at this level were 38.3 percent in 1985–1986 for the seventh year of school, 34.7 percent for the eighth year of school, and 26.6 percent for the ninth year. At this level, the enrollment rate for 1984–1985 was 37.1 percent for continental Portugal.

The second cycle is called *complementary secondary education*. It is not part of the system of compulsory education. It consists of three different orientations: teaching, which lasts three years (the tenth, eleventh, and twelfth years of schooling); technical-vocational, which also lasts three years; and vocational which lasts one year, followed by six months of training.

In 1986–1987 the percentage of students enrolled in the first orientation was about 95 percent of the total number of students in complementary secondary education. At this level, there is a clear difference, as far as objectives and curricula are concerned, because they were homogeneous at the previous levels.

Higher education consists of university education, which lasts four to five years, and polytechnical education, which lasts two to three years. In 1986–

1987, 24 percent of the total student population in higher education were registered in polytechnical education.

Nonformal Education

In the area of nonformal education there are various subsystems of training:

The apprenticeship system, which is an alternative training system for students between fourteen and twenty-four years of age who have a certificate in basic education. This training requires an apprenticeship contract between the student and the particular firm. The training period usually lasts three years.

Vocational training, which consists of many initial and continuous training sessions, some of which include compulsory practical training in the respective firms.

Nonformal education for young adults, which takes place within local organizations such as youth clubs and sociocultural and socioeducational associations.

Adult education, which is dedicated to adults who have abandoned the formal education system or have never had any education.

At nonformal level there are literacy programs and basic education programs that correspond to elementary and secondary education (both through evening classes).

THE LANGUAGE

Portuguese is the language of continental Portugal, the Azores, and Madeira. The total population in 1986 was 10,208,000, of which 5,280,000 were female and 4,928,000 were male. An exception to the Portuguese language is Mirandais which is the mother tongue of 15,000 people in the eastern part of Tras-os-Montes Department. Two preparatory schools in that region introduced this dialect into the school curricula in 1986–1987.

Reading and Educational Policy

Portugal's national educational policy is centralized and depends on the Ministry of Education; its main tasks are to study measures for effective education actions, their promotion, programming, and execution as well as the development of subsequent activities. The ministry's administrative system is very complex, consisting of eighteen general directorates or equivalent divisions, four regional directorates, and two advisory committees. These regional directorates, created for continental Portugal in 1987, facilitate the coordination and support of schools as well as the management of human, financial, and material resources.

The objective of the ministry's educational directorates is to give administrative support to teaching and educational activities, whereas the delegations of the general directorate for personnel manage the human resources of preparatory and secondary schools as well as the teacher training colleges.

At the local level, the municipalities have authority in matters of educational social matters, school transportation, and educational equipment. The municipalities have a very important role to play in adult education; they make classrooms available for adult evening classes.

In terms of reading policy, it is centralized and depends exclusively on the Ministry of Education. However, a process of decentralization began with the creation of regional directorates in 1987.

THE GOALS AND OBJECTIVES OF READING EDUCATION

The objectives of reading education are the same for girls and boys.

Elementary Education

The mother tongue program that has operated since 1980 has several objectives for reading and writing. With regard to reading, the student must be able to read both silently and in a loud and clear voice and to use reading in connection with different functions such as leisure and information. The student must also be able to distinguish the main characters from the secondary characters of a given text, separate the main ideas from accessory ideas, and to identify the logical sequence of the ideas contained in the text.

In terms of writing, at the end of elementary school education every student is expected to be able to write extemporaneously and to write topic paragraphs, letters, telegrams, and answers to questionnaires; to write the active vocabulary correctly; and to know how to use capital letters and punctuation marks.

Preparatory Education

In terms of reading, in 1975 Portugal established its objectives for this educational level as follows. For reading aloud, the improvement of diction, intonation, and rhythm of expression are encouraged. The students must be able to read texts while underlining the meanings and the purposes in such a way that those who listen to them can understand them. For silent reading, the readers must be able to read silently texts whose difficulty is adapted to their age and to show that they understand them. On the other hand, they must distinguish between the description of facts and the expression of opinions, and adopt a critical and personal position in relation to what they have read. At the elementary education level the main functions of reading are to encourage students to read for both pleasure and information.

As far as writing is concerned, the objectives are to develop personal expression, reasoning, and critical analysis. Great attention is given to the ability to write correctly and to transmit, with a certain rigor and originality, personal ideas and experiences. In particular, importance is given to reports and essays.

General Secondary Education

The following objectives of Portugal's reading programs at the secondary level were established in 1980–1981. In the seventh year of school, the main objective is to correct oral and written communication and to develop the student's sensitivity to the semantics and aesthetics of the language.

Value is given to analyzing texts, enriching vocabulary, and mastering orthographic rules and punctuation. Particular attention is given to verbal aspects by proposing that the student, at different levels of the language according to particular circumstances, interpret messages from other people and the oral and written communication with correctness and elegance.

For the first time, compulsory reading of a literary work is part of the program.

In the eighth year of school, the objective is to highlight the aesthetic aspects of communication and to sensitize the student to literature. The student must distinguish, then, literary from nonliterary works; recognize the richness of the language used; be aware of the multiple significances of that language; and understand that the elaboration of a text conforms to a certain structure.

The student is required to read six nineteenth- and twentieth-century literary works which are indicated in the programs.

In the ninth year of schooling, once the students are capable of recognizing the main characteristics of a literary text, the objective is that they be able to have a general view on Portuguese literature that will enable them to be sensitive to texts of given authors studied during these three years.

The compulsory reading textbooks are selected from works written during the sixteenth and twentieth centuries.

Complementary Secondary Education

As mentioned earlier, reading education is not part of the curriculum of the technical vocational orientation of complementary secondary education. It is a requirement only in the tenth and eleventh years of schooling. The programs set up for these two years distinguish three domains: written and oral comprehension, written and oral expression, and cultural training.

The objective of written and oral comprehension is to promote the student's comprehension of communication in relation to situations in which speeches are delivered, distinction between the objective and subjective content of a text, development of a critical attitude toward the written and oral text, and synthesis of different texts dealing with the same topics.

In terms of written and oral expression, the objective is to increase the student's knowledge of the language structure as a way of improving the capacity of expression. The students must be able to express their ideas with correctness and coherence, as well as to utilize a rich vocabulary. The capacity to elaborate schemes, summaries and syntheses is particularly recommended.

In the domain of cultural training, students are expected to become competent in the following areas: analyzing and reflecting on the moral, social, sociological, and aesthetical values of a literary text; familiarizing themselves with authors and literary texts considered to be the most important in the history of Portuguese literary culture; situating authors and literary works in time and space; and intervening through speech and writing on sociocultural problems.

Basic Adult Education

In 1987 educators set up the following goals for literacy programs: to learn to listen (to understand what other people say); to speak (to make yourself understood orally); to read (to understand graphic messages); and to write (to make yourself understood by using the written code and respecting its rules).

At the level of elementary education, reading aloud and silent reading are also valued competencies. The learners must be able to identify the main ideas of a text and to discover the meaning of words encountered in the text.

For writing, the student should be able to write legibly and correctly; to use correctly the punctuation signs and the capital letters; to express clearly ideas, opinions and experiences; and to adapt a message to various communication contexts and modify messages, taking into account the contexts in which they are delivered.

Adult Preparatory Education

At the level of preparatory education the objectives are, on the one hand, to enlarge the learners' communicative competence, and, on the other, to enable them to acquire conscious knowledge of the usage, structure, and function of the language. In this way students are expected to be able to choose the forms of verbal and nonverbal communication that might be appropriate to each context of communication.

In terms of discursive and textual competencies, the learners must be knowledgeable of the various types of messages and, therefore, different types of texts; to analyze them so as to understand the structure and functioning of the discursive and linguistic elements; to adapt the message to the communication situation; and to produce different types of texts.

At the level of linguistic competence, the learners should be able to interpret the different rules of the linguistic code and to apply them (phonetical, phonological, orthographical, morphological, syntactical, and semantical rules).

The oral text is the end product of the linguistic-discursive unity.

The teaching of the Portuguese language, of which reading education has been part since 1986–1987, has two components: (1) teaching as it is practiced in preparatory education with a curriculum and a specific time sequence; and (2) an interdisciplinary teaching ("Man and His Environment," "Complementary Training"). At this level, the objective of reading education is to read various texts connected with the issues at stake; to enrich the general and specific vocabulary of each domain; to use different instruments and work techniques (encyclopedias, dictionaries, files, etc.); to understand and analyze diversified texts; and to produce texts written about topics related to the themes under study.

ILLITERACY

Portugal adopted the following definition of reading literacy in 1988: the capacity to understand and use all the forms and kinds of written materials required by society and individually utilized. This dynamic and functional perspective of reading, which implies simultaneous competencies as well as practices and habits, yields a continuum that goes from the identification of graphic signs used in everyday life to the decoding of literary and philosophical texts. This definition has made obsolete the dichotomous classification (to be able to read or not to be able to read) and the research on "literacy levels and behaviors" classified and organized by reading tasks.

There are no available data on Portugal's illiteracy rate by sex. The last statistics published by the National Institute of Statistics date back to 1981 (see Table 16.1); moreover, at that time they used another criterion of illiteracy which is different from the one we have just defined: the illiterate are those who are not able to read whether or not they went to school.

Table 16.1 shows that, as of 1981, over 20 percent of the Portuguese population was illiterate and that the percentage of illiterate women was higher than that of men. An analysis of age groups shows that this difference appears at age thirty and increases with age.

READING DIFFICULTIES

At the national level no data are available on the nature and percentage of difficulties in reading and writing. All we have are statistics on school failure in general. Those figures that are concerned with elementary education may be useful, for they provide an indication on mother tongue difficulties. In fact, at the elementary school level, failure is due largely to difficulties in acquiring basic competencies, particularly in the domain of reading and writing.

In 1985–1986 the failure rate was 36 percent for the first phase and 25 percent for the second phase at the elementary education level. There were no failure rate differences between boys and girls.

On the level of preparatory education we have conducted a survey in a preparatory school in the region of Lisbon (Escola Preparatoria de Roque Gameiro) in an effort to understand the impact of difficulties in Portuguese. In 1987–1988, at the fifth year of schooling the failure rate was 25.5 percent and in the sixth

Table 16.1
Resident Population, Illiterate Population, and Illiteracy Rate, by Sex and Age Group, 1981

Age Group	RESIDENT POPULATION			ILLITERATE POPULATION			ILLITERACY RATE %		
	TOTAL	M	F	TOTAL	M	F	TOTAL	M	F
TOTAL	6978221	3298502	3679719	1415342	483579	931763	20.28	14.66	25.32
15-19	808,508	408,683	399,825	13,920	8,020	5,904	1.72	1.96	1.48
20-24	727,887	366,309	361,578	14,706	7,984	6,722	2.02	2.18	1.86
25-29	647,781	320,983	326,798	16,295	7,820	8,475	2.52	2.44	2.59
30-34	603,289	294,886	308,403	18,940	7,578	11,362	3.14	2.57	3.68
35-39	541,594	258,098	283,496	33,673	10,901	22,772	6.22	4.22	8.03
40-44	550,628	262,737	287,891	101,956	33,920	68,036	18.52	12.91	23.63
45-49	561,231	266,473	294,758	138,284	46,654	91,630	24.64	17.51	31.09
50-54	545,808	257,244	288,564	160,582	55,680	104,902	29.42	21.64	36.35
55-59	508,170	238,334	269,836	175,629	60,799	114,830	34.56	25.51	42.56
60-64	411,800	189,769	222,031	169,846	58,108	111,738	41.24	30.62	50.33
65-69	388,989	173,532	215,457	192,256	68,196	124,088	49.42	39.28	57.59
70 +	682,536	261,454	421,082	379,251	17,947	261,304	55.56	45.11	62.06

year it was 26.6 percent. The year before the percentages were, respectively, 31.5 and 23.5 percent.

In terms of adult education, the only available data concern elementary education in three regions of north Portugal (Braganca, Vila Real, and Viseu). In these regions in 1985–1986, a total of 277 adults registered to obtain the elementary school certificate and 257 succeeded, which corresponds to a 92.7 percent success rate.

In Portugal, difficulties in reading and writing are very large, and recently some legislative measures were taken to cope with these difficulties.

In 1987 an emergency measure (Law No. 19–A/87) was passed dealing with the teaching and learning of Portuguese. This law provides for the coordination of all subject matter in the curriculum so that they contribute to the full development of the student's capacities to learn Portuguese.

Many concrete measures have been taken for the first nine years of schooling, including the vertical and horizontal restructuring of the curricula with a clear and rigorous definition of the subject matter; the minimum objective to be achieved in the different levels of education of the Portuguese language and culture; and the promotion of action on the in-service training of teachers, taking into consideration the heterogeneity of their scientific training and the diversity of their professional training.

In 1987 a governmental resolution concerning a school success promotion program was adopted. Its objective was to improve quality education and teaching effectiveness and to promote the educational achievement of students and youngsters, in general, at the level of basic education, the priority being the first cycle of this educational level. However, there is nothing specific about reading and writing in this program. It is a program that emphasizes medico-social aspects rather than cognitive, pedagogical aspects.

Instruments Used in Diagnosing Reading Difficulties

Portugal has no formal test or instrument for diagnosing difficulties in reading. The different teams that work in this area use informal instruments that differ from team to team. The instruments used in evaluating competencies in the written language are essentially criterion-based tests that are constructed with reference to objectives defined in the school programs/curricula.

In terms of reading, the levels achieved are evaluated in diversified reading situations: texts by authors, texts by colleagues, and texts by a child. In situations of reading aloud, the type of reading realized is characterized in four ways: subsyllabic, syllabic, hesitant, and fluid and expressive. In silent reading situations, the level of comprehension of the text is analyzed, and the unities of meaning, words, syllables, and letters are pinpointed. The mistakes are analyzed: change of words but not meaning; change of words that modify the meaning; omission of words, syllables, and letters; the replacement of words, syllables, or letters.

In terms of writing, an evaluation is made of the level of writing achieved through different writing contexts: copying, dictation, essay, and free writing. Taken into account are semantic structure, logical structure, grammatical structure, orthography, and calligraphy.

Reading and writing difficulties have never been evaluated without consideration of each student's educational context. Therefore, many aspects are considered: at the family level, the type of sociocultural milieu, the social and personal adaptation of the parents, the characteristics of their personalities, and their educational attitudes; and at the school level, the teaching style and method used; the type of control and reinforcements used; class organization; and teachers expectations in terms of the students' difficulties.

No clear data are available on the effectiveness of support for children in difficulty, although there does not seem to be any difference between boys and girls at this level.

READING READINESS PROGRAMS

No official reading readiness program precedes elementary school education in Portugal.

TEACHER TRAINING AND QUALIFICATION PROCEDURE

Elementary Education

Teachers are trained in three kinds of schools: the School of Magisterio Primario (which is being phased out), the Higher School of Education (which will replace the Magisterio Primario), and the Integrated Centers for Teacher Training.

Access to these training institutions requires a certificate of complementary secondary education (completion of the twelfth year of schooling), and the training lasts six semesters. At the curriculum level there are three areas of training: expression-communication, mathematics, and physical and social milieu; education sciences; and practical pedagogical training. The final certificate, the so-called Bacharelato, is equivalent to the bachelor's degree.

Preparatory Education

Two training systems may be used as preparatory education for teachers. The first one is called the integrated system of training. The student acquires scientific and psycho-pedagogical competencies during the training session as offered by a single training institution. This training comprises specific scientific training, training in education science, and practice in pedagogy. It lasts eight semesters and the final certificate is the Bacharelato.

Different universities also offer teacher training. This training lasts five years, and the final certificate is called the Livenciatura (which is equivalent to a master's degree).

In the second system, which has existed since 1986–1987, the psycho-pedagogical training is conducted during the exercise of the profession and comes after the acquisition of an academic, scientific, and artistic certificate. It is not integrated into the academic training, and it is not offered by the initial training institute. This training lasts two years (or in rare cases one year) and includes components of the sciences of education as well as pedagogical practice.

Secondary Education

The training system for secondary school teachers is the same as that for preparatory education except for the case of the Bacharelato which is not allowed at this level of education. On the other hand, in 1987 a specific training system for secondary education was created in a few Portuguese universities, with the same teaching logic as the one described above.

Adult Education

No autonomous training system exists at the adult education level. The adult trainers consist of system-indigenous personnel and adjunct personnel. The great majority of these trainers at the elementary, preparatory, and secondary levels belong to the first group.

The adjunct trainers essentially teach at the level of basic adult education, and they are recruited locally. In general, adjuncts lasts three to nine months. They come from different professions and are selected according to the subject matter they teach. The training and social-professional area is almost exclusively their responsibility.

Thus, there are specific training systems for the different levels of education. The qualifications are the same for men and women.

At the elementary education level, the majority of trainers are women; In 1985–1986, 92 percent of the 38,817 trainers were female. In preparatory education, this percentage decreases, and yet the female percentage is always higher than the male. In 1985–1986, 69.6 percent of the 30,611 trainers were female. In terms of general secondary education, the statistics change drastically. Trainers are essentially male— 64 percent of the 30,006 trainers were men in 1985–1986. At the level of complementary secondary education, women again occupy most of the teaching positions. In 1985–1986, 61.8 percent of the 18,346 trainers were female.

If at the level of elementary education this percentage represents mother tongue teachers (at this level there is one teacher per classroom), this is not the case for the other levels of education. In the absence of available statistics on that particular question, we will say that, generally, reading education is taught by female teachers.

The statistics for adult education show that in 1986–1987 there were 364 teachers for literacy, 825 adjuncts, and 239 paraprofessionals. For preparatory education there were 443 teachers, 128 adjuncts, and 43 paraprofessionals. We have no data for distribution by sex.

MATERIALS USED IN READING EDUCATION

The reading textbooks used in formal education are produced by private publishers. Every school selects its own textbook from the choices available.

The Ministry of Education exerts control neither over the textbook publication process nor over the individual school's selection criteria. However, in a 1987 regulation, the ministry refers to "the necessity to legalize this issue not only by taking measures which safeguard the quality of textbooks but also, and this is fundamental, to allow for price control in accordance with the economic circumstances of the individual.'' According to that regulation, every textbook can be adopted for a period of only three years, and at the central level evaluation committees for textbooks exist in every subject matter and at every level of education. These committees select three textbooks by subject matter and by level of education. At this point, the pedagogical councils of every school make their final selection. This process has been adopted through the 1989–1990, 1990–1991, and 1991–1992 school years throughout the three levels of the educational system.

There are no textbooks for adult education. All teaching materials are designed and constructed by the trainers, sometimes in collaboration and cooperation with the learners.

The textbooks are always in Portuguese, and students purchase them from either the local bookstores or salespeople. This situation generates not only economic problems, but also problems of access in the isolated regions of the country.

FINANCING READING EDUCATION

Reading education is not financed as a separate subject area. The only data available pertain to the comprehensive (sum total) budget expenditures at the different levels of education: basic education, 43.4 percent; secondary education, 27.8 percent; higher education, 16.1 percent; and adult education, 0.9 percent.

RESEARCH ON READING EDUCATION

Research on reading education is almost nonexistent in Portugal. The Department of Education Psychology at the Higher Institute of Applied Psychology, which is a cooperative higher education institution, is the only institution that has a study group on the psychology of reading and writing. This group has been conducting research for some years at the preschool and elementary school level in the areas of (1) the conceptual activities and metallinguistical capacities of children before and during their entry to elementary school; (2) student knowledge of the support for written materials; (3) the student's approach to reading and writing tasks, and on his or her role as learner; and (4) the evaluation of written language comprehension during the elementary schooling process. There are additional research activities, two of which participate in illiteracy projects of the European Community.

CONCLUSIONS

For a long time the official Portuguese ministries gave priority to the essential role of reading in the struggle against school failure. However, the sociocognitive dimension of learning to read is not really taken into consideration. Rather, attention was paid to the sociomedical aspects (nutrition and health, etc.).

One can also notice the lack of congruence between official speeches and actual realization, as well as between the objectives claimed in school programs and those practiced in the teaching of reading. On the other hand, at the level of formal education, only the time spent in the formal schooling process is taken into consideration. That is, the acquisitions made during the preschool period are not considered in the process of reading education. At the level of adult education, however, these acquisitions are given serious consideration.

Educators in Portugal are showing increased concern for the training of teachers in this area. It would be interesting to coordinate some positive experiments conducted by local groups. The dissemination of results in reading education could help innovate and promote reading education in Portugal.

BIBLIOGRAPHY

Direcção Geral de Apoio e Extensão Educativa. 1987a, *Programas dos Cursos Nocturnos do 2 Ciclo do Ensino Básico*. Lisbon: Ministry of Education.

Direcçao Geral de Apoio e Extensao Educativa. 1987b. *Programas Referencias de Português, Matemática e Mundo Actual do 1 Ciclo dos Cursos de Educação de Base de Adultos*. Lisbon: Ministry of Education.

Direcção Geral do Ensino Básico. 1975. *Programas do Ensino Preparatório*. Lisbon: Ministry of Education.

Direcção Geral do Ensino Básico. 1980. *Programas do Ensino Primário*. Lisbon: Ministry of Education.

Direcção Geral do Ensino Secundário. 1979. *Programas do Ensino Secundário- Cursos Complementares*. Lisbon: Ministry of Education.

Direcção Geral do Ensino Secundário. 1980. *Programas do Ensino Secundário*. Lisbon: Ministry of Education.

Grupo de Estudos e Planeamento. 1989. *Análise Conjunctural 87*. Lisbon: Ministry of Education.

Instituto Nacional de Estatistica. 1988. *Estatistica da Educação. 1986*. Lisbon: National Institute of Statistics.

Instituto Superior de Psicologia Aplicada. 1986. *Análise Psicológica*. No. 1, Série V.

Instituto Superior de Psicologia Aplicada. 1987. *Análise Psicológica*. No. 4, Série V.

17

Republic of South Africa

Paul H. Butterfield

INTRODUCTION

Two basic problems are connected with the teaching of reading in South African schools. The first is that education is not compulsory for the largest ethnic group, the Bantu-speaking section of the population. This problem entails a concentration on studies of literacy rather than of reading readiness. A second major problem is that primary school teachers are trained in colleges of education, while secondary school teachers are trained in the universities. Thus, all secondary school teachers are graduates when they qualify, but no primary school teachers are when they complete their college courses. This difference creates a vast divide between primary and secondary school staffs. This separation is exacerbated by the fact that the university faculties of education are staffed almost exclusively by lecturers who possess secondary school teaching experience only. As a result, no South African university has organized a conference on reading in the last decade. The universities seemingly regard this aspect of education as unconnected with their activities. Adult literacy, however, has been thought worthy of considerable expenditure, research, and philanthropic endeavor. In sum, the South African universities apparently believe as a body that cure is better than prevention.

THE LANGUAGE BACKGROUND

The population of South Africa is 31,111,998, of whom the white population numbers 4,748,000; the Asian 870,000; the colored 2,765,000; and the black 22,372,850. In the early seventeenth century, when the coast of the present Republic of South Africa had become known to Europeans, the territory was inhabited by Bushmen and Hottentots. Merchant ships bound for India were utilizing the Cape as a halfway stop on their routes to India for the purpose of obtaining fresh vegetables, water, and any other supplies available. Dutch and English East India companies virtually monopolized this trade. In fact, two Englishmen actually annexed the Cape area for England in 1620, but the English king, James I, denounced this action as unauthorized. Subsequently, in 1652 the Dutch Company established the first European settlement at the Cape. Dutch farmers moved very quickly inland in their search for new acreages for ever larger farms until in the area of the present Eastern Cape they came face to face with the Xhosa group of the Bantu-speaking peoples. These confrontations occurred at the beginning of the eighteenth century and continued until the late nineteenth century. When Louis XIV revoked the Edict of Nantes in 1685, the vicious persecution of Huguenots in France resulted in these Protestants fleeing to Holland, England, and other European countries. A party of about 200 emigrated to the Cape where they introduced viticulture, but their language was slowly replaced by Dutch. Today many of the most prominent Afrikaners are the descendants of these Huguenots. These early white settlers treated both the Hottentots and Bushmen harshly and eliminated them whenever possible. The Bushmen were driven northward into the Kalahari Desert, and the Hottentots were suppressed almost to the point of extinction, so that today they do not exist as a separate group.

During the American War of Independence, the French occupied the Cape which they used as a naval base from which they interfered with the trade of the British East India Company with India. Thus, in 1792 when the Napoleonic wars erupted, the British government decided that the occupation of the Cape was vital to protecting the commercial link with India. A British expeditionary force occupied the Cape in September 1795, but under the Treaty of Amiens in 1802 the territory was returned to the Batavian Republic, the new rulers in Holland. When the hostilities were resumed in 1803, it was again deemed vital to occupy the Cape, and this was successfully achieved in January 1806. The Congress of Vienna in 1815 assigned the Cape permanently to Great Britain without ascertaining the wishes of the colonists.

While the new British administration required that a larger number of Britons be employed at the Cape, the total was negligible until Lord Somerset, the governor, decided to stabilize the turbulent eastern frontier by establishing a zone of settlers along the border. For this purpose the British government voted £50,000 to pay the passages of fifty-seven families comprising about 5,000 persons who were tempted by the offers of 100 acres of land free under certain conditions. These potential colonists were grievously misled because the land offered was not suitable for agriculture, even if the settlers had been selected for their farming skills, which was not the case. Nevertheless, these immigrants provided the first large English-speaking community in South Africa. They were a better class of people than the original Dutch settlers in that many were skilled; their contribution to the country of their adoption was invaluable.

After the British annexation of Natal in August 1845 by the governor of the Cape, Sir Peregrine Maitland, emigration from Britain was encouraged once again by the offer of the right of nomination of emigrants for free passage to all purchasers of Crown lands. Consequently, between 1847 and 1851 about 5,000 men, women, and children from Britain settled in Natal, motivated by the prospects of a new life in a country that, according to both official and unofficial (agents) sources, offered them wonderful opportunities to become wealthy farmers. At this time it was envisaged that Natal would become the source for the export of a variety of raw materials. Originally, ivory was the main product, but it was overtaken by wool. Although coffee and cotton were also exported to Britain, the sugar grown in the tropical coastal belt of Natal quickly surpassed all other exports from the colony. The planters were confronted with a major labor problem as they discovered that the black Bantu-speaking peoples were reluctant to work in the plantations and that when they were employed they were frequently unsatisfactory. Since indentured Indian laborers, called coolies, had successfully replaced slave labor in Mauritius and the Caribbean colonies, it was decided to utilize them in Natal. Originally, the Indian government refused to permit such a scheme, but eventually coolies were allowed to sail to Natal on three-year indentures, renewable for an additional two years. After this period they would be free to work and live wherever they chose, or, alternatively, they were provided with free passage back to India. In November 1860 these laborers began arriving in Natal, and within five years 6,500 of them were working on the sugar plantations. Thus, the third ethnic group was introduced into South Africa, but even today the bulk of the Asian population dwells in Natal and is largely English-speaking.

The fourth group constituting the population of South Africa is the Coloured peoples who originated from miscegenation between the original Dutch settlers and the indigenous Hottentots. The original party sent by the Dutch East India Company (V.O.C.) which landed at the Cape on April 6, 1652 consisted of 123 men and only 4 women. It is therefore certain that this miscegenation occurred fairly soon after the initial landing. As the Coloured people speak mainly Afrikaans and live in the Western Cape Province, it is not surprising that when the whole of the Republic is considered it is only the white-black relationship that extends throughout the four provinces.

When the Union of South Africa was established on May 31, 1910, it was an affair settled entirely between the British government and the white population of the four provinces. As a generalization, it can be claimed that the English-speaking white population opted for the financial rewards of industry and commerce, leaving the political aspects to the Boers. Today, as an approximation, the ratio of the Afrikaans to English-speaking sections of the white population is 3:2. This ratio is maintained among teachers, but with the exception of the old Eastern Frontier region, the English speakers are largely urban dwellers, whereas the Afrikaners (though increasing in numbers in the towns and cities) are totally dominant in the rural areas. This situation results in a series of anomalies. The first is that in schools for white pupils in rural areas English is taught by staff whose home language is Afrikaans. Second, in a large province such as the Transvaal, with its vast rural areas, an overwhelming number of the inspectors of education are Afrikaners. For example, in 1987 there was only one English home language speaker, for the teaching of English, in the whole province. Unfortunately, the English-speaking section of the white population of South Africa does not supply enough teachers to staff either its schools or its universities, but rather it depends on recruiting Afrikaners who nevertheless prefer to teach in their institutions.

The Department of Education and Training is responsible for the education of black children and students and is controlled mainly by Afrikaners. Because many black teachers are poorly qualified, white teachers are employed in secondary schools for black pupils. Most of these white teachers are Afrikaners, many of whom, being from rural areas, are able to speak one of the Bantu languages. Some black inspectors work for the Department of Education and Training, but most are Afrikaners. Since 1976 black parents have been allowed to choose the medium of tuition for the schools attended by their children as a result of the Soweto riots. The riots occurred when these Afrikaner inspectors attempted to force black teachers to instruct in Afrikaans in main subjects such as geography and history, leaving English tuition in minor subjects. Two methods, both very undesirable, supply teaching in schools for black pupils. The first, called double sessions, involves one teacher instructing two different classes in each day, one in the morning and another in the afternoon. The second makes use of platoon classes in which two teachers take two classes in the same classroom.

All but one of the universities for black students are situated in rural areas, and they are usually staffed mainly by Afrikaners who are prepared to live in these regions. Although the official medium of instruction is English, the administration is conducted in Afrikaans as are academic staff meetings. Once black students are admitted to these universities, they find themselves isolated in rural areas without access to any other university facilities. However, in January 1983 Vista University commenced operations with four decentralized campuses at Mamelodi (Pretoria), Soweto, Batho (Bloemfontein), and Zwide (Port Elizabeth), the first university for black students in or adjacent to cities in the Republic. It bears certain resemblances to the University of South Africa (UNISA), the largest university in the country and possibly the largest correspondence course university in the world. It is particularly designed for black urban students, and the sitting of the four campuses enables these students to utilize the library facilities of the cities concerned.

The official languages of the Republic of South Africa are English and Afrikaans. For all the population except the black people, these are the languages of instruction up to and including the tertiary level. There are ten different languages in the Bantu linguistic group: Zulu, Xhosa, Swazi, South Ndebele, North Ndebele, South Sotho, North Sotho, Tswana, Tsonga, and Venda. In the schools for black pupils, each tribal group uses these vernacular tongues as the media of instruction until the completion of the lower primary school course. Then from the senior primary school onward English or Afrikaans is used as the medium of instruction. Since the Soweto riots of 1976, black parents have been allowed to select the medium of tuition for their children, and the majority have opted for English.

READING INSTRUCTION POLICY

In South Africa the process of reading does not involve any overall acceptance of any special teaching method. Each of the four provinces, namely, the Transvaal, Cape, Orange Free State, and Natal, possesses for white pupils its own provincial Education Department which is authorized to prescribe its own policy for the teaching of reading. A similar situation applies to the administrative units charged with supervising the remaining three groups of the population, namely, the Department of Coloured Affairs, the Department of Indian Affairs, and the Department of Education and Training. Furthermore, there are the Homelands such as the Transkei, Siskei, Bophuthatswana, and Venda where the governments have been given control of their own schools but, as yet, have published nothing about reading policies.

In the primary schools for white pupils, reading is taught by the phonetic method but as is common in Western societies many children either enroll at school already able to read or, alternatively, supplement their reading at school by the loan of additional books from public libraries and the use of their own books at home or both. These additional sources are not generally available to the other population groups, many of whose schools do not possess electric lighting. Only within the last decade has Soweto, the huge black township on the periphery of Johannesburg, had electric lighting, installed at a cost far in excess of what it would have cost when the settlement was founded. The education of black children is not compulsory except for certain schools where the school committees have requested it. Hence, the attendance of these pupils is frequently spasmodic, and such pronouncements as "pupils who were twenty-one years of age or older and who had failed matriculation, and Junior Certificate pupils who were eighteen years of age and older, would not be allowed to repeat" are not uncommon. Obviously, blacks who attend schools for certain period of time and then leave to go to work to save the fees for another period at school do not receive a good education.

THE GOALS OF READING INSTRUCTION

No information is available on reading instruction; it must therefore be assumed that the aims of reading instruction are the same for both sexes. Unfortunately, for the black children with their irregular attendance at school, coupled with the teaching organization of double sessions and the platoon system, this means that few of them ever pass through their schools with what might be termed, in the

Western World, normal school days timetabled over a period of approximately five hours.

Asian and Coloured children have access to various types of pre-primary schools ranging from subsidized schools to creches. As in the education system for white pupils, the reading readiness programs for these pre-primary school Asian and Coloured pupils are strictly informal because no official guidelines have been published.

LITERACY AND ILLITERACY

The official calculations of illiteracy in the Republic of South Africa are based on the assumption that an individual who has completed Standard III is literate and, conversely, one who has not is illiterate. This definition has been criticized on the grounds that considerations such as the availability of textbooks; teaching standards; the number of hours spent in schools; the supply of stationery; and the physical conditions of pupils all influence the value of the time spent in schools. Nevertheless, the completion of Standard IV remains the yardstick of literacy, it being the equivalent of six years of formal education.

No statistics have been published covering the relative rates of literacy in either primary or secondary education. However, in the case of black pupils, the high dropout rates from schooling at all stages combined with the advanced ages at which many blacks enroll in the various grades ensure that it is virtually impossible to compile any valid statistics.

No specific statistics have been published for the levels of education after primary school.

Among the white adult population, literacy standards (see Table 17.1) have displayed a continued but slow improvement with the highest standards in the twenty- to twenty-four-year-old group where 98.95 percent are literate, the statistics for males being 98.90 percent and 98.99 percent for females. For the oldest age group of sixty-five or over, the overall literacy percentage was 96.07 percent with the figure for males being 96.54 percent and that for females 95.75 percent. However, for all age groups the literacy statistics were higher in urban areas than in rural districts.

For the Asian population the overall literacy figure was 84.81 percent, with the figures for males being 92.13 percent and for females 77.85 percent. There was a remarkable improvement in literacy among Asian women in the twenty to twenty-four years age group where 97.02 percent were literate compared with only 18.18 percent in the sixty-five or over age group. With males in this latter category registering only 56.26 percent literacy, however, the combined figure for this older age group was as low as 36.37 percent.

Colored adults ranked third in the percentages of literacy recorded, with the overall figure for the total population group being 73.37 percent. For the twenty to twenty-four years age group the overall figure was 83.81 percent as compared with 40.36 percent for the sixty-five and over years group. In the younger of

Table 17.1
Literate Persons (percentage)

White:		N.A.	Colored:		73.37
	Male:	N.A.		Male:	N.A.
	Female:	N.A.		Female:	N.A.
	Urban:	N.A.		Urban:	N.A.
	Rural:	N.A.		Rural:	N.A.
20-24 Year Olds:		98.95	20-24 Year Olds:		83.81
	Male:	98.90		Male:	83.24
	Female:	98.99		Female:	84.32
	Urban:	N.A.		Urban:	90.68
	Rural:	N.A.		Rural:	59.25
65+ Years:		96.07	65+ Years:		40.36
	Male:	96.54		Male:	38.32
	Female:	95.75		Female:	41.85
	Urban:	N.A.		Urban:	47.12
	Rural:	N.A.		Rural:	16.08
Asian:		84.81	Black:		53.05
	Male:	92.13		Male:	55.30
	Female:	77.85		Female:	50.83
	Urban:	N.A.		Urban:	N.A.
	Rural:	N.A.		Rural:	N.A.
20-24 Year Olds:		N.A.	20-24 Year Olds:		71.29
	Male:	N.A.		Male:	71.96
	Female:	97.02		Female:	70.65
	Urban:	N.A.		Urban:	84.14
	Rural:	N.A.		Rural:	60.49
65+ Years:		36.37	65+ Years:		16.06
	Male:	56.26		Male:	18.62
	Female:	18.18		Female:	14.17
	Urban:	N.A.		Urban:	29.89
	Rural:	N.A.		Rural:	9.27

these two groups, the figures were 83.25 percent for males and 84.32 percent for females as compared with 38.32 for males and 41.85 percent for females in the older group. There is, however, a marked discrepancy between the literacy rates recorded for the rural and urban sections of the Coloured population group. For rural areas the overall percentage for the twenty to twenty-four years age group was 59.25 percent as compared with 90.68 percent in the urban districts. Overall figures for the sixty-five or over years age group were 16.08 percent in the rural areas and 47.12 in urban districts.

All the lowest statistics for literacy were registered for black adults for whom the overall figure of all age groups was 53.05 percent, with the male figures being 55.30 percent and the female 50.83 percent. The overall figure for the twenty to twenty-four years age group was 71.29 percent, with males registering 71.96 percent and females 70.65 percent. For the sixty-five and over years age group, the overall percentage was 16.06 percent, with males recording 18.62 percent and females 14.17 percent. Once again there was an enormous discrepancy between the literacy rates registered for blacks in the rural districts compared with those in urban environments. Thus, in the youngest age group of twenty to twenty-four years, the overall figures were 84.14 percent for urban dwellers and 60.49 percent for rural inhabitants, but for the sixty-five and over age group the statistics were startling as the urban population registered 29.89 percent, whereas blacks living in rural areas registered only 9.27 percent.

READING DISABILITIES

Reading disabilities occur among 15 percent of the entire school population, but no statistics have been published for the other areas.

In 1975 the Lebowa Homeland Education Department initiated the first literacy scheme in South Africa when the Bureau of Literacy and Learning (BLL) was requested to prepare a suitable scheme for rapid implementation. The Department of Bantu Education (now renamed the Department of Education and Training), together with the Gazankulu Education Department, also sought the assistance of the BLL later in the same year. Although it had been operating in South Africa since 1946, the BLL had been registered as a not-for-profit association since 1964.

PRESCHOOL READING

For the white, Asian, and Coloured population groups several types of pre-primary schools are provided, mainly privately, although some subsidies are obtained. Only in the nursery schools are informal reading readiness programs implemented, but they depend entirely on individual initiative, and no official national or provincial policies have been adumbrated as yet.

TEACHER QUALIFICATIONS

The various academic attainments necessary to qualify as a teacher are laid down by the four administrative organizations that control the educational systems of the four racial groups, namely, the Department of National Education (whites), the Department of Indian Affairs (Asians), the Department of Coloured Affairs, and the Department of Education and Training (blacks).

For white teachers the requirements are a matriculation exemption plus a four-year diploma obtained from full-time study at a college of education for persons wishing to teach in primary schools. For those opting to teach in secondary schools, a degree followed by a one-year course under the aegis of university faculties of education is the basic requirement and entails a course of a minimum period of four years duration.

For the other three racial groups, the shortage of adequately qualified teachers is the biggest obstacle to better standards of education. This situation has been exacerbated by the drastic dropout rates of the pupils in these schools. Moreover, the shortage of suitably qualified teachers in these racial groups leads inevitably to the employment of underqualified staff, but even these individuals do not remedy the shortages. During the early 1980s the pupil–teacher ratios were 18.2 for schools for white pupils where all the teachers possessed at least the minimum qualifications; 24.3 for schools for Asian children where 17.75 percent of the teachers were underqualified; 27.3 in schools for Coloured pupils where 59 percent of the staffs were underqualified; and 39.1 for schools for black children where 77 percent of the teachers were inadequately qualified.

For black teachers in primary schools the "desirable" qualifications are the completion of a junior secondary school course of two years after the higher primary school course and then the completion of Form III, the lowest class, of the senior secondary school course. An examination is then taken, the object of which is to enable black pupils to obtain a senior certificate/matriculation qualification with or without university exemption. This certificate is the basic requirement for entry upon the training of a black primary school teacher.

Upon the completion of the full three-year senior secondary school course, black pupils sit for the same matriculation examination as white children. Success in this examination qualifies pupils for the four-year university course for secondary school teachers or, alternatively, a four-year college of education course for primary school teachers. Unfortunately, a number of intermediate steps operate adversely in all attempts to ameliorate the problems of teacher shortage. For example, a student completing the higher primary school course may be permitted to work as an unqualified teacher in lower primary schools. As a consequence, there are a multitude of different salary scales for black teachers depending on how far they have improved their educational standards by various methods such as registering for degrees at the University of South Africa (UNISA).

A comparable system exists for the supply of both Asian and Coloured teachers as for that of black teachers. Since the Soweto riots of 1976, there has been an influx of white teachers into schools for black pupils, but, in general, black people have opposed this movement. Most of these white teachers are Afrikaners whom blacks consider unsatisfactory for schools where the teaching medium is English, or, alternatively, they are believed to be attempting to control the teaching of English. In addition, some of these schools staffed with white Afrikaner and black teachers have two staff rooms, one for white staff where Afrikaans only is spoken and one, an inferior one, for black staff where the language spoken may be English or a Bantu language. Yet another cause of annoyance to the black population is that all the white inspectors of their schools are Afrikaners, although some, a minority, are black. It is extremely significant that since black parents have been permitted to select the medium of instruction in the schools their children attend, another result of the 1976 Soweto riots, the two most popular choices have been English and Zulu, with 2,824 parental groups opting for English and 2,103 choosing Zulu but only forty two of these groups selecting Afrikaans. The black parents are choosing English instruction for their youngsters in recognition of English as the major international language, and not as any indirect acknowledgment that the English-speaking section of the white population has afforded them better treatment.

Despite the blacks' resentment of the employment of Afrikaans-speaking teachers in their schools, such teachers dominate even in the school system for white pupils in the Transvaal where most blacks reside. This situation is entirely due to the fact that the English-speaking section of the white population fails lamentably to ensure that the English-medium schools of the province are staffed by teachers whose home language is English because the richer financial rewards offered by industry, commerce, and mining result in a total lack of sufficient interest in education in that community. Although the widespread criticism of the Afrikaner teacher among English speakers is not muted, the fact remains that in rural areas even the heads of the English departments of secondary schools are usually Afrikaners.

All appointments in tertiary education are the responsibility of the boards of governors and principals of these institutions. Nevertheless, the various administrative departments controlling the education of the four racial groupings retain the right to veto any appointments recommended, all of which require the confirmation of these bureaucracies. At least two notable examples of this veto have been utilized. The first occurred when Es'kia Mphahlele was appointed to a chair at the University of the North, and the second, when Andre Brink was offered a chair at the University of Stellenbosch.

Although experienced staff are preferred for appointments in adult education, some unqualified personnel are employed. In general, however, adult education is poorly organized in the Republic, and it is defective in both quality and quantity.

Literacy instructors are employed at the mines. The gold mines are particularly well staffed, but, although all the tutors have completed literacy instructors' courses, they do not usually possess any other academic qualifications. Another major obstacle faced by these literacy instructors is that many of the mine workers are contract laborers from other African countries, particularly from Mozambique, Zimbabwe, and Malawi, who speak different languages than the South African and Homelands workers.

No special qualifications are required for those who teach reading except that in primary and secondary schools teachers' certificates or diplomas are essential. Both male and female tutors need identical qualifications in this aspect of education in which the ratio of male to female instructors is approximately 6:4, with the number of female instructors increasing steadily.

READING MATERIALS

The provincial education departments order and store materials for reading instruction for white pupils. For the remaining population groups, the respective departments responsible for organizing the educational systems purchase and distribute books. Although some materials for reading education are imported, the majority are published by various South African companies.

All white primary and secondary school pupils utilize materials for reading education that are paid for out of general capitation allowances. For the other three ethnic groups, the respective administrative officials dictate what materials are available within the financial constraints imposed on them. The school inspectors of these institutions are also consulted, and, many being white Afrikaners, they frequently have disproportionate influence on the final decisions.

In 1984 the Department of Education and Training (the old Department of Bantu Education) instituted the program, Course Teaching Adults to Read and Write (CARW), which was a scheme for teaching illiterates to read. A year later seventy-four study teachers had been trained, and in just another year this number increased to 570. In 1986 the first program was completed, and all literary instructors in the field were then retrained to enable them to offer new courses. Subsequently, several posts for literary advisers were introduced in the various regions of South Africa. These advisers were given responsibility for adult literacy programs in their particular areas, the courses being available in Xhosa, Zulu, North Sotho, Tswana, South Sotho, Tsonga, Afrikaans, and English.

All educational programs for the Coloured community are administered by the Department of Coloured Affairs, with the exception of those provided by the University of the Western Cape and those of the Kromme Rhee Training Centre. Those from the Kromme Rhee Centre are administered by the Department of Coloured, Rehoboth, and Nama Relations in South-West Africa (Namibia).

For the Asian community, living mainly in Natal, the Department of Indian Affairs controls literacy programs, the reading policy, and the materials available. Although the original Asian immigrants came from the British Raj, they consisted of Hindus and Muslims, which today are the peoples of India and Pakistan. However, they are administered by the Department of Indian, not Asian, Affairs.

Reading materials at the lower primary level in the Bantu languages of Zulu, Xhosa, Swazi, South Sotho, North Sotho, South Ndebele, North Ndebele, Tswana, Tsonga, and Venda are provided, together with materials in English and Afrikaans for black children. For Coloured pupils, reading materials are available in Afrikaans and English, and for Asians in English. Financial limitations restrict the supply of such educational aids, although the most money is spent on white pupils and the least on black children.

In the Republic several groups operate independently of each other, with a variety of literacy programs financed from private sources. Among these groups the most prominent are the Laubach organization, the READ project, and the operations of Kenneth Baucom, an American. Although the black population in particular obviously benefits from the operations of these associations, they are basically concentrated on illiterate adults. In effect, the philosophy underlying the work of these groups is that the individuals are ready to begin learning to read when the tuition commences.

Once again the supply of reading materials is different for the various administrative departments controlling the education of the four ethnic groupings among the total population. For example, the Department of Education and Training controls the schools of Soweto, the vast black township near Johannesburg. It has introduced the Panel for the Investigation, Diagnosis, and Assistance program (PIDA) for students with remedial requirements. By contrast, the Transvaal Education Department possesses a central committee, whereas Natal has itinerant remedial teachers and the Cape Education Department provides remedial teachers in schools. Thus, the entire question of materials for reading education is departmentally controlled and, consequently, the actual practice differs for each administrative department.

FINANCING READING EDUCATION

Finances are allocated to schools by the various departments controlling general educational policies, but there are no specific budgets for reading education. However, since the passage of the National Policy for General Education Affairs Act (Act No. 76 of 1984), the minister has determined national policy on general educational affairs for all population groups. Thus, the present name of the department controlling the education of black children throughout South Africa is the Department of Education and Development Aid, and the earlier Department of Education and Training is under its aegis. For white children the Department of Education and Culture within the House of Assembly (Parliament) now administers education, to use official parlance, "as an own affair." Another Department of Education and Culture within the second House of Parliament, the House of Delegates, controls Asian education. Yet a third Department of Education and Culture exists within the House of Representatives (Parliament) to administer the education of the Coloured children of the Republic. Finally, on March 27, 1986, the state president promulgated an order under which the powers under the provisions of the Educational Ordinance, 1953, were transferred to the minister of education and culture (Administration) of the House of Assembly. By this legislation the education of white children, which had been under the control of the provincial educational departments within the purview of the provincial councils and administrations since 1910, was terminated and replaced by national control.

READING RESEARCH

Owing to the longstanding inadequacies of education for the black peoples of South Africa, many members of the present generation of black adults in the Republic are illiterate. Therefore, funds will likely yield a quicker economic return if they are expended on literacy training among adults over a short period of time than on school children for the minimum period of ten years. The Human

Sciences Research Council (HSRC), the official research body, has sponsored several major investigations on illiteracy but virtually nothing on reading research. Individuals have undertaken research into various aspects of reading in the field of primary education, but these studies have focused on achievement rather than on actual reading tuition. All the officially sponsored research has been in the adult education sector and has invariably related to literacy or lack of it.

One major exception to this general rule occurred in the 1970s when the HSRC sponsored a comprehensive investigation of reading instruction methods by publishing a digest of Western research on the teaching of reading. Basically, this analysis of overseas research was produced for the Afrikaans-speaking community, although an English translation was also made available. Since no empirical data were included, the report was a great disappointment, representing an opportunity missed. An attempt has been made to compare the advantages and disadvantages of electrical reading aids with traditional reading assistance methods, but the basic conclusions of the investigation may best be summarized by a quotation from the report. The report asserts that, "Of primary importance in the planning of reading assistance, is *the child* with *his* particular problem, and not a specific method or particular reading aid." It is contended that there existed a need to compile a justifiable handbook for reading assistance to be made available to all schools and that the aim of such a publication was to help teachers evaluate pupils' reading problems together with aspects important in planning a reading assistance program and methods of correcting inefficient practices by backward readers.

One obvious weakness of this investigation was that it was not basically a research project at all but merely a digest of all available educational literature concerned with the problems of retarded reading development among school pupils in Western societies where education was compulsory from early ages for all children whom the per capita expenditure per pupil was equal. As there were four distinct educational systems in the Republic, this report could, and should, have been the forerunner of a comprehensive investigation of the reading problems encountered in each of these four systems. It failed not only in this respect but also in its major aim of highlighting reading problems specific in Afrikaans teaching-medium schools for white pupils.

To summarize, the prospects for reading education will be considered unpropitious until it is officially recognized that the prevention of illiteracy is preferable to its cure, an acceptance that entails conceding that reading difficulties should be encountered and largely resolved in the primary schools of South Africa, so that the majority of children are reading competently when they enter secondary schools. At present, most of the available funds for reading education are absorbed by literacy programs. Ignored is the fact that if there were fewer illiterates additional finances could be diverted into the primary education of black pupils—provided, of course, education were made compulsory for all black children.

THE OUTLOOK FOR READING EDUCATION

As the end of the twentieth century approaches, education in South Africa is in a condition of near chaos owing to the multiplication of bureaucracies occasioned by the granting of "independence" to the Homelands. Although many other countries severely criticized the decision of the leaders of these states to accept this "independence," their basic motivation was to secure control of their schools, thus freeing them from the aegis of the old, hated Department of Bantu Education. That this independence was a sham is implied by the following official quotation: "Approximately the same amount is spent by the state on the education of Africans inside the self-governing territories as outside them." Until efficient compulsory education becomes a fact for black children, this requirement in itself entailing an adequate supply of suitably trained and qualified teachers, and not merely an announcement that such an innovation will be introduced on a certain date, the situation will remain unchanged. The dropout rates of black students in the primary schools are appalling; white children are not afflicted by this handicap. If a unified educational system were to be introduced for all four of South Africa's ethnic groups, the saving on the unwieldy, expensive bureaucracies would contribute additional financial resources for education and less rigidity in its operation.

SUMMARY

With the recent tumultuous upheavals in South Africa, it is difficult to prognosticate other than an eventual government by a black majority. When this occurs, the words of Dr. Motlana, a medical officer in Soweto and an implacable opponent of apartheid, may prove prophetic. In the *Jewish Students Journal* of the University of the Witwatersrand in 1983, Dr. Motlana maintained that when the black peoples finally obtained power there would be twenty years of chaos caused by the failure of the ruling Nationalist party to provide the majority of the population of the Republic with adequate education and administrative training to govern the country. If, however, the white population is prepared to assist the black peoples in overcoming these handicaps with greater tolerance than they have so far displayed, the collapse of the economy will be averted. However, if the assumption of power by a black government merely replaces a white authoritarian regime with its black counterpart, the obvious result will undoubtedly be the emigration of many white persons. Many possible difficulties could beset South Africa during the coming decade, the first being the declaration of a one-party state. Such an event has frequently occurred in Africa, but, in the Republic, it would lead to a mass exodus of the white population.

Education poses many such complications, although improving the qualifications of black teachers is of paramount importance but cannot be achieved quickly. As the majority of properly educated and trained teachers today is Afrikaans-speaking and is barely adequate for schools for white children, it is difficult to envisage any rapid increase in the supply of suitably qualified teachers for the compulsory primary school education for black children. Compulsory education seems inevitable but not, one hopes, creating a similar situation to that which at present exists for Coloured school children for whom education is compulsory but teachers are unavailable. The future happiness and well-being of all South African children depend on a policy of reconciliation of the four groups comprising the population without animosity and on soundly based long-term plans for sharing equally the economic benefits of a country so well endowed with natural resources.

BIBLIOGRAPHY

Arys, A., and Robertson, N. L. 1975. *Literacy and Numeracy Training in the Mining Industry—A Follow-Up Study*. Johannesburg: Human Resources Monitor. Chamber of Mines of South Africa.

Baucom, K. 1971. *An Introduction to Literacy Work*. Johannesburg: Bureau of Literacy and Literature.

Baucom, K. 1978a. *The ABCs of Literacy: Lessons from Linguistics*. Tehran: HALM/ Hulton Educational Publications.

Baucom, K. 1978b. *Report on Adult Literacy and Language Instruction in South Africa*. Johannesburg: University of the Witwatersrand.

Behr, A. L. 1982. *The Child and Educational Problems*. Johannesburg: South African Association for the Advancement of Education.

Bird, A. 1980a. "Black Adult Night School Movements on the Witwatersrand, 1920–1980." *African Perspective* 17 (Spring) 63–88.

Bird, A. 1980b. *Learn and Teach: An Evaluation*. Johannesburg: Learn and Teach.

Boshoff, H. 1984(?). *A Unified Preschool Movement in Southern Africa*. Johannesburg: Urban Foundation.

Butterfield, P. H. 1984. "Read, Educate and Develop, the 'Read' Project in South Africa." *International Review of Education*. 30 No. 4: 479–484. Hamburg: Unesco.

De Murray, H. C. 1969. *Report of the Committee of Inquiry into the Education of Children with Minimal Brain Dysfunction*. Pretoria: Human Sciences Research Council (HSRC). De Murray completed a follow up study ten years later, and this work was published under the same auspices in 1979.

De Wet, H. C. 1980. *From Illiteracy to Literacy*. Johannesburg: Informa.

D'Oliveira, C. I. 1977. "The Illiterate: An Untapped Source." *South African Journal of African Affairs*, No. 1: 59–64.

Ellis, C. S. 1982. *The Promotion of Literacy in South Africa: Numbers and Distribution of Literate Black Adults*. (Report TLK/Lit 2). Pretoria: HSRC.

Fourie, W. N. 1978. *Reading Assistance: Various Methods of Approach*. Pretoria: HSRC.

French, E. 1982. *The Promotion of Literacy in South Africa*. Pretoria: HSRC.

Frylinck, J. H. 1980. *Library Services for Africans in the RSA*. Capetown: South African Libraries.

Hauptfleisch, T. (ed.). 1978. *Literacy in South Africa*. Pretoria: HSRC.

Human Sciences Research Committee. 1981. *Report of the Main Committee of the HSRC Investigation into Education*. Pretoria: HSRC.

Kesting, J. G. 1978. "Formal education, literacy and the need for an adult library service in South Africa." *Skoolbiblioteek 10* (December).

Rodseth, J. V. 1978. *The Molteno Project: Mother-tongue Reading Instruction and English Language Teaching in African Primary Schools*. Evaluation and recommendations. Grahamstown: Institute for the Study of English in Africa.

Shillinglaw, N. 1981. "What can the public library do to increase literacy?" *S. A. Journal for Librarianship and Information Science 49*, No. 2 (October).

Verwey, C. T., et al., 1980. *Education and Manpower Production (Blacks). No. 1*. Research Unit for Education System Planning, University of the Orange Free State, Bloemfontein University Press.

Vink, C. M., and Frylinck, J. H. 1978. "Library services in the black states of the Republic of South Africa." *South African Libraries 46*, No. 2 (October).

Watkinson, J. 1981. *Pilot Survey of Adult Literacy Among Indians in the Durban Metropolitan Area*. (Occasional Paper No. 1). Durban: Institute for Social and Economic Research, University of Durban-Westville.

N.B. The best history of South African education, though heavy going, is found in the two volumes of E. G. Malherbe, *Education in South Africa*. Vol. 1. (1652–1922) (Cape Town: Jut & Co., 1925), republished 1976, and *Education in South Africa*. Vol. 2. (1923–1975) (Cape Town: Juta & Co., 1977).

18

Singapore

Vanithamani Saravanan

THE LANGUAGES OF THE COUNTRY

In Singapore, a multiracial, miltilingual country with a population of 2.5 million, 39 percent of the population is under twenty years of age. The population comprises three main ethnic groups: Chinese 76.4 percent, Malays, 14.9 percent, and Indians 6.4 percent. Other groups account for the remaining 2.3 percent.

The Chinese ethnic group is subdivided into dialect groups according to the language of both parents: Hokkien 43.1 percent, Teochew 22.1 percent, Cantonese 16.4 percent, Hainanese 7.1 percent, Hakka 7.4 percent and Foochow 1.7 percent. The Indian ethnic group is divided into several "community groups"; this division reflects the linguistic diversity of the Indian community: Tamils, 64 percent, Malayalis 8 percent, Punjabis 7.8 percent, Gujeratis 1 percent, and Others 19.2 percent. The Malay community groups are as follows: Malays 89 percent, Javanese 6 percent, Boyanese 4 percent, and Bugis 0.1 percent. Although more than twenty-five languages are spoken in the country (the Chinese dialects Hokkien, Teochew, and Cantonese are not mutually unintelligible), four languages—English, Chinese (Mandarin), Malay, and Tamil—have official status.[1] English is the main medium of education, but mother tongue competence is stressed to lay the foundations for a proper understanding and appreciation of indigenous cultural traditions.[2] The rationale for bilingual education in Singapore arises from the need to mold a unifying Singapore identity out of a multiethnic society. Bilingual education is seen as a response to the problem of linguistic pluralism[3] (Gopinathan, 1988).

Thus, English has been transformed into a "national" language and serves as a link language between the various ethnic groups. It is also the language of banking, trade, commerce, industry, and economic modernization. Therefore, a second rationale for societal bilingualism is the need to shape Singapore into a growth-oriented modern society without losing its fundamental nature as an Asian society (Gopinathan, 1988). On a more negative note, the government has expressed concern that proficiency in the English language has led to "undesirable" Western influences. Not all Western values are seen as compatible with Asian traditions and with Singapore's special needs as a developing nation, especially the Western emphasis on the individual as an independent center. A parliamentary committee was set up in December 1988 to identify the core values from the cultural heritage of the Chinese. Indians, and Malays which are to be incorporated into a national ethic (*Straits Times*, December 4, 1988).

THE GOALS OF READING

Pre-Primary and Primary Language Programs

The Institute of Education trains teachers who specialize in teaching pre-primary and lower and upper primary school children. These two-year full-time courses lead to a certificate in education in pre-primary and lower and upper primary teaching. Students are trained in a 120-hour and 150-hour language arts course in the lower and upper primary level, respectively.

Two other programs were developed to teach language and reading in the upper primary classes: the Active Communicative Teaching (ACT) and the Learning Activity Program (LEAP). These programs are being conducted with the assistance of the Curriculum Development Institute of Singapore, the British Council, and the Regional Language Center for the Ministry of Education. As of March 1987, a total of 1,248 upper primary teachers had attended the course. ACT promotes the use of communicative language teaching techniques, and LEAP prepares instructional materials for pupils who have difficulty coping with studies in the upper primary classes. Established in 1983 by the Curriculum Development Institute of the Ministry of Education, the LEAP team has developed multimedia, multilevel instructional kits for the language arts, mathematics, science, and prevocational topics. The language kits provide an integrated language arts program that highlights communicative language activities and books appropriate for learners with reading problems.

All the language teaching programs emphasize an integrated and communicative approach to language teaching. In the Shared Book Approach, children are exposed to English through enlarged print and picture story books (from New Zealand). The teacher reads the stories to and with the children in a simulated bedtime story situation. The approach is based on reading research studies that show that children who acquire the reading habit early are those who have shared stories with parents at home from an early age. As parents do not commonly read to their children in Singapore, the Shared Book Approach has been adopted in order to bridge the gap in early reading experience. The Language Experience Approach, complementary to the Shared Book Approach, integrates the four language skills of listening, speaking, reading, and writing. Children learn to use English through speaking and reading activities, which are first shared with the teacher. During conferencing these stories are then written down. This is followed up by reading and pupils' own words put into writing (Khoo, 1987).

Secondary School Language Programs

At the secondary school level, language programs are designed to increase proficiency and communicative effectiveness in school languages and to prepare students for their 0 level examinations. In order to help secondary schools whose 0 level English results are consistently below the national average and those who need specially designed reading and language programs, the Project to Assist Selected Schools in English Skills Education (PASSES) was set up in 1984. The project team together with the school staff develops and administers diagnostic measures, and conducts workshops in reading, writing, grammar teaching, and remedial programs. The PASSES team has introduced materials to teach inferential reading skills, Extensive Reading programs, and the Uninterrupted Sustained Silent Reading Program in schools. Beginning with twenty schools in 1984, PASSES has expanded to more than thirty schools.

The Curriculum Development Institute of Singapore (CDIS), established in 1980 as a branch of the Ministry of Education, has become the central agency for developing all curriculum materials for language teaching in English, Chinese, Malay, and Tamil, as well as for other subjects taught in both primary and secondary schools. The following instructional materials have been developed for language teaching in primary and secondary schools:

- PEP, NESPE, CUE, CLUE: English language materials for primary and secondary schools.
- CIPS, CLIMS: Chinese language materials for primary and secondary schools.
- TAPS, TASS: Tamil language materials for primary and secondary schools.
- MAPS, MASS: Malay language materials for primary and secondary schools.

All books for the teaching of reading, writing, tapes for listening comprehension and speaking skills, readers, workbooks, and teachers' handbooks are developed by the CDIS. The curriculum packages are multimedia and are accompanied by charts, audiotapes, slides and tapeslides, films, overhead transparencies, video cassettes, games, masks, and puppets. The Teachers' Guides give suggestions on integrating the four language skills and suggest pair and group work activities. Supplementary audiovisual materials on language kits to audio and video cassettes and films are available from the Instructional Materials Library (IML) which has a collection of over 40,000 such items, on language as well as on other curriculum areas.

Private publishing companies also produce a fairly large number of language textbooks, readers, and supplementary readers. Their quality varies, and schools are given the choice of choosing from the CDIS packages as well as materials produced by local companies and those published abroad.

ILLITERACY

The Census of 1988: Literacy and Language Use in Singapore

A large number of questions on language use was included in the census survey of 1980. The findings are summarized in Tay, 1983. Some of the findings on language use in the four official languages, English, Mandarin, Malay, and Tamil, are given in the following section.

In Singapore, the definition of literacy has been changed from "the ability to read and write a simple letter" (1957 census) to "the ability to read with understanding a newspaper in a specified language" (1970 and 1980 censuses).

The census report notes the greater use of Mandarin and English among members of the younger generation. The figures for English are 2.5 percent in speaking to grandparents, 9.3 percent in speaking to parents, and 15.4 percent in speaking to siblings, while 1.6 speak Mandarin to grandparents, 10.5 percent to parents, and 13.8 percent to siblings. These trends have been taken as indications of the success of the bilingual policy in education as the school or official languages are not home languages.

The census figures also show that English is of some significance as the principal household language for every ethnic group. For example, 7.9 percent of those with Chinese heads of households, 1.5 percent of those with Malay heads, and 21.1 percent of those with Indian heads reported using English, with the Indians using it much more than either the Malays or Chinese (Tay, 1983).

Study of literacy in the official languages for persons aged ten years and over showed the following: Chinese 58.5 percent, English 55.50 percent, Malay 16.9 percent and Tamil 3.4 percent (see Table 18.1). The changes in literacy in each of the official languages between 1970 and 1980 were as follows: Literacy in Chinese increased by 9.1 percent, in English by 8.3 percent, and in Malay by 1.1 percent; in Tamil it decreased by 0.4 percent. The increase in literacy in Chinese and English and the decrease in Tamil can be explained in terms of the bilingual policy in education. The increases in Chinese and English are the result of large numbers learning English and Chinese as either their first or second language in school. The drop in Tamil is the result of the decrease in numbers studying Tamil as a second language. Some Tamil students have opted to study Malay or Mandarin in school.

General Literacy Rates by Age Group, Ethnic Group, and Sex

Males aged fifteen to twenty-nine years showed high literacy rates. Those who were thirty years of age and over had a slightly lower literacy rate; a significant

Table 18.1
Literate Persons Aged 10 Years and Over by Official Language Literate in and Ethnic Group, 1980 and 1970 (percentage)

Official Language Literate In	Total	Chinese	Malays	Indians	Others
1980					
Malay	16.9	1.4	95.6	17.8	15.5
English	55.0	51.3	62.9	66.9	84.7
Chinese	58.5	77.2	0.3	0.4	2.4
Tamil	3.4	—	0.2	47.3	0.1
1970					
Malay	15.8	1.4	91.1	12.0	16.9
English	46.7	44.7	42.9	57.2	93.2
Chinese	49.4	66.0	0.2	0.1	1.4
Tamil	3.8	—	0.1	46.2	0.2

Source: Mary Wan Joo Tay, *Trends in Language, Literacy, and Education in Singapore* (Singapore: Department of Statistics, 1983), Table 3.8, p. 65.

drop in literacy was evident among males sixty years of age and over. (See Table 18.2 and Figure 18.1.)

In the case of females, the most significant difference in the general literacy rate was between those over forty years of age and those under forty. Thus, the difference between male and female literacy was marked in this age group. In the age groups ten to fourteen and fifteen to nineteen, females were more literate than males.

Language of Newspapers Read

The 1980 census in Singapore included questions on newspaper reading, television watching, and radio listening in the four official languages. As figures on newspaper reading reflect literacy trends in the population, they are summarized below.

A total of 78.5 percent reported reading a newspaper in one official language. Those who reported reading Chinese newspapers represented 36.9 percent, English newspapers 30.6 percent, Malay newspapers 9.5 percent, and Tamil newspapers 1.5 percent. A total of 21.3 percent reported reading newspapers in two or more official languages.

If the percentage reading newspapers in two or more official languages continues to increase, a greater proportion of the population will be exposed to the written language and in so doing will reinforce the languages learned in school.

Table 18.2
**General Literacy Rates per Thousand Population Aged 10 Years and Over by
Age Group, Ethnic Group, and Sex, 1980**

Age Group (Years)	Total	Chinese	Malays	Indians	Others
			Persons		
Total	840	826	865	898	977
10 - 14	919	912	941	934	970
15 - 19	966	966	967	964	983
20 - 24	959	959	960	965	968
25 - 29	946	944	943	957	983
30 - 39	885	879	879	919	989
40 - 49	733	717	721	843	981
50 - 59	619	580	642	799	966
60 & Over	428	400	469	676	928
			Males		
Total	915	909	932	928	985
10 - 14	912	903	941	927	969
15 - 19	964	963	967	967	985
20 - 24	964	961	970	975	970
25 - 29	965	963	970	974	985
30 - 39	951	947	954	968	991
40 - 49	894	881	927	933	992
50 - 59	837	816	868	875	991
60 & Over	695	685	679	757	975
			Females		
Total	762	744	793	857	967
10 - 14	927	922	941	940	971
15 - 19	969	970	967	961	982
20 - 24	955	956	948	953	966
25 - 29	925	924	916	938	981
30 - 39	817	808	805	862	986
40 - 49	567	551	530	716	965
50 - 59	384	363	356	584	929
60 & Over	196	177	207	431	884

Source: Tables 25, 26, 27, 28. and 29 of Census Release No. 3; Tay, *Trends in Language*, Table
    3.6, p. 61.

Language of Newspapers Read and the Student Population

The trends in the reading habits of the school-going population indicate the
need to encourage students to read from the elementary school level. Of all

Figure 18.1
General Literacy Rates per Thousand Population Aged 10 Years and Over by Age Group and Sex, 1980

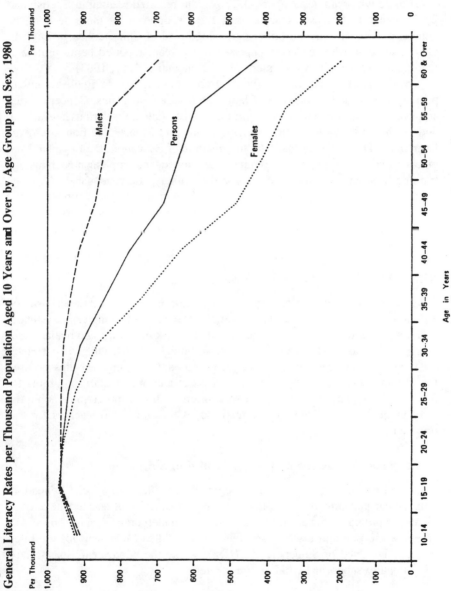

Source: Tay, Trends in Language, Chart 1, p. 62.

students aged ten years and over, 7.5 percent reported not reading any newspaper. (Eighty-five percent of these nonreaders were in primary schools and 15 percent in secondary schools.)

Of those who read newspapers, 33.7 percent reported reading in English and 25.5 percent in Chinese. These trends are the opposite of those seen in the general population where a larger percentage read in Chinese than in English. Of the students who read newspapers, 33.5 percent reported being biliterate, reading newspapers in two or more official languages (Tay, 1983).

A major shift in school enrollment from non-English- to English-medium primary schools led to a review of language teaching programs. Concerned that achievement and competency levels in English had fallen, the various educational and teacher training institutions in Singapore, the Ministry of Education, the Curriculum Development Institute, the Institute of Education, the Regional Language Center, and the British council developed and implemented language training programs to train teachers for the primary and secondary school-age population. All language training programs employ an integrated approach, that is, the teaching of listening, speaking, reading, and writing skills using a communicative approach. Special emphasis is given to the teaching of reading in all the language programs.

READING DISABILITY PROGRAMS

The Underachievers' Program funded by the Ministry of Education has started a pilot project in twenty schools to train 300 teachers in helping primary school children who are of normal intelligence but are weak in reading and mathematics in English in their first three years in school. Social and psychological correlates are used for identification and diagnostic purposes. No testing measures are used for identification. Teachers are trained to undertake remediation programs for reading and language with groups of five children, and this program is monitored throughout the year. By 1990 the team hopes to train 3,000 teachers for this program.

Movement for the Intellectually Disabled of Singapore

In 1984 the Institute of Education began the Certificate in Special Education, a three-year part-time training program. To date, thirty-four teachers have completed the program, and an additional eighty are undergoing training. Those who complete the program teach in specials schools called Movement for the Intellectually Disabled of Singapore (MINDS), where the blind, deaf, spastic, and educationally subnormal children are located.

Adult Education

The Vocational and Industrial Training Board (VITB) which was set up in 1979 provides vocational training through certification courses for adult industrial workers and early school leavers. In addition, provision is made for basic literacy courses through its language and numeracy courses and through the program Pre-Vocational Training (PVT), designed for primary school leavers from the slower than normal streams. On completion of PVT, the students enter the VITB's other vocational training program. The VITB has traditionally provided administrative backup for running part-time continuing education classes for workers and young school leavers.

In conjunction with the National Trade Union Congress, the VITB Continuing Education and Training Program is responsible for a national program for workers called Basic Education for Skills Training (BEST), to train workers in basic literacy, reading, and numeracy.

The government encourages private employers to view BEST as a long-term investment. Employers release staff for training programs and provide teaching facilities on company premises. The VITB arranges for instruction and textbooks with reading comprehension and communicative language activities, tapes, and videos produced with the help of teachers. BEST programs are funded by the government through its Skills Development Fund.

By early 1987 about 87,000 workers had participated in BEST, and more than 390 companies had organized BEST classes. Another program called Worker Improvement Through Secondary Education (WISE) began in 1987. This program aims to prepare successful students from BEST classes to sit for basic English and mathematics examinations at the national school-leaving exam level (which is taken by primary school students after six years of school) (Khoo, 1987).

The Extramural Studies Department of the National University set up twenty years ago provides continuing adult education through noncertification courses for both functional and advanced literacy, as well as various language courses ranging from basic speech skills, speed reading, reading comprehension, and language courses for Malay, Mandarin, and English. The enrollment in 1986 was about 15,000 in 824 courses.

The National Library

Other organizations in Singapore such as the National Library, the National Book Development Council, and the Society for Reading and Literacy are actively involved in promoting reading.

The National Library, established in 1958, provides loan and reference services at the Central Library and its six branches strategically located in densely populated public housing estates. The libraries provide reading materials and audio-visual materials in the four official languages in Malay, Mandarin, Tamil and English. National Library membership stands at about 840,000, and nearly 40 percent of its members are adults. Library services range from the general public to preschool children. Although adults' and teenagers' loans together amount to 54.7 percent of total loans, children's loans have reached 45.3 percent of the total. This is a result of its active campaign to provide books to match its readers. Its current initiatives include the organizing of a wide range of reading programs for children and young adults. The National Library promotes reading through story telling sessions for children, participation in national reading campaigns, and organizing book talks and films based on books for schools. Its other initiatives involve organized talks for parents and other age and interest groups. Between 1983 and 1985 the number of books on home loan increased five times.

The National Library's book collection stood at 2.7 million books for a population of 2.6 million people at the end of 1985.

School Libraries

The government provides all schools with school libraries and funds to build up their book collection. Currently, schools have a total of 4.2 million books, giving a ratio of ten books for each child. In the past four years alone, schools spent $17.5 million to stock up their libraries. In primary schools, the average number of books borrowed by each pupil in one year is 22, although the range for individuals varies from four to ninety books a year. The book collections in the four official languages largely consist of imported books from abroad. Some limited attempts have been made to introduce children's literature from Asia.

National Book Development Council

The National Book Development Council (NBDC) of Singapore was established at a 1966 Unesco meeting in Tokyo on book production and distribution in Asia; though not a government agency, it acts as a national agency. It represents all sectors of the book industry: authors, book designers, illustrators, translators, publishers, book sellers, librarians, and teachers. The NBDC's main roles are to promote reading as well as to coordinate all activities related to the book industry to conduct training courses on book production, publishing, and book distribution, and to conduct national readership surveys.

The Council has inaugurated book awards for books published in Singapore, publishes a Books in Print in Singapore and the Singapore Book World annually, and has started a translation and publication scheme for Singapore works that were originally available in one language only.

The ralson d'etre for a sustained promotion of the reading campaign goes back to 1980 when the first national reading survey commissioned by the NBDC revealed that the reading habit was poorly developed among Singaporeans. As a followup, the Council initiated the two-month-long National Reading Months (NRM) in 1982 and 1984. In 1986 the NRM was reorganized as the National Reading Fortnight, to be held every year. in 1988 the program became a government campaign, and major sponsorship came from Singapore Press Holdings and the Ministry of Community Development. Reading and book-related activities are organized for the public, which includes preschool children, students, adults, senior citizens, and parents.

The major event of the NBDC is the organization of the annual Singapore Book Fair. One of the main activities it initiated to promote reading and the book-buying habit is the Festival of Books and Book Fair. The Fair has a concurrent "Festival" of programs ranging from book talks, quizzes, meet-the-authors' session, to children's story telling. Some of its themes reflect the focus on reading through the slogans "Grow with Books," "Good Reading," "Give a Book a Child," "Towards a Reading Society," and "Reading for Excellence."

READING READINESS PROGRAMS

Preschool Programs

The increase in the number of working mothers in recent years has led to the establishment of training programs to train teachers for child care centers and kindergartens. In 1985 the Institute of Education started a 150-hour course for Child Care Center trainers and a 60-hour course for kindergarten teachers. Upon completion, the qualified trainers assist in the training of more Child Care Center personnel. To date, twenty such trainers are assisting in the training of other personnel. About one hundred additional kindergarten teachers are trained yearly. The training programs emphasize language learning through an integrated language arts approach. This approach features story telling, the Shared Book Approach, and the utilization of the children's own language to produce texts for reading (Khoo, 1987).

TEACHER-TRAINING PROGRAMS IN
READING EDUCATION

The Institute of Education, Singapore's main teacher training institution, is responsible for training teachers for preschool centers, as well as primary, secondary, and junior colleges. Its current programs are summarized below. The sixty-hour Diploma-in-Education English language methodology course for graduate teachers in secondary schools emphasizes the teaching of inferential and higher cognitive skills in reading comprehension, vocabulary development, text structure analysis, reading across the curriculum, and extensive adolescent reading programs related to reading interests and library-related activities.

The 150-hour primary methods course on integrated language skills emphasizes the teaching of inferential reading comprehension skills and vocabulary development, and recommends teacher-made materials such as big books and word games. Training is offered in dramatization for communicative language teaching and children's literature to introduce books to children.

Similarly, training for Chinese, Malay, and Tamil language teachers emphasizes the teaching of inferential reading comprehension skills, vocabulary development, and reading activities.

MATERIALS AND PUBLISHING IN SINGAPORE

The present situation of publishing shows an increase in the output of new Singapore titles, with 2,789 for 1987. This includes books published in the four official languages and ranges from children's books to textbooks and general books. About 70 percent of the printing and publishing industry's exports comprise printed books, 10 percent children's picture books, and 4 percent newspapers, journals, and periodicals. There are approximately 100 publishing houses and 200 printing firms.

Society for Reading and Literacy

Inaugurated in July 1985, the Society for Reading and Literacy (SRL) has established a role in Singapore as the Reading Association. The SRL promotes an understanding of reading processes and approaches to reading instruction. Workshops for parents and teachers such as "How to Put the Fun Back into Reading," "Understanding the Reading Process," and "Helping Children with Reading Difficulties" are popular with members and nonteachers. Its present membership is 200. In addition to its workshop series, resource persons give talks to child care centers, volunteer helpers, schools, and private companies. As a national affiliate of the International Reading Association and an affiliate of the NBDC, SRL is able to tap the resources of these other organizations.

RESEARCH THRUSTS IN LANGUAGE AND READING

The Institute of Education (IE) has undertaken a longitudinal study of kindergarten children. Begun in 1983, this study, the Project on the Cognitive and Social Development of Preschool Children in Singapore is funded by the Bernard Van Leer (BVL) Foundation of the Netherlands. The IE-BVL project completed its first three-year phase with data collection on aspects of the cognitive and social development of 2,000 children between three and six years of age. The study shows a need for improved English teaching techniques in the preschools. In 1986 it was decided to extend several integrated language teaching approaches, the Shared Book and the Language Experience Approaches, to more primary schools because more children in the lower primary classes showed that they had problems with reading and communicating in English.

The Reading Skills Project team at the Institute of Education undertook a three-year longitudinal-cum-cross-sectional study of Grade 1 to Grade 3 children ($N = 3,765$) to determine the progress patterns and skills which Singaporean children acquired in reading English in their first three years at school.

Testing began in March 1983 in twenty-four randomly selected Singapore schools. The instruments used for evaluation were the Neale Analysis of Reading Ability, the Burt Word Reading Test, Clay's Miscue Analysis, the Diagnostic Decoding Inventory (DDI), the Record of Oral Language (ROL), and Writing Vocabulary (WVOC). The results showed (1) that Grade 1 children lacked word-attack skills (including grammatical structure or syntax and contextual meaning); and (2) that one-quarter of the entire cohort were reading at the frustration level (less than 90 percent accuracy) (Ng, 1984).

A correlation matrix was marked out from the different variables, the Neale tests, the DDI, ROL, and WVOC; the Miscue Analysis indicated that the last three tests, the reading-related tests, were significantly intercorrelated. The study reported that if reading accuracy is correlated with the three other variables, DDI appears to have a higher correlation than ROL, an indication that oral language development is central to reading. On the other hand, if reading comprehension is correlated with these three variables, then ROL has the higher correlation, indicating the importance of decoding for reading accuracy. It also indicates that a command of syntax is just as important for comprehension of what is read. Thus, the study showed that all the skills of decoding, oral language, and writing are interdependent.

The work of this team led to the setting up of the Reading Skills Project. The Reading Skills Project team at the Institute of Education in 1983 and 1984 recommended the use of the Shared Book and Language Experience Approaches to improve pupils' language skills at the preschool and lower primary levels. In 1985 the Reading and English Acquisition Program (REAP) was jointly launched by the Institute of Education, the Ministry of Education, and the Curriculum Development Institute. All elementary Grade 1 teachers in thirty primary schools were trained to use this program. To date, 962 lower primary classes in 132 (out of about 200) primary schools are in REAP. Continued monitoring of the program indicates statistically significant differences between REAP and non-REAP children, with REAP pupils performing slightly better in all the listening, speaking, reading, and writing tasks tested (Ng, 1984).

Reading Habits Surveys

Several surveys on reading interests and habits have been conducted in Singapore. A questionnaire survey called A Measure of Reading (1978) surveyed 1,157 students (440 students were from non-English streams) in eighteen schools.[4] The amount of reading done by this sample of students was reported as follows: 33 percent read no story books, 41 percent read between one and two story books in the month previous to the survey, 43 percent read no magazines, 58 percent read no comics, and 24 percent read one to two comics.

The conclusion drawn was that the quantity of reading by students in English was small. The report noted that, if magazines and comics make less demands linguistically on the child, the low level of reading of these types of materials is significant. In comparison to books and magazines and comics, newspaper reading was high (95 percent), and this could be because they are readily available.

The National Reading Habits Survey (1988) had a random sample of 1,000 respondents aged twelve years and above and used face-to-face interviews. The survey examined the amount of time Singaporeans had for leisure and how they used the leisure time.

Reading ranked a close second to watching television as a leisure activity. The poll showed the following: 80 percent of the people read newspapers daily compared with 87 percent who watched television regularly; 80 percent of the literate population read magazines and 67 percent read books; and 94 percent of those surveyed could read and understand newspapers.

CONCLUSION

There is now greater awareness of the need to make Singapore a nation of readers. The government and the educational and teacher training institutions, the National Library, the National Book Development Council and the Society for Reading and Literacy emphasize reading education in their programs. Schools are given professional help to build school libraries, to implement a school library syllabus, to hold book talks and book-related activities, and to build up their book collections in relation to reading interests and various reading ability levels. Although there are no reading specialist teachers as such, all language teachers are trained to teach reading within the various language curricula, that is, in the teaching of Malay, Mandarin, and Tamil. The government recognizes the need for various literacy programs for adults and early school leavers, and basic literacy and numeracy programs have been mounted.

Although a great deal has been accomplished, much remains to be done to transform the children and adults into a nation of readers. The reading habits surveys conducted in schools show that students read in order to improve their grades or to help them with their school work. This attitude is prevalent right up to the tertiary level. Few students and adult readers read for pleasure and as a recreational activity. The crowded curriculum, and the pressures of learning two languages make demands on the students' time and leave little time for students to read for pleasure.

Yet other concerns relate to the availability of reading materials. Although a large amount of imported reading materials are available in English, few reading materials can be found in other languages. It has been noted that books that appeal to children in the Mandarin, Malay, and Tamil languages are inadequate. Few publishers and translators produce books for children and young adults.

NOTES

I wish to acknowledge two reports, Tay (1983) and Khoo (1987), which provided valuable information on literacy and reading education.

1. The status of Mandarin is given more prominence than any of the other Chinese dialects because of its greater prestige as a codified language and because the written script comes from Mandarin rather than the Chinese dialects.

2. A person's mother tongue was defined in the 1957 census as the principal language or dialect spoken in the person's home during the person's early childhood.

3. In line with the official language policy of Singapore, bilingualism is defined as proficiency in any two languages but in English and one other official language, that is, Mandarin, Malay, or Tamil.

4. This cohort of students had been exposed to six years of primary education in which English had been taught as a subject and as a medium of instruction for 35 percent of the curriculum time a week.

REFERENCES

Anuar, Hedwig, 1983. The Role of the National Book Development Council in the Promotion of the Reading Habit. In *The Reading Habit: Reading Seminar on the Promotion of the Reading Habit*. Singapore: National Book Development Council.

British Council. 1987. *Active Communicative Teaching (ACT)–Project Report*. Singapore. (Unpublished.)

Clay, Marie M. 1979. *Reading: The Patterning of Complex Behaviour*. Auckland, N.Z.: Heinemann Educational Books.

First National Readership Survey. 1981. Singapore: National Book Development Council of Singapore.

Gilmore, Alison, Croft, C., and Reid, N. 1981. *Burt Word Reading Test*. Wellington, N.Z.: New Zealand Council for Educational Research.

Gopinathan, S. 1988. Bilingualism and Bilingual Education in Singapore. In *International Handbook of Bilingualism and Bilingual Education*, ed. Christina Bratt Paulson. Westport, Conn.: Greenwood Press.

Gopinathan, S. 1979. Singapore's Language Policies Strategies for a Plural Society, In *Southeast Asian Affairs*. Singapore: Institute of South East Asian.

Hadijah, Bte Rahmat. 1984. *Children's Literature in Malay—An Inquiry into and an Analysis of Its Development and Functions as a Stimulus Towards Achievement*. Unpublished M.A. thesis.

Heaton, J. B. 1979. *Report on Reading Habits and Difficulties of Primary IV Pupils Singapore*. Institute of Education for the Associated Schools.

Khoo, Maureen. 1987. Country Report on Singapore. In *Proceedings of the Second International Conference on Literacy and Languages*. August 20–24, Thailand, pp. 317–328.

Kuo, C. Y. 1976. A Sociolinguistic Profile. In *Society in Transition*. Ed. Rias Hassan. Kuala Lumpur: Oxford University Press.

Lim, Pauline Keng. 1988. Publishing in Asia Pacific Today. In *Report of the Meeting of Experts for Planning Book Development*. Tokyo, ACCU, July 21–25, 1987.

A Measure of Reading. 1978. IE Survey of reading interests and habits. Singapore: Institute of Education.

Ministry of Education. 1980. *Education in Singapore*. Singapore Government Printer.

Neale, Marie D. 1969. *Neale Analysis of Reading Ability*. 2nd ed. New York: St. Martin's Press.

Ng, Seok Moi. 1980a. *Implementation of an English Language Programme. An Informal Method of Reading Assessment* Singapore: Institute of Education.

Ng, Seok Moi. 1980b. *The Status of Reading in Primary 1, 2 and 3 in Singapore.* Singapore: Institute of Education.

Ng, Seok Moi. 1984a. *Reading Acquisition in the Context of Communicative Approaches to Language Teaching.* Singapore: Institute of Education.

Ng, Seok Moi. 1984b. *Reading Acquisition in Singapore.* Paper presented at 10th World Congress on Reading. (Unpublished.)

Ng, Seok Moi. 1985. *Implementation Strategies for an Integrative Approach to Teaching Reading and Language.* Singapore: RELC Regional Seminar on Language Across the Curriculum, Singapore.

Ng, Seok Moi. 1987a. *Implementation of an English Language Programme for Young Singapore Children.* Singapore: Institute of Education.

Ng, Seok Moi. 1987b. *Research into Children's Language and Reading Development.* Singapore: Institute of Education.

Ng, Seok Moi, and Maureen Khoo. 1984. *Researching Early Reading Progress in Singapore.* Singapore: Institute of Education.

Papers of the Regional Seminar on the Promotion of the Reading Habit, September 7–10, 1981. 1983. Singapore: National Book Development Council of Singapore.

Parker, Richard L. 1987. The Functions of Reading: Singapore in an International Perspective. In *Proceedings of the Second International Conference on Literacy and Languages.* August 20–24, Thailand, pp. 317–328.

Pendley, C. 1983. Language Policy and Social Transformation in Singapore. *Southeast Asian Journal of Social Science* 2, No. 2: 46–58.

Rahman, Gail, Ng Seok Moi, and Diana Lew. 1985. *Use of the Burt Word Reading Test in Singapore Primary Schools.* Singapore: Institute of Education.

Report for the Society for Reading and Literacy. 1985. Singapore: Society for Reading and Literacy.

Report of the Committee on Literary Arts Advisory Council for Culture and the Arts, December 1988, 83 p.

Report of the Sub-committee on the Promotion of Reading. In *Report of the Committee on Literacy and Arts Advisory Council for Culture and the Arts.* December 1988, pp. 25–50.

Straits Times Survey of Reading Habits. Survey in conjunction with the National Reading Month 1988. Straits Times Research Department.

Tay, Mary Wan Joo. 1983. *Trends in Language, Literacy and Education in Singapore.* Singapore: Department of Statistics.

Wilson, W. E. 1978. *Social Engineering in Singapore: Educational Policies and Social Change.* Singapore: Singapore University Press.

Young, K. 1979. The Diagnostic Decoding Inventory. Unpublished manual. University of Hawaii.

19

South Korea

Byong Won Kim

INTRODUCTION

Korea is a peninsula of about 220,000 square kilometers protruding like a thumb from the land mass of Asia. The northern border is shared by China and Russia, and in the south lies Japan across the narrow strait. Korea was divided into south and north in 1945, when it was liberated from thirty-six years of Japanese control. South Korea occupies 45 percent of the peninsula with an estimated total population of 41 million.

According to *Education in Korea, 1987–1988* published by the Ministry of Education, South Korea, the enrollment rate of kindergarten-aged children is 60.6 percent and that of elementary school-aged children is 98.9 percent. In the elementary school, children learn how to read and write the Korean script, *Hangul*, in the Korean language course. Reading is not taught as an independent subject by reading teachers; it is taught by language teachers in the Korean course. Approximately 98.7 percent of the six-year elementary school graduates go to the three-year middle school, and 91.9 percent go to the three-year high school. Middle high school students learn 1,800 *Hanmun*, Koreanized Chinese characters and English as a foreign language.

According to the same report (Ministry of Education, 1988), there are 7,653 departments in 468 institutes of higher education 9 of which are for males only, 51 for females only, and 408 for both sexes. The institutes include 119 two-year junior colleges, 11 four-year teachers' colleges, 103 four-year colleges and universities, 209 graduate schools, and 26 others.

THE KOREAN LANGUAGE

The Korean language was uniquely developed by Koreans with no documented origin (C. W. Kim, 1983). The uniqueness, especially in contrast with Chinese and English, is characterized by four points. First, content words are combined into larger units like the sentence chiefly by means of agglutination of suffixes. For example, the Korean words *na*, *chag*, and *ig* (*da*) of three concepts, I, BOOK, and READ will be combined into a sentence with the help of three suffixes, *-nun* for the indication of topic/subject, *-ul* for object indication, and *nunda* for written sentence ending, as we can see below. The Korean sentence does not begin with a capital letter; in fact, there is no distinction of small versus capital letters in the Korean written language.

BOOK   I   READ
chag-ul   *na-nun*   *ig-nunda.*

Note: The three words, *na* (I), *chag* (BOOK), and *ig*(*da*) (READ) are agglutinated into a sentence by means of the particles *-nun* in *na-nun*, *-ul* in *chag-ul*, and *-nunda* in *ig-nunda*.

Second, the typical word order of the sentence is Subject (S) + Object (O) + Verb (V). Korean is a so-called S + O + V language. The verb always comes at the end of the sentence with one of several particles that function as indicators of sentence ending, like *-da* in the example, "*na-nun chang-ul ig-nunda.*"

Third, Korean is a context-oriented language (B. W. Kim, 1983, 1988). For example, the order of S + O, in the sentence S + O + V, can be reversed and either or both of them can be deleted according to the given situational or textual context. Thus, either *O* + *S* + V (*chag-ul na-nun ig-nunda*), or *S* + V (*na-nun ig-nunda*), or *O* + V (*chag-ul ig*-nunda) is by definition grammatically appropriate. The shifting of word order and the deletion of certain words (and particles) are usually determined within the situational or textual context. In the last case, for example, let's suppose someone asks you what you do, and you are going to say that you read books. In this context, the topic "I" in your answer is known to each other; so, it is not necessary to linguistically mark the topic for communicative purpose. You simply say: "*chag-ul ig-nunda*," meaning "read books." Koreans will not say "*na-nun chag-ul ig-nunda*" in that context. Use of Subject "I" (*na-nun*) in the sentence is not appropriate in Korean.

Finally, one expresses the interpersonal social position in the language by using a variety of sentence endings and relevant selection of certain categories of words (Dredge, 1983; Lukoff, 1978). Korean has honorific levels in the spoken language. Written Korean has an impersonal style (B. W. Kim, 1987; Nam and Ko, 1985). Newspapers, journals, novels, and books for education, including school textbooks, adopt the impersonal written form. If one employs a certain honorific level in the written language other than the impersonal written form, then the writing will appear to be a written record of personal speech delivered to the reader.

HANMUN CHARACTERS IN KOREAN

Old Koreans used spoken Korean that may be rather safely characterized by the above-mentioned four points: agglutination, word order of S + O + V, context-orientedness, and honorific levels. They do not seem to have had their own way of writing before they had access to the Chinese ideographic script, which is generally called Hanmun and learned how to pronounce the Hanmun characters and the fixed meanings of the characters. It is generally assumed that the earliest introduction of Hanmun to Korea was about 108 B.C., and some evidence shows that scholarly people began to use Hanmun characters proficiently by the fourth or fifth century (C. W. Kim, 1983; P. H. Nam, 1982; Pihl, 1983).

Hanmun cannot be a natural way of visualizing the Korean language because Hanmun characters have their own fixed meanings and pronunciations that have nothing to do with their Korean counterparts. The Chinese language is essentially different from Korean. Nevertheless, Koreans tried to use Hanmun characters with their original meanings and pronunciations to represent their thoughts and feelings, partly because they did not have their own way of visualizing spoken Korean and partly because they wanted to learn Chinese culture and thoughts, specifically, the Confucian philosophy (P. H. Nam, 1982).

We will see what happened to the Korean language when old Koreans tried to employ Hanmun characters to visualize their thoughts and feelings. The following explanations are unavoidably oversimplified, considering the scope and various sequences of what really happened to the Korean language when it came into contact with the Hanmun characters in 108 B.C., when we assume that Hanmun was first introduced to Korea. Nevertheless, the explanations will provide some background knowledge of the present Korean language and the traditional concept of reading in Korea. That knowledge may subsequently help elucidate the sequence of events in the field of reading education in Korea.

Let us suppose that one had a piece of thought that was represented by the spoken Korean: "*na-nun chag-ul ig-nunda*," meaning "I BOOK READ", or "I read books" in English. In Chinese, the meaning is expressed in the order of *ah* (S) + *dog* (V) + *So* (O). From these Hanmun characters Koreans borrowed *ah* for *na-nun* (or I in English), *so* for *chag-ul* (or BOOK), and *dog* for *ig-nunda* (or READ).

Korean sentence:	*na-nun*	*chag-ul*	*ig-nunda.*
Korean (content) words	*na*	*chag*	*ig*
Hanmun words	*ah*	*so*	*dog*
English words	I	BOOK	READ

Note: cf. Particles: *nun, ul, nunda.*

As noted above the Hanmun characters represent only the content words in Korean; they cannot represent the particles -*nun*, -*ul*, and -*nunda*. In Korean the particles agglutinate the content words into a larger unit like a sentence. The

Hanmun words *ah*, *so*, and *dog* have nothing to do with the Korean spoken words, *na*, *chag*, and *ig*, in the sentence, *"na-nun chag-ul ig-nunda."*

Together with the borrowing of each Hanmun character, the whole expression was also learned as it was: *ah dog so*, that is, S + V + O. The order of S + V + O is totally foreign to Korean whose basic word order is S + O + V. Still, the whole Chinese sentence, or part of it, was learned and used in Korea.

In spite of the unnaturalness caused by these and other points of inconsistency between Hanmun and Korean, the Hanmun characters were continuously used by rulers, and studied and taught by scholars at home or at school. Some Hanmun words were so widely learned and frequently used that they eventually became part of the Korean vocabulary. For example, the two Hanmun characters *dog*, meaning READ, and *so*, meaning BOOK, in the Chinese sentence *ah dog so*, formed a new word *dogso*, meaning BOOK READING or simply READING. Probably that is why Koreans now use two words for one meaning of "reading" in Korean: the pure Korean, *ig-nunda*, and the new word adopted from Hanmun, *dogso*. The new Hanmun word *dogso* is used as a noun in *"dogso-rul handa"* where the *-rul* is a particle. (The *-rul* is another object indicator like *-ul*.) The *handa* is a verb (meaning DO in English). The sentence *dogso-rul handa*, meaning DO READING, is an equivalent of the pure Korean *ig-nunda* which means READ, too. *Dogso* is also used as an independent verb when a verb suffix *-handa* is attached to it like *dogso-handa*, meaning READ, which is another equivalent of the pure Korean word *ig-nunda*. The Hanmun word *ah*, meaning "I" in English in the sentence, *ah dog so*, failed to survive within the Korean vocabulary.

The current total entry in Korean dictionaries is estimated at 140,000 or 165,000 words. More than half of them are the Hanmun words, like *dogso* and other types, and 40 or 45 percent are pure Korean (Huh, 1983; C. W. Kim, 1978; H. G. Kim, 1983). The remaining are the adopted words from languages other than Hanmun.

Thanks to Hanmun characters, leaders and scholars in the old days were able to enjoy life through written language. Their learning-teaching and use of Hanmun characters eventually enriched their knowledge of prescriptive philosophies of Confucian culture. New Hanmun words grew out of these and others, eventually being adopted as new Korean words.

In contrast to this bright side of the effects of Hanmun in Korean, two negative effects can be traced back to the days when Koreans had only Hanmun characters as their written media. These effects seem to form a major part of Korean reading culture today.

First, reading comprehension of Hanmun characters means to 'collect" the fixed meanings of the characters. This seems to lead people to believe that the individual character, or word, is the unit of meaning in the reading process and that meaning "resides" in the script. Some believe that the process of attaining meaning is direct and fast in reading Hanmun because the reader "immediately perceives the meaning of things at a glance of the Hanmun character" (C. H.

Oh, 1971, p. 33). These incorrect concepts of the unit of language and the locus of meaning appear to be prevalent as common sense among ordinary Koreans who strongly recommend that Hanmun characters should be used at school and in the society and that Hangul, the Korean phonetic script, should not replace the Hanmun counterparts.

Second, Korean leaders and scholars originally read books, especially Confucian classics, in order to learn the Confucian fundamentals of politics, morality, and gentlemanship (C. H. Choe, 1980; P. H. Nam, 1982). To Koreans, "reading" meant reading good books for such goals. This seemed to lead people to think of reading as prestigious and respectable. The greatest concern appeared to be a proper respect for *dog so* (meaning "book reading") that would lead people to read. The processes of reading comprehension did not seem to be as important as reading motivation; reading itself appeared to be a comprehension process because Hanmun characters themselves were thought to "possess' their meanings. The traditional concepts of reading as reading good books and as respectable activity appear to form part of the background of reading and reading education in Korea.

HANGUL, THE KOREAN ALPHABETS

Hanmun characters have brought about some formidable problems in language life in Korea. There are too many characters to learn in Hanmun. The total number of Chinese characters may be estimated at 80,000. Moreover, the characters have their own forms that uniquely symbolize their meanings. In addition to the forms and meanings, the characters have their own pronunciations which are totally different from the Korean spoken language. A Korean should also learn the forms, meanings, and their pronunciations in order to use Hanmun characters for communication. However, Koreans can hardly use Hanmun characters in place of their own language because the Korean language has its own unique characteristics, as discussed earlier. In the old days, Koreans must have faced these and other problems.

It became imperative that changes be made with respect to Hanmun characters to improve communication between people through written script. Thus, in 1443, King Sejong and his scholars organized Hangul alphabets, which represented a simple effective system of phonetic signs so that it would be possible to visualize the spoken Korean and record the pronunciations of Hanmun characters accurately. Ordinary people learned Hangul easily for their communication purposes. Hangul led people to the new world of literacy.

Scholars both at home and abroad seem to agree that Hangul is perhaps the most efficient alphabet in the world (Martin, 1972; Ong, 1982). Pihl (1983) names Hangul "The Alphabet of East Asia," reasoning that it was purposefully devised on the basis of sound phonological principles to serve the particular needs of a language and that it was the only successful attempt to invent a script for the practical use of the common people in a country where Chinese characters had to be adopted as their inconvenient writing system.

Hangul is characterized by three major strengths. First, a small number of basic consonants and vowels are systematically used to represent sounds and syllables. Second, consonant letters (C) and vowel letters (V) are combined into a limited number of equidimensional block patterns like OV, OVC, OVCC, CV, CVC, or CVCC, where the "O" stands for a circle-like zero that indicates there is no consonant in that position. For example, the OV pattern is used when there is only one vowel sound letter in the syllable. Each syllable block represents either one syllable in a word or a single-syllable word. Third, the sound and symbol relations show nearly perfect one-to-one correspondence. The basic Hangul symbols depict actual pronunciations of fourteen Korean consonants and ten vowels. From the basic symbols are derived some combinations that also depict their actual pronunciations. In contrast to Hanmun characters, each of the Hangul alphabets is a visual representation of each sound of the Korean language as it is naturally spoken right out of the Korean's mouth. Earlier we observed four characteristics of Korean—agglutination, word order of S + O + V, context-orientedness, and representation of honorific levels. These and other characteristics of Korean survived when the sounds were visualized in Hangul alphabets.

King Sejong with his scholars organized Hangul for two specified goals. First, he wanted to use the phonetic symbols for the appropriate description of the pronunciation of Hanmun characters. At that time, scholars wanted to learn the pronunciations of Hanmun characters as closely to their original pronunciations as possible. By means of Hangul alphabets, scholars could learn the one and same pronunciation of each Hanmun character that appeared the closest to the original pronunciation. Second, King Sejong wanted to teach Hangul to all of his people so that he could communicate with them by means of the Hangul alphabets that were easy to learn and convenient for the common people to use.

National acceptance of Hangul was very slow because the upper class continued to patronize Hanmun characters, the Chinese script, and ridiculed Hangul as "vulgar" or the "women's script," fit only for persons of little education, the common class, and women.

In 1894 a compromise between Hangul and Hanmun scripts began to be officially accepted when a code of official conduct in government was written in Hangul, too. It was known as the first Korean constitution, embodying the spirit of the Reform of July 1894, and it was the most significant event in the modernizing of Korea, promulgated by King Kojong. The code was written in three ways: in Hangul, in Hanmun characters, and then in the mixture of the two. It was the first official document written exclusively in Hangul in the history of Korea. At the same time, the government opened some modern educational institutes. Furthermore, the use and teaching of Hangul was legalized, not as a "women's script," but as the national script.

The official use of Hangul was supported by a new educational policy announced in 1895 in which the following statement was included.

Education has its own legitimate way; so, it is important to distinguish the vain knowledge and the practical knowledge we need. Those who are blind to the new world because they are fully engaged in reading and calligraphy to collect the remains of what ancient people wrote will remain nothing but simple minded student Confucianists even though their knowledge of Chinese classics appears superior to other scholars. (C S. Oh, 1964)

In the quotation, "reading" indicates the reading of Chinese classics written in Hanmun characters. This policy brought about a new world of the national language and Hangul in Korea.

The Christian missionaries played an active role in popularizing Hangul and in eradicating illiteracy. They translated the Bible into Hangul and succeeded in attaching some value to public literacy in order to make reading of the Bible possible.

In 1895 Yu Kil-Jun (Yu is his family name) published a book about his trips in the West. In it he used Hangul and Hanmun characters. Yu's book was the first in which Hangul was used. In 1896 Seo Chae-Pil began to publish a Hangul newspaper, *The Independence*; it was printed only in Hangul.

New schools for systematic education were established in 1895 for the first time in Korea. In 1906 the language course became an independent subject, and reading was one of three areas included in the subject. The other two were composition and calligraphy. Later, grammar was included in the language course. Hanmun was taught as an independent subject at school. Still, Hanmun was important and students had to spend more time learning Hanmun characters than studying Korean and Hangul. Generally, Hanmun occupied a more important position in the society than Hangul. Nevertheless, Hangul was now officially and educationally accepted as the Korean script. The two scripts, Hangul and Hanmun characters, were most frequently used in a mixed form.

In the same year, 1895, when Hangul became an official script by law, it was legally determined that school textbooks were to be organized either by the government or by nongovernmental agents who had to obtain the government's approval for publishing their textbooks.

In 1910 Korea came under the Japanese colonial administration, and the Japanese government began to oppress Koreans both politically and culturally. With colonialization, use of Korean and Hangul was prohibited. The Japanese language became the official language, and the Koreans were forced to accept Japanese as their national language. The teaching of Korean and its use at school was eventually prohibited by law in 1938. Nonetheless, the Korean language was spoken among the people, and the Hangul script, together with the language, was secretly taught and studied by some patriotic leaders and scholars.

USE OF HANGUL

In 1945 Korea was liberated from Japanese control, and north and south were separated. Events that took place in North Korea were not made known to South

Korea and the rest of the world. According to C. W. Kim (1978), in North Korea the use of Hanmun characters was abolished in 1946, and Koreanized Hanmun words were either discarded or replaced by newly coined pure Korean words in North Korea. By contrast, its language was not as simple as that in South Korea.

In 1945 the U.S. military headquarters, which temporarily assumed the governing power of South Korea, announced that Hangul would be exclusively used in school textbooks at all levels of elementary and secondary education, and Hanmun characters could be provided in parentheses when necessary for a better understanding of certain Koreanized Hanmun words. Hanmun characters were freely used in the society outside school classrooms.

The South Korean government, which was established in 1948, announced a law that prohibited any use of Hanmun in official documents and that allowed only temporary use of Hanmun characters along with Hangul, when necessary. This law was applied to official documents; it did not direct use of Hanmun characters in the daily life of people. Unofficial printed materials, especially newspapers, used Hanmun characters mixed with Hangul.

In 1958, governmental offices were handed further directives concerning the use of Hangul with no Hanmun mixed in. These directives were also recommended to those who worked in conjunction with government offices. Later, in 1969, the Korean association of journalists limited its use of Hanmun up to 2,000 characters. As a result of these and other historical efforts, today Koreans use Hangul nearly exclusively in their daily lives. For example, literary works, especially novels, are printed exclusively in Hangul, and most of the pages of the daily newspapers and nonprofessional journals are also in Hangul. In addition, Hangul newspapers have been to be published. As of 1988, two newspapers, a daily and a weekly, have used only Hangul. Their circulation has turned out to be successful. They won greater popularity among young adults and students who have been educated by means of school textbooks written only in Hangul since 1945.

From 1945 through 1964, textbooks were printed in Hangul, with Hanmun characters printed above certain Hangul words for six years and, in parentheses, attached next to their equivalent Hangul words, for thirteen years. For three years beginning in 1965, then, Hanmun characters were used along with Hangul, without any parentheses. That is, certain Koreanized Hanmun words were printed in Hanmun in the school textbooks for fourth, fifth, and sixth graders. Since 1970, however, all textbooks for elementary school have used Hangul exclusively. In secondary school textbooks Hanmun characters may be used in parentheses attached next to their equivalent Hangul words.

No Hanmun characters are taught in elementary school. At the secondary level some characters are taught in the Hanmun course. A total of 1,800 Hanmun characters are taught in middle and high school Hanmun courses.

Use of Hanmun characters has not yet been abolished in South Korea. For example, some college professors use Hanmun characters as part of their instructional media. Some Koreans use Hanmun characters freely in their scholarly papers and other publications. Many newspapers do not totally give up Hanmun characters in certain pages.

ERADICATION OF ILLITERACY AND
BEGINNING READING

In 1945 the illiteracy rate of South Korea was 78 percent. In order to eradicate illiteracy, the government, daily newspaper companies, the Hangul Association, and other organizations sponsored short-term Hangul Schools in every corner of the country.

Ordinary people can learn Hangul easily within a short period of instructional time. One report (B. W. Kim, 1985) revealed that twenty-one Korean-Americans who spoke English studied Hangul and became literate in forty-eight fifty-minute class hours in sixteen days. People who speak Korean may be able to learn Hangul in a much shorter time than that.

In 1958 a government report disclosed that only 4.1 percent of those above twelve years of age appeared illiterate. Compulsory elementary school education began to be provided in 1962. It has been so successful that the enrollment rate of school-age children steadily increased to 98.9 percent in 1987. According to some reports (S. H. Kim, 1986; Lee, 1986), approximately 10 percent of elementary school children and 5 percent of middle school students do not read Hangul. According to another report (Park, 1986), approximately 4 percent of elementary school children in the urban area and 10 percent in the rural area do not read Hangul. We assume that these illiterate children are slow learners who usually fail in subjects other than reading too. No official report of Korea's current literacy rate is available.

In Korea neither remedial courses in reading nor the concept of developmental dyslexia are known. Taylor (1981) believes that Koreans do not have need of that term, which means "difficulty in learning to read despite adequate intelligence" (Taylor, 1981, p. 32), because the alphabetic system of Hangul is simple and easy to learn.

Reading instruction begins in the first grade. Kindergarten children are not supposed to be directly taught how to read Hangul. They have a reading readiness program which consists of games that will help children get accustomed to the shapes that constitute the Hangul alphabets and grasp functions and uses of written words in life (Kim and Lee, 1986).

Until a new approach was adopted, the students were taught how to read Hangul by memorizing each syllable, the whole unit of the consonant-vowel combination, as they were supposed to learn each Hanmun character. In 1945 the Hangul Association adopted the new alphabetic approach to teach Hangul as suggested in the *First Step to Hangul* (Hangul Association, 1971). This work, the first school textbook compiled for the teaching and learning of Hangul, adopted the alphabetic approach in place of the traditional method. In this new approach, the instructor teaches the components of each syllable separately and how to combine them into certain syllables, so that the students can learn all twenty-four basic Hangul alphabets and their sixteen derivatives, as well as how to combine consonants and vowels into various syllables. Teaching of meaning and how to comprehend meanings are not emphasized in the alphabetic approach. It emphasizes the instruction of decoding skills.

The authors of the *First Step to Hangul* were aware of the difficulty of the alphabetic approach. The students were being required to memorize the forty alphabets and to learn how to combine them into syllables (Hangul Association, 1971). The authors explained, however, that the method would allow the students to learn Hangul as quickly as possible, which was a primary goal. Moreover, they did not have sufficient time to invent any other indirect method of teaching how to read and write Hangul (Hangul Association, 1971, p. 296).

In 1948, when the government began to provide the national textbook for Korean language learning, the authors adopted a text approach to replace the alphabetic approach. Since then, Korean children have learned to read sentences and stories in the Korean language textbook, which is provided by the government, and at the same time they learn how to read Hangul.

In the text approach the instructor first leads the children to grasp the meaning of the given text, whether it is a sentence or a story. The text is followed by the teaching of how to say the meaning in sentences. The text approach emphasizes understanding the meaning of sentences, and the children are expected to learn how to read and write individual words and syllables within the context of teaching and learning the whole unit of the text.

This approach remained the method of teaching Hangul at school until 1987 when the curriculum in South Korea was revised. This was the fifth revision since 1948. In the new curriculum which was to be followed beginning in Spring 1989, the alphabetic approach was added to the text approach. The instructor helps the children grasp the meaning of the given text and also helps them to learn individual alphabets and how to combine them into syllables.

Interestingly, the alphabetic approach was not treated as a reading method, but as a method of teaching the Korean language in the new curriculum. According to the curriculum, the Korean course is composed of six areas: reading, writing, listening, speaking, language, and literature. So, as usual, reading is to be taught as part of the Korean course. In the language area, the teaching of Hangul alphabets and their combination procedures is discussed; it is not included in the instructional objectives of the reading area.

Korea employs yet a third method of teaching beginning reading: the syllable approach. In this approach, the syllable may be the smallest unit of instruction, or the alphabet that forms the syllable may be the smallest unit. The instructor teaches specific words and syllables in terms of their alphabets so that the children may learn how to decode a syllable and a word as a whole unit.

READING IN THE LANGUAGE COURSE

The following goals are applied to Korean language education in elementary, middle, and high schools. The goals and instructional objectives that follow are quoted from *Elementary School Korean Course: Proposal of New Curriculum* (Korean Educational Development Institute, 1987) and the *New Curriculum of Middle and High School* (Korean Association of Secondary Education, 1987).

1. Students will learn how to understand and express thoughts and feelings appropriately through spoken and written Korean.
2. Students will learn knowledge of language and how to use Korean appropriately.
3. Students will learn knowledge of literature and how to comprehend and appreciate literary works.

The first goal includes the linguistic activities of reading, writing, listening, and speaking. These four areas, together with the second and third (that is, language and literature), add up to six areas in the Korean course.

The three goals, with six areas included, have been further developed into a list of instructional objectives. The objectives have been categorized into three stages in the elementary school education; the first and second grade stage, the third and fourth grade stage, and the fifth and sixth grade stage. The three goals have been further developed into instructional objectives for the three-year Korean course in the middle school, and the three-year high school Korean course I and II.

The middle school Korean course is required, and it is an extension of the elementary school Korean. The high school Korean I is required, and it is an extension of the middle school Korean. The high school Korean II is an elective course and covers current and ancient literature, grammar, and composition.

Next, we will list the instructional objectives of the three stages of elementary school reading. Certain objectives included in areas other than reading are added here when they are relevant to reading education; they are marked with asterisks. Their areas are indicated in the parentheses at the end of the statements.

First Stage

The first and second grade children will learn

1. To pronounce Hangul appropriately with good reading posture.
2. To read Hangul with a good understanding of the content with reading interests.
- To recognize and decode Hangul alphabets, syllables, and words (in Language).
- To recognize basic sentence patterns (in Language).
- To read verses and poems, written for children, with interest (in Literature).

Second Stage

The third and fourth grade children will learn

1. To read to understand the outline of the story.
2. To read to understand the content accurately.
- To recognize different types of words and their uses (in Language).
- To recognize different types of sentences and their organizations (in Language).
- To read literary works with interest and to understand the imaginative world in order to form an interest in it (in Literature).

Third Stage

The fifth and sixth grade children will learn

1. To read various texts effectively to realize different reading goals.
2. To appreciate the structure of the given text and to comprehend the main idea of the whole text.
- To recognize different types of words and their organizations (in Language).
- To recognize various forms and ideas that form textual cohesion in the text (in Language).
- To understand and appreciate the structure of the given literary work (in Literature).

Reading in the middle and high school Korean course is an extension of reading in the elementary school with an emphasis on comprehension. In the higher levels, reading is indirectly taught in the areas of writing, language, and literature, as well as in the reading area.

Hanmun is taught at the middle and high school levels. The instructional objectives of the middle school Hanmun course include the teaching of 900 basic Hanmun characters and an understanding of the structures of the characters, Hanmun words, Hanmun literature, and traditional culture. The instructional objectives of the high school Hanmun I course include the teaching of 900 new characters and an understanding of the structures of the characters, Hanmun words, Hanmun literature, and the thoughts of the ancient writers. High school Hanmun II is an extension of Hanmun I.

English is taught in both middle and high school. The instructional objectives of the middle school English include the teaching of practical use of English and understanding of the English language, together with the native speaker's life and culture. The high school English I course is an extension of the middle school English. The instructional objectives include the teaching of an additional vocabulary of 1,700 words. English II is an extension of English I. An additional vocabulary of 3,000 words is taught in English II. In addition to English, German, French, Spanish, Chinese, and Japanese are taught as elective foreign languages at the high school level.

Government statistics (Ministry of Education, 1987) show that 333,456 educators teach at all levels of educational institutes in South Korea. Among them, 37.57 percent are female educators. The following table shows the proportion of female educators at different levels of educational institutes, except for the universities and colleges. The proportions of female educators do not seem to indicate any sex segregation in education.

Educational Level	Total	Female	Percentage
Kindergarten	11,920	10,986	92.16
Elementary	130,142	59,417	45.65
Middle	74,858	30,497	40.73
High	45,976	9,317	20.26

Elementary and secondary school teachers are prepared through a four-year program at teachers' colleges and colleges of education, respectively. They take required courses for general education, courses for teacher qualification, and specialized courses for the subject the student elects to teach in the future. When they obtain the diploma and pass a national examination for future teachers, they receive the license that indicates their qualification. Students enrolled in a kindergarten education program participate in a two-year program. Those who receive the diploma can teach children at the kindergarten.

No reading teachers are produced in Korea. Korean language teachers learn how to teach in six areas, including reading. No textbook published specifically for reading instruction is available at this moment.

School textbooks for students are consumable. Each year elementary school children are provided with textbooks free of charge. Middle and high school students pay for the textbooks they use each year.

Public schools receive financial support from the national, provincial, and city governments, whereas private schools get support from their educational foundations. Through these funds, they purchase various materials that instructors and the students need for their educational activities in the classroom.

CONCLUSIONS

In ancient times Koreans adopted Hanmun characters for partial representation of the Korean language and for expression of their ideas and feelings. The difficulties in learning and using Hanmun characters led King Sejong and his scholars to invent Hangul.

The invention of Hangul did not immediately free the people from illiteracy. A new world of literacy in South Korea had to await the lifting of Japanese control, changes in attitude toward the use of Hangul in everyday life, and the success of language education in teaching students to prefer Hangul to Hanmun characters.

The reading culture that was formed in ancient times led Koreans to respect the reading of good books. Adults and school students are frequently encouraged to read good books both at home and at school. These reading campaigns are not directly related to teaching how to read at school.

Reading and reading comprehension are not taught as an independent course in the schools. No college department offers any course specifically designed for instruction in reading and reading comprehension. Nor have many research studies in the field of reading been produced.

These facts should not lead to any negative inference about literacy and reading culture in South Korea. Largely thanks to Hangul, all Koreans can read and write except for those who have general learning difficulties, including reading. Many of the children who begin to read the first Korean textbook in elementary school know how to read and write Hangul. Most of them learn to read at home, usually with the mother's help. Koreans believe in the importance of reading and value good reading habits.

Even so, there is space for further improvement in reading and reading education. In the areas of slow learners, teaching of reading comprehension, education programs for reading instruction, and reading research studies, no apparent development can bᴇ reported. It is not expected that these and similar areas, which are less developed than those in some other countries, will markedly advance in the near future. One reason for this negative outlook is that there is no particular problem in teaching how to read that may function as motivation for active development of any of these areas.

REFERENCES

Choe, C. H. 1980. Korea's Communication Culture. *Korea Journal* 20, no. 8: 1–12 (in English).

Dredge, C. P. 1983. What is politeness in Korean Speech? *Korean Linguistics* 3 (Journal of the International Circle of Korean Linguistics): 21–32 (in English).

Hangul Association. 1971. *First Step To Hangul*. Seoul, Korea: Hangul Association.

Hangul Association. 1979. *Fifty-Year History of the Hangul Association*. Seoul, Korea: Hangul Association.

Huh, W. 1983. Development of the Korean language. In the National Commission for Unesco, ed., *The Korean Language*. Seoul, Korea: Si-sa-yong-o-sa Publishers. Also, Arch Cape, Oreg.: Pace International Research, pp. 1–12 (in English).

Kim, B. W. 1983. Reading comprehension in Korea: a text-oriented linguistic approach. *The Horizon*, 24 (Journal of Hong Kong Teachers' Association): 137–147. Also ERIC Document Reproduction Series No. 233 331 (in English).

Kim, B. W. 1985. New understanding of the Korean language. In Association for Purification of Korean, ed., *Love and Understanding of the National Language*. Seoul, Korea: Chongho Books (in Korean).

Kim, B. W. 1987. Spoken and written Korean: a functional contrast. *The Bilingual Education*, 3 (Journal of the Korea Society of Bilingualism): 3–22 (in Korean).

Kim, B. W. 1988. Principles of teaching Korean as a foreign language. *The Bilingual Education*, 4 (Journal of the Korea Society of Bilingualism): 113–143 (in Korean).

Kim, B. W., and Lee, S. K. 1986. *Language Teaching to Pre-school Children*. Seoul, Korea: Tongmoon-sa (in Korean).

Kim, C. W. 1978. Divergence in language policies in Korea. In C. W. Kim, ed., *Papers in Korean Linguistics*. Columbia, S.C.: pp. 245–257 (in English).

Kim, C. W. 1983. The making of the Korean language. In the National Commission for Unesco, ed., *The Korean Language*. Seoul, Korea: Si-sa-yong-o-sa Publishers. Also, Arch Cape, Ore.: Pace International Research, pp. 13–42 (in English).

Kim, H. G. 1983. Chinese characters and the Korean language. In the National Commission for Unesco, ed., *The Korean Language*. Seoul, Korea: Si-sa-yong-o-sa Publishers. Also, Arch Cape, Ore.: Pace International Research, pp. 121–127 (in English).

Kim, S. H. 1986. Teaching of Hanmun characters will do harm to elementary education. *Hangul News*, 172 (December): 25–27.

Korean Association of Secondary Education. 1987. *New Curriculum of Middle and High School* (in Korean).

Korean Educational Development Institute. 1987. *Elementary School Korean Course: Proposal of New Curriculum* (in Korean).

Lee, T. G. 1986. Teaching of Hanmun characters at the elementary school cannot succeed. *Hangul News*, 172 (December): 18–19.

Lukoff, F. 1978. Ceremonial and expressive uses of the styles of address of Korean. In C. W. Kim, ed., *Papers in Korean Linguistics*. Columbia, S.C.: Hornbeam Press, pp. 269–281 (in English).

Martin, S. E. 1972. Nonalphabetic writing systems: some observations. In J. F. Kavanagh, and I. G. Mattingly, eds., *Language by Ear and by Eye*. Cambridge, Mass.: MIT Press, pp. 81–102 (in English).

Ministry of Education, South Korea. 1987. *Statistical Yearbook of Education* (in Korean with English).

Ministry of Education, South Korea. 1988. *Education in Korea, 1987–1988* (in English).

Nam, K. S., and Y. K. Ko, eds. 1985. *The Standard Grammar of Korean*. Seoul, Korea: Top Publishing Co. (in Korean).

Nam, P. H. 1982. Linguistic nature of the Koreanized Hanmun. In P. K. Hwang, et al., eds., *Introduction to Korean Literature*. Seoul, Korea: Chishig-sanup-sa, pp. 171–177 (in Korean).

Oh, C. H. 1971. *Critical Misunderstanding of the National Language*. Seoul, Korea: Tongmoonkwan (in Korean).

Oh, C. S. 1964. *New History of Education in Korea*. Seoul, Korea: Hyondae-kyoyuk-yangso (in Korean).

Ong, W. J. 1982. *Orality and Literacy*. London: Methuen and Co. p. 88 (in English).

Park, S. I. 1986. *Education of Slow Learners*. Seoul, Korea: Korean Educational Development Institute (in Korean).

Pihl, M. R., Jr. 1983. The alphabet of East Asia. In the National Commission for Unesco, ed., *The Korean Language*. Seoul, Korea: Si-sa-yong-o-sa Publishers. Also, Arch Cape, Ore.: Pace International Research, pp. 109–120 (in English).

Taylor, I. 1981. Writing systems and reading. In G. E. MacKinnon and T. G. Waller, eds., *Reading Research: Advances in Theory and Practice*. New York: Academic Press, pp. 1–51 (in English).

20

Soviet Union

S. M. Bondarenko, G. G. Granik,
V. I. Golod, G. N. Kudina,
Z. N. Novlyanskaya, and G. A. Zuckerman
Translated by John Poritsky

The USSR is a multilingual country, and in most of the Soviet and autonomous republics, reading is taught in the native language. Russian—the international language—is studied as a second language, beginning in the first or second grade. We will not discuss the problems peculiar to bilingualism here; further discourse will concern the general psychological principles of teaching reading that are applicable to any native language. Using the schools of the Russian Republic as our example, we will examine these problems.

THE GENERAL CHARACTER OF THE STATE SCHOOL

The fundamental range of psychological problems connected with introducing the child to written discourse was presented in the work of L. S. Vygotsky and his students. In all the work of the Vygotsky school, the central question seems to be whether the teaching of developmental literacy (in the most general sense of the word), giving the child a mastery of written discourse, will occasion new capabilities and improvement in other psychological functions, as particular skills of writing and reading are formulated as distinct skills in a series of many, having no significant influence on the systematic development of the child's consciousness and activity. The established position on the problem of developing language teaching in the USSR was reached as follows. In individual experiments conducted at educational establishments (less than 1 percent of the total number of schools in the country), ideas, facts, and concrete methods of enhancing children's written discourse, many of considerable potential, were accumulated. In the overwhelming majority of the schools, language teaching is at the tail-end of development, and school children consider philology their least favorite subject, boring and mindless. What is the reason for this state of affairs?

Historically, the skill (as opposed to development) orientation of writing and reading was conditioned in the first decade of Soviet power, when the government decided to eliminate illiteracy in the general populace. The problem of primary illiteracy in the Soviet Union has been resolved completely and finally. Today every child grows up among adults who have mastered writing and can show a child letters and read her a book. In kindergartens (attended by approximately two-thirds of all preschoolers), work is aimed only toward the preliminary preparation for writing and reading. Lessons in kindergarten are directed toward developing oral discourse, phonemic hearing, and overcoming the basic defects of articulation. Nevertheless, the majority of first graders go to school knowing many letters, and half the children (in the cities) can read between five and ten words a minute. Consequently, one objective has become not restricting the beginning elementary education to the practical task of training children in writing and reading. This objective, combined with the social necessity of developing reading, has led to compulsory eight-year education for all children in the Soviet Union. Public expectations of the elementary school have therefore been changed. Now the school must instill not only the basic skills of reading, writing, and arithmetic, but also a foundation for further learning. The child must be introduced to basic sciences (linguistics in particular) and, most importantly, must learn to learn (particularly to find new knowledge from books independently). Clearly, this goal cannot be attained without fundamentally restructuring the cognition of the child in the process of teaching.

Such a change in the sociocultural situation of children's development occurred at the end of the 1950s, when both the possibility and the necessity of building developmental teaching became apparent. The energetic cultivation of psychological principles of methods of developmental teaching was begun, namely, by L. V. Zankov, N. A. Menchinskaya, P. Y. Gal'perin, D. B. El'konin, and V. V. Davydov.

The achievements of science, however, were very slow to reach pedagogical practice. The basic reason stemmed from unlimited central management of elementary education. All schools in the Russian Republic have a common program for the teaching of language. This program specifies the basic concepts that must be studied in each grade, as well as their sequence; the number of hours devoted to each concept; materials through which a concept might be explored (for example, works of fiction); and the basic knowledge, abilities, and skills that pupils must master by the end of each year of study. All children, from the Baltic Sea to the Sea of Okhotsk, execute the same drills and the same uniform calligraphy, with the same textbook. For every textbook there exists a methodological plan for the teacher, deviations from which are permitted only within narrow limits. (For the right to change the subject matter of a course in the native language or literature the teacher must receive special permission from the administration.) School administrators and inspectors oversee the program.

This totalitarianism of the school is justified by the fact that government funding of national education precludes considering the local, distinctive features of every school, let alone the individual style of every teacher. All schools receive, without cost, an allocation of identical sets of textbooks, school equipment, and implements. In recent years schools have fully extended the free supply of all student textbooks, which children donate to the school library at the end of the year. The copy-books used by first graders are an exception, these notebooks are designed for a single use. On the one hand, this rigidly unified system takes into account the interests of children and parents, giving everyone the opportunity for education regardless of social, developmental, and nationalistic differences between children. Furthermore, for the child moving from one school to another, it is extremely comforting. On the other hand, the rigidity and the limitedness of the centralized system of national education make it sluggish, unamenable to new ideas and experiences. The preservation of the existing system of education is promoted by the nature of the teachers' education.[1] They study to work in today's school, using today's program and textbooks, which apply to today's method, and do not practically learn to learn independently, to supplement and restructure accepted pedagogical practice.

Therefore, regardless of the possibilities and keenly felt necessities, and regardless of the real achievements of Soviet psychology and the refinement of principles and concrete methods of developmental teaching schools, a mechanical, perfunctory method of teaching remains in both the school and the pedagogical institute. This leads to a fundamental conflict between the requirements of contemporary production and the graduates of Soviet schools. In the last year, however, the Soviet school has begun to be restructured, with the appearance of a new movement of teacher-innovators, who have new pedagogical ideas. Although individual, talented teachers comprise the movement at present, hope has arisen that its new ideas might be incorporated into mass pedagogical practice. The basic trends of the psychological-pedagogical investigation in the area of language teaching might, in the near future, offer tangible results.

THE LINGUISTIC DEVELOPMENT OF SCHOOL CHILDREN

This research trend is associated with D. B. El'konin and V. V. Davydov and their theory of developmental teaching in the elementary school. In the 1960s experimental evidence had already been published showing that the schools underestimate the growth potential of young school children.[2] Evaluating children aged seven to ten solely by means of a perceptible-empirical, rational cognitive model, the school in turn taught them empirical methods, without giving them the opportunity to develop a basis for reasoning, inculcating an imitative attitude toward learning, and barring the way for the child to realize creative initiative. Long-term experiments conducted in a series of experimental schools showed that under certain conditions young children are open to a genuinely scientific attitude toward the world (and toward the native language, in particular) and that such an aptitude is not an object of pedagogical influences, but a subject of educational activities. The entire focus of elementary education, which was previously restricted to teaching writing, reading, and computation, and broadening the child's perception of the surrounding world, was changed. The child's learning activity was now seen as a means toward self-development, with the goal of mastering general methods of action. What does this mean for the child?

A small child, solving a problem, for example, singling out the root of a word, is concentrated on a single word. The teacher might construct this assignment as a diversion: searching for the root of the word *biblioteka* (library), the child incidentally learns about the ancient city of Byblos and newly understands the word *biblia* (Bible); investigating the structure of the word hooligan, the child learns about a certain Irish family. . . .

In assigning children the task of searching for word origins, however, the teacher seeks not so much to broaden the children's horizons, as to teach the general means of analyzing any word from an etymological perspective. The teacher's task might become the pupil's task as well, if the pupil is not oriented toward a particular result, but toward a general course of action, and if the student sees a specific task as representative of a wide class of similar tasks. A preschooler will be content to learn amusing etymological history. If the pupil has a correctly developed learning attitude, he will go a step further; he attempts to ascertain that he has learned to find the roots of any given word. There is interest in the structure of the word, but, more importantly, the interest in the actual possibility of understanding this structure provides the child with a fundamental respect for himself as a student, a basic motivation for learning activity. The theory of learning activity also circumscribes methods of organizing teaching, molding the child's orientation away from isolated results, and toward a general method of correct activity.

Does it follow that the child, knowing how to do almost nothing, for example, familiar with only a few letters and reading her first words, already possesses the basic capability of reading any given word? For this to be the case she must make three fundamental discoveries along the way: (1) she must discover that a word is distinct from the object it represents; (2) she must realize that spoken language consists of sounds, which can be symbolized (drawn) by letters; and (3) she must realize a basic law of Russian orthography—the pronunciation of a consonant depends on the vowel following the letter.

Clearly, the six- or seven-year-old child does not make these discoveries verbally, by talking about words, but through practical activity with words. For instance, he sets out to travel to the country of words, where any object will materialize, if its name is correctly written. The child has to decide for which word he will need more letters (or sounds)—the word *train* or the word *car*. The child initially reasons according to the logic of the object: a car is smaller than a train; hence, it needs fewer letters. This helps him arrive at a material *model*, a *scheme* in which it is possible to place the elusive sound matter of the word, in which there are only the essential properties of the word, without the unessential elements that prevent the child from fathoming the linguistic phenomenon. (In the case of the words *car* and *train*, this is simply the diagram with which the child marks every sound in the word.)

Thus, the child's initial successes in the practice of reading guarantee the discovery of that primary law of Russian orthography, under whose guidance the child might read any given Russian word. All subsequent extensions of reading capability, and the child's accomplishments in language, can be construed as a deployment of the original knowledge in the system of linguistic concepts, as deductive knowledge, applicable to a wide range of practical writing.[3] Almost nothing is communicated to the child "in prepared form." Each time the teacher constructs a problem situation, in which the pupil arrives at the following conclusion: my knowledge is insufficient for solving this problem; I need to master this and that in order to write a new word, select an apt word for a given context, or understand a poem. The clear knowledge of his own ignorance leads the child to an active search for knowledge: at first, to take the initiative to ask the teacher cognitive questions, and later, to work with reference books, dictionaries, and other scholastic materials. The capacity to realize one's own ignorance, to clearly define the limits of one's knowledge and skills and to extend these limits, encompasses the basic ability to learn.

In the scheme of mental development, the appearance of this ability (the ability for discriminating metacognition) is central to the new psychic formation being cultivated in the early years of schooling, toward which learning activity is directed.

At the begining of elementary school, the cognitive interests of children are insufficiently developed for the search and intellectual effort needed to deduce, on their own, that knowledge of one's own ignorance is a means of solving a logical problem. This is reached only toward the end of elementary education. For the first two to three years of teaching, techniques are cultivated for creating and maintaining a dramatic intensity of research work in lessons. For first graders, this might take the form of stories in which the hero battles linguistic problems. Later, this becomes educational discussion, competition, different kinds of cooperative activities, and their tactics and etiquette are taught specifically to children. At the base of these techniques lies the procedure of polarizing different points of view, searching for truths in their conflicts, and attempting to reach mutual understanding. Such pedagogical techniques preclude authoritarianism and foster in children faith in themselves and interest in others. Hence, the problems of teaching can be narrowed down from the wider problems of education.

This logic of learning activity was implanted in the native (Russian) language for the elementary school (Aidarova, 1978) and a course for the high school (Markova, 1974). Teaching via these experimental programs showed that, along with the techniques of writing and reading, the ability to reflect on linguistic facts, steady cognitive interest in language, striving to perfect one's own discourse, and skills of self-development in this sphere might be fostered.

Practice showed that the principles of learning activity, devised to conform to the Russian language, can be carried over into other linguistical structures. However, within the theory of learning activity far from all the problems of teaching reading are resolved. In particular, the acute question of individualized teaching has been almost completely ignored. A textbook might become effective for individualized teaching, if it shapes a pupil's ability to work independently with a book.

THE ABILITY TO LEARN FROM BOOKS

Allowing highly capable, middle level, and so-called weak children to study under identical conditions is one of the negative features of modern school teaching. "Averaging" teaching impedes the development of all three groups of students.

For this reason one of the important tasks of modern school teaching is to create forms of teaching that assure all children conditions for developing their ability at their own level. Under such a framework of teaching, "interference" with the development of the most capable pupils will disappear, and the possibilities that the abilities of average children will "escalate," and that regressive children will develop normally, greatly increase.

In the USSR this problem area is most effectively addressed by the School Textbook psychological group (Bondarenko, 1975; Granik, 1976) leading both to optimization and individualization of the child's work with a text.

The entire work of this group reveals psychological principles that must be learned in order to compose good textbooks. To this end the group studied the processes of understanding and memorizing scholastic texts by children of different ages, and the formulation of these children's abilities and skills. Not only are the workings of these processes in the abstract studied, but also the causes of success and failure in their workings. Two areas are responsible for success and failure: (1) defects in the textbooks themselves, composed without taking into account the psychological principles of memory and understanding, and (2) insufficient development of pupils' ability to work with a text.

Hence, it becomes necessary to compose scholastic literature that not only contains cognitive material, but that is also conducive to understanding, memory, developing ability and skills, and formulating the ability to work with a book. Without this ability there can be no learning in school, no self-education in the future, and no success in intellectual labor. Moreover, this ability appears to be a characteristic of an intellectually mature personality; it can be argued that by developing this ability purposefully, we also develop the personality as a whole.

Research has shown, however, that the overwhelming majority of pupils do not possess this ability. The problem of learning to work with a book was never specifically posed, so there is no applicable pedagogical tradition. We therefore conducted special experiments, with the goal of determining the psychological components of the ability to work with a text. This resulted in the discovery of basic steps in the process that leads to understanding, and structural components entering into this process. In sum, the original standard was created—the "model of the ideal reader" whom we described in our works and whom we teachers and specialists address when composing textbooks. Work "for the ideal reader" generally has this structure.

The purpose of understanding is a basic premise that must be actively included in reading activity. From the first moment that the individual becomes engaged in a search for comprehension, the realization of an "information deficit" emerges; only as he realizes his own ignorance does an individual truly aspire to comprehend. In work leading to comprehension, an aggregation of mental processes contributes: thought, memory, emotions, imagination.

There are three stages in the mental processing of a text for comprehension and memorization. The first stage is the work preceding the actual reading of the text. It includes contemplating the chapter headings (and epigraphs, if there are any), "drawing on" reserves of knowledge about the subject indicated by each heading, and envisioning what will be said in the text.

The second stage is the most basic in the process of understanding. This is reading the text—not simply reading passively, but as if in a conversation, or dialogue, with the text.

The third stage is working with the text after it has been read. It includes deriving the main idea from the text and formulating it verbally; forming a frame of reference that takes into account other knowledge related to the given material; and paraphrasing, according to this frame of reference, while testing the completeness and accuracy of the paraphrase with the text itself.

Such a comprehensive structure of work for understanding and remembering texts presents its own hierarchical system of necessary and sufficient operations for the assimilation of scholastic material. Both teachers and authors of textbooks might work with this system. However, extant textbooks most often fail to further such active work on the part of the reader. Scholastic texts are structured as authors' monologues, addressing the pupil as a passive consumer relieved of the necessity of independent thinking.

The problem before us was to determine how textbooks could guarantee active work for understanding and remembering.

We consider the following one of the fundamental requirements for the scholastic text: it must anticipate conditions under which the reader can carry on a dialogue with it. What are these conditions? (1) The text must contain, either in plain or hidden view, a question (or a system of questions). (2) It must be possible to give a speculative answer to this question (to posit an hypothesis). (3) There are conditions for testing the hypothesis in the text, that is, conditions created for self-testing.

We established that the ability to carry on a dialogue was first of all formulated with the help of a fixed system of questions. Accordingly, the functional roles of questions varying in difficulty, position in text, and nature of intellectual activity stimulated were analyzed.

The place of a question in the text determines its functional role. Thus, questions before the text stimulate psychological interest in the work; they build toward resolution of the problem, helping both to correlate the question with knowledge already present and to bring forward hypotheses related to those contained in the text.

Questions posed in the course of reading stimulate probing, prognosis, and self-testing in any given fragment of the text. These questions are directed toward the consolidation and generalized self-testing for all the text.

We cultivated the individual view of the text, which created the possibility of teaching students to carry on a dialogue with it. With the aim of further improving textbooks, we also analyzed general expectations of the modern textbook.

The basic steps for composing and testing scholastic books were specified. We describe them briefly here. Composition of a textbook must be preceded by preliminary phases of work, falling into a series of interconnected steps. First, it is necessary to determine the functional load that the textbook will carry. At the same time, it is necessary to select a psychological theory, on the basis of which to propose to formulate these functions. Next, it is necessary to select (or construct new) methodological means of realizing the functions of the text. After this preliminary work the second step can begin—composing a textbook or a set of textbooks. The composition of the model is followed by the realization of its specific limits, after which its efficiency is tested. The textbook must pass this test in order to receive a limited mass circulation. We ascertained four stages in the testing of textbooks: (1) testing the program underlying the textbook; (2) testing every structural unit in the textbook during the course of its composition; (3) testing the completed but unpublished textbook in individual experiments and in class; and (4) mass testing through experimental circulation in a series of schools.

Analysis revealed that general expectations of textbooks show the necessity of considerably expanding their role in the scholastic process. The foremost of these expectations would revolve around those roles which the teacher, working with a full class, cannot fulfill for every pupil, as there are many pupils and only one teacher.

First, let us state that the functions of the individualization of teaching are the formation of a rational means of cognitive activity, including quantity and means of independent work with a book, formulation of interest in scholastic work and study material, and implementation of problematic teaching.

In accordance with these demands, our authors collective composed an experimental set of textbooks on the Russian language in which a problematic method of individualized teaching was implemented. For this task a basic structural unit was specifically developed, consisting of the following components: (1) a sequence (the sequence of the problematically individualized set is a specially organized aggregation of components, presenting a model combining activities for creatively teaching pupils with resolving problem situations); (2) problems and exercises for every sequence (or every few sequences); and (3) a set of test questions, also applicable to one or a few sequences. The aggregation of sequences comprises a textbook, the system of problems becomes a collection of tasks, and the quizzes become a collection of tests.

Authors of textbooks can utilize this structural unit to devise any scholastic course. It might be particularly advantageous for rural and underequipped schools to employ textbooks thus structured, in order to further the possibilities for pupils working independently.

At present, the group is developing a theoretical approach to composing language textbooks for Uzbek schools, English language for Russian schools, Russian literature, and mathematics.

EDUCATING THE READER OF LITERATURE

The teaching of reading cannot be considered completed if the person who possesses the techniques of reading is able to receive needed information from a book but does not develop aesthetically. Such a person does not enjoy literature, and does not see in literature an important source of self-improvement. Ten years in school is a sufficient period for educating readers of literature,[4] but not one year can be wasted! The unique experimental course in literature, developed by G. N. Kudina and Z. N. Novlyanskaya specifically for very young children, adolescents, and young adults, will be described at length.

The basic tasks of the scholastic course in literature are aesthetic education and the aesthetic development of the individual, and fostering in the reader the ability to appreciate a work of art. Such a reader might not only "discover" how an author sees the world in his text, but might also be able to judge, independently, its artistic merit and the view of life reflected in the work.

Unfortunately, the modern school is lax in addressing these tasks, culture is not conducive to reading, and interest in literature continually declines under the onslaught of television. For these reasons, the area of teaching literature remains particularly appropriate for psychological/pedagogical experimentation.

Such experimentation cannot be conducted without the presupposition that literature is being taught in the schools. Different points of view are possible here. In our opinion, the subject of literature should be presented in the school as practical literary activity in all its varieties—from readership through authorship. It is important to maintain the autonomy of the aspect being taught. This is in keeping with M. M. Bakhtin's theory of conceptualization, which treats the reading of a literary text as a specific dialogue between author and reader, maintaining autonomy and concluding with an "artistic model of the world." Bakhtin regards every link between "author–literary text–reader" only in relation to the others. In the process of reading a literary work, the reader does two things simultaneously: (1) he "becomes accustomed" to the author's world, "entering" it, vicariously living life as the hero; (2) at the same time he leaves this world and tries to view it through "the eyes of the author," with the author's vision and position. Moreover, in the process of reading, such a reader will formulate his own opinions of the fixed world of the author and compare his personal point of view with that of the author.

These theoretical positions allow us to describe a new scholastic course as "literature" through the initial relationship between "the author–the literary text–the reader." We suppose that the relationship might be reversible in the child's actual work and that by adequately "reading" for the author's position in the text that reader has himself found that position, that is, has experienced the author's work. Then the process of teaching might be viewed as a succession of resolutions to alternating creative problems. The pupil carries out creative work first from the position of the reader and then from the position of the writer, continually moving from one position to the other.

For successful advancement in each of these positions, the student must have a course in literary-critical appreciation. For the creative work to be ultimately successful and for the appreciation to be efficacious, knowledge of literary theory and of the principles employed by the author and the reader for composition of literary works are necessary.

In the work of the practiced reader, the positions of author, critic, and theorist are merged, and methods of work in these positions are internalized. In the beginning stages of teaching, however, these different approaches to literary works must be treated as different aspects of the work by different people. They must be addressed simultaneously, in practical interaction of the teacher with the children. The collectively distributed character of teaching lessons in literature is determined first of all by its different stages.

From this point of view, the task of the elementary school is to show pupils the positions of author and reader, place them in these positions, and help them realize that the principles of literary form contribute much to the process of resolving creative problems.

The first task of the reader, according to Bakhtin, is to understand the work as the author himself does. The basic direction of teaching must therefore be an orientation toward understanding the narrator and hero's point of view. From this it follows that in the first grade pupils must in practice assimilate the concept of point of view, learning to find and express, in works of various genres, the differences in point of view between the narrator and the hero.

In the second grade children might master, in practice, the basic means of construing a literary text as an interesting form. This task is addressed by means of work with the integral structures of indigenous works (counting songs, jokes, tongue-twisters, riddles, proverbs, fables, and tales).

In the third grade a specific task might be undertaken—a practical understanding of "types of literature" (epic, lyric, and drama) in folk tales, songs, and plays. Experimental tests show that this method of teaching is fully accessible to a majority of children and guarantees them depth and intensity of literary development in the years of study that follow.

This method of teaching gives fourth graders a foundation that permits them to build, in the middle grades, on one of the most prominent lines of study in the course of the historical-literary tradition.

In fourth through ninth grades pupils can be introduced to the context of culture and its historical development, namely, the beginnings of artistic sensibility in the eras of mythology, and subsequent manifestations of artistic sensibility in the folklore and literature of ancient peoples, medieval times, the Renaissance, and so on.

Engaging the modern youngster in a dialogue far removed from his or her own life experience and culture does not demand an exhaustive range of literature from all eras. It is necessary only to present the fundamental principles that allow such a dialogue to occur. To this end it is sufficient to compare literary phenomena from a few different, sufficiently distinct cultures.

Unfortunately, science does not at present have the means to show children different cultures in their entirety. Hence, the question of means of work arises. We consider it a distinct possibility for the older grades gradually to cross over into the lecture-seminar mode. This mode initially becomes possible if the young reader has had experience assimilating the positions of author, critic, and theorist, and has mastered the methods of working from these positions.

As a result of studying the author's position in historical-literary development—from the era of mythology through contemporary literature—at the end of ninth grade, we will already have fully developed readers. For these children the basic positions given in reading activities are in turn fused into the sole work of the "reader-critic." This allows us to structure a special course for the tenth grade.

In the tenth grade we would introduce a course provisionally titled Masterpieces of World Literature. In this course we would include the following works: Shakespeare's *Hamlet*, Cervantes' *Don Quixote*, Goethe's *Faust*, Tolstoy's *War and Peace*, Dostoevsky's *Crime and Punishment*, and Sholokhov's *Quiet Don*. These works are timeless and transcend the borders of art, making inroads into the realm of philosophy, with its universal questions. These questions are particularly meaningful for young people growing up. The lecture seminar format is replaced by the full seminar, in which the participants themselves do all the preparatory work. The primary mode of discourse becomes the readers' discussion, in which readers exchange their differing interpretations.

We formulated our proposals for a scholastic course of literature. These proposals were presented as a basis for experimental teaching, which was implemented in one first grade. At present these pupils have finished the sixth grade. Although the children in the experimental class have not yet gone through all the stages programmed by our course, the results already received confirm the productivity suggested by our system of developing holistic reading.

READING DISABILITIES

An analysis of reading disabilities, in the strictest sense of the term, depends on understanding the psychological character of this outwardly very simple form of verbal activity. Structurally, the psychological operations of reading include acoustic, visual, motor, and a series of other processes. As it is based on spoken discourse, the psychophysiological structure of the act of reading is defined by the type of written discourse used in a given language.

In languages with a phonetic system of writing, the process of reading begins with the perception of the letter and the establishment of its sound value. Insofar as a letter represents a sign it is a symbol, a universal designation for a sound of speech, and it is the basis for the ability to distinguish and isolate sounds in the process of reading. Obviously, the differentiation of sounds and articulatory indicators plays a decisive role. The presence of phonemes, formulated representations of the general sounds of speech, shows that the ability to isolate distinct indicators of oral sounds is an indispensable condition for reading to proceed normally. On the other hand, correctly formulated skills of isolating sound-articulatory complexes play no less substantial a role in attributing sounds to certain categories. Oral articulation guarantees a complex level of analysis and differentiation of sounds.

The process of perception is also defined by the activity of the visual-knowledge system. Graphic letters characterize a complex spatial arrangement of several elements, and the distinctive indicators of these graphic symbols of sounds must be easily identified in the process of reading. The differentiation of letters in this fashion presupposes the analysis of equally important elements, which depend on the presence of formulated spatial concepts. Finally, the letter must be firmly learned, independently of the individual peculiarities of its outline. This in turn shows the necessity of formulating a general visual image that will be etched in the memory.

In the following stage, in which the greatest difficulty in teaching has been noted, the process of confluence, or combining letters into syllables, emerges. The psychological content of this stage is determined by the necessity of abstracting the meaning of individual phonemes, sets of indicators that must be restructured and construed on another level, according to the position of the sound phoneme in the group that is under the influence of its particular surroundings. In the process of deciphering individual sound-letter correlations in sound-letter combinations, syllables form and emerge as a unit of reading.

The combining of syllables into words occurs in the next stage; as a rule, this process does not present excessive difficulty. The active character of the process of reading, and the reflexive determining, or ability to form a hypothesis or purpose, are determined by elements isolated in the act of reading: on the level of words, the meaning of letter complexes, on the level of word combinations, individual words, and so on. At this stage, the basic psychological content of reading activity is to devise, in practice, a search for anticipated meaning, and to compare coincidences and differences between hypotheses and the meanings of perceived material (Luria, 1969).

In this way, the structure of reading activity has a complex character and (in languages with a phonetic type of writing) depends on the process of phonetic analysis and synthesis, and on articulatory kinetics. It depends on the formulation of sound-letter correlations, with visual-recognition processes guaranteeing adequate spatial analysis of the elements of graphic signs; it is implemented immediately as a part of the mnemonic component of the activity; and it assumes the isolation of the meaning of perceptible elements of reading material on the basis of hypotheses, and ultimately testing them for truth. The fully developed act of reading is characterized by a high degree of automatism and a reduction of the symbolizing operations that guarantee immediate familiarity with words, word combinations, and entire sentences. From the psycholinguistic point of view, the entire act of reading "penetrates" the action of the semantic component of the individual's linguistic capability, which is realized on different levels of its operation, and assures the extraction of the meaning from the corresponding linguistic structure.

One of the most important characteristics of reading is that the psychological and concomitant physiological composition of its operation changes significantly in the process of ontogenic development. Sequential automatism of the reading process, in the course of ontogenic development, causes changes in both the psychological structure of the individual operation and the internal nature of the psychological process (Luria, 1969). The circumscribed structure of the act of reading is closely correlated with the process of assimilating the skills acquired from the process of teaching. In the following psychological framework, assimilation of reading skills is earmarked by the following stages (Egorov, 1953): the analytical stage, in which the assimilation of sound-letter correspondences is realized and a transition to syllabic reading occurs; the synthetic stage, combining mechanics to formulate a unified perception of printed material; and the stage of automatically formulating synthetic reading.

All evidence clearly shows that reading is a complex series of psychological functions, which might be disrupted, on the one hand, by disabilities in the process of formulating individual operations or components. On the other hand, dysfunctions might be caused by a break or weakening of links in an already formulated functional system. Fundamental (i.e., etiologically) isolated reading disabilities (alexia, dyslexia) are related to ontogenetic dysfunctions, inability or difficulty in mastering the skills of reading, and disintegration of a certain type of activity, caused by minimum brain dysfunctions. In analyzing reading disabilities, it is essential to understand that reading has a complex functional system and that different dysfunctions will surface at different links in the system.

Reading disabilities usually become apparent when it becomes necessary to master the basic skills of reading; they involve defects in reading technique, rate, and comprehension (Lalayeva, 1983; Spirova, 1965). The following mistakes of dyslexic children are among the most frequently encountered: the insertion of additional sounds, the omission of individual letters, the substitution of one word for another, mistakes in pronouncing letters, repetition of words, addition of words, and omission of words (Levina, 1940). In addition, transposition of sounds, skipping from one paragraph to another, confusing sounds, and letter reversal have been documented (Lalayeva, 1983). The differentiation of disability indicators is followed by an analysis of the degree and character of the mistakes, and of the systematic character of the disability, comprehension of nonwritten material, and other processes of verbal activity or other psychic functions.

Essentially, dyslexia may be typologically classified according to a disability of a physical function (or set of functions) comprising the complex structure of the act of reading itself. In classifying dyslexia, the cause of the affliction might be the visual-perception component, the oral-praxic area, mnemonic links, or difficulty in formulating symbolic functions for linguistic proficiency at different levels. Deciding on the significance of each will determine which factor plays the leading role in the structure of the defect.

M. E. Hvatsev's analysis of the mechanics of reading disabilities (1959) concentrates on phonematic dyslexia, which is characterized by difficulty in establishing sound-letter correspondences as a result of dysfunctional phonematic hearing, and optical dyslexia, conditioned by dysfunctional visual perception, which leads to difficulty in visualizing printed words as signs of phonemes. In addition to these forms, which in Hvatsev's opinion should be treated as disorders of childhood, he recognizes optical-spatial, semantic, and mnemonic dyslexias, which are rooted in damage to the cerebral cortex, that is, based on the distintegration of previously formulated mechanisms.

As a foundation for the classification of defects, diagnosticians should note acoustical dyslexia, conditioned by an inability to differentiate auditory perceptions, optical dyslexia, and motor dyslexia, in which dysfunctional eye movement affects reading (Tokareva, 1969).

In addition to the disabilities cited above, several authors have also discussed agrammatical dyslexia, which is caused by underdevelopment of grammatical facility (Lalayeva, 1983), mnemonic dyslexia, which is connected to difficulty in remembering sound-letter relationships, and semantic dyslexia, which is a dysfunctional understanding of words, sentences, and texts after they have been read.

Literal and verbal dyslexias may be distinguished by outward appearance. In literal dyslexia, defects are rooted in difficulties in recognizing individual letters (or complete inability in this area), whereas in the verbal, individual letters can be named or recognized, but difficulties surface at the word level.

Disabilities in the process of mastering the skills of reading are most often connected to errors in developing spoken language. Disabilities or difficulties in assimilating the sounds that comprise a language and, in the first place, its phonematic opposites lead to marked difficulty in mastering the skills of reading. Depending on the stage of teaching and the operation with which the difficulties are connected, the disability may be described as an inability to assimilate letters and difficulty in merging individual letters into words. This first defect becomes apparent with a large number of confusions and substitutions. Analysis derived from special experiments showed that mistakes of confusion, in this case, are not random in character; that is, they do not affect the entire system of sound-letter correspondence, but only those that present difficulty in syllabic differentiation.

Difficulty or disability in distinguishing the sounds of words leads to defects in formulating general differentiations of signs representing linguistic sounds. The results of this difficulty are inaccurate and incomplete phonematic concepts. While being taught reading, a child with these characteristics begins to experience severe difficulty in establishing the connection between the sound of speech and its graphic representation. If a sound image is inaccurately formed, its graphic symbol can easily be correlated with a whole series of different sounds. Typically, such a letter will not correspond with any given sound, but only with those sounds that do not differ, or that differ radically, in the process of syllabic analysis.[5] The absence of a precise sound image, or phonematic concept, leads to difficulty in formulating associations between the phoneme and its graphic symbol. Special experiments determined that the inability to assimilate a visual image—a grapheme—in such cases did not, as a rule, occur as a result of a mnemonic defect (Lalayeva, 1983; Levina, 1968; Spirova, 1965).

The question of the functional role of articulatory differentiation occupies a special place in the problem of formulating adequate sound-letter correspondences. The interdependence between adequate articulatory juxtaposition (the area most closely connected to the formulation of kinesthetics in general) and difficulty in assimilating graphic designations of corresponding articles has remained almost unstudied in the area of childhood dyslexia. There are only isolated indicators of the significance which this component of linguistic activity has for correctly assimilating the skills of reading (Lalayeva, 1983). As a rule, difficulty with articulatory differentiation is a hindrance to normal proficiency with sound-letter correspondences, emerging together with dysfunctional auditory differentiation, that is, disabilities with phonematic hearing.

Difficulty in assimilating sound-letter correspondences is most often noted at the stage of combining letters into syllables, and syllables into words (Levina, 1968; Spirova, 1965). The connection between difficulty in syllabic differentiation of juxtaposed phonemes and identification of syllables becomes most apparent here. The adequate combination of individual letters into syllables serves two parallel functions: (1) the realization of a definite connection between sounds of speech and letters, and (2) simultaneously abstracting meaning from isolated letters, that is, the realization that the sounds of designated letters are dependent on their immediate surroundings. In other words, there must be adequate understanding of the sounds of speech in the process of merging letters into syllables. Because of disabilities in this phase of verbal activity, the child does not develop, "reading by letters, enduring the 'torture of merging,' unable to move from letters and their meanings to the sounds of living speech" (El'konin, 1956).

This type of disability is most often characterized by letter-by-letter reading using alphabetical names for the letters and a pronounced instability in the process of recognizing syllabic forms. Under these conditions, syllables differing, for example, by one phoneme and one differential indicator might once be read as the same and another time as different. Subsequent difficulties in differentiating the sounds of speech impede the process of formulating semantic conjecture, which plays an essential role in the organization of reading words. Arising from previously made sound-speech automatisms, sound images are parts of words, in the process of reading, that serve as a foundation for assumptions about widely read words. As a result, the syllable is first read as one word and then as it is heard in spoken language. The process of combining letters into syllables, therefore, most accurately represents the pronunciation of sounds, as they are heard orally. In letter-by-letter reading, formulating sound images of words does not occur, and this defect in turn hinders normal imaging of entire words. As a result, inadequate images are formed, which causes replacement of one word with another, repetitions of individual letters and words, and transpositions. Slow rates of reading, distortions of widely read words, and dysfunctional comprehension result.

In addition to disabilities, underformulated mechanisms of phonematic analysis and synthesis characterize reading difficulty related to disability in the area of mastering the lexical-grammatical system of a language. Basically, the defect in such cases is rooted in difficulty with the general grammatical form of the word, its inflections. Adequate semantic imaging, which must occur in the process of visually perceiving a text, is closely related to morphological analysis of word elements. The absence of a firm knowledge of the composition of a word leads the child to begin orienting himself through such coincidental signs as, for example, letter similarities. Ignorance of the morphological elements of the word results. Difficulties of this type may be seen in the substitution of words, when in place of the word that is written, a word with the same root, but different morphological elements, is read. This most often occurs with parts of words, but occasionally with whole words.

Yet another condition of formulating correct reading skills is related to the transition from the perception of isolated words to the perception of units at a higher level, for example, word combinations. Because of the child's established proficiency in oral discourse, as well as the recognition of significant elements of words, the child can cultivate the skills of grouping words in syllabic unity. These skills mainly engender semantic conjecture: they are the basis for deciding on the meaning of a succession of widely read parts, which, in turn, exerts considerable influence on the perceptions of subsequent elements of the text. Disabilities in this link of the reading process are categorized as "non-contextual perception of phrases" (Spirova, 1965). The basic dysfunction in this disability is the perception of every word as an individual, isolated unit; every word read is granted equal importance, and is not distinguished in the structure of the lexical-grammatical connection. One of the most typical manifestations of difficulty in this linguistic area is revealed by an insufficiently formulated vocabulary. The absence of adequate linguistic experience in this case deprives the child of the capability of forming correct assumptions about widely read elements of the text. As a result, reading takes on a guessing character. The rate of reading slows, and comprehension suffers.

In a number of cases, reading disabilities might be connected to certain difficulties in assimilating the lexical meanings of words. Disabilities at the level of the lexical system of a language might have a wide range of manifestations—from a complete absence of verbal coherence in the child's vocabulary to imprecise, fragmented, undifferentiated meanings. As a rule, these disabilities surface simultaneously with general difficulties at the morpho-syntactical level. The child often sees the appearance of a word in an altered form, a suffixed/prefixed transformation, and the like, as a new lexical entity. In these cases, understanding of the text proves to be vastly erroneous.

Various mechanisms might comprise reading disabilities, and outwardly similar manifestations might hide different types of structural defects. The remedial teaching of children with reading disabilities takes into account peculiarities of a structural defect and its specific manifestations. Remedial work proceeds simultaneously in oral discourse and in reading. Correcting defects of oral discourse creates the necessary conditions for formulating adequate reading skills.

PERSPECTIVES ON THE DEVELOPMENT OF THE SOVIET SCHOOL

Soviet schools share a common perspective with schools in all countries: to graduate uniformly educated pupils, while creating different types of schools, alternative programs, and alternative texts; to create material and spiritual opportunities for unfettered experimental searches for new forms and methods of teaching and educating. Psychology has accumulated a sufficient supply of ideas for implementing these goals.

NOTES

We would like to extend a special thanks to Dr. A. M. Matuchkin at the Pedagogical and General Psychology Institute in Moscow for his involvement in this project.

1. Elementary school teachers train in three-year pedagogical programs and/or in departments of elementary education in five-year pedagogical institutes that have day, evening, and correspondence divisions. The teacher in an elementary school conducts classes in all subjects (except for music, art, and physical education, if the school has teachers who specialize in these disciplines). In the secondary school, education is by subject; a teacher–philologist conducts classes in the native language and literature in several different grades. The teacher–philologist trains in the philology departments of pedagogical institutes and universities.

2. At that time, school education began at the age of seven; now these conclusions are also applied to six-year olds.

3. In philosophy, this means of extending the theory is usually given the Hegelian name "the ascent from the abstract to the concrete."

4. The usual number of years in the Soviet system of education—there are now eleven grades in some parts of the country (Translator's note).

5. Shifts in stress alter the pronunciation of Russian vowels. For example, an unstressed *o* would be pronounced *ah* (Translator's note).

REFERENCES

Aidarova, L. I. 1978. *Psikhologičeskije problemija mladšikh školnikov rodnomu jaziku.* Moscow.

Bakhtin, M. M. 1979. *Estetika slovesnovo tvorčestva.* Moscow.

Bondarenko, S. M. 1975. *Počemu detjam trudno učit' sja?* Moscow.

Bugrimenko, E. A., and Zuckerman, G. A. 1987. *Čtenije bez prinuždenija.* Moscow.

Davydov, V. V. 1986. *Problemi razvivajuševo obučenija.* Moscow.

Egorov, T. G. 1953. *Psikhologija ovladenija navikom čtenija.* Moscow.

El'konin, D. B. 1956. *Hekotorije voprosi psikhologii usvoenija gramoti.* "Voprosi psikhologii," no. 5.

El'konin, D. B. 1974. *Psikhologija obučenija mladševo škol'nika.* Moscow.

El'konin, D. B. 1976. *Kat učit' detjei' čitat'?* Moscow.

Granik, G. G. 1976. *Učitel', učebnik i škol'niki.* Moscow.

Granik, G. G. (red.) 1979. *Psikhologičeskije problemi postroeija škol'nikh učebnikov.* Moscow.

Granik, G. G., Bondarenko, S. M., and Kontsevaja, L. A. 1987. *Kak učit' škol'nikov rabotat' s učebnikom.* Moscow.

Granik, G. G., Bondarenko, S. M., and Kontsevaja, L. A. 1988. *Kogda kniga učit.* Moscow.

Hvatsev, M. E. 1959. *Logopedija.* Moscow.

Kudina, G. N., Melik-Pašaev, A. A., and Novljanskaja, Z. H. 1988. *Kak razvivat' chudožestbenhnoje vosprijatije i škol'nikov?* Moscow.

Lalayeva, R. I. 1983. *Narušsenije processa ovladenija čteniem i škol'nikov.* Moscow.

Levina, R. E. 1980. *Nedostatki čtenija i pis'ma u detjei'.* Moscow.

Levina, R. E. (red.) 1968. *Osnovi teorii i praktiki logopedii.* Moscow.

Luria, A. R. 1969. *Visšije korkovije funkcii čeloveka.* Moscow.

Markova, A. K. 1974. *Psikhologija usvoenija jazika kak sredstva obšženija.* Moscow.

Melik-Pašaev, A. A., and Novlyanskaya, Z. N. 1984. *Stupen'ki k tvorčestvu.* Moscow.

Spirova, L. F. 1965. *Nedostatki čtenija u detjei' i puti ikh preodolenija.* // *Nedostatki reči u učašžikhsja nacal'nikh klassov massovoi' školi* Moscow.

Tokareva, O. A. 1969. *Rasstroi'stva čtenija i pis'ma (disleksii i disgrafii).* //*Rasstroi'stva reči i detjei' i podrostkov* /S. S. Ljapidevskovo. Moscow.

Vygotsky, L. S. 1982. *Mislenije i reč'. Sobr. soč., T.2.* Moscow.

Vygotsky, L. S. 1983. *Istorija razvitija visšikh psikhičeskikh funktsij. Sobr. soč. T.3.* Moscow.

21

Switzerland

Jürgen Reichen
Translated by Susan Sokolowski

LANGUAGES OF THE COUNTRY

Tiny Switzerland, which lies in the middle of Europe, is bordered in the north by Germany, in the east by Austria, in the south by Italy, and in the west by France. These neighbors have greatly influenced the language of the Swiss. Switzerland has four spoken languages. The largest percentage of people, 65 percent, speak German; in the west on the border of France, 18 percent speak French; and in the south, in the neighborhood of Italy, Italian is spoken by 10 percent. In addition, a small minority, 1 percent, live in the mountainous region of Graubuden and speak Rhaeto-Romanic dialects, which is a dying language. In addition, a large percentage of foreigners (approximately 15 percent of the inhabitants) live in Switzerland and speak Spanish, Turkish, Yugoslavic, and Greek. These languages do not play a role in school classes. (On the basis of bilateral international treaties with the mother countries of foreign workers, foreign students can attend classes for a few hours a week where their mother language is spoken and teachers of their own nationality preside.) German, French, and Italian are used in the schools according to region.

It seems obvious that this Swiss peculiarity creates a large problem. In Switzerland a major difference exists between oral and written use of the language because the standard languages have validity only in the written field while in oral communication the regionally modified dialects are spoken. This especially applies to the German-speaking part of Switzerland where the standard language corresponds to the standard high language in Germany. However, the various Swiss dialects of the language deviate so greatly that it is known as Swiss-German and is hardly understood in Germany.

This difference between the native dialect and the standard language that is expected in school classes has caused a lasting Swiss conflict. Pupils and instructors tend to use their dialect instead of the standard language. Therefore, school officials regularly issue a summons in favor of the standard language; that is, the instructors are reminded that in school classes the standard language is the official language. It is feared that the uninhibited use of dialect in instruction could endanger the main teaching goal of instruction—competent use of the standard language. Only the standard language is used in communication between the different speaking areas of Switzerland, and the standard language, therefore, has significance for domestic politics. On the basis of Swiss foreign dependency on Germany, it is also important to international relations, and, not lastly, to business as well.

READING POLICY

Switzerland like the United States is a federal state. Corresponding to the fifty American states, Switzerland is partitioned into twenty-six cantons that have final responsibility for school and instruction. Therefore, the reading instruction, like all instruction, is decentralized. In addition, within the individual cantons there is no centralized procedure. In Switzerland the instructors have a so-called method freedom, which means that the individual instructor is personally free in choosing a method.

In contrast to some other states, especially the United States, instructors in Switzerland are very well paid. Teaching salaries in Switzerland are among the highest in the world. Accordingly, the qualification demands are also high. The individual instructor in Switzerland has a large amount of freedom in organizing and executing the lesson. For the first reading instruction, for example, every instructor personally decides which of several different teaching methods to employ. It is principally open to the instructor to go ahead with "self-discovered procedures" and with "self-organized instructional material."

GOALS OF READING EDUCATION

In Switzerland, the goals of reading education are the same for girls and boys. In addition, there are basically no differing goal settings between the school levels. In the area of the whole schools, client schools as well as higher schools, reading instruction has only two goals: (1) the pupils should learn to understand at an age or level appropriate to a text; and (2) the joy of reading should be awakened and strengthened among pupils. They should develop, when possible, pleasure in and understanding for both prose and poetry.

Despite the schools' earnest efforts, these goals have not been sufficiently reached. The success rate is relatively small and has been steadily declining in recent years. In the education recruiting tests, young soldiers in the army are annually asked about certain subjects that also change yearly. In the tests administered in 1984, only 17 percent of young Swiss could give the general meaning of a simple abstract newspaper article. In addition, only 38 percent understood the description of the Swiss federal railways in regard to subscription tariffs. Such numbers awaken deep concern. Directions like "Entrance Around the Corner" are read well enough, but the reading ability is not sufficient to understand a somewhat harder context. The level was even higher one hundred years ago and significantly higher before World War I. In 1879 two-thirds of all recruits received satisfactory grades, and in 1913 the proportion rose to nine-tenths. In the light of such relationships, it comes as no surprise that only a few Swiss are true readers. Those who read for enjoyment find themselves in the minority; their count can be approximately set at 10 percent of the adult population.

The above-mentioned goal settings also include foreign language instruction in the high schools; even there a large part of the instruction is concentrated on English, French, Spanish, and Italian literature. Nonetheless, there has been little success in motivating reading. The only form of reading education in adult education classes is literature. A general lecture and discussion of a text, or seminars on a unionized educational topic like the theme, "How One Reads a Newspaper," are examples of adult education.

In the area of learning to read, considerable efforts have been made throughout German-speaking Switzerland to put the first reading class on a solid foundation. Most of the fables that were used earlier and were rigidly tied to the so-called letter method (synthetic) or the whole word method (analytic) were removed by the first reading courses which were scientifically sound. As a result, three teaching methods have crystallized and now dominate the first reading lesson:

1. "Reading, Speaking, Action" by Professor H. Grissemann. This work is a Swiss product that represents a method-integrating procedure by which, in addition to letters and whole words, word parts, for example (syllables, morphemes, signal groups, segments, etc.), play an important role.

2. "The Reading Mirror" by Professor Dr. K. Meiers. This work is the Swiss modification of a German teaching procedure that follows the letter method but requires a high demand level and in particular assigns great meaning to the simultaneous action of the children's own writing.

3. "Reading Through Writing" by Dr. J. Reichen. This work is a Swiss product and applies a new method whereby the children learn to write before they read and the ability to read develops as a byproduct of the writing.

ILLITERACY

Until a few years ago, literacy was not a recognized topic in Switzerland. Had someone questioned the expansion of literacy in Switzerland in 1980, the unanimous answer would have been that there were no illiterate people in Switzerland. Since then the figures have changed drastically. Shocked by an article in the German news magazine *Der Spiegel*, which itself shocked Germany in

1983 with the realization that even in the highly developed industrial nations there is adult illiteracy, Switzerland had to realize that, despite the well-developed school system, some children remain illiterate, or at least fall into illiteracy after leaving school. At the time of the economic boom in the 1970s, enough work positions were available that illiterate people could survive in business in their secure niches. With the decline of economic growth and the onset of unemployment in Switzerland, however, illiteracy for those affected by it became a severe handicap that could no longer be hidden. Illiteracy became publicly recognized. Today there are about 20,000 to 30,000 adult Swiss known to be illiterate, but when we include the estimated number of unnotified cases, the actual count may be considerably higher.

How the illiterate are distributed among the different school levels has not been established. It is known that boys are more severely affected than girls. But there are no certainties because the topic is somewhat of a taboo. Those affected represent an embarrassment to their environment and to the schools they attend; therefore, a coalition of silence has arisen behind which the illiterate can hide themselves. Only recently has this taboo been lifted, and it is now apparent that, in the vocational schools, a large percent of the students who wish to pursue a teaching career have enormous difficulties with proper writing and reading skills. At the initiative of Professor H. Grissemann (Institute for Special Education at the University of Zurich) local initiative groups have been formed recently whose courses are organized and presented for adult illiterates. Meanwhile, the demand has exceeded the supply three times over. But in the absence of clear rules for financing, chance often determines whether or not a certain course can be taught. The authorities have been holding back, and because there are no legal foundations there has been no success for regular financing.

DIAGNOSIS OF READING DISABILITIES

In the past thirty years, illiteracy in Switzerland has been diagnosed and treated under the name dyslexia. Both the diagnosis and therapy have been moving on shaky ground. Depending on the interpretation of the term *dyslexia*, about 5 percent of all students are considered dyslexic in a strict sense. If we consider all those who are receiving therapy or at least tutoring, however, then the figure rises to 15 percent. (This total includes children of foreign workers who are counted in because of their insufficient knowledge of German.) Among the dyslexics, there are more boys than girls, the ratio being about 6:4. This estimate represents all age groups, and is more or less stable. The only difference in the age groups is a strong declining preparation or readiness for therapy in the boys; with age they lose the motivation to fight the dyslexia.

About thirty years ago, researchers were more certain about the causes of dyslexia. Today they have reached the point that in reality they know absolutely nothing as to its origins. Recently, authorities like Professor Hans Grissemann or Dr. Heinz Ochsner (the leader of the project for Preventive Instruction/Education Direction in Zurich) have pointed out the many discrepancies in dyslexia management in Switzerland in both the Swiss Teachers Newspaper and in other daily papers. They have begun to depart from the term *dyslexia*.

When we speak about dyslexia in this chapter, we will restrict our discussion to how the term is understood vis-à-vis Swiss customs regarding it. In Switzerland dyslexia is equated with a disability whose treatment is financed or in part subsidized by the state disability insurance. Through this financing, a rather extensive dyslexia operation has been established in the country. There are approximately 6,000 to 7,000 reading teachers and dyslexia therapists in German-speaking Switzerland.

Children who are found to have difficulties in reading or writing, or both, are suspected of being dyslexic and are sent to the school psychologist for tests. This testing previously extended to sensory and motor functions, intelligence, and personality traits. When a discrepancy is found between IQ and performances on a reading test, dyslexia is diagnosed. The diagnosis involves no standard procedure. Each school psychologist uses those tests that seem suitable. The German tests are usually chosen, the only Swiss product being Grissemann's Zurcher Reading Test.

If dyslexia is confirmed, the child receives therapy from a fully trained reading teacher or, in cases of less severe performance inabilities, tutoring with a so-called dyslexia therapist (mostly former teachers with additional schooling).

The remaining therapy for dyslexia consists of tests that deal mainly with sensory-motor functions whose goal is to improve performance and confidence. However, therapy is successful for only some dyslexics; another portion seems to remain resistant to therapy. These erratic results suggest that the diagnostic and therapeutic instruments are faulty. At the end of the 1970s many researchers had concluded that current ideas and practices were not appropriate for handling dyslexic learning problems. At that time, dyslexia was spoken of as an empty stereotype. Since then, a distinction has been drawn between actual primary and secondary dyslexia; its cause is seen as bad instruction, which is then considered didactic dyslexia.

In this situation demand has arisen for precise diagnoses, clear therapeutic concepts, and improved education for therapists and tougher controls. In many places education of new dyslexia therapists has been inhibited. School psychologists are more reserved in their diagnoses, and the dyslexia therapists have shifted their focus from specialized training programs to the psychological promotion of children with slow reading and writing abilities. It is still hoped that improving visual and auditory perceptions of alphabetical order, place and time organization, eye-following movements, and the like will directly influence cases of primary dyslexia. Today the primary language problem is clearly not being resolved through simple function exercises, and researchers are turning away from the unclear term of dyslexia. Replacing that term, at least until 1989, was the phrase "difficulties in the acquisition of the written language," which didn't really yield any new perceptions. For want of better solutions, the present concepts are being retained, and efforts are being made to overcome the problems associated with reading and writing difficulties.

READING READINESS PROGRAMS

Dyslexia appears to be Switzerland's only difficult problem in reading education. Specifically, Switzerland has no need of reading preparatory programs for students who have not yet had primary education. In Switzerland the law requires the registration of all inhabitants and on the basis of that registration all registered children must attend school. Since there are no children without primary education, reading preparatory programs are not necessary.

TEACHER QUALIFICATIONS

Teacher qualifications and teacher education, like the whole school system, are set by the cantons. Elementary school teachers are required to have twelve to thirteen years of education—that is, to have completed a high school degree or diploma. In addition, teachers must obtain two to three years of vocational education in a teaching seminar. Teachers on the secondary or tertiary level must complete a university specialized study, which contains one to two semesters of didactic education in a teaching seminar.

Adult education in Switzerland is over 90 percent private; of course, no state qualification rules pertain to the private sector. The individual volunteer organizers of educational offerings for adults make appointments to the teaching positions. Most of these appointees are former or still employed teachers.

Switzerland has no true reading teachers. In the area of reading science and dyslexia therapy, some teachers have additional education that deals with the teaching of reading, but within the boundary of therapy hours rather than the framework of a class.

When we consider the term *reading education* in a broader sense, then of course all teachers who teach languages and literature in the higher schools can be called reading teachers. The prerequisite here is a specialized study of the appropriate language and the educational didactic as is generally expected for teachers on the secondary and tertiary levels.

With regard to the gender of the teachers, there are greater percentages of women teachers on the elementary than high school level. For example, in kindergartens almost all the teachers are women—99 percent—and approximately 60 percent of teachers in primary schools are women. In contrast, there are 45 percent female teachers in secondary schools, 27 percent at the tertiary level, and only 17 percent in adult education.

READING MATERIALS

In advanced reading courses, literary texts are used most often, followed by magazine and newspaper articles. The texts are collected in so-called reading books that are available to each student free of charge. In some areas, a complete class series can be borrowed; that is, the same book can be lent in thirty copies. With the expansion of photocopying and the revised copyright protection, practically all schools have begun to photocopy classroom text materials for the students.

Photocopying has increased so greatly in recent years that publishers are having to face reduced sales of text collections, and the publication of such books is only possible through considerable state publishing grants. Educational political considerations have led various school officials to enforce the use of such text collections, with the result that they are handed over to the students and are hardly, if at all, taught in the class by the teachers.

Photocopy texts are issued in considerable quantity and quality, as well as in all the languages that are taught. All materials have been made usable today through copying or are easily replaced. When a particular state text doesn't please a teacher (and that is often the case) the teacher simply copies texts that seem suitable.

FINANCING READING EDUCATION

Only state schools are obliged to set obligatory school time. Reading education in Switzerland is almost completely funded by public monies. Libraries are also publicly funded because most libraries are controlled by the state.

A different situation pertains to adult education, which is handled mainly by private entities. The largest organizations holding training classes for adult education are the food and merchandise chains. The individual user pays for adult education.

RESEARCH THRUSTS IN READING

Despite its small size, Switzerland is a rich country and is able to support research in many areas. It has thus gained international recognition. Unfortunately, this success does not extend to educational research and particularly not to research in reading. Switzerland has no school for education research, other than rudimentary beginnings, and research in reading does not exist at all. Only the University of Zurich has done in-depth studies in this area. For example, in the related Department of Psychology, Professor F. Stoll is interested in questions of reading, and some of his students have written their licenses or dissertations on a related topic. Among these topics have been questions of reading techniques such as perception psychology and physiological assumptions (eye movement) in reading.

Similarly, at the Institute for Special Education, Professor H. Grissemann is focusing on questions about dyslexia (that is, origin, prevention, and cure) and functional illiteracy. At the journalists' seminar, Professor U. Saxer is working on questions about reading in the area of media science, the influence of television on reading, and the disruptive effects of television on the reading habit.

In addition smaller literary studies are occasionally developed as papers for a diploma at educational institutes for teachers, holistic teachers, and social workers (for example, teaching seminars, schools for social work, and holistic education seminars).

In the permanent investigation of education research and development projects, which the Swiss Coordinating Office for Education Research in Aarau leads, only coincidentally have papers on the topic of reading appeared. Individual papers exist without having reference to each other, and so there are no true disagreements between them. Only in four area has more than one paper been issued: surveys of dyslexia; analyses of the content of reading books, especially in regard to sex role cliches; evaluations of new primary reading methods; and studies of the reading situation in the time of mass television viewing. But these papers have not received scholarly recognition and so have had no influence on reading education in Switzerland. The country has no "flowing focal points" of reading research because there is no reading research.

THE READING OUTLOOK

Reading education may become a viable research area in Switzerland in the near future, for the following reasons.

1. The revelation that Switzerland has adult illiterates, that is, the phenomenon of secondary illiteracy or late dyslexia, has challenged the national pride of many Swiss. Media unions like the Swiss Workers Group consider these findings a scandal and are working toward a remedy.

2. The reversal of reading competency has not yet shocked education politics, but it has alarmed the culture politic. For example, the Swiss Young People's Book Institute in Zurich has begun a large study of the reading behavior of children and teenagers.

3. The recognition that the established therapy has not helped those with primary dyslexia has caused the disability insurance sector to question whether or not it has financed a useless effort and whether it should stay that way. Education seminars and educational institutes and dyslexia therapists, as the main recipients of this money, were alarmed by this situation. Even they, however, considered the possibility that the theories about dyslexia therapy and about the reading process might not agree.

4. The totally new reading method, Reading Through Writing, has shed new light on reading in many schools.

Adult illiteracy, the reversal of reading competence, and the failure of accepted therapies to deal with primary dyslexia serve as criticism of Switzerland's present reading program. Reading instruction and reading learning will likely attract scientific interest in Switzerland in the next five to ten years, and there will be a paradigmatic change in the theory of reading learning in the sense that the

primary orientation of reading education will be given up to the grapheme–
phoneme correspondence.

SUMMARY

Switzerland's schools are in the hands of the cantons; therefore, school systems
and reading education are highly decentralized.

The public schools have high standards. They are well equipped, there are no
school fees, and teachers are well paid and well qualified. There are few private
schools, and practically all children fulfill their educational obligation in public
schools.

Reading classes in these public schools did not present a problem until the
past few years. Dyslexia was the only clear indication that German-Swiss reading
education was inadequate. Dyslexia was also the only area where scientific
methods and standards were used.

Recently, indications have arisen that Swiss reading education is more troubled
than was earlier thought. Fewer pupils can understand the content of a text, and
fewer pupils enjoy reading or have interest in literature, both poetry and prose
all of which were the goals of German-Swiss reading education. Despite the
schools' extensive efforts in this area, these goals have not been met. Success
has been extremely limited, and schools can no longer depend on self-taught
abilities to understand texts. This represents not only a personal/cultural loss,
but also a difficult social disability.

The clearly stated decline of reading ability in adults and the symptoms in
Switzerland of functional illiteracy have given rise to a concern that new approaches in reading research are needed. The question is, which ones should be
adopted.

Although a generally accepted answer has not been found, the old questions
are being more strictly researched with scientific methods. There is a stronger
sense of understanding children's learning in general, and in particular the language information process and language thoughts in the child's growing development. New forms of primary reading classes and a concerted effort to overcome
the phenomenon of dyslexia are pioneer topics in this field.

BIBLIOGRAPHY

General

Baer, J. R., 1979. *The Reading Process in Children*. Basel/Weinheim: Beltz–Verlag.
Bonfadelli, H. 1988. *Reading Behavior in Children and Teenagers in Switzerland*. Zurich:
    Jugendbuch-Institut.
Gruber, Ch. 1984. *Reading and Understanding*. Zug: Verlag Klett and Balmer.
Saxer, U., and Bonfadelli, H. 1984. *Reading, Watching Television and Learning*. Zug:
    Verlag Klett and Balmer.

Saxer, U.; Bonfadelli, H.; and Hattenschwiler, W. 1980. *The Mass-Media in the Lives of Children and Teenagers.* Zug: Verlag Klett and Balmer.

Stoll, F. 1978. "Towards a Theory of Reading." *Bulletin de l'Association Beige pour la lecture* 3.

Tauber, M. 1984. *Reading Understandability: The Influence of Reading Abilities Using Newspaper Articles.* Frankfurt/Nancy/New York: Lang–Verlag.

Dyslexia

Grissemann, H. 1984. *Late Dyslexia and Functional Illiteracy.* Bern/Stuttgart/Toronto: Huber–Verlag.

Grissemann, H., and Linder, M. 1980. *The Zurcher Reading Test.* Bern/Stuttgart/Toronto: Huber–Verlag.

Ochsner, H. 1988. *Dyslexia–What Is It?* Zurich: Padagogische Abteilung Erziehungsdirektion.

Wettstein, P. 1980. *School Attempts at Individual Research of Primary School Children with Reading and Writing Disabilities by Teachers and Parents.* Zurich: Heilpadagogisches Seminar.

Teaching Sources

Grissemann, H. 1980. *Reading-Writing-Business.* Lucerne: Interkantonale Lehrmittelzentrale.

Ochsner, H. 1977. *Better Reading and Writing.* Winterthur: Schubiger–Verlag.

Reichen, J. 1987. *Reading Through Writing.* Zurich: Sabe–Verlag.

Daily Papers

Schmidt, A. 1987. "Who Reads Today?" *Wochenendbeilage der Basler-Zeitung*, No. 40 (October): 3.

Ulrich, A. K. 1988. "No Reading Without Books." *Neue Zurcher Zeitung* No. 140, S. 25, (June): 18–19.

22

United Kingdom

L. John Chapman

INTRODUCTION

The shape and pattern of educational services in the United Kingdom has changed dramatically beginning in the 1980s. These changes have occurred in response to the central government's use of political power in ways that run contrary to established educational practice. For example, control of the curriculum and the teaching methods employed were once the prerogative of the school headteacher or principal in association with the school governing body. In the main, school governors were content to leave these matters to headteachers and their staff. Now the Education Reform Act has imposed a central or core curriculum with suggested content and a time allocation to various curriculum subjects. At the same time regional control has declined through the Local Education Authorities (LEAs) with moves to involve the schools themselves much more in their own administration. Thus, at the end of the 1980s the maintained section of education found itself with an entirely new set of regulations and relationships in the form of a national curriculum that was to be introduced by the National Curriculum Council in September 1989.

The predominant feature of the United Kingdom's educational scene today is the central government's determined drive for reform which it claims reflects the will of the people. Part of this reform effort is concerned with maintaining adequate standards of literacy and its teaching.

In addition to changes in educational provision, we will consider the effects of the changing theoretical perspectives that inform the study of reading and its associated skills. Although the focus of this chapter is on reading and the teaching of reading, it is impossible to disassociate reading from the other factors of language, namely, listening, speaking, and writing. In certain sections of the

Figure 22.1
Sizes of the Main Ethnic Groups Comprising the "Non-White" Population in Great Britain, 1983–1985

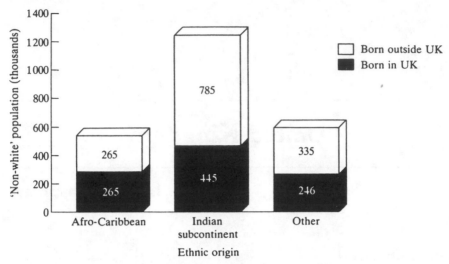

Source: From Statham et al., *The Education Fact File: A Handbook of Education Information in the UK*, 2d ed. (London: Hodder and Stoughton, 1990).

chapter, therefore, these will play significant roles. The term *literacy* is also used from time to time to indicate that both reading and writing are being considered.

THE LANGUAGES OF THE BRITISH ISLES

English is, of course, the dominant language of the British Isles, and it has almost become a world language. It is therefore easy to forget that there have always been other languages that reflect distinct cultures within the kingdom. Welsh is highly prized and robustly supported in Wales, as is Gaelic in parts of Scotland and to an extent in Northern Ireland. Welsh and Gaelic also have strong literary traditions that have played a significant part in their individual cultures for centuries. However, the largest proportion of the population—some 47.3 million out of the total of 56.8 million—lives in England and so English is the mainstream language.

A number of other languages have been brought to the country by the large number of immigrants who have settled in the United Kingdom since World War II (see Figure 22.1). The figure shows that immigrants into the United Kingdom were largely, though not exclusively, of Afro-Caribbean or Indian origin. However, there is lack of information as to the number of children speaking languages other than English in the home. In 1982, in response to a Department of Education and Science (DES) inquiry to Local Education Authorities (LEAs) concerning a directive from the Council of the European Commission about the education of migrant workers, it was found that of the total school population of children in the United Kingdom between the ages of five and sixteen years, approximately 4 percent (375,000 children) came from homes where English was not the first language, and more than half of these lived in just twelve LEAs. The geographical distribution was quite uneven; there were less than a thousand in Northern Ireland but one in seven in Greater London. The survey also showed that twenty-five different languages were taught to more than 43,000 children in the United Kingdom. Clearly, then, it is misleading to think that the Kingdom has a totally monolingual situation.

CENTRAL AND LOCAL ADMINISTRATION OF EDUCATION

The locus of control in education has shifted in recent years. The central government has brought in new legislation that has strengthened the control of the governing bodies of individual schools in the form of Local Management of Schools (LMS) and is in the process of introducing a central core curriculum together with new assessment systems. The governing bodies have been enlarged, and responsibilities for using resources, enrollment of pupils, and curriculum content are now much more their concern. This change has lessened the power of the LEAs, which were previously concerned more directly with the administration and control of the schools, and increased the responsibilities of the individual school. Indeed, after going through a number of important procedures, schools can opt out of local control altogether and become financed by a direct central government grant.

It would give a false picture, however, to allow the impression to remain that all schooling in the United Kingdom is in the government-maintained sector. There has been a long tradition of expensive private education in the United Kingdom and the misleadingly called "public" schools like Eaton, Rugby, and Harrow have educated a so-called elite of a nation whose people have long been stratified in a class system. Although there are signs that the rigidity of the class system is lessening, the public schools and the many smaller private schools continue to flourish. They are seen as sometimes being competitive and sometimes complementary with parents moving their children between the two systems as they seek "the best" education for their children (Johnson, 1987).

THE ORGANIZATION OF SCHOOLS

According to statistics supplied by the DES, in 1987 the United Kingdom had some 36,000 schools with 9.5 million pupils. These children are taught by a teaching force of 540,000 teachers. A certain amount of preschooling or kindergarten schooling is provided, but national coverage is by no means complete and there are considerable regional variations. LEAs are under no obligation to provide education below the age of five, but some do.

Some regions have centers for teaching English as a second language to children whose mother tongue was not English prior to their enrollment in the ordinary school system. In 1986 fourteen such centers catered for secondary- as well as primary-aged children.

Compulsory schooling begins at age five. Primary education, the first stage, begins at five years and continues in most schools until eleven years of age in England, Wales, and Northern Ireland. In Scotland children attend primary school from five to twelve years of age. Almost all primary schools are now mixed sex schools. "In 1985 there were nearly 25,000 maintained primary schools, including 648 middle schools, deemed primary. Almost all are mixed-sex schools. Between them they taught 4.4 million children. Non-maintained (or private schools) accounted for another 114,000 or so children of primary age" (Statham et al., 1989, p. 62).

The second stage of education continues until age sixteen years, but children can stay on voluntarily until they are nineteen years of age. In the maintained sector, following the 1944 Education Act, a tripartite system existed. Grammar schools provided mainly an academic education for those selected by ability; secondary modern schools offered a general education for those not attending grammar schools; and technical schools (only a few in number) had, as the name suggests, a technical bias. In Scotland the nomenclature is different (the term *grammar school* is not used there), with senior secondary schools and junior secondary schools covering the age range. In Northern Ireland, a selective system still operates, and the grammar secondary schools (with some fee-paying pupils) are nearly equivalent to the grammar schools in England and Wales. The secondary intermediate schools are similar to the secondary modern schools. This school organization has been disappearing in recent years until by 1985 84.5 percent of schools in England were selective comprehensive schools that accepted children of all levels of ability. In Scotland, 96.4 percent are comprehensive, and in Northern Ireland, which still retains its largely selective system, 88.3 percent of pupils go to secondary intermediate schools and 11.7 percent to grammar secondary schools. Some children go on to Sixth Form Colleges after sixteen years of age where these are available. These colleges educate young people for A-level certificates, which are needed for university admittance or entrance to other tertiary level education. In 1986 there were 108 such colleges with 64,000 pupils in the sixteen- to nineteen-year-old group.

Between 1971 and 1986 the number of grammar, secondary modern, and technical schools decreased, and a corresponding rise in the number of comprehensive schools took place. The period was also characterized by school closures as the number of children of compulsory school age fell.

Alongside this pattern of school organization some schools cater for children with special needs. In 1985 there were 1,958 special schools for the handicapped in the United Kingdom including 113 hospital schools and 103 assisted independent schools. Three-quarters of the 129,000 children attending these schools go on a daily basis with the remainder boarding.

THE GOALS OF READING INSTRUCTION

As indicated earlier, the central government's intervention in curriculum has had a marked effect on literacy education. Traditionally, central governments have set up committees of inquiry to investigate and report to the minister, now the secretary of state for education and science, on a number of topics concerned with the content and teaching of subjects in the school curriculum. These reports have been influential, and their recommendations have been implemented to a lesser or greater extent. If the recommendations have not been carried out, it is mainly due to the cost of the in-service training of teachers needed to implement the changes. Over the years a number of these official reports pertaining to literacy have been issued. Perhaps the most influential, until this year, was the report of the committee of inquiry into the teaching of English entitled *A Language for Life* (DES, 1975). This committee was chaired by Sir Alan, now Lord, Bullock and is often referred to as the Bullock Report. Before giving the committee's recommendations, it is important to point out that in the maintained sector of education in the United Kingdom there are no teachers whose only concern is the teaching of reading, apart from those who specialize in teaching children with reading or language disability. In the secondary school, reading comes under the purview of the English teacher whose main task is to teach English Literature. In the primary school there is little specialization apart from music and some physical education, although recent restructuring of teacher responsibilities requires each teacher in a primary school to have a subject speciality. However, primary teachers are responsible for all subjects of the curriculum. Until the late 1970s it was generally acknowledged that the teaching of reading was almost the sole job of the infant school teacher.

The Bullock committee made seventeen principal recommendations to the secretary of state for education. Among these was a proposal for a new monitoring system to be set up to assess "a wider range of attainments than has been attempted in the past and allow new criteria to be established for the definition of literacy." Another recommendation was the encouragement of preschool or nursery education where language could be encouraged to develop, and it was also proposed that every school should have "an organised policy for language across the curriculum, establishing every teacher's involvement in language and reading development throughout the years of schooling." Additional assistance was called for to help children who were "retarded in reading," and it was recommended that every LEA should have a reading clinic or center that provided a comprehensive diagnostic service and other expert advice. An increase in the provision for adults with low levels of literacy was called for, as was the need for substantial and sustained tuition in English for children from overseas. A recommendation for further in-service training opportunities in reading was proposed as was a national center for language in education.

The report tried to set the goals for reading instruction and while there is evidence of the effects of some of these recommendations, in the main most of them had substantial resource implications. Since finance was not forthcoming, few have been fully implemented.

The Kingman Report

One of the major concerns of the Thatcher government was to improve the teaching of English in schools. There was a strong feeling that modern progressive teaching had caused a drop in standards and that there should be a return to the more formal teaching of subjects like grammar and spelling of earlier times. The debate over the teaching of grammar has been long and is still raging, as the following rhetoric illustrates:

Among English teachers themselves, the battle is won—no one believes in teaching grammar to improve written composition. But what of others, . . . with power and influence over education, who loudly proclaim otherwise? . . . we cannot answer that, for to these people learning of grammar represents a disciplining of the flesh, a punishing of the rebellious spirit, and the ultimate guarantee of a stable society. In its very uselessness lies much of its value. (Wilkinson, 1986, p. 35)

The "back to the basics" movement is not unknown in other countries, but dissatisfaction with schools is particularly strong in the United Kingdom at the present time. Consequently, a committee of inquiry was set up in 1987 "to recommend a model of the English language as a basis for teacher training and professional discussion, and to consider how far and in what ways the model should be made explicit to pupils at various stages of education" (DES, 1988a, p. 1).

This official committee of inquiry into the teaching of English was chaired by a mathematician, Sir John Kingman. Its report (DES, 1988a) is much shorter than the Bullock Report and takes a different stance. The report has its problematic aspects, but the following comments are generally agreed to be in line with what is presently considered good practice in the teaching of English.

- there should be no return to formal, old-fashioned grammar teaching.
- the model of language which teachers and pupils need is one of language in use.
- knowledge about language should not be "bolted-on" to the curriculum, but should inform all language work in the classroom.
- teachers should use their own judgement in deciding how and when knowledge about language should be made explicit to students.
- the assessment of explicit knowledge about language should be largely the province of individual teachers and institutions.

- there should be funding for all teachers to undertake a course in knowledge about language.

- a National Language Project should be established.

- the model proposed in the Kingman Report is for discussion and debate, not instant implementation.

- to produce or use textbooks based on comprehension exercises or multiple choice questions would be to ignore the spirit of the recommendations. (*The English Magazine* 1988, p. 4)

As noted above, the report proposes a model of language that will, it suggests, inform English language teaching. The model is divided into four parts: (1) forms of language; (2) communication and comprehension; (3) acquisition and development; and (4) historical and geographical variation. In the report, the model is represented in tabular form, giving both the implicit knowledge of language (knowing how) and explicit knowledge about language. It also provides a series of attainment targets for children to reach at seven, eleven, and sixteen years. The detailed working of national testing is the concern of a task force appointed by the secretary of state for education and science. The proposals from this English working group are to be considered by the National Curriculum Council which has been asked to ensure that the attainment targets for the teaching of standard English ''are sufficiently precise for the purposes of assessment'' and ''to ensure that grammatical structure and terminology are appropriately reflected.''

Toward the end of 1988, the goals for the teaching of English were being specified by the central government as the national curriculum was introduced. As already observed, this is an entirely new experience for teachers in the United Kingdom. Some of the proposals for the age group five to eleven years follow as an example of these developments.

Proposals for English for Ages Five to Eleven

Another official report (DES, 1988c), which gives the proposals of the secretaries of state education and science and for Wales, outlines the attainment targets (ATs) for the age group five to eleven years. A further document for the secondary years was promised in 1989. It was envisaged that attainment targets would be set for the ages seven, eleven, fourteen, and sixteen. These would be grouped as profile components so as to make the teachers' tasks of assessment and reporting manageable. A ten-point scale covering the years of compulsory schooling was proposed as were national external tests together with the judgment of teachers. The document gives Profile components, attainment targets, and programs of study for the age range. Of the six ATs in speaking and listening, reading, and writing proposed, this chapter concentrates only on those that apply to reading. These are summarized as

ATTAINMENT TARGET I: The development of the ability to read, understand, and respond to all types of writing.

ATTAINMENT TARGET II: The development of reading and information-retrieval strategies for the purpose of study (DES, 1988c).

The associated program of study is divided into five levels for each of the ATs. As these will form the reading curriculum for primary schools in the near future, they are given in full below. The ATs for secondary schools were not available at the time of writing. (It should be noted that at present these ATs have the status of proposals only, but the Education Reform Act has established a national curriculum of which these will be a part.) It is clear that these ATs will become the goals of reading instruction in U.K. schools.

Attainment Target I

LEVEL	DESCRIPTION
1	Recognize that print conveys meaning (e.g. by turning to them readily, looking at, and talking about illustrations).
	Show signs of developing an interest in books.
	Respond positively to being read to (e.g., by listening attentively and by asking for more).
	Show a developing sight vocabulary (i.e., of words recognized on sight).
2	Demonstrate an interest in stories and poems (e.g., by becoming engrossed when reading to themselves and by enjoying listening to stories and poems).
	Say what has happened and what may happen in stories.
	Show some understanding of the feelings and motives of characters.
	Choose favorite stories and poems.
	Express opinions on what they have read.
	Read familiar stories and poems aloud with reasonable fluency and accuracy.
	Display increasing independence, confidence, fluency, accuracy, and understanding in reaching meaning in new reading material by using effectively more than one cueing strategy.
	Demonstrate a sight vocabulary drawn from all areas of the curriculum and from out-of-school experience.
3	Engage in sustained silent reading of stories.
	Read aloud from familiar stories and poems fluently with appropriate expression.
	Make confident and effective use of a variety of cueing strategies and reading experience to reach meaning.
	Make some use of inference, deduction, and reading experience to reach meanings that are beyond the literal.

Show developing understanding of the settings of stories, of how key events impinge on characters and of the reasons for their actions.

Continue to listen attentively to stories, showing an ability to recall details and a developing ability to discuss various aspects of stories.

4   Read regularly over a widening range of prose and verse.

Give reasons for establishing preferences.

Draw on reading experience to make comparisons and note parallels.

Show a developing familiarity with a number of basic kinds of narrative (children's fiction, legend, fable, folk tale, fantasy, science fiction, etc.)

Read aloud with increasing confidence and fluency from a range of familiar literature with appropriate expression.

Discuss aspects of a variety of books and poems in some detail, expressing opinions and providing supporting evidence from the text.

5   Read regularly and voluntarily over a still wider range of prose and verse.

Show developing tastes and preferences over an increased range of material.

Display fluency, adaptability, and accuracy when developing a range of reading strategies, whether reading to themselves or aloud.

Show through discussions that they can use text to infer, deduce, predict, compare and evaluate.

Attainment Target II

LEVEL   DESCRIPTION

1   Demonstrate awareness of language in the environment (names, labels, signs, etc).

Display interest in the information content of fiction and nonfiction.

Ask and answer questions on points of information.

2   Read accurately straightforward signs, labels, and notices.

Read and understand straightforward descriptions, explanations, or instructions in appropriate school books and in the environment.

Demonstrate knowledge of the alphabet and its application (e.g., in word books, dictionaries, and reference books).

3   Use well-selected information books in the classroom collection and in the school library.

Provide independently answers to simple questions when using appropriate preselected reference and information sources.

Select and use appropriate information and reference books from the class and school library to pursue a simple line of inquiry, showing their understanding that information is organized systematically.

Turn readily to printed information sources to answer their own questions, without verbatim copying.

4   Make effective use of alphabetical order, a list of contents, an index, and keys of symbols and abbreviations in appropriate reference books.

Select and employ appropriate reference books (from the classroom collection, school library, and public library junior section) sufficiently to pursue a reasonably sustained line of inquiry.

Use the classification system and catalogue of the school library.

Demonstrate when to skim, to scan, and to read closely.

5   Select and use appropriate referencing skills when pursuing an independent line of inquiry.

Respond to the flagging and organizational devices offered in information books (chapter titles, paragraph headings, italic and boldface print, diagrams, illustrations, etc.) and other printed matter.

Begin, in discussion, to evaluate information sources and critically to weigh evidence and argument.

ADULT LITERACY

In many industrialized countries, the United Kingdom and other European countries, the United States and Australia, there has been a growing concern for those in the adult community with low levels of literacy. Some employers have always complained about low literacy, at least since 1921, but getting help for this segment is a recent phenomenon, at least in the United Kingdom. Before 1975 apart from the help given to those in prison and in the forces, little was done about this problem. However, a national body, the British Association of Settlements, which represents many voluntary bodies, carried out a successful political campaign from 1973 to 1975 to raise public awareness of literacy problems among adults in the country. This campaign resulted in some action being taken, but the amount of money granted by the central government to help was limited and was granted for one year only. Nonetheless, it did assist those involved in setting up a central unit, and in 1975 the British Broadcasting Company (BBC) also became involved. It transmitted a series of innovative television programs called "On the Move" at peak viewing times on a Sunday evening. As a result of these programs and the referral service to which they were linked, some 55,000 adults (Wells, 1987) received help with reading and writing by March of the following year. The programs also helped lessen the stigma attached to being unable to read and write.

As this work continued, many began to realize that a problem of greater complexity and magnitude existed than had been appreciated before. It was found that many, often quite different, needs were being voiced. Some adults were almost completely illiterate, some could read haltingly, and others needed help with writing and spelling. As the needs varied, so did the motivation to improve.

One interesting feature of the composition of the groups seeking help was the small number of young adults involved. Wells (1957) expressed these two features, the many reasons for the underrepresentation of younger adults, and the growing size of the number seeking help, as follows:

Early BBC publicity . . . tended to feature older men (and) Sunday evening television was not likely to be watched by many young people. The memories of unsatisfactory school experiences were also likely to be strongest among those who had left compulsory schooling relatively recently and, clearly, many wanted to forget about reading-and-writing problems. . . . The mid 1970s was also a time of relatively low unemployment in the UK and, thus, most school-leavers found it fairly easy to obtain work that demanded little in the way of formal educational skills. Moreover it was relatively easy to change jobs. . . . . . between 1975 and 1978 the number of new students seeking help with literacy . . . were as follows:

1975/1976, 38,000 (estimated);

1976/1977, 46,119; and

1977/1978, 36,054.

By 1978, almost 70,000 adults were receiving help to improve their reading and writing at any one time in England and Wales (. . . provision in Scotland was different) (Wells, 1987, pp. 260–261).

As the program continued, more innovation and experiment and a concern for more than literacy skills were evinced. As a result, the Adult Literacy and Basic Skills Unit (ALBSU) came into being in 1980. At this time unemployment was increasing, and in particular young people were found to be very vulnerable. Those with low basic skills found their job position very precarious. Here it should be noted that many young school leavers in the United Kingdom tend to go directly into employment (in 1981 some 44 percent compared with 7 percent in the Federal Republic of Germany) and because of the worsening situation in the early 1980s the central government established the Youth Opportunities Program (YOP). This later became the Youth Training Scheme (YTS), which was designed to provide training and work experience, including reading and writing, over a two-year period.

A report issued in 1987 raised further concern about what appeared to be a growing number of adults with low levels of literacy and numeracy. This report was particularly interesting as it showed that the problem could not be regarded as a temporary one that could be solved by short campaigns. Evidence from the United Kingdom and other countries indicates that it is a cultural and not simply a remedial problem.

The data in the report were derived from the sample of the nation's population chosen for the National Child Development Study (NCDS). This is a longitudinal survey of all people born in England, Scotland, and Wales in the week March 3–9, 1958. Several "sweeps of interviewing" have been carried out on subsets of this important sample; the latest one, in 1981, was of a group of twenty-three year olds. Out of the 12,500 interviewed, some 13 percent reported difficulties with numeracy and literacy. These results were first published in a short report by Simonite (1983).

An outcome of this report was the decision to go further, and a follow-up study was designed to explore

1. the everyday practical problem that people with numeracy and literacy difficulties report most often. (Of obvious relevance to educators and trainers)

2. [whether there] are particular groups who report difficulties with basic skills but who are under-represented at the moment. (This having course design implications)

3. [predictions as to] who will have difficulties with numeracy and literacy in adulthood. (The NCDS having assembled a great deal of information about social background and educational experience) (Hamilton and Stasinopoulos, 1987, p. 5)

The report presents the findings in these three areas with some confidence, for on examining the NCDS data the project team found that practical problems had been very well documented. Therefore, they were able to go further with their own interviews using the NCDS as a firm base. The first query as to the practical problem experienced was, as expected, work related and referred mostly to men.

The second area of exploration asked whether particular groups were involved. The report separates out those who report difficulties and were having or have had help from those who reported problems and had not sought help. Unfortunately, this proved to be unreliable for the following reasons:

1. Tuition was not necessarily Adult Basic Education (ABE) tuition, but might have referred to some general course of education or training which might have had elements of literacy or numeracy within it.

2. Some people who had had individual tuition might not have identified this as a "course" and so these students would be under-represented.

3. Many people who did not report problems with basic skills said they had attended courses to get better at reading, writing and maths. In the case of maths this group was over 50% of those who had attended courses. This is further evidence that people were not always referring to ABE tuition (Hamilton and Stasinopoulos, 1987, p. 11).

Owing to the short time scale given for the research, the predictive value of the results is only touched on, but, given the size and detail available in the NCDS data, there are obvious important pressing reasons to pursue this line of investigation. Figure 22.2 illustrates the details of those reporting difficulties.

Another diagram in the report shows that of the 13 percent of twenty-three year olds reporting difficulties, more were men than women. Men were more likely to report reading and writing problems, but men and women were equally likely to report numeracy problems. The report also shows that "men were twice as likely as women to have received help with reading and writing difficulties and 4 times as likely to have received help with numeracy."

The economic situation of adults with low levels of literacy was clearly a

Figure 22.2
Distribution of 1,676 Individuals with Basic Skills Difficulties

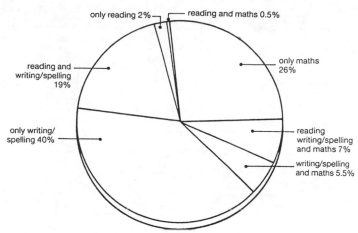

Source: M. Hamilton and M. Stasinopoulos, *Literacy, Numeracy and Adults* (London: Adult Literacy and Basic Skills Unit, 1987), p. 15.

factor in the findings. Research in the United Kingdom classifies occupational types according to the Register General's classification of socioeconomic groups. Although not perfect, this is a standard procedure in the United Kingdom and Tables 22.1 and 22.2 are organized using these classifications.

Table 22.1 shows that among women, personal service, that is, domestic and catering jobs and skilled and semiskilled manual jobs are involved more than those in the other categories. Of the men reporting difficulties, "personal service, foremen, all manual and agricultural workers are over-represented."

When the twenty-three-year-olds were interviewed about their difficulties, only one in three was able to articulate them as far as giving details of the practicalities of everyday work was involved. Several "hinted at . . . general feelings of failure and lack of confidence," and it is thought that more sensitive questioning would produce different results.

The literacy problems reported are set out in Table 22.2, and, as will be seen, the category with the largest percentage is that labeled "No Spec. Context." One of the interesting and perhaps unexpected findings is the extent of the writing and spelling problems reported. As noted above, the BBC has recently launched a series of programs to help with spelling problems. However, those with reading difficulties, the report points out, "appear to be a more seriously disadvantaged group than those with writing difficulties." Men and women appear to have different basic skills difficulties. Obviously, more information is needed to help solve the literacy and numeracy problems that some adults face. In addition, more information is needed on the problems faced by groups in the ethnic community.

Table 22.1A
Employment Experience: Current or Last Job of Men in the Cohort

	No Problems	Basic Skills Problems
Professional	649 (12%)	50 (5%)
Inter Non-Manual	655 (13%)	39 (4%)
Junior Non-Manual	701 (13%)	61 (6%)
Personal Service	101 (2%)	20 (2%)
Foremen Manual	325 (6%)	92 (9%)
Skilled Manual	1390 (27%)	333 (34%)
Semi-Skilled Manual	557 (11%)	180 (18%)
Unskilled Manual	235 (5%)	88 (9%)
Own Account	244 (5%)	41 (4%)
Agricultural Workers	126 (2%)	31 (3%)
Armed Forces	120 (2%)	22 (2%)
Never Employed	125 (2%)	19 (2%)
Total	5228 (100%)	976 (100%)

Table 22.1B
Employment Experience: Current or Last Job of Women in the Cohort

	No Problems	Basic Skills Problems
Professional	291 (5%)	16 (2%)
Inter Non-Manual	1414 (25%)	89 (13%)
Junior Non-Manual	2245 (40%)	202 (29%)
Personal Service	492 (9%)	90 (13%)
Foreman Manual	36 (1%)	8 (1%)
Skilled Manual	207 (4%)	35 (5%)
Semi-Skilled Manual	567 (10%)	176 (25%)
Unskilled Manual	83 (1%)	28 (4%)
Own Account	62 (1%)	12 (2%)
Agricultural Workers	40 (1%)	9 (1%)
Armed Forces	14 (1%)	—
Never Employed	106 (2%)	28 (4%)
Total	5557 (100%)	693 (100%)

Source: Hamilton and Stasinopoulos, *Literacy, Numeracy and Adults*, pp. 26–27.

Table 22.2
Difficulties in Everyday Life Caused by Literacy Problems

Type of Difficulty Reported	Number reporting difficulties
At Work	22%
Getting Jobs	10%
At Home - Children	2%
H-Hold Management	2%
Other Context	2%
No Spec. Context	74%
Leisure Arts	7%
Total	359 (100%)

"Missing Values": This question was answered "yes" by 29 percent of the group who reported problems with reading and/or writing.
Source: Hamilton and Stasinopoulos, *Literacy, Numeracy and Adults,* p. 18.

Adult Literacy Centers

People who need help are advised through BBC programs to make telephone contact with centers that hold regular meetings for adults requiring assistance. These centers are more often than not run by LEAs, although some centers are run by voluntary organizations. The tuition is usually given in the evening, and much use is made of volunteer tutors.

Once adults seeking help have overcome their initial embarrassment of attending a center, much of the stigma they feel is attached to their disabilities begins to disappear. The next problem faced by the center organizer is to match each of them with individual tutors; this matching together with the calibre of the tutor is of prime importance. On questioning a group of adults recently it was found that all named their individual tutor as the most significant factor in their progress. The conversation also made clear that the fact that another member of the community would give of their time and expertise voluntarily to help them made all the difference.

More will be done for those having literacy problems as the emphasis on training increases in the coming years. The Man Power Services and the Training agencies will place greater stress on these needs in the United Kingdom's workforce.

DIAGNOSIS OF READING DISABILITIES AND THE NATIONAL MONITORING OF READING

One recommendation from the Bullock Report that was adopted and resourced was the setting up of a national monitoring system to carry out surveys of language, mathematics, science, and foreign language performance across the nation.

The DES set up the Assessment of Performance Unit (APU) in 1975 ahead of the publication of the report. By 1983 the APU had made ten national surveys, five involving pupils aged eleven years and five of pupils aged fifteen years. The APU's terms of reference were to "promote the development of methods of assessing and monitoring the achievement of children in school, and seek to identify the incidence of underachievement." To carry out this charge, the unit saw its work in monitoring language performance as consisting of the four following tasks:

1. To identify and appraise existing instruments and methods of assessment which may be relevant for these purposes.
2. To sponsor the creation of new instruments and techniques of assessment, having due regard to statistical and sampling methods.
3. To promote the conduct of assessment in co-operation with LEAs and teachers.
4. To identify significant differences of achievement related to the circumstances in which children learn, including the incidence of underachievement, and to make the findings available to those concerned with resource allocation within government departments, LEAs and schools. (Gorman et al., 1988, p. 1)

Although the APU had a wider brief, in this chapter we concentrate on the work of monitoring language performance and, in particular, reading. A review of the surveys of language performance carried out by the unit over the years 1979–1983 gives some idea of the way in which the terms of reference were interpreted and the results that were forthcoming.

The unit acknowledged its origins in the report *A Language for Life* (DES, 1975) and set out to discover whether "the level of reading performance in schools was adequate to the demands of schooling and purposes outside it." Two important innovations in national assessment procedures came out of the discussions that the APU team and the Steering Committee had with Her Majesty's Inspectors of Schools, LEA advisers, and academics. These innovations were to collect information about pupils' attitudes and preferences and to collect writing from everyday classroom situations. While to leave out the writing and oracy assessment is to give only part of the picture, this chapter only has space to focus on the surveys of reading performance and attitudes to reading carried out by the unit.

The reading tests devised by the APU are unlike most previous reading tests given to children for similar purposes. Wherever possible the team attempted to make the reading passages used coherent in structure and content so as not to resemble the old-style sentence and paragraph tests. They noted that most of the material children are expected to read falls into three broad categories: works of reference, works of literature, and types of material read outside school for everyday life purposes.

The team produced a series of reference test booklets containing a range of materials organized so as to relate to a central theme. The passages in the booklets contained contents pages, an index, and page or chapter headings. Illustrations included graphs, diagrams, tables, and maps. The booklets were so designed as to involve increasing levels of difficulty, which, in turn, were reflected in the types of questions asked at each stage.

The reading material concerned with literature included reading that was, as far as possible, complete in itself. This included poems or short stories as well as extracts from a number of different sources. These collections led to a variety of question types.

The booklets reflecting everyday reading needs outside school contained extracts from comics, magazines, or newspapers and listings of different kinds. One such test, for example, was concerned with travel and included a brochure containing geographical and historical information as well as a description of amenities available together with a map and a booking form. Another test was in magazine format.

The team tried to vary the method of response. Although the majority of responses were the traditional question type, pupils were asked, for example, to fill in forms and tables and to label diagrams. In asking questions, the team's guiding principle was that the questions "should be similar to those that an experienced teacher would be likely to ask pupils taking account of the subject matter, the form and function of the reading material, and the context in which it is likely to be encountered."

Reading Performance at Age Eleven

Overall, the monitoring from 1979 to 1983 revealed that very few children were unable to decode familiar words, but many misunderstood what they read. The reasons the team gave for this misunderstanding are very informative and are consequently given verbatim.

We (that is the team) noted, for example, a tendency of lower-performing pupils to impose a literal interpretation on what they read, with a consequent failure to interpret a writer's unstated assumptions and beliefs. We noticed also a failure on the part of many pupils to understand the implications of variations in the style and tone of what was written, particularly in works of literature. In dealing with reference materials many pupils had difficulty in locating and selecting evidence that was relevant to issues in question, and in reconstructing such information and presenting it in a form appropriate to the purposes they had in mind. Good readers, in contrast, are generally willing to modify their initial interpretations of what they read, as they read, and to integrate information given at different points in the manner required by the tasks set. (Gorman et al., 1988, p. 7)

At eleven years of age, the surveys show that only one child in a hundred responded at a 10 percent or less success rate to questions about what they had read. However, as the team points out, this did not mean that the pupils understood the range of meanings the writer wanted to convey. In commenting on this matter, the team gave the following information:

- with both expository and literary materials children could locate and interpret accurately explicitly stated information at the 80–90% success rate.
- main themes were easily distinguishable by most pupils and about two-thirds could extract the gist of a passage.
- most could reject or confirm a proposition from evidence they had read as long as it was close to the wording of the original text.
- most (85%) could use an index to locate information and 70% could cross reference. Some 70% could use a page of contents and 65% a bibliography.
- most could interpret data presented in tabular form as well as information in maps and diagrams.
- one in ten could follow and recall sequences presented in narrative form and were able to recognise main characters.
- the same proportion of pupils i.e. one in ten were able to respond imaginatively to poetry with 80% able to deduce an unknown word from the context. Most recognised metaphor and 66% were able to understand the meaning of metaphor in description.
- between 40 and 60% of children could detect stylistic effects.
- 80% were able to form an opinion and justify it after reading expository prose and some 70–90% of primary children were able to identify points of conflict in evidence. (Gorman et al., 1988)

Reading Performance at Age Fifteen

The surveys at fifteen years showed that at this age the children had sufficiently developed reading ability to undertake all the tasks noted above but with more complex material.

In their survey the team made comparison with reading performance at age eleven years pointing out that the older children had "more insight into human character and motivation" and were thereby able to understand better their reading of literature. In general terms, the fifteen year olds were more aware of social, political, and moral issues raised by their reading.

In relating what reading activity the children found difficult, the team cites the focus of the question (that is, the type of meaning to be extracted) and the scope of the question (that is, the amount of material to be assimilated and the strategies required).

Here is an example of these difficulties (they are discussed in detail later in this chapter.)

When pupils at primary level were asked to answer questions relating to certain features of different types of whale, such as size and colour, the great majority had no difficulty in doing this, even though the material to be read was technically very complex. The evidence that had to be extracted was nevertheless relatively easy to locate and explicitly asserted. (Gorman et al., 1988 p. 9)

Misunderstanding appears to be the most serious weakness uncovered by the surveys, and this too will need further discussion as it calls into question the definition of reading (not simply to assess children's comprehension) that the team is working with for their surveys. The main problem reported for both age groups was not the density of the material but the nature of the questioning. Pupils found it difficult

- To recast information in a different mode.
- To read selectively for salient points and to record these succinctly without irrelevancies.
- To assess the satirical and ironic tone of a passage, or understand the attribution of particular viewpoints to fictional characters.
- To contextualize some forms of writing or to estimate the age/status of authors. This was due to pupils' lack of familiarity with different registers.

Attitudes Toward Reading Surveys

Among the interesting pieces of innovative work devised by the team are their surveys of children's attitudes toward reading. The team suggests that they show that "the patterns of response established at age 11 not only influence outcomes at age 15, but are likely to be in evidence from the earliest school years." We can likely rely on these findings inasmuch as they were gleaned from different methods of inquiry.

The following findings, as illustrated in Figure 22.3, are of particular interest:

- Differences in the way boys and girls develop interests in literacy.
- Differences in attitudes between primary and secondary pupils.
- The persistent finding of an association between reluctant or negative attitudes to reading and writing, and lower performance scores.
- Pupils' strongly expressed views about the nature of routine work associated with reading and writing.
- The fact that patterns of interest in reading are reflected in favoured types of writing. (Gorman, 1987, pp. 22, 23)

To give a flavor of the surveys, two figures from the 1983 survey are given below. These show the differences in the attitudes boys and girls showed toward reading at age eleven and fifteen years. The children were asked to say whether or not they agreed with statements about reading made by pupils of the same age. The pattern of response is said to have remained stable over the five years (Gorman, 1987, p. 22), and there was a strong association, positive or negative, with reading performance.

Figure 22.3
Primary and Secondary Surveys of Attitudes Toward Reading

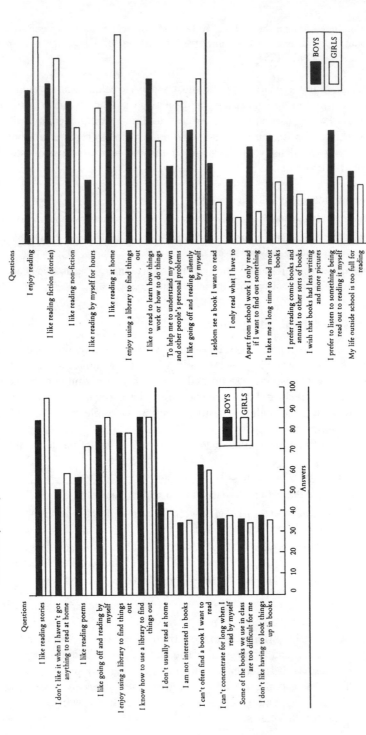

Source: T. P. Gorman, *Pupils' Attitudes to Reading* (Windsor: NFER–Nelson, 1987), pp. 22–23.

Gorman points out that there is a closer link between attitudes and performance than is often thought. The comments made about attitudes to reading are revealing and very important. These show that

good readers tend to be open-minded and show a willingness to revise or reconsider their preconceptions and opinions in the light of new evidence or information. They also show a willingness to accept and explore experiences and attitudes that differ from their own, and to learn from them. They are prepared to invest some intellectual effort in order to extract meaning from what they read; they tend to have inquiring minds; and they will have learnt to read what is presented to them selectively, according to the purposes or requirements they have in mind. In doing so they show an ability to distinguish between relevant and irrelevant information.

Poorer readers on the other hand often show an unwillingness to revise an initial judgement or opinion in the light of further evidence. They also tend to disregard the fact that an author's viewpoint may be at variance with the particular views attributed to characters or persons depicted. They sometimes have an ambivalent attitude to written sources of information. On the one hand they tend to regard what they read as authoritative when it deals with subjects that they are less familiar with, but they have a tendency to disregard written information when this deals with familiar matters or issues. They tend to impose a literal interpretation on what is read, disregarding meanings conveyed indirectly, or obliquely (Gorman, 1987, p. 24).

Criticisms of the APU

As with other attempts to test and monitor reading progress, the work of the APU has not been without its critics. One strong criticism of the overall wisdom of the whole of the APU's operation has been made by Rosen (1982). In his critique Rosen claims that it is not about language performance in schools as the reports claim, but about a series of tests of reading and writing. His concerns are that there is no discussion of the purposes of the exercise, and he comes to the conclusion that it follows the recommendation in the Bullock Report about monitoring literacy standards, which with little evidence, were thought to have been in decline. Rosen takes the team to task about their methods of assessing reading, pointing out in detail that the construction and content of the booklets, the questioning techniques, and the interpretation of the results are of little consequence.

Rosen is not the only critic. Chapman (1987a) has made the point that the team did not have a clear theoretical perspective, nor did it keep abreast of the extensive reading research effort in other countries, particularly the United States. He contrasted the opening statement of the framework for the APU's testing program with that found in the introduction to "Becoming a Nation of Readers," the Report of the Commission on Reading in the United States. The APU states that "little is known about the processes that underlie efficient reading" (Gorman, 1986, p. 5) and the Report of the Commission on Reading states, "the last two decades of research and scholarship on reading, building on the past, have produced an array of information which is unparalleled in its understanding of the underlying processes in the comprehension of language'' (Glaser, 1985, p. viii). It is clear that the APU team had paid little, if any, attention to the research work on schemata or prior knowledge, for instance, research that could well have informed their test construction. Many of the questions on the passages in the test booklets like the example on Whales cited above, could have been answered from prior knowledge as Tuinman (1973/1974) demonstrated with comprehension questions. In addition, the work on questioning, including multiple choice questions, and other assessment pitfalls such as those detailed in the section on assessment in the *Handbook of Reading Research* (Johnson, 1984) could perhaps have been avoided.

As a result of these shortcomings, the APU tests may seriously overestimate the reading ability of the children tested. Chapman (1987), working during the same years as the APU but using a different technique (see below), has shown that a large proportion of children from eleven to fifteen years in maintained schools are underachieving to a very large extent.

Whatever the criticisms of their work, the APU surveys represent the most sophisticated monitoring exercise into language performance in schools to have ever taken place in the United Kingdom. The findings of the Unit do not mention the need for models of language and grammars but rather propose that the debate should be about pedagogy and the need for teachers to understand the connections between language and learning. This in some ways echoes the American report mentioned above when it refers to the ''importance of studying good practice.''

QUALIFIED TEACHER STATUS

To be allowed to teach in maintained schools in England and Wales requires Qualified Teacher Status (QTS), and similar requirements apply in Scotland and Northern Ireland. A recent DES Consultation Document (DES, 1988) states that this requirement is to ensure that only those who possess appropriate knowledge and personal qualities and adequate classroom skills may teach in maintained schools. The majority of teachers in England and Wales become qualified by successfully completing a course of initial training approved by the secretary of state for education and science. Since the beginning of the 1980s, newly qualified teachers have been required to be graduates holding a Bachelor of Education degree or a B.A. or B.Sc. together with a Diploma in Education. Most of the courses provided for teachers now lead to graduate status with students being awarded a B.Ed. or B.Ed. (Honors) degree. Then, after a successful probationary year, they achieve qualified status. Before 1980, the main teacher qualification was the nongraduate Certificate of Education.

Other, so-called nonstandard routes to QTS are possible, but they are likely to be phased out if agreement is reached in the near future. In 1987 some 2,200 applications for QTS came from persons outside the United Kingdom, and these are very carefully scrutinized before QTS is granted. Only about one-third of

Table 22.3
Teachers as a Percentage of Finally Registered New Open University
Undergraduate Students, 1971–1977

Year	1971	1972	1973	1974	1975	1976	1977
New Students	19,581	15,716	12,680	11,336	14,830	12,230	14,971
Occupation (Education) As %	40.1	33.2	34.7	33.6	27.8	26.8	27.0
Teachers' certificates	31.4%	27.3%	29.6%	30.5%	27.3%	26.9%	27.3%

Source: Open University Digest of Statistics, 1971–1976, vol. 1, p. 26.

these applications were successful. The same Consultation Document gives the number of teachers employed by LEAs in maintained schools in England and Wales in 1987 as 427,000 with another 2,200 unqualified "instructors." The new scheme proposed in the Consultation Document will retain the present standard route to QTS but modify the non standard routes considerably.

In-Service Education of Teachers (INSET)

Before 1980, as noted above, many teachers had QTS but held nongraduate qualifications. Consequently, the provision of educational courses by the newly established Open University which was designed to serve the needs of part-time adult students in 1970 proved a great asset to serving teachers who wished to graduate. Prior to this, courses were provided for the education of teachers while serving, but these were few and far between for the certificated teacher.

Table 22.3 illustrates the takeup of the university's provision by teachers as they "topped up" their certificates to degrees.

The Open University Reading Courses

After this initial enrollment phase into general degree courses, perhaps the most significant development, according to Chapman (1979, 1987b), was the presentation of reading courses for teachers at different levels in the school system. It is only recently that the teaching of reading has been seen to be the concern of all teachers. The prospectus for the first course, called Reading Development coded PE261, shows that it was a leader in its time. The prospectus states that it was constructed so as

to help students to understand all levels and all aspects of the reading process and how to guide the development of reading competence throughout the school years. Opportunities will also be provided for the student to appraise and improve his own level of reading proficiency. Throughout the course students will be provided with a variety of

Figure 22.4
The Structure of the Reading Diploma

Level	Open University Diploma in Reading Development	
3rd	Module 3 P333 The Reading Curriculum and the Advisory Role 1/2 credit	Module 4 P334 Reading and Individual Development 1/2 credit
2nd	Module 1 PE231 Reading Development (rewrite of PE261) 1/2 credit	Module 2 E263 Language and Learning (from the undergraduate programme) (rewrite PE232 Language Development) 1/2 credit

activities integrating theory with practice. Although the course will concentrate on the middle years of school, consideration will be given to: (a) the early stages of reading; (b) special problems; (c) advanced reading. In the latter part of the course students will be given the opportunity to concentrate their studies on a particular area.

This course demonstrated that distance education could make a significant contribution to reading education. During the four years of its presentation, from 1973 to 1976, some 10,000 teachers took the course, most gaining a course credit. Indeed, during the evaluation procedures of the course, a demand for a more substantial course, or series of courses, on reading and the teaching of reading was revealed. The university team therefore decided to build a Diploma in Reading Development from the experiences gained during this first course for reading teachers. Its overall aim was "to raise standards of literacy by improving teacher performance in the classroom," and the whole diploma was conceived of as "an INSET vehicle for innovation and reform." The diagram of the structure of the diploma (see Figure 22.4) shows that it consisted of four parts or modules: Reading Development, Language and Learning (later Language Development), the Reading Curriculum and the Advisory Role, and Reading and Individual Development.

The first module dealt with "all areas of the curriculum emphasizing reading to learn as well as learning to read." It was intended for specialist teachers in subject areas as well as for teachers with more general curriculum responsibilities. The work fell into four main sections: developing fluent reading; developing independence in reading; using and abusing literacy; and organizing the teaching of reading.

The second module was taken from the undergraduate programme being an interdisciplinary course drawing on philosophy, psychology, sociology and linguistics. The course concentrates on the nature of language; how language organizes and structures the world; the process of language acquisition; teachers' use of language and how it effects pupils' learning; and the relevance of conceptual analysis of language in crucial development areas, for example, moral, political, literary and aesthetic judgment.

This module was replaced in 1979 by a new course, Language Development, which was written for the diploma's particular INSET needs. It was composed of six parts, each of which had a relevant developmental section. These were Understanding Speech, Patterns of Language, Words and Their Meanings, Communications and Context, Observing Classroom Language, and the Language Curriculum.

The third module was designed to

provide opportunities for the systematic application of theory to practice in organizing those aspects of the curriculum in which competence in reading and study skills can best be developed. The student looked at the wide range of skills required for effective and efficient reading in adult life and deciding how these might influence judgement about skill development in the age group with which the student is particularly concerned.

Module four extended the systematic application of theory to practice but

concentrated on monitoring the progress of individual children to help them develop all round competence as readers. In addition, this module aimed to provide insight into the role of literature in education and competence in developing in each pupil a wide range of reading interests.

The contribution to INSET made by the Open University's Reading Development Diploma can be best illustrated by giving the number of teachers taking its courses. Table 22.4 shows that over 37,000 teachers took the reading and language courses that made up the diploma between 1973 and 1985. This is a massive input into reading education in the United Kingdom as a whole, for the Open University (OU) operates in all provinces of the country. OU has a policy, however, of keeping its courses up to date; when the diploma courses became due for remake, unfortunately there were insufficient resources available to rewrite the diploma.

Recently, a new module, one on Language and Literacy, has been made for the master's degree program but does not have the classroom aspects that so clearly identified the original diploma.

As an addendum to this brief account of the part played by distance education in INSET in the United Kingdom, it is worth recording that a pilot research

Table 22.4
Language Development Courses

Course Code	Title of Course	Years of presentation	No. fully registered
PE261	Reading Development	(1973-1977)	9,427
PE231	Reading Development*	(1977-1985)	11,078
E262	Language and Learning*	(1973-1979)	10,433
PE232	Language Development*	(1979-1985)	3,386
P333	The Reading Curriculum*	(1978-1985)	1,807
P334	Reading and Individual Development	(1979-1985)	1,204
			**37,335

*Courses that made up the Diploma of Reading Development.
**Figures to 1985 (teachers only).
Source: L. J. Chapman, Multi-Media Programmes for Literacy Education. In M. Boonprasert and S. Nilakupta (eds.), *The Proceedings of the Second International Conference on Literacy and Languages*, Bangkok, 1987, p. 257.

project is underway in Zimbabwe, Africa, using the discontinued Language Development course from the Reading Diploma. The aim of this research is to find out what has to be done to make materials designed for literacy education in one culture applicable to another. If successful, this research will have great implications for literacy improvement in developing countries.

MATERIALS AND METHODS

Considerable efforts have been made to change the methods employed to teach reading during the past decade. Although some of the causes of the changes can be clearly stated, others are only just becoming discernible. As noted above, the research projects housed by the three universities had their effects, but other forces are also involved. In order to describe some of the more obvious changes, it is first necessary to relate the traditional methods involved in the teaching of reading in the majority of schools in the United Kingdom.

Book Supply: The Primary Sector

The publishers of materials for children's beginning reading instruction have, perhaps inadvertently, supported or advocated one particular method of teaching reading. For many years children starting school have had as their initial reader or primer the first book in a reading scheme or series. The process that followed was the well-known one in which children progressed from that book to the next prearranged reader according to the structure of the scheme. This system suited the teacher for a number of reasons. A reading scheme had a built-in structure so that teachers did not have to provide for reading growth. The reading scheme did their lesson preparation for them. The progress of the children could be easily recorded for the end of session report and could be clearly demonstrated to reassure anxious parents. The children quickly understood the way in which the books were organized, mostly by number and color, and soon appreciated that progress was gauged by teachers and realized by parents as the movement made from book to book in an ascending numerical order through the series.

One of the early signs that all was not entirely satisfactory with a one school/one scheme setup was the rapid growth in the number of schools that began to supplement the central scheme with additional reading material. Although the reading scheme publishers soon began to provide supplementary readers associated with their schemes, it became the practice for schools to have a number of schemes running alongside each other. Teachers were finding that it was necessary to enrich their pupils' reading diet. When the central scheme was completed the children went onto "library" books. This graduation released children from the closed reading environment of the scheme and also gave them the responsibility to choose their own volumes to read. These practices served as the pattern for teaching reading in the primary school for many years and remain so in most areas, as a recent survey in one large northeastern city in England showed. It was found that 79 percent of the primary schools in the city relied regularly on one scheme for their basic reading instruction. This was supplemented by other schemes but to a greatly reduced extent—from 19.4 percent to 27 percent (Rice, 1987, p. 93). This city is probably typical of most cities in the United Kingdom.

One way in which teachers "teach" reading is to hear individual children read regularly, preferably every day. This process was discovered to be an inefficient teaching method and in most cases served only as a progress-recording activity. The Manchester University research team criticized the procedure as being one that helped the young reader little, and so it suggested that it would be better to hear reading less often but for a longer time. The procedure would be more of a conferencing one after the conferencing notions of Graves (1983). A type of miscue analysis was proposed so that the teacher would be able to elucidate the strengths and weaknesses of the child's reading. Recently, however, there have been movements in thinking that are beginning to affect the practice of teaching of reading in more radical ways.

Changing Methods in the Infant Department

Toward the end of the 1980s, the writings of some leading authorities on reading like Goodman and Smith were sufficiently well known to begin to influence teachers' perceptions of reading and its teaching. The ground for accepting these views had already been broken by the findings of the research carried out at the universities of Nottingham and Manchester, and the courses presented to thousands of teachers of reading by the Open University. These views also coincided with the outlook of members of the London Institute of

Education who had long regarded reading schemes and their content as of dubious value for language work in schools. In essence, there was a strong belief that reading was not made up of a series of subskills that had to be mastered for reading to be successful. Rather, as the Nottingham project team proposed, reading was a unitary language process. Associated with this idea was the notion that for early reading the use of natural language, interpreted as the language of "real" or trade books, was paramount. Consequently, children's language development was thought to be degraded, and learning to read made more difficult by the type of reading material that most reading schemes provided. Furthermore, this impoverished version of English, which became known as primerese, was only to be found in reading schemes and was not encountered anywhere else.

The alternative to the subskills approach now being advocated has become known as the apprenticeship approach. This takes as its reading material the so-called real or trade book and tries to replicate the home situation where mother and child enjoy a book together. The author who most typifies the method is Liz Waterland (1985) who, in her book *Read with Me* shows how schools can break with the reading scheme and work entirely with story or other types of children's literature. Children, like apprentices, are encouraged to select their own books and to sit by the teacher, or other adult, and read. The child reads as much or as little as she can and the adult reads that which the child finds difficult. Gradually, as the child practices reading she will be able to read more and more until she is reading by herself.

Another characteristic of this approach is the absence of the teaching of phonics. Frank Smith's avowal that we learn to read by reading and that teaching phonics only makes it more difficult is taken very seriously; phonics is therefore avoided as a method of teaching reading. When phonics are taught, they are mostly for writing or spelling purposes.

Further changes were proposed as a result of the findings of the research carried out at the Open University (Chapman, 1987). In this work, problems arising from unfamiliarity with different genres of texts, which are met later in schooling, were addressed. It was suggested that children should make an early acquaintance with texts other than those in narrative or story form so that some of the problems associated with reading in the secondary school might be avoided. It was suggested that the "read with me" and the "reading to children" situations common in home and school were ideal situations for sensitizing children to different text types or genres. It is unclear at the moment how far these changes have gone, but they do seem to be gaining ground, particularly among teacher educators.

Changing Methods in the Junior Department

As described earlier, the primary years of education are in most cases divided between the infant department (five to seven years) and the junior department (seven to eleven years). The main indication of change in infant schools, as noted above, is concerned with teaching beginning reading. Indeed, the whole process of teaching reading was traditionally thought to be solely the job of the infant school. That is, it was assumed that learning to read was accomplished for most children before they came into the junior department, let alone the secondary school. In the same way as there have been changes in the infant school, so there have been changes in the junior departments. It is now common practice for direct reading instruction to take place in them. Much more work is now done to teach what are essentially study skills.

One method of developing these skills has been through what is termed Topic Work. In this method the children or teacher choose a central theme, and the facets of the topic are divided among members of the class. The children then work individually or in groups at their chosen or allocated tasks. Most of these involve reading for information of various kinds and reporting back to the class. This type of work has been heavily criticized in recent years (e.g., Tann, 1987, p. 62): Tann states that

There is little awareness amongst the children of what they are learning and there is little attempt by the teachers to analyse the potential and to identify what children might be learning. Having developed a way of doing Topic Work teachers then tend to stick with it. The children soon learn the knack of getting by. No wonder some of the children come to feel that it is boring and samey. However, this was also the feeling of many of the teachers! Many of them were dissatisfied and looking for change.

To advance and improve this type of reading, the methods advocated by the research team at Nottingham have been to the fore. Some of these, like group cloze procedure, have been found to be successful and a vast improvement on the erstwhile comprehension exercises which were in the main a series of un-connected comprehension tests that achieved little by way of improvement.

The process of hearing reading in the infant school as discussed above is also used in the junior schools where the situation is much the same. There is a need to make the occasion a more informative one for the reader.

Book Supply: The Secondary Sector

In a detailed review of research relating to voluntary and intensive reading, Davies (1986) presented the then National Book League with a substantial guide to reading about reading. In this very comprehensive survey Davies brings together research that has been carried out (inter alia) on voluntary reading, the criteria for evaluating and selecting books for subject or content area reading, textbook bias, textbook difficulties, and the availability of books in schools. Some of this research has been mentioned above, but that concerned with text-books in the secondary sector requires further comment.

As in other countries, the United States in particular, there has been concern about the effectiveness of textbooks for learning in the subject or content areas. That textbooks are a key resource and have an informative and supportive function is not in doubt. However, serious problems of reading and learning from text-books have been demonstrated. Some of these problems have been investigated, and a number of features that appear to facilitate comprehension have been detected. The use of objective linguistic criteria, like word frequency counts, including appropriate cohesion and register, are recommended. The review suggests that readability measures, owing to their "widespread use and misuse," should be restricted in future to initial surveys of textbooks. The review further advocates that schools should produce book selection policy documents, paying greater sensitivity to the criteria already available from research.

Since the publication of this survey, later research in the United Kingdom has shown that many children misperceive cohesion and register factors in their school reading materials. This has a detrimental effect on comprehension (Chapman, 1987; Chapman and Louw, 1986). Davies (1986) also shows that expenditure on textbooks continued to decline during the period under review and that even minimum quantities of books were not being supplied.

The following points arising from the survey by Davies and a companion volume *The State of Reading* by Ingham and Brown (1986) summarize their findings:

1. Textbooks are seen as central to school work by the majority of teachers questioned.

2. Many researchers, HMIs and curriculum development projects also support the text-book. The Cockcroft Report describes textbooks as providing a "structure within which work in mathematics can develop."

3. Criticism of the "impersonal language" of some textbooks ignores the work of researchers such as Halliday and the need for pupils to gain experience of subject-specific language.

4. Educational publishers are increasingly aware of the need to avoid bias or stereotyping in textbooks and such features, criticised in older books, are becoming rarer.

5. Worksheets used extensively as a substitute for textbooks are generally found to be unsatisfactory by researchers, teachers and pupils.

6. An effective textbook should be well written and designed, with clear "signposting" of features, previews and summaries. Its value is often reinforced by accompanying resource material of a flexible kind.

Overall, the greatest drawback is the decline in resources for the purchase of books. To this, however, a caveat must be added: many schools do not have a sufficiently well-thought-out policy for book selection on which to recommend purchases.

Changing Methods in the Secondary School

Although reading research surveys have been mixed in their findings regarding the level of reading attainment of secondary school pupils (e.g., compare the

APU monitoring exercise with Chapman's findings), one area in which progress in teaching has been noticed is the help provided for slow or failing readers.

During the last ten years, the same shift in opinion that characterized the changing methods in the primary schools has been taking place in some secondary schools. Most of the reasons given for reading failure that were prevalent earlier, such as perceptual failure, now appear unconvincing to an increasing number of teachers. Explanations are now being sought "outside the children rather than within them." Many now believe that there is not one single explanation why a child who has obviously learned to speak adequately is unable to learn to read. The explanations that have been offered are: reading not an enjoyable family habit, unpleasant early reading experiences, meaningless early reading material, and poor teaching. Absences from school, overlarge classes, and high teacher turnover are also given as contributory factors.

Plackett sums up the approaches taken to counteract the downward spiral that occurs with reading failure as being built around four principles for literacy learning:

1. The acquisition of literacy is a dynamic process for which we should not set limited goals. We do not want to commit some pupils to a lesser kind of literacy than others.
2. Reading is essentially to do with getting meaning rather than decoding; in writing, making meaning stimulates and controls the process of encoding.
3. Learning to read and write draws on the same strengths which pupils have already demonstrated in learning to produce and understand spoken language.
4. The most powerful explanations of failure to learn are social rather than clinical. (Plackett, 1986, p. 10)

Teaching according to these principles has led to concern for a secure learning environment in which the key is that children are expected to succeed. Moreover, much reading of "real" books takes place, and a considerable amount of support is given.

This account typifies the changes that are taking place from an erstwhile remedial approach, with some teachers calling on the work of the Nottingham University team which proposed a series of directed reading activities to enhance reading. These activities known as DARTS (Lunzer and Gardner, 1979, p. 308) consist of group cloze, group SQ3R, group sequencing, group prediction, and group reading for a variety of purposes.

READING RESEARCH IN THE UNITED KINGDOM

During the period being reviewed, apart from the national monitoring by the APU and the surveys of adult literacy there have been three major research studies in the United Kingdom. It is convenient to call these projects by the name of the university that housed the research teams, namely, the University of Nottingham, the University of Manchester, and the Open University. This reading research, as Chapman (1987a) suggests, is mainly about progress in reading, its teaching and its development. Its main characteristic is the collection of data in school rather than in laboratory settings. A further research development of more recent origin is that concerned with parental involvement in reading.

Reading Research at Nottingham University

The Effective Use of Reading project (Lunzer and Gardner, 1979) carried out research into three areas of reading and its teaching: (1) on the nature of comprehension; (2) a description of classroom practice in relation to reading; and (3) an evaluation of methods designed to improve reading to learn.

This project was the first major piece of research to shift the focus of the studies of the teaching of reading from primary to secondary school settings. Indeed, as noted below, the methods advocated for the later age groups have had a considerable influence on the teaching of reading. The research team was among the first to provide data showing that reading was better characterized as a holistic process rather than an amalgam of subskills. At the time this proposal was somewhat novel but it has since gained support and has influenced the growing popularity of the teaching of reading in the context of whole-language approaches. (These are reviewed below.)

In addition to providing evidence that reading was a single aptitude, Lunzer and Gardner also found no support for the idea that some children possess lower order skills like letter and word recognition and not higher order skills like comprehension. As a result of their studies, Lunzer and Gardner reintroduced the notion that comprehension was better conceived as a willingness to reflect on (think about?) what has been read rather than any other kind of cognitive activity.

Their recommendations for practice include the following:

1. reading situations designed to foster a willingness to reflect on what is being read.
2. a structure of instruction, guidance and reading practice which improves the quality of instruction.
3. a perusal of methods and materials aimed at creating the optimum opportunity for pupils to use reading purposefully. (Lunzer and Gardner, 1979, p. 301)

When the project team observed reading teaching in classrooms, they found a considerable difference in the patterns of teaching between primary and secondary schools. There was a decrease in the individual tuition carried on in the final year of the primary school and a corresponding increase in class teaching in the first year at secondary school. In addition, there was a considerable increase in the amount of time children spent listening, rather than reading, in the secondary school. The other main comparison was the marked increase in the use of textbooks in the secondary school.

Perhaps their most surprising finding was that more than 50 percent of all reading across all subjects at the secondary level was done in short bursts of 1 to 15 seconds. This, the team points out, mitigates against the reading of continuous texts. From these results the team went on to recommend procedures to be used by children to "interrogate" texts.

Reading Research at Manchester University

This research was essentially a fact-finding project that investigated the progress of children who had maintained at least average reading progress for two years. The research team, which concentrated on the seven- to nine-year-old age group, showed an awareness of recent developments in thinking about the reading process. Like the University of Nottingham team, they state that reading is best regarded as a thinking process; consequently, the team fixed attention on comprehension. Without themselves disregarding the notion advanced by Lunzer and Gardner that comprehension was a holistic or global process, they were careful not to dismiss traditional skill teaching methods.

Teachers involved in the project expressed two practical needs. They required greater knowledge of reading development and more information about assessment, diagnosis, and recordkeeping. The report states, however, that "only a small minority appreciated the need to ensure that a firm basis for both functional and recreational reading be laid down during the first two years of the junior school." The main recommendations of the report were of practical guidance for the teaching of reading.

Research at the Open University

This research differed markedly from the other two research projects, and as it has only recently been reported (Chapman, 1987a), it is described more fully here than the other two projects. The research had three interconnected aims. These were (1) to establish the educational significance of recently described textlinguistic features; (2) to trace, by a longitudinal reading research program, children's mastery of the linguistic features selected from the data provided by aim 1; and (3) to contribute to the theoretical debate on reading and textlinguistics drawing on the data provided by aim 2.

In essence, the research achieved these aims by employing recent advances in linguistics to identify text difficulty in school reading material. Then, using this as a basis, the research traced the reading progress of a large sample of children between the ages of eight and fifteen years. It was thereby a longitudinal study of children's reading development. Early in the research the superiority of the work of the systemic linguists Halliday and Hasan (1976, 1980) was clearly established. Their 1976 book on the description of cohesion in English was found to be particularly useful. The two principal linguistic concepts involved were cohesion and register. Cohesion allowed the internal organization of texts to be specified systematically, and register related the text to its external context or purpose. In effect, by using these newly defined linguistic features, the researchers had tools capable of describing the range of text encountered by children in schools for their everyday reading purposes. This enabled the research team to achieve maximum ecological validity by using texts drawn directly from those used by children in their classrooms and yet retain control of important text features.

The use of these particular linguistic concepts gave a further advantage, for the researchers were able to make proposals that clarified, they believed, certain features of the reading process. From this new perspective they were able to specify a methodology for reconsidering the growth of children's reading from eight to fifteen years. This development of the project's methodology was based on the following theoretical premise. Central to the concept of cohesion is the cohesive tie. This involves the easily demonstrable notion that one element in a text is not completely identifiable during reading without recourse to another in the text to which it is related in some way. So, for example, the pronoun "he" in a story gives only part of the information, but when "tied" to a proper name, say, John, it now gives the complete identification of the character in question. Halliday and Hasan (1976) go further. They suggest that many such ties can be organized into groups according to the way in which they work. However, while having these identifiable differences, they all have one essential characteristic in common: presupposition. The researchers suggested that this factor of presupposition causes a state of anticipation in the reader such that the onset of a cohesive tie presupposes that it will eventually be closed or tied.

Fitting this research into present-day notions of the reading process, it could be said that the anticipation or prediction that is a factor of fluent reading is, in part, the result of the presupposing process that is carried by the cohesive ties and, as they are so pervasive in texts, their effects will not be a trivial factor. Furthermore, the cohesive ties are seen to be chained through a text, and these chains carry the theme of the topic or action that is taking place in a story (Halliday and Hasan, 1980). Hence, it is possible to consider the use of a gap-making technique whereby one end of a cohesive tie is deleted and the reader is invited to complete it (Chapman, 1983). If the meaning relationship relating the two ends of the tie is perceived accurately, then the reader will replace the word or words that have been deleted. By examining their responses, it was therefore possible to discover the extent to which the children recovered the meaning of the text.

Unlike other deletion procedures, this one did not consist of a regular -*n*th, cloze-type deletion; rather, it was built on removing the ends of a small number of cohesive ties from strategic points in a chain.

Two kinds of analysis were performed on the data. The first was a quantitative type that took the replacement of the author's word as its only criterion. Perhaps the most innovative development was the new type of qualitative analysis that was devised. This involved examining every response against a linguistic base which included other features of systemic grammar as well as the cohesion and register concepts.

The research had many important results. In the first place it was shown that the use of systemic linguistics, including the concepts of register and cohesion, enabled the research to break new ground. In addition, the inclusion of these concepts into a model of the reading process gave new explanations of the on-going prediction capabilities of the fluent reader (MacLean and Chapman, 1989). Furthermore, when such a perspective was adopted, old ideas of reading attainment had to be abandoned in favor of the notion of a continuum of reading development along which each type of text category could be accommodated. This continuum enabled the researchers to produce reading development profiles for the children in the schools being used for the work.

As the research used everyday curriculum materials and not specially contrived passages for its reading explorations, the results had a good deal of teacher credibility from the start. In addition, the continuum profiles were also of direct relevance to teachers, who are hard pressed to produce assessments of their pupils.

The research also had implications for the teaching of reading, for the evidence produced showed that at least the bottom third of the reading ability range was not making the progress that might be expected in the secondary years.

A new account of vocabulary acquisition was forthcoming from the work, and it was found that some of the many facets of reading vocabulary could be identified giving important new insights as to the acquisition of words in context.

Parental Involvement in Reading

Traditionally, schools have been reluctant to involve parents in their work. However, during the 1980s several great changes occurred as a growing number of research projects exerted their influence.

Evaluation work of one such scheme began early in the decade in Inner London, and Tizard et al. (1982) provided evidence of the beneficial effects of parents listening regularly to their children read. These sessions were monitored by teachers who also gave regular guidance to parents.

Many differing types of parental involvement have developed such that, in 1986, Topping produced an article listing the many varieties then being used (Topping, 1986). This article gave an evaluation of the many schemes he had surveyed (Topping and Wolfendale, 1985). He listed them as follows:

Teacher's Guide

Best Buy	Paired Reading—Pure form
Good Value	Parent Listening
	Pause, Prompt and Praise
	Shared Reading—Original Version
Worth Considering	*Token Reinforcement
	*Precision Teaching
	*Direct Teaching
	**Paired Reading—Bryan's variant
	**Paired Reading—Young and Tyre variant

*For some children with particular difficulties
**For accelerating accuracy

Parent-teacher collaboration is now in a much healthier state, and this augurs well for the progress of reading in the future.

SUMMARY

During the years covered in this chapter fundamental changes took place in all facets of the maintained sector of education in the United Kingdom. The central government has assumed more control over both curriculum content and assessment, particularly in literacy teaching. Furthermore, the locus of control of schools has moved from the LEAs to the schools themselves.

The private sector, which coexists alongside the maintained sector, is seen as being sometimes competitive and sometimes complementary, with parents moving their children between sectors as they seek the best education for them.

While English remains the mainstream language, a multilingual situation is developing owing to migrants entering the country. This situation was at first viewed as a problem in some quarters but is now beginning to be seen as an asset from a language point of view.

The organization of schools into primary (five to eleven years) and secondary (twelve to sixteen years) age groups remains much the same, although some experiments have been done with middle school nine to thirteen year olds in some LEAs. During the decade a move took place from secondary selective education to comprehensive education. Regional variations of the English system in Scotland and Northern Ireland were noted.

The pattern of teacher pre- and in-service education is a system in which the Bachelor of Education degree has become the norm for qualified status, but this runs alongside another route of an arts or science degree plus a Diploma in Education. Perhaps the most important development is the move to an all-graduate profession. The Open University (OU), with its distance teaching operation, has played a large part in "topping up" nongraduate teachers to graduate status.

Furthermore, the development of the OU's provision of in-service courses for the teaching of reading was considered to be a significant factor. The concept of setting goals in objective terms was not even a feature in teacher preparation until thousands of teachers took these courses. However, government requirements for external assessment and greater teacher accountability will most likely establish teaching by objectives as a curricular mandate and this has caused considerable unease among some English teachers.

The practice of having select committees report to government departments on the state of teaching language and English was reviewed in the chapter, as was the setting up of the Assessment of Performance Unit (APU), which arose out of one such report. The APU monitors reading standards and other basic subjects.

The APU's surveys of reading performance at eleven and fifteen years, which were carried out between 1979 and 1983, used new procedures. These surveys produced some interesting findings as to the standards being achieved across the nation, and also revealed some of the characteristics of different levels of reading abilities. The attitudes to reading surveys, one of the more innovative tests devised, showed important relationships between attitude to reading and reading performance.

Recent research into adult literacy showed that the number of adults experiencing literacy problems was increasing much as they are in other highly industrialized countries. The latest research has the advantage of using a sample from the National Child Development program. Since this program has been in existence for a number of years, many demographic data were available to the researchers. Nonetheless, more research is needed to tease out the many problems involved in adult literacy.

Three reading research projects were reviewed, and particular note was taken of the work regarding the perception of textual cohesion and register variation during reading. When the results of surveys using cohesion and register were employed to test the reading performance of secondary school children, less optimism was found regarding progress than with the APU surveys.

Research and changing perspectives on reading and its teaching reveal that considerable shifts occurred in the methods being used to teach reading. Two main changes were discerned. The first, which has been taking place over an extended period, is the move from the teaching of reading being the sole concern of the infant school to one in which all departments are responsible for reading progress. The second is more recent and is not as yet countrywide; it involves a fundamental move in thinking about the conditions of early reading instruction within an emergent literacy paradigm. This reflects notions of using "real" books as opposed to reading schemes and of considering language to be a holistic rather than a subskills process. There are indications that this move in thinking is also present when slow readers are being taught in some secondary schools. There are fears that the resources needed for book purchase in the maintained sector are not sufficient to sustain reading improvement.

REFERENCES

Chapman, L. J. 1979. The Open University and the Development of In-Service Education Courses for Teachers. In J. Porter (ed.), *CERI Project on In-Service Education and Training (INSET) for Teachers*. Paris: OECD.

Chapman, L. J. 1983. *Reading Development and Cohesion*. London: Heinemann Educational Books.

Chapman, L. J. 1987a. *Reading: From 5 to 11 years*. Milton Keynes: Open University Press.

Chapman, L. J. 1987b. Multi-Media Programmes for Literacy Education. In M. Boonprasert and S. Nilakupta (eds.), *The Proceedings of the Second International Conference on Literacy and Languages "Literacy and Technological Development."* Bangkok, Thailand: Martin Benson, pp. 253–265.

Chapman, L. J., and W. Louw. 1986. Register development in secondary-school texts.

In B. Gillham (ed.), *The Language of School Subjects*. London: Educational Books, pp. 8–23.

Davies, F. 1986. *Books in the School Curriculum. A Compilation and Review of Research Relating to Voluntary and Intensive Reading*. London: The Publishers Association.

DES. 1975. *A Language for Life*. London: HMSO.

DES. 1988a. *Report of the Committee of Inquiry into the Teaching of English Language*. London: HMSO.

DES. 1988b. *Qualified Teacher Status. A Consultative Document*. London: HMSO.

DES. 1988c. *English for Ages 5 to 11*. London: HMSO.

The English Magazine. Summer 1988. London: The ILEA English Centre.

Glaser. 1985. Foreword. In R. C. Anderson, E. H. Heibert, J. A. Scott, and I. A. Wilkinson. *Becoming a Nation of Readers: The Report of the Commission on Reading*. Washington, D.C.: National Institute of Education, U.S. Department of Education, p. viii.

Gorman, T. P. 1986. *The Framework for the Assessment of Language*. Windsor: NFER–Nelson.

Gorman, T. P. 1987. *Pupils' Attitudes to Reading*. Windsor: NFER–Nelson.

Gorman, T. P, J. White, G. Brooks, M. Maclure, and A. Kispal. 1988. *Language Performance in Schools. Review of APU Language Monitoring 1979–1983*. London: HMSO.

Graves, D. H. 1983. *Writing: Teachers and Children at Work*. Melbourne: Heinemann.

Halliday, M.A.K., and R. Hasan. 1976. *Cohesion in English*. London: Longman.

Halliday, M.A.K., and R. Hasan. 1980. *Text and Context*. Sophia Linguistic V1. Tokyo: Sophia University.

Hamilton, M., and M. Stasinopoulos. 1987. *Literacy, Numeracy and Adults*. London: Adult Literacy and Basic Skills Unit.

Ingham, J., and V. Brown. 1986. *The State of Reading*. London: Publishers Association.

Johnson, D. 1987. *Private Schools and State Schools*. Milton Keynes: Open University Press.

Johnston, P. H. 1984. Assessment in reading. In P. D. Pearson et al. (eds.), *Handbook of Reading Research*. New York: Longman.

Lunzer, E. A., and K. Gardner. 1979. *The Effective Use of Reading*. London: Heinemann Educational Books.

MacLean, M., and L. J. Chapman 1989. The Processing of Cohesion by Good and Poor Readers. *Journal of Research in Reading* 12(1):

Open University. 1971. *Digest of Statistics*. Vol. 1. Milton Keynes: Open University.

Pearson, P. D., R. Barr, M. I. Kamil, and P. Mosenthal (eds.). 1984. *Handbook of Reading Research*. New York: Longman.

Plackett, E. 1986. Helping slow readers: Principles and practice. *The English Magazine*. No. 16 London: The ILEA English Centre.

Rice, I. 1987. Racism and reading schemes. 1986, The current situation. *Reading* 21(2): 92–98.

Rosen, H. 1982. The language monitors: A critique of the APU's primary survey report "Language Performance in Schools." *Bedford Way Paper*, No. 11. London: Institute of Education, University of London.

Simonite, V. 1983. *Literacy and Numeracy. Evidence from the National Child Development Study*. London: ABSLU.

Southgate, V., H. Arnold, and S. Johnson. 1981. *Extending Beginning Reading*. London: Heinemann Educational Books.

Statham, J., and D. Mackinnon, with C. Cathcart and M. Hales 1990. *The Education Fact File: A handbook of education information in the U.K.* 2d ed. London: Hodder and Stoughton.

Tann, S. 1987. Topic work: A mismatch of perceptions. *Reading* 21(1): 62–70.

Topping, K. 1986. W.H.I.C.H. parental involvement in reading? A guide for practitioners. *Reading* 20(3): 148–156.

Topping, K., and S. Wolfendale (eds.), 1985. *Parental Involvement in Children's Reading.* London: Croom Helm.

Tizard J., W. N. Scholfield, and J. Hewison. 1982. Collaboration between parents and teachers in assisting children's reading. *British Journal of Educational Psychology* 52, no. 1:1–15.

Tuinman, J. J. 1973/74. Determining the passage dependency of comprehension questions in five major tests. *Reading Research Quarterly* 9:206–222.

Waterland, L. 1985. *Read with Me. An Apprenticeship Approach to Reading.* Stroud: Thimble Press.

Wells, A. 1987. Adult literacy: its impact on young adults in the United Kingdom. Prospects xv, no. 11: 2.

Wilkinson, A. 1986. *The Quality of Writing.* Milton Keynes: Open University Press.

BIBLIOGRAPHY

Chapman, L. J. 1987, *Reading: From 5 to 11 Years.* Milton Keynes: Open University Press.

Davies, F. 1986. *Books in the School Curriculum.* A compilation and review of research relating to voluntary and intensive reading. London: Publishers Association.

DES. 1975. *A Language for Life.* London: HMSO.

DES, 1988. *Report of the Committee of Inquiry into the Teaching of English Language.* London: HMSO.

Gorman, T. P. 1987. *Pupils' Attitudes to Reading.* Windsor: NFER–Nelson.

Gorman, T. P., J. White, G. Brooks, M. Maclure, and A. Kispal. 1988. *Language Performance in Schools. Review of APU Language Monitoring 1979–1983.* London: HMSO.

Halliday, M.A.K., and R. Hasan. 1976. *Cohesion in English.* London: Longman.

Hamilton, M., and M. Stasinopoulos. 1987. *Literacy, Numeracy and Adults.* London: Adult Literacy and Basic Skills Unit.

Ingham, J., and V. Brown. 1986. *The State of Reading. A Report for the National Book League.* London: Educational Publishers Council.

Lunzer, E. A., and K. Gardner. 1979. *The Effective Use of Reading.* London: Heinemann Educational Books.

Southgate V., H. Arnold, and S. Johnson. 1981. *Extending Beginning Reading.* London: Heinemann Educational Books.

Statham, J., and D. Mackinnon, with H. Cathcart. 1989. *The Education Fact File: A Handbook of Education Information in the UK.* London: Hodder and Stoughton.

Topping, K., and S. Wolfendale (eds.). 1985. *Parental Involvement in Children's Reading.* London: Croom Helm.

Waterland, L. 1985. *Read with Me. An Apprenticeship Approach to Reading.* Stroud: Thimble Press.

23

United States

Jack Cassidy and Mary Ann Gray

[T]he reading problem [in the United States] is the direct outgrowth of . . .
The Great American Reading Machine—the interlocking mutual self-interest
created over the years among government agencies (local, state, and federal),
textbook publishers (particularly of basal readers), reading experts (professors in schools of education, reading specialists in the schools, and private
operators of reading programs), language arts coordinators, and classroom
teachers. They all have such high personal and financial stakes in the reading
business—in selling and defending their expertise—that they don't recognize
(and wouldn't admit) that they are the primary cause of the nation's reading
crisis. . . . The Machine is the culprit.
—D. J. Yarington, *The Great American Reading Machine*

INTRODUCTION

Yarington's *The Great American Reading Machine* is a little-known and poorly
received book that attacks educators, publishers, and government agencies for
causing the reading problems in the United States. While other more well-known
critics have made the same allegations, their criticisms are not as all-inclusive.
Certainly, this author's indictment has some validity. "The Great American
Reading Machine" has contributed to the reading problems in the United States,
but the book does not mention that it is this same machine that has contributed
to the great successes in literacy evident in the United States.

READING POLICY

Exactly how does "The Great American Reading Machine" operate in the
United States?

Control

Government agencies control all education in the United States except for private schools and clinics. There is little national control, however, since the U.S. Constitution relegates control of education to the states. National involvement tends to be focused on programs for students with special needs, such as those who have physical or learning handicaps, those whose first language is not English, and those who come from economically disadvantaged homes. Generally, these programs are partially or fully funded by the U.S. Department of Education whose chief administrator is the secretary of education. The most well-known special program is Chapter One or Title One (named for the statute that created it). This federally funded program provides additional instruction for economically disadvantaged students who are deficient in basic skills. Most often, these Chapter One programs focus on reading instruction. The U.S. government also occasionally funds reports that examine education in general (*A Nation at Risk*) or reading in particular (*Becoming a Nation of Readers*).

In addition to funding special programs and reports, the national government often sponsors a sample assessment of the reading ability of different age populations. Probably the most well known of these is the National Assessment of Educational Progress (NAEP) which was begun in 1969 and samples the achievement of nine, thirteen, and seventeen year olds. In 1983 NAEP also began assessing students by grade as well as age, and students in Grades 3, 7, and 11 were evaluated. Reading is one of the areas assessed by NAEP, and the goal is to obtain comprehensive and reliable achievement test data. Recently, NAEP also agreed to provide state-by-state comparisons of achievement and to attempt to ascertain the literacy level of adults ages sixteen to sixty-four.

Most of the control of education and reading instruction rests in the hands of the fifty state governments. Generally, these state governments yield the majority of their control to the local municipalities and counties which are generally known as local education agencies. These local agencies then take the responsibility for planning the curriculum, hiring teachers, and providing the needed resources. Most states, however, have some kind of standardized assessment to determine if the local education agencies are fulfilling their responsibility to the students under their jurisdiction. Although these state assessments may cover many areas of the curriculum, reading is always a prime concern (Valencia et al., 1989). Much of the funds for education come from taxes placed on real estate in the local school districts supplemented by state and federal funds.

The state of Pennsylvania with 501 local educational agencies is one of the larger states in the country and typifies the organizational patterns in the United States. The pupil population in these 501 districts ranges from 500 to 200,000. Each of these districts determines the scope and sequence of language skills and strategies for its students. However, these local plans should conform to the overall state plan (Lytle and Botel, 1988). In addition, the state assesses all students in Grades 3, 5, 8, and 11 with a test called the Test of Essential Learning and Language Skills. Students who fail to achieve the requisite score receive remediation, which is funded by the state government of Pennsylvania. Generally, this instruction consists of small-group instruction by a trained specialist in reading.

Population

Reading instruction in the United States generally focuses on Grades 1 through 6. Children range in age from five to seven years in Grade 1 and from ten to twelve years in Grade 6. This span roughly corresponds to primary education in many countries of the world. Increasingly, efforts have been made to start reading instruction in kindergarten (where the average age of children is five years) or even in preschool. This trend to begin reading instruction at an earlier age has caused concern among many educators.

For students in Grades 7 through 12, reading instruction for most pupils is incorporated into the subject areas (math, science, social studies, English, etc.). Students still experiencing difficulty with reading are often assigned to remedial classes or to easier subject area classes.

Adults with limited reading ability can get help in adult basic education classes (ABE) sponsored by local school districts or by literacy volunteers. The volunteer instruction is usually provided on a one-to-one basis.

In general, the reading goals of instructional practices are meant to be the same for males and females at all levels. Except in some private schools, males and females are taught using the same materials and grouped in the same class.

THE GOALS OF READING

Instructional Programs

Instructional programs in the United States generally include broad goals for all children, materials, assessment, and a variety of pedagogical approaches. Provisions for diagnosis and instruction are also made for students with reading difficulties. Many of the components of instructional programs generate a great deal of debate among authorities in the field.

Goals

The goals of students' reading instruction are generally determined by local education agencies. In practice, most of these school districts are so small that they lack the needed staff, time, and resources to develop definitive goals and objectives. Thus, there is a tendency to rely on goals and objectives developed by state or national governments or by those developed by professional organizations such as the International Reading Association and the National Council for Teachers of English. State agencies also provide guidelines in this area. See the accompanying list for the guidelines issued by the state of Pennsylvania.

Goals and Objectives of the Pennsylvania Comprehensive Reading Plan: Reading, Writing and Talking Across the Curriculum

1. Reading: Transacting with Text
   - Bringing prior knowledge and experience to construct/compose meaning.
   - Encountering texts that embody different purposes, concepts, and structures.
   - Using a repertoire of strategies for a variety of purposes.
   - Exploring similarities and differences in meaning and response.
   - Bringing creative and critical questions to the text and being willing to take risks.
   - Responding in a variety of ways: discussions, enactments, writing, and the use of other media.
   - Learning to read one's own texts and the texts of other students.

2. Writing: Composing Texts
   - Using a wide range of discourse: expressive, informational, and poetic.
   - Acquiring a repertoire of composing processes.
   - Selecting the strategies most appropriate for different kinds of discourse, audiences, and purposes for writing.
   - Learning about relationships between oral and written language.
   - Using writing to learn content and to engage actively in the study of discipline.
   - Using writing to make sense of and affect the world.

3. Extending Reading and Writing
   - Empowering oneself to become a more independent and self-reliant learner.
   - Choosing among options what to read and write, in and out of school, as part of the regular program.
   - Using reading and writing to satisfy personal and social needs.
   - Developing a variety of strategies depending on the text, context, and one's own purposes.

4. Investigating Language
   - Exploring language in the context of language in use, not as a separate set of skills.
   - Building on one's own prior knowledge and intuitions about language.
   - Acquiring metalinguistic awareness, that is, knowledge about language and how it functions, including knowledge of the structures of language (systems or parts and how they are related to each other) and knowledge of the social rules of language use.
   - Doing problem-solving tasks with whole texts; dealing with the parts only within a meaningful context.
   - Seeking information about language forms and functions in order to accomplish communicative purposes.
   - Understanding relationships between language and culture.

- Appreciating cultural and linguistic diversity in the classroom.
- Learning about different styles of language appropriate for different circumstances.

5. Learning to Learn
   - Building knowledge or awareness of one's own thinking processes and of what is entailed in the processes of reading, writing, listening, and speaking.
   - Using this knowledge to orchestrate one's own thinking and learning.
   - Developing a repertoire of strategies for different tasks such as note-making, studying, and generating questions.
   - Learning to function independently and interdependently.
   - Learning to pose as well as solve problems.
   - Taking risks in learning and learning from one's own false starts or errors.
   - Learning to collaborate with others.
   - Generating appropriate questions and responding appropriately to questions.

Another, more prevalent source for goals of reading instruction emanates from the publishing companies that produce sets of instructional materials. In the United States, these collections of books and other materials are called basal reading programs, and each of these generally contains an elaborate scope and sequence delineating the goals and objectives. Special editions of these materials are developed for teachers. In these teachers' editions, actual lessons are planned, and goals and objectives are given for each lesson.

Still another source for goals and objectives are the numerous standardized assessments of reading achievement available in the United States. The reading goals listed below are among the simpler and are from the Descriptive Test of Language Skills published by Educational Testing Service (1988). These objectives are for secondary students or college students who are just beginning their undergraduate study.

- Identifying word and/or phrase meaning through context.
- Understanding literal and interpretive meaning.
- Understanding the writer's opinions and tone.

Since these standardized instruments are being used to assess students, many educational agencies adopt the goals of the test as the goals of instruction.

LITERACY/ILLITERACY

A major problem in discussing literacy in the United States is that there is no agreed-upon definition of the term. Nor is there any agreement as to the populations to which this term should be applied (Venezky, 1990). Closely related to the definitional quagmire is the issue of assessment of literacy. Kirsch (1990) identifies three types of literacy assessment:

1. *The traditional approach*, which uses standardized multiple-choice tests and reports competency often in the form of grade level scores. Generally, the grade level definition of literacy or functional literacy has ranged from fourth grade level (Ahmann, 1975) to eighth grade level (Miller, 1973).

2. *The competency-based approach*, which assesses literacy using common materials generally read by adults and reports scores as to the percentage of adults who can master those materials.

3. *The profiles approach*, which again uses real-world materials, but also allows students to respond in writing or orally depending on the nature of the task.

Using the traditional approach, Fisher (1978) estimated that about 45 million adults scored below the eighth grade level on standardized reading tests, assuming that an eighth grade reading level constitutes literacy. Northcutt (1975), using the competency-based approach, estimated that there were approximately 23 million functionally illiterate adults. Currently, the National Assessment of Educational Progress is using the profiles approach.

Another criterion used to define literacy has been the number of years of schooling completed. UNESCO (Smith, 1977) has contended that maintaining permanent literacy requires at least four years of primary schooling. William S. Gray, one of the leading early authorities in reading in the United States, has also assumed that only four or five years of schooling are needed to gain enough skill to continue competent reading. In the United States 99.3 percent of the population has completed five years of elementary education; most of these who haven't completed four years of school are over fifty years old (National Center for Education Statistics, 1989c). Using number of years of schooling to define literacy is, however, a questionable practice (Harman, 1987; McCormick, 1987) since the skill level of individual students differs so markedly.

READING DISABILITIES AND THEIR DIAGNOSIS

The scientific study of reading disability and its diagnosis in this country began in the 1920s and 1930s with examination of clinical studies (Barr, Sadow, and Blachowicz, 1990). The fields of psychology and medicine were initially involved, but educators soon realized that their participation in more detailed case studies would provide insight into the reading process and how it is often disrupted. Special laboratory and reading clinics were established, generally at universities.

The incidence of severe reading problems in modern-day America has been estimated to range from 10 to above 50 percent of the school population, depending on how the term is defined (Rupley and Blair, 1989). Reading problems are sometimes the result of a learning disability, although a reading disability is often interpreted as just one of an array of specific learning disabilities. The approximate number of so-called disabled learners in the general school population is difficult to discover. Numbers range from 6 to 15 percent. This large range is due primarily to the arbitrariness of the definition of learning disabilities (May, 1990). Where once a child with a learning disability would be removed from the classroom and placed in a "special" setting, learning disabled students nowadays will often spend all or a good portion of the school day in the regular classroom. This is due to the passage of the Education for All Handicapped Children Act of 1975. The law, also known as PL 94–142, states that "no child between the ages of three and twenty-one can be denied a free, appropriate public education." The classroom teacher, along with the specialist, must be knowledgeable as to the best methods of diagnosis and instruction for these students.

Generally, a sequence of steps is followed in diagnosing a reading disability. The following types of diagnosis have been outlined by Wilson and Cleland (1989):

1. Informal on-the-spot diagnosis by the classroom teacher during instruction. The teacher pays attention to student responses to questions, writing activities, and general class participation.
2. Classroom diagnosis. In this more structured diagnostic effort, the teacher attempts to determine exactly what is causing the difficulty. In doing so, school records, past teachers, and health reports might be consulted. (See the accompanying list.)
3. Clinical diagnosis. If the above two efforts are unsuccessful, a reading specialist may be called in. A battery of tests will generally be administered to gather objective data on the student's reading skills. Sometimes, other specialists will be consulted, such as a speech therapist or a special education teacher. (See the accompanying list.)
4. Formulation of recommendations and referrals. The reading specialist develops a case study that could include recommendations for remedial treatment, further testing, or referral.

When a child is in need of remedial treatment, he or she will most generally receive help through a Chapter One reading program. Chapter One is a federally funded supplementary educational program, established in the mid-1960s, that services children who are experiencing educational difficulties, reading being one of the curriculum areas for which help is available. Chapter One teachers are usually reading specialists. The program does not replace the classroom reading instruction but supplements it. Chapter One teachers confer regularly with the classroom teacher so that instruction can "dovetail." Some schools in the United States who do not qualify for federal funds establish their own remedial reading programs, but Chapter One is by far the most widely used remedial program. A continuing concern of many reading specialists is the placement of learning disabled students in special resource rooms staffed by faculty with little or no reading background.

Partial List of Assessment Means Used in Classroom Diagnosis

1. Teacher-made informal reading inventories. These have the same features as commercially prepared inventories but are prepared by the teacher using the material from which the students will be taught.

2. Cloze test. This test indicates whether the material to be used is above a student's instructional level. A passage of 150 words from the book to be used is selected; every fifth word is deleted. The student supplies the omitted words.

3. Criterion-referenced tests. These reveal the student's ability to demonstrate a specific skill.

4. Curriculum-based measures. These are assessment techniques, such as teacher observation and teacher-made tests, that let teachers determine student progress before, during, and after instruction.

Partial List of Assessments Used in Clinical Diagnosis

1. Commercially prepared informal inventories.

   Tests: **Burns and Roe Informal Reading Inventory**
   Houghton Mifflin Company
   One Beacon Street
   Boston, Mass. 02108
   Qualitative Reading Inventory
   Scott, Foresman and Company
   1900 East Lake Avenue
   Glenview, Ill. 60625
   Classroom Reading Inventory
   Wm. C. Brown Company
   Dubuque, Iowa

2. Tests of mental ability.

   Tests: **Peabody Picture Vocabulary Test**
   American Guidance Service
   P.O. Box 31552
   Richmond, Va. 23294
   Slosson Intelligence Test, Revised
   Slosson Educational Publications
   P.O. Box 2802
   East Aurora, N.Y. 14052

3. Oral or silent reading of isolated words and some reading in context.

   Tests: **Botel Reading Inventory**
   Follett Publishing Company
   4506 Northwest Highway
   Crystal Lake, Ill. 60614–3397
   Slosson Oral Reading Test

Slosson Educational Publications, Inc.

P.O. Box 2802

East Aurora, N.Y. 14052

Wide Range Achievement Test, Revised

Jastok Associates

Durrell Analysis of Reading Difficulty

The Psychological Corporation

555 Academic Court

San Antonio, Tex. 78204–0952

4. Comprehension after silent reading.

Tests: **Woodcock Reading Mastery Tests,** Revised

American Guidance Service

P.O. Box 31552

Richmond, Va. 23294

Gates-MacGinitie Reading Tests

Riverside Publishing Company

Pennington-Hopewell Road

Hopewell, N.J. 08525

5. Word attack assessment.

Tests: **Doren Diagnostic Test of Word Recognition Skills**

American Guidance Service

P.O. Box 31552

Richmond, Va. 23294

Botel Reading Inventory

Follett Publishing Company

4506 Northwest Highway

Crystal Lake, Ill. 60014–3397

A program that was developed in New Zealand and begun in the United States in 1984 in a small number of Ohio schools is Reading Recovery. This early intervention program is designed for young readers who are experiencing difficulty in their first year of reading instruction. Designed to serve the lowest achieving readers in a first grade classroom. Reading Recovery is an individualized, daily supplemental program. Its primary goal is to help those targeted children catch up with their peers (Pinnell, Fried, and Estice, 1990). Arizona, Idaho, Illinois, Kentucky, New York, South Carolina, Texas, Virginia, West Virginia, and Wisconsin have joined Ohio in offering the program.

READING READINESS/EMERGENT LITERACY

The education of young children is a rapidly growing phenomenon in the United States. From 1970 to 1983, enrollment in preschool programs increased by 33 percent. These increases have been attributed to the increasing employment of mothers with preschoolers, a growing recognition of the importance of early education, and easier access to preschool classes. Indeed, the U.S. Department of Education predicts continued growth in enrollment figures for three- and four-year-old children, with the participation of five year olds rapidly nearing 100 percent (Plisko and Stern, 1985). Twenty-eight of the fifty states are currently funding or have earmarked funds for prekindergarten programs (O'Neil, 1988).

Going hand in hand with preschool education are reading readiness programs. Reading readiness programs have existed in this country since the 1930s (Durkin, 1987) but did not become firmly entrenched until the 1960s (Teale and Sulzby, 1986). Traditionally, these programs have focused on the acquisition of a specific set of skills that have been assumed to be necessary prerequisites to formal reading instruction. Specific types of readiness skills include auditory memory, letter recognition, visual and auditory discrimination, listening skills, and rhyming. These reading readiness skills are generally taught directly and tested formally, usually by using such tests as the Metropolitan Readiness Test, an instrument commonly given to kindergarten children. Every major publisher of a basal reading program in the United States includes a readiness level (Teale and Sulzby, 1986). This segment of the program tends to emphasize the skills described above.

Although a vast majority of kindergarten programs adhere to the reading readiness concept, a growing number of educators have begun to reconceptualize the practice. Research since the mid–1980s has challenged the notion of "getting children ready" to read, indicating that children begin the process of literacy development long before they enter the schoolroom, having learned about it through interaction with their home and community (Y. Goodman, 1986). The term *emergent literacy* is slowly replacing the concept of reading readiness as teachers recognize that "development takes place from within the child . . . emergence is a gradual process: it takes place over time . . . for something to emerge there has to be something there in the first place . . . things usually only emerge if the conditions are right" (Hall, 1987, p. 10).

Unfortunately, not all kindergarten programs in the United States adhere to this changing conceptualization of literacy acquisition. There continues to be some dichotomy between research and practice. Why is this the case? As was indicated previously, publishing companies supply easy-to-use, often attractive reading readiness materials. In addition, parents are pressuring schools for more academic kindergartens (O'Brien, 1989). In response, the National Association for the Education of Young Children issued a statement that decried the isolation of skill development from reading and writing development (Bredekamp, 1987).

In the United States, emergent literacy and the accompanying change of practice and methods that it implies will continue to be discussed and analyzed in the quest to refocus early literacy programs from preset skills to the children themselves.

TEACHER QUALIFICATIONS

Like the education of children, teacher education is for the most part controlled by the states. States license teachers and educators at all levels. For beginning teachers, four years of college is usually required, with a number of courses devoted to pedagogy. Forty-six states also require that prospective teachers take some sort of competency exam prior to licensing (National Center for Education Statistics, 1989a). In the mid–1980s several prestigious groups, including the Carnegie Forum on Education and the Economy (1986) and the Holmes Group (1986), recommended extending the college preparation of beginning teachers to five years, with most of the pedagogy courses to be taken in the fifth year. This extended training period would allow prospective teachers to attain a traditional liberal arts degree as well as eventual licensure in education.

In order to recognize high-quality teachers, these same prestigious groups proposed a higher level of recognition for those educators with three to five years of experience in the field who show real talent. This higher level of credentialism is known as certification, although some states still use the term *certification* to refer to the initial license. The National Board for Teaching Standards has been established to develop and implement the means to grant this advanced certification. In addition, several professional associations including the International Reading Association are either investigating or implementing certification procedures (Cassidy and Seminoff, 1988).

Specialists and administrators in the United States are also licensed by the state and are usually required to get master's degrees. The International Reading Association (1986) recommends certain courses in reading education for different positions. These requirements are summarized in Table 23.1.

The reading specialist operating in a school setting is one of the roles most unique to the United States. Generally, this person operates as a remedial teacher working with small groups of children who have reading difficulties or as a resource teacher serving all faculty and children in a school. In recent years, there has been a tendency to fill these positions with ill-trained people or to supplant the role with special education personnel who often have minimal training in the teaching of reading and language arts. The International Reading Association has taken some stands to thwart this threat to the reading specialist (Cassidy and Rickelman, 1989).

BASIC MATERIALS AND APPROACHES USED IN THE READING PROGRAM

Basal reader series are by far the most widely used materials for teaching reading in the elementary schools of America (Lapp and Flood, 1986). Basals

Table 23.1
Role Titles and Suggested Credit Hours of Training in Teaching Reading

Titles	Training
Classroom Teachers	
Early childhood & elementary	9 credits (6 in reading, 3 in related areas)
Secondary	9 credits (6 in reading, 3 in related areas)
Reading Specialists	
Diagnostic-remedial specialist	18-24 credits in Reading Education
Developmental reading-study skills Specialist	18-24 credits in Reading Education
Reading consultant/reading Resource Teacher	18-24 credits in Reading Education
Reading coordinator/supervisor	24-30 credits in reading plus 6 credits in supervision & administration
Professor of reading	doctorate in reading
Allied Professions	
Special Education Teacher	6 credits in Reading, 3 in related areas
Administrator	6 credits in reading, 9 in related areas
Support service provider	6-9 credits in reading and related areas

Source: J. Cassidy and N. Seminoff, Improving the status and training of the reading professional, *Journal of Reading* 32, no. 1 (October 1988): 20–24.

are complete reading programs, generally authored by reading educators, and published and distributed by private companies for sale to local school districts. The basal series usually consists of one or more readiness books, three pre-primers, a primer, a first reader, and one or two readers for each succeeding grade level through Grade 8. The student's reader is an anthology of stories, plays, poems, and biographies. Occasionally, some will include expository selections. Each basal reader is graded in difficulty; at the earliest levels, the vocabulary is strictly controlled (i.e., a select number of new words are introduced and reinforced in each story). Each reader details the scope and sequence for reading skills to be covered. A basal reading program deals with all phases of the reading program from word recognition and comprehension to vocabulary development and reading for pleasure.

A teacher's manual accompanies each grade level basal. The manual includes complete lesson plans for each reading selection, usually detailing for the teacher how to introduce the vocabulary, set the purpose, build background knowledge, and focus attention. The lesson plan is generally written in a Directed Reading Activity (DRA) format: The teacher motivates and develops background, and sets a purpose for reading; the students read orally and silently, and then respond to the teacher's directed questions. The manual also identifies for the teacher the specific set of skills to be taught through each selection. Comprehension questions, follow-up skill practice, and enrichment activities "round out" the lesson plan.

The student reader and the teacher's manual are the two primary items used in the instructional program. However, supplementary materials are available. These include consumable workbooks that children can complete to reinforce skills they have previously learned in class. They are designed to reinforce the skill taught in class. Other supplementary materials, such as duplicating masters, unit tests, enrichment activities, and reteaching worksheets, are also available from the publisher. These supplementary materials are often employed by the teacher as seat work for students when they are not meeting with the teacher in small groups for instruction.

An estimated 98 percent of U.S. teachers use a basal reader as the chief tool for reading instruction (Lapp and Flood, 1986). Approximately nine companies produce basal series. A few basal series—Houghton Mifflin, for example—publish in Spanish. In the 1980s development and production of a basal series generally cost $15 million to $20 million.

Other Approaches

Direct instruction is very similar to the DRA format in that the teacher controls the learning taking place by making decisions about the classroom environment, setting goals, choosing activities, and providing immediate feedback (Blair, 1984). Demonstration, guided practice, corrective feedback, and independent practice are recommended procedures in this kind of instruction. The Madeline Hunter Model of Teacher Effectiveness is a popular example of a direct instruction approach. Hunter's model contains seven elements or instructional processes that affect success in learning (Hunter and Russell, 1977). The accompanying list presents the seven processes in the model.

The Madeline Hunter Model of Teacher Effectiveness

1. Anticipatory Set. The teacher prepares the learners for the lesson by focusing their attention, motivating, and making positive transfer from previous and related learnings.
2. The Objective and Its Purpose. The teacher tells the students what is to be learned and why they are learning it.
3. Instructional Input. The teacher presents the students with the information to be learned.
4. Modeling. The teacher demonstrates what is to be learned while explaining what is happening.

5. Checking for Understanding. The teacher makes sure students understand the lesson and can perform the needed skills.

6. Guided Practice. The teacher directs and monitors the students' initial practice on the new learning task.

7. Independent Practice. The students practice without direct assistance from the teacher (Hunter and Russell, 1977).

Research on direct instruction indicates that it may be one of the most effective ways to teach most subjects, including reading (Lehr, 1986). Teachers must be cautious, however, not to overstructure and "overskill" their students, which can result in a loss of creativity, independence, and critical thinking.

A top-down, or meaning-centered, approach to the teaching of reading is the language experience approach (LEA), which has been used since the 1920s (Burns, Roe, and Ross, 1988). The essence of the language experience approach is use of the student's language and thinking as a foundation for reading instruction. The children's experiences become the basis for written text. LEA is an excellent approach when working with students who speak English as a second language since the material used for reading instruction is understandable (Moustafa and Penrose, 1985). Experience charts—individual or group-composed stories that are transcribed by the teacher on chart paper or the blackboard—and individual story books are the primary materials used in this approach. Typewriters or computers can be useful to the process. Although generally used in the primary grades, LEA can have many applications in higher grades, especially in content area instruction. The individualized, or personalized, literature program was espoused several decades ago by Willard C. Olson, a child development specialist, heartily supported by Jeanette Veatch and Walter Barbe, and most recently advocated by Kenneth Goodman and Frank Smith (May, 1990) and Bernice Cullinan (1987).

In the individualized reading approach, students move at their own pace through self-selected reading materials. Skill instruction is provided when the teacher deems it necessary. Extensive recordkeeping by both the teacher and the student is imperative. A primary element of this approach is the student–teacher conference. Once or twice a week, for approximately five to ten minutes, the two discuss the book currently being read. At this time the teacher can check for comprehension development, word attack skills, oral reading fluency, and the like. Obviously, reading materials—and lots of them—are the most important tools for this approach. Books, magazines, newspapers, and other texts must be readily available in the classroom. In addition, student book record forms, teacher-kept skill checklists, and a conference form, organized in a student folder, enable the program to be more manageable. Many teachers in the United States have turned to writing as an effective means of promoting and supporting the reading program. A process approach to writing, advocated by Graves (1983) and others, encourages students to take charge of their own development as writers. Like real writers, children move through five subprocesses of the writing process: planning, drafting, revising, editing, and publishing. Central to this approach is the writing conference in which students discuss their drafts with their teachers or peers. Within this structure the child's intended meaning is central, and written text is responded to with honesty and sincerity. Nancie Atwell (1987) reports that students succeed in a writing process environment because there is time for them to choose what they write, and they give, receive, and hear plenty of responses to written text.

Currently in the United States, many classroom educators are adopting a whole-language approach to reading and writing instruction that encompasses elements of language experience, individualized reading, and process writing. The whole-language approach is a philosophical set of beliefs about children and language (K. S. Goodman, 1986). It posits that reading and writing should be learned together in meaningful contexts (Shanahan, 1988). The creation of a language-rich, success-oriented, noncompetitive classroom environment that emphasizes process over product is an instructional must. Appropriate products of reading and writing will follow appropriate process instruction (Atwell, 1987). A whole-language approach includes whole books (as opposed to workbook pages and segmented stories) and daily journal writing. The language arts are taught across the entire, "integrated" curriculum. In a whole-language approach, subskill practice is minimized, while practice in whole-text writing and reading are emphasized. The pragmatic nature of language is never separated from the linguistic aspects of language (Weaver, 1988). Materials to support this approach are varied and depend on the students and the teacher. They might include a range of classroom trade books, both narrative and expository in nature; an available supply of writing materials: various paper types, pens, pencils, and markers; chart paper for group language experience writing; notebooks for daily journal writing; and other print materials such as reference books, brochures, catalogues, pamphlets, and the like. More and more classroom teachers are supplementing their basal reading program with elements from a whole-language approach. Although the basal continues to be the primary tool in the reading program, daily journal writing, individual reading of trade books, and group story sharing are adding a rich dimension to the total instructional picture.

Instructional Debate

The growing popularity of the whole-language movement in the United States has once again highlighted the instructional debates between various factions of reading educators. One of the most publicized areas of conflict in instruction has centered on the role of phonics in reading education. Since English is basically a phonetic language with about 84 percent of the words at the earliest levels conforming to some alphabetic principle (Hanna et al., 1966), some authorities have long argued that phonics instruction should occupy a more prominent place in the reading instruction of young children. Rudolph Flesch's books, *Why Johnny Can't Read and What You Can Do About It* (1955) and *Why Johnny Still*

Can't Read (1981) made the public aware of this concern. Perhaps because of the furor over phonics, the U.S. government sponsored a massive research effort known as the First Grade Studies. The results of these studies seemed to confirm that more variation existed within method than between method, but there was some small support for the phonics emphasis approach (Dykstra, 1968). Coming at the same time as the First Grade Studies was Jeanne Chall's scholarly book *Learning to Read: The Great Debate* (1967, 1983) which examined various instructional studies and concluded that an early phonics emphasis was preferable to approaches that did not emphasize phonics. This finding was again confirmed in *Becoming a Nation of Readers* (Anderson et al., 1985) and in later meta-analyses of existing research (Adams, 1990; Stahl and Miller, 1989).

These strong statements favoring phonics instruction invariably produced a reaction from opponents. Kenneth Goodman, a leading proponent of the whole-language approach, labeled phonics "the chicken soup of reading instruction" (i.e., a favorite remedy for illness that does not work). Later, K. S. Goodman (1986) attacked the authors of *Becoming a Nation of Readers*, calling them members of the "flat-earth society" for their refusal to consider more ethnographic research favoring a more language-based approach to reading instruction. Grundin (1985) also reexamined many earlier studies, including the First Grade Studies, and found that even the First Grade Studies could be reanalyzed and found to favor more language-based approaches such as the language experience method. Stahl and Miller (1989) criticized Grundin's conversion of statistics from parametric to nonparametric, claiming that much valuable information was lost. Stahl concluded from his meta-analysis that whole-language approaches are more effective in kindergarten and that more structured phonics linguistic approaches are best once formal instruction has begun.

Closely related to the instructional debates on phonics are arguments about the role of the teacher in reading instruction. In general, whole-language enthusiasts see the teacher's role as one of a "guide on the side" or a collaborator. Advocates of direct instruction are more likely to agree with the comments of P. David Pearson that

Whole language teachers arrange conditions and materials to allow literacy events to occur "naturally." They do not model the reading process for students, break reading into component processes, or correct "inventions" (what more conservative educators call errors). We have spent the last decade helping teachers move instruction off the wookbook page and into a dialogue with their students. And now we seem to be saying that we need to move it back onto a new kind of page, in a storybook. It is wonderful when children can discover the secrets of reading and writing on their own; when they cannot or do not, it is nice to have teachers around who can share those secrets.

The movement will have a positive impact on literacy instruction; in fact, it already has. But I think it would be ten times as effective if it allowed teachers a more central role in decision making and teaching. (Issue, 1990, p. 7)

TRENDS IN READING INSTRUCTION AND RESEARCH

The trends in reading instruction and research which emerged in the 1980s should continue to influence research in the future.

Comprehension

Much of the current research in reading has been affected by the relatively recent rearticulation of reading as an analytic, interactive, constructive, and strategic process (Pearson, 1985). Ever since Dolores Durkin's landmark study in 1978 which found that comprehension instruction was rarely being taught in elementary classrooms, comprehension has been the focus of much research and investigation. In conjunction with the new definition of reading, comprehension has come to be seen as a "dynamic interactive process of constructing meaning by combining the reader's existing knowledge with the text information within the context of the reading situation" (Monahan and Hinson, 1988, p. 2). The teacher assists the student in building bridges from the new to the known, from prior knowledge to new knowledge. More research is needed on ways to help students build these bridges.

Role of the Teacher

The teacher as collaborator rather than director of meaning-making is also being investigated in various studies across the United States. This image of teacher-as-cognitive-coach sees the educator and the student jointly sharing responsibility for meaning construction (Paris, 1985). Thus, teachers become helpers, mediators, monitors, and modelers. Think-Alouds, a strategy whereby the teacher verbalizes his or her thoughts while reading, has received much recent attention in regards to this shifting image of the teacher (Davey, 1983).

Cooperative Learning

Cooperative team learning is a generic instructional strategy that has found its niche in reading circles. It involves bringing together students of differing abilities to work together on learning tasks. Students are rewarded and recognized based on the group's performance. Individual accountability is also stressed (Johnson et al., 1984; Slavin, 1987). Since the new view of reading sees literacy acquisition as a social, interactive process, cooperative team learning works powerfully to support and uphold these principles. Research is currently being conducted to investigate how team learning can successfully be carried out in all types of reading programs.

Emergent Literacy

As has already been mentioned, recent research has provided new insights into how children develop as readers and writers. The result has been a growing understanding of "emergent literacy." The near future will see educators viewing literacy development more as an "in-head, not an in-hand phenomenon" (Schickedanz, 1989, p. 24). A readiness/prerequisite approach to reading development will give way to an emerging/scaffolding approach in which the teacher acts as a support, or "scaffold," for the child as he or she moves through the process of literacy attainment (Pearson, 1985).

Whole Language

Closely connected with the concept of emergent literacy is the whole-language approach to reading and writing instruction described earlier in this chapter. Educators are moving toward total integration of the language arts and its use across the total curriculum (Goodman, 1989). Connections between and among reading, writing, speaking, and listening are being made as teachers actively investigate what it means to empower their students to become literate members of society (Smith, 1989). Much research and investigation have been conducted to ascertain how educators can facilitate the natural literacy processes of children. In the coming years the battle over the nature of reading will surely continue as educators argue whether it is primarily "bottom-up" (reading begins with print and proceeds systematically to meaning) or "top-down" (reading begins with knowledge and hypotheses and proceeds to the print). However, the whole-language approach is influencing an increasing number of school programs (Issue, 1990, p. 7) and will very likely continue to do so.

Assessment

As reading educators face the decade, assessment will continue to be a key topic for discussion. Valencia et al. (1989) have pointed out that "knowledge of the reading processes and reading instruction is at odds with (current) assessment instruments" (p. 57). While the country's understanding of reading has advanced over the last ten years, tests have not. Current standardized reading assessment practices continue to rely predominantly on literal and sentence-level comprehension items and to test isolated skills. Forty-six of the fifty states have mandated state-regulated testing; all of them include testing in reading (Valencia et al., 1989). Unfortunately, most of the states that have developed their own reading assessments have modeled their tests on standardized assessments that do not reflect current understanding of reading processes. Some states, however, namely, Illinois, Massachusetts, Michigan, Maine, Pennsylvania, and Wisconsin, have designed or are designing tests that assess the multifaceted dimensions of the reading process. Background knowledge, the ability to construct meaning in order to comprehend text, the ability to use reading strategies, and students' reading habits and attitudes are just a few of the areas that will be tapped by these new tests.

Reading and writing assessment by the classroom teacher will also be examined in the 1990s. Performance-based assessment in the form of student portfolios will continue to be examined and developed. These portfolios will include a myriad of materials to better help the teacher, parent, and student understand the child's growing competence in various aspects of literacy. Daily writing selections, lists of books read, and personal reactions to literature are just a few of the items that might be collected over time and stored in the portfolio. These portfolios can then be passed along from year to year as a continuing document (Wolf, 1989). It is hoped that these new forms of assessment will narrow the gap between how readers read and how they are assessed.

Family Involvement

Family literacy, intervention programs, and parent education will also continue to be of primary concern in the United States. Several studies have indicated that parent involvement in their children's education has a direct effect on reading achievement (Shuck, Ulsh, and Platt, 1983). The notion of empowerment (Giroux, 1987) is central to school–home initiatives. Parents must be involved in the literacy development of their children—and not only involved, but also given choices and made equal partners with schools (May, 1990). The 1990s will see these home–school links strengthened and defined.

Computers

Finally, a word must be said about the role of computers in the future of U.S. reading programs. When computers first appeared on the education horizon in the early 1980s, many school districts moved quickly to obtain computer equipment. Indeed, many added "computer education" to the school curriculum in response to the fear of becoming a computer illiterate society (Rickelman and Henk, 1989). The initial enthusiasm for computer-assisted instruction and the frenetic energy that accompanied its arrival seem to have subsided. No doubt, computers will continue to be a useful piece of equipment in the reading instructional program. However, educators must decide on the direction in which to take this new technology. As computer technology evolves, so, too, must the computer knowledge base of reading professionals. Wepner and Reinking (1989) recommend that teachers rely, first and foremost, on their own beliefs and understanding about reading when making decisions about computers; that they consider how they will use the computer for instruction before making other decisions; and that they attempt to balance structure and flexibility when integrating computers into a reading program. If these recommendations are heeded, the use of computers is less likely to become an end in itself.

CONCLUDING COMMENTS

That, in a very few words, is "The Great American Reading Machine," a multifaceted interlocking operation involving government agencies, teachers, publishing companies, researchers, and, of course, children. For readers who want a more complete picture, the accompanying list of suggested further readings should prove helpful. Despite its complexity, the picture is nowhere near as gloomy as that painted in Yarington's 1978 book *The Great American Reading Machine*. Perhaps the following passages from *Becoming a Nation of Readers* (Anderson et al., 1985) more accurately reflect the beliefs of educators in the United States:

The more elements of good parenting, good teaching, and good schooling that children experience, the greater the likelihood that they will achieve their potential as good readers. (p. 117)

[The United States] will become a nation of readers when verified practices of the best teachers in the best schools can be introduced throughout the country. (p. 120)

Suggested Additional Readings

Becoming a Nation of Readers: The Report of the Commission on Reading by Richard C. Anderson, Elfrieda H. Hiebert, Judith A. Scott, and Ian A. G. Wilkinson. This very popular government report contains the interpretations of leading experts on the current knowledge about reading and on the state of the art in teaching reading in the United States. This report is a careful and thorough synthesis of an extensive body of findings on reading; it is written so that an educated layperson can understand it. Published by the National Academy of Education, National Institute of Education, and the Center for the Study of Reading; co-distributed by the International Reading Association (IRA), 1985, 147 pp.

Handbook of Reading Research, edited by P. David Pearson. This volume contains a current and comprehensive review of the research methods and existing knowledge base in the field of reading. Each chapter includes a historical overview and a careful breakdown and analysis of its topic. Representative chapter topics include a summary and a where-do-we-go-from-here section, plus bibliographies and subject and author indexes. Published by Longman; co-distributed by the IRA, 1984, 899 pp.

New Directions in Reading Instruction by Joy Monahan and Bess Hinson. This guide provides a quick summary of recent research ideas relating to comprehension instruction, cooperative learning, textbooks, questioning, and more than twenty other topics of current concern to teachers. The easy-to-use flip chart presents summarized nuggets of information on content area reading and learning strategies. Published by the IRA, 1988, 30 pp.

Teaching Reading in Today's Elementary Schools by Paul C. Burns, Betty D. Roe, and Elinor P. Ross. This volume is probably the most popular text in undergraduate reading courses; thus, it is one of the most often read reading methods books used by students preparing to be elementary teachers in the United States. Topics covered include major approaches to reading instruction, readers with special needs, assessment, and classroom management, as well as methods to develop word recognition, meaning vocabulary, comprehension, study skills, reading in the content areas, and literary and recreational appreciation of reading. Published by Houghton Mifflin Co., 1988, 639 pp.

Theoretical Models and Processes of Reading (3rd edition), edited by Harry Singer and Robert B. Ruddell. The theories, models, and research in processes of reading are covered in this comprehensive collection of important studies. Contributors focus on historical changes in reading, processes in reading, models of reading, and teaching and research issues. The authors describe issues related to meta cognition, schema interaction, knowledge use and control processes, substrata theory, and other related concepts. Published by the IRA, 1985, 960 pages.

What's Whole in Whole Language by Ken Goodman. This volume is an easy reading introduction to whole language for parents and teachers and is written by one of the most eminent authorities in the field. The author gives the underlying philosophy of whole-language instruction, as well as descriptions of whole-language classrooms. Included is some criticism of reading and language instruction as it is normally taught in U.S. schools. Published by Heinemann Educational Books, Inc., 1986, 80 pp.

REFERENCES

Adams, M. J. 1990. *Phonics and beginning reading instruction.* Champaign, Ill.: Reading Research and Education Center, University of Illinois.

Ahmann, J. S. 1975. An exploration of survival levels of achievement by means of assessment techniques. In D. M. Nielsen and H. F. Hjelm (eds.), *Reading and career education.* Newark, Del.: International Reading Association.

Anderson, R. C., Hiebert, E. H., Scott, J. A., and Wilkinson, I.A.G. 1985. *Becoming a nation of readers.* Washington, D.C.: National Institute of Education.

Applebee, A. N., Langer, J. A., and Mullis, V. S. 1988. *Who reads best?* Princeton, N.J.: Educational Testing Service.

Atwell, N. 1987. *In the middle: Writing, reading, and learning with adolescents.* Upper Montclair, N.J.: Boynton/Cook.

Barr, R., Sadow, M., and Blachowicz, C. 1990. *Reading diagnosis for teachers.* New York: Longman.

Blair, T. 1984. Teacher effectiveness: The know-how to improve student learning. *The Reading Teacher 38* (November): 138–142.

Bredekamp, S. (ed.). 1987. *Developmentally appropriate practice in early childhood programs serving children from birth through age 8.* Washington, D.C.: National Association for the Education of Young Children.

Burns, P., Roe, B., and Ross, E. 1988. *Teaching Reading in Today's Elementary Schools.* Boston: Houghton Mifflin Company.

Carnegie Forum on Education and the Economy. 1986. *A nation prepared: Teachers for the 21st century. The Report of the Task Force on Teaching as a Profession.* New York: Carnegie Forum on Education and the Economy.

Cassidy, J., and Rickelman, R. J. 1989. The importance of specialists in reading. *The Reading Instruction Journal*, 32, No. 2 (Winter): 3–7.

Cassidy, J., and Seminoff, N. 1988. Improving the status and training of the reading professional. *Journal of Reading* 32, No. 1 (October): 20–24.

Chall, J. S. 1967. *Learning to read: The great debate*. New York: McGraw–Hill.

Chall, J. S. 1983. *Learning to read: The great debate, updated version*. New York: McGraw–Hill.

Cullinan, B. E. (eds.), 1987. *Children's literature in the reading program*. Newark, Del.: International Reading Association.

Davey, B. 1983. Think-aloud—modeling the cognitive processes of reading comprehension. *Journal of Reading* 27, No. 1: 44–47.

Durkin, D. 1978–1979. What classroom observations reveal about comprehension instruction. *The Reading Research Quarterly* 14 No. 4: 481–533.

Durkin, D. 1987. *Teaching young children to read*. Newton, Mass.: Allyn and Bacon.

Dykstra, R. 1968. The effectiveness of code- and meaning-emphasis beginning reading programs. *The Reading Teacher* 22, No. 1: 23.

Educational Testing Service. 1988. *Descriptive tests of language skills: Reading comprehension*. Princeton, N.J.: Educational Testing Service.

Fisher, D. L. 1978. *Functional literacy and the schools*. Washington, D.C.: National Institute of Education. (ERIC Document Reproduction Service No. ED 151 760.)

Flesch, R. 1955. *Why Johnny can't read and what you can do about it*. New York: Harper and Brothers.

Flesch, R. 1981. *Why Johnny still can't read?* New York: Harper and Row.

Giroux, H. 1987. Critical literacy and student experience: Donald Graves' approach to literacy. *Language Arts* 64: 175–181.

Goodman, K. S. 1985. Becoming a nation of readers draws a variety of responses. *Reading Today* 3, No. 2 (October/November): 11.

Goodman, K. S. 1986. *What's whole in whole language*. Portsmouth, N.H.: Heinemann.

Goodman, K. S. 1989. Whole language is whole: A response to Huymsfeld. *Educational Leadership*, 69–70.

Goodman, Y. 1986. Children coming to know literacy. In W. H. Teale and E. Sulzby (eds.), *Emergent literacy: Reading and writing*, pp. 1–14. Norwood, N.J.: Ablex.

Graves, D. 1983. *Writing: Teachers and children at work*. Portsmouth, N.H.: Heinemann Educational Books.

Grundin, H. 1985. A commission of selective readers: A critique of *Becoming a Nation of Readers*. *The Reading Teacher* 39 (December): 262–266.

Hall, N. 1987. *The emergence of literacy*. Portsmouth, N.H.: Heinemann.

Hanna, P. R., Hanna, J. S., Hodges., R. E., and Rudorf, E. H. 1966. *Phoneme-grapheme correspondences as cues to spelling improvement*. (Research report No. 1991.) Washington, D.C.: Office of Education.

Harman D. 1987. *Illiteracy: A national dilemma*. New York: Cambridge Book Co.

Harris, A. J. 1968. Research on some aspects of comprehension: Rate, flexibility, and study skills. *Journal of Reading* 12: 205–210, 258–260.

Holmes Group. 1986. *Tomorrow's teachers: A report of the Holmes group*. East Lansing, Mich.: Holmes Group.

Hunter, M., and Russell, D. 1977. How can I plan more effective lessons? *Instructor* 87 (September): 74–75, 88.

International Reading Association. 1986. *Guidelines for the specialized preparation of reading professionals*. Newark, Del.: International Reading Association.

Issue: the "whole language" approach, which treats reading as a holistic process and de-emphasizes instruction in separate skills, is influencing an increasing number of school programs. Will whole language improve reading instruction? 1990. Association for Supervision and Curriculum Development Update (February): 7.

Johnson, D., Johnson, R., Holubec, E. J., and Roy, P. 1984. *Circles of learning.* Alexandria, Va.: Association for Supervision and Curriculum.

Kirsch, I. S. 1990. Measurement. In R. L. Venezky, D. A. Wagner, and B. S. Ciliberti. *Toward defining literacy.* Newark, Del.: International Reading Association.

Lapp. D., and Flood, J. 1986. *Teaching students to read.* New York: Macmillan.

Lehr, F. 1986. Direct Instruction in reading. *The Reading Teacher* 39 (March): 706–708.

Lytle, S. L., and Botel, M. 1988. *PCRP II: Reading, writing and talking across the curriculum.* Pennsylvania Department of Education.

McCormick, S. 1987. *Remedial and clinical reading instruction.* Columbus, Ohio: Merrill Publishing Co.

May, F. 1990. *Reading as communication.* Columbus, Ohio: Merrill Publishing Co.

Miller, G. A. 1973. *Linguistic communications: Perspectives for research.* Newark, Del.: International Reading Association.

Monahan, J., and Hinson, B. 1988. *New directions in reading instruction.* Newark, Del.: International Reading Association.

Moustafa, M., and Penrose, J. 1985. Comprehensible input PLUS the language experience approach: Reading Instruction for limited English-speaking students. *The Reading Teacher* 38 (March): 640–647.

National Center for Education Statistics. 1989a. *The condition of education, 1989: Volume one, elementary and secondary education.* (Publication No. CS89–650.) Washington, D.C.: U.S. Government Printing Office.

National Center for Education Statistics. 1989b. *The condition of education, 1989: Volume Two: Post secondary education.* (Publication No. CS89–650.) Washington, D.C.: U.S. Government Printing Office.

National Center for Education Statistics. 1989c. *The digest of education statistics, 25th Edition.* (Publication No. NCES89–643.) Washington, D.C.: U.S. Government Printing Office.

Northcutt, N. 1975. *The adult performance level project (APL): Adult functional competency* (Report to the Office of Education dissemination review panel). Austin: University of Texas.

O'Brien, S. J. 1989. But when is nap time? *Childhood Education* 65: 163–164.

O'Neil, J. 1988. Early childhood education: Advocates square off over goals. *Association for Supervision and Curriculum Development Update* 30: 1–6.

Paris, S. G. 1985. Using classroom dialogues and guided practice to teach comprehension strategies. In T. L. Harris and E. J. Cooper (eds.), *Reading, thinking, and concept development,* pp. 133–146. New York: College Board Publications.

Pearson, P. D. 1985. Changing the face of reading comprehension instruction. *The Reading Teacher* 38, No. 8: 724–738.

Pinnell, G. S., Fried, M., and Estice, R. M. 1990. Reading recovery: Learning how to make a difference. *Reading Teacher* 43, No. 4: 282–295.

Plisko, V., and Stern, J. (eds.). 1985. *The condition of education.* Washington, D.C.: U.S. Department of Education.

Rickelman, R., and Henk, W. 1989. Reading and technology: Past failures and future dreams. *Reading Teacher* 43, No. 2: 174–175.

Rupley, W., and Blair, T. 1989. *Reading diagnosis and remediation*.Columbus, Ohio: Merrill Publishing Co.

Schickedanz, J. A. 1989. What about preschoolers and academics? *Reading Today* (August/September): 24.

Shanahan, T. 1988. The reading-writing relationship: Seven instructional principles. *The Reading Teacher* 41, No. 7: 636–646.

Shuck, A., Ulsh, F., and Platt, J. S. 1983. Parents encourage pupils (PEP): An innercity parent involvement reading project. *The Reading Teacher* 36: 524–528.

Slavin, R. 1987. *Cooperative learning: Student teams*. Washington, D.C.: National Education Association.

Smith, F. 1989. Overselling literacy. *Phi Delta Kappan* 70, No. 5: 352–359.

Smith, L. 1977. Literacy: Definitions and implications. *Language Arts* 54: 135–138.

Stahl, S. A., and Miller, P. D. 1989. Whole language and language experience approaches for beginning reading: A quantitative research synthesis. *Review of Educational Research* 59, No. 1: 87–116.

Teale, W., and Sulzby, E. (eds.), 1986. *Emergent literacy: Reading and writing*. Norwood, N.J.: Ablex.

Valencia, S., Pearson, P. D., Peters, C., and Wixon, K. 1989. Theory and practice in statewide reading assessment: Closing the gap. *Educational Leadership* 46, No. 7: 57–63.

Venezky, R. L. 1990. Definitions. In R. L. Venezky, D. A. Wagner, and B. S. Ciliberti. *Toward defining literacy*, pp. 2–16. Newark, Del.: International Reading Association.

Weaver, C. 1988. *Reading process and practice*. Portsmouth, N.H.: Heinemann Educational Books.

Wepner, S., and Reinking, D. 1989. Integrating computers into reading/language arts instruction. In S. Wepner, J. Feeley, and D. Strickland (eds.), *The administration and supervision of reading programs*, pp. 290–227. New York: Teachers College Press.

Wilson, R., and Cleland, C. 1989. *Diagnostic and remedial reading for classroom and clinic*. Columbus, Ohio: Merrill Publishing Co.

Wolf, D. 1989. Portfolio assessment: Sampling student work. *Educational Leadership* 46, No. 7: 35–39.

Yarington, D. J. 1978. *The great American reading machine*. Rochelle Park, N.J.: Hayden Co.

24

West Germany

Franz Biglmaier

THE GERMAN LANGUAGE

German-Speaking Countries

German is the language of Germany, Austria, the German-speaking part of Switzerland, South Tyrol (Italy), Luxembourg, Alsace (France), and some smaller places at the borderline in Belgium and Denmark. German is also spoken in some ''language islands'' in Czechoslovakia, Poland, Russia, Rumania, and Hungary. Outside of Central Europe German is also spoken in parts of the United States, Canada, Brazil, Argentina, and Africa (e.g., South West Africa). Altogether there are about 100 to 110 million German-speaking people all over the world. In the rank-order of how many people speak a certain language, German ranges at the tenth position, with Chinese, English, and Spanish the most often used languages in the world.

German and English belong to the same Indo-Germanic language group and so have many features in common. Many basic words are similar: *Vater*—father, *Mutter*—mother, *Wasser*–water, *trinken*—drink, sechs—six, and so on.

Grammar

English grammatical forms are simpler than their German equivalent. For example, the English article *the* may be represented in German by *der* (masculine), *die* (feminine), or *das* (neuter) and some others (*dem, den, dessen*). On the other hand, spelling in German is in greater agreement with the spoken language than is the case for English and is therefore much less complicated than British or American English spelling. In order to represent a certain phoneme, only one or a few graphemes are used in the German language, whereas in the English language one phoneme may be represented by a dozen or more different ways of graphemes (letters, letter groups).

Dialect

The German language as taught in the schools and used by the educated classes, the newspapers, and the literary and professional publications is called High German (*Hochdeutsch*). But many Germans speak a language that is a mixture of standard language and dialect.

The three main groups of dialects spoken in Germany are Upper German, spoken in the south; Middle or Midland German, in the middle belt; and Low German or *Plattdeutsch*, in the northern area, the low-lying stretches of northern Germany. Plattdeutsch has many words similar to English. There are many distinct dialects within every group of dialects. The state of Bavaria (11 million people), for example, has three main dialects—Bavarian, Frankonian, and Aleman-Swabian—each with many different variations.

The main and official languages in Switzerland are German, French, Italian, and Rhaeto-Romance (Latin dialect). German is spoken by about 70 percent and French by about 20 percent. Schwyzer-Dütsch (Swiss-German) is spoken at home, whereas High German is taught in school and is used in public communication.

READING INSTRUCTION POLICY

Reading Instruction Policy Controlled by States

The Bundesrepublik Deutschland (FRG) or Federal Republic of Germany (FRG), often called West Germany in English, includes the states (*Länder*) of Baden-Württemberg, Bavaria, Bremen, Hamburg, Hessen, Lower Saxony, North Rhine-Westphalia, the Rhineland-Palatinate, the Saarland, Schleswig-Holstein, and West Berlin, which has a special status. As of 1981 more than 61 million people lived in an area of 248,700 square kilometers (density 246 people per square kilometer). About 4.8 million or 6.4 percent are foreign (Turkish, Yugoslavian, Italian, Spanish, Greek). West Berlin has the highest proportion of foreigners—13.6 percent—which is more than double the average of West Germany. This fact places a special burden on education in the city, for schools in general and reading in particular.

When the Federal Republic of Germany was founded in 1949, the Grundgesetz (Basic Law, Constitution) contained only one short article (Art. 7) on education regulating a few fundamental questions: state inspections of schools, religious instruction as a subject of the syllabus in state schools, and the right to private education. The responsibility for schools was placed with the eleven individual *Länder* of the Federal Republic. Each *Land* is autonomous in this respect and has its own constitution and its own Ministry of Education. This system favored the development of divergent educational practices and regulations. The constitutional law and the decrees of the respective *Länder* determine the aim of education, enforce school attendance, provide for the building and maintenance of schools, the training and in-service training of teachers, school inspection, administration and supervision, and the cooperation of parents in the life and work of the school. In order to overcome the hardships that might arise from differences in standards (especially for children whose families must move from one school district to another), duration of obligatory full-time school attendance, unequal requirements for admission to institutions of higher learning, and other issues have been regulated by the Kultus-Minister-Konferenz der Länder (KMK). Through agreements, resolutions, and recommendations at this conference of ministers, a uniform system for German education is sought. The agreements are referred to the separate state authorities or legislatures for adoption or, if no legislative action is required, are put into effect by decree. As a rule, the state legislature adopts such suggestions. The terminology of school types is standardized as follows. The junior division, attended in common by all pupils, is known as Grundschule (elementary school up to class IV or VI). The types of school continuing education beyond the Grundschule level are known as Hauptschule (main school, up to class IX), Realschule (secondary general school up to class X) or Gymnasium (secondary general school giving access to higher education, up to class XIII). Grundschule and Hauptschule were formerly called Volksschule. Schools for physically, psychologically, or mentally handicapped children or young people are known as Sonderschulen (special schools).

Compulsory education in Germany extends from the age of six to the age of eighteen. Full-time compulsory schooling lasts nine years. All pupils who at the end of nine years cease full-time attendance in a secondary school must attend a part-time vocational school, the Berufsschule, one day a week for three years. The vast majority of young people get their training simultaneously at their paid employment and in a vocational school. Apprentices must attend the vocational school until they have completed their apprenticeship, regardless of their age. The emphasis in vocational training is on specialization in the knowledge and skills necessary to carry out the young worker's particular type of work efficiently. The vocational school improves on the skill and knowledge gained on the job in the place of employment and gives insight into fundamental principles. At the same time, instruction in general academic subjects such as the German language and social studies is continued. The final examinations are set and judged by industrial administrative bodies (boards of industry and commerce and boards of handicraft) in collaboration with the vocational school.

In comparison with American schools, the German education system seems to be more specialized in the lower levels. For instance, in the fourth grade at the age of ten years, pupils may already be set on a college-bound school, the Gymnasium.

THE GOALS OF READING INSTRUCTION

Objectives in Beginning Reading

Reading instruction throughout all grades is part of the language instruction of the mother tongue (*muttersprachlicher Unterricht, Deutsch*). Every student must take German for four to six hours per week. In first grade several subjects are combined to *Gesamtunterricht* (united teaching: language, math, science, etc.), so that there is more time available to teach reading and writing and to integrate them with other subjects.

The goal for reading at the end of first grade is stated in the Berlin curriculum (1968): "Children should be able to read new texts of the same difficulty level as primers." The curriculum of North-Rhine-Westphalia (1969) says: "children should read texts which are within their comprehension and language abilities in a meaningful and expressive way." The Bavarian curriculum (1971) demands for the end of first grade: "After having read a text children should be able to recognize the essential content." The Berlin curriculum of 1988–1989 states: "The child applies his reading abilities independently in using texts." Specific criteria of reading are not mentioned.

Objectives in Primary and Secondary Schools

Reading in the following grades of the elementary school is called *Weiter-führendes Lesen* (continuing reading). The goals for reading are stated in general terms such as "to increase reading skills" or "to extend reading abilities." They are not specified. Only comprehension is dealt with in a more differentiated way. For the elementary school, reading can be specified objectively within the perceptive and cognitive domain according to accuracy, speed, fluency, and comprehension. In the emotional domain we look for motivation and interest.

Accuracy may be measured as the percentage of correctly read words. Speed can be calculated as the number of words read in one minute (words/minute). Fluency can be judged within a text as the percentage of coherently read phrases (which should be marked). Comprehension may be shown as the percentage of correctly answered questions.

For over thirty years Biglmaier has collected and published data on pupils from first to fifth grade (1960, 1973, 1990). These studies specify the reading goals for German-speaking children. A normally developed child should be able to read a text commensurate with his age and experience, as follows:

At the end of—	Accuracy	Speed	Fluency	Comprehension
Grade 1	80%	30 w/min	60%	60%
Grade 2	95%	60 w/min	80%	80%
Grade 3	95%	90 w/min	80%	80%
Grade 4	95%	120 w/min	80%	80%

Speed of oral reading increases constantly from first to fourth grade, whereas accuracy, fluency, and comprehension do not change greatly after the second grade. The topics are more challenging, the vocabulary load increases, but the criteria are quite stable. Speed of silent reading surpasses oral reading after the second grade, but the increase in silent reading among university students and teachers is not dramatic. Students and teachers in Munich and Berlin were checked based on informal methods. The average reading speed was 200 to 250 words/minute. The highest score recorded was for a secondary student who read 800 w/min with more than 80 percent comprehension. The range of reading speed in that class was 150 to 800 w/min.

ILLITERACY

Illiteracy means the inability to read and write. Everyone has the potential to learn to read and write, but not all have the opportunities to acquire it. Germany has always been among the countries with the lowest illiteracy rates; the estimate during the last four decades has remained steady at around 1 percent.

Of course, illiteracy rates depend on how we define the term and what method we use to decide who is literate. The manner of reporting illiteracy varies. In some areas the criterion of literacy is the ability to write one's name or to read or to read or write a letter, or the individual's mastery of at least the fourth grade of formal schooling (functional literacy). Germany uses a more complex term *Bildung*, which is hard to translate.

READING DISABILITIES

Legasthenia (Dyslexia) and Other Terms

Accuracy and error of reading are two sides of the same criterion: accuracy is the positive and error the negative. Messmer (1904) was the first German researcher to use a classification scheme of reading errors. E. Kirste (1926) used a similar causative error classification but with different subterms. To date many error classifications have been published: descriptive and causative. Descriptive classifications describe an error according to quantity, quality, sequence, and the like, whereas causative classifications look for the reasons behind the error: physiological, psychological, environmental, and so on.

Reading time was researched in the Laboratory of Wundt in Leipzig as early as 1886 by the American Cattell as well as by O. Messmer (1904), M. Beer (1910), Bobertag and many others. Biglmaier (1960) compared the results of former reading speeds with his own findings and established norms for oral reading speed at the end of the first up to the fifth grade. As mentioned above, he recently continued this research.

Accuracy and speed are the basic factors that determine whether a child reads above or below normal expectations. Percentile ranks (PR) and other statistical measurements can be used in order to determine the level of backwardness in reading. Quantitatively, we can differentiate between the following:

$$Leseschwierigkeiten = \text{reading difficulties (PR} < 25)$$
$$Leseschwäche \quad\quad = \text{reading "weakness" (PR} < 9)$$
$$Lesestörungen \quad\quad = \text{reading disability (PR} < 2)$$

In 1916 the Hungarian physician Ranschburg introduced the term *legasthenia*, meaning "weakness in reading." He used the term for children of all intelligence levels. Linder (1951) redefined the term as a special weakness in learning to read and (indirectly) in spelling found in children of comparatively good intelligence. The term *legasthenia* as used in Linder's definition is now widely accepted in Middle Europe. It is also called *Lese-Rechtschreib-Schwäche* (LRS = reading-spelling weakness), as Kirchhoff named it. Many other terms have been used in Germany, for example, *Alexie, Dyslexie, kongenitale Wortblindheit, angeborene Legasthenie, Bradylexie,* and *Schreib-Lese-Schwäche*.

In the 1950s several psychologists from German-speaking countries published experiences and tests that would diagnose and help those children: M. Linder (Zurich), H. Kirchhoff (Hamburg), L. Schenk-Danziger (Wien), and F. Biglmaier (Munich). In the 1960s and 1970s many publications appeared on legasthenia; among them were works by Angermaier, Atzesberger, Dummer, Eggert, Ferdinand, Grissemann, Klasen, Kossakowski, Kossow, H. Meyer, R. Müller, Niemeyer, Schlee, Schmalohr, Schubenz, Sirch, Valtin, and Weinschenk. Schlee and Sirch rejected the term *legasthenia* in "The Nonsense of Legasthenia" and "Research on Legasthenia at an End," but others advocated different approaches and institutional assistance. All the state ministries on education issued guidelines on how to help legasthenic students in school through screening devices and special groupings. A lot of materials have been developed especially for reversals that, according to Schenk-Danziger's definition, should constitute legasthenia. The quarrel over definitions, diagnosis, and therapy in connection with legasthenia (similar to that over the English term *dyslexia*) has stirred up public interest but it was not always in a very helpful way.

Problems of Diagnosis

In order to diagnose a child as legasthenic, both a reading test and an intelligence test have to be applied. There are no clear-cut borderlines stated on intelligence. Several German states offer their schools different measures (e.g., IQ 80, 85, 90, and 95). That situation was much debated, especially because a legasthenic child got several "privileges," for example, no grading in reading and spelling, promotion to the next grade despite language difficulties, and special small-group assistance. According to these differences, a legasthenic child in one state was not considered legasthenic in another state.

The term *LRS*—reading-spelling difficulties—avoided some of the shortcomings connected with the term *legasthenia* because intelligence was left out. The normal procedure for diagnosing LRS would be to apply a reading and a spelling test. The reading test should be an oral reading test, not a silent test for comprehension. An oral reading test furnishes data on accuracy, speed, and fluency which cannot be derived from a silent reading test. Several oral reading tests are available in Germany, both standardized and informal.

Spelling tests are offered for all grades in elementary schools and for some grades in secondary schools. Spelling is of great interest among German teachers and the public because a spelling test is more easily applied than a reading test. A whole group can be tested in one session, whereas oral reading has to be administered individually. Therefore some researchers diagnose reading-spelling difficulties with only a spelling test and omit reading.

Reading and spelling can be measured quantitatively and differentiated qualitatively. Biglmaier has suggested a classification of types of errors in reading (similar to Marion Monroe's procedure, 1932) and has extended it to spelling. Six categories with several subcategories are used; numbers 1–3 are for reading, and numbers 1–6 are for spelling:

1. Quantity. Addition and omission of phonemes or graphemes, syllables, and words.
2. Quality. Consonant and vowel errors; they are substituted by another phoneme or grapheme.
3. Sequence. Directional disorder of letters, reversed letter like *b-d p-q b-p n-u*.
4. Capitalization. Beginning letter incorrectly large or small.
5. Word articulation. Incorrect division of a word, contractions.
6. Sentence articulation. Punctuation omitted, added, or wrong.

Treatment

The treatment of children who are having difficulties in reading and spelling is provided either in elementary schools (secondary schools do not have such services) by special grouping and special lessons within the class or school (*Förderunterricht*), or, less frequently, for several schools in a special reading class (in some larger German cities). Reading clinics such as are found in the United States and Scandinavia were established in Munich and Berlin by Biglmaier and in Aurich by L. Schmidt. These are the only such clinics in Germany.

During the last twenty years, teachers, parents, and the public have become more aware of children with reading and spelling difficulties. Although the main job of helping these children has to be done in elementary school, much improvement remains to be encouraged at the secondary level. Too many students have to repeat classes or are sent back to *Hauptschule* despite their good capacities and intelligence. *Realschulen* and *Gymnasien* should help legasthenic students in several ways. Specifically, they should offer remedial programs, including diagnoses and successful correction of basic difficulties in word recognition, speed of reading, and comprehension.

READING READINESS

School Readiness Instead of Reading Readiness

Reading readiness is not a known term and therefore is not an issue in West Germany. Reading readiness is seen in a broader sense within the context of school readiness (*Schulreife*). Is a child fit for the school, or should the child be kept back at home or in kindergarten? This question was debated ten to thirty years ago. In the early 1930s, Arthur Kern found that about 40 percent of elementary school children up to the fourth grade failed and had to repeat a grade mainly because of failure in reading and writing. During the 1950s and 1960s many school readiness tests were used, and children were sent back to the families. This procedure was not very helpful, however.

Combined School Entrance Level

A better way to help children get a better start in school is to introduce a combined school entrance level. In Germany children go to kindergarten when they are three years old and continue up to their sixth year when they enter school. The five year olds in kindergarten get some additional training in language and other areas but not in reading. In West Berlin and some West German states the last year in kindergarten and the first year in school have been combined as the *Schuleingangsstufe*. A school teacher and a kindergarten teacher work together with a group of up to twenty-eight children. Each teacher is responsible for about half the group (eleven to fifteen children), and both halves work closely together. A child has a teacher for two years instead of one. Thus, the development of a child can be observed much more closely and receive better assistance. Reading results at the end of first grade showed a higher standard than normal first grades.

Beginning Reading Instruction

Methods of teaching reading have been used for two thousand years. Until the beginning of the sixteenth century, the alphabetic method was used all over Europe. In 1530 Valentin Ickelsamer wrote a book promoting sounding methods instead of using the names of the letters. But it took nearly 350 years until the last German Ministry of Education outlawed the letter-naming method. Since then, all German teachers have used the sounding methods.

Letter naming is still used in English-speaking countries, but English is not as regular as German. The use of phonics remains a much debated question. The knowledge of letters (not of sounds, which has not been investigated) is considered one of the best predictors of success in reading according to some research. Not all the ramifications of this question have been considered.

Phonics are used in German reading instruction from the beginning. Oral language—listening and speaking—is developed in every child who comes to school. Oral language should therefore be the starting point of reading instruction. The only trouble is that oral language can only be heard, not seen. To analyze a spoken word—that is, to divide it into syllables and sounds—is hard for a first grader. Visual and tactile assistance is necessary.

The great debate in Germany on reading methods during the 1950s and 1960s was concerned with old synthetic versus new analytic methods. Should reading instruction start with a letter or sound or, instead, with a word, sentence, or text? The single-unit approach versus the global approach! During the last two decades most of the teachers and authors of primers have agreed to use integrated methods: analytic and synthetic. They are also called methods-integrated approaches.

The present German primers can be ordered into four groups:

Analytic/**Global**	*Analytic*-**synthetic**	**Analytic**-*synthetic*	*Synthetic*
	some letters known	all letters known	all letters
word	word	word	letter
sentence	sentence		
text	text		

Global and *analytic*-synthetic methods start either with a whole word, a sentence, or a text. Synthetic methods start with a sound that is associated with a letter. Most of the teachers and authors using synthetic methods do not realize that in order to get a specific sound out of a series of pictures (which represent the spoken words) they do use analytic methods.

Stages of Reading Instruction

The analytic methods used in Germany mainly during the 1950s to the 1970s distinguish three main stages:

1. Preanalytic stage with primitive global reading, which means that children learn by heart a text (or poem or some part of a story) and remember a few words that will be repeated.
2. Analytic stage where similarities in words are recognized (= visual analysis). Auditive analysis is the same process with spoken words (syllables, sounds, position).
3. Synthetic stage, when several sounds and letters are known to the child and he combines sounds/letters to form new words.

These stages are not discrete but rather overlapping during the first year of instruction:

Analytic Stage

1. 2. 3. 4. 5. 6. 7. 8. 9. 10. month

Preanalytic   Synthetic Stage

Analytic-synthetic approaches do not use the preanalytic stage but start analyzing from the very beginning. Out of a text some words with a certain letter (-combination) are brought to the attention of the children. Visual and auditive forms are associated and differentiated. New words are built with known letters (synthetic stage).

Analytic-*synthetic* methods use only one word in the beginning. This is fully analyzed, every letter of the word is pronounced (analysis), and the sounds are combined to the known word (synthesis). This is also done with the same letters in different order to create new words.

Some Reasearch Results of Beginning Reading Instruction

In a study conducted during 1984–1988, we collected reading data for more than 1,000 individual first grade students in German-speaking countries on accuracy and speed and, for a smaller population, also on fluency and comprehension. We prepared oral reading checks three times a year, when a group had finished the study of twelve, eighteen, and twenty-four letters. This was about the third, sixth, and ninth month of first grade. Altogether there were fifteen different primers. Vocabulary lists and short sentences were given to the students. Reading accuracy was calculated in percentage and speed, in words per minute.

Accuracy of reading is the basic factor among all reading criteria. The process of decoding individual letters and letter groups, comparing the sounds with known words, and being able to speak the read word are prerequisites to accuracy. Most of the children reached the criterion of 80 percent accuracy.

The results of that research study for the German-speaking group showed considerable development, especially in speed of reading. After three months, the average pupil read about 10 words per minute, after six months, 20 per minute, and at the end of first grade 30 per minute was reached by more than 75 percent of the students. With a smaller group of second graders, we found that 60 words per minute was a good goal to be reached at the end of second grade.

Surprisingly, English-speaking children were significantly better in speed of reading at the end of first grade than the German speaking. The main reason for this result is that the English language teachers emphasize that reading is like talking, whereas German teachers ask their children to look at every letter and syllable and pronounce it accordingly. Over 75 percent of German children are able to read independently at the end of first grade and over 90 percent at the end of second grade. For English-speaking students it takes much longer.

TEACHER QUALIFICATIONS

Primary, Secondary, and Tertiary Teachers

All teachers in West Germany are required to pass two examinations: the *Erste Lehramtsprüfung* (at a state board in cooperation with the university) after six or eight semesters of study at the university or a teachers' college and the *Zweite Lehramtsprüfung* at the end of the preparational phase in schools which lasts about one and a half to two years. After these two examinations, a teacher is appointed to become a *Beamter* for his whole life, which means that he or she is a civil servant with all the rights the status brings until retirement.

The salary of a West German teacher is about one and a half to two times higher than the average salary of a working person. Therefore, a West German teacher has more income than most of his or her European colleagues. The salary is different according to the different office of a teacher and the time of training. An elementary teacher receives one level of his or her salary scale less than a *Studienrat* at the *Gymnasium*.

Elementary school teachers teach many subjects and in the beginning grades nearly all. They have to fulfill the role of all-round-teacher, but, of course, not all subjects can be taught in a qualified way. Teachers in the *Realschule* or *Gymnasium* teach only two or three subject matter areas. Their training at the university is quite intensive and long: eight semesters with about 160 weekly semester hours for their first subject. They are subject matter specialists and not so much concerned with the individual student. Elementary school teachers are better trained in teaching methods (didactic and psychology), and their education is more child oriented.

A professor at the university is required to have a doctorate and, in addition, a *Habilitation*, that is, a formal admission of an academic lecture into the faculty to which he desires to attach himself after having obtained, on the strength of a piece of original research, the *venia legendi*.

Other Teachers

Private schools and *Volkshochschulen* for voluntary adult education hire teachers with or without state examinations. Subject matter specialists or academically trained people offer their knowledge and skills for educating and training people in all kinds of subjects from philosophy, psychology, art, and languages to typewriting and other skills.

Private schools range from preschool institutions (kindergarten), elementary schools, *Realschulen*, to *Gymnasium*. There are also religious (Catholic and Protestant) and philosophically oriented schools like *Rudolf-Steiner-Schulen*. Both are supported and partly financed by the state. In cooperation with state authorities they can certify *Mittlere Reife* (after the tenth grade) or *Abitur* (after the thirteenth grade).

Volkshochschulen are adult educational institutions founded at the end of the nineteenth century following Scandinavian models. They are regarded as continuing education. In West Germany there are about 900 *Volkshochschulen* with more than 4,200 associated institutes in smaller places. Every year about two to three million people attend courses or lectures in languages, mathematics, sciences, technics, arts, and many other subjects. They do it in the evening; in some places, they spend a couple of days or weeks in *Heim-Volkshochschulen*.

MATERIALS IN READING EDUCATION

Primary Grades—Primers

Teachers of primary grades use primers mainly for introducing the reading process; this seems to be the case worldwide. But a closer look shows some big differences in Germany. Ludwig Reinhard reported the use of seventy primers in West Germany, Austria, and Switzerland in 1958. Currently, about thirty to thirty-five new primers are used in schools. During that time and even today East Germany has only one primer.

In Germany primers are used only during the first grade, which in general is for one year. In the United States about eight to twelve reading series are available. They are labeled from kindergarten to sixth grade and represent seven years of reading instruction in the United States and in German-speaking countries, only one year. If we compare the number of primers used in German-speaking countries in Central Europe with the U.S. reading series and take into account the population, then we can roughly say that twenty times more German primers have been published than U.S. primers. That is by no means an asset. Reinhard seriously questioned this "spring of primers" and criticized their use of language, the different kind of letters (print, script), old-fashioned methods (synthetic), and the big variation in difficulty levels (high vocabulary load).

The discussion concerning materials for beginning reading instruction in Germany has become more relaxed. The opposite methods—synthetic versus analytic—have become more or less united to analytic-synthetic methods. The term *method integrated* is used. Still, some are more analytic when they bring the pupil's attention to only a few letters of a word, within a sentence or a text, at the beginning of the reading process. Or they are closer to the synthetic approach when they analyze all the sounds and letters of one word. The first one uses language in a much broader way, whereas the other is more code-oriented.

Secondary Education: State-Funded Reading Books

From second grade until the end of secondary school, *Lesebücher* are used. These reading books for different grades are not so much concerned with reading skills as with literary education. Stories, poems, fables, riddles, and other kinds of literature are offered. No readability formulas are applied to the literature, but it seems that the materials in German reading books are much more demanding than those in U.S. primers and books. Oral reading is also used to some extent in secondary schools.

Tertiary and Adult Education: Libraries and Book Purchases

Students in colleges and universities have access to large libraries. Book production in West Germany is the third largest in the world, behind only the United States and the USSR. More than 300,000 titles are available.

FINANCING READING EDUCATION

Germany's educational institutions are financed by the federal and state governments and by local authorities (cities and communities). Except for the period of the Third Reich, Germany was always a federation (comprising more than 200 political units in the seventeenth century and now ten *Länder* and West Berlin). Cultural matters are mostly the function of the state (*Land*). A teacher is normally paid by the state.

READING RESEARCH IN GERMANY

Early Research: Reading Process

Reading research had its beginnings in France and in Germany according to William S. Gray in his international survey, "The Teaching of Reading and Writing," published by UNESCO. In his 1844 physiology textbook, G. Valentine remarked that the individual is able to fixate several letters at the same time. This observation might have been the starting point of the still controversial issue of whether the reading process is successive or simultaneous. In contrast, the psychiatrist Grashey (1839–1911) maintained that the letters successively pass the *macula lutea*, or yellow spot of the eye, and successively provoke relevant sounds. Contrary to Grashey's theory, James McKeen Cattell—an American scholar at the famous Wundt Institute of Experimental Psychology in Leipzig in 1886—found experimentally a large difference in the number of letters recognized in a single short exposure between nonsense material (only four to five letters) and meaningful words (twelve to fifteen letters). Erdmann and Dodge (a German professor and American scholar, respectively) confirmed this result in 1898, when they published their *Psychologische Untersuchungen über das Lesen auf experimenteller Grundlage*. These research results have stood during the last hundred years. The following summary of experimental reading research in Germany presents more specific details on the reading process.

In 1900 Zeitler found that dominant letters (high and low letters and capitals) were recognized more correctly than others and that the tachistoscopic span was increased if a consonant group had vowels in it. Such a group is more easily spoken. In 1904 Messmer conducted the first research on reading with children. In order to recognize a word, a visual simultaneous pattern of a whole word could be discerned and also single dominant letters, which are perceived successively.

Wiegand (1908) used the term *Gestaltqualität* in reporting his experimental study. He found that, first, high and low letters emerged and then the individual letters at the beginning and at the end of a word could be recognized. Last to be seen were the letters hidden in the middle of the word—the same pattern that has been observed in more recent times in the patterns of oral reading errors of dyslexic children. Kutzner (1916) mainly explored the effects of the quality of the Gestalt on word recognition. Korte (1923) experimented with factors of recognition within indirect vision. In his studies with different reading materials in Grades 1 to 8, Hoffmann (1927) found an increase in tachistoscopic span for familiar words with advance in school grades.

Heimann and Thorner (1929) demonstrated that pronounceable combinations of letters could be grasped more readily than nonpronounceable arrangements. The vowels require the company of consonants in order to gain high scores in experiments with a tachistoscope.

Research on Teaching Reading

In 1937 Bernhard Bosch wrote a prizewinning book *Grundlagen des Erstleseunterrichts* [The Foundation of First Reading Instruction]. He had studied the prerequisites of linguistic objectification within school beginners and found that six-year-old children, in general, cannot distinguish between the meaning and the length of words. However, in 1967 Katzenberger and Kluge, in their critical evaluation of Bosch's studies, found that children in Germany today appear to be better equipped linguistically than those of forty years ago.

Reading methods had been discussed in Germany both before and after World War II. In 1941 Hartmann published an experimental study comparing analytic or global methods and synthetic methods. His results favored global methods. Since 1948 global methods have been introduced in German schools on a broad scale. Outstanding authors of these primers are Brückl (1923), Wittmann (1929), Kern (1931), and after 1945, Reinhard, Walter Müller, Warwel, and many others. Schmalohr (1961) criticized the research procedure of earlier studies. In his own experimental study he found no differences between analytic and synthetic reading methods by the end of Grades 4 and 5. Heinrich Müller (1964) found that at the end of Grade 2 the synthetic method and the whole-word method brought better results than the whole-sentence method. Ferdinand (1970) compared two parallel groups taught by teachers who used the opposite methods (global and synthetic) in two groups. In the first year children taught by synthetic methods were better in all language criteria (oral reading, comprehension, spelling, and composition), but after two years globally taught students showed better results in composition. At the end of Grade 4 globally taught children showed better results in all language areas but reading.

Several research studies have been published during recent decades. Röbe (1977) documented several aspects of an analytic-synthetic reading method. Meiers (1977, 1978) did a correlative study on predictors, reading criteria, and teacher variables and a second study on organization, objectives, and media of first grade teaching of reading. Heinisch (1984) studied eye movements with a specific electro-oculographic camera and suggested detailed criteria for optimal measures of print for primers. Several studies had been conducted on reading and spelling difficulties (legasthenia, dyslexia).

Biglmaier (1960) compared oral reading rates measured by Messmer (1904) and Bobertag and Kirste (1916) with those of 300 German children in 1957 from the end of Grades 1 to 5. Children in Germany read faster today than those in the earlier studies. Better teaching procedures, based on more analytic methods, may account for this development.

A second result was surprising: The process of learning to read, in the sense of being able to decode and understand written symbols with a low error rate, is accomplished for German children at the end of Grade 2. In contrast, according to the norms of Monroe (1932), American children do not reach this stage until the end of Grade 4. The result may be attributed to the more regular grapheme-phoneme relations in the German language. However, development of the ability to read seems to follow similar patterns in every language, as can be deduced by the sequence of major error types.

In a study performed from 1984 to 1988, Biglmaier collected empirical data on the oral reading criteria (accuracy, speed, and, for some smaller groups, fluency and comprehension) of 1,430 German and 474 English-speaking children. The oral reading checks were developed for each primer and for three times a year. Children were checked individually. Both language groups showed the same level of accuracy at the end of the first grade. The English-speaking group scored significantly higher in speed of reading.

What does research say to the reading teacher? Research results are known by the researchers and are to a large extent confined within one language or nation; only a few books go beyond the national and language barriers. Research results should be published and disseminated so that teachers can understand and apply them. Many good ideas in research still await application, and many new questions remain to be solved. Research, national as well as international, must define, differentiate, and integrate the facts both for a comprehensive theoretical framework and for sound applications in schools and homes.

REFERENCES

Anderson, Irving H., and Dearborn, Walter F. 1952. *The Psychology of Teaching Reading*. New York.

Arbeitskreis Grundschule e.V. (1973, 1974). *Legasthenie—ein pädagogisches Problem*. Band 8. Frankfurt am Main 3. Aufl.

Arbeitskreis Grundschule e.V., *Fibeln und Erstlesewerke I*, II, E. 1976. Band 26/27. Frankfurt am Main. 1977. Band 30/31. Frankfurt am Main. 1980. Ergänzungsband 30/31E. Frankfurt am Main. 1986. Band 64. Frankfurt am Main.

Bergk, Marion. 1980. *Leselernprozess und Erstlesewerke, Analyse des Schriftsprach-*

erwerbs und seiner Behinderungen mit Kategorien der Aneignungstheorie. Bochum.

Biglmaier, Franz. 1960, 1971. *Lesestörungen—Diagnose und Behandlung.* Munich 4. Aufl.

Biglmaier, Franz. 1972–1973. *Westermann Lesebuch 1, Wir üben lesen,/Wir üben schreiben, Lehrerausgabe.* Braunschweig.

Biglmaier, Franz. 1990. Leselernentwicklung bei deutsch- und englisch-sprachigen Schülern. In 6. *Europäischer Lesekongress, Kongressbericht.* Berlin.

Bosch, Bernhard. 1984. *Grundlagen des Erstleseunterricht—Eine didaktische Untersuchung.* Ratingen 1937, 1961 5. Aufl. Frankfurt.

Cattell, James McKeen. 1885–1886. Über die Zeit der Erkennung und Benennung von Schriftzeichen. *Wundts Philos. Studien II/III.*

Erdmann, Benno, and Dodge, Raimund. 1898. *Psychologische Untersuchungen über das Lesen auf experimenteller Grundlage.* Halle.

Grissemann, Hans. 1984. *Spätlegasthenie und funktionaler Analphabetismus—Integrative Behandlung von Lese- und Rechtschreibschwächen bei Jugendlichen und Erwachsenen.* Bern/Stuttgart/Toronto.

Gümbel, Ruth. 1980. *Erstleseunterricht, Entwicklungen—Tendenzen—Erfahrungen.* Königstein/Ts.

Kern, Artur, and Erwin. 1930, 1952. *Lesen und Lesenlernen—eine psychologisch-didaktische Darstellung.* Freiburg 3. Aufl.

Linder, Maria. 1951. Über Legasthenie (spezielle Leseschwäche). *Zeitschrift für Kinderpsychiatrie,* Jg. 14, No. 4.

Meiers, Kurt. 1978. *Bedingungen des Lesenlernens—Eine empirische Untersuchung.* Kronberg/Ts.

Meiers, Kurt (Hrsg.) 1981. *Erstlesen.* Bad Heilbrunn.

Messmer, Oskar. 1904. Zur Psychologie des Lesens bei Kindern und Erwachsenen. *Archiv für die gesamte Psychologie.* Leipzig.

Monroe, Marion. 1932, 1948. *Children Who Cannot Read—The Analysis of Reading Disabilities and the Use of Diagnostic Tests in the Instruction of Retarded Readers.* Chicago.

Müller, Heinrich. 1964. *Methoden des Erstleseunterrichts und ihre Ergebnisse—Ein empirischer Beitrag zum Vergleich des ganzheitlichen und lautsynthetischen Lehrverfahrens.* Meisenheim.

Ranschburg, Paul. 1916. *Die Leseschwäche (Legasthenie) und Rechenschwäche (Arithmasthenie) der Schulkinder im Lichte des Experiments.* Berlin.

Reinhard, Ludwig. 1958. Fibelfrühling!—Fibelsegen? Eine kritische Sichtung des Leselernbücher für die Zeit 1945–1958, *Di Scholle 12.*

Röbe, Edeltraut. 1977. *Didaktik des Lesenlernens, Auswertung und kritische Erörterung der Unterrichtsdokumentation eines Leselehrgangs.* Arbeitskreis Grundschule, Forschungsbeiträge, Band 2. Frankfurt am Main.

Schenk-Danziger, Lotte. 1975. *Handbuch der Legasthenie im Kindesalter.* Weinheim.

Schmalohr, Emil. 1971. *Psychologie des Erstlese- und Schreibunterrichts.* Munich/Basel, 2. Aufl.

25

Yugoslavia

Petar Mandić

INTRODUCTION

The Yugoslav school system contains several levels: preschool education (age three to seven), elementary education (age seven to fifteen), secondary education (age fifteen to eighteen or nineteen), higher education (age nineteen to twenty-three or twenty-four), and post graduate studies (age twenty-four to twenty-six). The secondary level offers the student several possibilities to get general, vocational, and technical secondary education.

Yugoslavia also has highly developed and well-recognized schools for retarded children, schools for nationalities (ethnic majorities), adult education of different kinds, and nonformal education (education for self-management, self-defense, and protection of the environment). After World War II, Yugoslavia became one of the leading countries in adult education in Eastern Europe.

To understand and appreciate the diversity in contemporary patterns of schooling is in many respects to understand and appreciate the diversity of the cultures and structure of the Yugoslav population. Since the population is so small, visitors to Yugoslavia readily observe the similarities and diversities of the people, their customs and values.

Yugoslav authorities respect these differences when they set out to design the curriculum and organize the school system. According to the Yugoslav constitution, children have the right to obtain an education in their mother language. Consequently, many regions permit all kinds of schooling in two languages such as Italian and Serbo-Croatian, Albanian and Serbo-Croatian, and Hungarian and Serbo-Croatian. The present educational system was constituted in 1959 and was gradually perfected on the basis of initial reform documents issued in 1970 and

1974. Since that time educators have been working to improve the organization and process of education at all levels.

Compulsory education lasts eight years and is conducted in the mother language for all children, without exception. In addition to the three languages of the Yugoslav nations (Serbo-Croatian, Slovenian, and Macedonian), teaching is conducted in the nine languages of the Yugoslav nationalities (Albanian, Bulgarian, Czech, Hungarian, Romanian, Romany, Slovakian, Italian, and Turkish). All the textbooks and other materials for compulsory education are published in all twelve languages in which the teaching is conducted.

Pupils in nationally mixed regions may, in addition to their mother tongue, study the language of the other nation or nationality within which they live. The learning of second languages is encouraged. Some regions actually have compulsory bilingual schools. For most of the children of Yugoslav nationals employed abroad, teaching in the field of language is provided. A special textbook is published for such children.

Secondary education is also conducted in the mother language, in the three languages of the nation (Serbo-Croatian, Slovenian, and Macedonian), and in six languages of the Yugoslav nationalities (Albanian, Bulgarian, Hungarian, Italian, Romanian, and Slovakian). All of the students' textbooks are in their mother language.

Teaching at the nineteen universities in Yugoslavia is conducted in four languages (Serbo-Croatian, Slovenian, Macedonian, and Albanian), as well as in several languages of the nationalities at certain higher educational institutions and study groups at faculties (Hungarian, Italian, Slovakian, and Bulgarian).

Adult education of all kinds is conducted in the mother language for all participants. They have access to textbooks and other educational material published in their mother language.

These facts are very important for understanding the essence of Yugoslav education, the process of teaching, and especially reading education.

THE LANGUAGES OF THE COUNTRY

Yugoslavia is a multinational state, a community of equal Yugoslav peoples and other nationalities and national minorities. According to the census of 1981, Yugoslavia had a total of 22.4 million inhabitants, of whom 36.3 percent declared themselves to be Serbs, 19.8 percent Croatians, 8.9 percent Muslims, 7.8 percent Slovenians, 7.7 percent Albanians, 6.0 percent Macedonians, 5.4 percent Yugoslavs (an option provided for by Article 170 of the constitution), 2.6 percent Montenegrins, 1.9 percent Hungarians, and less than 1 percent Romanies, Turks, Slovaks, Bulgarians, Vlachs, Ukrainians, Italians, Czechs, Slovakians, Romanians, and so on. The Serbo-Croation language is spoken by 73 percent of the Yugoslav population (Serbs, Croats, Muslims, Montenegrins, and Yugoslavs), while the others usually speak their mother language as a first and Serbo-Croatian as a second language. As a result, Yugoslavia has no official language. In the

Table 25.1
Languages for the Medium of Instruction

| | Number of Students | |
Language	Primary Education	Secondary Education
Widely Used Languages		
Serbo-Croatian	1,937,354	789,824
Slovenian	226,460	82,767
Macedonian	273,108	80,813
Albanian	378,868	80,457
Other Languages		
Bulgarian	3,223	----
Czech	589	105
Hungarian	29,566	9,272
Italian	1,111	609
Romanian	2,372	410
Ruthenian	867	226
Slovakian	5,194	828
Turkish	6,833	633
Total	2,865,545	1,045,944

federal institutions people can use one of five languages (Serbo-Croatian, Slovenian, Macedonian, Hungarian, and Albanian). The full and complete equality of the members of all nationalities in Yugoslavia is also seen in the highly developed system of schooling in the different languages of nations and nationalities. In line with this policy, studies at university faculties in the autonomous provinces of Vojvodina and Kosovo, where most of the members of the nationalities live, are most frequently bilingual—in Serbo-Croatian, and the local minority language. This arrangement permits everyone to develop cultural identity, to develop their own culture, and to achieve the fullest possible realization of personalities. They also have the opportunity to learn about the other cultures and to establish active communication and interaction among different cultures.

In the medium of instruction in Yugoslavia, languages are used as shown in Table 25.1.

Most educated people in Yugoslavia speak and write in the Serbo-Croatian language, and they can use it in communication with other people. Of course, there are no political or legal measures that force people to use the language spoken by most of the population. It is permitted to use the mother language whenever one wants. With just one exception. The Yugoslav national army is the only institution where Serbo-Croatian is required.

Political and educational measures encourage young people to learn other languages in order to know their cultures and people, thereby leading to human communication and to an atmosphere of mutual understanding and appreciation.

Yugoslav schools teach mostly English, Russian, French, and German, and only rarely are Italian, Arabic, Spanish, and Esperanto taught.

Serbo-Croatian, the most frequently used language, is phonetic and has the basic rule, "Write as you speak and read as it is written." Thus, learning foreign languages that are not phonetic is very difficult for young people who are in the process of learning to read at all levels of the education system. To acquire basic writing and reading ability in the Serbo-Croatian language is easier than in any foreign language. So, for example, a person who knows thirty letters of the Cyrillic or Latin alphabet, who can read and write elementary things, can be considered literate. However, acquiring this basic knowledge in a foreign language does not mean that one is literate. Pupils in Yugoslavia meet special difficulties when they write a word in one way and read it in another.

In some schools in large towns, the foreign language is taught from the first or fourth grade in elementary school. Students are required to take one foreign language from the fifth grade of elementary school. A foreign language is studied in elementary and secondary schools for at least six years, but in some schools it is taught for eight years or more. Reading and understanding the material read in a foreign language is especially difficult for pupils.

Although phonetic, and therefore easy, the Serbo-Croatian language also has its problems and difficulties. First, there is the existence of two alphabets. In primary schools pupils learn both alphabets, and later they use them equally because books, materials, and literal works are printed in both alphabets. On the other hand, grammar and its rules cause many difficulties for pupils who are beginning to learn to read and write.

READING INSTRUCTION POLICY

In the decentralized Yugoslav society, education is under the authority of the republic units (there are six republics and two provinces), and equal rights of education are stipulated in the constitutions and laws of all these units. All peoples have the right to primary, secondary, and higher education as well as the right to be taught in the language of their nationality. The constitution of the Socialist Federal Republic of Yugoslavia and the constitutions of the Socialist Republics and Socialist Autonomous Provinces guarantee to all citizens the right to an education without discrimination as to sex, race, nationality, religious belief, or the like. The Yugoslav society seeks to promote education and culture and to enable all persons to use their right to obtain an education and to participate in cultural life. All nationals are guaranteed the comprehensive development of a free, creative personality.

According to the federal constitution, the republics and provinces are responsible for organizing and developing the educational system. The republics and provinces assure the uniformity of the nationwide system of education through mutual conventions and social compacts, which lay down the principles of a standard system of education from primary school to university-level studies. In recent years core curricula, which all the republics and provinces must incorporate in their programs of primary education, have been proposed. A similar agreement has also been achieved in regard to the curricula of secondary education, and a number of allied faculties (medicine, economy, law) in Yugoslavia have also established common study programs.

Yugoslavia espouses unique aims of education, basic principles for the development and functioning of the school system, and educational criteria that are the starting point in the process of teaching. These principles and criteria are applied in the teaching of all subjects and, thus, to reading education as well. The institutes for improvement of education take care of practical aspects of education. Methodic principles are successfully realized in all the languages, especially in Serbo-Croatian. Many experiments conducted by institutes for educational research and for the improvement of teaching, and by specialized experts from the universities who improve the process of teaching of the mother language, as well as foreign languages, have contributed to this success.

A lot of books have been written about methodics in teaching the mother language as well as foreign languages. These books focus on the problem of reading, especially its importance for successful learning in general and for the development of personality.

Since scientific experiments have a universal importance, their application cannot be limited within the republics and provinces. Therefore, we can say that scientific results reached in the field of improving the teaching process can be applied throughout Yugoslavia without limitation. This application has been possible because of the contributions of educational societies and unions of teachers of mother and foreign languages. At their meetings, symposiums, and congresses teachers try to find the best materials and methods that will help improve the teaching of reading. In particular, they discuss how to improve oral and silent reading (in both foreign and mother languages), how to accomplish correct and quick reading, and how to learn proper expressive learning.

Three fields in the teaching of reading are treated together and are almost identical in all Yugoslav schools. These are: preparation of pupils for beginner's reading and writing; the contents, treatments, and techniques of beginner's reading and writing; and the contents and methodic bases of raising so-called functional literacy. Instruments for evaluating the level and quality of a pupil's reading, instruments for diagnosing the causes of slow reading, and programs that give special help to certain categories of pupils who are lagging in beginner's reading and writing are universally applied. The permanent subject of the specialists' discussion and research is methods and treatment of beginner's reading and writing. During the last twenty-five years, the advantages and disadvantages of the following methods have been studied in relation to the beginner's reading: phonetically analytic and synthetic methods with a monographic approach to work with letters; phonetically analytic and synthetic methods with group work on letters, but including sound analysis in a beginner's preparation for reading (sounds are adopted together with identification of graphic symbols–letters); the global method, whereby the printed word as unity tends to become the real element of the beginner's reading and writing; and the global approach in the adoption of letters in reading education.

The leading theoreticians in the field of teaching (Cvitan, 1965; Demarin, 1965; Furlan, 1963; Mioc, 1950; Muradbegović, 1968; Šimleša, 1965; Stevanović, 1980) generally agree that in the first phase of the beginner's reading the teacher should apply global, and later, analytic and synthetic methods. Nevertheless, the specialist and scientific works acquaint teachers with the advantages and disadvantages of the above methods and treatments in reading education, and they are free to use whatever methods give the best results according to their own experiences.

THE GOALS OF READING EDUCATION

The goals of reading education in the compulsory schools are to promote the correct, quick, and expressive reading of scientific material and literature; to develop an interest in books and in lifetime reading; to expand vocabulary; to develop general linguistic and literary culture; to teach pupils to express themselves correctly; to foster interest in language as a device for communication and interaction; to encourage critical analysis of sources of knowledge and the development of pupils' creativity. Students are trained to read correctly and to interpret the material they read.

The goals of reading education in the secondary schools are to train pupils for correct, proper, and logical reading of given materials; to produce speed in oral and silent reading; to raise the culture of oral and written expression; to motivate students to improve their reading techniques, keeping in mind articulation of voice, diction, intonation, modulation, and color of words; to develop abilities for analytic and synthetic approaches to the contents and generalization of facts; to train pupils for logical thinking, critical approaches to the sources of knowledge, and creative interpretation of the material read; to develop a sense for aesthetic culture and encourage lifetime reading habits; to train pupils to use adequate reading techniques so as to learn different subjects; and to read as part of the process of permanent self-education. Especially emphasized is the aim to teach pupils to use informative or silent forms of reading in the secondary schools; at high schools and at universities it is important to develop functional literacy which is very important in an information era and in this era of knowledge explosion for everyone, regardless of education level, living conditions or duties. The development of reading abilities is an important condition in the process of learning to read.

At the high school and university level the goals of reading education are to encourage students to improve their speed, silent and oral reading, and oral and written expression techniques; to motivate them to approach the text seriously and to understand and interpret it correctly; to develop critical analysis concerning the sources of knowledge as well as critical opinion; to train students to use the book independently; and to develop an interest in books, in a rich vocabulary, and a wish for permanent education. The goal is to train students to use reading in their profession, to care for functional literacy, and to aspire to creative expression in professional work. Students at teachers' colleges are trained professionally, pedagogically, and methodologically in order that they may teach others (youth and adults) in the field of reading education.

The goals of reading education in institutions for adult education are to help adults, depending on previously acquired knowledge and kind of school attended to, learn about reading techniques; to develop their abilities of oral and written expression; to form a lifetime reading habit; and to develop interest in books and writing materials. Adults are encouraged to develop their abilities for oral and silent reading, for an understanding of materials read, and for a correct interpretation and critical analysis. This category of students receives reading education in order to prepare themselves for permanent education and for oral communication which is the most effective and usual way of spreading information.

At all levels of education reading abilities can be developed, the techniques of appropriate and logical reading improved and students trained to understand and interpret the materials they read. All schools seek to develop the students' love for books and to improve students' knowledge permanently.

In Yugoslavia both sexes have equal access to education, the only differences being in physical training and in home economics. The nation's teachers and psychologists believe there are no serious reasons to separate the sexes in education; tradition and social conditions are not an obstacle to consistent coeducation at all levels of schooling.

ILLITERACY

According to the criteria adopted by Yugoslavia's educators, an illiterate is one who cannot write and read both alphabets (Cyrillic and Latin) at an elementary level. With regard to functional illiteracy, no unique criterion exists for establishing it. Thus, it has neither been explored enough, nor has a body of reliable results been generated. For example, some people define an illiterate as one who can neither write nor read correctly and who has not learned to spell.

Others may define literacy in terms of adequate development of reading abilities, an understanding of reading materials, and correct interpretation; and adequate oral and written expression (paying special attention to the grammatical rules in writing and diction as well as articulation and intonation in oral expression). Yet others hold that a literate person is one who has acquired adequate knowledge in linguistic and literary fields. Recently, educators have been speaking of literacy in terms of basic literacy (a literate person being one who can read and write correctly), as well as historic, cultural, economic, political, and computer literacy. Basic literacy and the criteria for its evaluation have been common research topics among Yugoslav educators. Research on small samples, however, is not a reliable indicator of functional illiteracy in Yugoslavia.

Illiteracy has not been eradicated in Yugoslavia, but it has been considerably reduced. The level of illiteracy among the group up to forty years of age is 3 percent.

Established criteria and standardized tests have been set up to examine basic literacy. Functional literacy, or literacy at a higher level, is a universal world problem. Therefore, in Yugoslavia it is possible to talk about the functional illiteracy of a great number of youth and adults who have finished elementary and secondary schools. The special problem is literacy in a foreign language. According to our partial research work (using small samples), about 25 percent of the pupils are literate in a foreign language in primary school and 30 percent in secondary school, while the literacy of the average students at university (in foreign language) is a little bit better. Of course, partial research cannot be the basis for a reliable argument, but it can indicate an unsatisfactory situation and point to the problem.

READING DISABILITIES AND THEIR DIAGNOSIS

The Nature and Incidence Rate of Reading Disabilities

Reading involves the following mental processes: the appreciation of visual word wholes and their parts and sound wholes and their parts; the coordination of complicated movements of mouth, lips, and tongue; the binding of all these elements together into an intricate system of wholes and parts; and the linking up of all these mechanical symbols with their meaning, and the understanding of what is read. Since the causes of lagging in reading can be numerous, we will restrict ourselves to the best known: dyslexia, legasthenia, general linguistic disabilities, confusion of similar letters and words, difficulties in recognizing words similar in sound, difficulties in memorizing the visual or oral forms of a letter or word, disability in analyzing and synthesizing words and sentences, lack of self-confidence, changes in schools, teachers, and environment at the beginning of intensive reading education, and lack of continuity in work method in the lower and upper grades of schooling. Physical defects that have a negative influence on reading education have also been examined. The most frequent physical defects are hearing and sight disabilities and other problems concerning the speech organs (stammering, babbling, hard pronunciation of some sounds, etc.).

Problems can emerge when the methods applied in a beginner's reading are changed. Experiments have shown that some children learn better when analytic methods are used in reading education, while others do better when global methods are used. Experiments (Marković, 1971; Šimleša, 1965; Stevanović, 1980) have shown that reading is also influenced by other factors, including the student's general intelligence, richness of active vocabulary, keenness of sight, breadth of field of vision, perception of shapes and colors, type of perceptual activity, neurological factors, environmental factors, level of aspiration, emotional sphere of the psychic life and general health conditions. Reading difficulties are present at all levels of education, but many of the problems mentioned above occur at the primary school level. Experiments conducted by Ivica Radovanović in 1983 showed that every third pupil in primary school had some defects that hindered reading at a level expected of primary school pupils. In the secondary schools every fourth pupil had more or less expressed reading disabilities, while at higher schools and universities 12 to 15 percent of the students were unable to read and write successfully and to make optimal use of their books. Over 40 percent of the adults attending different kinds of schools also had reading and writing disabilities.

The most frequent difficulties found among primary school children are dyslexia, linguistic disability, keenness of senses (hearing, sight), speech disabilities, neurological factors, inability to recognize words similar in sound, and inability to analyze and synthesize words and sentences. In the upper grades difficulties of understanding and interpreting are present.

Secondary school pupils have the following problems: inadequate vocabulary, inability to understand and interpret reading materials correctly, difficulties in expressing themselves in writing and reading, lack of motivation, emotional disabilities, oral and silent reading rates, and inability to analyze and synthesize. In the high schools and universities, the main problems involve oral and written expression, lack of reading interest, inability to apply spelling and grammatical rules, and inability to read logically and aesthetically.

Adults' problems usually involve reading technique, reading speed, limitations in understanding and interpreting the read materials, difficulties in writing and oral expression, lack of good reading habits, and impoverished vocabulary. The adults' problems also included keenness of senses, emotional problems, and lack of confidence. Stevanović (1980) observed no important differences between the sexes that warranted special analysis. Experiments have shown that the sexes differ in the kind of literature they read and in their reading techniques more than in reading disabilities.

Diagnosing Reading Disabilities

In researching the problems of reading and the reasons behind reading disabilities, the survey research and case study methods are usually employed. The instruments used include an inventory questionnaire, and tests of general abilities, emotional maturity, and personality. These methods are used to conduct mass research works and to give detailed insight into the teaching process in general, especially in the teaching of the mother language, foreign languages, and reading education. Special instruments and procedures are available by which it is possible to examine reading disabilities in primary and secondary schools and in institutions for adult education. There are no special instruments that enable researchers to examine students' reading disabilities in high schools and universities.

First, reading readiness tests enable the measurement of the children's level of maturation, which is an important criterion for enrollment in the first grade. The pupil who fails the reading readiness test is either kept out of the first grade and made to wait to mature sufficiently to pass the test, or is given experiences involving the kind of tasks required both in the test and in learning to read. Special tests are administered to determine which children are unable to divide spoken words into separate sounds. In this case it is reasonable to conclude that this category of children will have trouble learning to read. In addition, other tests important for evaluating children's readiness to read are given.

Second, a number of diagnostic tests may be employed in the process of discovering reading disabilities. A diagnostic test breaks down a complex performance into many parts and thereby indicates the pupil's areas of strength and weakness. Depending on which problems are to be researched or whether a need to research them exists, an adequate number of instruments are available. So, for example, there are tests for examining the senses and the level of general linguistic development, for analyzing understanding of reading materials, for testing vocabulary level, and so on. Tests make it possible to examine all the specific aspects of the process of learning to read at school and university institutions. Diagnostic tests are so designed that it is possible to discover, for example, when pupils understand reading materials but simply read slowly; when their reading technique is well perfected but they have problems reading extraordinary words. These tests also reveal which special reading abilities remain to be perfected, even though the pupil has average or somewhat above-average success. It is also possible to examine why a pupil has a considerably better average grade in all subjects than in tests of either silent or oral reading.

Tests of readiness for learning foreign languages, tests for diagnosing the causes of poor reading in foreign languages, and tests for examining richness of vocabulary are especially created and used in practice. Of course, tests for examining the senses, tests of emotional maturity, and tests of general and special abilities are also used.

In the process of making and using diagnostic instruments, it is well to remember that reading is a complex conceptual and perceptual process, which involves knowing the human personality in whole, its general and specific abilities, its concrete skills, and the functions of the nervous system and senses. For example, dyslexia probably does involve some kind of minor brain abnormality, but it does not appear to be due to a simple lack of brain lateralization; or reading difficulties are seldom caused by an inability to discriminate the letters of the alphabet. Students poor in reading seem to have a problem with internal speech—speech that is thought rather than spoken.

Other Tests or Materials Used to Diagnose Reading Disabilities

Teachers, psychologists, doctors, and social workers own the instruments they use to examine physical health, mental health, social maturity, problems of success and failure, student behavior, social conditions, and so on. Most of these instruments, directly or indirectly, produce data that serve to evaluate some causes of lagging in reading, to discover problems that negatively influence general success or demotivate pupils to work more, to do their duties diligently, and to use books more as a source of knowledge.

From time to time, these experts conduct interviews with students who lag behind others in learning so as to discover the causes of their lagging in learning generally speaking and in reading education especially. Their research has shown that pupils who have problems in reading may very well have physical disabilities that are directly responsible. Otorhinolaryngologists and oculists for example, are able to directly evaluate the influence of hearing and sight difficulties on reading speed and comprehension. Similarly, speech therapists can test the influence of different speech difficulties on the student's ability to read effectively.

READING READINESS PROGRAMS

Each republic and province in Yugoslavia has its own program for preparing children for school. These programs are implemented in two ways: first, via regular preschool education, and second, via the so-called preparatory school. (The preparatory school is organized a year before the starting of school and lasts at least three months, under proper conditions.) The kindergarten program is designed to meet the interest of children, induce their development, help prepare them for the first grade, and motivate them to learn. The major purpose of all activities is to help children attain a readiness to learn by encouraging physical, mental, and social development through different kinds of activities such as organized observation, drawing, cutting, pasting, working with blocks, sand boxes, telling stories, playing with toys, and watching and discussing children's television programs. These activities give every child a chance to be mentally and physically active, to have visual and auditory experiences, to accomplish elementary motor and physical skills, to develop vocabulary, to acquire verbal communication ability, and to develop social abilities.

In some kindergartens children are prepared for reading and do indeed learn to read. However, learning to read is not the main purpose of the kindergarten in Yugoslavia; rather, the goals are to promote readiness to read and write, communication with others, following teachers' instructions, and taking care of their duties, all of which are important in the first grade. According to research results, kindergarten children normally have better readiness for the first grade than those who did not attend kindergarten because they had the proper stimulation to develop the ability to define words, to supply antonyms on demand, to find similarities between related things, and to detect and specify absurdities and incongruities in pictures and stories. Most of kindergarten activities are created to develop speech abilities and conceptual and perceptual abilities, to enrich vocabulary, and to accomplish readiness for reading and learning.

Preparatory school (infant school) is organized for children from six years. (Compulsory education starts in the seventh year.) It lasts from at least three months to one year. This kind of school is optional; it is not regulated by law. Its aim is to prepare children for school, for organized collective and individual learning, and for beginner's reading and writing. Programs to improve reading readiness are common in Yugoslav schools. The young child likes to be read to by someone and to look at pictures in books. Pupils make up stories, read picture stories, and listen to the stories read by the teacher. Children have the opportunity to exercise their senses (especially sight, hearing, and touch), to see things, and, even in a more concrete way, to talk with the teacher and other children, to express their own ideas and to enrich their vocabulary, and to develop basic skills and abilities important for readiness so as to transfer from preparatory (infant) school to primary school. Children who start the first grade of primary school do not start with writing and reading at once (if they did not finish preparatory school) but instead are prepared, getting prereading lessons for six to eight weeks. Preparation means exercises in speech and drawing and analysis of reading materials. In this period the child performs the necessary intellectual and motor actions important to starting reading and writing. When children learn to distinguish sounds in words and to pronounce (articulate) them properly, and when their hands become movable and precise, then they start reading and writing.

Children who have serious reading disabilities from the very beginning are organized in special sections where they are given more individual work and the concrete help of a specially trained teacher. On the other hand, children who have minor reading and writing difficulties get an additional one to two classes twice or three times per week, which are organized after regular school hours.

For children who have serious speech difficulties, a specialist (speech therapist) is engaged; they can also offer special help so as to lessen the effects of a certain speech defect on the normal success of children in school. Children with emotional problems that negatively influence success in reading have the help of teachers and psychologists; if their problems are severe, psychiatrists also help. Doctors are involved when hearing should be examined or when glasses or hearing aids must be prescribed.

All these measures are undertaken from the very beginning so that every child can develop according to his or her abilities. Special care is given to children who experience difficulties in reading. Reading experts have provided a large number of remedial programs and wide varieties of new teaching methods and materials. Still the problem has not been solved. Many children who have difficulties passing the reading readiness tests also lacked certain kinds of environmental stimulation in kindergarten or preparatory school.

Yugoslavia has no special program for the separate preparation of girls and boys for beginner's reading and writing. As mentioned above, racial, sexual, and social segregation is against the current law. Males and females are separated in school activities only in the presence of medical, educational, and psychological reasons and in exceptional cases. For example, physical education is separated for the reasons accepted all over the world. In addition, programs are the same for urban and rural areas. But besides a common curriculum, which is required for all and which should provide the minimum knowledge needed for further education, special programs are available for children who for various social reasons cannot prepare themselves for school. These programs are classified within what is called additional teaching, special additional courses, or extended teaching.

TEACHER QUALIFICATIONS

The personal qualifications important for the teaching profession include (1) native intelligence—the point that marks the average of the intelligence scores of the population at large; (2) social intelligence—capacities for leadership, tactfulness in working closely with others, and sensitivity to the needs and wants of those with whom one works; (3) facility of expression—expression and original thought, integrating an ability to advise and give directions; (4) special abilities—artistic, musical, verbal, creative, and the like; and (5) physical traits—physical vigor and good mental or physical health.

The teachers' principal functions center on (1) classroom instruction—planning, realizing, and evaluating all kinds of educational activities; (2) guidance and counseling—every teacher is a counselor to his or her pupils; (3) personal responsibilities and duties—self-management and the duty to prepare students for self-management; (4) staff functions—administration, meetings, work on improving teaching and introducing innovations, as well as community duties; (5) professional activities—work in professional organizations; and (6) to a great extent, independent decisions on how to arrange and perform duties.

Yugoslavia's teachers are prepared through training courses for a specialization in a certain subject or subjects; training courses in the field of philosophy of education, educational psychology, psychology of childhood and adolescence, and methodics (teaching aids and methods), as well as preparation for self-management and administration; professional training courses for primary and secondary teachers; and preparation for counseling and human relations.

With regard to teacher certification, the authority for certification is centralized in the state educational and staff management bodies. Certificates are issued for definite subject fields or a specified grade level and must be renewed through recurrent education and in-service training. Higher education for two to three years is a minimum requirement for the primary school teacher and a bachelor's degree for the secondary school teacher. A move has been made to require four years of professional training at institutions of higher learning for all teaching personnel–from preschool to secondary vocationally directed education.

Qualifications for Becoming a Reading Teacher

Clearly, there are differences in the content and duration of education for teachers, including the teacher in reading education. All teachers at all levels of education are required to teach reading. However, teachers in primary schools, teachers in secondary schools, and university teachers who teach both mother and foreign languages and are especially prepared to develop their students' writing and oral expression, motivate pupils for reading and evaluate achieved results in this field.

Primary school teachers take methods courses in teaching the mother language, as well as other special subjects (phonetics, syntax, and morphology). Such courses help train them to introduce pupils to reading and writing, to learn the techniques of reading, to understand and interpret materials read, to use the culture of speech in learning different subjects, and to develop an interest for books. They are also trained to identify and eliminate difficulties in reading, to evaluate the improvement of pupils, and to prepare the material students use in reading education. Teachers of mother and foreign languages in secondary school are especially prepared (in methodics, literature, phonetics, syntax, morphology) to raise the speech culture of their pupils, to help their pupils read quickly, to understand and interpret the materials they read, and to use proper grammar. They are also professionally trained to evaluate the results of their pupils' work, to diagnose reading problems, and to give help to pupils who need it.

University teachers of mother and foreign languages receive special preparation in the field of methodics, literature, phonetics, syntax, and morphology which helps them to develop the students' speech culture, to motivate them for reading, and to help them improve their techniques of reading and using written sources.

Since adult education teachers are recruited from the teachers of primary and secondary schools and from the universities, there is no special training for adult reading education. Additional education is available when needed.

Programs for the reading education of teachers are the same for males and females at all levels of preparation. They are taught together, receive equal degrees, and have equal salaries for the same jobs.

In Yugoslavia, the "field of education and culture" consists of 54.2 percent female and 45.8 percent male, while in primary and secondary education it is 57 percent female and 43 percent male. The greatest percentage (61 percent) of females work in primary schools, a lower percentage (47 percent) in secondary schools, and the lowest percentage of females at the university level. Beyond this there are no reliable data for the university level. There are also no official statistics regarding the number of male and female teachers of reading education.

MATERIALS USED IN READING EDUCATION

Several institutions prepare, print, and sell books, magazines, manuals, textbooks, cassettes, films, and other materials that pupils and teachers use in the process of reading education at all levels. Specialized publishing houses—institutes for publishing textbooks and teaching aids—prepare, print, and distribute to all kinds of schools and higher institutions textbooks for students, manuals for teachers, school readings, work notebooks, controlled tests, cassettes, films, tests, and other working materials that are used in the process of reading education and its improvement. General publishing houses print scientific works, literary works, and popular scientific works in all fields of human creativity and magazines. Publishing houses of daily and weekly editions print daily newspapers, temporary reviews, scientific publications, and children's newspapers and magazines. Some publishing houses also print scientific literature for teachers and other scientific workers who work in the schools. Of course, educational television and radio programs are made for the schools. In order to develop reading interest, some houses print books of anecdotes, fables, fairy tales, poetry, short stories, illustrated stories, and novels. Reading education is also encouraged by using computers, televisions, machines for learning, and video systems.

The Availability of Materials

The basic literature used by students at all levels of education (textbooks, manuals, practicums, working notebooks, and magazines) is printed according to need (textbooks each year); prices are modest.

Scientific books, monographs, and literary works are also printed according to need; their prices are very high, and school libraries buy them more often than pupils do. Each school usually has its own lending library which houses all the materials used by pupils and teachers in the process of reading education. The library sets its own regulations as to who can borrow books and other materials, including length of time and under what conditions. Each school also has its reading room where the student can take and use what he or she wants during the day. Pupils, teachers, schools, and faculties can also borrow books from the general library. Thus, many different materials needed to learn to read are at the disposal of pupils and teachers, and there exist adequate conditions for realizing reading education as planned by the curriculum and with the aims mentioned above.

Languages Used in These Materials

Materials for reading education in the primary school are printed in the twelve languages of the Yugoslav nation: Serbo-Croatian, Slovenian, Macedonian, Albanian, Bulgarian, Czech, Romany, Hungarian, Romanian, Slovakian, Italian, and Turkish. Printed materials are equally available regardless of language(s). The social community gives financial help to the publishing houses when only a small number of copies should be printed.

Materials for reading education in secondary schools are printed in nine languages of the Yugoslav nation: Serbo-Croatian, Slovenian, Hungarian, Italian, Romanian, Macedonian, Albanian, Bulgarian, and Slovakian. All materials needed for secondary education, regardless of language, are also available under the same conditions. Realistically, society is expected to help with the printing costs of small numbers of copies so that those publications can be accessible to all who need them.

For adult education at the primary and secondary levels, materials are printed in the languages of instruction which are given (see above) for regular primary and secondary schools. For the high schools and universities, materials are printed in Serbo-Croatian, Slovenian, Macedonian, Albanian, Hungarian, Italian, and Slovakian. These publications are printed in small quantities. Therefore, they are financed by the community and are thus available to all students.

Role of Consumable Versus Nonconsumable Materials

Almost one-third of the materials used by teachers and pupils at all levels of education are consumable. These are specially prepared materials for practicing and improving reading, for practical exercises, and for controlling achieved results. Nonconsumable materials include textbooks, balletristic literature, and scientific literature. Approximately two-thirds of materials used in the primary and secondary schools, and three-quarters of those used in high schools and universities are nonconsumable. These materials are designed to promote the systematic acquisition of knowledge, to help pupils learn independently, and to pass examinations successfully. Of course, the difference between these two types of materials is not great because all prepared materials are used in the process of teaching and learning reading. In preparing and printing consumable materials, it is necessary to keep in mind their volume, price, and educational function. At all scientific levels materials to be used by teachers and pupils are reviewed in order to ensure their scientific level.

FINANCING READING EDUCATION

In Yugoslavia the system of financing education is rather complicated. Resources that are pooled within the self-managing communities of interest are used on the basis of annual programs of educational institutions and organizations and the financial projects adopted by self-management organs—assemblies of self-managing communities of interest. Resources are fixed and distributed in accordance with the financial plan. The plan, adopted each year, is in harmony with the long-term plan and the annual plan of the relevant community.

The self-management system of educational financing should prevail over the budgetary financing of education. It is expected that the establishment of the self-management system of education financing will reduce the state's involvement in educational organization and activities. Specifically, this will reduce and eliminate mediation, prevent monopoly, and thus limit manipulation in the area of educational activities. Educational financing based on the delegation system, within self-managing communities of interest, provides the impetus for acquiring resources from the organization of associated labor, from the economic sector, and from other resources. This method is more democratic and thus socializes the distribution of resources.

The practice of exchanging and pooling labor and resources is multifarious and cannot be understood without knowledge of how the income system functions within the organizations of associated labor in the sphere of material production (economy) and other spheres of associated labor. Organizations of associated labor in the economic sector acquire income through free exchange of labor, the sale of products and services, various forms of compensation, and the like. When the resources for production and amortization are earmarked from the total income acquired, what remains is the net income of the organization of associated labor. Then the contributions (resources) for the social services and other amenities provided for by law (children's and social welfare, education, science, culture, etc.) can be provided.

Personal earnings are paid for from the individual and joint consumption fund; the workers earmark resources from these funds for their various needs, including their educational needs. Each year self-management agreements determine the rate of contributions earmarked from personal earnings or the income of working organizations designed for educational financing. Workers directly decide on their level. These resources are pooled in self-managing communities of interest, and the delegates representing all areas of associated labor make the decisions on their distributions. These include employees in the field of education, the economic and noneconomic sectors, state organs, sociopolitical organizations, and communities.

The personal income of each employee finances reading education on the primary level. Each year self-managing communities reach an agreement about financing. If the rate of inflation during a year rises above the planned maximum, the percentage for education is raised after the six-month financial report. Since the financial resources come from personal incomes, they are assured and thus guarantee that programs of reading education will be implemented.

High schools and universities are financed from the incomes of working organizations and other resources. Each year social agreements regarding financing are signed. The self-managing communities of interests decide on the percentage of financing.

Many schools and faculties have direct contracts with complex organizations of associated labor so as not only to educate the needed cadre, but also to obtain the adequate financial resources for that education. Faculties often conduct scientific projects for associated labor and so get additional financial resources. These resources finance reading education as well as all other educational work of teachers, schools, and faculties.

Adult education both as a whole and vis-à-vis reading is financed by self-managing communities of interests; students of different kinds of adult education; and working organizations which pay for the ordered education of their workers. If adult education is conducted within the regular programs of schools and faculties, then financing comes from regular resources with the possibility of using other resources. Courses and seminars sponsored by work organizations for the professional education of their members are paid for by the members themselves. Finally, the workers' incomes are also paid during the process of education.

THE CURRENT FOCUS OF READING EDUCATION

Research in the field of reading education in Yugoslavia is conducted by institutes for the improvement of education, universities, and some faculties within universities. Being a universal problem, reading education is frequently the topic of symposiums, seminars, and congresses.

Reading education at the primary school level has been the subject matter of much research during the last thirty-five years. The problems most frequently researched are: beginner's reading (Šimleša, 1971); beginner's reading and writing (Demarin, 1971); complex and monographic approaches in beginner's reading (Muradbegović, 1968); problems of literacy among primary school pupils (Marković, 1971); speech behavior of pupils (Vasic, 1970); critical reading (Krsmanovic, 1970); the psychological bases of learning to read (Ivic, 1973); reading and work on texts (Poljak, 1969); the possibilities of developing and exercising reading interests (Vasic, 1969); children's lexicon (Luloc, 1978); improvement of reading (Stevanović, 1980); and development and meaning of words.

Reading research at the secondary school level focuses on elevating the level of the speech culture, improving reading techniques, raising the literal culture of pupils, training youth to interpret materials they read, developing motivation for reading, and enhancing critical thinking. Much successful research has been done in the field of reading education in foreign languages. Over the last twenty-five years the following areas have been the focus of research: reading in the teaching of foreign languages (Dimitrijević, 1962); the development of creative abilities (Kvascev, 1974); literal work in teaching practice (Nikolić, 1975); neurolinguistics and reading (Dimitrijević, 1978); speed of reading in foreign languages (Prica, 1979); models of interpretation regarding home reading (Stevanović, 1979); cognitive abilities and reading in English as a foreign language (Prica-Soretić, 1983); psychological and social factors in the teaching of a foreign language (Ostojić, 1980); and modern teaching of foreign languages (Tanović, 1982).

No systematic research has been done with reading problems in adult education, but some researchers, either directly or indirectly, have worked on elements of this field. The subject matter of these books are the determinants of the adult educational system (Samolovčev, 1965); methods of adult education (Ogrizović, 1966); rationalization of educational work (Babić, 1979); individual and life-long education (Savicević, 1983); program learning in adult education (Andrilović, 1984); and innovations in teaching (Mandić, 1987). Of course, problems regarding the motivation of adults for learning, as well as some aspects of the difficulties in elevating the speech culture, reading interests, and level of reading and writing in adults, are also being researched.

THE OUTLOOK FOR READING EDUCATION

Based on the above research on reading education and actual experience with students at all levels, some analysts have concluded that reading education should have been researched more deeply than it has up to now. Furthermore, it is necessary to invest in teaching and in the education of teachers, to provide different printed materials that will be available to all categories of readers, and to motivate students to read books that are not part of the curriculum.

The programs adopted for the next five years recommend that financial resources be invested in the training of teachers. Books on teaching methods will help teachers to train pupils in reading and writing, and in techniques of proper writing, and to develop the abilities to understand and interpret the materials they read. Concentration on an understanding of reading materials represents a quick, automatic use of reading techniques, rapid identification of graphema, correct articulation, accepted tempo and rhythm, and correct accent—all of which means a synchronization of visual and acoustic perception, and a connection between meaning and adequate intellectual activity. Further research work will be done in this field, especially with regard to techniques and approaches to perfect informative or silent reading. Research activity will also be directed toward finding the solutions for reading disabilities, improving reading, and the like. Well-thought-out plans have been made for preparing and publishing materials to satisfy the modern teaching of reading. Teachers will receive systematic preparation for all these tasks.

Ambitious plans are being laid to raise the speech culture of pupils at higher levels of education; to intensify the reading and use of books; to develop the technical and semantic aspects of reading; and to achieve the use of reading skills with materials that have a solid educational base. The following measures have been undertaken for the preparation and professional in-service training of teachers: thorough encouragement of the scientific research of reading problems in secondary schools; development and publication of materials that will enable the consistent realization of reading aims; and the introduction of technological improvements in teaching.

This field of education has not been researched enough in the past and, so, many questions remain to be answered. Future plans will focus on research, the creation of teachers, and the preparation and publication of materials that will help to improve reading. Teaching will be directed toward the intensive development of reading abilities, understanding the meaning of reading material, and the correct interpretation of materials read. Since a great number of adults use silent reading skills in their professional lives, special care will be paid to appropriate techniques and approaches for this group. Improvements will also be sought in the field of methods. Since adults are at different ages, experiences, levels of knowledge, motivation, and aspiration, the teacher should adapt method and content to these differences. Finally, in order to understand the needs and interests of adults, research is needed in this field.

SUMMARY

Reading education in Yugoslavia is taught in primary, secondary, and higher schools, and in adult education courses as well. Reading is taught in twelve languages in the primary schools, nine languages in the secondary schools, and five languages at higher schools and faculties. The process of reading instruction is decentralized. The aim of reading education is to develop reading abilities, to understand and interpret reading materials, to cultivate both speech culture and an interest in books and logical thinking; and to develop critical thinking skills. Illiteracy in the population aged over ten years is 9.5 percent. Functional illiteracy is over 30 percent and represents a greater problem than elemental illiteracy. The inability to read could be the result of sense disabilities, speech defects, difficulties in color and shape perception, width of the field of vision, neurological difficulties, inadequate methods of learning to read, and environmental factors. Different methods and diagnostic tests are available for examining why lagging in reading occurs; there are various techniques to lessen or remove their influence on personality development. Reading readiness programs can be found in all schools and compensatory courses. The publishing houses prepare materials for the teaching of reading, and materials are published in all the languages in which reading is taught.

Reading education is financed through agreements with self-managing communities of interests each year. Research in reading and reading problems is being conducted in the areas of primary, secondary, and adult education. Prospects for the further development of reading education are very good within the context of currently adopted plans.

REFERENCES

Brujić, Marinko. 1966. Govorne vjezbe u nastavi stranih jezika, izdavac, Pedagosko-knjizevni sabor. Zagreb,

Bujas, Ramiro i Zoran. 1938. Citljivost latinskog i cirilskog pisma, izdavac. University of Zagreb, Zagreb,

Dimitrijević, Naum. 1974. Istrazivanja u nastavi jezika, izdavac Naucna knjiga. Belgrade,

Dimitrijević, Radmilo. 1969. Osnovi teorije pismenosti, izdavac, Vuk Karadjic. Belgrade,

Furlan, Ivan. 1963. Citanje u svjetlosti teorije informacije, casopis Pedagogija. Belgrade,

Furlan, Ivan. 1978. Jednominutni ispit glasnog citanja, izdavac, Skolska knjiga. Zagreb,

Janjušević, Desanka. 1967. Nastava pocetnog citanja i pisanja, izdanje, Zavod za udzbenike Srbije. Belgrade,

Jovanović, Magdalena. 1959. O nekim pitanjima ucenja pismenosti, Savremena skola. Belgrade,

Kobala, Alojz. 1977. Unapredjivanje citanja u osnovnoj skoli, izdanje, Skolska knjiga. Zagreb,

Kvaščev, Radivoj. 1974. Razvijanje stvaralackih sposobnosti ucenika, izdanje, Zavod za udzbenike Srbije, Belgrade,

Lukić, Vera. 1982. Decija leksika, izdanje, Institut za pedagoska istrazivanja. Belgrade,

Mamuzić, Ilija. 1967a. Carolija citanja, izdanje, Mlado pokoljenje. Belgrade,

Mamuzić, Ilija. 1967b. Nastava usmenog i pismenog izrazavanja u osnovnoj skoli, izdanje, Mlado pokoljenje. Belgrade,

Mandić, Petar. 1987. Inovacije u nastavi, izdanje, Svjetlost. Sarajevo,

Mandić, Petar, and Gajanovic, Nedeljka. 1982. Teorijske i prakticne osnove prijema djece u skolu, izdanje, Svjetlost. Sarajevo,

Marjanović, Sanda. 1962. Moje dijete i knjiga, izdanje, Narondna knjiga. Belgrade,

Markovic, Zika. 1971. Putevi skolske prakse, izdanje, Zavod za udzvenike Srbije. Belgrade,

Muradbegović, Muhamed. 1968. Kompleksni i monografski postupak u pocetnom citanju, izdanje, Zavod za udzbenike Srbije. Belgrade,

Nikolić, Ljiljana. 1973. Problem citanja u nastavi srpso-hrvatskog jezika, izdanje, Zavod za udzbenike Srbije. Belgrade,

Ostojić, Branka. 1980. Psiholoski i drustveni faktor u nastavi stranih jezika, izdanje, Svjetlost. Sarajevo,

Peruško, Tone. 1972. Materinski jezik u obaveznoj skoli, izdanje, Pedagosko-knjizevni zbor. Zagreb,

Poljak, Vladimir. 1969. Citanje i rad na tekstu, u casopisu Pedagoski rad broj 7–8. Zagreb,

Prica-Soretic, Mirjana. 1978. Brzina citanja na stranom jeziku u svjetlu novih istrazivanja, izdanje, Prosveta. Belgrade,

Prica-Soretic, Mirjana. 1983. Kognitivne sposobnosti i citanje na engleskom kao stranom jeziku, izdanje, Prosveta. Belgrade,

Šimleša, Pero. 1965. Metodika, izdanje, Pedagosko-knjizevni zbor. Zagreb,

Stevanović, Mirko. 1980. Metodika nastave srpsko-hrvatskog jezika, izdanje, Djecije novine. Gornji Milanovac.

Tanović, Mustafa. 1972. Savremena nastava stranih jezika, izdanje, Svjetlost. Sarajevo.

Tanović, Mustafa. 1978. Savremena nastava stranih jezika, II izdanje, Svjetlost. Sarajevo,

Težak, Stjepko. 1964. Govorne vjezbe u nastavi hrvatsko-srpskog jezika, izdanje, Pedagosko-knjizevni zbor. Zagreb,

Vasić, Smiljka. 1967. Govor vaseg deteta, izdanje, Zavod za udzbenike Srbije. Belgrade,

Živković, Dragisa. 1965. Teorija knjizevnosti sa teorijom pismenosti, Naucna knjiga. Belgrade.

26

Zaire

Dianzungu Dia Biniakunu

THE LANGUAGES OF THE COUNTRY

As in many black African countries, the linguistic situation in Zaire is very complex—so much so that, despite recent efforts, its languages are not known with certainty. For decades the number of the country's languages has been estimated to be over 400 (Massiala, 1984). The most recent study has determined that the number of the country's languages fluctuates around 221 (Alac, 1983). But this number is by no means final because of the ambiguity of the concept of language as used in the study. Indeed, as Ngalasso (1986) points out, Alac's use of the word *speeches* instead of *languages* makes this 221 figure simply tentative since language and speech do not necessarily coincide.

While we do not know the exact number of languages spoken in Zaire, it is important to recognize that the country is a highly multilingual one and that this state of affairs is attributable primarily to the 1885 Act of Berlin. By this law Africa was divided by the European colonial powers—France, England, Germany, Portugal, and Belgium—without taking into account either the political or the sociocultural entities that then existed on the continent. Instead, as Dianzungu and Mbuyi (1987) point out, the 1885 Berlin act either divided existing kingdoms and empires in different colonies—such as the ancient Kingdom of the Kongo which then included parts of today's Angola, Zaire, and the Congo—or united kingdoms and empires that were then different and sometimes ignored each other if they were not hostile. The ancient Kingdom of the Kongo, for example, was united with, among others, the ancient Empire of the Lunda, both having their own and different languages. Zaire is thus an amalgam of numerous ancient kingdoms and empires which, in terms of language, were and are still heterogeneous.

Table 26.1
The Four National Languages of Zaire

Language	Number of People Speaking The Language
Kikongo	3,000,000
Lingala	6,000,000
Kiswahili	8,000,000
Tshiluba	3,000,000

The numerous languages of Zaire are not, of course, of equal importance; many are spoken by millions of people, whereas others are spoken by only a few thousands. Consequently, until now it has been impossible to promote any of them to the status of official language. As a result, French, one of the two languages of the former colonial power, Belgium, has not only retained its prevalence over indigenous languages as Dianzungu (1980a) has indicated, but has also become the leading official language of the country. That is, it is the language used in formal life: government, justice, commerce, education at its secondary and higher levels, and so on. Thus, at both the national and international levels, problems and transactions in such fields as politics, economy, finance, trade, communication, and secondary and higher education are dealt with in French.

How many Zaireans speak this official, albeit foreign, language? It is impossible to give an exact figure for no serious official statistics exist. Ngalasso (1986) gives an estimate of below 3 million stating, "With regard to French, it is generally estimated that the number of French-speaking Zaireans is below ten percent of the total population, that is below three millions, whose competency is extremely variable." Be that as it may, the fact is that only a trifling minority of Zaireans can speak the language in which the most important affairs of the country are conducted. As a result, the vast majority of Zairean people are excluded, as it were, from the decision-making process, at least in the area of basic issues.

Aside from the official language, Zaire has four major indigenous languages that enjoy the status of national language. These are Kikongo in the southwestern part of Zaire, spoken by about 3 million people; Lingala, in the northwestern part of the country, in Kinshasa, and along the Zaire River between Kinshasa and Kisangani, spoken by about 6 million people; Kiswahili in the east and the east-southern part of the country, the most widely spoken language of Zaire with about 8 million speakers; and Tshiluba, in central and southern Zaire, with about 3 million speakers (See Table 26.1). These national languages are in fact regional lingua franca: they are the media of regional interethnic communications and transactions.

With regard to education, the situation is a twofold one. At the kindergarten and primary school levels, in principle and depending on the geographic school location, one of the above languages or, in some cases, an important ethnic language having no national status—such as Kimongo in the Equatorial region or Kitetela in the Eastern Kasai region—is used as the instructional medium while French is taught as a subject matter from third grade. It follows that the language of the curriculum Grades K–6 varies depending on the school location within the country. Actually, that is theory; the practice is quite different in urban milieus where high-fee private schools attended only by children from the elite portion of the population teach in French, which is also the true medium of socioeconomic promotion and power. Many of these private schools, which are not illegal, often use imported curricula.

At the secondary level, French is the language of the curriculum. Not only is it taught as a subject matter, but it is also the language in which the teaching is done. This explains why only a minority of Zaireans are French-speaking citizens: only those very few who go through secondary education can speak the official language of the country.

THE PROCESS OF READING INSTRUCTION

On the basis of the language situation in Zaire, one would expect its reading instruction policy to be decentralized, at least in kindergarten and primary schools and, to a lesser extent, in secondary schools as far as national languages as defined above are concerned. On the contrary, the process is highly centralized. Reading curricula, whether in French or in indigenous languages, are made by the Ministry of Primary and Secondary Education. No local initiative is allowed. There is no exception to this regulation. For example, in 1986 the minister (Educateur, 1986) of primary and secondary education sent a circular to the country's schools about the "strict prohibition for schools all over the country to use textbooks that are not approved of by the Ministry." It reads:

I remind you that the use of the Republic's schools of textbooks which have not been approved of by the Ministry of Primary and Secondary education is strictly prohibited. Only the Direction of Curriculum and Instructional Materials is qualified to proceed to the necessary approval. Thus any textbook that hasn't been approved of by the Ministry must be immediately discarded from our schools.

The prohibition also holds for methods used in reading instruction.

To be sure, at the general political level, steps are being taken to decentralize the political process and, consequently, to give local and regional governments and authorities more decision-making power. Whether or not this political decentralization will have some impact on education in general and on the process of reading instruction in particular is not known yet. For the time being, centralization is the strict rule, which is really detrimental to the development and promotion of relevant literature in indigenous languages and, thus, of reading instruction. Since the languages termed national languages are in fact regional and local languages, one would think that both the development of literature and the teaching of reading in these languages would be facilitated and made more relevant if they could take place where they are needed, that is, at the local and regional levels. Unfortunately, that is not the case.

On a regular basis, the central government issues lists of reading textbooks that are to be used in schools. One of the consequences of this stringent centralization is poor production and thus scarcity of reading materials. This in turn results in poor reading education. In fact, the Ministry of National Education is aware of and complains about this poor book production in terms of both quantity and quality. Since the main criterion for approving a reading textbook is conformity to the government-made curriculum, most manuscripts submitted to the Ministry of National Education for approval, the Ministry complains, "are alike, deal with the same contents, and use the same presentation and teaching methods, so much so that the authors seem to be copying one another" (Lwamba, 1985).

THE GOALS OF READING EDUCATION

The goals of reading education in primary education were defined in 1963, three years after independence in 1960. Since then, they haven't really changed. Learning to read is said to be "one of the most important functions of primary education" (République Démocratique du Congo, 1970). Theoretically, reading education in primary schools is aimed at

1. Helping every child, during the first two years, to acquire the necessary knowledge and skills involved in the reading process.
2. Helping the pupil, during the intermediate years, to start turning reading into a process through which he or she gets access to information and knowledge. Thus, at this stage reading is designed to become little by little a spontaneous activity that enables the pupil to enjoy stories, tales, and legends. This means, among other things, that pupils are encouraged—or rather are supposed to be encouraged—to read books spontaneously other than those assigned to reading classes. To make this possible, one needs to have plenty of books to choose from, which is not generally the case. So as far as daily practice is concerned, this goal is hardly achieved.
3. Making reading in the last years of primary education a multipurpose process, namely, an extraordinary way of getting new information, knowledge, and skills; an important study skill; an opportunity to enjoy different kinds of writings; an important research and documentation tool; and so on. As a result, official regulations read: "The reading book is not enough at this stage. A number of school tasks will require that the pupil read newspapers, reviews, magazines so that he may engage in discussions, thinking, judgments, and so on." But here again, that is theory; daily practice and realities tell a very different story. Most Zairean children, especially in city slums and in rural areas, graduate from or leave schools without ever having read in full one single book, magazine, review, or whatever piece of writing.

During the last six years, Zaire's condition has been worsened by the country's debt crisis and by the structural adjustment program imposed by the International Monetary Fund and World Bank, a program that has made drastic budget cuts in education, health, and other social programs. Not only is the book industry poorly developed (Taubert, 1984), but also the country cannot afford to import enough books for schools under today's economic circumstances. As a result, most goals for reading education are not achieved; one can even affirm that some of the goals of reading education cannot be achieved simply because minimal conditions are truly not there.

Theoretically, in order to achieve these goals, the Ministry of National Education recommends that libraries be set up in primary schools in general and in each classroom in particular. However, for the time being and, for most schools, that is simply daydreaming.

In secondary schools, reading education is supposed to achieve the following goals:

1. As a major learning skill. Most modern knowledge is stocked in books and periodicals. Therefore, the systematic use of textbooks in secondary schools, many of which are "imported in massive numbers from other francophone countries" (Taubert, 1984), is expected to achieve this purpose. That is why, as Dianzungu (1982) puts it, "one of the reading objectives of Zairean eighth grade is to teach students to identify the main ideas and supporting details in passages, and to determine the relationships between ideas."

2. As an opportunity for students to get to know and appreciate some of the world and especially the best African literary works. By African literary works, one really means "the literary works written by Africans in European languages" (Ngugi, 1986) since real African literary works, especially masterpieces, written in African languages have yet to be produced.

3. As a means of cultural enrichment through the reading of diverse literary works, namely, drama, fiction, and nonfiction.

In secondary schools, too, libraries are recommended. To be sure, secondary schools are more likely, generally speaking, to have some books for students to borrow from once in a while. A few schools do have some kind of libraries; these schools are usually church-operated institutions that sometimes receive books as donations from the outside. In most schools, however, either there is no library or there are very few books about which the use of the term *library* might be misleading. For one thing, to realize these goals, one has to secure large numbers of books of all kinds, which is not the case under today's socio-economic circumstances characterized by the foreign debt crisis yoke.

Aside from specialized departments such as literature and language departments, the country's universities and other institutions of higher education have no formal reading education. Where it is taught, reading in tertiary education aims either at making students able to understand different kinds of foreign language texts both literally and critically, which also contributes to their literary and cultural enrichment, or at providing students with the opportunity for an in-depth knowledge and appreciation of a wide range of national, African, and world literary works.

Adult education is poorly developed in the country. There are no statistics available. The few centers that offer programs in this area, aside from literacy program centers, are located in big cities such as Kinshasa, Lubumbashi, Kananga, and Kisangani. They are primarily vocational or technical and offer such courses as accounting, secretarial, and sometimes computer programming. More and more companies are requiring that employees be knowledgeable in foreign languages, especially in English. As a result, foreign language centers, especially English centers, are being set up in big cities, where reading naturally takes place. In this case, reading education aims primarily at helping students to meet professional needs.

Because of the churches' involvement, the most important kind of adult education is by far the one that is provided through what is termed *social promotion centers* within which exist "literacy cells." These centers in general and their literacy cells in particular are attended mainly by women simply because women are the portion of the population that suffers more from illiteracy. It follows that this is the area of adult education where reading education is relatively important and aims at. (1) "weeding out illiteracy that is steadily spreading" (Département des Affaires Sociales, 1985); (2) giving an opportunity to those who never benefited from schooling or never attended school to get to read and to acquire new knowledge and skills through reading; and (3) meeting one of the basic human rights and the country's commitment to fulfill it.

Up to this point no mention has been made of males versus females with regard to the goals of reading education. It is a deliberate omission. Indeed, at no level would this apply. There is no such thing as male or female reading education goals in Zaire. To be sure, there are sometimes girls' or boys' schools, which are mostly if not exclusively operated by the Catholic Church. However, whether girls and boys attend the same or separated schools, the goals for reading education are the same. By the same token, secondary schools might include programs designed primarily for girls; this is the case in such programs as home economics. Under these circumstances some books are read only by students involved in these programs, but this is true in the teaching of reading in all secondary school subject matters and doesn't mean girls would have particular reading goals.

In brief, then, there is no difference between male and female in terms of goals for reading education at any level whatsoever.

ILLITERACY

There is no official way of determining illiteracy. There is only a general and popular definition of illiteracy, namely, the inability to read, whatever this means.

Such a way of determining illiteracy is not very helpful because it surely doesn't carry an unequivocal meaning. This is actually understandable because in Zaire, despite the number of speeches and statements made by various officials, weeding out illiteracy has never been considered a priority. There has been no program aimed at nationally and within a predetermined period of time eradicating illiteracy.

It follows that illiteracy in Zaire is extremely high. As always, however, statistics about illiteracy are not available. Thus, the rate is not known, not even within the Ministry of Social Affairs which is responsible for literacy policy and management. The number of times literacy policy and management have been moved from one government ministry to another is indicative of the insignificant attention paid to the whole issue by the country's authorities. Indeed, the Ministry of Social Affairs once wrote (1985):

The General Management for Literacy and Adult Education was first established in 1966 within the Ministry of National Education as a response to one of the resolutions of the Teheran, Iran Congress on literacy organized in 1965 by UNESCO. In 1971 it moved from the Ministry of National Education to the Ministry of Social Affairs, then in 1974 to the Ministry of Civil Service, and finally it went back to the Ministry of Social Affairs in 1980.

Today's situation and location of the general management doesn't satisfy. Indeed, many people think that the Ministry of National Education would be more appropriate to conceive of and manage literacy policy rather than the Ministry of Social Affairs. Nonetheless, the illiteracy rate in Zaire is very high. The Ministry of Social Affairs gives an estimate of 40 percent. Actually, this is definitely too optimistic a figure. For one thing, official figures indicate that "more than 40% of school-age population are not attending any school" (Aluma, 1986), which means that more than 40 percent of children of that age are illiterate. Now if we consider that the majority of those who attend never graduate from primary schools and are illiterate, then it becomes understandable that the true rate of illiteracy is worse than it is thought to be.

For another thing, since 1973, copper, the heart of Zaire's economy, has been selling very poorly. Consequently, the country has known its toughest economic crisis and has been unable to meet its financial commitments in favor of educational development and improvement. Obviously, this has had a negative impact on literacy programs. For yet another thing, because of the government's inability to meet its financial commitment in favor of education, parents' financial contribution to education has been made legally mandatory. The minister of primary and secondary education now determines—from kindergarten to twelfth grade—the annual amount of school fees to be paid by every pupil or student attending any Zairean school. On the one hand, the country's wages are among the world's lowest and, on the other hand, unemployment is very high. Accordingly, most parents simply cannot pay those fees, all the less since a large proportion of them have several children in schools.

All this means that the last fifteen years have not eased illiteracy in Zaire. On the contrary, as an official at the Department of Social Affairs recognized in July 1988, it can be argued that illiteracy is rather on the rise. A representative of the Kimbanguist Church at the National Seminar on Literacy Staff Training held in Kinshasa in 1985, talking about literacy within his church, recognized that "the rate of illiteracy among the Kimbanguist Church devotees was steadily increasing" (Département des Affaires Sociales, 1985). What is true for the Kimbanguist Church devotees is certainly true for the whole population, namely, that illiteracy is not diminishing; rather, it is increasing.

The official population in Zaire is 35 million. If the official estimation of Zairean illiteracy rate were true, namely, 40 percent, there would be about 14 million illiterate Zaireans in the country, but it is almost certain that this is an optimistic figure. How are all these illiterate people distributed among males and females and among the different levels of education? Again, statistics are not available, so that this question cannot be answered with precision. At least in urban areas there should be no difference between boys and girls at the elementary school level. This is not the case at the other levels whatsoever. At these levels, illiterate females should outnumber illiterate males by far, because if it is true that today almost all boys and girls go to school for at least a few years, in the past many more boys went to school than girls. This is still true at both the secondary and tertiary education level where females are outnumbered in terms of school attendance, which means that there should be many more illiterate females than males.

READING DISABILITIES

As for reading disabilities, in whatever respect they are examined—their nature, their distribution in terms of males versus females, instruments and methods used in their diagnosis, efforts in remediating them—the simplest way to address the issue would be to say it doesn't apply; that is, the issue is almost never dealt with for the time being. It might be taught in universities, and to be sure, "the necessity for schools to have specialized resource people capable of dealing with this aspect of reading education" (Kazadi, 1988) is sometimes recognized and voiced. It is also true that students with serious reading problems are likely to be numerous. However, the schools are not equipped to deal with these problems. They have neither the qualified resource people nor the necessary instruments to do that. It follows that the whole issue of reading disabilities is almost unheard of as far as policy, action, and daily practice are concerned.

In today's state of Zaire's affairs, such a preoccupation is almost a luxury in comparison with the most urgent needs, such as giving every Zairean child a chance to learn to read (one is reminded that more than 40 percent of Zairean school-age children have no chance to attend any primary school), providing schools with reading materials and qualified teachers, and so on. If efforts to politically and administratively decentralize the decision-making processes that

are underway can materialize, reading education in general and reading disabilities in particular might become matters of greater attention and preoccupation,
which they are not now despite much pompous rhetoric.

READING READINESS PROGRAMS

Before 1986 kindergarten education existed in big cities like Kinshasa, Kananga, Lubumbashi, or Kisangani. However, in most instances the existing preschool programs were an outgrowth of private initiative. In 1986 Zaire passed
legislation regarding preschool education which today is recognized as part of
national education. It is neither mandatory nor well developed. In rural areas,
it is almost nonexistent except in very few areas where factories with important
manpower sometimes organize such facilities in favor of employees' children.
But this is exceptional and needs no mention. In cities, preschool programs are
in great demand, despite their high cost, because, among other things, of the
steady increase in the number of working mothers.

Since 1986 the public school sector has been involved in preschool education
whose purpose is "to prepare the pupil to undertake primary education" (Educateur, 1986). It is thus safe to say that some reading readiness programming
is taking place, although it would be misleading to speak of systematic reading
readiness programs per se. As for whether there might be different programs for
males versus females, that is not the case. As was said about goals for reading
education, no difference is conceived of between male and female reading readiness programs.

TEACHER QUALIFICATIONS

The procedure for becoming a qualified teacher in Zaire is rather complex
because qualified teachers have to be distinguished according to levels of schooling. In primary education as well as in secondary education, there are two levels
of teacher qualification. At the primary school level, there are, on the one hand,
four-year teacher training courses after primary education (ten years of schooling
altogether) for those destined to teach in either first or second grade and, on the
other hand, six-year teacher training after primary education (twelve years of
schooling in all) for those teachers destined to teach in Grades 3 through 6.

At the secondary school level, the country has also conceived of two levels
of teacher qualification. First, teachers undergo a three-year training program
after graduation from secondary education (fifteen years of schooling altogether)
if they want to teach in the first four years of secondary education, that is, Grades
7 through 10. Second, teachers with a five-year training after graduation from
secondary education (seventeen years of schooling in all) can teach in both the
eleventh and twelfth grades. As can be seen, whether at the primary or the
secondary school level, the higher the grades the teacher instructs, the more
training he or she gets.

To become a qualified teacher in tertiary education, a candidate must hold at least a master's degree (or an equivalent degree), while to be a qualified teacher in adult education, a diversity of training is necessary depending on what one teaches. In the particular case of literacy-related adult education, it is a common practice that, as the Department of Social Affairs put it, "teachers who have been trained for primary education . . . receive additional training in andragogy, literacy, literacy methods, group dynamics, demography, community development, adult social psychology, evaluation and laboratory activities" (Département des Affaires Sociales, 1985).

With regard to reading teachers, the country has no such teachers; no teachers are specifically trained and used to teach only reading. Every teacher in primary schools is ipso facto a reading teacher for both French and whatever national language is used as the teaching medium and taught as a subject. In secondary schools, any language teacher (French, English, or Zairean) is also a reading teacher. In tertiary education, the same is true: whoever teaches a language or literature is also a reading teacher.

Statistics on the proportion of males to females among teachers are not available. It is a fact, however, that in secondary and tertiary education male teachers outnumber female teachers by far. In primary education, the proportion of female teachers is high, though not as high as that of male teachers. In adult education dealing with women-related matters such as home economics, female teachers outnumber male teachers. Unfortunately, it is not possible to give any figure.

MATERIALS USED IN READING EDUCATION

The government is the primary source of materials used in reading education, at least as far as primary and secondary schools are concerned. Although reading materials are also available from private sources, the government must approve them before the schools can use them. For instance, I am the author of a book—*Na Nsesi, Na Nzau ye Na Nguvu*—which is used in third grade in the Kikongo-speaking region of lower Zaire. But before it could be introduced in the schools, it needed government approval. In tertiary and adult education, there is a greater diversity of sources, with private sources playing the most important role. As noted earlier, anyone can submit a manuscript to the government for approval.

Reading materials are not often available for all levels and all languages. The lack of materials is probably the chief obstacle to the whole business of reading education. To give only one example, reading materials in Zairean languages (Kikongo, Kiswahili, Lingala, Tshiluba, etc.) were not available beyond the second grade at the beginning of the 1988–1989 school year. Indeed, the nineteenth issue of the government-published *Educateur* published a list of available reading materials and their prices at the beginning of the school year, but nothing on that list can be used beyond second grade. The situation is better in French for which there is at least one reading textbook for every grade from first to twelfth, even though some of those reading books, like those used in seventh and eighth grades, have not been used for the last twenty years! Literacy reading materials in all languages represent by far the worst situation. As long as book production is not regarded as a top priority in the country's educational policy, education in general and reading education in particular will not be enhanced.

Although the situation is far from satisfactory, French reading materials do exist for both primary and secondary schools. However, much more needs to be done because, if there is at least one reading book for every grade in both primary and secondary schools, many of those books should be considered outdated, having been in use for more than twenty years. Poor book production in Zaire is not due to any lack of printing facilities; it is due to the lack of any policy in terms of reducing both production costs and delivery times, as well as to the lack of any system of book distribution not only within the country but also within cities and towns. In 1989 Taubert wrote something that is still true when he stated,

The inability of Zaire book industry to satisfy demand is not due to any lack of printing facilities: in Kinshasa alone, there are one hundred printing works, some of them equipped with the very latest equipment. The real problem lies in the lack of qualified staff . . . , they do not have the skilled personnel needed to typeset and print a scientific or technical work.

In addition (and this too constitutes a real obstacle to book production), Zaire has no professional body that regulates the situation and protects the rights of publishers and authors, despite the existence of the Union des Ecrivains Zairois (UEZA), the Zairean Writers Union.

For economic reasons—such as low wages and high unemployment—most books published in the country (about 250 titles a year), even textbooks, are in the form of consumable materials regardless of the area of reading education. Moreover, since reading is an uncharacteristic feature of Zaire's culture, the price of books must be the lowest possible if they are to be bought. Consequently, it would be very uneconomical and risky to publish books in forms other than consumable materials because the chance of selling them would be very slim.

FINANCING READING EDUCATION

As stated above, aside from adult education dealing with literacy programs, reading education is not treated differently from any other school subject matter. Hence, it does not require particular financing. Only reading education within literacy programs requires some particular—but actually poor—financing. So across the whole school system, reading education is financed in part by the government and in part by parents. At the beginning of each school year the government determines the amount of money to be paid by every pupil or student, part of which is intended to buy books. For instance, at the beginning of the present school year (1988–1989), kindergarten and primary school pupils have to pay, respectively, 200 Z and 300 Z, while in secondary schools students have to pay 1,000 Z or 2,095 Z, depending on the student's particular department—humanities, sciences, technical (U.S. $1.00 = ± 350 Z). In tertiary education as well as in adult education, students have to buy most of or even all their books.

THE CURRENT FOCUS OF READING EDUCATION

It would be exaggerated to talk about the current focus of reading research in Zaire. Research in general and educational research in particular are in a state of crisis, as is the country itself. Back in 1980, I wrote in my doctoral dissertation, "Literature in general and research literature in particular are not important in Zaire. One can even assert . . . that research literature is growing scarce" (Dianzungu, 1980a). Things haven't changed much since then. If they have changed at all, then they must have worsened because, as said earlier, the country has been undergoing its toughest economic and social crisis in the last fifteen years. This crisis has resulted, among other things, in drastic budget cuts in general and in educational research in particular.

Ten years ago, talking about higher education in Zaire, Verhaegen (1978) wrote, "Despite the favourable factors and conditions just mentioned, the situation of research at the end of this decade can be summed up in a lapidary judgment: there is no Zairean research for Zaire development. In such key areas as agronomy, demography, medicine, ecology, Zairean research is nonexistent." Reading education is no exception. This is so true that periodicals such as *Revue de Pédagogie Appliquée*, a publication of the Kinshasa-Binza Teacher Training Institute (IPN), which used to publish works on reading education and other educational matters, have either ceased to be published or continue being published but on such an irregular basis that no one expects them any more. One periodical, however, has come back to life—*Educateur*, a publication of the Department of Primary and Secondary Education. It was first published in 1964 but was discontinued for a number of years. Its publication resumed in 1984. From time to time *Educateur* contains articles on reading or on reading-related matters such as the language issue. Three such articles were published by Lwamba (1985), Masiala (1984), Apumbi (1984), which discuss the language issue with its implications for reading; another such article was published by Ikete (1986) and deals with textbook readability. There are a few doctoral dissertations on reading such as the one by Kabuya (1980) on reading education evaluation and one by Dianzungu (1980a) on reading programs. Dianzungu has also published on primers in Kikongo language (1980b) and on reading comprehension (1982). But again, it would be an exaggeration to talk about the current focus on reading research because there is no such thing for the time being. There is too little research to speak of any real focus.

THE OUTLOOK FOR READING EDUCATION

In light of the foregoing discussion, we would expect a grim outlook for reading education in Zaire. Indeed, in the short run that outlook is not brilliant because there will be no significant improvement in the foreseeable future in terms of publishing, teacher qualifications, reading incentives, school budget, cost of living, and so on, which have a direct impact on reading education. Besides, if the political and administrative decentralization passed by the Zairean Parliament can be accelerated, then the short-run grimness of reading education can be shortened.

In the long run, there seems to be little doubt that the outlook for reading education in Zaire is promising. In the last few months, a lot of television and radio shows have talked about human rights, and it is now recognized that the ability to read is a right and that "the Government is obliged not only to insure that every Zairean child gets at least primary schooling but also every Zairean adult can read, write, and compute." As a result, although no special steps have been taken yet, talks about moves to end illiteracy and to improve education in general and reading education in particular are expanding. In addition, Zaire is probably the only country on earth whose government includes a full Ministry of Human Rights. Moreover, proofs of adults wishing to be able to read are cumulating. I have personal experience with this fact. On the one hand, as mentioned earlier, I have published a Kikongo language reading textbook designed for third grade—*Na Nsesi, Na Nzau ye Na Nguvu* [The Gazelle, the Elephant, and the Hippopotamus]—which has since been translated into the Lingala language. People have such a profound desire to read that not only many adult people are asking for the book, but also it is being used in adult literacy programs, especially church literacy programs.

On the other hand, as I described it in a recent paper (Dianzungu, 1989), I did an experiment on scientific popularization for a book, *Nsi yankatu ngongo eto* [We want no desert here], in the Kikongo language (Dianzungu, 1987). The book was especially designed for peasants. Indeed, the peasants are to a large extent, and mostly by ignorance, accountable for the ecological decay in the Lower Zaire region because they burn the land on an annual basis (bush fire). The book thus deals with ecological and agricultural matters, and it gives scientific explanations and analyses of the region's ecological and agricultural troubles: low soil fertility, erosion, drying out of small streams, steadily decreasing rainfall, poor harvests, and the like. Despite the classical difficulties of book distribution in Africa, especially in Zaire, and the lack of any advertising in the country—not to mention the fact that peasants almost never read—the 10,000 copies were sold out in less than two years. Never, according to the publisher, had a book had such a success. Those who read it and many others are asking for new books on a diversity of matters and issues. Better yet, illiterate peasants are now asking for literacy programs. I myself have been asked to write a primer for adult people.

Last July I asked tens of peasants who had read the book why they enjoyed it. Most of them replied that they had enjoyed and valued the contents of the book, that they had particularly appreciated the first book written for them in their own language, that it was the first time they had read a book that provided them with sound explanations and analyses of issues of real concern to them, and that, as a village chief put it, "for the first time the university has come down to the village!"

Thus, in the long run, the outlook for reading education appears to be bright because people, including peasants, are increasingly realizing that books and periodicals can discuss highly valuable, vital matters and issues. They are becoming aware that books and periodicals can play a significant role in the whole process of development. If efforts in the book industry and in teacher training can be pursued and intensified, if decentralization can be achieved as passed by the Parliament, if intellectuals can increasingly engage in book production, especially in Zairean languages, and if books can be produced in great numbers that provide grass-roots citizens with answers to their problems and needs, then undoubtedly the brilliant long-run outlook for reading education can be hastened.

CONCLUSION

In view of the foregoing analysis and discussion, it is clear that reading education in Zaire is characterized, in part, by tremendous shortcomings owing to a number of unfavorable political, economic, geographic, cultural (linguistic), organizational, and management factors. The inconsistent linguistic policies, especially with regard to education; the too centralized reading instruction process, particularly in terms of language management and reading materials production; the steadily high illiteracy rate among adult people owing to the still high percentage of school-age children who have no opportunity to benefit from reading instruction; the lack of qualified teachers, reading materials, and money—to mention only a few difficulties—make the whole reading education situation in Zaire a very intricate one. In the short run, it is highly desperate for alleviation. Unfortunately, there has not been any national project or program with timed implementation and precise means, designed to eradicate illiteracy, to motivate people to read, to make book production and thus reading a significant part of the development process. The country's economic crisis makes the enhancement of reading education appear hopeless.

And yet, Zaire is undoubtedly one of the richest countries in Africa, and even in the world, in terms of human and natural resources. It should be a leader in most areas, including education. It has the necessary printing facilities, the potential writers, and scientific and technological popularizers. All it needs is a more humane and democratic (thus decentralized) political process, a more generous and just social organization that considers illiteracy as both hindering social progress and impeding the whole development process.

Things may be starting to move: the political process though timidly and too slowly, is being democratized and decentralized; the mass media are becoming freer while criticism of the political and social system is on the rise; the need and demand for more reading education and more literacy programs are equally on the rise; book production, which is far below the country's capabilities, seems to be looking for a new start; the newly passed law on education and the present insistence on human rights seem to be pushing in that direction; and so on. In any event, the country may well be heading toward new horizons, and reading education is expected to be enhanced.

REFERENCES

Alac. 1983. *Atlas Linguistique du Zaire. Inventaire Préliminaire*. Paris: ACCT–CER-DOTOLA, Equipe nationale zairoise.

Aluma, Lifeta. 1986. "Diagnostic de l'Enseignement Normal." *Educateur*, No. 11: 56–58.

Apumbi, Lomema. 1984. "Les Langues dans l'Enseignement au Zaire." *Educateur*, No. 4: 33–35.

Arboleda, Amadio A. 1983. "Distribution: The Neglected Link in the Publishing Chain." *Asian Book Development* 14, No. 4: 42–53.

Dianzungu Dia Biniakunu. 1980a. "Design and Evaluation of a Beginning French Reading Program: The Case of Third Grade Program in Zaire." Ed.D. dissertation, State University of New York at Buffalo.

Dianzungu Dia Biniakunu. 1980b. "Learning to Read Kikongo: A Primer Makes a Difference." *The Reading Teacher* 34, No. 1: 32–36.

Dianzungu Dia Biniakunu. 1982. "In-service Teacher Training Improves Eighth Graders' Reading Ability in Zaire." *Journal of Reading* 25, No. 7: 662–665.

Dianzungu Dia Biniakunu. 1989. "Vulgarisation Scientifique et Développement: Cas de l'Education Ecolgique et Agricole en Langue Africaine en Milieu Paysan." Paper presented at the Research Week at Marien Ngouabi University, Brazzaville, Congo, April 17–23, 1989.

Dianzungu Dia Biniakunu, and Mbuyi, Dennis. 1987. "African Languages and Education: Two Perspectives on Language Policy. Paper presented at the 31st Annual Meeting of the Comparative and International Education Society, Washington, D.C., March 12–15, 1987.

Educateur. 1986. "Loi Cadre No. 86/005 du 22–9–1986 de l'Enseignement National." *Educateur*, No. 11: 10–36.

Ikete, Ebale Belotsi. 1986. "La Lisibilité des Manuels Scolaires." *Educateur*, No. 12: 23–27.

Kabuya, Lumembele. 1980. "Assessment of Reading Abilities of Zairean Students at Ages 12 and 18 Years." Ph.D. dissertation, State University of New York at Buffalo.

Kazadi, Betukumesu. 1988. "Rôle et Importance d'un Service Psychologique dans une Ecole." *Educateur*, No. 19: 36–37.

Krieger, Milton. 1988. "African Policy Linking Education and Development: Standard Criticisms and a New Departure." *International Review of Education* 34, No. 3: 293–311.

Lwamba, Lwa Nemba. 1985. "La Problématique de la Langue d'Enseignement au Zaire." *Educateur*, No. 5: 33–42.

Massiala, Ma Solo. 1984. "La Problématique de Langue Nationale dans l'Enseignement." *Educateur*, No. 4: 25–32.

Ngalasso, M. M. 1986. "Etat des Langues et Langues d'Etat au Zaire." *Politique Africaine*, No. 23: 7–28.

Ngugi, Wa Thiongo. 1986. *Decolonizing the Mind: the Politics of Language in African Literature*. Nairobi (Kenya): Heinemann.

Ngulugu, Kakesa, and Alex, Michel. 1986. "Le Français en Première et Deuxième Années Secondaires: Activités des Classes." *Educateur*, No. 8: 47–66.

République Démocratique du Congo, Ministère de l'Education Nationale. 1970. *Programme National de l'Enseignement Primaire 1963*. Kinshasa. Editions Saint-Paul, pp. 43–44, 51–52.

République du Zaire, Département des Affaires Sociales, Direction de l'Alphabétisation. 1985. *Séminaire National de Formation des Cadres de l'Alphabétisation et de l'Education des Adultes*. Kinshasa: DAEA-Unesco, p. 45.

Verhaegen, Benoît. 1978. *L'Enseignement Universitaire au Zaire: de Lovanium à l'UNAZA 1858–78*. Paris: L'Harmattan.

"Zaire Republic." 1984. Sigfried Taubert, ed. *The Book Trade of the World: Africa*. Munich: K. S. Saur, pp. 324–334.

Index

About the Editors and Contributors

RAMADAN A. AHMED Professor, Department of Psychology, College of Arts, Kuwait University. Dr. Ahmed received his Ph.D. in Psychology in Leipzig in 1981. His dissertation topic was "Concept Formation in Children Cross-Culturally." His interests cover the fields of developmental psychology, cross-cultural psychology, especially cross-cultural cognitive psychology, and school psychology.

NOUCHINE ANSARI Past president of the Children's Book Council of Iran in Tehran.

FRANZ BIGLMAIER Professor of Education at the Freie Universitat in Berlin. Dr. Biglmaier received his Ph.D. in Psychology and Education from the University of Munich. He was a Fulbright Scholar and the first president of the German Reading Association.

S. M. BONDARENKO Reading Scholar at the Institute of General and Educational Psychology in Moscow.

PAUL H. BUTTERFIELD Late of the University of the Witwatersrand, Johannesburg, South Africa.

JACK CASSIDY Professor of Education at Millersville University of Pennsylvania.

L. JOHN CHAPMAN Professor of Education in the School of Education at the Open University in England.

DIANZUNGU DIA BINIAKUNU Reading Scholar in Brazzaville, Congo.

JOHN ELKINS Professor of Education at the University of Queensland in Australia.

WILLIAM ELLER Professor in the Department of Learning and Instruction at the State University of New York at Buffalo. He is coeditor (with John Hladczuk) of *Literacy/Illiteracy in the World: A Bibliography* (Greenwood, 1989—a *Choice Outstanding Academic Book for 1990*) and *Comparative Reading: An International Bibliography* (Greenwood, 1987).

WARWICK B. ELLEY Professor of Education at the University of Canterbury, Christchurch, New Zealand. Dr. Elley teaches courses in Reading, Language, and Measurement, and has conducted research in vocabulary acquisition and on evaluation of book-based reading programs.

DINA FEITELSON Professor of Education at the University of Haifa in Haifa, Israel.

ELIANE FIJALKOW Ph.D. in Psychology (1987) at the University of Toulouse (France). Dr. Fijalkow's doctoral dissertation was entitled ''Reading, Writing and Inner Speech with Deaf Children,'' Chargee de cours et Attachee de Recherches (Universite de Toulouse-Le Mirail).

ROSHAN S. FITTER Professor of Education at the University of Lesotho.

V. I. GOLOD Reading Scholar at the Institute of General and Educational Psychology in Moscow.

FRANCISCO GOMES DE MATOS Professor of Applied Linguistics (Portuguese as a native language; sociolinguistics; psycholinguistics; evaluation of literacy materials), Universidade Federal de Pernambuco, Recife, Brazil.

CHRISTINE GORDON Associate Professor of Reading/Language Arts in the Department of Curriculum and Instruction at the University of Calgary and the co-editor of *Reading-Canada-Lecture*. Dr. Gordon's teaching/research interests include cognitive and metacognitive aspects of the reading/writing process.

G. G. GRANIK Reading Scholar at the Institute of General and Educational Psychology in Moscow.

MARY ANN GRAY Associate Professor of Education at Millersville University of Pennsylvania.

JOHN HLADCZUK Director of the Center for Interdisciplinary Studies in Knoxville, Tennessee and East Amherst, New York. He is coeditor (with William Eller) of *Literacy/Illiteracy in the World: A Bibliography* (Greenwood, 1989—a *Choice Outstanding Academic Book for 1990*) and *Comparative Reading: An International Bibliography* (Greenwood, 1987).

CHRIS HOPPER Associate Professor at the University of Montreal. Dr. Hopper teaches French language arts courses for preservice and in-service teachers. His teaching/research interests include writing with computers and software development.

PAUL KIDSTON Professor of Education at the University of Queensland, Australia.

BYONG WON KIM Director of the Center for Applied Linguistics at the Pohang Institute of Science and Technology in Pohang, South Korea.

G. N. KUDINA Reading Scholar at the Institute of General and Educational Psychology in Moscow.

MARGARET MACLEAN Associate Professor at the University of Ottawa and coordinator of the Computers in Education program. Dr. MacLean's teaching/research interests include literacy in vocational classrooms and the use of computers in language arts.

PETAR MANDIĆ Professor of Education at the University of Sarajevo in Sarajevo, Yugoslavia.

MARGARIDA ALVES MARTINS Head of the Educational Psychology Department at the Instituto Superior de Psicologia Aplicada in Lisbon, Portugal.

VICTOR R. MARTUZA Chairperson of the Department of Educational Studies at the University of Delaware, Newark, Delaware.

MIAO XIAOCHUN Associate Professor in the Department of Psychology of the East China Normal University in Shanghai, China.

LARRY MILLER Associate Professor in Language Arts at Queen's University. Dr. Miller's teaching/research interests include the use of technology in schools, children who read and write prior to school entrance, and the translation of reading/writing theory to practice.

TOURAN MIRHADY Reading Educator in Tehran, Iran.

Z. N. NOVLYANSKAYA Reading Scholar at the Institute of General and Educational Psychology in Moscow.

ABIOLA ODEJIDE Senior Lecturer and Acting Head of the Department of Communication and Language Arts (1987–1989), University of Ibadan, Ibadan, Nigeria.

YOUNGSOON PARK Professor of Education at Korea University.

JÜRGEN REICHEN Reading educator in Basel, Switzerland.

JOHN RYAN Coordinator of the International Literacy Year Secretariat.

TAKAHIKO SAKAMOTO Professor of Educational Psychology at the Women's College of Fine Arts, Tokyo, Japan. Dr. Sakamoto is a past president of the Japan Reading Association.

VANITHAMANI SARAVANAN Lecturer in the English Studies Department of the Institute of Education in Singapore.

MARIA DEL CARMEN UGALDE Professor at the University of Costa Rica.

G. A. ZUCKERMAN Reading Scholar at the Institute of General and Educational Psychology in Moscow.